RHUBARB & CUSTARD

Luton Modern School & Luton Grammar School for Boys

UBI SEMEN IBI MESSIS

James Dyer

THE LUTON MODERN SCHOOL FOR GIRLS & BOYS
VOLUME ONE

The Book Castle

In memory of
Kenneth B. Webb
(1904–2004)
Headmaster 1940–1966

and
Ronald Phillips
(1900–1995)
Assistant Master 1927–1964,
who asked me to write this book.

First published September 2004
by
The Book Castle
12 Church Street
Dunstable
Bedfordshire LU5 4RU

The right of James Dyer to be identified as the Author
of this work has been asserted by him in accordance with
section 77 of the Copyright, Designs and Patents Act 1988

ISBN 1–903747–54–6

Printed by Antony Rowe Ltd, Chippenham, Wiltshire

Contents

Chapters prior to 1919 contain material by Anne Allsopp and James Dyer

	Foreword by Sam Whitbread, Lord Lieutenant	iv
	Preface	v
	Acknowledgements	vi
Chapter 1	**Beginnings – Luton Secondary School**	1
Chapter 2	**Luton Modern School – 1908–1919**	21
Chapter 3	**The Great War and its Aftermath**	51
Chapter 4	**Sanderson's Later Years – 1919–1933**	69
Chapter 5	**The New Broom – 1933–1938**	107
Chapter 6	**To Bradgers Hill at Last – 1938–1939**	147
Chapter 7	**Notes of Discord – 1939–1940**	163
Chapter 8	**War and Peace – 1940–1942**	177
Chapter 9	**The Lost Boys**	201
Chapter 10	**Business as Usual – 1943–1944**	211
Chapter 11	**Luton Grammar School – 1944–1950**	227
Chapter 12	**The Challenge of the Fifties**	265
Chapter 13	**1956 to 1960**	313
Chapter 14	**The Final Years – 1961–1964**	347
Chapter 15	**The Bombshell – 1964–1966**	383
Chapter 16	**Epilogue**	413
	Roll of Honour	430
	Index	431
	List of Subscribers	440

Foreword

by Sam Whitbread, Esq, JP,
Lord Lieutenant of Bedfordshire

The Luton Modern Schools opened a hundred years ago in Park Square, in a 'curious-looking building ... of a temporary character' in the words of *The Bedfordshire Times and Independent*. Four years later a new, purpose-built school was opened, also in Park Square.

Two leading figures in local education were present at both opening ceremonies. One was Rowland Prothero (later Lord Ernle), Chairman of the Higher Education Sub-Committee of the County Council, becoming Chairman of Governors of the new School. The other was my grandfather Samuel Howard Whitbread, formerly Member of Parliament for South Bedfordshire and, by 1908, Member for South Huntingdonshire, while at the same time being Chairman of the County Council's Education Committee from its formation in 1903 until his retirement in 1928.

The first school (the Luton Secondary School and Technical Institution) was opened by Mrs Wernher of Luton Hoo (her husband Harold did not succeed to the Baronetcy until 1905) and the aim of the school was to provide secondary education for boys and girls from the age of twelve upwards. The curriculum for the four-year general course included English, Geography, History, French, German, Mathematics and Physics, as well as domestic hygiene, botany, drawing and needlework. In the final two years, book-keeping, shorthand 'and other specialised commercial subjects' would be added.

In his address, Rowland Prothero emphasised the co-operation between the County and Borough Authorities. 'Luton has taxed itself for the school maintenance to the limits which the law allows; the County has responded to the appeal with conspicuous generosity.' He described the ages of twelve to sixteen as 'the most critical period of our existence' and urged parents to make every effort to find the fees of £6 a year 'including all extras', accepting that 'the wages that the boys and girls might earn are a temptation.'

The new Luton Modern School, opened in 1908 just across Park Square, could accommodate twice as many pupils as its predecessor. The opening ceremony was performed by the Duke of Bedford, Chairman of Bedfordshire County Council, whose wife, Duchess Mary, had been a Governor of the School from its foundation. He said that the school provided 'a fresh and striking proof of that spirit of cordial co-operation for the general good, which animated the County Council and showed that Bedfordshire could unite to promote the welfare of every class.'

In proposing a vote of thanks to the Duke, Howard Whitbread highlighted the difference in Higher Education provision between Bedford and Luton. 'In Bedford there existed venerable, well-tried and efficient institutions for the promotion of higher education; in Luton they had to fend for themselves. Yet it is characteristic of Luton that it was always entering into friendly and vigorous competition with Bedford in order to show that it was the more vigorous portion of the county.'

Do we detect in these words a hint of the divisions between Luton and the rest of the County which emerge from time to time, even in our own day?

In any event it is right and proper that the centenary of the Luton Modern Schools should be marked by the publication of this comprehensive history and I can think of no more suitable authors than Dr Dyer and Dr Allsopp.

Sam Whitbread, Southill, 2004

Preface

Ronald Phillips died on the last day of 1995. I had spoken to him only four days before. We had previously talked at length about the School and his 37 years there, and I had promised him that I would try to write its history. He gave me his collection of School Magazines, and after his death, his nephew, Hugh, sent me numerous other mementoes. Unfortunately, pressure of work prevented me from getting started.

In 2002 I was introduced to Anne Allsopp, who had plans for a history of the Girls' High School, to celebrate the 2004 centenary. It seemed a good idea to work together to produce a history of the original Luton Modern School and the High, Junior Technical and Grammar Schools that grew out of it. Neither of us realised the enormity of the work, and it soon became obvious that two volumes would be needed. The first, by James Dyer, would cover the Modern and Grammar School for boys, whilst the second, by Anne Allsopp, would cover the Girls' High School and Junior Technical School. It was also clear that if both books were to be complete in themselves, it would be necessary to duplicate most of the pre-1919 section. This we have written together.

From the beginning we ran into a major difficulty. The early Log Books for the Schools were missing. When the Sixth Form College came into being, the Log Books should legally have been deposited either in Luton Museum or the Luton and Bedfordshire Archives at Bedford. It is rumoured that they were thrown away. Only the Grammar School Log from 1947 was available to us. In *Rhubarb and Custard* I have had to rely heavily on the School and Old Lutonian Magazines, *The Luton News*, and the Minutes of some of the earlier Governors' Meetings.

I have talked and written to many old students who have given freely of their time and memories. Where they have not been quoted directly, the information they have given has been important in helping to build up a picture of a particular event or time. Many have a strong love-hate relationship, with tales of enduring friendships, inspiring teachers, sporting battles grown bigger with the years; or memories of indifferent teaching and insidious bullying. Happily the former far outweighed the latter.

It is surprising how many generations of the same family, like the Gethings for example, passed through the Schools, and as a result, traditions, which Mr Sanderson claimed were non-existent, were born and passed on. Nicknames of staff and boys persisted through the years, such as those of the Whalley brothers, T.B.W. (1927–28) 'Pop', P.C.W. (1932–36) 'Big Pop', and R.D.W. (1938–45) 'Little Pop'.

In writing this book I have seen familiar people in a new light, and hope that the reader will do so also. Boys are cruel animals, and generally speaking Modern and Grammar School boys were no exceptions. Some of their more original non-conformist colleagues, as well as some of the finest masters, were treated abominably. I hope that I have shown that they were also human beings who deserved far better.

I am conscious that I have left out far more people than I have included. Whole swathes of boys whose lives were normal, decent and ordinary, get little mention. As in all walks of life it is only a handful of the more colourful ones that have been chronicled. But none began more or less important than the others. They were the seed that the school nourished, and from the seed grew the harvest. Most Old Lutonians agree that theirs was a good school; a great school, that gave them a real start in life. Sadly, it is no more. These pages are a tribute to the sixty-two years of devoted teaching and fraternity that were the Luton Modern and Grammar School for Boys.

Acknowledgements

I would like to thank the Editors of the School and Old Boys' Magazines, whose editorials, school notes and sports reports, written over sixty years, I have plundered most liberally. Although all now deceased, I must particularly mention E.W. Edmunds, F.W. Findlater, G. Clarke, E. Jones, C.W. Parry, H.E. Woodcock, J.A. Muse, and Arthur B. Allen. Many of the sentences in this book are really theirs, not mine. I must also thank the Editor of *The Luton News,* John Buckledee, who has watched this project with interest, and allowed me to quote from news reports, and to use many photographs taken by his papers' photographers (notably George Gurney) during the life of the School. Many of the negatives are now stored in the Luton Museum where Chris Grabham, the Museum's photographer, has spent many hours digitising them for me. They are acknowledged (*LN-LMC*) 'Luton News', Luton Museum Collection, in the captions. I am most grateful to Chris Grabham, and to Dr Elizabeth Adey, the Museum's Keeper of Local History, for their constant support.

The School's centenarian Headmaster, K.B. Webb, spent what was for me a most rewarding afternoon answering queries and loaning me photographs. The late Mr C.E. Wareham was also most helpful when interviewed four months before he died. His son P.H. Wareham kindly loaned me some of his father's photographs. The Principal of the Luton Sixth Form College, Mr Simon Kitchener, and his staff (especially Sally Leech) have given me every assistance and allowed me access to the surviving Modern and Grammar School records. John and Pat Gillespie, Bob Norman, R.D. 'Jim' Whalley and Melvyn Butcher have been invaluable in a thousand ways, and I thank them most sincerely.

A work of this sort could only have been written with the co-operation of hundreds of people in many parts of the world who have answered letters and telephone messages over the past two years. It seems invidious to single out any, but the following have answered my demands and queries at length: I thank them all:

Jack Adams, M. Bagshaw, Donald J. Burrows, the late J.H. Burgoyne, Matthew Butcher, M.V.W. Chote, M.J. Clark, G.P. Eden, D.L. Farr CBE, Michael Freedland, Phillip Gething, D.C. Glover, A.C. Hauke, Colin J. Humphreys CBE, Sir Alec Jeffreys, Ivan Jones, R.W. Joyner, D.H. Kennett, D.R. Oldroyd, A.T. Redman, David Renwick, B.D. Robinson, M. Root, Tom Smalley, T.P. Smith, J.M. Southgate, F.E. Stygall, the late Eric Taylor, A.W. Thorpe, J. Waller, J.R. Walters, D.G. Wick, D.J. Wood.

A number of people unconnected with the School have given their valuable time to help me with this project. In particular I would like to thank Ken Abbott, John Burley, James Collett-White, Eddie Grabham, Eric Meadows, Hugh Phillips, James Sparham, Beryl J. Whipp and Stewart Woolsey.

My co-author, Anne Allsopp, has been a considerable support, with a fund of information about the history of education. Without her enthusiasm this project might still be waiting to be written! Sally Siddons and Paul Bowes at 'The Book Castle' have been patient and understanding with a project that hasn't stopped growing.

In conclusion, I would like to thank the Lord Lieutenant of Bedfordshire, Sam Whitbread, for writing a Foreword to our work. Without the foresight of men like his grandfather, S. Howard Whitbread, the Luton Modern School might never have come into existence, and there would have been no centenary to celebrate.

James Dyer, June, 2004

Aerial view of the Modern School, dominated by the College of Technology (now Luton University), prior to its demolition in 1959. St Mary's Church and the electricity cooling towers beyond. (*LN-LMC*)

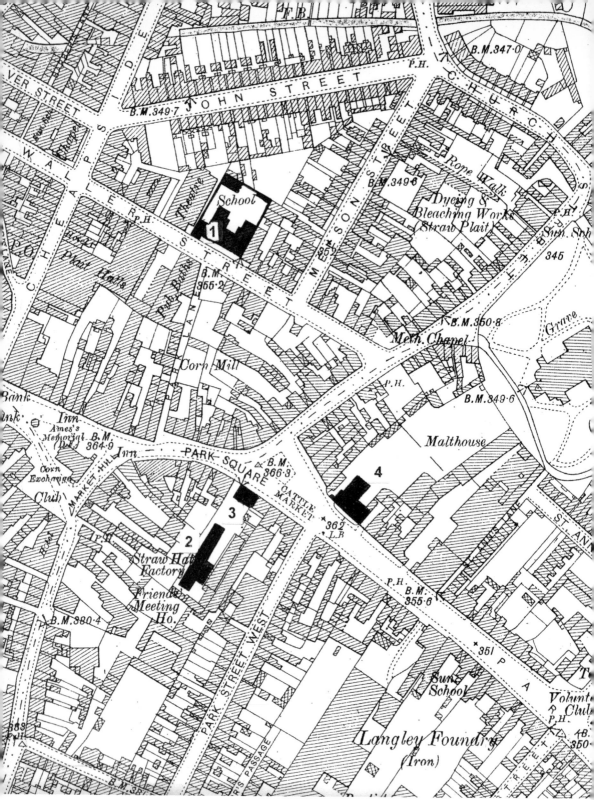

Section of Ordnance Survey map of 1901, showing the position of 1) Higher Grade School, Waller Street; 2) Luton Secondary School 1904-08 in Vyse old hat factory; 3) School Office and Headmaster's Study; 4) The White House.

Chapter 1

Beginnings –
Luton Secondary School

I was waiting for my train on Stroud Railway Station, which is dominated by the tall chimney of the local brewery, and I could smell the unmistakable odour of hot malt. It was then that I experienced a curious sinking feeling in my stomach, and my mind went back to 1904.

My first day at School at the Luton Secondary School, a *new* school, housed in an *old* disused hat factory, a gaunt brick building in Park Square, some hundred yards from the street and almost adjacent to Green's Brewery. Having suddenly been transferred from a Board School, I attended prayers conducted by the Head, in cap and gown, and supported by a small staff, also similarly attired. Overawed somewhat by this display of academic splendour, and feeling a little home-sick (and possibly school-sick, too), I was in no way comforted by the sickening pungent smell from Mr Green's malt, which permeated the whole neighbourhood, and that crowded the room.

It is authoritatively stated that the sense of smell is the most evocative of memory, and I well believe that this is so, for over a span of 56 years I could recall vividly my first day in that strange school. [C.C. Bennett, 1904–09]

Luton in 1904 bore very little resemblance to the town we know today. It was a prosperous, somewhat grubby, little market town with a population in the region of 36,000. Most of its wealth came from the manufacture of hats, its labour force dominated by women. Local businessmen, aware of the dangers of basing an economy on one industry alone, and of the presence of a surplus of unemployed male workers, invited other manufacturers to the town. Among the companies

which responded were Hayward Tylers, Laportes, the CWS Cocoa Factory, Vauxhall Motors, George Kent Ltd. and The Skefko Ball Bearing Company. The running of Luton was mainly in the hands of the business and professional classes, although the Crawley and Wernher families, of Stockwood and Luton Hoo respectively, showed a real interest in the welfare of the town.

From the 17th century education in Luton was only available to a small number of boys and girls. Cornelius Bigland and Roger Gillingham both left bequests for the schooling of poor children from Luton, though there is no evidence that a school actually existed there. The 1706 *Episcopal Visitations Returns* for Luton record 'a free-schole within the parish, the endowment of which is about £15 a year.' In 1709 is added 'John Swonell Master. About 50 boys.' By 1717 we are informed of 'One publick school. About 70 children well taught in it, and well Instructed in the principles of the Christian Religion, and duly attend the Service of the Church of England,' and three years later 'about 30 Boys taught therein.' John Richards in 1731 and Thomas Long in 1736 left further generous endowments for the education and apprenticing of Luton boys.

Luton had no long-established Grammar School, or things might have been different. In a will made in 1537, John Norrys of Luton left £20 to his brother Edward, with the proviso that if Edward died before the will was proven, '30 shillings is to be used for his burial, and the remaining £18 10s. is to be used to build a house for a grammar school, the house to be near the church, and the parish to decide where it shall be set.' Sadly for Luton's children Edward didn't die, and the school was never built!

With the introduction of Forster's Education Act of 1870 all children in Luton, as well as those in the neighbouring villages and hamlets, who had come from a labouring or working class background, had the right to elementary schooling. Even so, although Luton made attendance compulsory in 1874, it was still possible for a boy or girl of 11 to leave school before reaching the age of 13. To do this they only needed to apply for a Labour Certificate, which could be gained either by passing an examination or by attaining at least 250 attendances each year for five years [350 after 1900]. The test was intended for children of 13, but if an 11-year-old passed it, he or she could leave school. Tragically for the child and the nation, it was the clever youngster who did so. Luton provided elementary education in some eight denominational schools and also in the nine schools set up after 1874 by the Luton School Board. There was little doubt that most children brought up in the elementary system were likely to spend the rest of their lives in it.

It was not considered appropriate for the children from the professional classes or the sons and daughters of hat factory owners or managers to attend the local elementary schools. A few might take the train each day to one of the Bedford public schools, but the majority were more likely to be enrolled locally in private schools. For boys there was some choice: Norton House School (or College) in Havelock

Road with the adjacent facilities of Bell's Close and People's Park, Grosvenor College in Rothesay Road, St Gregory's School in Downs Road, St John's College off New Bedford Road or the larger Dunstable Grammar School founded in 1886. Girls could attend St Dominic's Convent School in Rothesay Road, described as 'a Boarding School for the daughters of Gentlemen', Luton High School in Cardiff Road (not the one described in this book), or travel to Moreton House in Dunstable, established since 1864.

It was accepted that some boys needed business skills and many of them had been able to take commercial subjects in classes held under the auspices of the County Technical Instruction Committee. It was also recognised that, in order to keep the schools running, there was a need to train teachers under the old pupil-teacher system. Luton's attitude to education was essentially utilitarian and, for most children, a basic education in the 3Rs was all that was expected.

Although elementary schooling was available for every child, secondary education was only accessible to a few in the Public and Private Schools, which were 'locked, bolted and barred' against any but wealthy parents, and a few endowed Grammar Schools. The latter often granted scholarships to elementary school pupils, but these were a mere drop in the ocean. Many local authorities started Higher Grade Schools like that in Waller Street, Luton, which offered boys a wider curriculum. It was highly regarded in the town, but was, strictly speaking, illegal because it was funded with money specifically allocated by the government for elementary education. There were several unsuccessful attempts to set up a Higher Grade School for girls from more 'respectable' families, but, on the whole, the education of girls in Luton was confined to the traditional 'female' 4Cs: cookery, clothing, church and children.

Government Provision

In 1902 the Balfour Education Act transferred overall responsibility for education to the County Councils. Luton, however, was large enough to be a Part III authority. This meant that the Town Council was allowed to keep control over the elementary schools but Bedfordshire County Council became responsible for rural schools and secondary education. The wider concept of secondary education was familiar to the people of Bedford, who had enjoyed the benefits of the Harpur Trust, but was new to Lutonians. The Bedfordshire Education Committee and Luton Town Council lost no time in preparing plans to open a combined Day Secondary School and Technical Institution to serve Luton and the south of the County in September 1904. This was to provide secondary education for boys and girls during the day and technical classes for older students in the evenings. The setting up and running of the school was to be funded by Government Grants, School Fees, and a one penny rate to be raised each year by the Luton Town Council.

For some years Evening Classes had been successfully conducted in Luton under

the direction of the Technical Instruction Committee. In future they would be co-ordinated into a definite Institute under the direction of a Principal, who would also be the Headmaster of the Secondary School. The joint Institution would be managed by a body of Governors constituted as follows:

Elected by the Bedfordshire County Council:
    Her Grace the Duchess of Bedford
    A.J. Hucklesby Esq. Hat Manufacturer, JP, Mayor (5 times)
    W.T. Lye Esq. Plait Dyer, JP
    R.E. Prothero, Esq. MVO, (Chairman) Chairman, Higher Education Committee
    R.Richmond Esq. Pharmacist, JP, (from Leighton Buzzard)
    H.O. Williams Esq. Builders' Merchant, Brickmaker, JP, Mayor

Elected by the Luton Town Council:
    E.Oakley Esq. Hat Manufacturer, JP, Mayor (3 times)
    A.A. Oakley Esq. Provision Merchant, Mayor
    C.H. Osborne Esq. Hat Manufacturer, Mayor
    J.H. Staddon Esq. Hat Manufacturer, JP, Mayor
    G. Warren Esq. (Vice-chairman) Hat Manufacturer, JP, Mayor
    A. Wilkinson Esq. Architect, Mayor
Co-opted
    W.R. Hawson Esq. Banker
    Miss Amy Walmsley Principal, Bedford Training College
    Mrs Alice Wernher (later Lady Wernher, then Lady Ludlow)

The school in Luton was to be a mixed one; this was not an ideological decision but one of convenience. 'It was always intended to have separate schools as soon as circumstances warranted them, but the project was delayed by the first World War, after which a separate school for girls was provided.' The town greeted the idea of a new school with mixed feelings. The official prospectus claimed that 'the education [to be] offered was for both professional and commercial life and [would] prepare the way for a University and Higher Technical Education and also for prospective teachers.' The local Chamber of Commerce welcomed 'the desirability of Luton lads (not lasses!) receiving a special training for commercial life' but, as was to be expected in the early days of the twentieth century, there seems to have been some resistance towards giving girls a better education, especially in a town where they were likely to become a life-long part of the local hat industry. This was demonstrated by a piece in the 1905 *Luton Year Book* entitled *Are College Girls Marrying Girls?* which pointed out that only 22 per cent of college girls marry after graduation, compared with 80 per cent of non-college girls who marry and have children.

Setting up the School

For its first four years the school was housed in a temporary building which stood back from the western side of Park Square and had formerly been a straw hat warehouse run by Messrs. Vyse and Sons. £600 was spent on renovations which allowed for three classrooms, with a laboratory on the ground floor and an assembly room 57ft long and an art and mechanical drawing room 60ft long on the floor above. The adjoining Brewery yard served as a playground. The Headmaster's study and school office were housed in an old cottage which stood on the frontage of the factory site, some distance from the school itself and facing onto Park Square (it subsequently served for a time as the United Omnibus Company's Office). Three rooms on the ground floor were used for Woodwork instruction. The stairs in one of these led up to the stationery sales office and the Head's room which overlooked the street. It can be imagined what noise the Head had to endure from hammers and saws inexpertly wielded by potential craftsmen. Bicycle sheds were provided at the back of the school. It seems that in 1904 these buildings were owned by Mr Joseph W. Green, the brewer, who later demolished some of them in order to extend his brewery. He negotiated a rent of £80 a year while also subscribing £100 towards the initial cost of establishing the school. Mr Green's business was also on Park Square and the earliest scholars remembered that their 'senses of hearing and smell' were 'deafened and tortured by the buzzing and odour which emanated from the Brewery' next door.

A major consideration was the appointment of a suitable staff, and in particular a strong Headmaster or Principal. Local expectations probably favoured H.C. Middle from the Higher Grade School (a non-graduate), or J.H. Hargreaves from the Pupil Teacher Centre, but the Governors looked further afield and chose T.A.E. Sanderson. Thomas Arthur Edwin Sanderson, aged 36, was born at Litlington near Royston, Hertfordshire, where his father was the Vicar of St Katherine's church. The family moved to Hampshire when he was four. Educated at the City of London School, he obtained a Beaufoy Leaving Exhibition and Major Mathematical Scholarship at Trinity College, Cambridge. He graduated in 1890 with a 1st Class degree in Mathematics. He achieved high marks, earning the distinction of being 21st Wrangler (a person placed in the first class of the mathematical tripos). Before coming to Luton Mr Sanderson had done a certain amount of coaching at military establishments, including Sandhurst. Perhaps the innumerable forms that were a feature of his organisation were the result of the time he spent at these. More probably they were the signs of a neat and orderly mind.

Mr Sanderson has described the events leading up to his appointment.

'Early in the summer of 1904 appeared an advertisement stating that the Bedfordshire County Council was about to open in Luton a Secondary School for

girls and boys. I decided to apply for the Head Mastership. At that time I was on the staff of Bath College, a school run by a private company on public school lines.

'For various reasons I did not apply till the last moment. When called for interview illness in my family made it desirable that I should not leave Bath before it was absolutely necessary. So I took a night train to London, arriving in Luton about breakfast time. Making my way through damp streets to the George Hotel I formed the impression that Luton was rather like the suburbs of Manchester. At the hotel, having asked for a room in which to change, I was shown to No. 13 – a bad omen. Many of the other candidates wore frock coats with silk hats; I had a boater, which in a straw hat town may have been one of the reasons why I was selected.

'Of the ten or twelve candidates interviewed in the morning, three of us were asked to return after lunch: Mr R.S. Haydon, Mr C.C.H. Walker and myself.

'The afternoon proceedings were short, and after being offered the post I was asked whether I had any special remarks to make. I replied that I hoped no school rules would be made except such as could be strictly enforced. This remark seemed to make little impression on the committee, but perhaps accounts for the fact that later on I was sometimes regarded as an ultra-strict disciplinarian.'

Ronald Phillips, who joined the staff in 1927, said that 'in his earlier years, to his pupils Sanderson was a formidable figure with a striking head, a fierce dark moustache, a fresh complexion and wavy hair, but later he shaved off his moustache and assumed a more benevolent aspect.' F.M. Edwards spoke of 'his piercing eye, which could make a boy feel extremely 'small', also a powerful voice which could make the rafters ring.' Another of his first pupils, C.C. Bennett wrote, 'The Head, 'Puggy' Sanderson, was rather a terrifying figure and a strict disciplinarian. I cannot remember anyone being caned – it was not necessary. His dominating personality was quite sufficient to tame the wildest spirits.' Among the tributes paid to him on his retirement in 1933 was 'his complete impartiality . . . he never harried the delinquent with a nagging tongue, nor pursued the clever boy with fulsome praise.' His devotion to the school was well-known: 'it is common knowledge that even during the holidays he was to be found at his post and, somehow, it seemed natural to find him there.' He was also remembered for 'a certain sternness that has sometimes led to his being misunderstood.' Sanderson admitted that he found running a mixed school very difficult and it seems that his empathy lay more with the boys than the girls.

'One of my greatest reliefs was the opening of the Girls' School – not that the pupils gave any trouble, but I found a male staff far easier to deal with than a mixed one.'

Thomas A.E. Sanderson, MA, Headmaster: 1904–1933. (*H.F. Thurston*)

During the summer of 1904 Staff were appointed whose services would be divided between the Day and Evening classes at the Headmaster's discretion. Sanderson observed, 'This arrangement led to many difficulties, for when members were not actually teaching they could not be expected to remain on the premises and so no duties outside the classroom could be insisted upon. After the first year the day and evening work were separated, and the staff were treated as full-time teachers in the day school, with extra pay for any evening work they did.' Apart from Messrs Edmunds, May and Otter, who had been instructors under the Technical Instruction Committee, the staff all appear to have been appointed from out-of-town, since none of the names is familiar from the time of the Luton School Board.

Principal: T.A.E. Sanderson, MA (Maths)   Salary £300 p.a.
Senior Assistant: E.W. Edmunds, MA, B.Sc.(Classics, Science)   Salary £200 p.a.
Assistants: J. Bygott (English, Maths, Geography)
               Miss Clara S. Gardner, LL.A (History, English, French, German)
               J.B. Hoblyn, ARCS (Chemistry, Physics)
               C. Wesley Hutchinson, BA (General subjects)
               W.E. Llewellyn, (Modern Languages)
               Frederick F. May, ARCA (Art and Design)
               Miss R.E. Moylan (French, English)
               William Otter (Manual Instruction, *i.e.* Handicraft)

Admissions

An advertisement was placed in *The Luton News* on 1st September 1904 which informed its readers that:

The **Luton Secondary Day School** will open
for the First Term on Wednesday, September 14th, 1904.
Boys and girls who desire to become pupils at the above school
must pass an entrance examination. Fees £1 10s 0d per term.
A Second Admission Examination will be held
on Saturday, 17th September, 1904.
Full Particulars and Entrance Forms may be obtained
of the Headmaster, at the School, or of the Undersigned.
Special Contract Tickets at reduced rates
are issued by the Railway Companies
to Scholars journeying daily to the School.
FRANK SPOONER
Director of Education, Shire Hall, Bedford

The *Prospectus* for the new school included these rules:
- No pupil could be admitted below the age of ten and none could stay beyond the age of 18 without special permission.
- Day pupils must live with parents, guardians or near relations or at a house approved by the governors.
- No pupil was to be admitted unless of good character and sufficient health, and who had been found fit for admission in an examination under the direction of the Headmaster. (Health certificates were introduced in 1907).
- Preference was to be given to children who resided within the Borough of Luton and the County of Bedford.
- Examinations were to be held three times a year in December, April and September. Dates to be advised in the local newspaper.
- Compulsory examinations in Arithmetic, Dictation, Composition, Reading, English Grammar, Geography or History.
- Optional examinations in Elementary French, Elementary Science and Elementary Mathematics.
- Fees – £1 10s 0d per term, Stationery and textbooks to be supplied by the authority but paid for by the scholars, as were fees for games.
- Free scholarships. These were held for two years and were renewable for the remainder of the course subject to good conduct and satisfactory progress.
- A Report concerning the pupils' progress and conduct was to be sent to parents or guardians at the close of each term.

The fees were prohibitive for the ordinary working classes but a whole new world was about to open up for children who passed the examination for free places, although the money had to be refunded if the pupil left within two years. 25 per cent of these places were offered by the Governors to Luton children in the school's first year and Bedfordshire made County Scholarships available for out-of-town children. The first scholarships were awarded to:

> R.J. Aldred; C.C. Bennett; G.L. Bond; Nellie Breed; F. Buckingham;
> Edith Fensome; G.W. Fensome; L.T. Few; Eveline Fletcher;
> Mabel Hawkes; J. Hunt; Leila King; A.E. Perry; Hilda Pilkington;
> A.T. Reeve; Marion Robinson; F.R. Simpson; W.C. Waldock;
> A.T. Wheeler; E.C. Wright.

From December 1906 all scholarships awarded by the Governors included free books and stationery, and this applied retrospectively to the scholarships already operating. In 1908 the Board of Education insisted that all fee paying Secondary Schools must provide a proportion of free places. This was usually about 25 per cent of the total pupils on roll. Failure to comply could lead to substantial cuts in grants. Bedfordhire responded by introducing Junior County Scholarships in 1908. Over the years,

money was also made available from certain local charities, notably Chew's, Bigland's and Richard's. The Bigland, Long and Gillingham trusts were combined in 1915 to provide Secondary School Exhibitions, Technical Exhibitions, University Exhibitions or maintenance allowances for 'necessitous boys and girls resident in the Borough of Luton, who have attended public elementary schools for at least the last two years.' These were still being awarded by the Bigland, Long and Gillingham Foundation after 1966 when the Schools became the Sixth Form College. In 1918 the Bedfordshire County Council began to give Leaving Scholarships for further education based on a set examination, school records and a personal interview. These covered tuition fees and a contribution towards maintenance.

At the time of his retirement from Luton Grammar School in 1964, Dr John G. Dony wrote:

> 'The School was started when I was five years old, and in its early days it was intended mainly for those who were financially better off rather than those who might benefit from a higher education. As a child I was resigned to the fact that I could not go to the School, but got a little consolation in doing the homework for some of those who did. I was lucky as the school to which I went was not cursed with the homework abomination. Looking back, I feel that it is probably the strangest feature of my life that I taught for so long (23 years) in the school that I was unable to attend, and as I leave it the first impression of my childhood remains, namely that there are scores of boys in the school who would be better educated elsewhere and as many boys in the town who could well replace them.'

There is some evidence to show that the elementary school Headteachers were biased towards which of their pupils they entered for the entrance examinations, favouring, as Dr Dony said, those from the relatively better off homes, rather than poorer children with good brains. As late as 1919 A.J. Mander, Head of Old Bedford Road School, chose half a dozen of the better class boys to sit for the Modern School Entrance Examination. These did not include Fred Dyer and Frank Potts who believed that they could do better. Together they went to the Modern School and talked with a friendly teacher who gave them application forms. These were filled in, and in due course they both took the exam and passed. Fred's father said he could attend if he wanted, but thought he would do better with an apprenticeship. Other relatives also urged him to get apprenticed, and so he did. Frank was also talked into an apprenticeship. For Fred, it was a mistake that he regretted for the rest of his life. Although Mander knew that the two boys had passed, he never acknowledged the fact to either of them.

The First Students

The early Admission Books make interesting reading. According to these, 47 boys and 38 girls were admitted to the school in September 1904 and many names familiar in the history of Luton can be recognised. It would take up too much space to name them all, but, as a token, the names of the first three on the list (all scholarship holders) are included here.

1. Arthur Edward Perry, 30 Victoria Street, Luton.
   Previous School: Waller Street
2. George William Fensome, 41 Waller Street, Luton
   Previous School: Waller Street
3. Nellie Breed, School House, Stopsley
   Previous School: Stopsley (Her father was C.H. Breed, the Headmaster)

Waller Street Higher Grade School was well represented, 27 of the first 85 pupils having been educated there. Other Luton elementary schools sent children, and boys and girls also came from Leighton Buzzard, Eggington and Dunstable (all conveniently close to the Great Northern Railway line). Private schools lost a few pupils but it looks as though parents were hesitant at first. However, once the new school had proved its worth, the trickle became a flood and some of the private schools went out of business. Even Waller Street began to feel the impact on its older pupils.

The Admission Books give 'father's occupation'. As has been noted, few of the ordinary men in the street could afford the fees, so it is not surprising that occupations listed are teaching, clerical posts, managers, farmers, ministers of religion, retail, etc. Owners and managers of hat factories took top place; this was only to be expected in a town where the manufacture of hats was the main source of wealth. This situation had altered only slightly by 1960 when a sociological survey of class 4a at Luton Grammar School carried out by David H. Kennett indicated that the only real change showed many fathers employed on the managerial staff at Vauxhall Motors replacing the declining hat industry's senior executives.

Students had to travel from all over Luton and south Bedfordshire. When places were available students also came from north Hertfordshire. There were two convenient rail links: one was the Great Northern Railway from Leighton Buzzard, through Dunstable, to Luton and Welwyn. The other, the London, Midland and Scottish line, followed the present Thameslink route.

F.M. Edwards travelled:

'twelve miles daily to and from school. The train left Flitwick station at 7.40am. School was reached at 8.15am, long before the playgrounds became crowded. The

morning train was always crowded with young men and women employed in the straw hat trade; on one occasion twenty-three souls were crushed together in our compartment, normally seating ten.

'Only once in four years did I miss the train. Cycling some twelve miles against a stiffish head-wind, I arrived in time for morning prayers, but unfortunately some two minutes late. Some five days later I received the white card summons to attend the headmaster's study at once. After much ranting and threats of expulsion, I was advised of dire penalties if ever it occurred again.

'Lessons ended at 4.20pm and my train left at 4.47pm, giving me ample time to collect goods – ironmongery, hardware or grocery items for my parents who ran a country store. They found my school journeys most convenient in giving customers prompt service.

'Trains were very fast in those days and they were very punctual. We often covered the home journey in thirteen minutes. This could not be bettered by modern engines.'

The railway companies made deals concerning fares, but they were not always so accommodating in response to requests to change their timetables. On the contrary, after the first two years the school hours were changed from 9am–12.40pm and 2pm–4.30pm, to 9am–12.20pm and 2pm–4.15pm to make life easier for the pupils who travelled by train, particularly those from Leighton Buzzard. In 1908 trams were introduced; they ran from their depot in Park Street to Dunstable Road, New Bedford Road, High Town Road and Hitchin Road up to Round Green. No doubt some families could afford the £7 or £8 for a bicycle, but many children would certainly have walked to school.

'Feeling rather like David Copperfield,' Rex Clayton made his 'first journey to the new Luton Secondary School in a village carrier's van. It was a cold January morning in 1908. The journey from Markyate, four miles of hilly country and over flinty roads, took over an hour. A few minutes before 9am I was put down on Park Square to make my lonely way into the converted hat factory which for ten terms had housed my predecessors. After a week or two I was allowed to cycle to and from school.

'About that time Luton's new tram system came into service. We boys who cycled to school were longing to ride in those shiny tram-lines. We learned our lesson the first morning!'

The Luton Secondary School and Technical Institute Opens

On Tuesday, 13th September, 1904, members of the Bedfordshire County Council, Luton Town Council and numerous Civic and Religious dignitaries met for an inaugural ceremony at the Luton Corn Exchange, which was performed by Mrs Julius Wernher, later Lady Ludlow.

It was not until a week later, on Monday, 19th September, 1904, that 'Luton Secondary School met for the first time in a room the bareness of whose walls was solely relieved by an engraving of G.F. Watt's *Sir Galahad*, most kindly presented by Miss Walmsley (Governor).' There were 85 children present, 46 boys and 39 girls.

'From the opening morning, – when groups of excited girls and boys assembled on Park Square and discussed the possibilities of the new life on which they were about to enter – to the end of the school year, when those same scholars listened with excitement, mingled with awe, to the reading of the form lists, our first year at the school was one long round of novelty and pleasure. Firstly, we had the delight of criticising the mistresses and masters, and it is only fair to add that our criticism – though quite impartial and candid, as all schoolgirl and schoolboy criticism is – was decidedly favourable. The same cannot be said of the school building, I fear.'   [E.B.]

'It was, I think, surprisingly well adapted, bearing in mind the original function of the place. There were four or five classrooms, a good chemistry laboratory, a large Art room, and a cloakroom [toilet] so well equiped that I was filled with wonder, after having experienced the contraptions which then graced the streets of Luton.'   [C.C.B.]

'We were initiated into the mysteries of many new and interesting subjects. We learnt of angles and parallel lines; made the acquaintance of the mysterious x; were delighted with the truly wonderful results we were soon able to obtain in the chemical laboratory (results as marvellous to our instructor as to ourselves, one would imagine!), and were soon deep in the study of Specific Gravity, and of Weights and Forces.

'The Art Room was the scene of our first drill lesson, though afterwards we were promoted to the dignity of the Plait Hall.'   [E.B.]

Games were at first held on a field in Crescent Road belonging to Model Farm, lent by Mr John Facer, father of one of the first pupils, H.H. Facer. Unfortunately, the field was soon required for building. The pupils were then invited to subscribe to a voluntary games fund which enabled them to hire a meadow belonging to Faunch's Farm, on the east side of Old Bedford Road almost opposite Wardown House

(Museum). During the summer of 1906 the Governors purchased a plot of land together with some buildings, from the Wesley Guild, for use as a playing field, in Dunstable Road. This land was sold in 1909 to build Beech Hill School. At that time the town ended near Waldeck Road and there were three miles of open country between Luton and Dunstable.

Miss Jane Macfarlane joined the staff in 1907 to teach German and French. She later recalled:

> 'the pungent, but not unpleasant, smell of hops from Green's Brewery, the Headmaster's Study and the Common Staff-room. There was, of course, no 'sick room', and I have a vivid recollection of looking after a casualty, and stretching the girl out upon a hard form – the only thing upon which she could lie down.
>
> 'We formed a Hockey Team among the girls and entertained our first visiting team to tea in the Woodwork Room, perched precariously upon stools and benches. We enjoyed ourselves tremendously. The boys played football, but had no teas as far as I can remember.'

There was little attempt to establish a school uniform in the early days. Sanderson said that during his years in office he 'always aimed at avoiding window-dressing and at keeping the essential expenses of pupils as light as possible, for in the early years pupils often came from homes that were far from affluent. Except for a school cap there were no restrictions about dress.' Even so, when the first whole school photograph was taken in 1908 there was a definite uniformity in the boys' and girls' clothes, seen again in the celebration of King George V's coronation photographs of 1911. The earliest recorded caps were black or navy-blue with a small school badge and motto at the front. The football team had their own maroon-red cap with long gold tassel, and an LMS monogram on the front in gold and blue. There was also an all-white cricket cap with the LMS monogram and coloured braiding round the edge. By the time Edith Webb started at the school in 1917, something more was expected of the girls:

> 'The uniform consisted of a navy-blue gym-slip with braid girdle, white or cream blouse, navy-blue bloomers with linings and a straw boater complete with band, embroidered with the school badge. Other items requested were indoor shoes, shoe bag and a dictionary and a satchel.'

When the boys' and girls' schools separated in 1919 both schools had adopted distinctive uniforms, of which more will be said later.

The Curriculum and Relevant Examinations

From the beginning it was hoped that all pupils would take the General Course, which, the prospectus stated, should last for four years. In the first two years all the pupils worked together and the subjects offered were:

English, Geography, History, German, French, Mathematics, Higher Arithmetic, Geometry, Chemistry (theoretical and practical), Physics (theoretical and practical), Domestic Hygiene, Botany, Drawing, Manual Training and Needlework.

During the next two years some degree of specialisation was permitted and pupils were allowed to choose two subjects from the following: Book-keeping, Shorthand and specialised commercial subjects, Higher Mathematics and Advanced Science.

After four years pupils could take the London University Matriculation Examination or the Junior Certificate of the London Chamber of Commerce. In July 1907, the first 30 pupils were put in for the Cambridge Local Junior Examination and 29 gained certificates. These were the school's first public examinations. A few pupils went on to do the Cambridge Local Senior exams. Matriculation was an important step up the academic ladder. It was originally intended to be a qualification for a degree course but became more and more used as a school-leaving exam and could be demanded by employers. Most issues of *The Luton Modern School Magazine* meticulously listed the name of everyone who passed these examinations. So keen was the Head Master to record pupils' progress and to ensure their academic success, that tests were rigorously held at the end of each week. Those who failed to reach the required standard were severely chastised, and persistent offenders were threatened with expulsion!

Unfortunately, many of the people in Luton were out of tune with the concept of secondary education and successive Headteachers attempted to persuade parents to keep their children at school rather than let them leave early to take up some form of employment. Later, agreements had to be signed and fines were imposed on parents who allowed their children to leave. This was a serious problem and concerned the Education Committees, the governors and the staff throughout the life of the school.

It appears that German was the first foreign language to be taught. An article in the school magazine noted how the subject both interested and appalled the pupils. 'How we struggled with the unfamiliar guttural sounds, and sighed in despair as we made the acquaintance of 'das kleine Madchen, Anna' and 'der gute Knabe, Karl'. French came onto the curriculum in the second year and then the pupils struggled 'to produce French vowels correctly . . . faces underwent various contortions until the shape of the mouth was considered passable.' By 1909, there was a demand for Latin and pupils began to struggle with the complexities of its grammar:

O genie of the Grammar Land,
Take thy pupils now in hand,
Lead us to thy dread abode.
Teach us now the rules of prose,
And verbs that govern every clause,
Make us understand.

[Balbus]

At the end of the First World War, with anti-German feelings running high, and following the recommendations of a Board of Education report, the Governors declared:

'That, as from the Autumn Term, 1918, French shall be the first foreign language taken in the Luton Modern School,' and 'That for a second foreign language the pupil shall have the choice of German or Latin, but, as a general rule, a second language cannot be taken before entering Form III, and only then on showing aptitude for languages, and providing the pupil is remaining at school for at least a further two years.'

Readers will notice that religious education is also omitted from the school syllabus, and remained so until 1920, by which time the Boys' and Girls' schools had separated. When challenged, Sanderson replied,

'I am not in favour of introducing Scripture teaching, because I am very much afraid of introducing hypocrisy. My experience of the instruction in boys' schools is that it has done more harm than good. There is the fact that some who are teaching it are not doing so from conviction, but simply because they are more or less compelled. Then I think Luton is a more ethical place than others, and there is a stronger sectarian feeling in Luton than in many other places.'

At the Girls' Modern School in 1920 Miss Sheldon held different views, stating that she was strongly in favour of some kind of Biblical teaching. Following a lengthy debate the Joint Governors decreed that religious education should be introduced into both schools from September 1920.

In the early days drill, which was traditionally thought to improve discipline, was on the timetable. There was no particular place for teaching this. If the weather was fine it might be in the Brewery yard, but classes could also find themselves in the Art Room, the Plait Hall or the Corn Exchange. On rare occasions space was even found in the Town Hall (the one burnt down in 1919).

'It mattered little to us pupils in which building it was held. Either involved a few minutes' walk which was eagerly looked forward to. Then these public buildings were not so secluded as the Town Hall; little surprises inevitably occurred. Once in the Town Hall the girls were considerably startled to see a man emerge from a small recess in one of the corners. It was afterwards discovered that he had been attending the clock; but at the time, he was regarded as a most mysterious person, and naturally our nerves, and consequently the steadiness of our drill, suffered from such paralysing shocks.'

The children had no objection as the few minutes extra walk meant shorter lessons.

'Yes, drill it was then and one prepared for it by simply removing the coat, and possibly even the waistcoat, in the case of the more enthusiastic.'

'Weird and wonderful garments' were fashioned in Needlework classes and 'many a test tube and beaker were smashed in the Laboratory.' In the Art Room 'drawing lessons seldom occurred without many distractions. Desks would suddenly tilt, pots of water would be accidentally upset, and sometimes singing lessons were conducted on the other side of a curtain.'

From this account and from the reminiscences of Edith Webb and other pupils, it appears that behaviour was not always exemplary. Apart from the usual writing out of lines, punishments included detention and suspension.

C.C. Bennett has written: 'The School was co-educational, and we got on well with the girls. We had two or three women teachers with whom we did not get on quite so well . . . I recall my embarrassment and anger on being ordered by one of them to brush my hair before coming to class.'

Starting a Tradition

Sanderson noted that 'One of the main advantages of starting a new school was the absence of tradition. I was able to introduce my own fads such as weekly examinations, one-way traffic, and so on, without treading on the heels of precedent.' Rowland E. Prothero, Chairman of the Bedfordshire Higher Education Committee and of the School Governors, who was later described as 'the father of this great school', explained the part he played in this by giving the school its badge and its motto.

'The badge consists of three ears of corn loosely bound together. I meant it to connect this new foundation with an ancient monastic establishment in the neighbourhood, which had been conspicuous for keeping alight the lamp of learning during the Dark Ages. In the fine parish church of St Mary's in Luton is the tomb of one of the abbots of St Albans, Abbot John of Wheathampstead. From this monument are taken the ears of corn which were his canting arms. But

monastic institutions were unpopular in Luton, and the ears of corn, with their stalks, might have been unacceptable, if they had not also represented the material

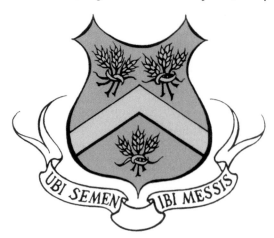

of the straw-plaiting industry on which the commercial prosperity of the town had been founded. The motto links together badge and school, by the reward which awaits the labour alike of sower and teacher. Without a sowing, neither soil nor mind will yield harvest. This is tensely expressed in the Latin motto: *Ubi semen, ibi messis.* (Where the seed, there shall the harvest be.)'

Since Prothero wrote this it has been shown that the arms in the church are not those of Abbot John of Wheathampstead, but are in fact those of William of Wallingford, Abbot of St Albans from 1476 to 1492.

At first the words *Luton Secondary School* were written below the badge but, in 1908, these were removed and the motto took their place. This idea of sowing seed and reaping a harvest became a recurring theme in the ethos of the school. However, academic success was not to be the only harvest; the school was expected to produce good citizens who would always place public duty before private interests and should encourage real sportsmen and women who would always play the game. These were certainly high ideals and they well suited the spirit of the age.

Ronald Phillips has written:

'Among the many features of Mr Sanderson's administration one or two may be noted here. He instituted the unusual system of weekly examinations, whose chief merit was that it eliminated the end-of-term rush for the masters and the end-of-term inactivity among the boys. Another feature, which also eased the burdens of the teaching staff, was the system of coded reports, which made it possible for a master to do the whole of his reports in one period. Noteworthy too was his absence record system whereby a check was kept every period upon attendance. This proved so effective and easy to work that it still [1960] remains in place.'

The efforts to establish a successful school were appreciated by His Majesty's Inspectors, Mr Westaway and Miss Crosby. After the first inspection in 1906, they congratulated Sanderson on the excellence of much of the work. They also took up the idea of building a tradition and hoped the pupils would develop their 'social instincts' by sharing in the corporate life of the school.

Two pupils at the new school when it opened in 1904 were Fred Buckingham and Dora Middle, daughter of the Higher Grade School Headmaster. Although the school entered no pupils for public examinations in 1906, the year that they left, they were to become the first old boy and girl of the school to obtain degrees. He gained a BSc. in Engineering at London University in 1913 and she a BA in 1914.

The School's temporary buildings in the hat factory were overcrowded and inconvenient, and work began on a new building in Park Square.

On 6th April, 1908, just a month before the new School was due to open, the old School was burgled. The Headmaster's office had been closed for the night, soon after evening classes finished. The Caretaker, Mr T. Hooker, (known as 'Policeman' to the boys), locked up the premises and made his way home. In the meantime, the burglar, who clearly knew the layout of the building intimately, hid himself in the Woodwork rooms below. He then let himself into the Headmaster's room, without tampering with the lock. He rifled the drawers of the Head and his Clerk, taking money and stamps, and he then broke into the Stationery Office. Having acquired about £4 9s. including 30s. collected by the pupils for the Bute Hospital Fund, he slipped the catch of the front door, let himself into the street, and closed the door behind him.

OPPOSITE The School Badge, based on the arms of William of Wallingford: *Gules, a chevron between three clusters of wheat each of three ears banded Or.*
BELOW Sedelia on south side of Sanctuary in St Mary's Church, Luton, showing the arms of William of Wallingford, Abbot of St Albans (1476-1492) at either end. (*Eric Meadows*)

Chapter 2

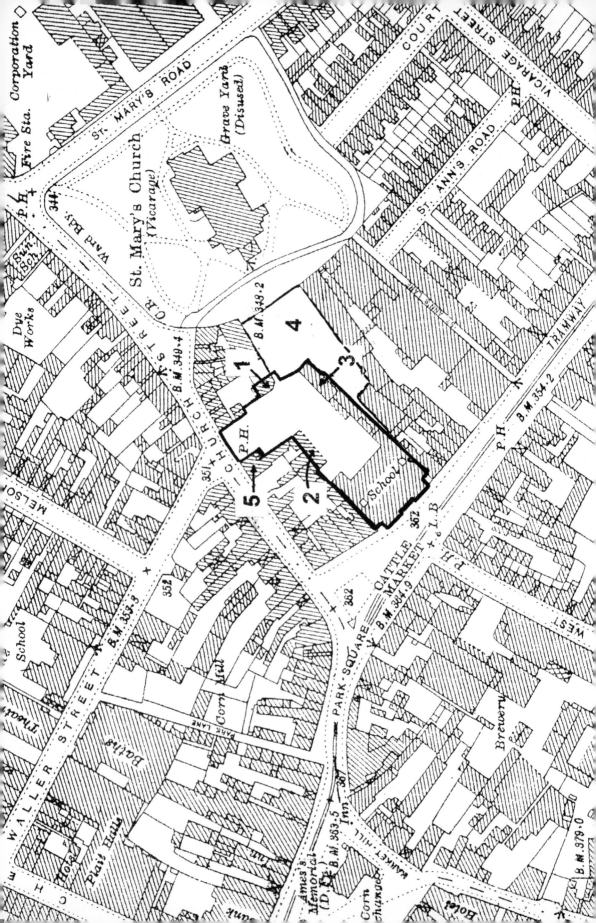

Luton Modern School
1908–1919

The school had rapidly outgrown the temporary premises. Back in 1903 the Bedfordshire County Council had obtained a mortgage for a new building on the eastern side of Park Square, some fifty yards from its junction with Church Street, on what is now the Luton University frontage. This had been the site of 'Park Square House' or 'The White House' as it was more commonly known, with its extensive garden backing onto St Mary's churchyard. It was purchased from the old established local brewing family, the Burrs, whose brewery adjoined it to the south. The County Council invited architects to submit outline design proposals for the new school. Some 200 were submitted, but only six were chosen to compete for the contract. The trade magazine, *The Builder*, criticised he Council for limiting the competition, asserting that the best interests of the Bedfordshire public were not being served. A minority of Councillors agreed and some architects complained, to no avail. The architects Spalding and Spalding were chosen, and they produced plans for a three-storey building, designed to accommodate 300 pupils. During the day this would house the Secondary boys and girls, and in the evening the Technical students. A chestnut tree survived from the old 'White House' garden, and stood in the new school playground, providing shade and conkers for a generation of pupils, until it was unceremoniously uprooted in 1936 to make way for engineering workshops. In 1938, after all the Secondary children had moved either to Alexandra Avenue or

LEFT Section of Ordnance Survey map, 1924, showing the layout of Luton Modern School.
1) the 'Ark'; 2) bicycle sheds; 3) woodwork, music, etc; 4) girls' playground pre-1919;
5) 'The Wheatsheaf' public house.

Bradgers Hill, only the Technical pupils remained at Park Square.

The formal opening of the new school was by Herbrand, 11th Duke of Bedford, on Friday, 1st May, 1908. He was accompanied by Mary, Duchess of Bedford, who had been a Governor of the school from its inception. The ceremony was described at length in *The Luton News* for 7th May, 1908. We quote:

'The buildings have been erected by the Bedfordshire County Council, under whose jurisdiction in all matters of higher education Luton remains and in whose control the school is vested. No better indication of the fact that the new school is a county institution could be needed, perhaps, than the presence at the opening ceremony of representatives from all parts of the county.

The large central hall of the new school (measuring 64 feet by 36 feet), provides seating accommodation for some hundreds of people, but it was not large enough to seat all who had obtained invitations to the ceremony, and, when the Duke of Bedford, attended by representatives of the County Council, the Borough and the School Governors, stepped on to the platform prepared to hand over the keys to the Governors, the two circular galleries, in addition to the body of the hall, were crowded. His Grace took the chair, and was supported by the Mayor (Cllr. Harry Arnold), Mr S. Howard Whitbread, MP (Chairman of the Beds. Education Committee), Mr Rowland E. Prothero (Chairman of the School Governors), Councillor George Warren, JP, Mr W.W. Marks (Clerk of the Beds. County Council), Mr T.A.E. Sanderson, MA, (Headmaster), and Mr Frank Spooner, BA (Secretary to the Governors).'

The newspaper recorded the names of more than a hundred special guests, which included Bedfordshire and Luton councillors, local dignitaries, clergy, headteachers and representatives of the architects and contractors (Messrs. A. Lewin and Son of Kettering). The scholars and teaching staff filled the galleries. After a brief speech the Duke of Bedford declared the building open and handed the key to Mr Prothero,

'In the confident expectation that the Governors would administer the School, on behalf of the County Council, with energy and with success to the very great profit and advantage of the inhabitants of the southern portion of the county.'

In reply, Rowland Prothero observed that:

'They had spent some four years in temporary premises. In that time they had gathered around them a staff of teachers who were second to none, even in Bedfordshire, which was famous for its educational establishments. The organising power and directing ability of the Headmaster and the zeal and enthusiasm of his assistants had laid the foundations firmly for their future advance.'

Prothero explained to the pupils that it was within their power to 'create an atmosphere in which nothing mean, cowardly, despicable, nothing that could not bear the light of day should thrive or find existence.' He hoped that they would remember the school with gratitude 'for the strength and firmness it had given to their moral character.' He told the parents that giving their children a sound education was the 'best commercial investment' they could make and he pleaded with employers to give the young people a chance to develop their talents, to become better sons and daughters, husbands and wives, fathers and mothers, citizens 'of no mean city' and custodians 'of a mighty Empire'.

Councillor George Warren noted that this was a high day, something some of them had been dreaming about for a number of years, and now their dreams had been realised.

'He was glad it had been pointed out that the institution was erected not only for Luton but for South Beds. There seemed to be an idea that the Modern School was intended specifically for Luton, but that was not so. Facilities had been provided for scholars to come in from the villages and towns outside Luton. He hoped it would be well understood that they did not desire in the least to injure the excellent work that was being done at the Dunstable Grammar School under Mr Thring.'

'After the opening ceremony the principal guests were entertained at the Town Hall by the Governors of the School. Slaters, the well-known caterers of Park Square, were entrusted with the arrangements, and the manner in which they carried them through reflected upon them the greatest credit. The entrance hall was very prettily decorated, and, in the Council Chamber, the effective arrangement of a buffet along the whole length of the Chamber, and the placing of charmingly decorated tea tables about the room, gave it a very inviting appearance. The Duke of Bedford and a large number of out-of-town visitors enjoyed the dainty spread.'

The New Building Described

From *The Luton News*, 7th May, 1908:

'A large number of the guests then took advantage of the opportunity given to all to inspect the buildings, and on every hand expressions of admiration were heard. The great central hall, which stands in the heart of the Park Square block, and covers quite half the ground floor, was greatly admired. Few members failed to ascend to the first and second balconies which surround the hall, and from those eminencies gained a bird's-eye view of the animated scene below. The splendid

lighting of the hall also called for much comment. Daylight pours in through glass in the slopes and in the ends of the roof, and yet further streams of light filter in through the glass doors and partitions that shut off the class-rooms from the central hall.

'Great interest was also taken in the class-rooms which surround the central hall. A full description of these may be interesting. In the front of the building, on the ground floor are the physical laboratories, the physical lecture room, and a class-room. To the rear are also three class-rooms of similar type, two of which may be thrown into one by opening double, sound-proof sliding doors. On the floor above, the arrangement of class-rooms is almost identical, but the rooms open on to a spacious balcony instead of on to the floor of the central hall. Similarly, on the next floor, there are six class-rooms. Four of them, however, are for special purposes. Two of the three overlooking Park Street are fitted with a chemical laboratory and a chemical lecture-room. The laboratory is fitted with a heavy concrete floor, and is fitted with benches for chemical experiments. Two of these three class-rooms, which overlook the rear playgrounds, and have a north-easterly aspect, have been fitted especially as art rooms.

'Without exception the class-rooms throughout the building are splendidly lighted by extensive windows. But, in this respect, the art rooms have been very specially favoured. Massive plate-glass windows provide the maximum of north-easterly light – the light most favourable to art class work – and ensure a minimum of shadow.

'Experts, who were certainly well represented amongst the visitors, were struck mostly by the fact that everything has not been sacrificed to provide a school of well-lighted class-rooms. In a truly extraordinary manner, every inch of space has been utilised, and the Headmaster, the male and female teachers, the stationery and general office staff, and the caretaker, are all provided with suitable rooms for their special purposes. There are also separate boys' and girls' entrances, leading from Park Street by lengthy corridors to washing-rooms, cloak-rooms, and lavatories.

'To illustrate the methodical attention to detail in the new school, every class-room has been fitted with a bell, attached electrically to the school clock, which will ring automatically at the beginning and end of every lesson.

'Much attention was also given to the playgrounds, at the rear of the main block of buildings, in which a manual block has also been erected. This block consists of four rooms – two on the upper floor for cookery and needlework, and two on the ground floor for woodwork. The upper rooms are only accessible from the girls' side of the main building by an asphalted, covered way. Similarly, the woodwork rooms can only be approached from the boys' side.'

By 1933 the ground-floor of an out-building known as the 'Ark' had been relegated to hold the school's entire stock of text-books, with, above, a mixture of class-room, museum, library and secondary dining-room.

At the end of 1908 the insurance for the new building and its fittings was set at £8,000, with the movable furniture, books, maps and utensils, etc., insured for £2,000. The premium for the £10,000 being £7.10s.0d. per annum.

The Headmaster summed the new building up succinctly when he observed that 'It was designed for use rather than beauty, and proved a great boon after our temporary home which had by that time become inconveniently crowded.'

The children moved over from the old temporary building on the opposite side of Park Square on the following Monday, 4th May, 1908, and it is recorded that on that opening day every one of the 170 pupils on the books was present. The report in *The Luton News* added: 'The children all wore the regulation head-gear, the girls in their wide-brimmed 'boaters', each trimmed with a black band and badge, looking very smart. The boys, all wearing dark caps and badges, also looked much smarter than in the old days, when any kind of tweed cap might be seen. Most of the girls wore cream blouses and red scarves ornamented with the school crest. Parents present at the opening ceremony on Friday probably noticed the effectiveness of this costume.'

Although the new school opened in May, the school kitchen was not ready until September. Regular cookery lessons then began for girls of certain forms, and school dinners were cooked by the girls for about twenty out-of-town pupils at a weekly cost of half-a-crown for four dinners. Casual diners were charged at 9d. a meal. These meals consisted of meat and two vegetables followed by a sweet or pudding of some sort. Grace was always said in Latin by the Headmaster.

At the first assembly of every new term Mr Sanderson read the lesson from *Ecclesiastes* which reminds the over-zealous student that 'of making many books there is no end and much study is a weariness of the flesh.' F.M. Edwards and C.C. Bennett had clear memories of Prayers in the Assembly Hall,

'An electric bell rang for morning assembly, when all the scholars filed out of their classrooms into the main Hall. Girls occupied one half of the Hall, the boys the other half, lady teachers flanking the girls and the masters in their gowns with the boys. When all were in position and steady – and complete silence reigned – the headmaster entered in mortarboard and gown.

'The girls did most of the singing, the boys only joining in when obscure references to football, such as "Our defence is sure" were noted. A powerful American organ, or harmonium, was operated by a master named Jordan, a musician of no mean ability, with a flair for dramatic illustrations. Suitable effects were introduced for "Chariots of Wrath the deep thunderclouds form", which were deeply appreciated. But when a hymn, one line of which ran, "And Jordan rolled

between" was to be sung, a pre-arranged effort engineered by the boys, resulted in a sudden and terrific shout which quite drowned that organ . . . !'

[Mr Jordan taught geography, science and maths at Park Square from 1908–16]

What is it in the morning
Makes such a pandemonium,
An instrument of torture? Why
The jolly old harmonium.

[E.O. Payne]

Miss Jane Macfarlane, (teacher 1907–19) wrote in 1961:

'Memories of those days are innumerable – an elderly mistress with a high lace collar kept up by a wicked piece of whalebone behind each ear [Miss Gardner perhaps?]. How difficult it was to persuade the girls that tunics should only reach just to the knees. Black woollen stockings were worn, with a real Luton 'boater' on top of long hair. No boy was to be seen without his school cap.

'Now physical training began in earnest, the girls in the Hall, and the boys in the playground under the traditional sergeant-major.

'Before long the school acquired a playing field in Trapp's Lane (Cutenhoe Road), part of this is now the Memorial Park. Here the girls played tennis and hockey, and the boys cricket and football. When a match was 'away' we travelled by train or by horse-drawn brake, the driver of which often had some mysterious and urgent business at the various inns along the route! Alas, when World War I began, part of the field was ploughed up for potatoes and we spent hours clearing the ground of stones.

'You were very fortunate if your form-room was at the back of the school, where you could fling windows open wide and all was quiet. Although there were few motors then, the front of the school was very noisy, especially on Market Day. Then the various stall-holders vied with each other in selling their wares – a china plate would smash – cattle would be driven by – horses' hooves clattered along the road – all very disturbing.'

Luton's new tram system had opened only three months before the new School, on 27th February, 1908, and the cars clanked past the building all day. A street and cattle market were held in Park Square every Monday, and the annual cattle fairs held on the third Mondays in April and October. His Majesty's Inspectors visited the school in March 1909, and also observed that:

The whole School photographed at the rear of the new building in 1908.

'The great noise made by the electric tram-cars and other vehicles passing along in front of the school tends in a serious degree to impair the effectiveness of the teachers' work. It would be a very great advantage if the roadway in front of the school and to a distance of thirty to forty yards on either side could be paved with wood blocks. Perhaps the Governors would approach the Town Council on the question . . . The school is much in need of a general library and of a teachers' reference library; both should be regarded as indispensable. The books might be accumulated gradually . . . It is unfortunate that more liberal provision for storage purposes was not made when the new school was built.'

Looking back in 1951, Arthur B. Allen asked:

'How many now recall old Lucas, standing outside the school gate, selling ice-cream in the summer and hot roast chestnuts in the winter, and in that betwixt and between period, when it was neither hot nor cold for more than two days together, Old Lucas with his barrow – divided carefully into two, with ice-cream at one end and baked chestnuts all piping hot at the other? The days of initiative and enterprise have gone.'

In 1959 Rex Clayton recalled his forty-three years association with the School. He expressed his amazement that boys no longer indulged in playground games like 'truss' and 'pokey-eye'. Only football seemed to have survived the generation gaps.

'During the dinner hour we enjoyed our football. Between the boys' and girls' playgrounds was a cleft oak fence in the middle of which was a gate, which for obvious reasons was never opened, but which made an admirable goal at that end. At the classroom end was an ancient acacia tree which did quite well for one post of a goal, but we had to improvise another. Just junior to me was a tall boy, "Nanny" Calder, who was a real sport but played no games. We persuaded him to stand throughout the dinner hour and act as the other goal post, which he consented to do provided he could read. On many occasions we collided with our human goal post and down he and his book would go, yet he continued to oblige us.'

Prior to the move to the new building the school had always been known as the Luton Secondary Day School. In February 1908 Alderman Rowland Prothero persuaded the County Council to seek permission to amend the name of the School to 'King Edward VII School, Luton', although some, like Cllr. Osborne, thought that 'Luton Modern School' would be preferable. It was agreed to seek royal consent, with the proviso that if it was not forthcoming, 'Luton Modern School' would be chosen. It was generally assumed that the King's name would be adopted, and it

The exterior of Luton Modern School, Park Square, photographed prior to its opening in 1908, by T.G. Hobbs. (*LM*)

came as something of a shock when the formal invitations to the school's opening bore the name 'Luton Modern School'. It was stated on good authority that the refusal was the outcome of a belief among the King's advisers that there were already a sufficiency of King Edward's Schools. Unfortunately, the enterprising local publisher and photographer T.G. Hobbs jumped the gun in 1907 when he published, in his picture book *Luton and its Neighbourhood Illustrated*, a photograph of the unopened building, captioned 'King Edward VII School Building, Park Square'.

In the summer of 1908 the School Fees were changed to £2 per term inclusive of Books, Stationery, Games, etc. The Headmaster tactfully reminded the Governors that when he was appointed, they had promised to review his salary once the new School had opened. He requested an increase to £400, rising by annual increments to £600, in line with London County Council salaries.

Staff and Governors in the Early Years

Over the years staff came and went. Some stayed for a short while but others were there long enough to make their mark and to become part of the history of the school. Of the original staff, the Headmaster, Thomas A.E. Sanderson (1904–33), Mr Frederick F. May (1904–36) and Mr William Otter (1904–33), stayed for the longest time. Mr Otter came out of retirement from 1941–44 to help during the wartime staff shortage. Also from the original staff, Mr John B. Hoblyn, Head of sciences, left in 1915 to become chief chemist for Vauxhall Motors. A report by HM Inspector Mr F.W. Westaway of September 1915 observed that 'an investigation into the teaching of languages is needed', and in April 1916 a further report indicated that heads had to roll: Mr Edmunds was asked to leave; Miss Gardner's position to be reviewed, and Miss Macfarlane allowed to stay. Not a word of this leaked into the public domain. Mr E.W. Edmunds and Miss C.S. Gardner left in July and December 1916 respectively. Edmunds, the Second Master, specialised in sciences and English, and was described as a 'black-bearded, slim, scholarly gentleman. His voice was gentle and he was inclined to lisp. He could also be very angry.' John M. Forbes came to teach mathematics in 1909 and remained until 1939, except for a period of military service during the 1st World War. He succeeded Mr Edmunds as Second Master. Miss Jane Macfarlane taught French and German at the school in 1907 and left in 1919, rejoining the following year and transferring to the High School. Miss E. St S. Poulton, who joined the staff in 1908, taught English and was made Senior Mistress in 1910, leaving in 1918. Miss Daisy C. Rose began in 1912 and moved to the Girls' Modern School in 1919. Mr Ernest J. Taylor came to teach German and French from 1912 to 1930. Born with a silver spoon in his mouth, well read and travelled, but not trained for teaching, Sanderson saw his appointment as something of a gamble that paid off. 'During the war he worked strenuously at cultivating the School field, so strenuously that I thought he enjoyed the work though I found out afterwards that it was done much against the grain.' Mr A.P. Frost, known to the boys as 'Happy', came to help the Head teach mathematics in 1913 and stayed until 1942. James W. Findlater joined the staff in 1916 to teach history and English. Officially retiring in 1945, he taught part-time at the Grammar School until 1950. Other members of staff who moved to the girls' school were Miss V.M. Barnes (1917–19), Miss M.M. Netherwood (1917–19) and Miss A.L. Price (1918–19). Miss F.M. Jackson (1918–20), the new Senior Mistress, was an unsuccessful applicant for the headship of the girls' school and was the only female member of staff given permission to remain at the Boys' School. She went on to take up the post of Senior Mistress at Redlands School, Bristol. From 1916 to 1918 former pupil Lucy Stafford returned to teach Maths, Latin and Botany at the School.

Edith Webb's reminiscences of the staff in 1917 are more colourful:

The Staff, 1908. *Standing*: F.F. May (art), Miss E. Webb, Mr W. Otter (woodwork), Mr G.J. Denbigh (science), Miss J. Macfarlane, Mr J. Bygott (English, mathematics), Miss E. St S. Poulton. *Seated*: J.B. Hoblyn (science), Miss C.S. Gardner (senior mistress), T.A.E. Sanderson (headmaster), E.W. Edmunds (senior master), A. Kirsch (French, German). (*LMC*)

'Since it was wartime, the staff had been very much depleted and places were filled by rather unusual characters. Geography was taught by an Irish clergyman, M.W. Thompson, nicknamed 'The Parson', whose temper was very uncertain and who constantly threatened 'to put you down in the book' (detention). 'Granny Wheeler' was a little old lady who crept around. (Miss E.S. Wheeler was only at the school for two months during 1917). In their classes discipline was very lax – a favourite trick of the boys was to make pellets of blotting paper dipped in the ink wells and to catapult them onto the ceiling from the end of a ruler. Other members of staff were of sterner stuff. 'Ma' Bell (Miss C.B. Bell) taught Geometry. She wore a green velvet dress, had flaming red hair and a temper to match. Mr E.J. Taylor taught German. He was red-haired also and had a violent temper. I heard much later that he 'came into money' and was taken to school in a chauffeur-driven Rolls

Royce! Miss C.K. Thomas (languages) was a diminutive Welsh woman – a strict disciplinarian who had even the tallest boy under her thumb. Freddie May taught art and was invariably dressed in ginger-coloured Harris tweed. Miss C.D. Rose took gym in the hall. The equipment consisted of a few balls, bean bags and benches. Needlework and cookery classes taught by Miss H.G. Forsaith were held in a small building in the playground known as the 'Ark'.'

Looking back in 1954, T.A.E. Sanderson wrote in *The Bedfordshire Magazine*:

'What I owe to the staff would take too much space to describe in detail, but I must mention Mr. J.B. Hoblyn who was responsible for our early scholarship successes, and Mr Forbes who was able to imbue his colleagues with a co-operative spirit which before his time (1908) was sometimes conspicuously absent. I was lucky, too, in the chairmen under whom I worked. First Lord Ernle (R.E. Prothero), whose principle was that the man at the wheel should be interfered with as little as possible; then Mr H.O. Williams, who always consulted me before each Governors' meeting; and lastly Mr Harry Arnold, who never gave me any trouble at all. Then there was HM Inspector, Mr F.W. Westaway, whose visits I always cordially welcomed. Discussions with him usually ended with one of us converting the other to his point of view; in the rare cases where we failed to agree he would always leave the final decision to me, saying that I knew more about local conditions than he did. Last, but by no means least, I must mention my secretary, Mr H.J. Jeffs, who came to me straight from school and served me faithfully for some 25 years. No hours were too long for him, no tasks too exacting. I owe him more than I can say.'

Charles Wareham added a postscript: 'No one ever got to see Mr Sanderson without passing John Jeffs' scrutiny!'

Mention should perhaps be made at this point of Mr Andrews, the second School Caretaker, and Skylark, his deaf and dumb assistant. The latter's Emporium was the broom-and-bucket shed by the rear entrance to the boys' cloakroom.

In January, 1908, a revised Scheme of Management was drawn up for Luton Secondary School. It contained some 27 clauses, which ranged from defining the School's function: 'for the supply of education, other than elementary, to boys and girls,' to setting rules for the Governors. It listed the Governors who were to serve until 31st March, 1910 as follows:

Appointed by the Bedfordshire County Council:
Her Grace the Duchess of Bedford
W.T. Lye, Esq.
R.E. Prothero, Esq.

W.R. Phillips, Esq.
R.Richmond, Esq.
H.O. Williams, Esq.

Appointed by Luton Town Council:
    Ald. E. Oakley, Esq.
    A.A. Oakley, Esq.
    C.H. Osborne, Esq.
    J.H. Staddon, Esq.
    G. Warren, Esq.
    A. Wilkinson, Esq.

Co-opted:
    Mrs Pilling
    Miss A. Walmsley
    W.R. Hawson, Esq.

- On 21st April, 1910, and in every third year following, the representative Governors are to hold a meeting for the purpose of appointing the co-optative Governors, and a retiring Governor, whether representative or co-optative is to be eligible for appointment or co-option.
- If in any year the Town Council fail to contribute the proceeds of a 1d. rate towards the support of the School, the Governors appointed by the Town Council are to cease to hold office.
- Five Governors are to form a quorum and the Chairman is to have the casting vote.
- The Director of Education is to act as Secretary to the Governors.
- The Governors, (subject to approval by the County Council), are to prescribe the general subjects of instruction, the fees to be paid by scholars, and the age for the award of scholarships and for admission of pupils.
- The appointment of the Headmaster is to be determinable by three months' notice on either side, but the notice, when given by the Governors is only to be given in pursuance of a resolution of two-thirds of the Governors present at a meeting.
- The Governors are to frame their financial estimates in November for submission to the County Council at the end of November.

The staff of the Modern School were naturally concerned about their salaries. In 1913, certain members of staff had attended a meeting with the Governors in order to appeal for a rise. Mr Edmunds spoke on their behalf. He reminded the governors of the importance of the school to the life of the town and claimed that the standard

of work done there was as high, and measured by average was probably higher than that done at the Bedford Modern School (where some masters were said to earn more than £250 p.a.). Edmunds then went on to ask them to recognise the dignity of the teaching profession and the high standard of personal life and character which was expected of them, pointing out that the next generation would reap the benefit of their 'high character' and 'expert knowledge'.

The following salary scales will not make happy reading for women of the 21st century, but unequal pay for teachers was par for the course until the middle of the 20th century.

			Minimum	Maximum
1908				
Men	graduates		£150 x £5	£180
	non-graduates		£120 x £5	£150
Women	graduates		£120 x £5	£150
	non-graduates		£100 x £5	£125
1914				
Men			£150 x £10	£200
Women			£120 x £10	£160
1917				
Men				£220
Men with special responsibilities				£280
Women				£180
1918				
Men			£200 x £10	£360
Women			£160 x £10	£300

(These amounts included special War bonuses)

Teachers in Training

At the beginning of the twentieth century the pupil teacher system was still the main route taken by girls and boys who wished to become teachers. The first step was to become a monitor in an elementary school. Those who were judged to be competent could then be apprenticed as pupil teachers. This meant that they would have to teach for up to 25 hours a week, but were also to receive tuition themselves. From 1897 instruction was provided at the Pupil Teacher Centre in Waller Street, Luton, at first under Mr T.E. Wargerison, MA, and from 1899 from Mr J.H. Hargreaves.

At the conclusion of their apprenticeship, pupil teachers could become uncertificated teachers or, if they had obtained the Queen's (or King's) Certificate, progress to a Training College.

One of the criticisms of the pupil teacher system was that boys and girls received all their instruction within the elementary school system and then went on to work in that same system. Critics claimed that a secondary education would produce a better class of teacher and everything began to change when secondary education was provided. The first effect was that monitors were admitted to the secondary school on half fees; in 1904 three boys and 11 girls were allowed this concession. A concession it may have been, but parents whose children had been earning ten shillings a week as monitors, were now faced with the need to feed and clothe them as well as finding fees. Nellie Breed, whose father was Headmaster at Stopsley, and had himself come up through the pupil teacher system, was one of the first pupils to benefit, and passed her London matriculation in July 1908.

In 1908 the Bedfordshire Education Committee complied with government legislation and began the student teacher scheme. Instead of trainee teachers coming through the elementary system, they had to come from secondary schools. Maybe this was an improvement in some respects but the door was firmly slammed in the faces of girls and boys who were unable to go to the secondary school for whatever reason. From 1908, Luton Modern School was involved in this scheme. Pupils who committed themselves to teacher training became Bursars. This meant that they received grants during their last year at school and then began their training as student teachers under the auspices of the Bedfordshire County Council.

In July 1908 the Pupil Teacher Centres in Bedford and Luton were closed. During the eleven years of its existence, the Waller Street Centre had taken 200 students, of whom 168 were known to be teaching, including 44 who had also had College training.

Sports and Games 1904–1919

Recalling the opening years of the school, Mr Sanderson observed: 'The school curriculum made no provision for games: they were not even mentioned. This did not trouble me. I held, and still hold the opinion that games and classroom work should be quite distinct, and in no circumstances should the former be allowed to interfere with the latter.' Later he claimed that this was a mistake and looked forward to a time when games would form an integral part of the school curriculum, where everyone would be obliged to take part unless they had an exemption on medical grounds. In a retrospective article written twenty years after his retirement he seems to have reverted to his original opinion. He noted that 'soccer was started, mainly because the father of one of our boys, Mr Facer, was kind enough to lend us a field for the purpose.' In spite of Sanderson's misgivings, games, which were played on

Wednesdays and Saturdays, soon became an established part of school life. They were compulsory on Wednesday afternoons, (officially designated a half-holiday), but not on Saturdays unless you were part of a school team. Ronald Phillips has recorded that on Sports Day the Head was keenly interested in the timing of the various events and did not approve if the programme was not completed in its allotted span. With other out-of-school activities he had little sympathy, so that during his regime very few clubs or societies existed.

As already mentioned the school's first official playing field from 1906 was at Beech Hill, (Dunstable Road), but in 1908 Sir Julius Wernher of Luton Hoo provided a site, on favourable terms, off Trapp's Lane (now Cutenhoe Road), in West Hill Road. This was to be the School's recognised Sports Ground until 1922, when Lady Wernher gave the land to the Borough of Luton as a Park, in memory of her son Alexander Pigott Wernher, of the 1st Welsh Guards, who was killed in action in 1916.

> 'Games at Trapp's Lane (West Hill) made steady, if slow, progress. Tennis courts were laid; and a cricket pitch was levelled; and for several years we were able to engage a cricket professional for the summer months.'

Drill Instructors were appointed for the first time in September 1910: Miss C. Howland for the girls, and Major J.H. Plummer for the boys. Previously Physical Exercises had been superintended by various members of the teaching staff.

> 'At one time a pompous old fellow whom we addressed as "Major" took us for drill. Endeavouring to "give the boot" to one lad named Merritt, who failed to put enough sparkle into his drill, the "major" fell backwards on his posterior. Our squad spluttered with laughter.'

The First World War upset the sports programme for several reasons. The masters who took the keenest interest in games were the first to enlist: Drill Instructor J.H. Plummer, Mr J.M. Forbes, and Mr Ernest I. Barrow who was killed in France in 1916. Sergeant Major C. Kitchener was appointed Drill Instructor from 1917–18 on the grounds that since he had been a machine-gunner during the War he would be better able to control the boys!

Speaking at Speech Day in March 1919, Mr Sanderson observed:

> 'In 1914 the military took possession of our field for trench-digging, and of the hut which served as a cricket pavilion. This hut came to an untimely end, being mysteriously burned to the ground one Saturday evening. The President of the Board of Agriculture was appealing to the Country to increase food-production, so a portion of the field was ploughed and planted with potatoes. Many of the boys

did good work, first in erecting a fence, and later in trenching a part of the ground. The venture didn't appeal to them quite as forcibly as I could have wished, but we succeeded in lifting some five or six tons of potatoes; enough to supply the school kitchen for a year and leave a considerable quantity for disposal. Thus for a time games have been practically in abeyance. Moreover the restricted train-service necessitated the abandoning of the mid-week half-holiday; and this alone did much to dampen athletic enthusiasm.'

After the War there was no man on the staff officially responsible for boys' drill, physical education or games until the appointment of Mr H.H. Horseman in 1924. The girls were not effected; Miss C.D. Rose being responsible for their sporting activities from 1912 to 1919.

School Houses
From 1913 the boys were divided into four Houses for inter-house sports: these were somewhat innocuously named Bees (yellow), Grasshoppers (green), Hornets (brown) and Wasps (red).

How these names were chosen remains a mystery. C. Wynne Parry, writing in 1954, quoted 'one popular theory, that during a discussion on naming the Houses one Governor said: "My name begins with a B; let's call one house the Bees." Upon this the other Houses are said to have received their names by analogy.

'Such stories are usually apocryphal. There may be more in the unflattering theory that someone, believing that schoolboys are unpleasant creatures, found the names of hostile creatures to suit them,' – though one can hardly call grasshoppers hostile!

The girls had three Houses for hockey named after birds, Pelicans (purple), Eaglets (green) and Ravens (orange).

Football
The School opened its doors in September, 1904, and before the end of October had formed its first football club. Difficulties were swept aside: a school without a football team was somewhat anomalous, a character and reputation had to be made, and on a precious but diminutive piece of ground in Crescent Road the boys set about their task. How long, they wondered, would it take to match themselves against the older schools in the district?

S.J. Stone was the first school football captain; but he left the school early, and was succeeded by A.L. Gilder who left a good name behind him both as a player and as a captain. He had a keen and capable vice-captain in A.T. Wheeler; and as club secretary O.E. Hart was superb. The first elevens that represented the school set a good standard to their successors, playing the game cleanly and pluckily.

Very few matches were lost in the first season, though Dunstable Grammar

The School Football Team, 1910-11. (Staff) E.W. Edmunds, A. Jordan, G.J. Denbigh, W. Otter, (back) H.G. Brightman, R.W. McAdam, J.H. Ireland (goalkeeper), L.A. Maynard, E. Allen (waistcoat), (middle) A.J. Bazeley, T.L. Few, G.L. Bond, F. Smith, W.L. Turney, (front) R.E. Otter, H.W. Few. (Mrs Cheesborough)

School 'A' team beat them thoroughly three times. As a contrast they went to St Albans and trounced the school there 24–0, everyone in the team scoring except one of the halfbacks!

In the 1905–6 season they succeeded in beating Dunstable Grammar School 'A' team on their own ground, but lost to Dagmar House School at Hatfield by 4–3. When the return match with Hatfield was played at Luton in driving rain, the opponents walked off the field halfway through the second half because they disagreed with one of the referee's decisions!

The following season the move to the sports ground at Beech Hill, with the luxury of a small pavilion, gave the team a new impetus. This became evident in 1907–8 with the best season to date. More boys began to take part, perhaps helped by the first official School jerseys: blue with red and gold collars and cuffs.

In September 1908 the School moved to the new ground in West Hill Road and there was ample room for expansion. A Form Competition was introduced and a

The School Football Team, 1913–14. Mr G.J. Denbigh; boys (not in order) F.J. Lacey, C.T. Barnard, A. Farrar, A.W. Brodie, W.M. Summerbee, G.A. Powell, R.C. Morsley, R.S. Clayton (captain), F.M. Leighton, R.J. Verran, C.E. Robinson (front left), C.F. Coles.

School 'league' formed in which almost every boy in the School took part.

In the 1909–10 season, the school team was led by S.J. Simpson and was rather on the light side, the opposition invariably being bigger and heavier, resulting in many defeats. 'What boy who played against St Saviour's, when the School lost by 11–1, could ever forget the size and weight of the men who administered such a heavy defeat? In the match with the Old Boys the School was overweighted and defeated. But this match provided another landmark. For the first time it was celebrated by a tea, generously provided by the Headmaster!'

In 1914 the team's defeats were the lowest on record. They only played one game during the season, and that was stopped by rain! Although there were many boys keen to play, it appears that there were not always enough enthusiastic supporters, judging from this appeal from Frank Facer in the *School Magazine* in 1913.

'It is not the boys who play who are at fault; because who can deny that the play is generally full of enthusiasm? But where are the supporters? Why, even at the last

match there were not half a dozen boys down at the pitch; and again at the Hitchin match there were, in fact, more masters than boys looking on . . . Now, this is not the state of affairs which should exist, and I think it is quite time the lower school should rally and help the School to obtain as good a name on the sports-field as it holds for school-work.'

The War was to have a devastating effect on the School's football. Someone signing himself "Passiton" wrote a scathing article for the *School Magazine*:

'The Art of football at School has disappeared since the War began. Matches arranged at School have been played only amongst the "Inner Circle". No encouragement has been given to the Juniors, therefore it is not likely that they would care anything for the game. During matches there have generally been about five of six captains to a side, and each wants his own way. According to this, the way to become an XI Captain is to have a big voice, strut about showing yourself to the youngsters (who do the voting) and generally well-advertise yourself. The way to obtain a place in a team is to hang around the Football Committee, calling them by their Christian names, and propose other fellows as being footballers, then they will remember you.

'The "Old Boys" were the fellows who founded our School football; they began badly at first, and triumphed later. They succeeded because they agreed to play together, and not for themselves alone. Let not their efforts be in vain. Come Moderns, buck up, let us have the old fighting spirit back again. Nowadays boys have done nothing but slack. And what is the alternative use a fellow wishes to make of his time? Getting on a bike armed with a muslin net, and catching "bugs"! Is this a true picture of a Modern boy? I fear that it is, and it makes the outlook for school games, such as cricket and football, a very gloomy one. Come, it is not too late; let us turn into the old and proper paths, and above all, learn to put "the School" before our own miserable selves.'

One cannot help but sympathise with those hundreds of bug-hunters who, throughout the school's existence, found kicking a bladder of air around for an hour, an utterly futile and mind numbing exercise!

It is probably unwise to name names because it is impossible to do justice to everybody, but perhaps a few boys who made an impression on the football field could be mentioned: F. Facer, R.S. Clayton (later to join the school staff), G.L. Bond, F.M. Leighton, C.E. Child, F.C. Creak, J. and D. Grice, and H.F. Small. Apart from inter-house games and matches against Old Boys, the school XI also played against Dagmar House School at Hatfield, Hitchin Grammar School, St Albans Grammar School, Dunstable Grammar School, Westbourne Football Club, Vauxhall Juniors, Crescent Football Club, as well as other clubs.

Cricket

The beginnings of school cricket were fraught with difficulties. The lads were all 'new boys' and the first task was to find out who could play. In many cases, theirs was not always cricket of the orthodox style! A major difficulty was to get equipment and to find a ground. The first season in 1905 consisted mostly of practice on the Moor with the aid of a few stumps and borrowed bats. Surprisingly, by the end of the summer they had developed into a very fair side. The next year they were able to play at Faunch's Farm in Old Bedford Road with better equipment. The boys put in hours of hard labour to get the pitch into good condition, and benefited from the coaching of Messrs. E.W. Edmunds, J.B. Hoblyn and C.W. Hutchinson. The team was well assorted, with fast and slow bowlers, sloggers and stone wallers, and all madly keen on their cricket. Actual matches were few, their main opponents being Bury Park Club and Dagmar House School at Hatfield.

Cricket was soon taken very seriously and, prior to the first World War, the services of a professional coach were made available. Accounts in the *School Magazine* give blow-by-blow records of matches and there are detailed lists of batting averages. The masters were also keen and played in their own team against the boys. Although the school had a cricket pitch at Trapp's Lane (West Hill) until about 1920 and from 1925 at Chaul End, they quite often played home matches on the better prepared upper sports ground at Wardown Park. During the wet summer of 1912 they had net practice for the first time, with extra evening coaching. Also that season the Chairman of the School Governors, Mr Prothero, invited the team to his home beside the Ouse at Oakley to play cricket against his village team, and enjoy an afternoon of boating, swimming and refreshments in a beautiful garden.

By 1916 the war was having an adverse effect on the cricket season. The team had no professional coach and the boys had to do the best they could for themselves with help and advice from the masters. It was observed that 'as a whole the boys are small in size and possess little knowledge of the finer points of the game. However there is no lack of energy and enthusiasm, and many of the house matches have proved extremely exciting.'

As well as house matches, the boys also played against St Albans Grammar School, Hitchin Grammar School, Forman's Cricket Club, Luton Town Cricket Club and the Old Boys.

Athletics

Sports Days tended to be held on Wednesday or Saturday; sometimes the boys' and girls' sports were held on the same day, but as more and more events were introduced different days were often selected.

The first detailed record of the Modern School Boys' Sports Day was 3rd May, 1913, at which Frank Facer won the Senior Championship Medal by winning the 100 yards, 440 yards and long jump. He came 2nd equal in the mile:

'Five started in this event and ran in very close order until the last lap; then on rounding the dip every one made a fine spurt and in a splendid race home Lacey stayed longest and won by three yards, while the proverbial hair separated the next three. Seamark ran very pluckily and was not far behind. (Time: 6 min. 14 secs.)'

The full programme of events that year consisted of:
100 yards, 220 yards, 440 yards, one mile, long jump, high jump, throwing the cricket ball, slow bicycle race (50 yards), obstacle race, Old Boys' race, House relay, and house tug-of-war.

Better weather the following year allowed the Boys' and Girls' Sports to be run on the same day. W.F. Summerbee was the Senior Boys' Champion, and for the second year running Dorothy Burley the Girls' Champion.

'The boys' obstacle race provided much amusement; the custard supplied with the apples proving rather too burnt for most of the competitors, seemed to be the most difficult obstacle; indeed the first arrival at these choice dishes could not make up his mind to partake thereof for quite a considerable time.' Winner: H.S. Rentell.

Athletics seems to have got short shrift at the school during the War and there is no record of any special Sports Days being held. As part of the Peace Day celebrations on Thursday 18th September, 1919, all the Luton Senior Schools were invited to 'an excellent Tea' in Luton Hoo Park, followed (somewhat unwisely) by a Sports Day, in which Modern School pupils excelled.

Cross-Country Running
Cross-Country at the Modern School is first recorded in 1914, when it was still known as a 'Paper Chase'. Readers may recall the famous paper chases featured in *Tom Brown's Schooldays* and *The Railway Children*. Two boys, the 'hares', run a course known only to themselves, scattering scraps of torn paper at intervals to mark their route. After a short time a pack of boys, the 'hounds', follow in pursuit and endeavour to catch the hares before they can return to base.

On 21st January, 1914, Rex Clayton and Frank Facer were chosen as hares and wrote in the *School Magazine*:

'We decided upon a circular track, and took our followers between eight and nine miles. We crossed Stockwood Park both on our outward and homeward journeys, and the sprint through the 'Lawn' home was perhaps the most enjoyable part of our run. We arrived home in good time, about half an hour before the first hound – Mr E.I. Barrow.

'One rather amusing incident occurred, when about two miles on our way, we were crossing a ploughed field and were running direct towards a spinney. As we

approached the latter, we ran across a farmer and his son, who were spending the afternoon in their hut pigeon shooting. Naturally enough, the farmer was most indignant at our sudden appearance together with the disappearance of his feathered friends. He commanded us to retreat, which of course would have been disastrous for us and the chase. We entreated him to let us pass, but he was insistent, whereupon we struck off at right angles, and left our 'friend' busily picking up our trail – (a somewhat tedious task, as the trail somehow seemed thicker than usual at that spot,) – he no doubt knew that no sooner had his sport begun again, than the hounds would put in an appearance. His efforts however did not prevent Mr Barrow and his pack from paying him a visit; and intending to pay us out, he unfortunately, (although fortunately for us), sent them off in an opposite direction to the way we had gone. Had it not been for this, no doubt the chase would have been a closer one.'

Hockey

Not to be outdone, the girls played hockey although, if the accounts in the school magazine are to be believed, the standard of play in the early days was not high. Matches were played between the three houses, Pelicans, Eaglets and Ravens.

The School Magazine

A number of references have already been made to the School Magazine, which provides unique material for a history of the establishment. The first issue, called somewhat unimaginatively, *Luton Modern School Magazine*, appeared in December 1912, in a red paper cover, which incorporated the crest with the motto, '*Ubi semen, ibi messis*', and a list of its contents. It then appeared half-yearly, cost sixpence, and was approximately A5 in size. There were advertisements for local firms on the other three cover sides, W. Lacey & Son for clothing, H. White for boots and shoes and S. Farmer and Co., for music. The Editor's name is not given, though it is reasonable to assume that it was E.W. Edmunds, the Senior Assistant and English Master. Printed locally by W.F. Bunker, it was initially published termly, but in order to save paper, no editions were published in 1918, 1921 and 1922.

The aim of the Magazine, as defined in the first issue, was 'to be a record of the life and doings of the school from year to year, so that every pupil shall have a souvenir of his or her school life, which shall be pleasant to look at in after years.' The earlier issues made somewhat confusing reading in that the first 2 or 3 pages were devoted each time to the 'history' of the years before the first publication, *i.e.* 1904–1911. It didn't get sorted out until 1919! Every issue contained brief accounts of each year's progress, the names of new and leaving staff, scholarship winners, and other important items of news. Articles and poems were written by members of staff or pupils, but it is not always possible to identify contributors as initials were used

instead of full names and some were anonymous. When names do appear, girls are given their Christian names, but boys receive only a surname and initials. There is a general impression that more articles were the work of boys than girls.

Articles were often rather long and carefully written. School games and societies are well reported, especially the activities of the Literary and Scientific Society (from 1926). During the First World War military matters were prominent; in themselves providing a powerful social history of the war. There is a strong flavour of patriotism which tends to evaporate in the later years. C. Wynne Parry, reflecting on the magazines in 1978, noticed 'a marked preference for prose rather than poetry. Some of the poetry is, interestingly enough, translation from French poets. Charles d'Orléans: *Le Temps a laissé son manteau*, Villon's *Les Chansons d'Antan*, some Gautier, and Hugo's *Extase*. This fondness for translation returns briefly in the 1940s, with, this time, some odes by Horace.' An article of 1917 on caring for teeth reflects the initiatives which were being introduced into schools to monitor aspects of children's health. Copies of every issue were deposited in Luton Central Library.

Throughout the Magazine's history there seem to have been problems with its marketing and a malaise amongst its intended readers. An Editorial written in March 1913 lamented:

> 'Too many of our pupils are slow in realising their duty to the school. They take little or no interest in the games; they take as much interest in the school magazine. They say it is not worth sixpence! No argument will ever convince such boys or girls that patriotism is one of the highest of human traits; but those who cannot confess to a feeling of loyalty to their school now will never know the larger patriotism of the citizen in after-years.'

That was written only a few months before the outbreak of the First World War, when thirty-nine old boys and three masters would make the ultimate sacrifice!

When the girls moved to Alexandra Avenue they produced their own Magazine, *The Sheaf*, and in due course the Junior Technical pupils had *The Shell*.

Some Administrative Matters

The School received its second Inspection by the Board of Education on the 1st, 2nd and 3rd of November, 1910. This was the first inspection in the new building and was conducted by three HMIs, Mr F. Spencer, Mr F.W. Westaway and Mrs M. Withiel, all of whom seem to have been suitably impressed by what they saw.

By 1912 the number of children on the School Roll stood at 297, compared with 85 pupils in 1904 and 207 in 1908. Numbers were rising rapidly and Sanderson anticipated that there would be more than 300 children within the next two years. It was clear that further accommodation would be urgently needed. With this in

mind in 1913 the Governors, through the County Council, entered into negotiations with Luton Suburban Estates to purchase ten acres of land in Alexandra Avenue, (named after Queen Alexandra) and plans were prepared for a new School for the girls. The outbreak of the First World War brought progress to a standstill and delayed any move until 1919.

Numbers of pupils on roll each September:

Year	Boys	Girls	Total
1904	46	39	85
1905	46	67	113
1906	53	61	114
1907	76	70	146
1908	121	86	207
1909	149	88	237
1910	147	96	243
1911	149	127	276
1912	161	136	297
1913	189	145	334
1914	197	153	350
1915	204	148	352
1916	223	158	381
1917	208	176	384
1918	209	181	390
1919	265		

Most years more boys than girls joined the school. By 1919 the school population of Luton was 7,791, of whom 555 were receiving a secondary education, and of those 474 were in the two Modern Schools.

For the first time since the Modern School was opened, a system of Monitors was established in the Spring of 1915. This was chiefly due to the fact that Major J.H. Plummer, the Drill Instructor, had enlisted, and was no longer available to maintain discipline. Six boys and seven girls were chosen for the task. Mr J.E. Anderson, writing in the *School Magazine*, commented that 'There is much to be said of the value of putting boys in control of boys; the old saying, "set a thief to catch a thief", applies very well in this instance.' At first the Monitors had little power, their duties being mainly confined to traffic control in the Hall and on the staircases. Later they were allowed to give impositions for insubordination. The Monitorial system was deemed a success and in 1916 a further three girls and seven boys were promoted. Sadly one of the boys, David McL. Johnston caught a chill and died of pneumonia on 22nd December, 1916. After the girls had moved to Alexandra Avenue in 1919,

both schools replaced Monitors with Prefects and chose a Head Prefect each year.

> 'The prefects swank. Thompson says that his father says all prefects are the same. Thompson says his father was Head prefect in his school. Perhaps he was and perhaps he wasn't. Anyway, his father says we will be just as bad when we are prefects.'
>
> [Prep. Form]

Discipline in the School seems to have been very strict, largely maintained by the strong personalities of the Head Master and his staff. An imposition or after-school detention seems to have been a suitable deterrent for most pupils, coupled, if very serious, with the threat of a visit to the Head's study for a lecture. There is little indication of the use of corporal punishment. Impositions usually consisted of writing a hundred lines or conjugating French verbs.

Social Life

Concerts and entertainments featured early in the School's life. To celebrate George V's Coronation, on Thursday, 22nd June, 1911, children from all over Luton processed to Luton Hoo, where pupils of the Modern School performed scenes from *A Midsummer Night's Dream* on a temporary stage set-up amongst the trees in the Park. Unfortunately few records exist of this and other performances, and it is not until the publication of the first *Luton Modern School Magazine* in 1912 that we get any comprehensive details.

A series of annual winter concerts began in 1911, of which the second, held in the School Hall on Saturday 16th November, 1912, was described at length by Alice Knight.

> 'For some time prior to the 16th November, we had been delighted during evening preparation by the practising on the piano, by songs and violin solos, by the jingle of tambourines and the tripping of country dancers on the hall platform . . . At last the great day arrived . . . The galleries around the Central Hall were festooned with banners bearing the School badge, and the platform was also tastefully decorated. By 6.30 pm the Hall was packed and our masters were still flitting about in their university caps and gowns when the first item, *The Dance of the Demons*, a pianoforte duet by F.M. Leighton and A.L. Matthews, was announced.
>
> 'Miss C.S. Gardner accompanied two German songs sung by a number of boys and girls. It is hoped that these songs showed the visitors that German is not the harsh and unmusical language most English people think it to be. The first was *Das Ringlein*, and the second a German carol, *Stille Nacht*, which brought visions of Christmastide and thoughts of holidays into the minds of those of us who understood it. The tambourine dance, *Lurline*, which followed, performed by five

Modern School girls and boys (left and centre) gather for the Coronation celebrations in Luton Hoo Park, 22nd June, 1911. All are wearing straw boaters specially provided for the occasion.
(A.E. Bodsworth)

girls, was the liveliest item on our programme . . . and according to the remarks heard on every side it was thoroughly appreciated.

'A scene from Sheridan's *The Rivals* was next presented to us. It was rather a short scene – in fact too short for most of us, who would fain have seen the great duel enacted. Frank Leighton as Bob Acres, and Rex Clayton as Sir Lucius O'Trigger, both acted their parts extremely well. Clayton looked a born fighter of duels and appeared most threatening when pointing the pistol at Bob Acres.'

At this point the Headmaster made a short speech, as did Mr Prothero, the Chairman of the Governors, while Mrs Prothero distributed examination certificates.

After more songs and dancing and a further scene from *The Rivals*, in which:

'Pamela Stafford, as Lydia Languish, proved stubbornly loyal to the lover of her own choosing. Her bosom friend Julia was acted by Marthe Schefer. Gwendolen Amos as Mrs Malaprop was exceedingly good; her 'malapropisms' evoked much laughter. Frank Facer as Sir Anthony Absolute looked an ideal country squire. We shuddered to think of the drastic methods he would employ to force his daughter – if he had one – to comply with his wishes. The National Anthem brought to an end the best concert which has yet been held in the School.'

The following year (1912) the concert was performed twice to some 600 visitors. After a musical introduction, Hilda West:

'Very demurely and with a pretty accent recited one of La Fontaine's fables. The puzzled appearance of some of the younger scholars, as they vainly endeavoured to gather the drift of this piece would have formed a fine study for the camera. The "pièce de résistance" took the shape of a German play by eight boys and girls in Ia. It was not only the easy way and fluency of speaking German that was noticed in *Grossvaterchen und Grossmutterchen*, but also the very natural manner of acting. It was worth a long wait on the Gallery to see Barbara Slatter and C.A. Mowse dressed in their antiquated costumes; and Mowse's fall over the chair, to the great harm of his "churchwarden", was received with loud applause and laughter.'

Mr W.W. Marks, Clerk to the Bedfordshire County Council, was Guest of Honour on that occasion. After he had distributed prizes, an all-girl cast performed scenes from *As You Like It*.

'From the outbreak of War in 1914 all annual school concerts ceased. My memory of these is that the girls looked extremely becoming in their white dresses and red ribbon sashes. Juniors were generally perched on the top galleries at the school and had difficulty in hearing the words of the performers.' [F. M. Edwards – 1912–16]

It is, perhaps, remarkable that in a co-educational school very little is heard of schoolboy and schoolgirl romance. But it was there: F.M. Edwards again:

'During my second year I fell madly in love with a certain young maiden (not in my class). My lessons must have suffered a good deal from lack of concentration. Every day I was happy if only I caught one glimpse of her as we changed classrooms. She was younger than I. Even now as I write I can picture that figure in neat school dress, carrying her books with handkerchief in hand, and dark curled locks. I wonder if life has been kind to her or otherwise. Her school number was 572. At that time I was very shy and sensitive.'

The Modern School gave boys the opportunity to attend the Secondary School-boys' Camp which was held under canvas each year on the Isle of Wight:

'The site,' according to M.S. writing in the *School Magazine* for July 1915, 'leaves nothing to be desired. The ground at the top of a cliff is level and affords good pitches for football, cricket, hockey and squash-racquets. One of the greatest attractions is the bathing, generally held five times a day. I strongly advise those who can to take bicycles because the roads are good, and excellent rides may be had to Sandown, where noted ices and American iced-stone-ginger may be obtained. When you arrive the bicycle is also a great aid in finding a passably smooth place on which to sleep at night: the rule is "first arrive, first choose", and there you have a great advantage over those who have to walk.'

The previous summer G.B. Walkerly had described how the campers had watched the preparations for War, observing crowds of sailors congregating around Portsmouth, where 'two wicked-looking destroyers were coaling.' They watched soldiers digging trenches around a fort near Sandown:

'dashing about with a machine-gun, placing it here, pushing it there, and then digging furiously until they had their gun nicely commanding the bay.

'One evening a friend and I were coming back to camp, and suddenly, "Halt! Who comes there?" and we saw the glint of a bayonet. As we answered correctly, we were allowed to proceed, but only to be challenged twice more in about twenty yards.

'Every day mine-layers were to be seen in the bay, and sometimes torpedo-boats would plough across, but no Germans appeared.

'At night searchlights would come peeping over the hills from Portsmouth, and wander along the coast, while many a sentry strained his eyes for the Germans who never came.'

Another activity during the First World War was the Holiday Competition which was organised because 'doubtless many find that they have a good deal of time to spare during the summer holidays.' Members of the Staff offered book prizes. In 1916, the categories for Senior Pupils in Forms V, IV, IIIa, b, IIa, b, c. were:

1. A sketch of a tea-table (ready laid) or a landscape, in pencil, pen or colour.
2. An original story or poem.
3. (a) *For Boys only*: The wooden part of a Tangent Galvanometer. A model can be seen in Room 17, on application to Mr Denbigh.
   (b) *For Girls only*: A collection of wild flowers, stating their names and where found. All specimens must have been collected during the summer holidays.

The categories for Junior Forms 1a, b, c, d; Pa, b. were:

1. A landscape in pencil, pen, or colour.
2. A description of any entertainment at which the competitor was present.
3. (a) *For Boys only*: A jig-saw puzzle.
   (b) *For Girls only*: A holland workbag of original design, size 16in. x 12in. when finished; or: A doll's hat or bonnet made and trimmed by the competitor.

During the Christmas holiday the tasks were similar but boys could make a 'burette stand' or a piece of fretwork, while the girls might grow daffodil bulbs. The written task for the Juniors was to expand the following story and also choose a suitable title:

A lion casts hungry eyes upon a donkey. A cock, standing by, sets up a vigorous crowing; the lion is startled and runs away. The donkey pursues the lion, and is devoured.

A class in the Art Room (1908), showing a selection of their work, with F.F. May at the rear. The boys at the front of the picture are Claude Bartlett and Fred Morris.

Chapter 3

The Great War
and its Aftermath

When war was declared on 4th August, 1914 a surge of patriotism swept through Britain, engulfing everyone from the youngest children to the oldest citizens. It was to have a profound effect on all those connected with Luton Modern School, who were at that time enjoying their summer holidays.

As soon as War was declared, troops were called up and billeted in schools across southern England. The Modern School was no exception and was occupied until mid-September. The building was left in a filthy and damaged state and it was some days before the children could be re-admitted. There was considerable delay before the School eventually received £99 17s 3d in compensation.

The Editor of the *School Magazine* wrote passionately in the December 1914 issue congratulating the first fifty Old Lutonians who had hastened to respond to their country's call:

> 'The sacrifice which they make, and the danger they incur, are great; but the honour and the privilege are great also. It is rare for an Englishman to have such an opportunity of striking a blow in a cause so just, and so necessary to the welfare of the world.
>
> 'Our enemy . . . has shown himself an unscrupulous and brutal soldier, as well as arrogant and grasping in his international dealings. The German name will be associated for ever with deeds as foul and atrocious as the worst in modern history: the violation of treaties; the devastation of Belgium and the massacre of the civilian population; the barbarous outrages at Louvain, Termonde, Senlis and Rheims; the wholesale looting of private residences; the submarine attacks on hospital ships;

the strewing of mines in neutral waters – these are but a few items that the civilised world has against Germany.

'We shall not, as our Prime Minister has said, sheathe our sword until Germany is compelled, by the only process she can understand, to recognise her duties. Our part in this very necessary task is an important one, and we hope to hear of still more Old Lutonians joining in it.'

To so many boys, in the first few months, the War was a great adventure, and they faced the future with eager anticipation:

'We saw Lieut. Frank Facer, looking fit and well, bowling along on a brand new N.U.T. motor-bike. He pulled up and informed us that he had that very morning made his first official flight in an aeroplane. Facer was always a first class man on the football field and if his flying is anything like his football was, he ought to be able to show the Huns a few tricks.

'We are sorry to hear that Cpl. W.H. Wooding, had a nasty fall from his motor-bike. It appears that he was riding in the neighbourhood of the Suez Canal, when the ground suddenly caved in and Wooding went with it, breaking the frame of his bicycle and experiencing a severe shaking. We hope there were no permanent injuries.'

The Board of Education made it clear to all teachers that in the eyes of the Army Council, teaching was a public service, and therefore grounds for *not* enlisting. In spite of this at least six members of staff felt compelled to join the Old Boys at the front, possibly encouraged by one of the girls, Doris Garside, who wrote this verse for the *School Magazine*:

> O'er England's shores is cast again
> A cloud of strife and war:
> Yet not of war for greed, for gain,
> But justice to restore.
> Your duty and your country call:
> Why tarry then, I pray?
> Why let your comrades for you fall,
> Whilst you at home do stay?

One of the first Masters to rush to the Colours in August 1914 was Ernest I. Barrow, BSc, who had taught maths and science at the school since September 1911. He had entered enthusiastically into school life, taking part in concerts, chairing debates, and playing for the staff football team. When he left to join the Army, he told Sanderson to do what he thought best with his post, but the County Council decided to hold

it open and paid him a salary of £80 a year to supplement his Army pay. He fought with the 2nd East Lancashire Regiment, becoming a Lieutenant.

The *School Magazine* for May 1915 has a piece written by Barrow and called *The Life of a Recruit* in which he describes, with some humour, his Army training.

'We have learnt very thoroughly, and some of us at our cost, that the old adage – "an army fights on its stomach" – is true in more senses than one. To be running and then fall flat, with lightning celerity, while burdened with rifle and pack, needs practice if it is to be done without a severe shaking up.

'One unhappy sight, after a shower of rain, was to be seen scampering madly up a hillside, with a rifle in one hand and a greatcoat in the other. On the word of command to drop, the coat went down first, then the rifle, and lastly the man on top of the coat.

'We know (some of us) what it is to be on night guard, with the rain coming down in sheets, wet through to the skin, with mud over the boot tops, and ¾ of a mile of delightfully slippery mud, traversed by deep trenches, to plough through on the way to and from the guard-hut.

Later he wrote:

'I was slightly wounded the other day, but it is nothing to worry about. A piece of shell casing hit me on the chest. It was considerate enough to hit me flat side on, which was lucky for me. As it was, it knocked me head over heels, raised an enormous bump, and broke a rib. I refused to go into hospital and am still "carrying on". Apart from this little dent in the frame-work I am very fit.'

Rex Clayton wrote in the 1959 issue of *The Lutonian*:

'Mr Barrow, a young Manchester graduate who was as full of mischief as any boy and incidentally was most popular with us all, was left alone in the staff room for the last period on a Friday afternoon where, unseen, he could remove an electric light bulb and put a piece of metal across the terminals, blowing the main fuse, and plunging the whole school into darkness. This continued for the whole of one winter. Boys were suspected but the culprit was never discovered. Knowing Mr Barrow as well as I did, I can imagine how he would enjoy doing it and never being suspected. It was the same enjoyment of living dangerously that caused him to lose his life in the First World War.'

Lt. Barrow died during the Battle of the Somme on 23rd October, 1916. He was 27 years old.

Two other former members of staff also died during the war. Captain Thomas

Huffington, MA, who taught History and Languages from 1913 to 14, died of wounds on the Somme on 8th February, 1917, aged 24. James H. R. Lendrum became a Chaplain 4th Class attached to the 8th Battalion, Kings Own (Royal Lancaster Regt.). He had taught Languages and Maths at the school from 1910 to 12. He died near Bienvillers in the Pas de Calais on 22nd August, 1918, aged 31.

> 'Two of our masters were killed, one a particularly handsome young man, with features like an Adonis. He was extremely popular with the whole school, and I believe caused many heart flutterings among the senior girls. The other was the most easy-going of any of the school's masters though he rose to the commissioned rank of Captain. Such was the passing of Isaac Barrow and Thomas Huffington.'
>
> [F.M. Edwards]

Three teachers who fought and survived the war were J.M. Forbes, Connaught Rangers, (3rd Batt.); H.W. Gilbert, 3/1st East Anglian Division, Signal Company, R.E. (in other words a motor dispatch rider!); and A. Jordan, Royal Engineers. G.J. Denbigh was rejected for Active Service so volunteered for chemical work and was sent by the Ministry to Brotherton's in Leeds, manufacturing picric acid.

The first Old Lutonian to die during the war was Private Ernest Allin of the 24th County of London (Queen's) Regiment. Allin attended the Modern School between 1907 and 1909. He left to become a technician apprentice at the Vauxhall and West Hydraulic Engineering Company. 'He worked hard and was a regular student at Evening Classes. His ready wit and unfailing good humour made him a general favourite; he was an indispensable singer at the Old Lutonian entertainments.' He was badly wounded at Bethune by a stray bullet while leaving the trenches to draw the day's rations, and died two days later, on 1st May, 1915. A characteristic cheery letter from him had been published in the *School Magazine* the previous December:

> 'Many of you will agree that Old Lutonians who enlisted, did so for the one outstanding reason that His Majesty's Army would not and could not be complete without some O.L's. in its wake. Those of us in the Queen's Own Rifles have, since joining, found that it was not merely for the meagre 7/- a week that they became soldiers, but absolutely for the honour of being able to serve their Country.
>
> 'What tales we'll have to relate when we return to our one and only Luton.'

In all, 42 old boys and staff lost their lives as a result of the war; 36 in the Army, four in the Royal Flying Corps and two in the Navy. Many acts of heroism and courage were recorded, both of those who died, and those who lived to tell the tale.

Private Frank Rimmer joined the school with a free place in September 1906, and left in 1909, after which he worked in the straw trade. He served in the 5th Battalion, the Bedfordshire Regiment and 'died in the terrible charge in which the

Regiment received their fire-baptism' after landing at Gallipoli on 16th August, 1915, aged 21:

> 'Captain Cumberland called for two volunteers to scout, previous to the advance on 15th August, which proved so fatal to the battalion. Frank Rimmer and a friend went and had an exciting time, as the bullets were flying thickly around. When they got back the battalion stormed the hill in fine style. Frank Rimmer ran on ahead with the leaders. That was the last that was seen of him. His body was found near that of Lieut. Brighten – he lies buried with him in 'Lone Tree' valley.'

A fellow Old Lutonian, Private Harry Berry, aged 21, died on the same day and in the same campaign. At the Modern School from September 1906 for less than a year, he was on the staff of *The Luton News*.

Arthur D. Gladwin had been in Horton War Hospital at Epsom for three months with gunshot wounds in the hip, from which he happily recovered. He wrote to the *School Magazine* in March 1917 to say:

> 'Whilst in France last Summer, I met Second Lieut. Arthur Haworth, who was a close friend of mine at the 'LMS', and we had many happy talks of school days. I saw poor Haworth last a few days before his death, and managed afterwards to secure a button from his tunic – a token of remembrance which I shall always treasure. He was a fearless, gallant soldier, and met his death whilst operating his machine gun in an exposed position with an utter disregard of danger.'

Arthur Haworth served in the 16th Battalion, The King's (Liverpool) Regiment, attached to the Machine Gun Corps (Inf.) and died near Laventie in the Pas de Calais on 19th July 1916, aged 20.

Sergeant F.G. Harmer was the first Old Lutonian to receive the Military Medal and happily survive the war. Lance Corporal John Hayden Healey was not so lucky. He died in Belgium on 17th July, 1918, aged 29 and was awarded the Military Medal for outstanding bravery. Lieutenant Sidney Charles 'Squizzy' Squires received the Belgian Croix de Guerre. He had rallied his battalion when it was pushed back on Vimy Ridge, and had taken them 'over the top' again. He was later accidentally killed on 28th October, 1918. 'Whilst his spirit is among us, we have something to live for and something to hope for.' Sergeant H.C. Hunt, attached to a fighting squadron in France, was awarded the Distinguished Flying Medal for bringing down nine German aircraft and one observation balloon. On one occasion he brought down three machines in one patrol.

Edith Webb described her joy on 11th November, 1918, when she saw the Town Crier, Charlie Irons, on the top of St Mary's Church tower, ringing his bell and declaring that the Armistice had been signed. In 1930, a poem to recall the occasion,

written by a teacher, H.H. 'Froggy' Watson, was published in the *School Magazine*:

Twelve years have passed since that November day,
When sick of carnage, strife and clash of steel,
Hardly believing war would ever cease,
We heard the bells ring out a joyful peal.
The end had come, now men had ceased to slay
Their fellow-creatures, and at last was peace.

Comrades, whose merry laugh once rang out clear,
Though Death, with icy hand, was ever nigh,
No longer do you tread this earth below,
But your brave souls, will never, never die.
Smile down on us, who toil and struggle here,
Until we reach the goal, that one day we shall know.

At Speech Day on 24th March, 1919, Mr Sanderson listed the contribution which boys from the Modern School had made to the War effort:

'More than 250 have been serving in the various branches of HM Forces; and of this number at least 40 were awarded Commissions, many of them after a period of service in the ranks. According to our present information the highest positions were gained by Captain P.G. Horsler, Captain F.M. Leighton, Captain R.E. Oakley, Captain B.A. Smart and Major C.G. Hyde.'

Foreign Distinctions

The Belgian Croix de Guerre	S.C. Squires.
The French Croix de Guerre	B.A. Smart

British Distinctions

Mentioned in Despatches	F.F. Biggs (2), T. Dickson, E.F. Foster (2), H.W. Gilbert, C.E. Hayward, C.G. Hyde (2), R.E. Otter, W. Sharp (2), W.J. Twidell (2), A.G. White.
Meritorious Service Medal	A. Gilder, W. Sharp, W.J. Twidell.
Military Medal	H.W. Child, C. Farr, E.F. Foster, G.F. Harmer, J.H. Healey.
Military Cross	W.W. Brown, P.G. Horsler, F.M. Leighton, R.E. Oakley.
Distinguished Flying Medal	H.C. Hunt.
Distinguished Service Order	with a bar – B.A. Smart.

We may, perhaps, be forgiven for finishing this solemn section on a lighter note. The *School Magazine* for July 1915 records the following military howlers from the School's Entrance Examination:

'A *billet* is a place where they put on soldiers.

A *liner* is a man who puts up telefon poles.

I want to tell you about the war that is going on in this letter.

We see the Red Cross full of wonded soldiers from the trances.

A *Zeppelin* is something like a sausage filled with gas.'

Cadets and Guides

In May 1918, with the War in its final phase, it was somewhat belatedly decided to form a School Cadet Corps. At the instigation of Cllr. W.J. Primett, and with prompt and generous donations from 18 Governors and friends, an Establishment Fund amounting to over £120 was soon forthcoming. 71 boys initially mustered each Saturday for drill and parades, led by Sergeant-Major C. Kitchen and Sergeant Sanders. Voluntary parades, held after school and during the holidays, proved less popular, and attendance was distinctly poor for Tuesday afternoon lectures on map-reading and musketry.

Early in the summer term the Corps received an issue of rifles, belts, etc., which gave the boys a chance to drill with arms, as well as keeping equipment clean. Messrs. Day of St Albans supplied caps free of charge, but it wasn't until the middle of December that khaki uniforms became available. Their effect on the smartness and keenness of the Corps was immediately apparent. A secure room in the Church Street premises was used as an armoury. From the start the Luton Modern School Corps was affiliated to the Bedfordshire Territorial Division of the Royal Engineers, in line with the Corps of Bedford Grammar School and Bedford Modern School. Major Cumberland Brown offered the use of the Luton Rifle Club range in Dallow Road, which was gladly accepted.

Mr W.H. Ovenell, the classics master, took temporary charge of the Corps until January 1919 when Lieut. H.H. 'Froggy' Watson joined the school staff and was immediately made Commanding Officer of the Corps. The initial Roll of NCOs, drawn from the senior boys, consisted of *Company Sergeant-Major* H.E.L. Punter; *Sergeants*: J.S. Briars, S.G. Gregg, D.A. Sim, L.H. Simmons; *Corporals*: R.J.F. Brown, D. Grice, F.T. Chamberlain, G. Johnson, T.F. Skillman; *Lance Corporals*: A.M. Sim, J.L. Sim, E.T.W. Day, E.O. Payne, J.W. Jones, A.S. Otter and W.F. Harmer.

The School Governors formed a Cadet Corps Committee, chaired by Clr. Primett, which laid down the following regulations:

'Boys of 12 years and upwards are eligible for membership. Boys between 11 and

12 years of age who intend to join the Corps on attaining the age of 12 years may attend drills and parades provided they pay the usual fees; such boys may not, however, wear the Corps uniform until 12 years of age. Boys leaving school may retain membership until 18 years of age subject to finding their own uniform and attending the necessary drills to maintain efficiency. Boys wishing to withdraw from the Corps must give at least one term's notice; a boy may be dismissed for unsatisfactory conduct or failure to maintain efficiency. Cadets must attend a minimum of 40 parades during the year, and be officially recognised as efficient at the annual inspection. The terms of subscription are: an entrance fee of 10s 6d, with an annual subscription of 10s 6d, payable 3s 6d per term. Uniform will be provided for members of the Corps. Members desiring to provide their uniform privately may do so on condition that such uniform is of the same pattern as supplied to the Corps.'

By the summer of 1919 the intricate movements of Company Drill had been mastered, due to the energetic efforts of Sergeant-Instructor Kitchener (who received a salary for his efforts), and Lieut. Watson had managed to introduce 'a touch of novelty into the awful experience of physical jerks.' The Corps had caused something of a stir in the town when they marched from School to Leagrave, thence Dunstable Road and back to School again.

The December 1919 issue of *The Luton Modern School Magazine* lists newly promoted and appointed NCOs, but there is no further reference to the Corps in subsequent issues. With the First World War over and the disclosure of its horrors, the desire to participate in matters military seems to have lost its appeal, and we must conclude that the School Cadet Corps was finally wound up within a year or two.

It is worth noting that not all the School Governors were in favour of the formation of the Cadet Corps. Henry Latchmore was a prominent Quaker and member of a well-known local banking family who found difficulty in accepting most objectives of the Corps. He would have liked to see the boys and girls interested in such subjects as the League of Nations, international courts of arbitration for the settlement of disputes by peaceful means instead of by the sword, and the gradual elimination of militarism for human relationships. Having felt unable to subscribe to the establishment of the Corps, he offered instead to fund, for at least three years, prizes for essays on the subject of dealing with international disputes.

With the formation of the Cadet Corps, the girls were naturally not willing to be outdone, and during the Autumn term, 1918, the School formed its own Girl Guide Company composed of members from Form IIIb upwards.

Before leaving the Cadets and Guides it is worth quoting from an account of Speech Day in 1919:

'On the evening of the 28th March, the girls and boys gathered in the Great Hall

of the School, and, headed by the Girl Guides, marched down to the Winter Assembly Hall, the Cadet Corps, commanded by Lieut. Watson, bringing up the rear.'

'. . . The majority of the girls in the hall wore becoming white frocks contrasting effectively with the dark blue uniforms and red ties of the Girl Guides, who sat in a body near the platform. Opposite the Guides were seen the boys of the Cadet Corps, whose khaki uniforms helped to introduce a military touch to the proceedings and perhaps reminded many of the Great War which had just ended, and of those who had gone forth to return no more.'

Social Conscience

Boys and girls at the School were encouraged to support selected charities each year. One of the earliest was for the maintenance of the 'Modern School Cot' at the Bute Hospital in Dunstable Road. It had been in use almost continually since 1910 and in December 1916 was occupied by a little girl who called herself 'Topsy Lily', who had had an operation on her neck. The parents of each little patient who occupied it paid half-a-crown a week, although the full cost was nearer £1. The rest of the cost was paid for from the School fund which raised about £50 each year. From time to time pupils were encouraged to visit the child in the cot.

In 1919 Mr Sanderson was able to report that the money collected by the School towards a variety of charities since 1907 came to £388. Of that sum about £150 was allocated to the Bute Hospital, nearly the same amount to the Children's Home and most of the balance being expended in purchasing materials for the girls to work up for the benefit of those suffering through the War. In all, 1,253 garments and other useful articles were made and distributed to various hospitals and other institutions; without counting 500 hospital bags sent in response to Lady Smith Dorrien's appeal. Special collections were held during the First World War for *The Over-Seas Club* (£1 9s. 10d.), *Belgian Relief Fund* (£25), *Blinded Soldiers' Children Fund* of the National Institute for the Blind (£112 13s. 11d.), *Dr Barnardo's Homes* (£45 7s. 0d.). A letter from the Director of Dr Barnardo's to the Headmaster said 'It may interest you to know that it was by far the largest result from any School visited last term.'

In November 1916 a War Savings Association was formed. Pupils were able to buy coupons which could be exchanged for War Savings Certificates. Friends, relatives and former students were included in the scheme and, by February 1917, there were 145 members who had bought a total of 288 certificates. By 1919, a total of £2,000 had been put into War Savings.

After the War the School continued to give generously and between 1925 and 1930 almost £500 was collected for local charities. At Christmas 1930 £37 8s. was raised to help the dependants of those who lost their lives in the R101 airship disaster.

One interesting project was the support of Mr J. Foster Stackhouse's British Antarctic Expedition which left England in August 1914. Its aim was to explore that part of Antarctica lying between King Edward VII Land and Graham Land. It was pointed out that the cost of a tent was £21, a sledge cost £12 12s., a cooking stove £10 10s., a dog £7 7s., a sleeping bag £6 6s., and a pair of fur mittens £5 5s. The School collected £8 8s. and it was decided that the money should be used to buy a dog. A girl in the Fourth Form suggested that the dog should be called Lumo, made up from the first syllables of 'Luton' and 'Modern'. One pupil wrote a letter of advice to the dog, which appeared in the April 1914 issue of the *Modern School Magazine*:

> My dear Lumo,
>
> Before you set foot upon your expedition to the Antarctic Regions, I should like to offer you a word of advice. We have adopted you into our ever-increasing family: we have given you your name; you have now to prove that you are worthy of such a distinction. Remember that you are working for the honour of the School, my boy. When the sledge is too heavily laden, when the weather is at its worst, and when food is reduced below the minimum, remember that we in England are thinking of you. Then pluck up your spirits, fight with renewed strength, and never give up hope.
>
> But if you die worsted in the struggle, then die like a hero, and prove to all the world that we Lutonians are game to the end.
>
> On the other hand, if you return, although the world may not notice you, we shall give you a welcome, and your name shall go down to posterity in the annals of the School.
>
> So here's good luck to you, old fellow, from
>
> A Sister Lutonian.

Sadly, there are no further references to Lumo in the School Magazines, and his fate remains unknown.

Future Success

How can success be defined? It would not be possible to trace the life of everybody who went to the school, and who is to say that one life is worth more than another? Sanderson himself expressed similar thoughts at the first post-War Speech Day on 28th March, 1919:

> 'There is some danger of mistaking for the true harvest such visible signs of progress as Examination successes, Athletic distinctions and promising careers. These will be useful indications that the crop is making healthy growth, but they must not be confused with the real harvest. This will ripen slowly and gradually.

We ourselves must not expect to be the reapers. We must be content if we catch occasional glimpses of the ripening corn. It will be indeed a harvest which requires no reaping, though its fruits will be enjoyed by future generations: A harvest of good citizens who will always place Public Duty before private interests; of real sportsmen who will always play the game; of men who will swear unto their neighbours and disappoint them not even though it be to their own hindrance.'

So, in order to enlarge on the history of the School, and with apologies to the many who have been omitted, we will note the successes of just a representative few during Sanderson's Headship.

With the opening of Luton Modern School in 1904, for the first time, ordinary boys and girls in Luton had been given a realistic chance to take advantage of a college education, and the School was rightly proud of the pupils who succeeded in the academic world. It does appear that more attention was paid to boys but Sanderson said that, although there were always more boys entered for examinations than girls, the girls more than held their own. Their results compared very favourably, and in the summer term 1919 six pupils sat their London Matriculation

A woodwork class. The boys are smartly dressed with no concession to health and safety.

and passed, and only one of them was a boy.

Amongst the first pupils to achieve university success were;

Fred Buckingham, (1904–6) who gained one of the first free places when the School opened in 1904. He was given an Allen Scholarship with the W.H. Allen Engineering Company of Bedford, where he succeeded in obtaining all the First Class Prizes offered for competition among the firm's apprentices. He was the first Old Lutonian to graduate when in 1913 he gained a London University BSc in engineering. He was also awarded the Associateship of the City and Guilds Institute. He returned to the School on 28th March, 1914, to lecture to the Old Lutonians' Club on 'The Problem of Flight', 'despite strenuous opposition in the shape of a particularly noisy Salvation Band outside the building!'

Arthur Thomas Reeve (1904–10) won a scholarship from the Beaudesert School, Leighton Buzzard, to Luton Modern School in 1904. He showed such unusual ability that he was awarded a Royal Scholarship from the Royal College of Science, South Kensington. He passed examination after examination, obtaining his BSc, the ARCS, and winning the Forbes Medal for Botany, and the Diploma for the Imperial College. In 1914 he went to Ceylon and spent seven years with the Rubber Growing Association as a research botanist. When the Association's work was taken over by the Government Department of Agriculture, he became the Inspector of Plant Pests and Diseases. He died suddenly at Galle in Ceylon on 2nd April, 1925 aged 32.

Essie Keating left the School in 1909, and went to University College, Reading, where she gained a BA in 1914.

Lucy Stafford (1906–1912) was the daughter of Edward Stafford, manager of the CWS Cocoa Works in Dallow Road, Luton. Her sister, Pamela, and her brother, M.E.A. Stafford, were also pupils in the school. Lucy was hockey captain both for the School and for Pelican house. She went to University College, Reading, where she was awarded a London BA. In January 1916 she returned to the Modern School as a member of staff, remaining there until 1918. Not long afterwards she married Mr Chell, [possibly James Henry Chell, MA, Curate of Caldecote ?] and, as was usual at that time, seems to have given up her teaching career.

Frank Milner Leighton (1906–14) was the first pupil to be awarded an Open Scholarship to Selwyn College, Cambridge, worth £40 per annum, and later in 1913 an Open Scholarship worth £60 to Trinity Hall, Cambridge. He obtained a First in Chemistry after five years' war service, followed by a BSc at London University. C. J. Nixon was awarded a Mitchell Scholarship (value £40) at the City and Guilds Technical College, Finsbury, in 1914. The following year Dorothy Currie and A. E. Perry received BA degrees from London University.

There were other pupils who did not go to university but obtained bursaries before becoming student teachers. They learnt their teaching skills at classes held by the County Council and also at the chalk face. One of the first of these was Hilda Puddephatt (1904–09). Other trainee teachers found sufficient financial support to

pay for tuition in Teacher Training Colleges. Amongst these were Nellie Breed (1904–08) and Margareta Harris (1904–08) who obtained Teaching Certificates in 1911, from Homerton College, Cambridge. Ethel Janes and Constance Breed emulated them in 1913.

Alec H. Squires (1907–1910) was a student at the Guildhall School of Music. He wrote a hymn tune called 'Lutonian' which was used in the School.

Harry Berry (1906–1907) was on the staff of *The Luton News*.

Charles Barnard (1911–1914) became an articled chartered accountant to Mr Bernard T. Crew of George Street West, Luton.

Ernest Allin (1907–1909) attained a good position at Vauxhall Motor Works.

Henry P. Dunkley (1907–1910) and W. A. 'Billy' Gething (1908–12) took exams for entry to the Civil Service. W.A. Gething was at the School with Blanche Burgoyne, whom he married. Their daughter Joan attended the High School (1936–40) and son Phillip, the Modern School from 1939–46. Phillip's wife Helen Slater attended the High School, and both her parents, Wallace Slater and Doris Edwards were pupils of Luton Modern School!

In an age of Empire, it is not surprising that several ex-pupils sought adventure overseas, Canada being particularly popular:

Walter W. Brown (1907–1911) wrote:

> 'Taking things all round Canada has been very good to me and has taught me that all the education in the world is absolutely no use without sound common sense. I've worked real hard both with my hands and head ever since I arrived here: my experiences have been varied and I already feel amply repaid for the sacrifice I made in leaving my home and friends.
>
> 'Canada is a grand country for a worker but no good for a shirker . . . I have been Farmer, Cook's Assistant, Marble Worker, Labourer and Boiler Attendant and now I am a soldier with a Maple Leaf for my emblem.'

There were also sacrifices to be made as this obituary of Charles Johnson Wing, (1906–8), who went in 1911 to take up farming in Canada, explains:

> 'He was still engaged in farming at Fort Qu'Appelle when he was stricken with what proved to be a fatal illness, appendicitis. To be cut off in the springtime of youth, far away from all his relatives, renders the circumstances peculiarly sad, and we offer our deepest sympathy to his parents, brothers and sisters, in their bereavement.'

Douglas M. Christian from St Albans (1904–1908) went to Canada in 1910, served for a time on the Staff of the Toronto *Globe*, and then became 'editor of an enterprising newspaper' in Redcliff, Alberta, and A.E. Rackham, who 'took a farm in

Manitoba'. A lengthy anonymous article in the 1916 issue of the *School Magazine* paints a poetic picture of winter in Newfoundland, which can be very cold and bleak.

'By January the Frost King has set his seal upon the land, the Storm Fiend wheels in mad career, and snow lies piled upon snow. The usual marks are no longer visible, and the sleigh tracks cross by the shortest routes, passing over frozen lakes and sometimes topping what was not long since a fence or a green-leafed hedge. Safe beneath her fleecy mantle Nature sleeps, till the voice of Spring again calls to her in leaping streams, freed from its frost-forged fetters, and in the awakened life of the woods, and then the silent earth once more resumes her robes of green.

'But if wild Nature sleeps the winter out, human nature is very much alive. To the fishermen and their families, living in the lonely outposts scattered along Newfoundland's far-flung shores, winter is the season of enjoyment. Social pleasures, out and indoor amusements, games, shooting, hunting, trapping – these, and many other recreations are freely and enthusiastically indulged in. Dancing is a favourite winter amusement. To the music of flute, or fife, fiddle or even Jew's harp, the lads and lassies dance for hours with a whole-hearted vigour and honest enjoyment not obtainable, perhaps, in fashionable ballrooms. It does not seem to matter to these people at what hour of the night or morning they disperse. Guests will drive or walk long distances in the crisp frosty air, with light hearts and sometimes lighter pockets, for these meetings are often held for some charitable purpose.'

Edgar Elvey wrote from Cottesloe in West Australia in 1928 in favour of emigration:

'After six years in Victoria, we have moved to West Australia. Trade has been good in the Eastern States in the past few years. The number of motor cars owned by people is amazing. Owing to people over-spending and buying luxuries on the hire-purchase system, money was tightened up by the banks. Last season the wheat crop was bad, which was reflected in the city, and the result is a great slump.

'The Government of West Australia helps land settlers and emigrants better than the Governments of the Eastern States. At the present time huge areas of land are being thrown open for selection. The settlers are aided by a grant, a few hundred pounds capital being sufficient to start with.'

Although the colonies probably attracted most of the pioneers, many chose other lands. Basil M. Joyce (1910–12) wrote from Bahia in Brazil, whilst another letter was received from a former scholar (unnamed) living in Pakhoi, China in 1917:

'I suppose you want to know what our home is like? We are well off for physical

comforts, and can boast of having electric light. All around the house is a large veranda; the servants' quarters and our kitchen are outside. We have four servants, viz., a cook, his wife, and two coolies. The cook's wife washes and mends all the clothes, one coolie looks after the house, and the other tends the garden.

'We have to use tinned milk, but can obtain fresh butter from Hong Kong: the latter comes from Australia! But it is fresh compared with tinned butter.

'One of the drawbacks to life out here is the flies. No matter how one tries to keep them out of the house they seem to get into the rooms in thousands, and this in spite of having sieve-like doors and windows.'

The Old Lutonians' Club

A strong community spirit soon grew up amongst the old boys and girls of the School. On the evening of Saturday, 23rd March, 1912 about 150 old pupils attended the inaugural meeting of the Old Lutonians' Club, which was held in the school hall, at the invitation of Mr Sanderson.

'Prompt to time the Head took the chair, supported by Messrs. Edmunds, Denbigh, Jordan, May and Otter, whilst Miss Macfarlane and Miss Poulton welcomed the old girls and kept them in order.'

Six months later, on 28th September, 1912, the First Annual Meeting was held, with Mr Edmunds in the Chair. He outlined the hopes of the organisers as to the Club's aims. It was proposed that meetings would be held during the winter months which would afford valuable opportunities for socialising and the exchange of ideas amongst old pupils resident in the town. It was believed that the new *School Magazine*, being launched that winter, would keep Old Lutonians in distant countries in touch with their friends at home, as well as providing an opportunity for literary expression. Mr Sanderson was unanimously elected the Club's Chairman, G.L. Bond its first Secretary, and Mr Edmunds, the Treasurer. A Committee of eight ladies and seven men were also elected. The evening ended with a musical programme arranged by C.C. Bennett, which was to set a precedent for innumerable future meetings.

Almost immediately the old boys formed a Football Section of the Club, but the old girls were somewhat slower in getting a Hockey Section going. 'We hope that age does not yet bar the way,' observed an unidentified writer in the *Magazine* for 1912! It didn't, and soon they were playing against the school teams. Tennis and cricket sections were formed the following year, and membership was marked by the conspicuous appearance on the streets of Luton of coloured hatbands and ties.

The Club became a focus of the old pupils' social life for many years to come. The *School Magazine* also served its purpose and we owe it a great deal, for without

the wealth of material contained within its pages, this book would have been much more difficult to write.

The pattern of Club meetings was set in the first two or three years. Whist Drives were an immediate success with as many as 70 members taking part. Christmas Parties became an annual event, and tended to bring in new members. The first on 28th December, 1912, was a great and enjoyable occasion.

> 'In spite of rough weather, dark muddy roads, and in many cases inconvenient train services, at about half-past six the hall contained at least one hundred former pupils, many of whom had travelled some distance. Several members of the school staff were present and the Headmaster presided over the gathering.
>
> 'All shyness and reserve that some of the old boys might perhaps have felt at once more meeting their old school-girl acquaintances, who to them seemed to have undergone some strange metamorphoses since those by-gone days, was soon overcome. In a short time even the most timid were walking bravely towards old boys and girls whom they perhaps had not seen for years and were soon asking all kinds of questions in a most unconventional manner.'

Interspersed between intervals for conversing with old friends, were games and charades, a musical entertainment, refreshments, further games, dances and competitions. Before leaving 'all the members clasped hands and sang several verses of *Auld Lang Syne* with but little consideration for tone, yet with a vast amount of good feeling.'

The Old Lutonians' Club was certainly very active. At first, lectures and concerts were held fortnightly. In March 1913, Fred Buckingham, the first Old Lutonian to gain his BSc degree lectured on 'The Problem of Flight'. Pointing out that knowledge of bird flight must be applied to the solution of artificial dynamic flight, he spoke 'of balloons of the present day, giving us a classification of modern dirigibles, a branch of aviation as yet in its infancy' and using many blackboard sketches, the full theory of how an aeroplane 'lifts and drifts' 'till our poor benighted heads buzzed, and we gaped in bewildered wonderment.'

The Debating Society proved very popular. The subjects chosen are interesting because they indicate that, while some things have changed in the last hundred years, there are others which have remained much the same. 'Has science or art benefited the world most?', 'Capital Punishment should be abolished', and 'Vivisection' were all debated. In support of the last, R.E. Oakley pointed out the scientific benefits while Christine Roberts called for its discontinuance on the grounds of cruelty. Those who supported vivisection as 'a means to a beneficent end' won the day. A fortnight later the majority of members were in favour of 'The Nationalisation of the Railways.' All these topics are relevant today, but the subject for March 1914, 'Should women engage in Commercial pursuits?' is much more contentious and

would be quite unacceptable. Lizzie Forsyth stated that it was necessary for a large proportion of girls to support themselves, but W.H. Wooding in reply said 'that business on the whole spoils a girl, it makes her deficient and coarse, and these are not the sort of girls men want to marry.'

With the outbreak of War many old boys enlisted, and the old girls rallied to the cause, meeting on Tuesday and Friday evenings in the school Needlework room to make warm clothing for the children of the town who were in distress, and also to make such items as warm gloves, scarves, and caps for the troops.

Members who could not immediately join the Forces formed the Old Lutonians Rifle Club 'to prepare themselves in some way so as to volunteer later on.' The Hon. Sec. of the Luton and District Rifle Club offered the Club special facilities, and the Headmaster guaranteed the fee for affiliation. Forty members joined and firing practice commenced three days later on the Winter Range, which was situated behind the Royal Hotel in Mill Street.

The *School Magazine* devoted a number of pages to news from Old Lutonians, and soon it began to report marriages between members, such as that of the Club's first Hon. Secretary, G.L. Bond to Committee member Miss Hilda Morsley in 1915. This was a trend which continued throughout the life of the school and which earned a humorous comment from Peter C. Vigor (an ex-Waller Street Higher Grade School pupil) in his book *Memories are made of this* (1983):

> 'Luton Modern School boys had a wider field for girl friends but a narrower marriage choice. They could have affairs with elementary school girls, Modern School girls [after 1919] – always assuming that the headmistress did not know about it – and girls from the Convent. If marriage was their aim only the more refined type of girl was eligible according to their parents. This adolescent discrimination caused jealousy and snobbery and was one of the reasons why Waller Street became the scene of many a mêlée rivalling those between the Montagues and the Capulets. We had no rapiers or bright swords, and had to resort to cap-snatching and satchel swinging (a deadly enough weapon if it contained a wooden pencil case), or, in season, snowball throwing.'

By this time the epithet 'Rhubarb and Custard' had become a common cry of abuse directed at any Modern School boy or girl displaying an elite red and yellow scarf or other distinguishing mark, by the non-Secondary youth of Luton.

It will save confusion later if we note that although the Luton Modern School for Girls opened in 1919 the Old Lutonians' Club nominally represented the old boys and girls of both schools until 1934. However, in October 1927 some old boys formed their own breakaway, all male, Old Luton Modernians' Club. In the summer of 1921 the girls had formed their own Old Girls' Association, leaving the Old Lutonians' to become, in fact, an all male institution.

In May 1930 Tom Smalley applied to join the Old Luton Modernians' Club. His letter of acceptance from the Club Treasurer, L.F. Hunt reads, 'The subscription to the Club is 5/- per annum, with the option of Life Membership in the second year for a compound subscription of one guinea (£1.05). Club ties are 4/- each (20p) and blazers £1.15s. (£1.75), (supplied by W. Bell and Son., Chapel Street) and silk scarves 12s. (60p) each.' The ties were in the Club colours: Cambridge blue and gold stripe on a maroon background. 'With regard to sports, Rugger, Cricket and Soccer are now going strongly, while on the Social side there are the Annual Dance in December and Annual Dinner in January.'

In an extraordinary joint general meeting held in the Boys' School hall on 21st June, 1934, it was unanimously decided to amalgamate the Old Lutonians' Club and the Old Luton Modernians' as "The Old Luton Modernians' Club, incorporating the Old Lutonians' Club".

'Park Square is filled with ghosts; friendly, happy ghosts for the most part. It was half-filled in those earlier days with girls too, some of whose loveliness still lingers in the memory. Then the girls went into "another place" and the school lost much of its savour, for with the girls went Polly Poulton, one of the finest characters that ever graced the teaching profession [Miss E. St S. Poulton]. I do not know whether the Old Girls remember Polly, but some of the Old Boys do, for to her and her help we owe much, and the world was the poorer when she passed on.'

[Arthur B. Allen]

Chapter 4

Sanderson's Later Years
1919–1933

'The great Hall was silent and, except for murmuring sounds that came from the surrounding rooms, there was no sign of life anywhere.

'Suddenly a bell shrilled above me, a door rattled and a flood of boys poured out. More doors opened and more boys poured out. The corridors were filled with seething masses while the Hall resounded with the tramp of many feet. It was as if a beehive had been stirred up.

'The boys lined up outside doors. These opened and the boys filed in, exchanging remarks (and other things) with those coming out. The masses gradually thinned and melted away. A bell rang; a few doors banged; and except for the varying tones of masters' voices, silence descended once more. Another change of lessons had taken place at the Luton Modern School.'

[R.B. Salmon, 1934]

The great Hall was at the centre of all that happened at Park Square. All juvenile traffic walked in single file anticlockwise (to the right) around it, never across it; unless it was serving its function as the assembly hall, a concert hall or the gymnasium.

'The Prefects don't have to walk in single file but can stand and gossip outside Room 16. They can also turn to the left when they leave a room. They like to do this if we are looking. They stalk past us as much as to say, "Look at me". So we do, but if they turned round quickly they would sometimes see us laughing.'

[Prep. Form]

It was in the Hall that the annual Prize Day or Speech Day ceremonies took place. No Speech Days were held during the War years, 1914 to 1918. They resumed on 28th March, 1919, and Mr Sanderson explained that the former gatherings had been arranged on his initiative, but when the War cloud burst he felt that all public gatherings of a festive nature should be deferred. In the general interests of the School they were now being revived. He went on to say:

> 'At the time when the School was opened there was in Luton no Public Secondary School either for boys or girls; it seemed appropriate therefore that ours should be a mixed School. I mention this to emphasise the fact that a mixed School was provided merely as a matter of expediency, not at all because its founders considered such an arrangement preferable to separate Schools for boys and girls. By the year 1912 our numbers were close upon 300, and it became clear that further accommodation was urgently needed. Ten acres of land were purchased, and plans were selected for a new School for girls. At this point of the proceedings the outbreak of War brought progress to a standstill.'

The guest was H.A.L. Fisher, President of the Board of Education, who said:

> 'Your school, run with spirit and enterprise and initiative ought to be the centre, the source of all kinds of intellectual and artistic movements spreading through the whole community. It ought to be the intellectual capital of Luton, make it so.'

Six months after that Speech Day, on 30th September, 1919, Cecil Harmsworth, MP, performed the opening ceremony of the new Girls' School, in the Modern School Hall, before travelling with the rest of the guests and some of the girls on specially hired trams, or walked to the huts in Alexandra Avenue that were to serve as the Girls' Modern School for the next eleven years.

In 1919 most educationalists favoured coeducation at infant and junior levels, and at university, but recommended the segregation of boys and girls in adolescence. For Sanderson, the girls' departure was something of a relief, although he was unstinting in his praise of their achievements and said that in examination successes they had certainly had more than their share. Looking back to the School's beginnings, he wrote in *The Bedfordshire Magazine* in 1955:

> 'During those early years I found the post exceedingly trying. Some of the Governors were apt to object if I took any action without first consulting the Board. Others with children in the School seemed to think that they need not adhere strictly to school rules. The mixed staff was not easy to manage, and sometimes there was what I considered undue interference from the Shire Hall. I would have taken some other post had I found the opportunity to do so. However,

Drawing of the interior of the School, showing one half of the central Hall.

by degrees the difficulties disappeared. In fact, as soon as the Girls' School was being started, I felt that the Board was losing interest in mine and would have welcomed more interference. One of my greatest reliefs was the opening of the Girls' School – not that the pupils gave any trouble, but I found a male staff far easier to deal with than a mixed one.'

With the departure of the girls and their staff imminent, Sanderson had to select new teachers for the Boys' School. Amongst these was 32 years old Harold Hugh 'Froggy' Watson, BA, appointed to teach French, German and English, and destined to remain at the School for thirty-four years. R.H. Pilling, MA came to teach history and Latin. Rex S. Clayton, BSc, 'Jelly-belly', one time Captain of soccer and cricket, returned as a member of staff in September, 1919, to teach science. He became the School's first Careers Master in 1940. Cyril J. 'Piggy' Godfrey, BSc held a temporary teaching post from December 1918 to July 1919, but returned in July 1921 to teach mathematics. In 1940 he became Second Master; a post he was to hold until his retirement in 1964. As has been said earlier, Miss F.M. Jackson, BA, the recently appointed Senior Mistress, was the only lady to remain at Park Square after the girls had left. In January 1920 Mr A. Henry Tyers joined the staff temporarily, to teach English and Latin. Mr Harold Hunter was appointed at £260 per annum to teach Geography and Singing, – this was the School's first official music post, 'so that the Board will not need to appoint a visiting master.' A very popular man, Mr Hunter emigrated to Australia in 1925. In April 1921 Mr H.T.L. Lees, BSc and Mr A. Moore, BSc both joined the Science Department, and in September Mr H.G.N. Ashby, MA took responsibility for Latin and some English.

In July 1921 the Board of Education confirmed provisional recognition of plans for teaching Advanced Courses at the school and agreed that an additional master would be appointed in connection with it. These courses were planned for teaching what was known as post-matriculation work, and roughly covered the years from 16 to 18, linking the pupil's previous school work with that of the Universities. The County Education Committee agreed to allot two Leaving Scholarships annually, valued at £50 each, to students undertaking post-matriculation studies; a further Scholarship of the same value was in the gift of the Trustees of the Bigland, Gillingham and Long Foundation.

In January 1920 the Governors had approved an all round increase in staff salaries of £20 to the men at the Boys' Modern School and £10 to the lady teachers at the Girls' Modern School. 'Councillor Primett said that if they wished to get and keep good staffs they must pay them what they were worth in the market.'

During 1920 the Government accepted the Burnham Committee's proposals for standardising teachers' pay throughout England and Wales. The Bedfordshire County Council was faced with an immediate increase of £1,400 for the two Luton secondary schools. From 1921 all teachers would be moved to their appropriate

places on the new scale and some would get a rise of over £100. Mr Sanderson's salary rose from £700 to £800, and Miss Sheldon's (who started on £400 in 1919, and had received an increment of £100 at the end of her first year) now rose to £550. Mr Forbes was appointed 2nd Master with an extra £50.

In March 1921 the County Council approved a grant of £3,000 to the boys' school for the current year, with a supplementary grant of £500 to cover the Burnham rises.

Miss Amy Walmsley, Principal of Bedford Training College, who had been a Modern School governor since its inception in 1904, tendered her resignation in January 1921 due to increased pressure of work at Bedford. Mrs Mahon, another energetic governor, and wife of E.B. Mahon, Minister of King Street Congregational Church, resigned in April 1923 when the family moved away from Luton.

A stalwart of the Governing Body, Alderman H.O. Williams, died on 19th May, 1931. He had been a member of the original Body, formed in 1904, and had served continuously, latterly in the capacity of Chairman from 1921 until his death. His keen interest in the School never flagged, and with his passing it lost one of its warmest supporters and benefactors.

Prospectus of Boys' School

Mr Sanderson presented a draft of his proposed Prospectus of the Boys' School to the Governors' Meeting held on 15th July 1919. It was passed with little alteration and is worth quoting almost in its entirety.

> 'The aim of the School is to provide for boys from the age of 10 to 18, a sound general Education, which shall fit them for the needs of professional and commercial life, and which shall form a step in the passage from the Public Elementary Schools to the Universities or to the Higher Technical Institutions.
>
> Parents are advised to enter their boys at the earliest possible age. The full benefit of the School cannot be obtained if entry is deferred much beyond the age of 12.
>
> It is perhaps as well to emphasise the following facts:
>
> (a) The School is a Secondary School, and as such, its work is arranged to suit the requirements of boys who are to remain in attendance for not less than four (preferably 5 or 6) full School Years.
>
> No boy will be admitted to the School till his parent, or guardian has signed an undertaking in the following form:
>
> I request you to admit ....as a pupil at the Luton Modern School, and in consideration thereof I undertake:

1. That he shall be subject to the School Regulations as sanctioned by the proper authorities.

2. That he shall remain in regular attendance as a pupil until the end of the School Year in which he attains the age of 16 years, unless the written permission of the School Governors for earlier withdrawal is obtained.

3. That in the event of his leaving prior to that time without such consent I will pay to the Governors on demand such sum as they may determine, but in no case exceed a sum of £5.

(b) The School Year begins in September and ends in July. It is therefore most desirable that boys should join in September rather than at any other time; and they should never (unless quite unavoidably) leave at any time other than at the end of a School Year, i.e. in July.

Admission. At the annual examination for admission in September a certain number of Free Places are offered for competition. This examination is usually held about May or June, the exact date being advertised in the local newspapers. The subjects of examination are English (Spelling, Grammar, and Composition), and Arithmetic, special attention being paid to handwriting and general neatness.

If accommodation is available boys may be admitted at other times provided they can at a special test satisfy the Headmaster that they have reached the standard necessary for admission.

The Preparatory Course, which should be commenced at the earliest possible age, includes instruction in English (Reading, Grammar and Composition); English History; Geography; Arithmetic and Algebra; Practical Geometry; Nature Study, or Elementary Science; Drawing; Woodwork; Singing; Drill.

The General Course, which should be commenced at the age of 11, covers 5 years. It includes instruction in English (Grammar, Composition, and Literature); History; Geography; French; Latin or German; Mathematics; Theoretical and Practical Science; Drawing; Woodwork; Singing; Drill.

French must be studied for two years before a second foreign language is begun; even then this second foreign language may be taken by those boys only whose progress in French satisfies the Headmaster that Latin, or German, may be added with advantage.

At the end of the General Course whole Forms are entered for the Cambridge Senior Local Examination, for which no fees are charged.

A certain amount of specialisation will be allowed after the General Course is completed, and the Senior Local Examination is "passed". Boys may then be

recommended to give particular attention to subjects bearing more directly on their future careers.

Home Work. All pupils are expected to perform certain tasks at home. At the commencement of term they are supplied with time-tables stating the nature of the tasks allotted to each evening, and the time each should occupy. This time should be about forty minutes each evening for those in the preparatory classes, increasing to about 2 hours for those at the top of the School.

Fees. These will be £2 per term payable before term commences. This sum includes the supply of all necessary books, stationery, etc. It also includes membership of the Games Club.

School Hours. The School is open from 9 am. to 12.20 pm. each morning; and from 2 pm. to 4.15 pm. each afternoon except Wednesday and Saturday. Boys should arrive 10 minutes before School opens.

School Year. The School Year commences in September. It is divided into three terms of about the same length. At the close of each term reports on the progress and conduct of pupils are posted to parents.

Dinners and Teas. Dinners and teas are provided for those pupils who come from a distance. Particulars as to charges may be obtained on application.

Games. Organised games are arranged for Wednesday and Saturday afternoons, and it is hoped that parents will assist in securing regular attendance.

Cadet Corps. Boys wishing to join the Cadet Corps may obtain particulars at the School Office.

The School Rules

At the same Governors' Meeting the School Rules were approved. They numbered just eleven, and were in keeping with Sanderson's remark at his selection interview, that he 'hoped no school rules would be made except such as could be strictly enforced.' (From 1942 onwards, when the Rules were first printed in the *School Lists*, they numbered 23.) Here are some of the 1919 list:

(For breach of Rules the Headmaster has authority to suspend boys from attendance at School.)

1. School Fees (£2 per term) must be paid at the office in Park Square not later than the day preceding that on which term commences. Treasury notes, if sent by post, should be registered. Cheques should be made payable to "T.A.E. Sanderson".

2. No boy may be absent, except when unwell, without the previously-obtained permission of the Headmaster. Such permission is granted only in the most exceptional circumstances. Leave will not be granted for purposes of mere pleasure.

4. At the beginning of term each boy must bring the prescribed form of Health-certificate duly completed.

6. When journeying to and from School, and when taking part in any School function, boys must wear the recognised School cap or School hat. The recognised cap is a plain black or navy-blue cap with School badge. The recognised hat is a plain white "boater" with black ribbon and School badge. Badges (price 6d. each) may be obtained from the School Office.

7. Each boy must be provided with a suitable bag for carrying books to and from School. The School authorities provide bags to contain drill shoes; each boy must purchase one of these (price 1/6) at the School Office.

8. When drilling, all boys must wear suitable shoes; they must not wear braces, but belts not less than three inches wide.

9. Boys who are unable to return home for dinner are not allowed, without special permission, to leave the premises during the interval. Those who do not take the School Dinner may bring their dinners with them. Leave will be given, at the request of parents, for boys to dine at private houses in the town, but not at restaurants.

10. All hats, caps, overcoats, cloaks, shoes, note-books, and other articles must be clearly marked with the School number of the owner.

A system of punishments was in place for breaches of the rules or unacceptable behaviour. Minor offences usually resulted in impositions (impots) which might consist of conjugating French verbs or writing lines, to be completed within a set time. Jack Adams (1929–32) remembered a bright individual trying to invent a 'multiple nib' pen to speed up the process. More serious offences were punished by evening detention, normally lasting an hour after school, and spent in completing unfinished work, solving cube roots, or some menial domestic chores. The worst

criminals were called into school for Saturday morning detention, which, if you were lucky, might involve working for Andrews, the caretaker, or less happily written school work. Saturday detention took precedence over every other engagement. Corporal punishment by the Headmaster was seldom practised; his charisma was sufficient to quell most malefactors. A number of lesser masters were known to use physical punishment, sometimes quite maliciously, and almost certainly without official permission. Foremost amongst those was Bourlet, the Physics master, who was alleged to have punished boys with electric shocks, and to have dangled one lad over the hall gallery railing. Few boys would dare to complain for fear of getting even more. The red and yellow Card System was a disciplinary measured introduced by Mr Sanderson when pupils were not working as expected. They had to be signed by each master or mistress at the end of every period. Woe betide anyone who failed to get a full card of signatures. At that time Prefects had little power.

'One prefect was a strange fellow indeed. He was wedded to the giving of lines, and imagined that the more lines he gave the better was his discipline. Poor fellow, he never learned. Not even when he gave me an impot of one thousand times – 'I am intoxicated by the exuberance of my own verbosity' – to be handed in within an almost impossible time limit. The lines were done in five different styles of handwriting, and he never said a word. The clearest memory of the prefects one has is of their making Oxo or a Bovril drink in the Chemy. Lab., boiling the water in a beaker over a Bunsen burner. The only time I ever discovered any sense in the Chemy. Lab.!'   [Arthur B. Allen]

Serious breaches of the school rules, including expulsion, had to be dealt with by the Governors, a task that some of them felt wasted a lot of their time. In March 1924 they passed a resolution that 'Cases of breach of school rules be referred to a sub-committee of the governors, who shall present recommendations to the General Committee.'

The School's 'Great War' Memorial

On the morning of Friday, 11th November, 1921, the whole school gathered in the Hall to witness the unveiling of the War Memorial, which had been placed on the wall at the back of the stage. They were joined by many old boys, former staff, civic dignitaries and relatives of those who had died.

Designed by Luton architect Basil C. Deacon, FRIBA, at a cost of £120, the memorial took the form of a triptych, carved from East Indian teak, with satin wood panels, surmounted by a carved laurel wreath, which enclosed the school crest, picked out in coloured enamels. Carved on the central panel were the names of the master and boys who were killed. The inscription read:

Lest we forget.
In ever grateful and proud remembrance of the master and old boys of
this school who so nobly laid down their lives in the Great War.
1914–1918.

The thirty-nine names were carved on the inner faces of the two doors. The memorial was unveiled by the Revd. E.B. Mahon, of King Street Congregational Church, whose only son, Arthur's, name is one of those on the memorial. Amongst the visitors present at the ceremony with the Headmaster were the Chairman of the Governors, Councillor H.O. Williams JP, The Deputy Mayor, Alderman Harry Arnold JP, Councillor A. Wilkinson, Messrs. George Warren, W.J. Primett, Basil C. Deacon and the Revd. D. Jenkins.

The last Speech Day at Park Square, 4th April, 1938. Mr V.E. Goodman, Chairman of the Bedfordshire Education Committee is presenting the prizes. Lady Keens is in the background. The War Memorial is clearly displayed. (LN-LMC)

'A noble panegyric of the dead was delivered by the Revd. Mahon, and after the names had been read by the Headmaster, the memorial was dedicated with the following words: "To the undying memory of the men and lads of this school who laid down their lives in the Great War, we dedicate this memorial, that it may be a reminder and an example of heroism and of sacrifice in all times to come."'

The whole company then stood in silence for two minutes, after which many floral tributes were placed by the memorial, before all the boys filed past.

When the school moved to Bradgers Hill, the memorial was placed on a wall in the Office Lobby Entrance, to be joined in 1946 by one commemorating the dead of the Second World War. Both now face each other in a corridor of the VIth Form College.

More New Staff

A number of excellent staff, who were to give long term service to the school, were appointed in the last ten years of Sanderson's Headship. In January 1923 Harold E. 'Timber' Woodcock, MA, came to teach French. Alex F. Bourlet, BSc, was appointed in 1924 to teach Physics. Arriving a year later John A. 'Jock' Cleaver, MSc, was to specialise in Geography. Ronald 'Pills' Phillips, MA, joined in 1927, and taught English, PT, and Religious Instruction. George R. 'Growler' Howard, MSc, (1928) Maths, Chemistry and Physics. Albert C. 'Birdie' or 'Fezz' Partridge, BA, (1929) French. From 1930 Thomas P. 'Nobby' Clark, BA, taught History; Enyr 'Jonah' Jones, BA, German and Basil J. Cooke, BSc, Physics. Arriving in 1931 Charles E. 'Pants' Wareham, BSc, taught Physics, Chemistry and PT, whilst Arthur 'Spud' Root, BA, was responsible for Latin.

The inclusion of Religious Instruction on the School syllabus was made compulsory in 1920, but no one was given responsibility for the subject, and teaching it seems to have fallen onto Willy Otter's not unwilling shoulders. Ronald Phillips' appointment in 1927 included Religious Instruction, and he carried the bulk of the subject until 1941 when C.W. Parry joined him. Canon Eric Jones (LMS: 1934–39) has observed 'the atmosphere in my day was unrelentingly secular – and, indeed, so was mine at that time. I do remember that the lower three years had a weekly period of so-called bible study – appallingly badly taught, and consisting of reading round the class verse by verse, without any comment or explanation. It was obvious, even to my naïve eye, that the master was an unwilling conscript. 'Somebody's got to do it!' Looking back, I think that accorded with the general atmosphere at the school at that time.'

Although there were new masters, there were considerably more new boys, who formed their own opinions of those that taught them: views that changed little throughout the School's existence:

'This is our first term in the School. It must have about twenty masters. They differ in dozens of ways. Some are tall and some are small; some are bold and some are old; some with moustaches, some clean shaven; some with curly hair, some with it brushed back, some have frizzy hair, some have grey hair and some have no hair at all. Some wear glasses which make them look gentle and kind, but remember you cannot always tell by their looks.

'Every morning we have Prayers in the Hall, and the masters wear long black gowns. Some of the masters' gowns are a disgrace; they are very ragged and hang in ribbons, but they wear them just the same. After Prayers the names of the detention victims are read out in front of the whole School. When a boy has a tickle in his throat, he thinks Prayers a long time. We wait to see if he will splutter. If he does, he goes red like a beet-root.

'Some masters have extraordinary sayings; others give you impots or keep you in till half-past five. One master fires off cubes and impots like a machine gun.'

[Form 1c, 1930]

Other, older boys had more positive views of the staff. Alan E. Silvester (1940–47) spoke of James 'Finny' Findlater as the quiet, gentlemanly elder statesman who promoted an interest in English Literature in the most hearty of Sportsmen. Whilst to Willy Otter and Sidney Pointing (1933–1948), the denizens of the woodwork and metalwork shop, we irreverently ascribed the motto: 'Give us the job and we'll finish the tools.' For Frank Stygall (1937–1944) 'Hugh 'Froggy' Watson was a small man with a large personality. Pigeon-chested, middle aged, his eyes twinkled and his little moustache twitched when someone or something amused him. He had an extremely keen sense of humour and was entirely loveable – my friends and I were very fond of him.' Stygall adds 'Harold Woodcock was a typical Yorkshireman of the best kind. Tall and good-looking with a charming personality. He taught French but frequently digressed and talked about anything and everything. We didn't learn much French, but we learnt a good deal else during those interminable digressions. He assisted with music and possessed a conductor's baton. When a boy transgressed he would order him to come to the front and bend over. He then performed a 'train ride' with the baton on the lad's posterior: di-di-di-dum, di-di-di-dum, etc. The boy wouldn't know whether to laugh or cry!' There was no malice on either part.

G.C. Hay recalled the day when a certain Squires entered the Physics Lab. on the top floor at Park Square and spied a very tight pair of trousers in the doorway of one of the under-bench cupboards. The temptation was too much for him, and he landed a mighty wack with the edge of his rule. It was however, only to wish the floor would swallow him up, for whose wrathful face should emerge from the cupboard but that of Mr Bourlet, so much feared for his varied forms of physical punishment.

Findlater again – Arthur B. Allen (1917–21) wrote: 'Finny is enshrined for ever in the memory of those who were fortunate enough to have him. He came into the

classroom, when the writer was standing on the top of his desk, clad in his gown and beating time with a pair of blackboard compasses . . . and all the form singing "I'm for ever blowing bubbles". Beautiful, soul-uplifting harmony . . . and then the choir died out suddenly. In the door stood Finny. His face completely expressionless, except for his twinkling eyes. "Allen," said he, "when you have earned the right to wear cap and gown I shall be proud to lend you mine." That was all. He turned and withdrew into the Hall for a moment. It was long enough. The gown was restored to its proper place and I was off the desk like a shot rabbit. That was so typical of Finny. He ruled by winning intense loyalties; small wonder we loved the man, and still do.'

Most boys (and some Staff) regarded the Headmaster with awe. Sidney A.P. Jackson (1932–36) was 'frightened to death by him.' One boy nearly choked trying to supress a cough in assembly for fear of being chastised. Jackson remembered one of Sanderson's Saturday morning maths lessons. "With what do you draw a line?" he asked. "A ruler, Sir." "No! A ruler controls people. You draw a line with a rule!"

Ronald Phillips has written: 'Having been a Wrangler at Cambridge, Mr Sanderson was intensely interested in the teaching of Mathematics. He held very strong views about how the subject should be taught and carefully instructed in his methods the masters who taught it. Woe betide anyone who ventured to diverge therefrom! It is not for me to judge the efficiency of these methods, but many of those who came under his tuition spoke very highly of his abilities as a teacher.'

One of those was J.H. 'Jack' Burgoyne (1923–1931) who had the highest regard for T.A.E. Sanderson, both as Headmaster and as a mathematician. Finding himself too young to go to University, he spent an extra year in the Sixth Form, where the Head taught him Advanced Mathematics on a one-to-one basis. A strong rapport developed between them. Burgoyne was a serious student who enjoyed hard work, and was inclined to agree with Sanderson that sport was rather a waste of time. In spite of that, he enjoyed tennis, and came first in the 220 yards in 1931! He thought very highly of C.J. Godfrey who had taught him chemistry and maths at form level and prepared him for higher work. He considered G.R. Howard's Advanced Chemistry teaching outstanding, and he could not fault J.W. Findlater's enthusiasm for history and literature. Although the school prepared him well academically, he very much regretted that in 1931 there was no kind of careers guidance for higher education. Indeed, Burgoyne turned to Edward Hoblyn, two years his senior and already at Imperial College, as his mentor.

Jack Burgoyne excelled as an organist, and must have found the harmonium in the school hall something of a pain. One of his colleagues, G.K. Impey, wrote in 1931:

> Struggling one morn at the organ, I was worried and far from pleased,
> As my fingers blundered wildly over its dusty keys;

The boys knew what they were singing, what hymn 'twas supposed to be'
As I played some cacophony that was meant for harmony.

The stops they refused to function, the bellows groaned and squeaked,
The back fell off with a clatter, blown off by the wind that leaked,
The boys almost left off singing in their efforts to hide their mirth,
While the masters looked impassive but rippled along their girth.

It may be that some kind governor will leave us a legacy
That will get us a decent organ to utter sweet harmony,
Or perhaps a Christmas Collection or some other Charity –
Or it may be that only at Chaul End shall we get real Euphony.

It was to take almost twenty years and a tragedy before the School got a real organ.

Two Old Modernians who Faced Disasters

Britain was shocked by the news, on 5th October, 1930, of the loss of the Airship R 101, over a lonely hill-top in northern France. The airship had started on an official flight to India, but ran into turbulence over Beauvais and was completely destroyed when its hydrogen gas exploded. 48 of the company of 54 were burned to death, including Flying Officer Maurice H. Steff, RAF, who was Second Officer of the airship. Steff was born in Luton in 1896, and entered Luton Modern School in 1908 and left at Easter 1910. He worked for R. Laporte Ltd. until September 1914, when he joined the Royal Navy. Serving in *HMS Inflexible*, he was one of the two Old Boys present at the Battle of Jutland in 1916. A Flight Officer in the Kite Balloon section of the Royal Naval Air Squadron in 1918, he served in the Adriatic Barrage Kite Balloons in Italy. In 1920 he was appointed to the instructional staff of the School of Balloon Training, and from there went in 1925 to the Royal Airship Works, and was appointed Second Officer of R 101 in 1929. He was lent to R 100 for her trial flights, and flew with her as Second Officer to Canada and back in July 1930.

In honour of Maurice Steff, the Modern School boys collected £37 8s. at Christmas, which was sent to the Fund raised to help the dependants of those who lost their lives in the R 101 disaster.

D.F.R. Bussereau, who was at the Modern School from 1925 to 1930, was a surviving member of the crew of the *S. S. Watford*, which was wrecked off Cape Percy, Nova Scotia, in September 1931. He was the senior of seven cadets, and with 37 others, was rescued by life line and breeches buoy by a party of Royal Canadian Mounted Police, assisted by the local rum-runners. Six hours effort in a fierce gale were necessary to complete the rescue work, but, sadly, two of the crew were swept away. His younger brother, E.V.R. Bussereau, was killed in the 1939–45 War.

The Sporting Life

From the autumn term of 1919 until 1922 the Trapp's Lane (West Hill) playing field was being turned into the new Memorial Park and the boys gradually lost their games facilities. Fixtures were played on a variety of sites, including Faunch's field in Old Bedford Road that they had previously used in 1905–7, which now belonged to the Luton Amateurs' Football Club.

An anonymous writer in the *Old Luton Modernian* commented that:

> 'The introduction of PT [physical training – in place of drill] was a radical change and it took some time for shorts and slippers and no neckties (athletic vests were not compulsory even then) and the use of apparatus to be regarded as the usual thing. Yet this was a great advance, despite the obvious handicaps and disadvantages of using the Hall – memories of an enormous splinter from the floor rise at this juncture. One day a master [C.E. Wareham] was giving a vigorous and repeated demonstration of a particular exercise, when he seemed in danger of coming adrift from his beautiful white nether garments. To the secret chagrin of thirty boys the apparently interminable repetition did eventually cease – short of the point at which confusion might have followed for the instructor on the platform!'

This may be an appropriate place to mention Charles Wareham's unfortunate nickname – 'Pants'. When questioned about it in September 2002, six months before he died, he said that although he was well aware of it, he did not know its origin. Eric Taylor, who was at the School from 1926–32 was in no doubt that it came from the lines of a popular song:

> Father's pants will now fit Willy,
> Will he wear 'um? Wear 'um? Will he?

In 1925, after several years without a proper ground, the Governors leased 5½ acres of 'beautifully-situated' land from Chew's Foundation at Chaul End. It lay to the west of Chaul End Lane at its junction with the Dunstable Road. On Monday, 20th June, 1927, a new pavilion was opened there by Ald. A. Wilkinson, the Mayor, whose speech provoked a little controversy. He suggested that the love of sport might be carried too far, and expressed the hope that the boys' interest in the battle of life would not be prejudiced by too much sport. Mr J.B. Hoblyn, whose job it was to thank the Mayor, said that he was amazed to hear him damn sport by faint praise. He thought it was a very important thing in the life of the nation. The lad who played his cricket with a straight bat, and who shot straight for goal, learned to live straight, and he hoped that in the future the school would build up a record for sport

equal to that it had obtained in the past in the fields of scholarship. An Editorial in *The Luton News* wondered if his Worship was not confusing sport with pleasure. 'Is it not as true today as ever it was, that "all work and no play makes Jack a dull boy?"'

> 'The new pavilion, a very pleasing one, 50 feet by 22 feet has been erected by Mr C. Jeyes at a cost of about £650. It is constructed of wood on concrete foundations, and roofed with fibrous asbestos tiles. The upper portion of the exterior is roofed with rustic elm boards, and this gives the whole an air in keeping with the surroundings. The ceilings and the outside are painted white, and the interior stained and varnished. The accommodation comprises two rooms, the home changing room and the visitors' changing room, with lockers that can be used as seats, lavatories, and storage beneath. The front of the building forms a balcony and stand, built up on posts; and the segment arches thrown over this add to the general effect.'

The writer of the Cricket Report for the *Luton Modern School Magazine* in 1932 had a message for every reader, but there were many who would not agree with him:

> 'It has often been said, with some justice, that your years at school are the happiest of your life. Whether that be true or not, there can be little doubt that the pleasantest hours of school life are spent on the playing fields. Whenever Old Boys meet, whenever in after life they indulge in reminiscences, the most common topic of conversation is the games and the matches in which they played. A boy who leaves school and has taken no part, or only a small part, in this branch of school activities, has missed not only most of the joy of school life but also valuable training for his future.'

The *School Magazine* for Summer 1931 records that 'The School will be pleased to know that its one representative in County Cricket, C. Bray of Essex, is in great form with the bat. After a series of 40's and 50's, Bray scored 100 against Northamptonshire, on 30th May, helping his County to win by 135 runs. *The Observer* of 31 May, made the following comments: "Bray completed a very fine hundred out of 164, in three hours five minutes, before being caught in the slips. He hit with certainty all round the wicket reaching the boundary ten times."' Bray left the School in 1912, having played in the First XI, under the captaincy of R.S. Clayton. He was a prisoner of war in Germany in 1915.

For eight years between 1922 and 1930 Association Football was officially abandoned at the school, to be replaced by Rugby Football at the request of the staff and some of the boys.

During the summer term of 1922 members of the 1st and 2nd Football XIs, together with the Fourth, Fifth and Sixth forms, were informed by Mr Sanderson

Rugby Football Team, 1924-25. Dr J.M. O'Meara; boys (not in order) D.M. Broughall, M.F. Hunt, J.H.F. Harmer, S.C. Faunch, D. Harrison, C.A. Gregory, F.F. May, H.F. Stratton, J.A. Jackson, R.D. Ward (captain), S. Emerson, E.C. Hawes, L.E. Prosser, K. Bolton, H.N. Barnes, F.H. Hawes.

that a growing number of Grammar Schools all over the country were changing to Rugby, including Dunstable and the Cedars, and this would leave Luton with very few football fixtures. Consequently Luton would also play Rugby!

'During that summer holiday many of us who were destined to form the first ever 1st XV that played in Luton were put through our paces and the Rules of the Game of Rugby by J.F. "Ginger" Friend, an enthusiastic Rugby player and Master. I can still here his cry of "Come on you forwards – up, up, UP!"

'We played the Cedars at Leighton Buzzard in a very memorable game. After leading by 20 points to nil after ten minutes, and even though we allowed them to play 3 Masters as we were obviously much stronger than they, things began to happen. First, as I was racing their full back for the ball he attempted to fall on it, but instead put his head on my knee, splitting his head and doing my knee no good. Then Charlie Smith tackled one of the Masters who fell awkwardly and broke his leg, and finally a second Master had a rib broken in a tackle. In the end we were so frightened of doing further damage that the final score was only 29–0.

'The Cedars Head Master alleged that we had played a rough and dirty game, and we were all called to Mr Sanderson's room to explain our behaviour. Fortunately Dr J.M. O'Meara, a keen Rugby enthusiast, had watched the game, and reported that far from being rough, we had in fact been a bit too gentle, there had been no dirty play, and the accidents happened because of our opponents' ignorance of the game. It was many years before we played at Leighton Buzzard again.'

[L.F. Hunt]

By 1930 opinion had swung back in favour of football, and at Speech Day that year spontaneous applause greeted Mr Sanderson when he announced that in future, Rugby would be played before Christmas, and Association Football afterwards, 'so that all parties may have an innings.' *The Luton News* devoted an Editorial to what it called 'Mr Sanderson's predicament'. It observed that:

'Luton is essentially the home of Association football, but it has become the custom of schools that rank above the name of elementary to foster Rugby, rather than Association football, and it therefore follows that, to have the opportunity of taking part in the best and most enjoyable of all school sporting contests – meetings with other schools – it has become necessary for the Modern School to take up Rugby.

'All who have played the game, or have learned sufficiently of its intricacies to be able to follow it, will appreciate the devotion of the Rugbyite to the handling code, but the fact remains that it is too complicated for the crowd to follow, unless you happen to be in an area where it has been nurtured.

'Luton Modern School is now [1930] to have a playing field of nearly fourteen acres, instead of only five, and this will give ample room for both Rugby and Association football to be accommodated simultaneously. Why not cater for both games through the season, and give the boys the chance of deciding for themselves which they prefer?'

On 24th November, 1923 a team made up of 'Past and Present' players from the School played the Queen's Works 'A' team at Bedford. Two of the Luton players, G.G. Wain and A.M. Sim were enjoying the novelty of motoring to the match when their machine skidded; Sim was thrown to the ground and was so dazed that he was unable to play in the match; Wain was also cut but was able to turn out. The match went to the Bedford team, 7 points to 0. A postscript adds that at half time the appalling news came that the lemons had disappeared from the pavilion, but as it was a raw day nobody missed them much!

The *School Magazine* does not refer directly to the opening of the new Sports Ground at Chaul End, but oblique references in match reports indicate that although the pitches were in pretty good order when they first came into use in the

1925 season, they were not ideal: 'We decided to kick up-hill.'

A number of old boys have referred to playing football at Chaul End some ten years earlier, but we can find no official confirmation of this and can only assume that they were playing on Chew's ground by permission of the Foundation, prior to its purchase by the Governors.

At first the sloping field at Trapp's Lane was adequate for athletics, but during the early 1920s the school used the more varied facilities of the Vauxhall Sports Ground. In 1924 the new lower sports ground in Wardown Park opened and it became possible for the first Inter-School athletics meetings to begin.

The first recorded post-War Modern School Boys' Sports Day was held on the Vauxhall Sports Ground on 20th June, 1923, and the names of two brothers appeared for the first time: these were Brian C.V. Oddie (LMS, 1916–23) and his younger sibling Geoffrey J.W. Oddie (LMS, 1917–24), sons of the Headmaster of Christ Church School, Luton. Brian won the high jump (4ft 8in), the half mile (open) and the 1 mile (open – 5 min. 12 secs.) and Geoffrey the long jump (open – 16ft). On 5th June, 1924, in the Bedfordshire Athletics Championships Brian Oddie won the 3 mile race and his younger brother Geoffrey won the long jump and came second in the 120 yds. hurdles. Later that year, after Brian had left for Queen Mary College, London, Geoffrey achieved 17ft 3ins. in the open long jump, and also won the 220 yards in a dead-heat with G.T. Ekins. He followed Brian to Queen Mary College, where they both graduated with first class honours in physics, and both joined the Meteorological Office. Brian became a research assistant at the Airship Meteorology Station at Cardington. The work came to an end in 1930 when the R101 Airship disaster occurred and his leader, M. A. Giblett, together with his Old Modernian colleague M. E. Steff (LMS, 1908–10), were killed. Brian Oddie took a major role in producing the official report of the enquiry into the tragedy. He served as a Wing Commander in the RAF during the War, and then spent the final years of his career as Deputy Director of the Meteorological Office, for which he was rewarded with a CBE.

Brian Oddie's interest in athletics earned him international distinction as a long-distance runner. He twice finished second for Britain in the 5,000 metres against France (1927, 1929) and was individual winner of the 3 mile team race against Germany in 1929. He represented Britain in the 5,000 metres at the 1928 Amsterdam Olympic Games when he came 4th in the 2nd heat with a time of 15 min. 16 secs. He earned an international vest in Paris in 1929 when he finished 29th in the international Cross-Country race. He was placed 5th in the 3 miles in the 1930 British Empire Games which were held in Ontario. It is recorded in the quarterly *Journal of the Royal Meteorological Office* that 'Whilst working at Lerwick in the Shetland Isles in 1931 he took part in a 10 mile road race and, with a mile to go, was so far ahead of the other competitors that he had time to stop for a cup of tea at the Observatory and still win comfortably!'

Geoffrey Oddie did not seriously continue his athletic activities. He joined the staff of the Meteorological Office, Air Ministry, in 1928, working in aviation meteorology. During the War he served with the RAFVR in Europe, and afterwards was responsible for building up the Meteorological Office at Heathrow Airport. In 1952 he joined the secretariat of the International Civil Aviation Organisation in Montreal, becoming Chief of the Meteorology Section until his retirement in 1967.

After the departure of the Oddies, Sports Days seem to have been quieter affairs. That of 20th May, 1925 was held at Chaul End. A 'ding-dong' struggle was recorded between L.E. Prosser and R.D. Ward in the mile, in which the former's superior condition just turned the scale in his favour. The final Tug o' War between the Grasshoppers and Hornets roused the onlookers to great enthusiasm, the Grasshoppers winning after a great struggle. Later reports state:

'The sports began on Wednesday, 5th June, 1929, but the rain soon drove everybody to the shelter of the pavilion, leaving the obstacle race buns to face the downpour uneaten. We understand they were last seen in somebody's chicken run. As it was hopeless to continue, the events were postponed till 13th June.'

'The sports were held on Wednesday, 21st May, 1930, under ideal weather conditions. Consequently, somebody's chickens were deprived of buns which they might pardonably be expected to regard as an annual treat.'

Sadly the competition in 1930 did not live up to the weather. The times for the Mile Open and the Half-Mile Open were not as good as in the previous year, with the competitors merely ambling round the track for most of the race.

By 1930 the Playing Field had been enlarged to 14½ acres, allowing plenty of space for new games pitches. The running track remained in the same position. Sports Day was brought forward to the afternoon of 18th March, and in almost ideal conditions Richard Dillingham won the Mile and broke the 880 yards Open record in 2 mins. 23 secs. Dillingham was to have a distinguished amateur athletics career and became a stalwart of the Bedfordshire Schools and County Athletics scene throughout his life.

The Modern School swimming club commenced a boisterous career on the first Monday of the summer term, 1919. Meeting at the Waller Street baths, each Monday from 4.20 to 5 p.m., some 124 boys of varying abilities were coached by Messrs. W. Otter, H.H. Watson and C.J. Godfrey. Mr Otter wrote:

'It is with difficulty that these [124 boys] are squeezed into the limited number of dressing booths available; many boys find it quite a task to finish their dressing by 5.30; while the congestion round the looking glass is a thing that could not have been foreseen!

'The swimming is progressing satisfactorily. It is gratifying to see an increasing

number of boys venturing on their first few strokes. An interesting lesson given by Mr Watson in swimming on land has proved a great help.

'The popular method of entering the water is still by stepping gingerly down the ladder and "ducking" as far as the eyebrows. Bolder spirits jump in; but it is seldom that one can see any attempt at diving. It is a pity that more boys do not take advantage of the spring-board and the graduated diving boards to learn this graceful art.'

In 1932, H.H. "Froggy" Watson reminded the non-swimming boys:

'That it is not fair or right that other people, often perfect strangers, should be called upon to risk their lives just because you have been too slack and lazy to take the trouble to learn to swim yourself. It really is too absurd that you should boast about belonging to a great island race, and go about singing "Britannia rules the waves", when you can't swim a stroke in the aforesaid waves.

'At least one master has set a good example to the non-swimmers by mastering (sorry!) the art of swimming this term. To those boys who have not quite managed to learn this term we offer a few words of encouragement. Persevere and you will surely succeed!'

Watson's words had not fallen on deaf ears. During the summer of 1933 one of the school's best swimmers, P.A. Sjogren, was on holiday at Teignmouth. A man bathing about a hundred yards from the shore got into difficulties, Sjogren heard his cries and, although fully dressed, went immediately to his rescue. Then, after bringing the drowning man to the shore, he successfully applied artificial respiration.

In recognition of his bravery, the members of the Luton Amateur Swimming Club presented Sjogren with a silver wrist-watch.

Some Administrative Matters

During 1920 a new agreement was drawn up between the Bedfordshire County Council and the Luton Town Council for the administration of the Luton Modern Schools. The main points were an increase in the number of governors from 15 to 21, an increase in the limit of expenditure the County Council would be called on to provide from £5 to £10 per head, and the Clerk to the Governors (at present the Director of Education for the County) to be appointed by the governors. The governors also wanted children to be admitted to the schools from the age of 9, but after much discussion at County and Town Council level it was agreed that the age of admission would remain at 10.

His Majesty's Inspectors visited the school in 1920 and gave it a most satisfactory report. They did, however, include some candid comments on the attitude of Luton

people towards education generally. The Board pointed out how seriously the work of the school was affected by the present short school life of the pupils. They recognised that the governing body had given attention to the matter, but there was clear evidence that local opinion had to be better informed. The Report also drew attention to the poor state of the library and the lack of pictures in the school: only the single picture presented by Miss Walmsley in 1904 of *Sir Galahad* graced the walls.

The school library was a constant source of worry for Mr J.W. Findlater, who went to great lengths to persuade leavers and Old Boys to donate books, and to induce the younger boys to borrow and read. Slowly things improved and, by 1932, the librarian R.C. Iles was able to report 380 books in the Reference Library and 1,249 in the Lending Library. Amongst them he quoted *The Brethren* by Rider Haggard, *Windsor Castle* by Harrison Ainsworth, *The Woman in White* by Wilkie Collins, *The World of Sound* by Sir William Bragg and *Europe since the Renaissance* by Brett. He also thanked J.H. Burgoyne, B.W. Gregory and S.W. Odell for their donations.

The Governors decided that from 1926 boys would be expected to supply a more detailed medical certificate than that already required. It was considered necessary for the school to know of any medical problems, since a few boys were unable to cope with some aspects of their work due to ill health. It was not intended as any kind of bar to their entry to the school.

In 1930 the County Medical Officer of Health inaugurated a system of annual medical inspections for older children, giving parents advice about such things as eyesight and dental care, which might easily escape notice.

In April 1933 the Bedfordshire Education Committee, following a Government directive, decided that they would standardise the fees for all Secondary Schools funded by the County Council. This applied to Luton Boys' Modern School, Luton Girls' High School and the Cedars School, Leighton Buzzard. Pupils admitted on or after 1st April, 1933 would be required to pay £12 per annum. This included the provision of stationery and games, but not books. The fees for pupils coming from out of the county would be £20 a year. Fees would reduce by £1 per term for those pupils over 16 who had passed an approved examination, and a reduction of 25 per cent would be made for a second child from the same family. The rises would not effect pupils already at the schools.

On the 31st March, 1933, the Bedfordshire Education Committee approved the budget for 1934 for the Luton Secondary Schools, allotting £8,500 to the Modern School, £8,250 to the High School and £1,250 to the Technical Institute.

A Question of Hats

In 1927 Mr Sanderson approved the introduction of a conspicuous new school cap. It was maroon-red in colour, with a yellow band around the rim, an inch wide at the back, narrowing to half an inch above the red peak. Three gold ears of corn were embroidered on the front. This rapidly revived the insult, 'rhubarb and custard', which had been hurled at Modern School boys and girls ever since the School had first chosen red and yellow as its colours.

In 1931 Eric Taylor (1926–32) and two friends, R.P. Muller and K.L. Parrot, thought it was time the School supported the local hat industry. They took it upon themselves to revitalise the dull straw boaters and persuaded their mothers to decorate them with variations of red and yellow bands. When they arrived at school wearing them they were soon called to Mr Sanderson's room, where they naturally expected the worst. Instead the Headmaster summoned John Jeffs, his secretary, and they inspected all the hats thoroughly. Choosing Eric Taylor's design, they persuaded Charles Mares, the School Outfitters, to make a hundred! Sadly, Mrs Taylor got no remuneration! The escapade was hugely admired by the other boys, who were soon calling themselves the Boater Brigade and sporting the new head gear.

Eric Taylor's photograph of his class-mates playing 'Truss' in the playground at Park Square, 1931. The boys facing the camera are (l. to r.) Sjogren, Roberts, Barnes in foreground, Smith, Garratt, Burns, Canham, Holmes, Garratt, Rawsthorne, Clarke, Chambers, Goodman, Coles with back to wall.

'The Boater Brigade were out in the yard,
And were finding their life exceedingly hard,
For, "O, look at the sight!" was th' unmusical tune
On everyone's lips, on the 17th of June;
But don't be afraid,
Join the Brigade,
The jeering has ceased,
In some forms at least;
So, fill up your tumblers (with lemonade),
And drink the good health of the Boater Brigade.'

[Ian E. Tweedie]

Whether boys wore caps or boaters, certain strict rules applied. Headgear was worn at all times when journeying to and from school, or on official school business. When meeting a lady or a member of staff the wearer was expected to raise his hat. If a funeral cortège happened to pass, he would remove it completely. Boys spotted without a hat could expect a punishment. On the other hand, if they were causing trouble, they should make sure their identifiable caps were not in evidence! The author was 19 when he left the Sixth Form, and had surreptitiously avoided wearing a cap for the previous few years. On his last morning at School in 1953, the Second Master, C.J. Godfrey, informed him that he had long been well-aware of the misdemeanour, but, in view of his age and height, would have done the same had he been in a similar position!

Whilst writing of what were considered 'good manners', it was the mark of a Modern School boy that he always stood up when a master or a lady entered a room, opened doors for them and allowed them to pass through first, and gave them their seats when travelling on crowded trams or buses.

So what was life like for the average Modern School boy during Sanderson's time? Jack Adams from Kimbolton, transferred to Luton (1929–32) and wrote:

'Nothing very interesting happened there, one boy killed his friend with a 12 bore shotgun, but not in school hours; a Master lost his temper and knocked a boy unconscious. [*The Master was dismissed.*] Willie Otter, the handicrafts master, lost his temper and threw a half-made bookcase at someone, considerably damaging the bookcase; we put silver paper in the electric-lamp holders so that when the light was switched on it blew the fuses; we dropped stink bombs during prayers and sang rude words about Auntie Mabel when we should have been singing 'Through the night of doubt and sorrow' – and we also wore red and yellow caps and tried to ignore the nasty council school boys who shouted 'rhubarb and custard'.

'During my time at the Modern School a disastrous fire occurred at Vyse's Hat

Factory near the school. This started one lunch-time, and the streets became jammed with people and vehicles. I well remember standing in the street watching people jump out of windows, and getting caught up in the general pandemonium. Clifford Punter, who was a close friend of mine, had an uncle employed at Vyse and was worried for his safety. He had good cause to worry, for his uncle was badly burned and died in hospital next day. I recall poor Punter sitting at his desk with tears running down his face, and I was astounded that the master showed him so little sympathy and told him to 'stop snivelling'.'

Speech Days, Prize Days and Guests – 1919 to 1933

This chapter began with the first post-War Speech Day, the last in which girls as well as boys took part. Held on 28th March, 1919, Mr Sanderson gave his celebrated sermon on the school motto, which expressed very well his ethos for the school and his belief in life-long learning, (a supposedly modern concept), though it was directed almost exclusively to the boys present. It has been quoted in Chapter 3, but began:

'Our School Motto reminds us that Education is frequently likened to agriculture. Education is a life-long process, and it is only with the early stages of this process that we schoolmasters are directly concerned. We are in fact the sowers. But it stands to reason that our sowing will be inefficient unless we constantly bear in mind the nature of the harvest at which we aim.'

One wonders what the Head thought of C.A.L. Farmborough's irreverent quip in *The Modern School Magazine* of 1931:

'The arms of the School are three *wheat ears, or* [gold]*, on carmine*; but it has been suggested that they should be altered to *masters many, azure,* and *prefects, supine*, surmounted by *pupils, rampant*.'

Although Mr Sanderson inspired awe in his pupils, he himself seemed to stand in awe of no one. Ronald Phillips has recorded that on Speech Day, 1923, the chief guest was to be Sir John Hewitt, the local Conservative MP. The Head was infuriated to receive at the last moment a telegram from the special guest saying that urgent work in the House of Commons prevented his attendance. The Mayor of Luton, Ald. Murry Barford, to Mr Sanderson's further annoyance, not very willingly consented to act as Sir John's deputy. Seated in the front row of the audience among the VIP.s was J.W. Green, the local brewer and a prominent Tory.

The proceedings had not long been under way when a commotion occured. Sir John had turned up after all. The local brewer became wildly excited, threw up his

hands and cried, "Sir John!, Sir John!" and Sir John was ushered on to the platform. T.A.E.S., however, turned his back on Sir John and went calmly on with his report.

On 23rd May, 1924, Mr Sanderson drew attention to the fact that the number of boys attending the School had fallen from 330 to 287 in the past year. The following year it was to drop to 265, and in 1926 to 263. He attributed this in some measure to the increased school fees, but chiefly to the period of depression through which Luton and the country was passing.

Happily admission numbers began to rise again from 1927, but Sanderson was quick to point out that the number of boys over sixteen had decreased. He also bewailed the fact that too many boys left before the time specified in their agreements. Parents did not seem to think it mattered, so long as they paid the penalty. It was abundantly clear that the best work was done by boys over sixteen, and it was disappointing that more did not take advantage of the Advanced Courses, and the much greater choice of careers available to them.

Speech Day guests varied enormously, as did their messages, which were usually long and tedious. Dr Gordon Fowler, CBE, a distinguished marine biologist and historian, talked in 1924 of the need to set 'this poor old topsy-turvy world' right again. That could only be achieved by everyone working soundly and putting their best into it. If each boy carried on like that the poor old world would soon be spinning on its axis again. The Lord Lieutenant, Mr S. Howard Whitbread appealed to both masters and boys to develop an affection for their own language, and to try and speak it and write it clearly and effectively. With all the money spent on education, boys and girls went out into the world singularly incapable of writing a letter in English, and very often incapable of properly addressing an envelope. Another guest, Mr Hugh E. Seebohm, a banker and Chairman of the Luton Water Company, also took the subject of language and its everyday abuse. How they cut it, they clipped it, they left out words and they mispronounced others. It was wonderful, really, that they got along as well as they did. The address by Sir Frank Dyson, the Astronomer Royal, in March 1928 was eagerly awaited by the boys, but was as exciting as a wet weekend. Instead of the stars he gave them yet another lecture on working hard! Mr H.C. Hambro was the guest in 1929, and endeavoured to introduce some humour. That morning he had been appointed High Sheriff of Bedfordshire. He told the boys that he might not be able to hang them all, but he could summon them on a grand jury, and that, in his opinion, was a lot worse – (laughter). 1930 saw the Vicar of Luton, Revd. R.T. Howard, deliver a homily on life being divided into three parts – work, games and leisure, each requiring as much attention as the others. Lord Ernle, (formerly R.E. Prothero), who had done so much for the school in its earliest days, was the most appropriate guest for Speech Day, 1933, which also marked the retirement of the Headmaster. As Chairman of the Bedfordshire Secondary Education Committee in 1903, it was he who drafted the report urging the establishment of a Modern School at Luton. Speaking to the boys,

Lord Ernle said that there was one matter in which every one of them could help and which no one else could do for them – to see that the tone and the atmosphere of the School was such that nothing degrading, nothing despicable, nothing dirty, could thrive in their midst.

Examination Successes – 1919 to 1933

Speech Days concluded with prize giving, and special attention was always given to those boys who had achieved high academic honours. Their success usually resulted in the pupils being given an extra holiday. In July 1920 S.J. Gregg passed his Cambridge Higher School Certificate, gaining a distinction in Chemistry, and was awarded a State Scholarship. He went on to London University where he became the first Old Modernian to earn the title of Doctor of Philosophy. D.E. Lambert left school in 1920 to enter King's College, London, and gained a BSc in engineering. In 1921 T.S. Skillman won a State Scholarship for distinctions in Chemistry and Physics, and the following year was awarded an Open Scholarship worth £80 a year at Clare College, Cambridge. A.M. Sim left in 1921 for Downing College, Cambridge to study Natural Sciences, and later worked in West Africa. Alfred Caress (with distinctions in Chemistry, Mathematics and Physics) gained an Open Scholarship of £60 a year at Trinity Hall, Cambridge in 1922. In 1926 he was 'diligently researching in the mysterious gloom of the Physico-Chemical Laboratory. The exact nature of his work being beyond the comprehension of his fellow Old Modernians, who had it on his own authority that it was of the first importance.' Shortly afterwards he received the Gordon Wigan Prize for chemical research at Cambridge, and a Salters' Company Fellowship of £250 per annum for research. He obtained his PhD in 1928 and joined the Headquarters Staff of Imperial Chemical Industries, Ltd., rising by 1960 to become a Director of the Company. He was one of the first (of two) men to make corrugated Perspex sheets. In the same year R.J. Connell graduated with a BA in Divinity from Manchester University. He became a Methodist minister, and in later life was General Secretary of the Methodist Homes for the Aged.

The Oddie brothers, Brian and Geoffrey, were awarded Leaving Scholarships of £50 per annum in 1923 and proceeded to Queen Mary College, London. L.E. Prosser received a Leaving Scholarship worth £50 and in 1925 an Open Scholarship of £40 tenable at King's College, London. S.G. Smith was given a Leaving Scholarship of £40 a year by the Cowper and Bennett Trust in 1924. State Scholarships were awarded to Herbert R. Barnell and William H. Wheeler in 1925. Barnell was also awarded a Governors' Leaving scholarship of £50 per annum. In 1931 he received the Frank Smart Studentship in Botany at Cambridge University, one of the most coveted botanical awards. With a PhD he was appointed Plant Physiologist and Lecturer in the School of Agriculture in Cambridge in 1932. He

went to Trinidad in 1937 to work on the storage and transport of tropical fruits. On his return in 1943 he worked for the Ministry of Food becoming Chief Scientific Adviser. W.H. Wheeler won an Open Exhibition of £30 a year tenable at East London College; and later on an Open Scholarship of £60 per annum at St Catherine's College, Cambridge. He obtained 1st class honours in the Cambridge Natural Sciences Tripos, Part 1 in 1928, and was later awarded a Beit Fellowship at London University. A census of Old Modernians at London University in June 1927 showed three Chemists, one Dentist, one Economist, two Physicists, one Pharmacist, one Engineer – 'and there ought to have been another, but B.C.V. Oddie has been captured by the Air Ministry, who needed a cross-country runner.' C.W.W. Read got a first class in Physics in his final BSc (Honours) degree at the end of two years at London University. L.E. Prosser's first-class BSc (Honours) in Engineering was also notable for being obtained at the end of his second year in 1927. An Entrance Scholarship of £60 a year, tenable at the Imperial College of Science and Technology, London, was awarded to W.G. Wren in 1928. The following year E.T.H. Hoblyn (son of the Head of Science, J.B. Hoblyn) received an Open Scholarship to the same College, where he obtained the ARCS, and BSc (London), with 2nd Class Honours in Chemistry. In 1932 he was awarded an Industrial Research Fellowship of £300 by the Salters' Institute of Industrial Chemistry, and in 1933 a PhD for research work in chemical engineering at Imperial College, London. J.H. Burgoyne, who gained his School Certificate with a distinction in mathematics at 14, was awarded an Open Scholarship to Imperial College, London in 1931, where he studied chemical engineering. There he worked for his BSc, his PhD, and was the first Old Modernian to become a DSc for his research into fuel technology. In later life he was to hold visiting Professorships at City University and the University of Sheffield. He received a CBE in 1980. H.R.V. Meakin was also awarded a Governors' Leaving Scholarship of £50 a year. That same year, P. Scanes, took his London BSc (Hons.) in Mathematics whilst working for his living at the same time, and F.F. May qualified as a Licentiate of Dental Surgery at the Royal College of Surgeons. At Queens' College, Cambridge, Laurence A. Brown was awarded the degree of BA, Class II of the Theology Tripos, and was ordained deacon in Southwark Cathedral in 1932. He held curacies in Kennington and Luton, before becoming a Vicar in Welwyn Garden City. In 1960 he was consecrated Bishop of Warrington. Also in 1933, Herman E.W. Chalkley, the son of an Old Boy, obtained a Leaving Scholarship of £50, and an Open Exhibition to study biology at Imperial College, London. In 1948 he joined the School staff to Head the Biology department.

The School Building

During the summer holidays in 1920 the interior of the school, which after 12 years was looking rather tired, was redecorated at a cost of £344. The whole building was beginning to prove rather inadequate, not only due to overcrowding, but also because of a lack of foresight in its design. In 1908 the County Council had tried to get as much value as possible from their architects, whilst spending as little as possible. The result sacrificed any attempt at an attractive working environment, for stark utility. In an article on 'Luton's Architecture' in *The Luton News* for 20th May, 1920, V.G. Lewis wrote:

> 'Why should we have such blots upon the face of the town as that horrible building in Park Square – the Modern School? I never glance at the place without a shudder to contemplate such ugliness. What a temple of learning for young Luton!
>
> 'What could have commended it in the eyes of those who caused it to be erected has ever been a mystery to me. It is neither particularly convenient nor very practical inside, while outside it is soul starving and horrible and a cross between a county gaol and a block of a lunatic asylum.
>
> 'There is hope for the new Girls' School when the time comes for it to be built. It is fervently to be desired that the design will be more worthy than that for the Boys' School.'

A visit from HM Inspectors in 1922 stressed the need for better laboratory accommodation. Architects were called in who devised a scheme for enlarging the existing elementary physics room by removing the gallery and fitting four benches and one common sink bench. This would provide room for a whole class instead of only half of one. They also planned to turn the metalwork shop into an advanced chemistry laboratory. In July 1923 the County Education Committee approved the changes at a cost of £400, and the work was carried out during the summer holiday. At the same time £141 was spent on painting the exterior of the building.

In October 1929 the County Council purchased about 24 acres of land at Chaul End from the Chew's Foundation. This included 14 acres that they already rented from the Foundation for the Modern School playing fields. It was the Governors' intention to erect a new boys' school there in the not too distant future to replace the buildings in Park Square.

Although the school was occupied for adult technical classes each evening, the Governors were anxious that the school should be used by as many other organisations as it could accommodate. For example, on Tuesday evenings in the spring term of 1921 the Workers' Educational Association were offering a course on Industrial History run by Canon Hibbert. On 21st March that year a Luton Branch

of the Historical Association was set up at the school. Although the Association was open to anyone, one of its aims was to improve the teaching of history in schools. Miss Tanner, BA, Head of Bedford Girls' High School presided over an inaugural meeting, during which Dr J.E. Morris (a Bedfordshire man who had helped form the original Historical Association) addressed the meeting on the need to study history. A committee was formed consisting of Miss H.K. Sheldon; T.E. Maw, the Borough Librarian; Mr Storey; Miss Green; William Austin (the Luton historian) and Mr Sanderson. In June Dr Morris led the Branch on a field excursion to Dunstable Priory, the Downs and Totternhoe Castle, and in October, William Austin spoke to them at the school about 'The Common Lands of Luton'. John G. Dony (aged 24) led an outing to St Albans in May 1923 and 'proved himself to be exceedingly well-informed on historical matters.'

In November 1923 a report of the Bedfordshire Education Committee observed:

> 'The establishment of separate schools for the sexes at Luton was undoubtedly responsible in some degree for their steady growth, and had also proved beneficial in the development of the corporate life of these schools, more especially in the realm of sport.'

School Activities

One noticeable feature of Sanderson's Headship is the apparent scarcity of 'out of school' activities. Work and pleasure were kept strictly apart, and it wasn't until his later years, that one can detect even a partial breakdown of this dictum.

On 23rd February, 1921, the veteran actor, Sir Johnston Forbes-Robertson (1853–1937), visited the Grand Theatre and addressed a large audience of senior pupils and staff from Luton schools on 'The British Theatre'. Children from the Modern and High Schools were prominent, as were Mr Sanderson and Miss Sheldon. The experience clearly proved stimulating, and later in the day the two Heads joined other prominent Lutonians in criticising the lack of literary and artistic societies and other outlets for the arts in Luton.

At close of school on Friday, 2nd December, 1921 all the boys, and 150 girls from the High School, together with the Mayor of Luton, Ald. Murry Barford, Mr A.R. Bird, (Secretary of the Luton Branch of the Union of the League of Nations), Miss Sheldon and Mr Sanderson, gathered in the Modern School hall to listen to Mr Fred Wheelan describe the work of the League of Nations, and 'appeal for the support of younger generations in the work of the League'.

It wasn't until the autumn of 1929 that a Modern School Branch of the League of Nations was formed under the watchful eye of Ronald Phillips. It was open to all boys on payment of 6d per annum, half of which went to Headquarters. 175 members were recruited in the first year.

With enthusiastic masters like J.W. Findlater on the staff, it is surprising that the school had no regular Literary and Scientific Society before 1926. There had been a Debating Society which met somewhat irregularly. Clearly there were obstacles to meetings held after school: many boys had trains to catch, and the school buildings had to be cleaned before evening classes began after 6pm. These were often taught by tired masters who had been teaching all day. Even so, it should have been possible to fit in a regular programme of lectures or debates. If they took place there is little record of them.

The first recorded meeting of the Literary and Debating Society was 9th December, 1924, which elected officers (Mr Findlater: President) and set down rules. Membership was restricted to years IV, V, and VI, although applications from boys in other forms would be considered. On 20th January, 1925, they debated the motion: 'That this house deplores the wireless craze and especially its effect on School work.' The motion was defeated, as were the subsequent ones: in February 'That this house is of the opinion that the powers of the monitors should be curtailed' and in March: 'That this house is of the opinion that civilisation is degenerating'. Speakers in the latter debate included two members of staff, Messrs H. Hunter and A.W.H. Woodward. R.J. Connell, reporting in the *School Magazine*, observed 'Apart from our natural glee on seeing division in the ranks of the common enemy, we gained valuable hints on the art of debating. We shall always be delighted to have masters at our meetings.'

The following year, meeting at 4.30pm in Room 6, the first topic for debate was 'That the world owes more to its writers than to its scientists'. In proposing the motion, Mr J.W. Findlater developed the argument that through science we have become an artificial civilisation. He saw instances of science being positively harmful, as in the case of doctored foods. He spoke of the work of science as being spectacular, which made it more impressive than it really was, whereas literature worked unobtrusively, giving ideas to the world, which were quite as explosive as gunpowder. After quoting the influence of Luther and Rousseau, he played his strongest card, the influence of the Bible. He maintained that this one book had had more effect than all the sciences put together. E.J. Chennells seconded the motion.

The senior Science Master, Mr A. Moore, maintained that scientists were just 'coming into their own'. Writers had had hundreds of years start but science was catching up. He argued that literature was of little use to a starving man, only science could help him; again, only ships – invention of the scientist – could deal with an overcrowded population. He said scientists were like hermits, working quietly and steadily for the sake of human beings. Science, with its wireless, ships, canals and trains, had annihilated space and would end war by making it too terrible. He was supported by W.H. Wheeler, after which a general discussion ensued. Amidst great excitement the motion was carried by 22 votes to 17.

On 11th October, 1925, a Scientific Society was formed and Mr H.H. Watson

gave its inaugural lecture on 'The History and Development of Wireless'. This was followed later by visits to Waterlow's Printing Works at Dunstable and the Rothamsted Experimental Station at Harpenden.

At a meeting of Forms V and VI in October 1926 it was decided to amalgamate the Scientific Society with the Literary and Debating Society under the title of the Luton Modern School Literary and Scientific Society, with the Head Master as President and the senior Science and English masters as Vice-Presidents. During the next forty years, until the school's demise in 1966, it was the only society to continue its activities without a break. The Society heard lectures by visiting speakers, staff, old boys and senior pupils, continued to debate, and enjoyed visits to a variety of establishments of mutual interest. Visits to J.W. Green's Brewery, Cadbury's, Meltis Chocolate Works, and anywhere that finished with 'a jolly good tea' or 'a handsome souvenir' were greatly favoured.

Mock Elections were very popular, and usually preceded a General Election. That held on 23rd October, 1931, was a highly serious and consequently relatively tame affair, compared with some of those held in the 1950s and 60s. One could, perhaps, feel the restraining hand of the Headmaster. R.P. Hawkins (Lab.) was pledged against inflation and wage 'cuts' and proposed to balance the Budget by abolishing the Sinking Fund and by War Loan conversion. E.R. Roberts (Con.) pointed out that the present Labour government's free trade policy enabled Germany to undersell us both at home and abroad. In his view tariffs would not increase unemployment. J.R. Sears (Nat. Liberal) intended to stabilise the pound and increase exports. He did not believe in the nationalisation of banks. The ballot resulted: Roberts, 31; Sears, 31; and Hawkins, 7. Mr Roberts was elected by the chairman's casting vote.

Some subjects for debate came round again and again. Probably the most popular being 'That in the opinion of this House Blood Sports should be made illegal'. In January, 1932, the motion was carried by 27 votes to 9.

School visits, an everyday occurrence nowadays, were a distinct rarity. It was only in the final years of Mr Sanderson's reign that Mr John A. Cleaver, the geography master, was allowed to take the boys out in school time. At first they were short visits to local lanes and fields where they practised simple surveying. On Empire Day, 24th May, 1932, the third and fourth year Geography Sets visited the Alma Cinema to see films produced by the Australian Government, 'Life in Australia' and '5000 miles in 15 minutes' (a talking film), which were clearly intended to attract immigrants, and from the letters of Old Modernians written in later years, they clearly had the desired effect on a not insignificant few. Wednesday 1st June, 1932, began wet, but a large party of boys and staff set out optimistically for Kew Gardens, where the sun came out, and after gaining free admission they enjoyed an informative 'sports' afternoon. The following Wednesday, 31 boys from Form II, again with John Cleaver, spent a whole day at the Imperial Institute in South Kensington studying the African Galleries, and visiting the Institute's cinema to see films on Australia and New

J.A. Cleaver's first class, surveying in Gypsy Lane, October 1926. (back) Griffiths, Hobbs, Gilpin, Mead, Bonner, Burgess, Gazely, Bates ?, Whitworth, Maskell, Muller, Smith, Storey, (front) Adams, Brown, Parrott, Green, Eric Taylor, Clarke, Barker, McGeorge, Sjogren, Jones. (J.A. Cleaver)

Zealand. They also managed to fit in an hour at the Science Museum to complete a very full day. They returned to the latter in November 1932, unfortunately arriving late, and missing the guided tour that had been booked for them.

A Time of Change

In many ways the 1930s marked a turning point for Luton and the School. The war between China and Japan was seriously affecting supplies of straw plait to the local hat industry, forcing it to look in a new direction to felts, braids and sisal. The Girls' High School had opened in 1930, the new Town Hall was growing in George Street, and a museum to celebrate the town's history was emerging at Wardown House. There was a strange peace outside the School in Park Square. The open air street market, that polluted the School with its noise and smells for most of the year, had moved in 1925 to the covered Plait Halls, and no longer would Luton's trams:

> From Wardown's sunny pastures
> To London Road on high,
> Old Luton's rumbling tram cars
> Rock on from side to side.
> [M.V. Bates]

They had clanked their way past the School for the last time, to be replaced by buses.

One unfortunate incident was to spoil Mr Sanderson's last weeks at the school. On the afternoon of Monday, 13th March, 1933, the school Caretaker, Edward Enticknap, aged 41, attempted to murder his wife Edith, who was the school Cook, whilst she was working in the Modern School kitchen. He had seized her round the waist and beat her on the head with a poker, at the same time saying, 'This will be the finish'. She managed to get away and cried out to some of the masters to come and help her. They found Enticknap lying on the floor with his throat cut, having attempted suicide. The Police and an ambulance were called, and he was rushed to hospital. He survived the ordeal, but was arrested for attempted murder and suicide, (the latter was still a criminal offence in 1933).

The couple had married in 1908, and had two children, but they had not been happy together. He had fought in France for the duration of the War, and on his demobilisation they had patched things up for a time. She left him for a period in 1919, and they had finally separated in November 1932. She had been having an affair with a man at King's Walden for some years and admitted not being honest with her husband about money. In 1933 he had tried to persuade her to come back to him, as the empty house was getting on his nerves, but she had refused. She nagged him incessantly and he wrote 'It is hell working in the same place with her'.

He was committed for trial at Bedford Assizes where he pleaded guilty to maliciously wounding his wife and attempted suicide. A number of masters from the school were called as witnesses, together with Dr E.J. Crarer and Det. Sgt. Frost. A medical report showed that Enticknap was suffering from shell-shock and was unbalanced through no fault of his own. It was considered absolutely essential that he should receive medical treatment. He was sentenced to twelve months imprisonment, with the proviso that if he responded completely to treatment the sentence might be reconsidered by the Prison Commissioners at a later date.

The Old Order Changes

But there were greater changes afoot. Two of the School's most stalwart members of staff were retiring.

Born in 1868, William Otter joined the staff of the Higher Grade School in Waller Street in 1897. He was appointed to the Modern School as Woodwork Instructor at the time of its foundation in 1904. He was already serving as an Instructor under the Technical Instruction

LEFT Willy Otter, as seen by A.W. Martin.

Committee, and gave invaluable help in the preliminary arrangements for opening the new School. He worked part time in each of these institutions until 1919, but in that year he became a full-time member of the School staff. The teaching of Scripture was one of his great joys. He and his wife spent many pleasant hours watching School cricket, and year after year he had coached the Wasps tug-o'-war team to victory.

His three sons were educated at Luton Modern School; and all were treated impartially. They were Raymond E. Otter (1907–10) who emigrated to Australia; L.M. Otter (1911–15); and Alan S. Otter (1916–23).

When 'Willie' retired at Easter 1933, the Head Boy, J.R. Coles, presented him with a gold watch on behalf of the boys. This was complemented with a gold chain and the best wishes of the staff; and on behalf of the Old Boys, Mr E.J. Chennells and Mr. L.B. Hunt presented him with an electric standard lamp and shade. Another Old Boy, G.L. Bond, observed that Mr Otter had made an impression on him at a very early age. He was bending over at the time and was doing his best with a mortice and tenon!

During the Second World War, and at the age of 73, Mr Otter came out of retirement to teach at Bradgers Hill from 1941 to 1944. In May 1944, whilst visiting friends in Sheffield, he unexpectedly died, and was buried in Luton General Cemetery after a service at Christ Church, Luton. On 7th December 1944 his eldest son, Raymond Otter, visited the School and presented the Otter Cup for junior Inter-House Football in memory of his father.

At the end of the summer term 1933, Thomas A.E. Sanderson ('Timmy') completed 29 years as Headmaster of Luton Modern School, and at the age of 65 began his well-earned retirement. He was getting tired, and although he still ran a good school, his lack of vitality was beginning to show. He did not encourage his younger staff members to initiate new ideas, and many felt his regime oppresive. The school was marking time. By a curious coincidence, 1904, the year he began teaching at Luton, was the one in which the school's last Headmaster, K.B. Webb, was born.

Speaking at Prize Day on 1st June, 1933, Lord Ernle said that in Mr Sanderson they had been fortunate in obtaining a man, reserved perhaps in speech and manner, always loyal to his Governors, preferring the interests of masters and students to his own, and so compelling them to a recognition of his efficiency and power of organisation, and winning throughout a great town respect as people gradually realised what incessant and unselfish labour he had bestowed on the School.

When Mr Sanderson was starting on his difficult task, Lord Ernle had wished him "God-speed"; now he was laying down his burden, he was glad to say: "Well done."

The boys of the school presented him with a set of golf clubs with chromium-plated steel shafts. H.E.W. Chalkley, as Head Prefect, made the presentation, prefacing it with a short speech of praise for what the Headmaster had done for the

school. Afterwards, Mr Sanderson went round and said Good-bye to each form in turn, and it was wonderful to see the way the boys showed their unaffected good-will towards him.

The staff's gift, from both past and present members, consisted of a silver salver, and was presented by Mr Otter, who, having just retired, formed a link between the two.

The Old Boys held a dinner in Mr Sanderson's honour at the Red Lion Hotel. The President of the Club, Mr E.J. Chennells, spoke of their admiration and esteem for him and mentioned his faculty for instilling knowledge without killing the love for it, as witness of which there was the long record of Old Boys' successes. He then gave him a suitably inscribed gold watch. In addition to these gifts the Governors of the School presented Mr Sanderson with a typewriter.

Interviewed by a *Luton News* reporter in August 1933, Mr Sanderson said that his life had centred on the School. Its work and its human material occupied his physical energies and his meditation. He allowed himself only one diversion. That was his garden. He had a big garden at his Harpenden home, but he expected to be moving to Bedfordshire during the next twelve months.

He was asked how the boys of 1933 compared with those of 1904. "There is one distinct change. Their memories have gone. They cannot remember so well. It is probably because of more outside interests. They have not such retentive memories as they had in the past."

Of the education system, he thought that the general tendency of recent years had been to put too much into the curriculum. "If one has to cover a wider field it is impossible to do it thoroughly."

"Discipline is much more relaxed. It began during the War when fathers were away. People say that I have been much more lenient than I used to be, that is the same with everybody when they get older."

"Physically, boys are bigger now; they grow much taller than they did in 1904. It may be because they have more games than they used to, but at the same time they have more pictures [*Luton had six purpose-built cinemas in 1933*]. I do find that they think they cannot do without the very latest appliances. That is a great mistake."

Speaking at an Old Boys' dinner in December 1935 Sanderson said that since retiring he was busier than ever, and had even done a fortnight's teaching at his old school, the City of London School – which he found a very interesting experience.

He and his wife settled in Westoning in south Bedfordshire, where they continued to enjoy gardening. He came out of retirement for a brief period during the War to teach at Bedford Modern School. He died on 4th November, 1960, aged 92, 'peacefully after a long illness patiently borne.'

A Memorial Service was held in the Grammar School Hall on 11th December, and was conducted by the Revd. Arthur B. Allen, Vicar of Bisley in Gloucestershire, and a former pupil (1917–1921). Lessons were read by Leslie W. Button, President

of the Old Lutonians' Club, and by Mr Kenneth B. Webb, the Headmaster. Dr Jack Burgoyne, another Old Boy, played the organ.

Accompanying Mrs T.A.E. Sanderson and her daughter Euna were the High Sheriff of Bedfordshire, Ald. H.G. Brightman (a former pupil), the Mayor and Mayoress of Luton, Ald. and Mrs J. Couldwell, the Deputy Mayor and Chairman of the School Governors, Ald. F.W. Bates and Mrs Bates, Dr J.A. Corbett, the Borough Education Officer, Mrs Eileen Evans, Headmistress of Luton High School accompanied by her school prefects, and Mr Edward Hoblyn, son of the first chemistry master. Mr J.M. 'Jimmy' Forbes, Miss Jane Macfarlane and Miss Daisy Rose, contemporary members of staff were also present.

In a tribute, Sir John Burgoyne, a former Governor of the school, said:

'When we refer to him as the founder of secondary education in Luton, that is literally true. When he came here 56 years ago, no secondary education was being provided in Luton, and there was no school into which he could be put for the commencement of his work.

'He took on a great task, and he brought to that task great gifts. He was a most efficient and excellent leader of young people. His legacy to Luton was two fine schools, where the work done was of such high grade that they were considered eligible for a new name, and were designated Grammar Schools. Meanwhile the Evening Institute had developed under his encouragement, and after his retirement, it was designated Luton Technical College. The way was open and the road was clear for what we have today.'

Revd. Arthur Allen paid the second tribute, saying:

'The Headmaster was of all things faithful. He was never a half-and-half man, and you knew exactly where you stood with him. That is an essential quality demanded of the office of headmaster. I remember, as a boy, being absolutely terrified when I first met my Headmaster. This huge character bore down upon me, and asked me what my name was. He could see how afraid I was, so he left me alone for two or three minutes, and then came back. From that time onwards I had no fear of the Head.

'It was never the man that mattered; it was never the boy or the girl that mattered; it was the School, of which we were all component parts. I remember that when we got into trouble while we were wearing our school caps, it was always the School we were given to understand that suffered. Nothing must damage the reputation of the School.'

The memorial service ended with the singing of the hymn "Lord dismiss us with Thy blessing", which always closed the School Year at Park Square.

The G. O. M.

He builded better than he knew.
A mighty man, he. Senior wrangler.
Amid the noise and Stingo stench
On Monday morn, he logarithms taught,
Square roots and probabilities.
Interlarded with "Bosh!" and "Fiddle-sticks!",
When minds like yours and mine
(Inclined to "muck about" too frequently)
Refused to function adequately
Mathematically.
Like Sanderson of Oundle, he
Laid claims to immortality.
Inspite of mien austere,
And discipline enforced
By Red and Yellow card,
There was, beyond the quantitative
Aspect of things,
A human and a kindly heart.
And when there comes the final climb
He'll measure Infinity all right!
Elysian climes, Olympic heights,
Will whisper, as we used to do,
"Soft! Here comes the Boss!"

         [E. M. O., 1914–1920]

Chapter 5

UBI SEMEN IBI MESSIS

The New Broom
1933–1938

At a meeting of the County Education Committee on 22nd January, 1933, the Clerk read a letter from the Governors of the Luton Modern and High Schools, informing them that Mr Sanderson would be retiring at the end of the summer term, and asking them to advertise for a successor as soon as possible. The appointment carried with it a salary of £700 per annum, rising by annual increments of £25 to a maximum of £850. The commencing salary might be increased to £750 in the case of a candidate with previous experience as a Head of a Secondary School. The Committee agreed to advertise at once, as they felt that six months was not too long a period in which to find a suitable man. They subsequently agreed to pay the travel and out-of-pocket expenses of not more than three members of the selection sub-committee of Modern School Governors who would meet to short-list, interview the candidates and appoint the new Headmaster.

The Committee received 236 applications for the post, and eventually short-listed four candidates. These were J.H. Barkell, MA, Headmaster of Daventry Grammar School; F.E. Gauntlett, MA, Headmaster of Chorley Grammar School; L.C. Soar, MA, Headmaster of Henley-on-Thames Grammar School, and A.E. Wilson, MA, D Lit, Senior History Master at Brighton Grammar School.

From those they appointed Frederick Edward Gauntlett, MA, a 41-year-old Londoner. He was married, with two children, Hugh, (7) and Christine (4): (Hugh later attended Dunstable Grammar School). Educated at Haberdasher's Aske's School, New Cross, London, from 1904 to 1910, Gauntlett had then proceeded to King's College, London, where he achieved a BA degree in modern languages in 1913, his Associateship of King's College, and his Teacher's Diploma from the

Mr Gauntlett at the table, addressing the boys in the Central Hall, on Mr May's retirement. May was the last remaining member of the original 1904 staff. (*LN-LMC*)

London University Institute of Education. In 1921 he was awarded his Masters degree in medieval and modern languages.

From September 1913 to 1921 Mr Gauntlett had been employed as an assistant master at Southend High School for Boys. Subsequently he became chief modern languages and games master at Haberdasher's Aske's School, and in 1927 he was appointed Head of Chorley (co-educational) Grammar School in Lancashire.

He had played association football for his college, and devoted much time to athletics and the Officer Training Corps cadets at both Southend and Haberdasher's Aske's School. He was wounded during the Great War, whilst he was serving in France with the Sherwood Foresters, and where he attained the rank of Captain. In

1917 he transferred to the RAF, and became a Flying Officer. He was injured by a machine gun bullet whilst flying over Ypres, but, before he was fit to resume service, the Armistice had been signed.

Gauntlett's appointment must have seemed like a breath of fresh air to many of the Staff who had become rather frustrated by Sanderson's refusal to move with the times. The old man's Headship was described retrospectively as one of 'tyrannical government' in an Inspector's Report published in 1940. As a traditionalist he had been exemplary, but as a visionary he was somewhat blinkered. By the 1930s education was moving out of the classroom and taking a much wider look at the world. The traditional subjects on the curriculum needed to be extended to meet the boys' out of school interests. Mr Gauntlett, it would seem, was prepared to meet this new challenge, and give the school freedom to explore the post-War world.

With the exception of Mr Sidney Pointing ('Tin tacks') who taught Handicrafts, and joined the School at the same time as Mr Gauntlett, the new Head inherited an enthusiastic and loyal staff, and during his time at the School he made only five new appointments. Notable amongst these were Mr Henry B. Williams, MA, (1935) to teach English, and Mr Arthur W. Martin, (1936) for art. The latter made an immediate impression by designing a bold new cover for *The Lutonian*.

Once ensconced in Luton, Frederick Gauntlett decided to make broad sweeps with his new broom. Apparently on his first visit to the school he had taken an immediate dislike to the boys' colourful but obtrusive caps. He told the boys of his dislike and invited them to vote on the matter. He was backing a winner, for many of the boys hated the cap's 'rhubarb and custard' image. Apparently every boy was in agreement with him, and they were allowed a voice in the choice of a new design. With almost undue haste 'the new caps came, were seen and instantly conquered' in the spring of 1934, and as Mr Findlater observed 'they have met with universal approval and the new fashion has been adopted with almost feminine rapidity, abridging considerably the period of grace allowed for discarding the old cap. The distinctive nature of the prefects' cap should add a new dignity to that important office.' The cap was navy in colour, with the school badge and motto embroidered in gold wire on the front. The prefects had a larger version with a red triangular insert beneath the badge at the front. The red football cap with gold tassel, introduced before the 1st World War, seems to have disappeared, but the all white cricket cap with the LMS monogram on the front, and a coloured braid edging, survived. Charles Mares Ltd.'s advertisement for summer 1934 carried the line: 'The Regulation School Cap, guaranteed real Indigo Dye, all sizes, at 3/9d. Bears the 'Chasmar' label.' The boys continued to wear grey or navy suits, with grey or navy raincoats or overcoats for another year. There seems to have been less consultation about the rest of the boys' clothing. By January 1934 a full school uniform was in place, and the Spring issue of the School Magazine, *The Lutonian*, carried an advertisement placed by Lacey's of Wellington Street announcing:

To every boy and his parents at
THE LUTON MODERN SCHOOL
We are in a position to clothe every boy to conform with the
regulations at a moderate cost to every parent

Navy Gabardine Raincoats, Guaranteed Fast Colours,
rising 1/- per size, 21/-, 25/-, 30/-
Blazers (including Badges), with lined sleeves, 12/6 on size 6.
Rising 6d. per size.
Grey Flannel Knickers [short trousers], 2/11, 3/11, 4/11, 5/11
Grey Flannel Trousers, 5/11, 6/11, 8/11, 10/6, 12/9
Cream Flannel Cricket Trousers, 10/6, 14/11, 18/11
Regulation Caps with Superior Wire Badges, 3/9
Grey Shirts, 2/6, 3/11, 5/11
Regulation Socks, 2/6, 3/6
Ties in Knitted Art Silk, 1/-, Wide End Silk, 1/11
White Gym Vests, 1/6. Black Gym Knickers, 1/6

Charles Mares carried a less detailed announcement, with comparable prices, and a photograph of a dummy wearing the uniform, complete with satchel. For mothers, grandmothers and aunts, the new uniform was a licence to knit grey socks, pullovers and scarves, all trimmed with the school colours, as birthday and Christmas presents!

From September 1933, morning assembly, traditionally the sole domain of the

The boys at Assembly, July 1936. (*LN-LMC*)

Headmaster, included seats for all the staff on the platform, and a Lesson read each day by one of the Prefects. On 15th November a group of five boys who were being taught the violin by a visiting teacher, Mr L. Dawson, LRAM, MRST, accompanied the singing of the hymn. 'The School found it a pleasant change from the harmonium.' The lesser of two evils, perhaps? There was certainly musical talent in the school. S.M. Earle, aged 12, was placed first in playing the Solo Violin at the prestigious Sunday School Eisteddfod, held in the Central Mission, Luton, in October 1934.

Staff, as well as boys, probably heaved a sigh of relief when it was announced that the weekly system of exams, which had been in place since the school opened, was to be abolished in favour of holding them in the last fortnight of each term.

On the 18th and 19th December two Socials were held, one for forms I and II, and the other for the rest of the school. In addition to various competitions which were keenly contested, numerous entertainments proved highly successful. 'One

LEFT Spectators at the 1938 Sports Day. Most boys are wearing regulation blazers and grey trousers. Prefects and sub-prefects were allowed to wear navy or grey lounge suits. Navy or black caps were compulsory. (*LN-LMC*)

special feature were the decorations by Mr May, of the School Hall, which gave it a very festive charm. A performance by Form IIa of Eden Phillpotts' play, *Something to Talk About*, came in the nature of a surprise and was a really fine effort, greatly appreciated.'

The following Christmas, on the 17th and 18th December, the Hall was again decorated with flags, paper chains and balloons. Before school and between lessons boys could be seen leaning over the balconies and ignoring the prefects in order to admire these novel attractions.

> 'The day came. When all Forms I and II were seated in the Hall, a violin solo was rendered and plays were performed. After this we were allowed to roam the bottom floor of the School at will. On this one day of the year we could *cross* the Hall, turn *left* or *run* where we liked. Games were soon in progress and the noise of the ping-pong ball was heard as the last play was ending. In the classrooms many games were organised, such as bagatelle, table tennis, rings, darts and others.
>
> 'Tea followed, but as all the forms could not have tea at once, the Camera Club showed films to the waiting throng. Then there were more plays, competitions organised by Mr Forbes, the sweet music of the orchestra and many other jolly events. At the end of a happy evening the Headmaster distributed prizes to the lucky ones in the competitions; we lustily sang "Auld Lang Syne" and then went home, tired perhaps, but very contented.'
>
> [H. M. Kilby]

In the above extract, the writer refers to the Camera Club. This was only one of a number of after-school societies and clubs that suddenly appeared after the arrival of the new Headmaster. Indeed, some, like the Music Society, began at his express wish. Its activities fell into two main categories: the Choir and the Orchestra. 'The latter is still a very frail flower, but it shows promise of future development.' Beginning with only four or five violinists, it soon had 26 boys taking up the instrument, with lessons once a week from Mr Leslie Dawson. There were also two cornets, an oboe and a double bass, all conducted as an orchestra by Mr Harold E. Woodcock.

By the summer of 1935 the Choir and Orchestra were confident enough to perform on Speech Day. Mr Woodcock would have liked to increase the orchestra's strength by including some of the Old Boys, but they were not available for rehearsal until the evening, by which time the building became the Luton Technical Institution:

> 'It ought to be possible to rehearse in School hours, but the extensive curriculum of the modern secondary school appears to leave no time for aesthetic pursuits since every moment must be devoted to the task of placating that inexorable enemy of true education which is worshipped under such various titles as School Certificate, Higher School Cert. and Matric.!'

On 10th March, 1936, the Junior Orchestra, conducted by Leslie Dawson, competed at Bedford against other orchestras from various parts of the county. This was the first time they had appeared in any musical competition. The test piece was "Peasant Dance" by Charles Woodhouse. They were delighted to be placed second with 77 points, the top score being 80.

By 1937 descant singing by a section of the Choir with violin accompaniment became a regular feature of Thursday morning Assemblies. 'The general effect will be much improved when all members of the "congregation" are prepared to do their part and "raise the roof" in opposition to the descant voices.'

Members of the Music Society did well outside school. At the Leighton Buzzard Eisteddfod held in February 1937, A.R. and G.A. Emery were bracketed first in Class 2 (ages 12–14), Pianoforte Duets, with 91 marks out of 100. They were taught by Miss E.M. Toyer. D.A.N. Bradshaw passed with honourable mention in the Grade 1 (Violin) examination of the Associated Board of the Royal Schools of Music. Like many other boys in the School over the years, he was a pupil of Mr Leslie Dawson.

The Literary and Scientific Society had been in existence since 1926, but now it began to play a much more vibrant part in the life of the School, with lectures, debates or visits every fortnight. The Dramatic Society, with a membership of about fifty boys, grew out of the one act plays that individual classes had performed from time to time. Some sixty of the more serious boys joined the Chess Club under the watchful eye of Cyril Godfrey. The Stamp Club encouraged the swapping of duplicates and the exchanging of magazines. There was also a Meccano Club, Ping-Pong Club and Model Aeroplane Club. The Field Club was formed in 1934.

During the summer of 1933 two members of the Model Aeroplane Club achieved local notoriety by building a full-sized glider. D.F.J. Arnold and his friend D.F. Cook had begun making the glider the previous summer. The machine had a wing span of 30 feet and was 13 feet 6 inches in length. On launch day Arnold (who won the toss) actually glided some distance before disaster supervened. He happily survived, not only to tell the tale but, along with Cook, to make another.

On 11th November, 1936, the Table Tennis Club (formerly Ping-Pong) played its first match against an outside team, the Christ Church Boys' Club. Although they were defeated by 13 games to 7 they learnt some valuable lessons for future tournaments. R.A. Widtman was the only Modern School boy to win all his games.

As there seemed to be a genuine desire on the part of many boys to pursue athletics further than running a few races on Sports Day, it was decided in February 1935 to form a Luton Modern School Athletics Club. The school were lucky to engage the services of Mr J. 'Jock' Dalrymple as their coach. Father of Malcolm J.W. Dalrymple, (of whom more later), he was the Scottish National javelin champion, and worked for the LMS Railway at Bedford.

Athletics training over Easter 1936 prepared the athletes for the new season. They

participated in the County Championships at Bedford on 25th April, but they were not strong enough to outclass the two Bedford Public Schools.

That bastion of female insularity, the Girls' High School in Alexandra Avenue, was to weaken very slightly after the appointment of Mr Gauntlett. On 16th October, 1933, Miss Sheldon invited the Fourth Form boys to attend a performance of Sheridan's *The Rivals*, given by the 'English Classical Players'. The invitation was to be repeated in subsequent years, with the boys watching the same Company in *The Merchant of Venice, Julius Caesar*, and other School Certificate plays. In February 1935, Mr Phillips took members of Form IV to the 'Theatre Royal' at Bedford to see a performance of *The Merchant of Venice* performed by the Benson Company. In the Autumn term of 1937 Miss Sheldon invited a number of boys to the Girls' High School to see a Marionette play, *Dr Faust*, presented by Herr Paul Brann, of Munich, who was on tour in England.

The relationship between Helen Sheldon and Thomas Sanderson had always been courteous, but neither seems to have gone out of their way to encourage very much contact between their schools. Indeed, Miss Sheldon seemed positively antagonistic towards any form of socialising between the pupils of either school, or indeed of any other male establishment. They had shared the same Governors for many years and worked together when it was in the interest of their schools, but there was always a certain coolness about their approach to each other. Miss Sheldon was 37 years old when she became Head of the Girls' School, a year older than Sanderson when he was appointed to the Modern School. By 1919 he was 51. As a Cambridge scholar, at a time when neither Oxford nor Cambridge granted degrees to women, irrespective of their ability, it is possible that he instinctively regarded her as inferior. She certainly exhibited a broader, more 'modern' approach to education. One cannot help feeling that she enjoyed 'scoring' points in his later years, making sure that all her School's most positive achievements were recorded in the local press: something that did not seem to interest Mr Sanderson.

Frederick Gauntlett was, as yet, an unknown quantity, with excellent qualifications and a fine military record: everyone wanted to meet him. On 13th December he was invited to present the prizes at the Girls' High School Speech Day, and Luton Rotary Club and Luton Services Club both invited him to speak at their Annual Dinners. He soon found himself on numerous out-of-school committees, and it wasn't long before the pressure of work began to tell. For example, in 1935 he had to resign from the Luton Public Libraries Committee that met on Tuesday evenings. He was by then in control of evening classes with more than 800 members, and Tuesday was one of his busiest evenings at the Technical Institute.

One innovation of the new Headmaster was the School List. First introduced in 1933, the Lists eventually recorded the names and degrees of staff, the House allocations of staff and prefects, the names of prefects, sub-prefects and monitors, and also those of form captains, and the house, school number, name, age, and form

of every pupil, in alphabetical order. For some years from 1941 the Lists contained all the School rules. Later the rules were sold separately, price one penny. Lists continued to be printed after the School became the Sixth Form College.

Every boy who passed through the School had his own individual *dossier*, containing all his records throughout the time he was at the School, often to well beyond the day he left. Most of these are still preserved in the Archive Room at the Sixth Form College, filed under the pupil's School number.

The Golden Thirties

On 24th February, 1934, the poet, Walter de la Mare visited the school, and read one of his fairy-tales and some of his poems to a number of the younger boys. Before Mr de la Mare began, the Headmaster, perhaps rather audaciously, explained the characteristic features of the poet's work, hopefully enabling the audience to enjoy the readings with greater understanding.

Summer holidays were times for the older boys to get away from home. Hugh 'Froggy' Watson was a great advocate of the Youth Hostel Movement, and tried to persuade some of them to join. Although it started in Germany before the First World War, an English Youth Hostel Association had been operating from Welwyn Garden City since 1930. It cost 2/6 a year to belong, or 5/- if you were over twenty-five. All sorts of buildings had been adapted as hostels all over the country where you could stay for 1/- a night. 'Froggy' was clearly impressed by what he had seen on his travels in Germany:

'Two hostels in the most romantic situations are the Loreli Hostel, perched upon the Loreli Rock, and Burg Stahleck, on the other side of the Rhine, above Bacharach. The latter hostel is a new building fitted into the ruins of an old Rhine castle. A night spent here is unforgettable, especially if it is a warm, moonlight night, and one has joined with the 150 odd youths and maidens singing their national and folk songs on the ancient battlements overlooking the Rhine.

'The leaders of the Hitler Movement, recognising the great value of the Association with its network of hostels, have not hesitated to give their approval and encouragement. They recognise that nothing is more likely to inspire in young Germans a greater love of their country than intimate knowledge of it gained by wandering on foot, touring on bicycles, or travelling by canoe throughout the length and breadth of the land. This, then, is a legacy they have accepted with great satisfaction from their predecessors.'

On the 23rd July, 1938, Mr Enyr Jones led the first party of boys from the Modern School on a journey abroad. Twenty-five of them sailed from Hull on a cruise to Norway on board the brand new *M.S. Dunera*. The trip was held under the auspices

of the School Journey Association. Altogether there were 850 boys and 1350 adult passengers on the ship, including fifty more Luton boys from Beech Hill, Denbigh Road and Old Bedford Road schools.

'The weather throughout the cruise was quite good, the last day at Stavanger especially being hot and sunny. During the voyage concerts and films were arranged for the adults and schoolboys, as a result life on board was very rarely dull.

'The first place to be visited was Bergen, a quaint city, surrounded by steep hills on the landward side. Wonderful views could be obtained from the summit of the funicular railway. We went to see the Svartisen glacier extending from snowfields to the sea, and we watched reindeer swimming from our ship. At Bodø, eighty miles inside the Arctic Circle, the whole town turned out to greet us with a civic welcome as it was the first time so large a ship had visited the port. A local band did its best to play the two National Anthems. The Mayor made a speech in exceptionally good English, and in the evening he and other leading townsfolk were entertained to dinner and a concert on board the ship. That night everyone stayed up to watch the midnight sun: it was only below the horizon for ¾ of an hour. [Two years later invading Germans razed Bodø to the ground; it has now been rebuilt.]

'One of the highlights of the cruise was the wonderful train journey from Åndalsnes to Bjorli. For thirty-six miles the railway rises in a steady gradient of one in fifty, and is a marvellous example of engineering skill. At Stavanger, the centre of the fish-canning industry, we made a fascinating visit to a canning factory. From Stavanger the ship returned to dock at Tilbury on 6th August, and so ended a splendid fortnight's holiday.'   [A.R. Emery and G.A. East]

When *M.S. Dunera* arrived at Tilbury a party from Luton Technical College were waiting to begin a repeat of the same cruise.

Societies and Clubs

The new Headmaster was to find himself elected President of most of the School's Clubs and Societies. He told the Literary and Scientific Society that he would follow their proceedings with interest and would do his best to be present at some of them. On 18th October the Lit. and Sci. visited Messrs. Waterlow's printing works at Dunstable, where they watched all the stages of book production from setting the type on the Linotype machine to the application of gold leaf to the bindings. The first debate of the year considered the motion that 'In the opinion of this House modern dress needs reforming'. It was defeated by 34 votes to 18. Other debates included 'This House considers Dictatorship a better form of government than

Society and Club Officials, 1935–36. (back row) I.L. Cameron, G.C. Brandon, W.J. King, J.A. Pyper, R.D. Chapman, (middle) R.A. Newham, R.G. Sinfield, P.A. Neville, P. Andrews, R.G. West, W.A. Morton, R.J.C. Hazleton, G.R. Crouch, (front) R.B. Birchmore, H.A.W. Clarke, I.E. Tweedie, P.C. Whalley, R.R. Flint, G.E.K. Walsh, R.C. Janes, B.P. Connors, C.H. Collins.

Democracy' (defeated 27 votes to 5); 'That the Cinema is a menace to society' (carried 22 votes to 17); and 'That the Cave-man was happier than the Man of Today' (carried 20 votes to 18). In November 1933 the Revd. E. Scott illustrated his lecture on the recent Scout Jamboree in Austria with lantern slides made from his own photographs. Later in the month Mr Gauntlett talked about his summer holiday in Canada. In December, one of the boys, J.P.C. Seale, showed lantern slides of a journey he had made to the upper reaches of the Thames. Two members of staff, Mr Enyr Jones and Mr Hugh Watson, talked about 'Cowboys in the Pampas', and 'Tramping in the Rhine valley'. During the year, four of the senior boys gave talks on subjects as diverse as Astronomy, Witchcraft, Television and Cubism. In 1935 Mr Henry B. Williams' talk was called 'Peeps at Samuel Pepys'.

In February 1936 the first of what was to become an Annual Joint Debate was held at the High School with the High School Literary Society. Chaired by Mr Gauntlett, the motion: 'That England is on the Downgrade' was debated by Margaret Knight and G.E.K. Walsh who were for the motion, and R.R. Flint and Marjorie Thorogood who opposed it. The motion was defeated by an overwhelming majority. The subject for 1937: 'That it is justifiable to keep wild animals in captivity' was carried by 89 votes to 60. In 1938, the motion 'That newspapers are

a harmful influence' was defeated; and in 1939, with Miss Sheldon in the Chair, 'That the progress of science is a menace to civilisation', was defeated 113 to 42.

Over the years the Lit. and Sci. made visits to the Foster Instrument Company in Letchworth, Vauxhall Motors, Naylor Brothers in Slough, the Skefko Ball Bearing Company, the Shredded Wheat Co, Laporte Chemicals, Bovril Ltd, the Gramophone Co at Hayes, Electrolux Ltd, Meltis Chocolate Company at Bedford, Murphy Radio at Welwyn and numerous other companies.

On 18th May, 1934, the Dramatic Society presented four one-act plays before the School in the School Hall. The first was *The Bishop's Candlesticks* (Norman McKinnel) adapted from Victor Hugo's *Les Misérables,* and produced by Mr Partridge. Mr Thomas P. Clark produced *Evidence for ....,* by Harold Simpson. The third play was Clemence Dane's *Shivering Shocks,* produced by Messrs Cleaver and Watson, and the performance ended with *The Old Bull,* by Bernard Gilbert, produced by Mr Jones. Ronald R. Flint reviewed the plays for *The Lutonian* and observed that '*Evidence for....* showed the disadvantage of hero Brown making love to heroine Smith. In future it would be advisable to present plays with no love-making and several stage fights.' He concluded by mentioning: 'the realistic effect of the fire – which burned continuously, but squeaked – and the School Orchestra, yet in its infancy, which filled the intervals most pleasantly.' The School's newly acquired grand-piano and hall chairs made their first appearance on this occasion. No longer would it be necessary to hire them for School functions.

The highlight of the Dramatic Society's summer term in 1935 was 'The Mock Trial', written by R.R. Flint and G.E.K. Walsh and produced by Mr Jones:

'Hezekiah Percy Snell was charged with wilfully, maliciously and of his malice aforethought failing to do three tasks imposed upon him: to wit (1) some mathematical calculations, (2) certain impositions, and (3) some French prose corrections.

'Many and witty were the references made on that afternoon to the Luton Modern School, its staff, its prefects and its dinners. It will surely be agreed that every part was played admirably. And what a cast! It will be some time before we forget the sulking prisoner, his tearful mother, the stern judge and the charming Miss Luvaduck; not forgetting the somewhat cosmopolitan jury and Sir Ebenezer Flint and Sir Gekko de Walsh, the persistent counsel.

'The prisoner was found guilty and sentenced to take School dinners for the remainder of the term. On hearing the sentence the prisoner fainted and was carried away by the two warders.'

In December 1935 the Dramatic Society provided three plays for the Christmas Socials, *The Crimson Coconut,* by Ian Hay, *The Dear Departed,* by Andrew Lang and *The Man in the Bowler Hat,* by A.A. Milne. *The Dear Departed* was produced by Mr

Jones, the other two plays by Mr Williams. R.B. Salmon, who played the waiter in *The Crimson Coconut*, was awarded a prize for Best Actor.

At the Socials in December 1936 *The Grand Cham's Diamond* by Alan Monkhouse, *Eldorado*, by Bernard Gilbert, and *Pyramus and Thisbe* from *A Midsummer Night's Dream*, by Shakespeare, were produced by Mr Jones, Mr Martin and Mr Williams respectively. D.G. Stanghan and R.H. Rainbow were the outstanding actors.

The Dramatic Society's plays for the Christmas Social in 1937 were *The Oak Settle*, by Harold Brighthouse, produced by Mr Jones, *Excerpts from Henry IV, Part I*, produced by Mr Williams, and *St. Simeon Stylites*, by F. Sladen-Smith, produced by Mr A.W. Martin. Messrs. M. Holdsworth, R.S. Newman and S.E. Richardson managed the lighting. The Society repeated the last play at the Girls' High School on 2nd March 1938, and, whilst the girls attended in large numbers, the actors did not get the support they expected from their own School.

When first formed The Camera Club was interested in both moving and still photography. In 1934 it attracted an audience of 250 when it screened Fritz Lang's 1926 German silent film *Metropolis,* set in an underground city in the year 2000. Club members visited the projection boxes of both the 'Alma' and 'Palace' cinemas, and began to make their own film. In 1935, with the formation of the Film Club, the Camera Club concentrated on still photography. Encouraged by Mr Harold Woodcock, boys learnt how to develop their own films and to take portrait and flashlight photographs. In the autumn of 1935 the School managed to find them space for a small dark-room. Much of the Club's work was entered in the Luton and District Camera Club's Christmas exhibition, which had been held in the School hall for the past 10 years; and photographs of School teams taken by Club members appeared in *The Lutonian*.

The Field Club, under the guidance of Messrs Cleaver and Clayton, made visits to Kew Gardens, the London and Whipsnade Zoos, and Dr Macklin's aviaries at Ampthill where, after hearing the life histories of his foreign birds, 'the sumptuous tea he gave us wound up a most enjoyable afternoon.' Interspersed with lectures by masters and boys were cycle rides to Lilley Hoo and the Dunstable Downs, and the making of scrap-books of nature photographs for a competition. In 1936 they were shown round Letchworth Museum by its naturalist curator, W. Percival Westell, and the following year they cycled to Verulamium to gaze down into Dr Mortimer Wheeler's excavations of the Roman city.

Throughout its life the School was always short of library books. Boys at School would pass on titles they had outgrown, like *Comrades on the Nile* and *Pathfinders of Today* or back-numbers of the highly popular *National Geographic Magazine*. Each year Mr Findlater would beg leavers to donate a volume that could be inscribed with their name. A number left popular works like Boys' Annuals or outdated and badly printed 'classics'. A small number left books of real worth that would still be of

educational (and sometimes financial) value if they survived today. Old Boys proudly sent copies of their published works, though they were often well above the heads of their young readers, and probably of some of the staff as well. In 1937 for example P.G. Bond's popular *Rambles around Luton* (2s.6d.) and A.S. Long's short stories of air combat, *War Patrol* (2s.6d.) rubbed shoulders with J.H. Burgoyne's *The Combustion of Aromatic and Alicyclic Hydrocarbons* and S.J. Gregg's *Examination of Patrick's theory of Adsorption.*

Literary works of another kind were stored in a little book in the Masters' Common Room. They were all genuine home-made products, and represented the only type of mistake masters enjoy.

Chloroform is stored in dark bluebottles.

Cheap glue is sometimes used in pork pies and is called coltsfoot jelly.

In Hinduism there are four castes – priests, warriors, farmers and unbearables.

Many people from England hibernate in the winter and go to Switzerland.

Question: Frame a sentence to explain the expression: 'As the crow flies'.

Answer: As the crow flies it caws.

The Ageing School Building

In December 1933 the Governors approved a £1,000 extension to the School for use as a woodwork block. The Buildings Committee had inspected the room in which handicraft instruction was given and found the accommodation totally inadequate. In many cases three boys had to work at one bench. It was decided that the block of buildings in which the craft centre was situated should be enlarged to provide additional accommodation on the ground floor for handicrafts, and an upper floor for the school library. There semed to be no other room in the school that could be used as a library or where VIth form boys could undertake private study. A plan had been prepared which provided for an external staircase, and a timber store at one end of the block. Some Governors questioned whether it was worth spending money on an expensive extension when the whole building was inadequate, and should be replaced by a new school as soon as possible. A new school, they were told, was in the distant future, but a handicraft block was needed urgently.

During the Christmas holidays the School Office was redesigned, allowing Mr Jeffs, the Headmaster's secretary, to operate from a spacious room, but reducing the public view of him to an occasional glimpse through a small window labelled 'Enquiries', thus giving him a new air of mystery. At the same time the playground was repaired, and the pavilion on the playing field was renovated.

During the 'depression years' of the 20s and 30s, there was comparatively little unemployment in Luton; about 4% compared with 80% in the north-east of England. Thousands flocked from the north and Merseyside, to find work in Luton's

light engineering industry. Most had young families, some of whom in due course entered the Modern and High Schools. At the same time refugees fleeing from Nazi persecution sought refuge in Britain and came to Luton where they found employment in the hat and clothing industries, and their children sought education. All these diverse peoples brought new ideas and cultures into a somewhat staid old market town, and contributed towards overcrowding at Park Square and Alexandra Avenue.

From 1933 a number of Governors and Old Boys began to press for the building of a new School. When the land for the Girls' High School had been purchased in 1913 it had been the Governors' intention that a boys' school would be built next to that of the girls. This scheme was dropped when the acquisition of the land at Chaul End offered a larger site for both a School and playing fields, conveniently sited beside a major bus route between Luton and Dunstable. With this new site in mind, L.B. Hunt, writing in *The Old Luton Modernian* for December 1933, delivered a scathing attack on the building at Park Square:

'There can be little excuse for the sacrifice of so much in the way of dignity and amenities for so little in the way of pounds, shillings and pence. At the time they were opened the buildings were described in the Press as having been erected at a cost per pupil far less than the figure generally accepted for similar school buildings. Would this wretched unit, this paltry cost per pupil, have increased materially had some of the acres of asphalt at the rear been exchanged for a few blades of grass at the front? Would the price have risen by more than the cost of half-a-dozen pupils had an adequate entrance hall been a feature of the design, or had two or three comfortable rooms been provided? Did no-one think of a library, a gymnasium, a prefects' room, or a civilised dining room when the plans were under consideration?

'Immediately official school hours are over, the place is as comfortless as an Underground station, and there we come to the main point of our argument. The difference between a public school education and a secondary school education is due largely, if not entirely, to the contacts made other than during class-room hours. More often than not there is nothing to choose between the actual school work in the two types of school. But for school life to be really attractive and valuable there must be an adequate range of after-school activities, and suitable accommodation for the pursuit of these activities, and even for the humble operation of eating, must be provided if a corporate spirit is to be fostered. In order to bridge the gap between a day school and a public school training it is necessary to impart to a school an atmosphere of comfort and homeliness which will promote a full and vigorous school life and outlook.

'With the present buildings the position is hopeless. The solution is obvious – the School needs and deserves a more comfortable home.'

In a debate on the provision of Technical Education in Luton on 11th May, 1934, Alderman Harry Arnold referred to the lack of facilities at the Technical Institution, and to the fact that the Modern School buildings were out of date. 'While they may not be as suitable as they should be for a boys' secondary school,' he said, 'they might be of very great utility for a Technical Institution.' He went on to say that letters had been received from various people regarding the technical instruction given at Luton, and the lack of facilities for that area. There were communications from Sir Walter Kent, CBE of George Kent Ltd, from the Luton section of an association of engineers, and from the Chamber of Commerce, in relation to trade schools.

On 30th November, 1934, the County Council approved plans to convert the Luton Modern School into a Junior Technical School and Senior Evening Institute, and to build a new school on the Modern School playing field at Chaul End. Mr Hunt and the Old Boys were delighted 'although our pleasure is somewhat dimmed by the weary resignation provoked by the long period of waiting for this obviously inevitable development. Certainly the site is healthy, and a school building will forestall the prospect of ribbon development along the Dunstable Road.'

However, the Governors were soon having second thoughts. The land that the Education Committee had bought ten years previously at Chaul End, off the Dunstable Road, would not be big enough for a school of four or five hundred pupils, together with the necessary recreational facilities for such a number. Another point against the site was the change in the pattern of traffic since the land had been bought. Road traffic had increased enormously, with buses passing every five minutes and private vehicles and goods traffic extremely heavy. To turn such a large number of boys, many of them on bicycles, onto a main road was not a good idea.

Because of these considerations and the lack of any extra available land at Chaul End, the Governors had decided to look elsewhere. Fortunately an area came to their attention, and had been visited by almost all the Governors, who unanimously came to the decision that it was desirable to buy the site which was offered them.

The new site was at the junction of the Old Bedford Road and Bradgers Hill Road, in Stopsley Ward. Addressing the County Education Committee on 6th February, 1935, Alderman Harry Arnold said that this was nearer to the centre of Luton than Chaul End Lane, if George Street was taken as the centre. It was an area of twenty-three acres, and an ideal location not only for a school but also for recreational facilities. The land was available at £300 per acre, which was considered very reasonable, and he thought they could sell the Chaul End site, which was only 12¾ acres, at considerably more than they would give for the new one. They would be under no liability for road charges as Bradgers Hill was an old existing road, whereas Chaul End Lane would have to be made up at a cost of around £1,000.

The Editor of *The Luton News* commented rather prophetically in 1935:

'Ten years ago our county and city fathers would have regarded as ludicrous a proposition to build a new Luton Modern School at the foot of Bradgers Hill beyond Wardown. There may be some who still regard it so, but in ten years time the new school will be just as much surrounded by residential estates as the High School is now.

'One's only regret is that Luton loses the chance of a good advertisement, because another dignified and impressive school will be tucked away out of sight. But back land is cheap, and that accounts for it.'

On the Sports Field

During the Easter holidays of 1934 two concrete batting pitches for use with the nets were made on the playing field at Chaul End. The work was carried out voluntarily by some of the boys, with Mr W. Roberts, the groundsman, supervising and adding the final touches. Mr Roberts worked loyally for the School from 1925 until his retirement at 65 in 1949. It was during the 1934 season that a distinctive new cricket blazer made its appearance, together with the newly designed cricket cap. Mothers, once more, turned to knitting white pullovers and jerseys, with 'V' necks trimmed in bands of red and yellow.

In a cricket match played against St Michael's College at Hitchin on 4th July, 1934, K. J. Lambert scored 100 not out. The School made the fine score of 187 for 4 wickets (declared) and then dismissed St Michael's for 47. According to T. Brian Whalley, writing in *The Lutonian*, 'Lambert gave a magnificent display of forceful batting, his total including 13 boundaries. He is the first to qualify for the bat offered by the Headmaster to a boy who scores a century in a school match.' Brian's younger brother, L. C. 'Peter' Whalley's score of 57 not out was the 2nd highest of the season.

At Sports Day on 10th May, 1934, J.F. Wilsher broke the records for the one mile open (5 mins. 17 secs.) and the half-mile open, and K.S. Hoar beat the existing time for the half-mile 'under 14'. E.R. Roberts, for the third year in succession, was *Victor Ludorum*, and was the first to receive a new cup presented by the Old Luton Modernians' Club. A notable feature of the day was the first appearance of the competitors in their new athletics outfits. These consisted of white shorts, and white singlets trimmed with the competitor's house colour at the neck and shoulder, and with the School badge sewn onto the left front. Boys who had been awarded their red and yellow athletics 'colours' wore them vertically on the centre of the vest.

On Easter Monday, 1935, the Athletics Club competed in the Beds. County AAA Junior and Colts Championships and returned with three Cups, six Silver Medals and four Bronze Medals. J.F. Wilsher again excelled with one Cup, a Silver and two Bronze medals. 'Crusader', who wrote the weekly 'Sports Chat' column in *The Luton News*, had recently chastised the School for failing to take part in athletic activities outside the School; now he had to eat his words and compliment the boys on their

Sports Day at Chaul End, 5th May, 1937. This appears to be the 100 yds. Open, which was won by E.B.D. Jenkins. (*LN-LMC*)

achievements: 'They were conspicuous on the track, and also in field events, though they had had only six weeks preparation for these, and as the instruments they used were not the same standard as the other competitors, they were discounted. Some of the Luton boys had not handled a javelin or discus until last month, but they are to take it up seriously next year.' Mr J. Dalrymple continued to coach the boys, ably assisted by Messrs. Cyril Godfrey and Albert Partridge. The latter had been a fine athlete and all-round sportsman in his youth. In November 1935, Flight-Lieut. R.C. Jordan, the Midland Counties AAA Hurdles Champion, stationed at RAF Henlow, held the first of a series of coaching sessions at the School.

Sports Day, 6th May, 1936 dawned unusually bright, the weather gods smiling as activities commenced at 10 am. in brilliant sunshine. By the afternoon, however, more usual conditions prevailed, with a thunderstorm adding its volume to the cheering and loudspeakers. The Marconi Public Address Apparatus was provided as usual by the kindness of Mr Welch of Biscot Road. The Grasshoppers won the House Championship Cup and R.A. Newham retained the Victor Ludorum Cup.

Three weeks later the Athletics Team set off for the County AAA Junior Championships at Bedford in two coaches:

'Everything was going smoothly until we reached Streatley when the peace was shattered by a roar from Mr Godfrey. We had left all last year's trophies behind at School! The coach came to a genuine "screeching halt" and the sister coach in front was frantically hooted.

'"All first event runners in the first coach," shouted Mr Godfrey, and back roared our coach at full speed towards Luton. Everyone knows the crowded main street on a Saturday afternoon – but the driver performed miracles and hurtled us back to Park Square.

'Out jumped Mr Godfrey. In a few seconds he reappeared, arms laden with silver cups, tumbled into the coach, and off we sped again.

'Once more all went well until Barton Cutting. They were at that time making the new road – result, one-way traffic, and of course the signs were against us. Everyone, by this time, was reduced to a state of nervous collapse – Mr Godfrey's almost purple face was enough for me!

'It was then discovered that Jumbo Lawrence was in our coach and he was a first race man – well, anyone who has seen Jumbo eat up 440 yards with his lope, can well understand Mr Godfrey's desire to get him there in time. So to save precious minutes, it was ordained that Jumbo change in the coach! We reached the Bedford outskirts, and never flinching under the amazed gazes of a number of good Bedfordians, Jumbo gallantly changed into his running kit!

'Well, to round off, we arrived just in time, Jumbo Lawrence dashing out and just making his race and winning it! How Mr Godfrey survived without a double Scotch I don't know – but now I come to think of it, was it closing time when we arrived?'

[D.L. Price]

Sports Day, 1937, passed with little of note, save for the presentation of a new Challenge Cup for field events, given by Cllr. H. Richardson, and the first appearance on the athletics scene of 12-year-old M.V.W. Chote, who won the (u.13) Long Jump, and of whom more will be heard later.

On 9th April, 1938, the County Junior Championships were held at Bedford, and despite a cold, easterly wind, a fine day's sport ensued. The School team scored a brilliant success by winning the County Championship Cup from Bedford Modern School by a margin of 13 points. Bedford School was placed third. The Cup had been held by either of the Bedford Schools since 1927. It was the first time that it had been won by Luton, and well repaid the work of Messrs C.J. Godfrey and A.C. Partridge, and some extra tuition from a Finnish coach, Mr Valste. V.C. Farr set up a new County Record in the 800 yards (1 min. 57.12 secs.) and J. Lawrence scored a 'double first' in the 100 yards and 400 yards. M.V.W. Chote came 1st in the Colts' Long Jump.

Edward D.B. Jenkins, who was the School *Victor Ludorum* in 1937 and 1938, took part in the Junior AAA Championships at the White City in 1937. Chosen to

ABOVE The winners of the Junior Championship Cup at the Bedfordshire County Athletics Championships (Juniors and Colts), 9th April, 1938. Bedford Modern School and Bedford School came 2nd and 3rd respectively. (*LN-LMC*)

The Rugby Team, 1933–34. (back) D.J. Craig, T. Carruthers, A. Hopkins, J.C. Merrett, (centre) P.M. McConnell, R.G. Woodwards, A.H.D.S. Machen, P.A. Neville, A.J. Southwell, P.C. Whalley, (front) D.S. Walsh, R.F. Austin, J.P.C. Seale, G.R. Crouch, R.A. Newham.

put the shot, he was injured during the meeting and failed to score.

In 1936 the School took full advantage of the Football Association's coaching scheme. Eric F. Tomkins, the new coach for the Bedfordshire FA, who had captained the English Schoolboys against Wales in 1906–7, paid three visits and gave the boys some valuable instruction, both by advice and demonstration, and showed the staff the lines on which they might base their future coaching.

According to Mr Ronald Phillips, 1936 saw a revival after a severe depression lasting – as far as the senior teams were concerned – several years. The 1st XV after a poor start pulled together well, and although winning only a third of their matches made a good showing in some of the others. The 2nd XV were also much better than usual, though they won no matches. But the finest team of all would have been the Under 15 XV if six of the best of them had not been wanted to make up the 1st XV!

The 1937–8 Rugby season was marred by the death of a promising young player,

LEFT Modern School footballers receiving advice from the County Football Association coach, Mr E.F. Tomkins, at Chaul End, February 1936.

(LN-LMC)

Peter J. Gilpin, aged just 13, who had already begun to make a name for himself on the sports field with his enthusiasm, vigour and cheerfulness. In November he was playing for the 'Under 14' team and apparently received a knock on the head when he collided with another player. He died in the National Hospital, Queen's Square, London on 8th March, 1938. Three masters and a number of his school friends were present at his funeral.

In 1933 the Old Boys had given the school a cup for the House Swimming Championships, and two other cups were presented in 1934. Mr F.G. Harmer gave the Harmer Cup for House competition in Association Football. The Squires Cup was presented by Mr J.R. Squires in memory of his son, Sub-Lt. Eric William Squires RND, a pupil from 1904–9, who was killed in action on the Somme in November 1916. This was to become the major trophy for which the Houses would compete until the School's dissolution in 1966. The cup was awarded annually to the House which scored the highest number of points in both classroom work and sports. A rather cumbersome system for allocating the points was devised: 500 per term for classroom work, 300 allotted to each of the three major games, 200 to athletics, 200 to swimming, 50 per term for contributions to the school magazine, and 50 at the discretion of the Head Master

The following table shows the results of the competition for 1934:

	Bees	Grasshoppers	Hornets	Wasps
Rugby	119	108	64	9
Association Football	86	108	31	75
Cricket	99	66	70	65
Athletic Sports	71	47	30	51
Swimming	31	97	8	64
Magazine	39	30	31	50
Class-work	300	432	395	373
Grand Total	745	888	629	687

Speech Days

The first Speech Day under Mr Gauntlett was held on 27th June, 1934, when the main thrust of his report concerned the problem of overcrowding in the School. 'You will have heard rumours,' he said, 'of the proposal to build a new Modern School. Nothing definite has been decided, and it may be a long time before anything happens. Nevertheless, we look forward to having some day a building which will have all the amenities our present building lacks, and none of its faults.' He also talked of the many clubs and societies which provided scope for the non-athletic boys.

The Guest of Honour was Dr Leslie Burgin, the M.P. for Luton and Parliamentary Secretary to the Board of Trade. In his speech, he said, 'one of the greatest things which all schools in the western countries are teaching boys today, is that they need not turn to books of reference or to governments to settle their difficulties. They have in their own minds a 'book of words' which will show them how to deal sensibly with any problems which may arise.'

An innovation at Speech Day on 26th June, 1935, was an address of welcome to the guests by the Head Boy, Ronald R. Flint. The Headmaster, in his annual report, stressed the importance of well-educated boys in the development of Luton. 'Already we are unable to supply adequately the demand for boys with a secondary education, and many applications by employers for boys have to be refused for the sole reason that our supply becomes exhausted. Secondary education is really the touchstone of our whole educational system, and on which depends in a remarkable degree the destiny of our country.'

Sir Felix Cassel, Bart, KC of Putteridge Bury, presented the awards and spoke of the School motto. He likened the Headmaster to the farmer, the other masters as agricultural labourers, and the education disseminated at the school as the seed. The boys were the soil upon which the seed was sown, and it depended very largely on them what sort of harvest resulted. He went on to offer the boys a riddle, which was received with polite laughter and muffled groans: 'Why am I like this school?' – Answer, 'Because my wife is a Governor of this School, and she also governs me.'

The promise of a new School was again one of the Headmaster's talking points on 2nd April, 1936. 'Our accommodation here is severely overtaxed, and the noise outside seems to increase every day.' He mentioned that there were 390 boys in the School that term and he had had to send a hundred of them to the playing field because there was insufficient room for them during the ceremony in the Hall.

Mr Charles J. Bartlett, managing director of Vauxhall Motors, Ltd, distributed the prizes. He observed that 'there was never a time when opportunity was greater in the world than now, nor when the human understanding and knowledge of the other fellow's feelings was more important to the nation than at present. The world was changing rapidly, and during the career of the boys was going to change a lot more than the older people could foresee or even imagine. Prospects of a successful career were not limited to professors or commerce, because there were great opportunities open to them in industry. They should remember that there would be no stain on their character through getting stains on their hands, or even their noses.'

Opening the Speech Day on 10th March, 1937, Mr Gauntlett summed up the school year as quiet and uneventful, marked chiefly by the achievements of Ian E. Tweedie, and the feeling of anticipation inspired by the prospect of a new school building. Thirty-seven boys had passed their School Certificate examinations, and seven had gained their Higher certificates.

Sir Thomas Keens, Chairman of the County Council, presented the prizes,

certificates and other awards, and then addressed the gathering. He urged the boys to take an interest in contemporary events and read their newspapers, to look at Europe and beyond. 'Here in this country, almost alone, we have preserved liberty and constitutional government. In other states we have seen the totalitarian form of government in which free expression of opinion is not allowed, where obstruction is not brooked, and the simplest method to get rid of people who do not agree with you is to put them in prison or concentration camps.'

He continued, 'If you are going to preserve liberty it is perfectly obvious you will have to know how to exercise it to the full. But the very exercise of it means tolerance, and tolerance means putting up with people you do not agree with.'

He reminded the boys that the three greatest forces in the world were intangible things – love, nationality and religion. As to the future, he said that life was not going to be easy, but the educational facilities at the boys' disposal should be of great assistance to them.

More Examination Successes

In 1933 and 1934 two Luton Modern School boys, E.R. Roberts and E.J. Whitmore, gained between them no fewer than five University Scholarships. Roberts won an Entrance Scholarship to the Imperial College of Science and a Free Studentship at the same College, where he gained his BSc (Honours) in chemistry in 1936. In 1938 he was awarded a Fellowship by the Commonwealth Fund of New York, which enabled him to do two years research in agriculture at the University of Minnesota. Whitmore won an Entrance Scholarship to the Imperial College of Science, a Royal Scholarship at the same College, and finally a State Scholarship, the highest award a schoolboy could win. He also gained distinctions in mathematics and physics at the Higher School Certificate Examination, and both he and Roberts were awarded Leaving Exhibitions by the Governors. Whitmore achieved his BSc in 1936. J.P.C. Seale sat a Civil Service Examination in 1935 and was placed 16th in the whole country out of 3,000 candidates. In 1936 Ian E. Tweedie was awarded a State Scholarship and a Royal Scholarship to the Imperial College of Science. He also gained distinctions in mathematics and physics at the Higher School Certificate, and received a Leaving Exhibition from the Governors. By 1938 he had gained his BSc (1st Class Honours) in mathematics, the first Old Lutonian to gain a 1st class degree in that subject. Ronald R. Flint was the first boy of the School to be awarded a 'Reserve' State Scholarship for an Arts subject, all previous successes had been in science, but unfortunately it did not materialise. He went on to University College, London, where he obtained an Honours degree in history, together with a Teacher's Diploma. Cyril Reid won a Royal Scholarship in Botany in 1936, tenable at the Imperial College of Science. He had left the Modern School in 1932, and worked for the examination privately, whilst he was employed as a laboratory assistant at

Rothamsted. In 1938 he was awarded a BSc with honours, and ARCS, and later awarded a Ph.D. In 1937 R.D. Kitchener gained a Royal Studentship to the Imperial College of Science and a Leaving Exhibition. He was the first student to receive the Old Boys' Prize, to be awarded to the Head Boy annually. Also in 1937 L.J. Norris was placed 75th among 1,911 candidates in the examination for RAF Aircraft Apprenticeships and was accepted for Cranwell. M. Holdsworth gained a Royal Scholarship to the Imperial College of Science to study biology and a Leaving Exhibition in 1938. Together with R.S. Newman he also qualified for the executive group of the Civil Service, the first time that members of the School had entered for that group.

Health and Social Matters

In February 1934 the County Council's Higher Education Committee were asked by the governors of the Modern and High Schools if the same privileges regarding medical treatment of children attending elementary schools could be extended to their scholars. Parents were often advised to get medical treatment for their children, chiefly with regard to teeth and eyes, but some of the parents could not afford to have such treatment given. The Committee considered it a good idea and it was approved. The first fruits were seen the following Spring when a Dental Inspection took place. For some days one of the masters' Common Rooms became a dental surgery, equipped with all sorts of dread instruments and apparatus of torture. Medical inspections were held in the School during the autumn terms of 1935 and 1936. They continued on a smaller scale after that, most medical care being transferred to the new School Clinic which opened in Dallow Road in January 1938, and was expected to serve the medical needs of all of Luton's 11,000 school children.

Social and Medical Services as we know them were still quite rudimentary in the 1930s and boys with psychological problems were easily missed. On Sunday, 13th September, 1936, a fourteen-year-old Modern School boy, Colin E. Thomson, took his own life. Described as a clever, scholarship pupil, he left a heart-rending note that *The Luton News* published in full, in which he wrote 'I know I am mad, for what sane person would make the mistakes and be as clumsy as I am? I am subject to awful maniacal fits. I kick and damage things. I am afraid they will lead to me murdering someone.' His school medical report said that he was well-developed, well grown and apparently healthy. The Coroner concluded that he had taken his life by coal gas poisoning, by giving way to a sudden impulse, at a time when his mind was temporarily unbalanced.

A recurring item in the Minutes of the Modern and High School Governors was the withdrawal of children before they reached sixteen. When children were admitted to the School their parents signed an agreement stating that the child would remain at the School until the end of the school year in which they became

sixteen. When this agreement was broken the parents were required to pay a fine of £5. In cases of hardship repayment could be made over a period of months. Where it was not paid at all, legal action was taken against the parents.

If parents took a child away from either of the Schools, contrary to the agreement, most Governors considered that the headteachers should not give the child a testimonial. Some governors considered this unfair to the child. It put a handicap on those who had to leave school through no fault of their own, and it was thought that the Governors might be accused of levying blackmail by telling parents that it would prejudice the child's future. Lady Keens considered that it was the parent who was penalising the child, not the headmaster or headmistress. In Miss Sheldon's opinion children who were taken away from school at fourteen could not claim to have received a proper education, and yet this was what the testimonial was intended to confirm. In special cases where the Governors agreed to a child leaving before the agreement had been fulfilled, the matter was left to the discretion of the headmaster or headmistress.

The School continued its long tradition of collecting for charity, realising £27 11s. 7d. at Christmas 1933, £25 of which was forwarded to the Luton Guild of Service, and £2 2s. 0d to the local branch of the RSPCA. The following Easter £28 14s. 7d. was collected. From that £10 10s. 0d. was sent to the Bute Hospital, £10 10s. 0d. to the Children's Home, and £2. 2s. 0d. to the NSPCC. At Christmas 1934 the collection reached £30.10s.0d.

Deaths, Retirements and Rejoicings

The end of 1933 was marred by the death of John B. Hoblyn, ARCS, FIC, at the age of only 53. 'Johnny' Hoblyn had been the School's Senior Science master from 1904 to 1915, when he was head-hunted by Vauxhall Motors and became their Chief Chemist and Metallurgist. In later years he was a member of the Board of Governors and President of the Old Lutonians' Club. His son Edward Hoblyn was a pupil at the School from 1921–28 and elected President of the Old Lutonians' Club in 1934–5.

On 2nd July, 1937, Lord Ernle died at the age of 85. He had been the first Chairman of the Governors of Luton Modern School, and had been largely responsible for the School badge and motto. Born Rowland Edmund Prothero, he was educated at Marlborough and Balliol College, Oxford. Called to the Bar in 1878, he did not pursue a legal career due to serious eye problems. In 1898 he became chief agent to the Duke of Bedford, and in 1904 a member of the Bedfordshire County Council. It was at this time that he played such a large part in the beginnings of Luton Modern School. He was elected Member of Parliament for Oxford University in 1914. Two years later Lloyd George appointed him President of the Board of Agriculture and Fisheries, where his tremendous energy and ability

Presentation of a wireless set to Mr F.F. May, Art Master, on his retirement on 24th July, 1936. Note the chestnut trees and bicycle sheds in the background. (*LN-LMC*)

were of great value to the country during the War years. In 1919 he resigned, and was raised to the peerage. His cricketing skills were recognised in 1924 when he became President of the MCC. He was a Vice-President of the Old Luton Modernians' Club for many years.

Alderman Murry Barford also died in 1937, aged 66. He had been a Governor of the Modern and High Schools for many years, serving as Chairman of their Finance Committee. He entered municipal life in 1909, and in 1921 became Mayor of Luton on the first of four occasions. A national figure in the photographic world, he was a Fellow of the Royal Photographic Society and President of the Luton Camera Club, whose annual exhibitions were held in the School Hall each Christmas. He inspired many members of the School Camera Club, to whom he lectured and gave advice.

Mr Frederick F. May, ARCA, retired in the summer of 1936 after 32 years' service as Art Master. 'We all looked forward, however poor in artistic ability, to the periods spent in the two light and airy rooms where he presided, to be initiated into the mysteries of perspective and "light washes", and to hear some example of his characteristic dry humour.' He and Mrs May were responsible for the School banner which was prominently displayed on every Speech Day. He died at Boscombe on 30 December, 1952, aged 77.

John H. Jeffs, the Headmaster's Secretary, left the Modern School in July 1937, and was appointed Secretary to the Principal of the Luton Technical Institute and Junior Technical College at a salary of £320 per annum. An Old Boy of the School, and known to all as 'Jeffs' of the School Office, he became office boy when he left school in 1908. 'Except for war service in Africa he has been "on duty" almost continually ever since, although, of course, in a higher capacity later, and indeed has come to be regarded as an institution almost as permanent as the School itself. No more shall we be able to go to him for information (and home truths). He has a faculty for memorising many particulars of almost every boy who has passed through the School.' Mr Jeffs was succeeded as Headmaster's Secretary by Miss J.M. Oakley, at a salary of £120 per annum. She occupied that post until she left to marry at Christmas 1944.

Occasionally national events touched the life of the School. The Education Committee declared 6th May, 1935, a holiday for all local schools to celebrate the King's Silver Jubilee. Unfortunately the Modern and High School were already on holiday that day, so they both missed out! On the morning of 28th January 1936, the day of the funeral of King George V, a short service was held after morning school. The Headmaster was authorised to spend £10 decorating the School for the Coronation of King George VI and Queen Elizabeth. To celebrate the event the boys received three days holiday from 12th May, 1937, plus the Whitsun holiday, and returned on 19th May. A few of them made the journey to London to watch the proceedings, although the majority stayed in Luton and listened to the radio broadcast.

In February 1936 the County Education Committee gave approval to plans for an engineering workshop, two engineering laboratories and a drawing office to be built in the school playground for use in connection with the Luton Technical Institute at a cost of £6,000. Until then Vauxhall had placed accommodation at the School's disposal, but now it was needed for its own purposes. As the new premises were required by September, H.C. Janes Ltd. began to build almost immediately, not without some sadness on the part of the Modern School boys:

> 'One cannot but notice with regret that in order to make way for "progress" at the bottom of the yard it has been found necessary to uproot the chestnut tree. Apart from sentimental recollections, the tree itself has always fulfilled a purpose – if it were only to "right-wheel" round, or to supply "conkers". It seemed a permanent institution, one which defied "winter and rough weather". It once lived in a beautiful garden and survived the change when that garden became our playground. The fact that it has passed away shows us that even the most stable objects are frail and fleeting and that "progress", alas, too often demands the sacrifice of beauty. We suppose engineering laboratories are essential, but we are sorry to lose our chestnut tree.'
>
> [Ronald R. Flint]

'The Lutonian'

With the new Head Master, there also came a better name and a new size for the *Luton Modern School Magazine*. From number 42, Autumn term, 1933 it appeared as *The Lutonian*, and although it retained the same red paper cover as its predecessors, it was now larger: an awkward 9 by 6¾ inches. After only three issues this was increased to a standard quarto size, 7¼ by 9¾ inches, a size it retained until 1939. From Number 45 it was printed on luxury paper by the St Christopher Press at Letchworth. It appeared every term and contained photographs which were printed on glossy paper and 'tipped' onto pages reserved for them alone. It had a striking cover design by Alfred Martin, the art master, on the theme of the School motto. Illustrations by the boys, mostly lino-cuts, were used regularly.

From soon after he joined the Modern School in 1916 Mr Findlater, as Head of English, was the natural Editor for the Magazine, and one can detect his hand correcting spellings and grammatical expressions throughout the ensuing editions. Each year he was assisted in his task by Mr Woodcock as Sports Editor, and three senior boys. One of these, the Head Boy, Ronald R. Flint, wrote the Foreword in 1936 with an uncanny foreboding:

> 'How many and important are the events that have taken place in Europe, in Asia and in Africa since the last issue of this Magazine. The whole world has been and still is hurrying at an accelerating pace towards some crisis, the issue of which lies on the knees of the gods. Life at school begins to appear rather insignificant in comparison with world problems, and our enthusiasm for school life and all that it implies is apt to dwindle. But we must always remember that it will fall to us to play a part in guiding the New World, whatever it may be like, that will be born out of the present chaos.'

Advertisements increased, to help defray the printing costs. Regulars included Mares, Laceys, Partridge's, Blundell's, Wild's, Perring's and Farmer's. Items for sale in 1936 included 6ft. asbestos slate bedded Billiard Tables at £4.19s.6d., three piece suites for £8.19s.6d., bedroom suites for £6.6s.0d., upright pianos for 52 guineas, Raleigh all-steel bicycles from £4.19s.6d. and Lester's, next door to the School, would cut your hair for 3d!

A regular feature of the School Magazine until the 2nd World War was the 'Letter from .....' feature, written by an Old Boy at one of the Universities. These were usually filled with news of fellow Old Lutonians, university sporting fixtures, and advice to aspiring students, reminiscent of a 'benevolent older brother'.

The custom grew of exchanging copies of *The Lutonian* with other schools, including all those who played against the boys, and every issue acknowledged the receipt of 'contemporaries'. The list includes *The Albanian, The Buzzard, Dunstable*

School Magazine, The Elizabethan, The Georgian, The Goldonian, The Hertfordian, Hitchin Grammar School Chronicle, The Magpie, The Sheaf, St Christopher Magazine, The Stevenage Alleynian, and of course *The Old Luton Modernian.* With the outbreak of the Second World War in 1939 the Magazine temporarily ceased publication, and in the Winter of 1940 and 1941 the school only produced two broadsheets duplicated at the School itself.

The New School

Having, by July 1935, acquired a new site for the Boys' Modern School at Bradgers Hill Road at a cost of £7,019 3s 2d., the Governors tried to work quickly to get things moving. But first, designs had to be drawn up. The Bedfordshire County Council decided to 'invite architects willing to compete in a limited competition for a new Secondary School for Boys, proposed to be erected in Luton, to send their names to the Clerk of the County Council before 26th October, 1935.' From the names sent in, six would be selected and invited to submit designs. This was the method followed when the Girls' High School had been built. But there were to be snags.

The proposal to limit the number of designs to six to be judged by members of the County Council did not conform to the regulations of the Royal Institute of British Architects, which considered that in order to attract the most innovative designs the competition should be open to all, with a professional assessor appointed to make a final choice. A letter from the RIBA warned that if their regulations were not met, they would have to advise their members not to compete. It was added that the usual fee paid to an assessor was 50 guineas, plus one-fifth per cent of the cost of the building, although that might be modified in this particular case. Ald. G. Wistow Walker pressed the Committee to support an open competition. He had experience of limited competitions in Luton and he claimed that no satisfactory conclusions were ever reached, particularly as most architects had no special experience of school planning and knew nothing of the modern requirements for schools.

Walker pointed out that he had gained much experience from the competition for Luton Town Hall. That had been an open competition, for which people with the necessary experience could enter, and he thought the new Modern School should be seen as a similar case. There were a number of architects in Britain specialising in secondary school planning, and he thought it was better to get experienced people from all over the country to submit their ideas. The Committee accepted his recommendation and amended their advertisement accordingly. They also agreed to ask the President of the RIBA to appoint an assessor on their behalf.

Whilst this was taking place authority was given to the School Governors to take action to seed the ground bought for the new school as soon as circumstances were

UBI SEMEN IBI MESSIS

THE LUTONIAN

THE MAGAZINE OF THE
LUTON MODERN SCHOOL

No. 52   SPRING TERM   1937

The cover of The Lutonian designed by Mr A.W. Martin in 1936

convenient. Ald. Arnold pointed out that until the field was suitable for playing purposes, the land at Chaul End used as a sports ground could not be vacated. A note in the School Magazine for Summer 1936 jumped the gun when it observed that the boys had spent their last term on the Chaul End playing field. The Bradgers Hill field was barely ready for use when the new building opened in September 1938!

Professor William G. Newton, FRIBA, was appointed the assessor for the new School design, entries for which had to be submitted by Wednesday, 27th May, 1936. The Conditions of Entry required the design of a secondary school to accommodate 500 boys, with allowance for a 20 per cent. expansion in classroom and laboratory accommodation. The new building should have the 'dignity of simplicity.' It must also have the simplicity of economy, for although 'a building is desired worthy of its functions and the site, the greatest importance is attached to economy.' The cost of the building was not to exceed £45,000, including fences, roads, paths, playgrounds, playing fields, garden work and everything except movable furniture.

The competitor was given considerable freedom as to planning style and construction. The only reservations were that the accommodation was to be mainly on two floors, and that the upper floors must be of fire resisting construction. [The specifications for Luton's new Town Hall were fresh in the minds of the Councillors!] It was suggested that the outside walls should be of brick, but no form of construction or material was ruled out. The requirements of the Board of Education had to be complied with.

The site was described as an open area of treeless arable land of about 23 acres, lying on undeveloped agricultural land and protected on the east by a ridge of downs. The western boundary bordering the Old Beford Road was reserved for private houses, amongst them 'a pleasantly coloured modernist villa, a solitary outpost of a Brave New World.' The main entrance was to be from Bradgers Hill Road, at that time little more than a cart track, which bounded the site on the south. It marked the present line of suburban development. South of it were Elmwood Crescent and Wychwood Avenue, where half timber jostled mock modern, an embarrassing choice for the competitor who insisted on courtesy to his neighbours.

No fewer than 102 sets of drawings were received from registered architects all over the country. All were placed on public display at Shire Hall in Bedford from 17 to 22 August, 1936.

Announcing the winners of the competition, Professor Newton congratulated the Education Committee on creating the opportunity to build a school which he considered should prove an example and an incentive to other authorities.

The design placed first, and awarded a prize of £200, was submitted by Messrs. Marshall and Tweedy, FFRIBA of Newcastle and 9 Cavendish Street, London; the second award worth £100 went to Messrs. Taylor and Davidson, of Sheffield; and the third of £50 to Mr Paul Pascoe, ARIBA.

In making his choices, Professor Newton explained, there were two problems that had to be overcome: aspect and access. As far as possible all rooms occupied by pupils or staff should have an aspect allowing sunshine during some period of the day, and teaching rooms should have it in the morning rather than the afternoon. Access involved the ease of distribution of 500 boys both on arrival and departure, simplicity of movement around the building, and ease of supervision during the working day.

The site was unusual and interesting, falling away somewhat steeply in a north-westerly direction from Bradgers Hill Road, where the main entrance had to be placed.

The solutions submitted divided themselves into those which had the main axis of the building parallel to Bradgers Hill Road and those which conformed to the land contours, and were placed at an angle to the road. The first solution had certain disadvantages, including waste in excavation and in building.

Professor Newton went on to remark on particular features of the chosen design. 'The Headmaster and offices are self-contained, yet accessible, and the Headmaster's room is sunny and quiet. The dining room and kitchens are well thought out, but a little more room there would be an advantage. Other points to note are the roomy locker bays in the ground-floor corridor, the changing room, the roof terraces for the staff common-room and the school library [the latter was not constructed], the prefects' room overlooking the playground, the class-rooms' outlook onto gardens and grass, and not onto a paved space. The whole scheme seems a smiling, gay, well-working arrangement, full of sunshine.'

The Architects' Journal for June 25th, 1936, reviewed the winning design, and wrote:

> 'The assembly hall is placed on an axial line at right angles to Bradgers Hill Road, and practically the whole of the class room accommodation is placed on a line running north-east from the assembly hall group with the teaching rooms facing south-east. The drawbacks which have been repeated *ad nauseam* in the planning of State aided schools in this country – the closed quadrangles, classrooms facing in almost any direction but south-east, halls placed so that all their noise is reflected into the working rooms – all those are swept away; in addition the assembly hall becomes what progressive education authorities have for years been saying it ought to become; both the dominant feature of the whole plan and the fully equipped centre for all types of intelligent education in its widest sense.
>
> 'In their single class-room block the winners have considered that simplicity, compactness and good aspect outweigh the advantages of a full separation of all the units. The one drawback of the plan would seem to lie in the "smelly rooms" being intermingled with ordinary class-rooms; but with the ample, one might almost say the maximum, window area incorporated in the winning scheme,

smells will have little chance of reaching rooms less offensively occupied.

'Apart from this mingling of the laboratories with the ordinary class-rooms the winning scheme observes the division of the accommodation into separate groups with great compactness and success. The gymnasium group adjoins the playing fields, whilst the changing rooms are admirably placed to serve as retiring rooms for the assembly hall. The dining room and its service accommodation is placed well out of the way of the general traffic of the building, but immediately accessible from the main entrance hall and forming a block on one side of the main entrance which is balanced by a compact administration unit on the other.

'In this plan the sequence of movement of the boys – entrance hall, cloakrooms and lavatories, assembly hall and thence to class-rooms and special rooms – is arranged for in a way that compels admiration. Even movement from the class-rooms to the gymnasium is arranged for without scholars repassing the administration and assembly hall by a by-pass path across the re-entrant angle of the plan.

'In the past few years it has rarely been possible to be jubilant over the result of a competition, but for once Messrs Marshall and Tweedy have done something in the way of planning which is really worthwhile. Their elevational treatment proves how informal plan arrangements offer really interesting architectural possibilities.'

The Education Committee accepted Professor Newton's decision and agreed to appoint Marshall and Tweedy as their architects, and the plans were referred back to the Modern School Governors for their observations and amendments. It was estimated that the scheme, without taking into account any revision of the plans, would fall within the specified cost of £45,000.

A number of alterations were made, details of which were given to the Governors in July and October, 1936. These included redesigning the art and handicraft areas, provision for a sound proof music room [craftily placed over the Staff common-room!], a biology laboratory with small greenhouse for growing botanical specimens, a geography room, accommodation for cars, and provision for an open-air swimming pool. It was noted that if the Board of Education insisted on a covered pool, the Governors would have no objection! They did, however, hope that work could proceed on the main building without delay. They were prepared to consider the less urgent position of the swimming pool, an oval-shaped, single running track and squash racquets courts at a later date. The Governors agreed with Professor Newton that the kitchen area needed to be larger: as planned it would only accommodate 100 boys, but there were 410 on roll, with the likelihood of more in the future.

Messrs. Prove Bros. of Watford fenced the site in November 1936, and a scheme for the layout of the grounds and the planting of trees and hedges around the

perimeter was drawn up with the help of the County Agricultural and Horticultural Organiser. Most of this was not expected to take place until the building work was completed. On the east and western boundaries as far as the School buildings extended, hedges of *Cupressus Macrocarpa* [Golden Monterey cypress] would be planted. The remainder of the boundary would be of beech.

Meanwhile, the County Education Committee received seventeen tenders for building the new School, and in March 1937 they accepted one of £56,727 presented by H.C. Janes Ltd. of Luton. This was a significant reduction on Janes' original tender of £66,660 6s. 4d. 'made by certain modifications in the planning, and savings in other directions.'

Building work started in May 1937, and the new school was eagerly anticipated, though with a hint of nostalgia for Park Square.

> There's a new-fashioned school in a new-fashioned street
>   Being built in a new-fashioned way;
> With a new-fashioned hall where new scholars will meet
>   On that far distant opening day.
> New-fashioned classrooms and new-fashioned labs,
>   With everything new that we need –
> New stones and new sticks, new cobble and bricks;
>   Modern boys will be modern indeed.
>
> There's an old-fashioned school in an old-fashioned street
>   In a town that seems not quite so old;
> There's a hall in that school trod by thousands of feet,
>   And where thousands of tales have been told.
> And although to the new school I may have to go,
>   I wonder if it will compete,
> When all's said and done, with the old-fashioned one
>   In that noisy but old-fashioned street.
>
>   [D. G. Champkin]

In December 1937 the Governors decided to abandon further action regarding the provision of a swimming pool due to the excessive extra cost it would entail.

The local Press kept a watchful eye on the progress of the new building. When *The Luton News* reporter went along to the site on 10th June, 1937, he found workmen busily engaged marking out the ground and laying concrete foundations. He was pleased to observe that 'Mr W. Owen Wilkins, well known for his work with the building of Luton Town Hall, is clerk of works.'

On 1st August 'anyone who passes the site now, first of all notices the high steel work of the assembly hall, which will be about 86 feet by 46 feet, and will have a

stage and gallery. Progress has not been affected by the present steel shortage, as arrangements were made well in advance.

'Work on the boiler house is well in hand, as all the steel framing for this part has been delivered. This will house two automatically-stoked coal boilers which in winter will also heat the domestic supply through a chlorifier. When in summer the two boilers are not needed the domestic supply will be heated from a smaller boiler.

'Behind the assembly hall is a gymnasium, 60 feet by 30 feet. This will be wood floored and equipped with all the latest apparatus. It will be finished with white facing bricks.'

The Governors accepted a tender from Messrs. Spencer, Heath and George, Ltd. amounting to £280.18s.6d. for the provision of gymnastic apparatus and equipment. Some of this had to be built into the gymnasium during its construction. Tenders were also sought to provide furniture for the rest of the school.

Visiting the school in April 1938, *The Luton News* reporter found it well on the way to completion. 'Its rustic yellow bricks [hand-made Leighton Buzzard whites] and white stone facings reflecting their newness to the sun. Piers between the windows, and flower-boxes, are in brown brick. Roof and balcony projections, copings and steps are in reconstructed stone aggregate.'

With the building nearing completion, consideration had to be given to the appointment of new caretaking and grounds staff. The Head Caretaker would be required to live in a special house built in the School grounds. He would be paid £3 10s 0d a week, less 10s per week in respect of the tenancy of the house. Mr Albert R. 'Bob' Killick was appointed, out of 200 applicants, from 15th August 1938. Mr P.P. Higgins, one of the caretakers at Park Square, was transferred to Bradgers Hill as Assistant Caretaker at £3 0s 0d. per week. Four lady cleaners were employed part-time at 18s 0d per week.

Mr R.G. Currington was appointed Head Groundsman at a salary of £3 0s 0d. In addition to ordinary maintenance work on the school grounds, he would have responsibility for the haulage unit, gang mowers, rollers and other machinery. Mr W. Roberts was transferred from the Chaul End playing field where he was earning £2 10s 0d a week, and his wage was increased to £3 0s 0d from 1st October, 1938.

The Governors accepted a tender from Fairland Cleaning Services to clean the outside windows of the School each term for £3 15 0d.

In September 1937 the Junior Technical School came into being at Park Square, housed in a variety of unsuitable locations. Within a year they would be occupying the premises evacuated by the Modern School boys. A friendly rivalry was soon established between the two schools, particularly on the playing field.

One of Mr Gauntlett's last acts at Park Square was to introduce a system of House Prefects. The importance attached to the office was seen in the fact that it ranked immediately after that of Head Boy. There was no Second Prefect at that time. The first House Prefects to be appointed in January 1938 were: Bees, J.E. Carr;

The new School at Bradgers Hill, well under construction by H.C. Janes in October, 1937. This view was taken from above the toilets, looking east along the playground side of the lower corridor towards the hills. (*LN-LMC*)

Grasshoppers, A.S. Moorey; Hornets, N.G. Smith; and Wasps, J. Lawrence.

The final Speech Day in the old building was held on 4th April, 1938. Alderman Harry Arnold, who presided, looked back over the past thirty years and said that he thought everyone associated with the School had abundant cause for satisfaction and pride in its achievements. He hoped that even better work would be done at the new School.

The Headmaster reported that in all School activities the standard had been well maintained and in some departments had improved. Out of 55 boys who took the 1937 School Certificate, 36 had passed, and in the Higher School Certificate the 8 candidates were all successful. R.S. Newman had taken four Higher School Certificate subjects, although only two were required to secure a pass. He succeeded, and accomplished something never before attempted in the School, or, as far as Mr

The School Staff at Park Square, 1936-37. (back row) R.S. Clayton, H.B. Williams, A.F. Bourlet, A. Root, T.P. Clark; (middle row) E. Jones, A.C. Partridge, C.J. Godfrey, C.E. Wareham, B.J. Cooke, S.J. Pointing, R. Phillips, J.H. Jeffs (Secretary); (front row) J.A. Cleaver, A.P. Frost, J.W. Findlater, J.M. Forbes, F.E. Gauntlett (Headmaster), F.F. May, H.H. Watson, G.R. Howard, H.E. Woodcock.

Gauntlett knew, in any other. In addition two boys passed the London Intermediate Examination in Science, while one boy, R.D. Kitchener, gained a Royal Studentship to Imperial College. The Headmaster concluded by saying that it had always seemed to him unfortunate that the fine record of scholarship successes gained by the School during the past 25 years had never been displayed on an honours board. He intended to rectify the omission when they moved to the new School.

Before presenting the awards, Mr V.E. Goodman, Chairman of the Bedfordshire Education Committee, exhorted the boys to become decent citizens, and live their lives to the fullest extent possible. The proceedings concluded with a musical programme by the School choir and violin class, after which visitors had the opportunity to visit an exhibition of the boys' work.

In *The Lutonian* for Summer, 1938, Henry B. Williams wrote a valedictory piece entitled 'Farewell to Park Square':

'This is the last term we shall spend in our present building. For thirty years the address of the Modern School has been "Park Square;" now it is to be "Bradger's Hill"[*sic*]. Such an occasion would seem to call for some comment, and we all know the flowery manner in which our public men might refer to such a change: "We now write *Finis* to a chapter of the School's history . . .", "the beginning of another phase . . .", "the dawn of a new era . . ." Politicians and history text-books have made us familiar with such phrases.

'But what will it mean to us who are to experience the change, to see the School's history in the making, to be the makers of that history? With us lies the responsibility of starting the life of the new School worthily. Transplanting should mean new life, fresh vigour, a sturdier growth. By September the new building will be ready for us, with playing fields on our doorstep. What use are we going to make of them?

'For fine buildings and elaborate equipment do not mean everything. A school is the aggregate of all its members and is judged not on its bricks and mortar but on the boys who pass through it. How do the people of Luton judge us now? Not only by our examination results or the number of scholarships we win, but by what they see of us every day – our behaviour on buses and in the streets, our interests, our ideas, our everyday way of living, our development from boys to young men as we pass through the School, and what we are when finally the time comes for us to leave.

'"Everything will be fine at the new School" only if we see that it is. Not many boys have such an opportunity as is ours. We are the few who are to take what is best in the School at present and give it fresh life in its new surroundings. And missed opportunities make sad reading.'

An aerial view of the new School, showing its location in open countryside, with Stopsley Common Farm (upper left) and Common Farm – the Black Barn – in the distance. (*LN-LMC*)

Chapter 6

To Bradgers Hill
at Last

The final weeks of the summer holidays were very busy for Mr Gauntlett and a number of his staff, making sure that everything was in place for the opening of the new School on 15th September, 1938. A certain amount of science equipment had been transferred from Park Square at the end of July, but books, stationery and furniture had to wait until the new building was practically completed. For the most part, the desks and other furnishings would be brand new.

On the evening of 7th August a terrific thunderstorm broke over the School and lightning struck the clock tower, knocking off a corner of the concrete coping. Two lumps of concrete estimated at a total weight of 5 cwt. fell into the passage leading to the projection room, damaging steps in the passage. Although there were workmen nearby, fortunately no one was hurt.

Workmen were still putting the finishing touches to the building on the night before it opened. At 10.30pm that evening, two men were cleaning the floor in the lower corridor with rags and turpentine when one of the rags caught alight and flames spread quickly. A large container of turps caught fire, as did the rubber flooring. The caretaker, Bob Killick, dashed down the corridor and put out the flames with a large dust sheet. One of the men, who had been smoking and possibly caused the fire, was taken to hospital with burnt legs.

Next morning, Thursday, 15th September, some 417 boys made their way to Bradgers Hill and for the first time took their places in the Assembly Hall where a brief opening ceremony took place. It had been hoped that the Minister of Education would perform this ceremony, but he was unable to attend. On the platform were the Headmaster, Alderman H. Arnold (Chairman of the Governors),

Lady Helen Cassel, Lady Keens, Mrs Harden, Alderman J.H. Staddon, Alderman C.H. Osborne, Councillors J. Burgoyne, G. Brightman, A. Day (Governors), the Mayor of Luton, Alderman J.T. Harrison, the Vicar of Luton, the Revd. W. Davison, Alderman G. Wistow Walker, Mr H.C. Janes (Builder) and the Director of Education for Bedfordshire, Mr H.E. Baines.

Alderman Arnold told the boys that it would have been strange indeed if they had simply entered the School and begun work without something being said about the new premises, which he described as 'wonderfully efficient'. With the boys in them, they now became a living entity, pulsating with life, instead of just an example of the artistry of architects and craftsmen. He congratulated the architects and builders, and told the boys, 'Your School is beautiful this morning. Keep it beautiful and don't do anything to tarnish it.'

Alderman J.H. Staddon, High Sheriff of Bedfordshire, said that in spite of anything that might be said to the contrary, he considered that that morning was the proper time for the official opening. The Mayor of Luton wished the boys every success and said, 'May some of you in days to come wear the chain I am wearing today.' In conclusion a dedicatory prayer was offered by the Vicar of Luton, the Revd. W. Davison. By 10 o'clock the boys were in their classrooms and the first day of term had begun.

A special feature in *The Luton News* displayed pictures of the School and wrote in glowing terms of:

> 'The entrance hall with its majestic sweep of Indian silver greywood panelling, and the Terrazzo steps of a spiral staircase rising very gently to the floor above. A corridor, the length of the School, with linoleum to deaden sound, and gloss paint in pastel blue covering the walls. The classrooms have jarrah wood-block floors and the laboratories oak block floors. The Library is wood-lined, with pictures on the wall, a homely fireplace and polished cork floor. Suitably sited and toning with the rest of the scheme is a wooden sports pavilion with all the necessary accommodation.'

For a more considered and mature opinion of the building we can turn to Dennis L. Farr, CBE, (LMS, 1939–47), Director of the Courtauld Galleries (1980–93), who considered it an extremely distinguished design for its date. In his book *English Art 1870–1940* (Oxford History of English Art, volume XI) he wrote:

> 'Another school in the more relaxed manner of [Walter] Gropius and [Maxwell] Fry is Luton Modern School, (now Luton VIth Form College), Bedfordshire, which was the prize-winning design in an open competition held in 1936. The design was submitted by Marshall and Tweedy, but it was actually the work of their senior assistant, G.L. Turok, ARHA, and their assistant architect, J.E. Moore,

The western side of the Entrance Hall with the terrazzo steps of the spiral staircase rising very gently to the Balcony Parade above. Below was a brass disc, listing the names of the architects, builders, governors, etc. present at the opening on 15th September, 1938.

ARIBA, who supervised it from the drawing-board to the final stages of its completion in September 1938. The competition assessor, Professor W.G. Newton, singled out for special praise the open plan of the school, which marked a complete break from the centuries-old tradition of collegiate and school architecture characterised by enclosed courtyards and cloisters . . . Predominantly in yellow brick, with concrete coping-stones and detailing, the Luton school is planned so as to utilise a gently sloping curved site to great advantage. Its splay-fronted assembly-hall, which links the dining room with the administrative block, is punctuated by a clock tower that marks the transition to the long two-storey classroom wing, sited along the main north-south axis. Later insensitive additions have spoilt some of the distinction of this building.'

Farr adds in a footnote that G.L. Turok was apparently an Hungarian refugee, who came to England during 1934 from the State Architect's Department (Staatliche Bauabteilung Oesterreich) in Vienna, but the RIBA have no record of him. He left Marshall and Tweedy soon after the competition to set up his own practice.

There was one feature of the new School that was not mentioned on its opening

day. As the boys arrived they noticed workmen beginning to dig trenches beside the playground. These were air raid shelters. Although it was September 1938, the national and local newspapers were preparing their readers for a possible war. As early as November 1936, responding to a Home Office warning, the local Fire Brigade began making plans in case any of Luton's factories were bombed. They had been told they would have 'only 7 minutes to prepare.' Efforts were made to persuade people to join the ARP, but most folk were too complacent. By March 1938 the main fear seemed to be of a possible poison gas attack, and *The Luton News* carried articles on how to wear a gas mask and prepare a gas-proof room. In May calls were being made for fit men to help dig public air raid shelters, and in September the newspaper published detailed plans for digging and building an air raid shelter in your own back garden. It was announced that Luton was to receive 90,000 respirators as soon as they could be manufactured, and by October the first 8,000 gas masks had been received and distributed to Luton school children. Adults were to be supplied later.

A feature of the School's design was the simplistic long curved cycle shed at the eastern end of the site. It was expected that many of the boys would travel to school either on foot or by bicycle. This was all very well if you lived within a reasonable distance, but some boys came from Leighton Buzzard, Toddington or Harpenden. It was relatively easy for them to get to the centre of Luton, but less easy to get to Bradgers Hill Road. A number of letters from parents appeared in the local press:

> 13th October, 1938. 'A No.7 bus sets the boys down in Stockingstone Road, over half a mile from the School, and a No.8 just under half a mile. Most of the children have had a walk – in some cases a long one – before joining the bus, and a few have had journeys of up to 8 miles before arriving in Luton.
>
> 'These children leave home before 8 am in the morning and do not reach home again until 11 hours later. It is bad enough in summer, although even on a summer's day torrential rain is not unknown in Luton. In winter these boys will sit about day after day in wet clothes that would not have been so wet had the bus continued its journey for another half mile.'
>
> '*Editorial Note*: The traffic commissioners have to be satisfied that there is a public demand before they can change a route. We are told that they have received no such demand.'

Mr Gauntlett wrote to the Luton Corporation Transport Committee asking them to consider providing buses to and from Bradgers Hill, but they made it clear that they were not prepared to grant additional facilities. The Governors were equally unlucky, and were told that the neighbourhood was already well provided for. J.H. Staddon observed 'I thought they wanted more income?', to which Harry Arnold replied, 'They do, but they also want less expenditure!' An unexpected side-effect was that

The lower corridor, with classrooms on the right and a continuous bench on the left. Most old students will remember it filled with columns of boys, all keeping to the left, and dominated by Mr Godfrey's majestic figure. The corridor no longer exists, nor does the porthole window at the end, which was echoed in the design of the classroom doors. (C.E. Wareham)

members of the orchestra who now had to cycle to School, found difficulty in transporting their instruments, and frequently failed to attend practices.

The matter of public transport was not resolved for twenty years. The School's nearest bus stop was opposite Wardown Cricket Ground in Old Bedford Road, close to the junction with Stockingstone Road. Over the years thousands of bored schoolboys waited outside 230 Old Bedford Road and discovered that if you twisted a coin in the soft sandstone wall, it left a neat cup-mark. Today, more than sixty years later, the pock-marked wall still stands to tell the tale!

The Old Luton Modernians' Club was quick to make use of the new premises, and held their Annual Dinner there on Saturday, 3rd December, 1938, ably prepared and served by the School's catering staff. Alderman John H. Staddon, JP, the High Sheriff of Bedfordshire, toasted 'The Club' in an interesting and humorous speech. He observed that he had been down to the old school in Park Square and seen desks being smashed and distributed to the unemployed for firewood. "It was a great pleasure," he added.

Outside organisations were also taking an interest in the new school and its

facilities. Particular interest was shown in the gymnasium, and permission was granted for it to be used by the Luton and South Bedfordshire Schoolmasters' Association who organised Physical Training Courses for men teachers in Senior Schools on Thursday evenings, and for an Instructor-Leader's Course on Wednesdays.

As they approached the end of their first year in the new School, two boys, E.W. Jones and D.W.H. Sharp, took a retrospective look, and asked if life had become more enjoyable. They thought it had. They particularly appreciated the cheerful classrooms and long, spacious corridors. The better catering facilities were universally welcomed, both at lunch time and in the evenings. It was a welcome change to go out at lunch time and see organised games in progress on the green grass of the playing field – a pleasant contrast to the drab asphalt of the yard at Park Square. And what did they consider were the highlights of the year? The first public production of the Dramatic Society clearly ranked as one of them (see below). Hitherto they had lacked the facilities for such an ambitious project, but now they were well on the way to heights undreamt of. Speech Day seemed more impressive, with its bigger audience and the dignity and beauty of the new Assembly Hall.

The only new member of Staff to be appointed in September 1938 was Mr Eric F. Harvey, who was to teach physical education and games.

On 19th January, 1939, a letter appeared in *The Luton News* objecting to the employment of 15 or 20 Luton Modern School boys by the Post Office, over the Christmas period, at the full-rate for men. The writer observed that there were plenty of unemployed men to whom the work would have been a godsend. The Editor observed that it was not every man amongst the unemployed who could quickly adapt to rapid and accurate sorting, and that might have some bearing on the matter.

Speech and Drama

The first Speech Day in the new School building was held on Wednesday, 22nd March, 1939. Mr Gauntlett described the occasion as a memorable day in the history of the School. 'One could enumerate a long list of the benefits the change in building has brought us,' he said. 'We are very grateful to the County Council and the School Governors for having provided us with one of the most up-to-date schools in the country. I feel that the boys educated here have a wonderful opportunity, if they will only take advantage of it.' He went on to say that he was not one of those who thought that modern youth was decadent, a charge which was levelled at every generation. The same charges had been levelled at their fathers, and probably their grandfathers too, when they were boys. The lad of today, he continued, was certainly born into a more complex world. He needed a sound body, an alert mind, courage and loyalty as implied by the expression 'not letting the side down', and the cultivation of these qualities should, Mr Gauntlett thought, permeate

The first Speech Day at Bradgers Hill, 22nd March, 1939. Admiral Sir Lionel Halsey is seen presenting a House Championship trophy. (LN-LMC)

the whole of the training given in the School.'

Admiral Sir Lionel Halsey distributed the prizes and certificates and in his speech, the key-note of which was 'play the game', he told the boys that they had to fit themselves to carry on the work of the Empire, a great work that offered room for every one of them. They had a far greater chance in life than their predecessors ever got and he urged them to make the most of it.

On the 27th and 28th April, 1939, the School Dramatic Society gave its first public performance, when it presented Dorothy Sayers' three-act detective comedy *Busman's Honeymoon*. The Mayor and Mayoress of Luton, Cllr. and Mrs John Burgoyne, and Alderman Harry Arnold, chairman of the School Governors, were in the audience.

Both the ground floor and the balcony of the Hall were filled to capacity by parents, Old Boys and friends. Acting on the whole was excellent, and the boys who had to take female roles acquitted themselves admirably.

Ronald Phillips wrote: 'To reproduce the frivolities of Dorothy Sayers' famous detective, Lord Peter Wimsey, with his unfailing high spirits was no easy task, but J.E. Carr rose nobly to the occasion. His reconstruction of the murder in the third act was particularly well done. It seemed unbelievable that Harriet, his wife, was being portrayed by a boy – D.W.H. Sharp. His mellow contralto voice, his action and appearance, the ease and grace of his carriage, all contributed to the general excellent ensemble.

'J. Gray earned most applause in the difficult role of Mrs Ruddle, the charlady. Woe betide anyone who fell foul of such a Mrs Ruddle as this. Much amusement was caused by G.H. Grover, who had obviously found his vocation, playing Mr Puffett, the chimney sweep.'

The augmented School Orchestra provided the incidental music, under the direction of Mr Leslie Dawson. The play was produced by Mr A.W. Martin, and Mr H.B. Williams was the stage manager.

The joint debate of the Literary and Scientific Society and the Girls' High School Literary Society was held on 13th February, 1939, when the motion 'That the progress of Science constitutes a menace to Civilisation' was defeated by 113 votes to 42. Miss Sheldon was in the Chair, and the principal speakers were: for the motion, J.E. Carr and Betty Linger; against, Megan Evans and S.E. Richardson.

On 20th May, 1939, members of Forms IV and VI, accompanied by Messrs. Findlater, Phillips and Williams, paid a visit to the Winter Garden Theatre in London to see the E.S.T. production of Shakespeare's *Macbeth*.

At the Annual Soccer Match on Saturday, 25th March, 1939, the School was

The Rugby XV, 1939. (back) M.V.W. Chote, W.H. Bass, D.P. Swain, K.G. Henson, D.M. Williams, H.H. Barker, D. Clifford, G.K. Lines, F.J. Mullinger. (front) P.S.J. Adkins, D.J. Bland, T.W. Shepherd, G.H. Grover, D.E. Matthews, D. Heley, W.A.C. Lee. Shepherd founded the Old Lutonians' Rugby Club in 1946. (H.E. Woodcock)

Sports Day, 30th March, 1939, when wet weather had made the track heavy going. The rural setting of Stopsley Common Farm and Warden Hill, with only three semi-detached houses in Bushmead Road, would remain undisturbed until after the war. (*LN-LMC*)

trounced by the Old Boys to the tune of 7 goals to nil, but both teams were overwhelmed by a violent snow-storm and the second half had to be abandoned.

The O'Meara Shield for Senior Rugby was won by the Wasps, and the Brightman Cup for Junior Rugby by the Grasshoppers, who also won the Harmer Cup for Association Football.

The first Athletic Sports at Bradgers Hill, scheduled for 29th March, 1939, had to be postponed due to inclement weather. It took place the next day in brilliant sunshine, although there was a biting wind, and the track was very heavy, which tended to prevent any records being broken.

G.H. Grover was the *Victor Ludorum*, with P.J. Hunt as runner-up. Hunt, however, won the Richardson Cup for Field Events. J.E. Carr, last year's winner in the mile open, was again the winner, but was disappointed in failing to break the school record of 5 mins. 9 secs., set up by J. F. Willsher, in 1935. His time was 5 mins. 16 secs. M.V.W. Chote won the under 15 Javelin, with a throw of 89 ft. 4 in.

In spite of having no swimming pool, greater interest was being shown in the sport. P.J. Hunt was the first boy at the School to gain the Royal Life Saving Society's highest award, the Silver Medal for Life Saving. A match with Bedford Modern School 2nd Team at Bedford on 14th June, 1939, resulted in a close contest, which the School won by 27 points to 22.

The Field Club was active with visits to Flitwick Moor, Maulden Wood and Rowney Warren. Two boys, Hunter and Cain, gave talks on Bees and the School had its first well-stocked bee-hive.

Academic success was at a low ebb in 1939. Although 54 boys gained Cambridge School Certificates, only 4 boys obtained Full Higher School Certificates, and ten in Subsidiary subjects. It was not a good time to enter University, and no places were offered to boys from the School.

Canon Eric W. Jones left the School as a Sixth Form boy in 1939. He was articled to a London architect:

'but the experience of walking the streets of Westminster surrounded by uniforms was too much for my young instincts, and as soon as I reached eighteen I joined the RAF, aiming at aircrew. I had to wait for training and sat out the blitz on an airfield in County Durham. Eventually I was sent to America for training, and started on a course that would eventually lead to my ordination. The local pub Landlord's barman-son took me to church with him and got me confirmed. (In how many English pubs would I have had that experience?). On release from the Air Force in 1946 I went to Lincoln College, Oxford, and was, in due course, ordained. I spent eight years in theological education in the Pacific – three years at the new ecumenical Pacific Theological Centre in Suva, Fiji, and then five as Warden of the Patteson Theological Centre in the Solomon Islands.'

The Shadow of War

In May, 1939, both the Modern and High Schools were warned that in the event of a national emergency they would be expected to take Secondary children from the London area who would be evacuated to Luton. The Education Committee had to reassess the impact this would have on air raid protection at the schools. By July they had decided that more air raid shelters would be required, and the Buildings Committee were given executive powers to prepare the necessary scheme for the extra accommodation and to carry out the work.

When the School broke-up in August almost every master and boy sensed an uneasy air of expectancy and foreboding; the summer holidays were subdued, and a feeling of unreality pervaded the whole country. On 3rd September, 1939, Britain declared War on Germany. By that time, a mass exodus of women and children from London to the country had begun.

A report in *The Luton News* for 19th September, 1939, informed its readers that because adequate protection against air raids was not yet available, Luton Modern School would remain closed until further notice. It went on to say that it was not yet known whether boys from other Secondary schools would be attending the Modern School, but if so, it would probably be necessary to work a shift system.

The clock tower and south front of the new School at Bradgers Hill. The Headmaster's room, with staff room and balcony above, are in the foreground. A blast wall shelters the main entrance to the left, and all the windows are covered with splinter-proof gauze. There is a poison-gas detector board by the front wall. The white biology lab 'greenhouse' juts out in front of the main run of classrooms, with the geography room at the far end. (LN-LMC)

At a meeting of the School Governors on the 3rd October, 1939, it was announced that the Chief Constable of Luton considered that adequate Air Raid Precautions had been made for the School to re-open on Monday, 9th October. This included two concrete-lined air raid shelters, or trenches, as they were initially called. One ran the length of the playground, whilst a second lay behind the cycle sheds. A brick blast wall was built across the high, glass fronted Assembly Hall entrance, and sand bags were strategically placed around the hall windows. Gauze was pasted onto all the other windows to prevent the glass shattering into the rooms. Fire extinguishers, brooms and sand buckets were stationed around the building. Due to the cost, and with the exception of a few specialist rooms, the Head's study and the Staff Room, there was no blackout in the rest of the school, including the Hall, until the end of 1942! This made it impossible to hold after-school activities, meetings or concerts in the building after dark. In March 1940, boards, looking like bird tables,

with a painted surface that could detect poison gas, were set up at the front of the School.

Every one in the country had been issued with a gas mask, and these had to be carried at all times. Woe betide the boy found without one!

'I started at LMS on 4th September, 1939, the day after war was declared, quite an auspicious beginning. One of the first things we had to do after general assembly, was to practice air raid drill, and file out by forms into the dark smelly shelters dug into the field adjoining the playground. With our gas masks, of course, contained in square cardboard boxes, until some bright manufacturer started to make cylindrical tins for them.'   [Dennis L. Farr]

On 10th October, 1939, the Governors were informed that the Junior Technical department attached to the North Western Boys' Polytechnic School would be evacuated to Luton Modern School for theoretical work, commencing in December. This school is no longer in existence as a Junior Technical School, and records of its stay in Luton have proved elusive. The boys and their masters lived in local homes until Whitsun 1945 when they returned to their school in Prince of Wales Road, Kentish Town. One Old Polytechnican, Harry Frost, was actually evacuated to Letchworth, but travelled by bus each morning to Round Green, from where he walked down Stockingstone Road to the School. Like most boys at the time, his clearest memory is of Monday, 6th November, 1944, when a V2 rocket landed beside Commer Cars at 10 o'clock in the morning, with a tremendous explosion that caused everyone, masters and boys, to dive under their desks. Frost recalls that the Polytechnic had six masters, including Mr Flemming, who taught English, and whose son Michael became a Modern School pupil in IIIa in 1940; Mr. Woodward, nicknamed 'Puffer', who taught Science and had written a popular textbook; Mr Hughes who taught maths and PT, and the Headmaster, Mr ? , known to the boys as 'Tapper', who was a short, jolly little man, with side whiskers. Boys who were at school at the time, say that the two Schools lived together amicably enough, but that there was no very close association between them. Morville Chote recalled some of them playing for the School cricket team when he was Captain, including a brilliant bowler called Crasman. A few of the older Polytechnic boys and members of their staff joined in Fire-Watching duties.

The North Western Girls' Polytechnic School was also evacuated to Luton, but seems to have had no contact of any sort with the boys. About 100 girls were taught in a large house (now demolished), formerly the YWCA, at the south-western end of Brook Street. For some commercial subjects they walked in a crocodile to the Junior Technical School on Park Square, where they were taught on alternate days to the Luton pupils. Physical education was taught in a nearby Church Hall in Bury Park There were some six teachers at Brook Street, under the Headmistress, Miss

Gertrude Armstrong, who took an active part in local affairs. Amongst the staff were Mrs Brierly who taught English, Miss Fuller ladies tailoring and Miss Spry, who ran a training course for nursery 'nannies'. Beryl Whipp (née Smith), who was a pupil from 1943, remembers the teachers' voices being drowned by steam trains passing behind the school. She returned to Kentish Town with the School in 1945, but later came to live in Luton.

The School Must Go On

Every new building has its teething problems. After only three months the ruboleum and wood flooring in parts of the School were showing alarming signs of wear, and the Architects were asked to rectify the problem during the Christmas holidays. The School was not a year old when cracks began to appear in the plaster in various parts of the building, and the flat roof began to leak over the Library and Art Room stores. In October 1939 Messrs. S. and F. Contracting Co. Ltd., were instructed to treat the whole of the flat roof with a green camouflage paint to Air Ministry specifications at a cost of £112 11s 2d. The final account for building the School was published in March 1940. It came to £60,741 0s 8d as against the estimate of £58,600. Messrs. R.J. Eve and Son and the Rating Authority assessed the rateable value of the School at £1,090. This was based on 500 scholars at £2 each: £1,000 and 23 acres (18 acres net) of playing field at £5 per acre: £90.

In October 1939 the School Caretaker, Mr 'Bob' Killick, was called-up for military service as an Army Reservist. The Governors agreed that he would continue to be paid such a sum as would bring his military service pay, including marriage, family, and other similar allowances, up to the level of his civil pay whilst serving in HM forces. Mrs Killick would be allowed to occupy the Caretaker's house for the duration of the War. Mr P. Quenett was appointed temporary Caretaker at a salary of £3 per week. In February 1940 the full-time caretakers and groundsmen at both the Modern and High Schools were given a temporary increase in wages of 3s 0d a week. The wages of the women cleaners was also increased, to 10 old pence an hour.

Mr A. Talbot, BA, joined the staff in September 1939, to teach mathematics, and Mr M. R. Barker, BSc came for one term in April 1940 to teach biology.

In October 1939, permission was granted to Mr E. Jones and Mr H.H. Watson, with their foreign language skills, to enter their names on the Central Register of persons with special qualifications which was being compiled by the Ministry of Labour, for use in the event of emergency. Two months later it was announced that any staff of the Modern and High Schools who wished to undertake Voluntary National Service duties outside school hours were permitted to do so.

D.W.H. Sharp was appointed Head Boy for the 1939–40 School Year. He was assisted by ten other prefects, who helped to maintain order in the crowded School. A popular punishment amongst prefects and staff in the first years at Bradgers Hill

was filling one or two buckets with stones from the School field, which seemed to have more than its fair share of very sharp flints. Copies of the School rules were issued to new boys on duplicated sheets until 1941, after which they were printed in the *School Lists*. A few unwritten rules seem to have existed, such as not riding bicycles through 'Nanny Goat Alley', the footpath opposite the School that led into Elmwood Crescent, where goats in the adjoining paddock were easily frightened, and where Mrs Richardson kept an unofficial 'tuck-shop'.

Mr Gauntlett, unlike his predecessor, made use of his cane. Two boys, Beale and Impey, were caught fighting; one told his father who complained to the Head. The other lad was caned. The class set about the boy who had complained, and as a result Mr Gauntlett caned the whole class in his study. Derek E. Wood (1938–46) fell foul of him when arrived he at School one morning without his obligatory gas-mask:

'I calculated that I could cycle home to Marston Gardens, collect my gas-mask, and get back to School before morning assembly started. As I sped out of Bradgers Hill Road I saw the Headmaster walking towards me. I judged it expedient to greet him, "Good morning, Sir". He didn't answer, but stared at me intently. I got back to School in good time, and joined my class-mates in the Hall. When Prayers were over and before School was dismissed, the Headmaster came to the edge of the stage and pointed in my direction., and bade me to "Stand up, boy. I am awarding you a detention . . . you know what it's for . . . !" For at least an hour after the Assembly I was a sort of School hero. What was the misdemeanour that justified such a public rebuke? My School-mates, when they heard, were as unimpressed as I was. That was my only encounter with Mr Gauntlett.'

Other masters used the cane, but treated it much more lightly. Mr B.J. Cooke, the Physics master, had problems with two boys called G.A. West and G.A. East. When they played him up, he gave one of them a metre rule and made him whack the other, and then the roles were reversed! A number of Old Boys have referred to Mr Bourlet, the Physics master, who one might be led to believe, spent most of his time throwing chalk at anyone and everyone. Even the placid Ronny Phillips might take a boy's nose between the knuckles of his first and second fingers and turn it upside down, bringing tears to the victim's eyes.

The activities of the School Societies were necessarily curtailed owing to the War, but the Literary and Scientific Society, the Musical Society, the Chess Club and the Athletics Club still carried on.

Sports Day was held on 1st May, 1940, and competition between the Houses was very close, the Bees finally managing to win. The *Victor Ludorum* Cup was won by D. Heley, with H.H. Barker runner-up. Three records were broken. P.H. Gilder broke the half-mile (u.14); D. Heley took two-fifths of a second of the 100 yards (open) event at 11 secs., and the junior relay record was broken by the Hornets.

M.V.W. Chote was placed third in the javelin (open), to S.G. Booth (1st) and K. Lines (2nd).

At the end of the Summer term, 1940, School Report Books were introduced for the first time. These books, with their Post Office red covers, gold badge and lettering, became a familiar sight to all subsequent pupils at the School, who were instructed to take them home and cover them with brown paper. Apart from containing the termly reports, there was a page for physical training progress. Another showed certificates gained in public examinations, offices held in the School, and a record of games and other activities. The final report by the Headmaster basically ranked as a testimonial. The book was taken home at the end of each term for the boy's parent or guardian to sign. It then had to be returned to the Form master, together with a signed health certificate, on the first day of the following term. It was stated that boys failing to do this would not be admitted.

In July 1939, to the regret of most of the School, Mr J.M. 'Jimmy' Forbes retired. The son of an Irish Archdeacon, he had been educated at the Portora Royal School, Enniskillen, and later at Benston College, Staffordshire. He graduated at Trinity College, Dublin, and after a brief spell of teaching in a preparatory school, joined the Modern School Staff in 1909. During the First World War he served as a Captain in the Connaught Rangers, and on his return to the School after the War was appointed First Assistant Master, (or Second Master), a position which he filled with assiduity and unfailing tact.

Mr Sanderson described him as 'always the most ideally loyal colleague anyone could have.' James W. Findlater wrote: 'It is no exaggeration to say that, especially during the last twenty years, the School was one of the main interests in his life. On the playing-field, especially, he was a familiar figure and his interest in the games side of the life of the School must now be bearing fruit in the lives of scores of Old Lutonians. In the class-room, his work was not only characterised by thoroughness, but owed much of its success to his keen sense of humour and his obvious liking for young people. It must be a source of satisfaction to know that he carries with him into retirement the warm feelings and thanks of so many people.'

At Assembly on the last morning of the summer term the School paid its farewells to Mr Forbes, and he was presented with a set of Dickens' novels and a standard lamp by the staff and boys respectively. The Old Boys gave him a gold half-hunter watch, suitably inscribed, and asked him to accept a writing set for Mrs Forbes.

Arthur B. Allen remembered 'Jimmy' with his re-iterated 'D'yu see?'

'We didn't, but we said we did. It made his life easier somehow . . . and there was that one unforgettable incident during a visit from an HMI when the Inspector unexpectedly asked him to explain how logarithms could be applied in everyday life. If ever a master flashed an SOS to his boys, Jimmy did at that moment. He picked up a book and balanced it on his hand. "Now boys," he began. "This book

is a steamship. The top of my desk here is Southampton. The top of the cupboard over there is New York. We are sailing from Southampton to New York." And he flung the volume from desk-top to cupboard-top. P. F. Stone half-turned in his seat and said in a stage whisper to Tiggy Barnett, sitting just behind, "That ain't a steamship. That's a ruddy aeroplane!" The HMI gave a shout of laughter and hurriedly left the room. Jimmy watched him go, then he walked across the room to where Stone was sitting and held out his hand. "Stone," he said. "Shake hands, sir, you're a gentleman!" There was a moment's stillness and then a great roar of laughter. There were no more logarithms that afternoon!

'So many tales were told about him. In the classroom "What is a narc, boy? A narc is a part of a circle! Remember the digits, you idjit!" and "as soon as I open my mouth some fool begins to speak" were repeated again and again . . .'

Mr A. Talbot, BA (Hons), Cambridge, was appointed to succeed Mr Forbes in the Mathematics Department.

Chapter 7

Notes of Discord

On the face of it, Mr Forbes' retirement seemed natural enough. Although in his 61st year he was eligible to retire, he might have been expected to teach for a little longer. But an ominous undercurrent was developing within the School.

In December 1938, Mr Gauntlett had asked the Governors for a review of his salary. He had successfully completed the move to the new School and felt this deserved some recognition. Miss Sheldon, at the High School, had just had her salary increased, creating a precedent. In view of the various opinions expressed by members of the Governing body, however, the Chairman, Harry Arnold, was instructed to inform the Headmaster that, for the time being, they could not see their way to granting his request.

Why was this? Ever since the move to the new School it was said that the Headmaster had begun to behave strangely. He would not see parents when they needed to see him. He refused to see Governors, thus alienating them against him. Old Boys who called at the School were not welcomed, although he was President of the *Old Luton Modernians* during 1938–39. At times he would shut himself off from most of the staff and would only communicate with them through Miss J.M. Oakley, his secretary. He would take important decisions without consulting those members of staff who should have been involved, particularly Mr Forbes. He no longer seemed interested in discipline either in or outside his School, and he failed to back-up his staff when it was required. One Old Boy has described him at this time 'as a slight, rather sinister figure with piercing eyes who seemed to creep around the school'. He appeared to spy on staff as they taught. Many boys remember seeing him hovering in the corridor outside classrooms, peering through the port-holes in the doors, and listening but seldom entering. He believed that the Staff talked about him behind his back, and indeed the more oddly he behaved, the more they *did* talk!

It should be remembered that in the old building at Park Square the Head had been surrounded by the School's activities, and he only had to open his door to see what was going on, but at Bradgers Hill his Study was well out of sight and ear of the action.

Mr Ronald Phillips said that the Head had become very unpopular with the staff and had 'changed' in his final years. K.B. Webb had been told that he had lost the confidence of the masters, boys and parents, and that he had ignored an accident in the road, turned away from it and wouldn't have anything to do with it, although it was one of his boys. He failed to hold Staff meetings, and in the end they were held without him, or with him sitting at the bottom of the table. In September, after Mr Forbes' retirement, the Staff elected Mr B.J. Cooke, the Head of Physics, to take the Chair. (Mr Godfrey, who had hopes of becoming Second Master, did not wish to jeopardise his chances of being appointed.)

In March 1939, the Headmaster had reported to a meeting of the Governors that, although Mr Forbes received extra remuneration in respect of his appointment as First Assistant Master, he did not consider that he acted as such, and in view of the fact that he had now reached retiring age, Mr Gauntlett requested that Forbes' retirement should be expedited. There is no record of what passed between Mr Forbes and the Governors. There is no doubt that he and the Headmaster were at loggerheads. In consequence, as has already been said, in May 1939, Mr Forbes tendered his resignation to the Governors with effect from 31st August.

With the imminent departure of Mr Forbes, the Headmaster turned his attentions to other masters whom he considered were under performing, were having problems with discipline or were not teaching in what he thought to be the most effective manner. He may have been right, but his methods of correcting them were far from tactful. The immediate cause of trouble were Mr Arthur Root's disastrous School Certificate Latin results. Instead of considering how he or his colleagues might help the situation, Mr Gauntlett advised Mr Root to seek another post.

Memories of the period are somewhat hazy and conflicting, but it is clear that the Staff were not prepared to tolerate this treatment, and persuaded Mr Root to seek the advice of the Assistant Masters' Association. Security of tenure had never been recognised in Luton, and after the tyrannical way in which Mr Sanderson had ruled his School, the Staff, who had become more belligerent, made up their mind to resist any future dismissals by Mr Gauntlett. In Ronald Phillips' words the Staff decided to 'gang-up on him'. 'Froggy' Watson said that the Staff sent a round-robin of complaint to the Governors, using the threatened dismissal of Arthur Root as the catalyst. Unfortunately, Mr Root never spoke of this incident to his sons Michael and Richard, and we do not have his views on the matter. With the approval of the AMA the Staff sent a letter, dated 22nd September, 1939, to the Governors, who convened a Special Meeting on Tuesday, 3rd October to consider it. Fifteen Governors were present, with Ald. Harry Arnold in the Chair. The observations of

the Headmaster, dated 26th September, on the communication from the Staff were also submitted to them.

The Governors resolved that a special Committee be appointed to fully investigate the contents of the Staff's letter, collect all the evidence appertaining to the communication, and any other evidence that they considered should be investigated, and submit their report on the whole matter to a Special Meeting of Governors on Thursday, 19th October, 1939, at Luton Modern School. They further resolved that the special Committee should consist of the Chairman of Governors (Ald. H. Arnold), Mr G. Brightman, Mr O.E. Hart, Mr T. Skelton and Mr J.H. Staddon.

Mr Gauntlett said that he was summoned to appear before the special Committee without any prior notification and was taken quite unawares by a barrage of hostile questions, against which he defended himself as best he could. He felt that the Governors had been set against him mainly by Henry Baines, the Director of Education for Bedfordshire. As a result of this stormy meeting, he rather naively accepted the situation and agreed to set about rectifying the grievances of the Staff, believing that all trouble would now be over.

There is no minuted record of a meeting being held by the Governors on the 19th, but at 7.30 pm that evening Mr Henry Baines telephoned the Headmaster and 'asked him to place in his hands, his (the Headmaster's) written resignation dated 31st March, 1940, by 2 pm the following day at the latest. If the Head failed to do this he would be dismissed the next day.' The Headmaster, unfortunately, yielded to the threat, although Mr Baines denied that he influenced him in any way to resign his post.

Twelve Governors were present the next afternoon, 20th October, when the Chairman reported orally that the special Committee had met four times and gone into the dispute very carefully. They had interviewed a deputation from the Staff arranged by the AMA and consisting of Messrs. Godfrey, Cooke, Clayton and Jones. The masters had not only defended Mr Root but brought charges against the Headmaster, accusing him among other things of not holding Staff Meetings and of being indifferent to the maintenance of School discipline. The Committee had discussed the matters arising in connection with the School in all its various relations and had arrived at a number of unanimous recommendations to be placed before the Governors. Mr Arnold said that certain developments had supervened which made it unnecessary to submit to all their recommendations. What these developments were is not recorded. The full report would be presented early in 1940.

The resolutions that were proposed give us some idea of what had been discussed: a) The Governors would defer the appointment of a Second Master for the time being, it being understood that the Chairman and Director of Education would be making frequent visits to the School as occasion served.

b) A Careers Master would be appointed for the School. Such a post would be

regarded as a post of Special Responsibility in terms of the Burnham pay scale. The Girls' High School had had a Careers Mistress for some years, and specialised courses adapted to future careers.

c) The teaching of Latin at Luton Modern School was to be reorganised.

d) That Staff meetings at the School should be held regularly.

Nowhere is there any reference to the demand for, or receipt of, the Headmaster's resignation.

The Chairman of the Governors, Alderman Harry Arnold, aged 76, and by that time a rather weak character, gave Gauntlett some encouragement, by saying that once the Staff's recommendations were in place, his letter of resignation would eventually be withdrawn and all would be well. In December 1939 Gauntlett approached the Head Masters' Association for help and they advised him to withdraw his letter.

At this point in the proceedings the Board of Education announced that they would conduct a Full Inspection of Luton Modern School during the week ending Friday, 8th March, 1940. Whether this was prompted by news of the unrest within the School is unknown. It was 12 years since the previous inspection, and was certainly overdue.

Mr Gauntlett seems to have deliberated for some time before writing on 19th February, seeking permission to withdraw his letter of resignation. He was asked to appear before a Special Meeting of the Governors which was held at the School on Tuesday 5th March, 1940. This, it is worth emphasising, was the first day of the Board of Education's Full Inspection. At the Governors' meeting the Secretary read out the full Report of the Special Committee that had been appointed on 3rd October, 1939. The Headmaster gave the Governors his reasons for requesting that his letter of resignation be returned to him. This was declined, and without even waiting for the Board of Education Inspectors' report upon the School, it was decided then and there to dismiss him, resolving 'that notice be given to Mr Frederick Edward Gauntlett terminating his engagement as Headmaster of Luton Modern School at the end of the summer term, viz. 31st August, 1940'.

The Governors agreed that if Mr Gauntlett voluntarily resigned his post, an advertisement for a new Headmaster for the School would be issued as soon as possible, offering a salary of £800 per annum, to be increased by annual increments of £30 to a maximum of £1,000 per annum.

Before taking any further action Mr Gauntlett contacted his Union, the Incorporated Association of Headmasters, who wrote to the Governors, asking if they might be informed (in confidence) of the grounds on which the Governors had based their decision to terminate Mr Gauntlett's engagement. In their reply the Governors provided the information requested and informed the IAH that, in accordance with the Articles of Government of the School, Mr Gauntlett had the right of appeal against his dismissal if he so desired. The Headmaster must have

realised that his position was becoming untenable, and there is no record of any appeal.

It must be stated at this point, that all the six Inspectors concerned with the Full Inspection of the School between 5th and 8th March were of the opinion that, although the Headmaster was not in any way a strong, outstanding personality, he appeared to them to have done good work and certainly, as far as they could judge, not to have merited the harsh treatment meted out by the Governing Body. Mr C.J.R. Whitmore, who had previously been the District Inspector for the School, and was a member of the Full Inspection Panel, had never observed anything approaching a lack of discipline in his many visits to the School. If the Headmaster did not call frequent Staff Meetings he certainly worked through his Heads of Departments in order to equip the new building. When the Chief Inspector, Mr Duckworth, met the Governors, he told them 'We are quite at a loss to understand your action!'

The only public announcement of the Head's resignation was a brief paragraph in *The Luton News* for 9th May, 1940, which stated that:

> 'Mr F.E. Gauntlett, MA, headmaster of Luton Modern School for the past seven years, is resigning, and applications have been invited for the appointment of a new Head, which will take effect at the commencement of the autumn term.'

The Staff, too, seem to have regretted the outcome of their action. On Sunday, 10th March, Mr Rex Clayton and Mr Ronald Phillips called upon HM Inspector Mr H.F. Collins and asked on behalf of the staff what action the Masters could follow in order to save the Headmaster from dismissal. During the conversation that followed it transpired that the staff were adamant that they would resist all future dismissals, and it emerged that as well as Arthur Root, Charles Wareham and Enyr Jones felt that their posts were insecure. Mr Collins suggested that the Masters should get in touch at once with the Assistant Masters' Association and the Governors. The Staff envoys were emphatic about the unjust treatment of the Headmaster.

How did the boys find Frederick Gauntlett? Derek Page (1938–44) wrote 'To say that Mr Gauntlett was unpopular with the boys is a serious understatement, as I think we all went in fear of him.' Jack Waller (1936–40) 'never recalled seeing him smile, he had no rapport with the boys nor with his masters – an impression gained more from what was not said, rather than what was said.' To Phillip Gething (1939–46) 'he was a small, rather sallow and scholarly man who was certainly not a natural leader or mixer. I heard later from a Chairman of the Governors, that he was so shy he would cross the road to avoid meeting a governor.' Frank Stygall (1937–44), Head Boy in 1943–4, knew him slightly better than the rest but described him as 'a boorish ignoramus, totally unfitted to be a Head.'

He left, a bitter man, almost unlamented, and there is no record of his final School Assembly on 26th July. Jack Waller says that no collection was taken for a leaving present for him, although it was usual to give all staff a gift, however small. As there was no School Magazine published that year, nor a mention in the local Press, we have no contemporary confirmation. Only a note in *The Old Luton Modernian* for December 1940, recorded that 'Mr F.E. Gauntlett has resigned from the Headmastership of the School, and the Committee has presented him with a fountain pen as a parting gift from the Club. It is with pleasure that we record the Club's warmest thanks for Mr Gauntlett's ready co-operation with the Committee and his many efforts on behalf of the Club.' Mr Gauntlett and his family moved to Cheltenham, where he taught modern languages at the Grammar School.

In January 1941 the Governors granted Mr Root permission to visit the Royal Grammar School, Worcester, to observe recent teaching methods in Latin. The French teachers were also given permission to attend a short course at St Hugh's College, Oxford.

As a result of a Governors' meeting on 20th October, members of the staff were invited to apply for the post of Careers Master. Four applications were made and, as a result, Rex S. Clayton, then aged 42, was chosen. It was agreed that he would receive a special allowance at the rate of £50 per annum, commencing in January 1940. As well as advising boys on University entry, his job was to help less brilliant boys to take their places in the professions, in industry and trade; and to help local industry avoid placing square pegs in round holes. *The Luton News* recorded that 'Mr Clayton plans to investigate the records of boys before they enter the School, and to endeavour to get to know each boy individually. He hopes to encourage an early choice of career, and to help each boy equip himself for that chosen career.'

Early in 1940 the father of one of the older boys died and his mother was faced with the prospect of having to stop his promising career, because she could not afford it. The staff and the Old Modernians' Club took up the matter: so did a mother who sent an anonymous note to Rex Clayton. It read:

> 'Dear Mr Clayton, Your interest in a boy who has recently lost his father has come to my notice. If you have been able to arrange for his school fees next term, will you use the enclosed 5 shillings for his book fees. If he is unable to remain at school, perhaps you can find some way of using the money for him. From a mother who, if placed in similar circumstances, would be able to let her son complete his education. Best of wishes.'

Another more crucial appointment was made in the summer of 1940, that of Second Master. Cyril J. Godfrey was the Governors' and Staff's unanimous choice, and he took up his post on 1st September, 1940, receiving an additional £25 per annum. Having first joined the staff in 1918 he had a thorough knowledge of the

working of the School, and was in a strong position to guide a new Headmaster when appointed. He taught maths, and at one time chemistry. He had lost an eye, and the glass one which replaced it caused confusion to every boy who stood before him, each unsure as to which eye was looking at them. 'He was a strict disciplinarian: young boys feared him, older ones respected him. He was stern but fair with a leavening of compassion.'

The Full Inspection, March 1940

The Board of Education's Inspection of Luton Modern School took place over four days from 5th to 8th March, 1940. It was carried out by a team of eight Inspectors, and from it we can get a fair impression of the School at that point in time.

There were 435 students in the School, and with their ages reckoned as on 31st July, 1939, 43 were under 11 and only 8 over 16 years of age. 85% of the boys were resident in Luton, the remainder coming from places in the near vicinity. A steady annual intake of about 85 boys made it possible to have a three Form entry. The heavy admission of 108 pupils in September 1939 was explained by the inclusion of 22 privately evacuated boys. At the other end of the age range, conditions were not so good. Most boys left as soon as they reached the end of the academic year in which they became 16. This was explained by the relative ease with which remunerative juvenile employment could be obtained in Luton.

In recent years there had been a praiseworthy increase in the number of boys who were entered for the Cambridge School Certificate examination. In July 1939 out of 68 boys entered, a creditable 54 obtained a Certificate. At the time of the Inspection there were only 22 boys working at the post-Certificate stage, and of those 16 were in the first year. Higher School Certificate results, though not outstanding, represented a steady level of achievement. In 1939 only five candidates were entered and four Certificates were gained. During the past three years two Open awards, tenable at the Imperial College of Science, had been won, and over the same period one boy had proceeded to Oxford University, four to London University and two to Training Colleges. A scrutiny of the limited occupational statistics that were available showed that, as at the time of the 1928 Inspection, the majority of boys took up some form of engineering or clerical work when they left school.

Of the 448 pupils in attendance on 1st October, 1939, 108 were totally exempt and 55 partially exempt from paying fees; the remainder paid full fees which, for boys resident in Bedfordshire, amounted to £12 per annum, and for out of county pupils £32 per annum. In addition a charge of 5s. a term for the loan of books was made to all pupils including the 33% who were awarded Special Places.

It was obvious to the Inspectors that the new School, with its spacious and satisfying surroundings, was already exerting a stimulating influence upon the efforts of everyone who was fortunate to work there.

The Library in 1938 provided a relaxed atmosphere for study, but was extremely short of books.
(*LN*)

For the first time in its history the School had something approaching proper library facilities. A liberal grant of £100 for new books in 1938–39, and £40 for 1939–40 meant that there were now some 2,603 fiction and other books for lending, as well as a good reference section. 'An especially interesting feature are the file of papers and articles written by Old Boys and a copy of *The Times* newspaper published at the time of the Battle of Waterloo.'

Reviewing the Staff, the Inspectors found the Headmaster an able teacher of German, who, during the seven years he had been in office, had shown an organising ability adequate to his responsibilities and had secured for the School a broader curriculum and a quickened social life.

There were 20 full-time Masters, providing a ratio of 1 Master to 21·75 boys, which was not considered numerically excessive. Of the Masters, 17 were University graduates, 14 held Honours degrees and 3 were suitably equipped to teach Art, Handicraft and Gymnastics. As a team they represented an experienced, competent, hardworking body of men, who, almost without exception, could be relied upon to do justice to their particular subject in the classroom and make some contribution to the corporate life of the School.

The school curriculum was organised upon the lines of a three Form entry and

offered three courses, A, B and C, for the School Certificate Examination, which might be taken from any of the four Forms, Upper IV, IVA, IVB, IVC. The appearance of a fourth Form at the first Examination stage was explained by a desire to create smaller forms for the School Certificate candidates, and also to make room for boys who wanted to take the Examination for a second time. An additional Form, Form IIIR, had been created for slower boys who wanted more time to work for their examinations.

During their first year all pupils were taught Religious Education, English Language and Literature, History, Geography, French, Mathematics, Science, Art, Music, Handicraft and Gymnastics. In the second year all boys had a choice of a second foreign language, either German or Latin. From the third year onwards, Geography, an increasingly important subject, was taken only by those boys who decided to drop German or Latin in its favour. One other variation occurred in the School Certificate Forms; there, Art and Handicraft became mutually exclusive.

The Inspectors questioned the wisdom of allowing all boys to attempt a second foreign language; they thought it was better reserved for the abler pupils. They cautioned care in the choice of Latin or German lest at some future time it might handicap a boy's career. They also criticised the lack of Music after the first year, and they felt that all boys should receive some Geography after the second year.

At the time of the 1928 Inspection the Higher School Certificate courses were in Mathematics and Science. Now there were also opportunities for boys to study English, History, Latin, French and German, although some of the courses were perhaps tentative rather than well established.

The preamble to the Inspectors' Report concluded: 'the School as a place of learning is sound and, with the exception of Latin, satisfactory work is done in most departments. Nor is this condition of affairs merely static. In many branches of the curriculum aim and achievement appear to be on the upward grade.'

The Report then devoted ten pages to discussing the Subjects in detail.

Scripture

This subject received a weekly lesson taught by Ronald Phillips during the first three years, and then ceased. Such teaching as was observed created a favourable impression and it was felt that, given greater scope, he could teach the subject adequately throughout the School.

English Language and Literature

This was well organised and effectively carried out, resulting in a standard of attainment that was very creditable. James Findlater, the Master in charge, was described as a skilful teacher of mature experience, admirably suited to his post by temperament and knowledge. He was assisted by Ronald Phillips and Henry B. Williams with the older pupils, and Arthur Root and Hugh Watson in the three

lower Forms. Only four boys were studying English beyond the First Examination stage, one in a third year of advanced work. Boys on the Science side had one period of English to prepare them for the General Paper in their Second Examination. It was felt that a second period should be introduced for all members of the Form irrespective of their special studies. The spoken word, though not neglected, required more systematic care. It was felt that the encouragement of a clear and confident delivery should be a matter of general school policy.

History

James Findlater was also responsible for the work in History and until recently had taught the senior classes. This he had now relinquished to Thomas P. Clark, an Honours graduate, appointed in 1930, who was keen and competent but lacking in experience, and rather out-of-date in his methods. The syllabus began with a brief sketch of Ancient and Medieval history, and devoted the following three years to a consecutive account of English history from 1485 to 1914, accompanied from 1830 by the parallel study of European history. Local history and current events were only referred to when occasion arose. The Inspectors suggested setting aside a special room for History teaching where wall illustrations, maps, models, specimens and so forth could be displayed. For the first time, there were six boys studying history for the Higher School Certificate. There was also an experiment in progress, in collaboration with the Art Master, in making historical models.

Geography

This was studied by all boys in Forms I and II with an allowance of three and two periods a week respectively. After that it was an alternative to either Latin or German, and it was suggested that C stream boys should take the subject to the examination stage. The Inspectors considered that other boys would benefit from studying geography in their final main school year, even if only for one period a week, so that they could leave school with sufficient up-to-date knowledge to allow them to intelligently interpret current world affairs. John Cleaver, the Master in charge, was adequately qualified for his work and was enjoying a well-furnished and equipped Geography room. 'Although his keenness may be leading him to talk too much on occasions and to question his class too little, he may be expected shortly to settle down to a really sound teaching technique on modern lines. He has the gift of making the work interesting and at the same time instructive, and the recent examination results show that his pupils attain a sound knowledge when they complete the full course.'

French

The organisation of the French department fell to Hugh Watson, the senior Modern Languages Master, who, by temperament and linguistic equipment, was admirably

fitted for that responsible task. He was fortunate in the support he received from two well qualified specialist colleagues, Albert C. Partridge and Harold Woodcock. The Inspectors considered that there was insufficient time given to studying the subject properly and that it was essential for the boys to have continuity with the same teacher for at least two years. French had still to establish itself in the post-Certificate Forms.

German

German could be studied to School Certificate level over a three year course. There was a refreshing keenness about the boys taking this subject which the Headmaster and his two colleagues, Hugh Watson and Enyr Jones, had done much to inspire. Very few boys dropped German in favour of Geography, and over the past three years 112 candidates had offered German in the School Certificate Examination.

Latin

The standard of attainment was below average. The Master in Charge, Arthur Root, an Oxford Honours graduate appointed in 1931, came to the post without professional training and virtually without experience. His lessons lacked the skill and vigour necessary to keep all the members of a class purposively occupied; in consequence learning was uncertain and most of the boys lacked confidence in attacking their work. The standard had been low at the time of the 1928 Inspection and examination results implied that it had failed to improve subsequently.

Mathematics

This subject was entrusted to an efficient team of three Masters, two of whom, Archibald P. Frost and Cyril Godfrey, though not well qualified on paper for their tasks, had had long experience of teaching the subject in the school. The third, Alan Talbot, was a young, brilliantly qualified Cambridge mathematician, who showed every promise of becoming a successful teacher.

The standard of work in the Main School was very satisfactory, especially when the difficulties imposed by a short four year course were borne in mind. The post-School Certificate work was very promising, but in some respects, for example algebra, where a new text-book was needed, it was hardly yet on modern lines.

Science

Four Masters shared the Science teaching, George Howard (chemistry), Bernard Cooke (physics), Rex Clayton (botany and elementary chemistry) and Charles Wareham (lower school physics and chemistry). The first three senior Masters were competent teachers and the work in their respective subjects reached a good standard. The junior Science Master was not so effective as his colleagues, and it was necessary to point out a mistake he was making in the practical work of one of his

Form IIIR in the new science laboratory, September, 1938. (*C.E. Wareham*)

physics classes. The Inspectors suggested that botany might be replaced by biology; and they lent their support to the Headmaster and staff, who were considering adopting General Science for work in the Main School.

Art

Arthur Martin, the Art Master, had planned a useful course, of adequate range and suitable content. The work generally reached a satisfactory standard of achievement, with some good work, and the Master gave evidence of his desire to relate his subject to the general education given in the School.

Handicraft

The spacious workshop was considered well equipped for teaching woodwork and metalwork. The layout of the machines and benches, the neat, orderly storage of the hand tools, and their excellent condition reflected credit on Sidney Pointing, the Master concerned. He was a capable and keen teacher who, by precept and example, secured his pupils' interest and co-operation; and their excellent behaviour clearly indicated the cordial relations that existed between Master and pupils. The Inspectors felt that some of the higher Forms might specialise in the craft to be offered in the Certificate Examination.

Music

Music did not fulfil its proper function in the life of the school community; indeed after a boy's first year, unless he was a member of the school choir or orchestra, his musical education ceased. Harold Woodcock, the Modern Languages Master, succeeded in making the work interesting. No song books were available and the repertoire was meagre; the practice of writing down the words of a song was uneconomic and wasted valuable time in the Music lesson. A visiting teacher took a violin class once a week, and his pupils were encouraged to join the school orchestra. The Inspectors thought that it would help the orchestral work if the School purchased a few string instruments of the larger type. A small room at the top of the building had been provided, but apart from the presence of a good piano, there was little to indicate that it was a Music Room.

Physical Education

Every Form received two gymnastic lessons weekly, but games were voluntary and played out of school hours. The majority of boys took part. There was no gymnastic tradition for Eric Harvey, the Master in charge, to build on, and the general standard of work remained low, especially in the upper forms. A more dynamic method of teaching would have added verve to the lessons and authority to the instruction. The Gymnastics Master laid commendable stress on the hygiene aspect of the work and all the classes now changed into gymnastics kit and made full use of the showers after exercise. He was also making a welcome effort to develop an interest in athletics, and success had resulted from his initial attempts.

Within the limited opportunities of a four-day visit, the Inspectors formed the opinion that the Luton boys, by their behaviour in and out of classrooms and by their general neatness of appearance, compared favourably with pupils seen under similar conditions elsewhere. The general impression produced was that, as far as the boys were concerned, the School could be described as a friendly, hard-working community.

The Report of the Board of Education Inspectors was sent to the Chief Education Officer and the School Governors on 13th May, 1940. The Governors did not meet until the 9th July, and they then decided to defer any detailed consideration until the autumn when the new Headmaster took up his duties.

Advertisements for a new Headmaster appeared in May 1940, and 162 applications were received. From these a short list of eight was drawn up, which was eventually reduced to three. After interviews on 5th June, 1940, Kenneth Burgess Webb was selected. The appointment was to take effect from 1st August, 1940.

Kenneth B. Webb, MA, BSc, Headmaster, 1940–1966. (October, 1954)

Chapter 8

War and Peace

Kenneth Burgess Webb was born on 10th March, 1904, at 30 Crofton Road, Peckham. His father, John Henry Webb, was a Civil Servant and a Methodist Lay-Preacher who lived to be 90 years old. His mother and two aunts were all teachers, whilst his sister became a missionary in China, living until she was 95.

Webb won a scholarship from his local elementary school to the Whitgift Middle School in Croydon. From there scholarships took him to King's College, London, where he obtained a First Class Honours degree in Physics and then Trinity College, Cambridge, where he got a First Class Honours Part 2 in Natural Sciences. Whilst in Cambridge he met his future wife, Eva, who was a student at Homerton College.

The Revd. Harry Bisseker, Headmaster of the Leys School in Cambridge (a Methodist foundation), was looking for someone to replace his senior physics master, and, hearing of Webb's academic success, offered him the job, which the young student accepted with alacrity. 'So with no teacher training, I was allowed to borrow a handcart from the Porter's Lodge of Trinity, put my few possessions on to that, and go down the road to the Leys School and initiate myself into their bachelor staff quarters as an assistant master in charge of physics. Their new J.J. Thomson Laboratories were being built, and I was allowed to dictate certain fairly obvious requirements to the builders, Holloway Bros., such as all benches requiring a water and electricity supply. I did seven years there as Head of Physics.'

In 1933 K.B.W. became Head of Science at Epsom College, Surrey. There he began his life-long interest in Current and World Affairs, which he was to develop further at Luton. As he got older, he wanted to become a Headmaster and put back into the national system something of which he had taken advantage.

In April 1940 the Headship of Luton Modern School was advertised at a starting salary of £800 per annum, increasing by annual increments of £30 to a maximum of

£1,000. Such a salary was the limit of expectations in those days, and Webb had no hesitation in accepting the job. He commenced duties on 1st August, 1940.

By this time he was married to Eva and had two small sons. His only contact with Frederick Gauntlett was in buying his house in Old Bedford Road. His first experience of the new School was to tour it with the Chief Education Officer for Bedfordshire and the Medical Officer for Health. The latter was sizing it up for use as an emergency hospital, and, by October, dozens of beds and mattresses were delivered in readiness and stacked on the balcony parade. Similar deliveries were made to the Girls' High School. Three months later they were all removed again, due to the potential danger from incendiary bombs.

There had been a big unexplained decline in the number of children who took the entrance examination in 1940. Only 256 boys applied for the Modern School, and 265 girls for the High School. In 1939 the numbers had been 330 and 341 respectively. It was thought the drop was due to apathy on the part of the local Elementary School Heads who didn't want to lose their best pupils.

There were only three weeks summer holiday in 1940, the autumn term beginning on 19th August for 309 pupils already at the School and on 1st September for 109 new boys. There had been a three-form entry for some years, leading to classes of around 36 pupils.

On the first day of the new term, Mr Webb recalled, 'The place seemed a riot to me. There were no rules about direction in corridors or on the stairs, so there was congestion every time there was movement.' His first task was to get to know his new Deputy, Cyril Godfrey, who from 1st September would be the Second Master.

At first the Head was reluctant to give Mr Godfrey an entirely free rein on discipline, although it was a specification of his appointment. Matters soon came to a head when Mr Godfrey told Mr Webb, 'You don't buy a guard dog and then bark yourself!' From then on it was agreed that Godfrey would be responsible for all the day to day running of the School, and that the Headmaster would deal with the administration; an arrangement that seemed to suit them both, and the School, admirably. Order was very soon instilled in the pupils.

The boys returning after the summer break were not only to be met by a new Headmaster. Over the next few months there were to be many new faces on the staff, whilst a few of the older ones left for the Forces. In August Ronald Bridger, LRAM, joined to teach music and mathematics, and Francis C. Minns, BA, taught biology. In January 1941, Conrad Wynne Parry, BA, AKC, came from Swindon to teach geography, religious instruction, French and English. A month later Professor Hans L. Hamburger arrived and taught mathematics for six months before moving on to Southampton University. He seems to have made a great impression on many at the time. A refugee, with a string of German degrees and formerly Professor of Mathematics at Berlin and Colgne Universities, he was probably the most highly qualified member of staff ever to enter the Modern School staff-room. He was

reputed to have worked with Einstein. Although he was ragged unmercifully, when he left, one form gave him a rather fine propelling pencil: he was totally overcome. William Otter came out of retirement to teach handicraft in February, 1941. A genial Scot, Lothian Small, MA, who had worked with the International Federation of League of Nations Societies, came from Gordonstoun School, to teach languages. A local man, Dr John G. Dony, BSc, was a teacher with the North Western Polytechnic. In September 1941 he transferred to the Modern School staff to teach history and general subjects; he was joined by Mr James D.C. Grayston, BSc for mathematics; Mr Dennis F. Gallimore, MA, mainly for English and French; Mr Ronald Ridout, BA, for English; Mr Joseph Magoon, BA, for Latin and English; Mr Samuel Finlay, BSc for mathematics and general science; and Dr Frederick W. Pick, a young German Liberal, who had lived in Britain since 1935. He was the author of two books and numerous articles, and taught history at the School for only a month before he was interned in '45 P. Camp, Liverpool'. The Headmaster went to great lengths to try to prevent his internment and secure his release, which eventually happened in September 1942, when he went to teach in Buxton. Dr Pick suddenly died of a heart attack in 1949 (aged 38), and Mr Webb again intervened to help his wife, Helene Pick, and their two small children to emigrate to the USA in 1951. Three men who came to teach Physical Training briefly during this early period of the War were A.H. Brewer; L.A.W. Moss (who also taught history); and B.A. Roberts. They were each paid £5 per week.

Six masters went to War. Mr W. Bailey (PT) joined the RHA. Mr Thomas P. Clark went to the RAF, as did Mr Eric F. Harvey (PT). Mr Alan Talbot joined the Army, Mr Arthur Root was with the Pioneer Corps, and Mr Henry B. Williams joined the Royal Navy.

Daylight air-raids on England were mainly concentrated between the Spring and Autumn of 1940. Fortunately there were not too many occasions when the boys had to file to the trenches even at that time. A.W. 'George' Thorpe recalls:

> 'The disruption was minimal. At first the sirens were taken seriously and well-organised classes were led to their appropriate stations by anyone in control and handy, form monitors, any grade of prefect or even teachers. It was soon apparent that most teaching was too difficult to continue or be taken seriously and the boys' spirits only lifted when they were allowed to use their pocket chess sets and the like, and, in the case of the seniors, bring out their packs of dog-eared playing-cards. I cannot recall the shelters being used much (for legitimate causes at least) by the time the war ended. I clearly remember the day when a well-placed stink-bomb brought about a hasty evacuation. I wonder if we would have evacuated so rapidly had bombs been dropping all around?'

In spite of the large number of boys and staff making use of the School's well-built

air-raid shelters, the Governors agreed to allow access to members of the public living close by, particularly after dark and at weekends, when not needed by the School.

Mrs F. Sankey was appointed School Cook in October, 1940, in place of Mrs Elliott. She was to be paid £1 10s 0d per week, and all the Kitchen Staff had their wages increased to 1s. an hour (23s 0d per week) from 28th March, 1941. At first Mrs Sankey was not able to produce all the dinners required, and boys living within walking distance of the School were encouraged to go home or to bring sandwiches. By the summer of 1941 things had improved somewhat and it was possible to serve two relays of boys with more than 200 hot meals every day. The back of the Assembly Hall was used as an additional dining area, unfortunately leaving a lingering smell of stale food.

One of the best known slogans of the War years was 'Dig for Victory'. To make the School self-sufficient in potatoes about an acre of land (now built on) at the corner of Old Bedford Road and Bradgers Hill road was ploughed, and the biology master, Francis Minns, took charge of the planting. More potatoes were planted in the north-east corner of the School field. All these had to be dug up by the boys. Arthur T. Redman has never forgotten the day someone put a fork through one of his toes: he still bears the scar! Other boys helped Mr Roberts with gardening on the future Memorial Tennis Courts site, and general grounds maintenance.

On a lighter note, during the holiday season in August and September 1940, the School's cricket table, which had not proved very satisfactory, was re-laid by senior boys at a cost of £27 15s 0d. A contribution of £15 towards the cost was gratefully received from the Old Boys, whose team had full use of the table. Unfortunately, it wasn't the success hoped for, due to a combination of adverse weather conditions and the tenacious local clay.

The autumn term ended on Tuesday, 17th December, with what was to become an annual Carol Service for the boys of the School. It was held in the morning, and the pupils were joined by a number of Governors, parents, and boys from the North Western Polytechnic. Among the many favourite carols sung was 'Good King Wenceslas', during which appropriately-dressed characters acted the scene. A quintet composed of members of staff – one from the Polytechnic – played a medley of carol tunes, and lessons were read by boys from years III, IV, and V and P.R. Franks, the Head Boy. For the first time the service ended with 'God be with you till we meet again'; a hymn that would be sung at the end of every term for the rest of the School's existence, and all round the world, in places wherever Old Boys were gathered together.

During the Headmaster's speech a small figure dressed in a red cloak and hood, and complete with a white beard, climbed onto the platform carrying a bag. From it Mr Webb took small parcels containing photographs of the School which he presented to the Governors. In thanking him, Alderman J.H. Staddon, said 'The Governors are very pleased with the work you have done in your first term at this

School, and we would like to congratulate you on this wonderful ending.' After three cheers for the Governors and three heartier ones for Christmas, the School broke up for four weeks. The long holiday saved the School's fuel ration for the coldest months of the year.

60 members of the School choir met again during the holiday to sing carols at the Children's Hospital in Tennyson Road, and at the new Luton and Dunstable Hospital.

The Orchestra, which included several masters, began to accompany Assembly every Wednesday morning.

By the autumn of 1940 there was a constant threat from incendiary bombs, and in October a massive 'bread-basket' of them fell harmlessly to the east of the School, up on Stopsley Common. The Chairman of the County Buildings' Committee authorised the School to purchase all the necessary ladders, buckets, pumps, rakes, shovels, sand, etc. for the protection of the building against such bombs. Fire Watching posts were set up all over Britain, and from January 1941 Luton Modern School and the Girls' High School were no exception. Nationally, any able bodied person aged 18 or over, who was not engaged in other military activities, was eligible for Fire Watching. At the Boys' School every night, weekends and holidays included, at least one master and several senior boys (over the age of 16) patrolled the School building at intervals during the night. They were joined in this task by staff from the North Western Polytechnic. In between patrols they 'slept' in the Staff Room. Morville Chote's memory is typical of many: 'Fire watching on the school roof and being allowed to share the staff room with the duty master. Mrs Sankey in the kitchen supplied very good cold evening meals too! Bread and butter pudding was great!' Frank Stygall remembers that 'when entering the *sanctum sanctorum* it was not easy to see the far end for cigarette smoke; most of the staff were heavy smokers: the harmful effects were not then known. We slept on camp beds and had to get up, ready for action, when the air-raid sirens sounded. This was a rare occurrence, thankfully. We never had to fight a fire.' Another Old Boy recalled 'groping his way back to School through the smoke screen for fire watching duty.' The smoke screen was produced by some 25,000 generators that were dispersed around Luton and on moonlit nights burnt rags soaked in filthy sump oil producing a dense, foul smelling, oily smoke.

Instead of the usual evening dinner the Old Luton Modernians' Club held a luncheon at the School on Saturday, 18th January, 1941. This gave many old boys the opportunity to look round the building and meet Mr Webb for the first time. Before the meal the company stood in silence in memory of those Old Boys who had lost their lives whilst serving with the Forces. In after-lunch speeches, the Mayor, Cllr. John Burgoyne, said he hoped that Mr Webb would help to make Luton Modern School second to none in the country. In reply, the Headmaster said how deeply touched he had been by the welcome he had received in Luton. His first term

The Old Luton Modernians' Club luncheon, held in place of the Annual Dinner, at Bradgers Hill on Saturday, 18th January, 1941. The Mayor of Luton, Cllr. John Burgoyne, addressing the gathering. (*LN-LMC*)

had been a most enjoyable one. He thought the Old Boys' Club was a marvellous organisation. 'I understand,' he went one, 'that there are 2,800 Old Modernians in Luton, and the present membership of the Club is 300, so there will have to be a big round-up before we have to take Olympia for this event.' He concluded by saying that he was quite willing to see old boys at any time they liked to call at the school.

It was reported that the Club had held no dances since the outbreak of War, but the usual cricket and rugger matches with the School had been played. It had not been possible to play the annual soccer match. The Athletics and Cricket Clubs both suffered from a dearth of fixtures, and were handicapped by their own and opposing team members having to work on Saturday afternoons.

Mr Webb's First Speech Day

On the afternoon of 12th February, 1941, Mr Webb presented his first Speech Day. His Guest of Honour was the Mayor of Luton, Cllr. John Burgoyne, who said that he looked forward to the time when education would come into its own, and it would be used as a means of exploring spiritually, morally, and intellectually the

Speech Day was held on 12th February, 1941, when Luton's wartime Mayor, Cllr. Burgoyne, gave an address and Mrs Burgoyne presented the prizes; in this case the O'Meara Shield for Senior Rugby to the Grasshoppers. (*LN-LMC*)

resources of every boy and girl, whether the child lived in a cottage or a mansion, and when all these resources would be used to the full for uplifting and ennobling our civic and social life. 'The future of England,' he went on, 'can be guaranteed by uplifting, developing, building and enlightening the mind of every man and every woman.'

Mr Webb made the point that 'If the School Certificate is ever allowed to be the be-all and end-all of secondary education in this country, this country is doomed, and secondary education is damned. The mind is not an attaché case to be filled, but a young plant to be tended and nourished. In fact, boys are so resilient and nature so strong, that with hobbies of one kind or another, various school societies, and his outside interests, no boy's life is dominated by the need to pass an examination.

'Boys know that whilst there are lessons to be learned there is a life to be lived; that they come to school not only to learn something but to be something.

'And it will be the constant endeavour of my colleagues and myself to quicken the 'life to be lived' without diminishing by one iota the success with which the 'lessons are learned. Education is not only information. It is more akin to inspiration.'

Reporting on sporting achievements for 1940–41, which had been much

curtailed by the War, Mr Webb said that of eight Association football matches played, one was won, one drawn and six lost. In cricket the 1st XI played eight matches and won seven. Other School XI's had played 15 and won 10. At Rugby the 1st XV played 10 matches, winning 3 and drawing 2. At the annual athletic sports in May 1940, three colts School records were broken.

Amongst the academic achievements were five full Higher School Certificates and nine for Subsidiary Subjects. The Governors' Leaving Exhibition went to the Head Boy, D.W.H. Sharp. P.R. Franks and A.R. Emery were awarded Open Scholarships in maths, physics and chemistry at University College, Hull.

When the County Education Committee met in February 1941 they were told of a large number of cracks that had developed in many parts of the School roof. The defect seemed to be an unforeseen one arising from the ambitiousness of the design. The roof was so large in area that it was unable to take the great amount of expansion and contraction which followed. The problem was to occur repeatedly in flat-roofed buildings built subsequently. In July the final cost of building the new School was revealed to be £6,580 above the original estimate, mainly due to quantities of materials being altered. The total cost, with land, was just over £70,000. The Education Committee agreed to pay the Quantity Surveyor the amount still due to him, but decided to leave the Architect's fees for later agreement.

Each year during the War special Savings weeks were held, when Luton, Dunstable and Luton Rural District banded together in a concerted effort to raise a million pounds in one week as their contribution to the War effort. In March 1941 'War Weapons Week' was inaugurated by Sir Nevile Henderson, the pre-war British Ambassador in Berlin. The target was easily exceeded and a sum of £1,420,423 was collected. Modern School boys raised £350. Apart from money raising schemes within individual schools, children played a part, by producing posters for a 'War Weapons Week' School Posters competition. The First Prize winner in the Boys' 13½ years and over class was Eric Rowley (14) of the Modern School, whose design showed a destroyer advancing beneath a rainbow. The girl winner in the same age group was Jean Alexander (18) of the High School. Two Modern School boys, Alan E. Impey (14) and Geoffrey Williams (15) had between them made 18 models of Wellington bombers, Spitfires, and other aircraft, that were used as part of Luton's War Weapons display. Later the models were exhibited at Stoke Newington Town Hall as part of London's War Weapons Week, where £115 was collected.

In the 1941 Annual Soccer match with the Old Boys, the School XI won by 3 goals to 2. Sports Day that year was held on Saturday, 17th May, when three records were broken. A.N. Grice ran the 880 yards (u.14) in 2 minutes 33.12 secs; J.D. Ward broke the long jump (u.14) record by 1 ft 5 ins with a jump of 16 ft 2½ ins; and M.V.W. Chote, who held the javelin (open) record of 139 ft., had three extra throws and attained 146 ft. 2 ins. The *Victor Ludorum* was P.S.J. Adkins, the Powdrill Cup for Athletics was won by the Bees, and the Richardson Challenge Cup for Field

Morville Chote, winner of the Richardson Cup for field events, demonstrating the javelin in May, 1941. He was chosen to represent England in the 1948 Olympic Games. *(LN-LMC)*

Events went to Chote. In Cricket T.R.R. Whittaker scored 100 not out against St Christopher School.

In July Mr Godfrey organised the first of a number of Annual Invitation Sports Meetings at the School in aid of the Red Cross. It took the form of a triangular match between the Old Boys, the RASC and the School and resulted in a win for the School. They aimed to raise £70 and managed to exceed it. The highlight of the afternoon was a demonstration of Javelin throwing by Morville Chote, when he broke his own record and threw 158 ft 1½ ins.

Throughout the War the boys also contributed to the 'Penny-A-Week' Red Cross Collection, raising £20 in 1940–41.

The School Secretary, Miss J.M. Oakley, worked single-handed in the School Office and as the Headmaster's Secretary. At the beginning of the Autumn Term, 1941, Miss Marjorie Hartley, a High School girl, was appointed Assistant Secretary.

Soon after Ronald Bridger joined the Staff, interest was shown in purchasing an organ for the School. A Concert was held on the afternoon of Saturday, 22nd November, to try out the organ they were contemplating buying. Taking part in the

The first full-scale use of the School stage. In December 1941 Mr Martin produced *A Child in Flanders*, with choir and orchestra conducted by Mr Bridger. (*LN*)

concert were Augustus F. Lowe, a distinguished local music teacher and organist; Henry Cummings, a BBC baritone; and the School choir. The Concert was a great success and raised £107 towards the purchase of an organ.

Twelve years old Michael Marsh-Edwards reflected glory on the School when he took the Examinations of the Associated Board of the Royal Schools of Music, London, during 1941, and passed Grade 2 Piano, Grade 4 Viola, and Grade 4 Violin, all with distinctions. At the local Music Festivals he gained one Silver Cup, two Silver Medals, and twenty-five Certificates!

The School year closed for Christmas in 1941 with three performances of a Nativity play, *A Child in Flanders*, performed by members of the Dramatic Society assisted by the Choir and Orchestra, and produced by Mr A.W. Martin. The play opened with a prologue set during the Great War, and showing three British soldiers seeking shelter on Christmas Eve in a French peasant's cottage. This was followed by a series of tableaux showing the subject of their dreams – the Annunciation, the Adoration, and the coming of the Three Kings. In the epilogue the scene returned to France during the Great War. The atmosphere of the play depended on awe and

reverence, achieved in full measure by the tableaux and in the leave-taking of the Tommies when each in turn took a last glimpse of *la mère et le fils.*

Chief praise for the acting went to F.J. Mullinger, P. Panton and C.J. Titmus, and to G.W. Pearson who performed the dual role of peasant and Virgin. Mullinger made an excellent Cockney soldier and his halting French was well managed. Panton, gifted already with a rich Scottish brogue, made an equally good Highlander, while Titmus performed his part as an Indian soldier with credit. Pearson deserved special commendation on his versatility. In gesture and accent as a French peasant, in decorum as Virgin, he was a great success.

Mr Bridger composed a special prelude, and the production included music by Walford Davis, Sibelius and Fibich, together with appropriate carols. These were played and sung by the School orchestra and choir.

During the Christmas postal rush a number of boys and a master were employed by the GPO as sorters and postmen.

And into 1942

On January 1st, 1942, Alderman Harry Arnold resigned from Luton Town Council after forty years service. He agreed to retain the Chairmanship of the Modern and High School Governors, a position he had held since 1931.

Young people were being drawn more and more into the War. On 31st January, 1942, all boys of 17, born between 1st February 1924 and 31st January 1925, were required to register for war work or military service. A month later boys of 16 followed suit. It was announced that girls of 17 would register on 28th March. Young folk in full-time education were deferred, but could expect to be called-up as soon as their education ceased. Only a few escaped for a temporary respite at University, and most of those soon found themselves on manoeuvres with the Officer Training Corps.

The School made a minor contribution to the War effort, when its iron gates were removed, ostensibly to be recycled into munitions. As the gates were left permanently open, they served no useful purpose, and the cost of repainting them would be saved. This was all seen as part of a morale boosting campaign. In truth, most of the ironwork collected was considered useless for recycling and dumped into the Thames estuary. The School paid a local firm £10 to remove the gates carefully, so that the walls would not be damaged.

In February 1942, plans were in active preparation in the Luton area to form a Cadet Corps from which boys would pass into the Home Guard when they became 17. Luton Modern School was in the forefront, followed closely by the Luton Boys' Club. The Modern School Cadet Corps, which included a platoon from the North Western Polytechnic, began training on 19th February. Capt. S.J. Pointing was the acting CO, with Lieut. J. Flemming of the Polytechnic as 2nd in command. They

were actively assisted by 2nd-Lieuts. Gallimore, Magoon and Grayston, (L.M.S.) and Moss and Hughes (N.W.P.). By March, some 120 Modern School boys and 50 Polytechnic boys had joined.

During the Easter holidays four platoons took part in attacking and defending a farm at Lilley. Although the attackers managed to infiltrate through the opposing patrols, their attack failed due to the defenders having posted themselves in the most advantageous positions. A short route march, to Streatley and back, resulted in several members, including CSM Jacobs, suffering from sore or blistered feet.

Speaking to parents at Speech Day on 25th February, Mr Webb said that:

> 'Not many parents will find my decision to encourage a Cadet Corps within the School really incompatible with the atmosphere engendered in the play *A Child in Flanders* produced at the end of Christmas term, if you have regard to the part would-be Christians can play in a non-Christian world. I hope that Cadets will join because they wish to add their quota of force to actions which, on the wide canvas of humanity, are opposed to slavery, injustice, fraud and hate, and in support of freedom, justice, truth and brotherliness.'

In his report the Headmaster stressed the importance of remaining at School:

> 'A boy is not "due to leave", nor is "his time up" – as if he were about to be let out of prison – when he completes the school year in which he turns 16. A boy's secondary education cannot achieve full stature if it is cut short at two-thirds of its intended duration. And secondary education will not make its proper contribution to the life of the community, that is, bring enrichment, just criticism, and true creativeness to our daily living, so long as boys are swept away from all consciously directed educative influences just as the doors and windows of their human capacities are beginning to open.'

The Government had initiated at least three schemes to strengthen the upper end of the school. The first was to promote scientific and technical training A State Bursary was offered to any lad passing Higher Certificate in certain combinations of physics, mathematics and chemistry if he was over 17. This defrayed all expenses to a University for one or two years and would permit some boys to take a degree.

There was also a plan for the boy not mentally equipped to take Higher Certificate or who for financial or other reasons must leave. Training for the radio industry was offered to any who had reached School Certificate standard physics and mathematics.

For some years the State had offered 360 scholarships each year to boys and girls who did most brilliantly in the Higher Certificate examinations. Another plan offered to Higher Certificate linguists the opportunity to learn Turkish, Persian,

About 70 Old Boys and friends attended the Annual Luncheon on Saturday, 24th January, 1942. Amongst those at the High Table were R. Parker, B. Grey (Old Dunstablians), H.R. Waller, the Mayor, J.H. Burgoyne, D.C. Earle, K.B. Webb, T.E. Smalley, T.A.E. Sanderson. A few men are in uniform. Staff wives joined kitchen staff to prepare the meal. (LN)

Chinese and Japanese, to take a commission and to be at the Government's disposal for five more years.

'Facts such as these,' Mr Webb concluded, 'prompt me to tell the School that they can render one kind of service their country needs by doing their school work well.'

Mrs A.C. Powell presented the certificates and prizes: 48 School Certificates, 10 Higher Certificates, 14 in Subsidiary Subjects. The Governors' School Leaving Exhibition was presented to J.H.S. Kent, who was also awarded a State Scholarship held at Emmanuel College, Cambridge; Open Exhibitions to University College, Hull, went to A.R. Emery and P.R. Franks; and State Bursaries held at King's College, London University to A.R. Emery, and at City and Guilds College, London, to his brother G.A. Emery. Amongst younger boys, J. Heley (13) gained a Scholarship to Dartmouth College; and E.B. Dawson (14) Navy Artificer; and D.P. Clements (15) an Aircraft Apprenticeship.

Early in 1942 the Old Modernians formed a Careers Sub-Committee to help the Careers Master, Mr Clayton. Its aim was to advise boys leaving school of the prospects, method of entry, and courses of study for various trades and professions. One of the objects was to discourage boys from entering 'dead-end' jobs, even if they seemed to offer good pay prospects at the commencement. In the past many boys

had complained of a lack of career guidance. The Careers Sub-Committee consisted of D.C. Earle, H.R. Waller and H.O. White.

During 1941 groups of boys under the wary eye of Mr A.W. Martin, designed and began to paint a series of murals of local, historical and scientific subjects on the bare walls of the corridors. Due to Mr Martin's illness the work became protracted, and some were never completed. Dennis L. Farr recalls 'painting a mural opposite the Biology laboratory on the Evolution of Coal! Francis Minns, the head of biology, was highly critical of the fauna and flora we invented on the slenderest of geological and archaeological evidence. I'm not sorry they have disappeared; they were pretty dire, and the technique in which they were executed would have ensured that they flaked off anyway.'

School Clubs and social activities were seriously curtailed during the first years of the War, largely due to lack of blackout in the building and Cadet Corps training.

In September 1941, the Literary and Scientific Society had a lecture from refugee teacher, Dr F.W. Pick, on 'Goebbels at Work'. Pick was an acknowledged expert on Hitler's Minister of Enlightenment and Propaganda, and in 1942 published an influential book *The Art of Dr. Goebbels*. An innovation in the form of a 'Brains Trust' met with particular success. The panel was made up of K.B. Webb, F.C. Minns, C.W. Parry, L. Small and H.H. Watson, who dealt manfully with such questions as 'Is space infinite?' and 'Upon what does the humour of Tommy Handley rely?' The only visit the Society managed to make in 1941 was to J.W. Green's Brewery and Malt House.

Mr Dennis Gallimore was in his element when he enlightened the Lit. and Sci. on the finer points of his hobby 'Swing Music' in February 1942. Another staff 'Brains Trust' was held in October, and, in November, Dr E.W. Russell from Rothamsted delivered a brilliant lecture on 'Post-War Agriculture'.

The Field Club made a number of visits during the year, though mainly in small groups. Led by Mr Minns, Dr Dony and Mr Cleaver they explored the Whipsnade bird sanctuary, Flitwick Marsh, Wheathampstead Common and Fancott, and a senior group spent a day in Cambridge.

In response to a memorandum from the Ministry of Agriculture the School formed a Rabbit Club in June 1942. It began with about 50 members who shared equally in the work and profit according to the amount they had invested in the club. The initial stock consisted of one pair of Dutch rabbits, and one English doe, with ten young. By the end of the year several hutches had been built and the number of does had been increased from two to ten. Some 20 lbs. of rabbits had been killed for meat, providing a small but useful supplement to the meat supply of the School.

The musical life of the School seemed to flourish during the War. Choral and instrumental work increased, and a Male Voice Choir consisting of senior boys and staff was formed and performed publicly at Speech Days and in various concerts. The orchestra was augmented with clarinets, a double bass, a second 'cello and a

Ronald Bridger conducting the School Choir 1941–2. A few members of Staff (including the Headmaster) and senior boys are in the back row. (*LN*)

number of very young and keen violinists, under the leadership of Dennis Gallimore.

On the last afternoon of the Easter term a 'Form Singing Competition' for Years I, II, and III was held in the Hall. Each form choir was conducted by its boy conductor and Mr Parry accompanied at the piano. By way of introduction, J. Berridge (IIIc) gave a short talk on Folk Songs. Form Ib was the winner of the 1st Year group, IIc and IIIa the winners in their groups. The conductor awarded most marks was Michael Marsh-Edwards of IIIa. A competition for the recitation of humorous verse or stories followed, together with various solo musical items.

The winning Form Ib choir performed again at the breaking-up ceremony on 1st April, together with a vocal quartet from IIIc comprising R.W. Cox, J.F. Edwards, A.F.W. Pakes and A.G. Warren; and a quintet formed by F.E. Stygall, piano, P.D. Southgate, violin, V.E. Raymond, violin, M. Marsh-Edwards, viola and J.M. Southgate, 'cello.

The Luton News reported that 14 years old Michael Marsh-Edwards conducted

the King Street Junior Orchestra at Easter to raise funds for the Children's Hospital.

Another Concert to raise money for the School Organ Fund was held in March, featuring Miss Grace Nevern, soprano, with Augustus F. Lowe at the piano, an Instrumental Octet arranged by Mr Haydn Roberts, the School Male Voice Choir, and the School Choir (85 voices). Proceeds from the concert amounted to almost £50, bringing the Organ Fund total to £150 2s. 6d.

For the first time in the School's history a broadcast was made from the Hall on Saturday, 26th September, 1942. The occasion was a concert of songs by British composers, performed by the Luton Choral Society, conducted by Arthur E. Davies.

Luton's special Fund Raising week in 1942, named 'Warship Week', was enlivened when a knight in armour threw down a gauntlet at the foot of the Mayor, Ald. John Burgoyne. He brought a challenge from the Mayor of Watford, claiming that his town would collect more money than Luton. In the event, Luton raised £1,421,724 as against Watford's £1,203,040.

Members of Mr Martin's Art Class and a number of other boys were invited to design Warship window displays for six of Luton's more important shops in the centre of the town. The work consisted mainly of huge painted backgrounds and plywood cut-outs. Dennis L. Farr remembers painting a poster exhorting the Luton public to buy a warship and defeat a Hun. The School's Savings effort during the week amounted to £439 10s, a considerable improvement on the previous year's War Weapons Week total.

The War effort was helped in another way when the Board of Education gave permission for boys over 14 to help farmers during either the morning or afternoon sessions, as well as during the school holidays. Modern School boys found themselves helping in the cultivation of kale and sugar-beet.

> A farmer sits in his spacious hall,
> Drinking his home-brewed ale,
> 'Oh where shall I get some braw lads,
> To weed my goodly kale?'
>
> 'The Modern School lads are broad and strong,'
> Quoth the foreman at his knee.
> 'And I will write you a braid letter,
> To get you two or three.'
>
> Be it wind, be it weet, be it hail, be it sleet,
> This field we've got to weed;
> We've got to bend till our backs are sore,
> And the tear blinds our e'e.
>
> [A. F. Trendall, IVa]

Some boys preferred engineering to farm work, and local factories were keen to give them the opportunity to follow their particular interest. A register was drawn up between the School and employers, and when the latter were short-handed they could call on the School for help.

Between 15th and 20th June the School took part in 'Religion and Life Week'. Mr Appadurai Aaron, an Indian Christian, visited the School and talked about India's friendship with Britain. He made a passionate yet very reasonable plea for India's independence, pointing the way to lasting goodwill between the two nations. At the end of the week a Youth Conference was held in the School Hall on 'Youth, Religion and the New World Order'. There were two sessions, in one of which Christian Citizenship was discussed, and, in the other, Social Reconstruction. The leaders were Revd. E.A. Willis, the S.C.M. Schools' Secretary, and Sqd-Ldr. Dowell. Together with these two, Mr Webb and Revd. Wilfred Wade co-operated in a Brains Trust, which attempted to deal with some of the questions submitted by Study Groups.

1942's sporting activities began with cross-country running in January. With the co-operation of Mr Shaw at Manor Farm, Stopsley, a course was designed to lie almost entirely on grassland, muddy lanes and a bit of ploughland. The oldest boys would run as far as Warden Hill, whilst the younger lads would face a shorter circuit turning at Common Farm, the 'Black Barn'. The School soundly defeated an Army team, E. Hobbs coming in at the head of the first eight places, all won by the school. The inter-House competition took place immediately before the Easter holidays and was won by the Bees. In September the age limit ban on boys under 14 years of age was lifted, encouraging a high proportion of junior boys to join the Club.

Continuous frost confined the Association Football season to just six weeks. Twenty-one School matches were played at different age levels, ten being won, seven lost and four drawn. The Ist XI was above average and under normal circumstances would have been a good team, but the late start to the season and the curtailment by other school activities of after-school practice prevented the development of good teamwork. Colours were awarded to the Captain and Vice-Captain, B.V. Sealy and J.C. Crabtree, and to P.S.J. Adkins, F.J. Mullinger, and I.E. Norman.

The 1st Cricket XI had an outstanding record. Not a single School match was lost and only one drawn, a record due entirely to the keenness and friendly team spirit of all members of the XI and to the able captaincy of M.V.W. Chote.

Sports Day was held on Saturday, 31st May. F.J. Mullinger broke the School Mile Record in 5 minutes 6.48 secs., as did A.S. Tweedie who came second. Mullinger also broke the Long Jump Record with a leap of 18 ft. 7½ ins. M.V.W. Chote again broke his own School Javelin Record with a throw of 157 ft. 6½ ins. The *Victor Ludorum* Cup was once more won by P.S.J. Adkins. Chote was awarded the Richardson Cup for the most meritorious performance in Field Events. The Powdrill Challenge Cup was won by the Hornets with 251 points.

The School Athletic team that competed in Mr Godfrey's Red Cross Sports in July 1942.
(back) C.M. Jacobs, P.H. Gilder, – , – , J. Irvine, A.S. Tweedie, K.G. Adams, (front) I.E. Norman,
J.C. Crabtree, F.J. Mullinger, M.V.W. Chote, P.S.J. Adkins, J.D. Ward, P. Heanue. (*LN-LMC*)

The Second Annual Red Cross sports was held on Friday, 26th July, when Mr Godfrey persuaded five teams to take part, including the Old Boys, Vauxhall and a team calling themselves Nondescripts. The event raised £113 1s. for the Red Cross.

Luton's 'Holidays at Home' included the Bedfordshire Junior and Colts AAA Championships, which were held at Wardown on Saturday, 1st August. Ten teams from Luton, Dunstable and Bedford took part, including the Luton Modern School, the Junior Technical School, the North Western Polytechnic, Vauxhall, and the Luton ATC. Luton Modern School won the Championship Challenge Cup with 166 points, Bedford Old Goldroadians were second with 59 points and the Old Luton Modernians third with 12 points.

The 1st Rugby XV, managed by Messrs Phillips, Bridger and Bailey, had a number of promising players. After vigorous training and the usual misfortunes, the team more than fulfilled expectations and won nine of their ten matches, making it

one of the most succesful teams ever. Colours were awarded to the Captain and Vice-Captain, K.G. Henson and M.V.W. Chote, and to P.S.J. Adkins, F.J. Mullinger, J.C. Crabtree, E. Hobbs, J. Irvine, and I.E. Norman.

During the Easter holidays the School kitchen was replanned and new equipment installed. At the same time the price of dinners was reduced to sixpence.

On Monday, 1st August, 1942, the School Hall hosted a Brains Trust organised by the Luton 'Holidays at Home' committee. The great attraction was the appearance of Professor C.E.M. Joad, Head of Philosophy and Psychology, at Birkbeck College, London, and the most popular 'star' of the BBC's weekly radio 'Brains Trust' programme. He was joined by a panel consisting of Dr E. Leslie Burgin, MP for Luton, Mrs Tate, MP, and Mr C.J. Bartlett, Director of Vauxhall Motors.

Prof. Joad caused much amusement for the men and considerable annoyance to some of the ladies present, when he responded to one question by saying, 'If I married a woman with brains I should expect her to find housework dull. If my wife

The undefeated 1942 Rugby XV, with Ronald Bridger and Ronald Phillips. (back) G. Mullinger, G.A. Hawkins, D.B. Fensome, B.G. Brightman, B.V. Sealy, D.R. Cook, C.M. Jacobs, A.R. Jeffs, P. Panton, H.G. Lynn, (front) J.D. Ward, E. Hobbs, F.J. Mullinger, J.C. Crabtree, J. Irvine, P. Heanue, M.J. Barber. (*LN-LMC*)

The School hosted a 'Brains Trust' in August 1942, when the principal speaker was
Prof. C.M. Joad (left) of Birkbeck College, a popular radio personality, seen here with the
headmaster

had essentially practical abilities I should expect better results than if I had an intellectual woman in the house.' He was, of course, only joking, but those who took him seriously have probably never forgiven him.

Red Tape

Until October 1942, Luton Modern School was almost totally without any form of blackout. The Governors had long ago refused to pay the enormous costs involved in its installation. Consequently, in the winter months the large building lay idle after dark, leaving Mr Webb conscience stricken, knowing that groups like the Home Guard and the ATC were desperate for accommodation and had funds to pay for it.

In order that the building could be made ready as an emergency hospital,

permission was given by the Governors for the Ministry of Health to install and fit blackout curtains at a substantial cost to itself. The work was completed by mid-October, but it was made clear that the blackout material was the property of the Ministry of Health and *not* the Governors, and the latter had no authority to use the curtains for school purposes, however tempted they might be. The School was 'itching' to make use of the amenity, but it was not permissible! Any organisation wanting to use the building at night had to pay for the use of the blackout.

This ludicrous situation lasted for weeks whilst letters passed between Governors and various Government Departments. Eventually, early in 1943, the Home Office intervened and the School was at last given the go-ahead to use the blackout.

From September 1942 the Wednesday half-holiday, that had existed since the School began, was switched to Saturday morning. This had the advantage of helping the Kitchen staff, and saving rubber and fuel for special buses on two half-holidays. It seemed to have everyone's approval.

At Christmas the Junior Dramatic Society presented a dramatised version of *A Christmas Carol*. Three performances were given to the School, parents, friends and Governors. The Choir and Orchestra, under the direction of Mr Woodcock, contributed greatly to the performances. An anonymous reviewer in *The Lutonian* wrote: 'J. Berridge's portrayal of Ebenezer Scrooge, the miser, was restrained but powerful. D. C. Arnold did well as the tyrannised clerk, Bob Crachit, but found it difficult to unloosen as the cheerful father. S. Mullins as Marley's Ghost was most convincing when the lighting was finally perfected, and J.R. Dony (Mrs Crachit) looked the part, but must learn to do nothing with more conviction. R.H. Burgess (the Messenger Boy) must now try something less obviously made for him!'

110 boys and 80 girls from the Modern School, the High School, the Technical School, the North Western Polytechnic, the Convent School and Dunstable School were all recruited to join the delivery staff at Luton Post Office over the Christmas period. They were able to provide two letter deliveries each day and a parcel service. Another group of boys found Sunday morning employment at Electrolux and other factories around Luton.

There were a number of Staff changes during 1942. Mr L. Small, who had joined in April 1941 to teach English and French, left at Easter to become a Supervisor of French Broadcasts at the BBC. In July Mr L.A.W. Moss (History) and Mr J. 'Danny' Magoon (Latin and English) left to join the Forces. Morville Chote recalled his interview for entry to Emmanuel College, Cambridge. This was dependent on his sitting an entrance exam in three weeks time, which included Latin: a subject that he had not studied. The Headmaster freed Mr Magoon's timetable, and for three weeks he and Chote concentrated on the one subject, which Chote passed without difficulty. He was forever grateful for this special attention.

It was with regret that the School said 'goodbye' to Mr A.P. Frost, who had joined the School in 1913 to teach mathematics, English and French. Educated at

Westminster City School and London University, he came to Luton from the Junior School of Manchester Grammar School. Between 1916 and 1919 he was absent on military service, but returned to Luton on being demobilised. Known to the boys as 'Happy', he was a quiet, unassuming man. He was an excellent teacher who saw to it that his classes consumed as much mathematics to the hour as was comfortably possible. Nearly all his lessons were punctuated with examples of his great sense of humour, and perhaps that was what appealed to the School more than anything else. He left to take up a post as Mathematics master at Bodmin County School.

Amongst new teachers who arrived in September, usually for only a few months, were two who stayed much longer. William H. Chapman, BSc, came to teach general subjects, though he specialised in mathematics. Robert H. Squire took over the Physical Training department. He is remembered either with affection or loathing, depending on one's liking for physical exercise. Born in 1887 in Brixton, he attended the LCC Higher Grade School from 1896–1902, and after numerous jobs joined a circus as a tumbler. He spent some time in Germany and gained a Teaching Diploma from the Kaiser Frederick Teachers' Gymnasium in Berlin, and later a Teaching Certificate from the LCC Physical Instruction College in Paddington. Alan Silvester has commented: 'He compensated for his lack of PT theory with abundant energy, enthusiasm and theatrical flair!' To Dennis Farr he was 'a Cockney fru and fru; he must have been pushing seventy [actually 59], and loved to tell of his circus days, and how, as a youngster, he had to sleep with the 'orses, until one day in the gym, a bored voice from the back enquired, 'What, rocking horses?' Most boys remember him for organising a series of PT Spectaculars that will be described later. A.W. 'George' Thorpe was not alone in considering him 'a physical and mental clown in all respects. Synchronised cycling, and marching while someone stands atop the cricket pavilion bellowing out advice and encouragement, was not my idea of how best to illustrate school physical success.'

Dr John G. Dony, 'Doc', published his PhD. thesis *A History of the Straw Hat Industry* in March 1942, and it immediately became a standard work. He was soon recognised as the leading authority on the subject and was frequently consulted by politicians, trades unionists, and anyone seeking information on the industry. For the next fifty years he contributed articles to trade journals, directories and the *Encyclopaedia Britannica*. Born in Luton in 1899, he was educated at Surrey Street School, where his Standard VII teacher was Frederick Mander (later Sir Frederick). Mander's fascination for wild orchids brushed off on John, thus beginning a life long passion for botany. Apprenticed as an engineer, and after brief service in the Navy, he became an uncertificated teacher at Norton Road, and later Queen's Square School, Luton. In 1931 he moved to a London Church of England school, and spent his evenings studying for his BSc (1935) at the London School of Economics. He joined the Modern School staff as an historian in 1941, where he found R.S. Clayton teaching botany. There was always an uneasy tension between the two men, but

Dr John G. Dony (centre) taught history and economics at the School, but was internationally known as a botanist. He is seen here with Sir Frederick and Lady Mander. (*LN*)

Dony had no desire to usurp Clayton's position. 'Never teach your hobby,' he told the author. 'It will spoil it for ever.' How true that was. He had been the Honorary Keeper of Botany at Luton Museum since 1936, and in 1953 published another major work, his *Flora of Bedfordshire*. This was followed by a *Flora of Hertfordshire* (1967), *Bedfordshire Plant Atlas* (1976) and posthumously, with his wife Christine, *The Wild Flowers of Luton* (1991). He was internationally famous for his botanical work, and after many years as Secretary to the Botanical Society of the British Isles, he became its very active President from 1967–1969. In 1964 he joined with two former students, Frank Stygall and James Dyer, to write *The Story of Luton* and in 1970 *A History of Education in Luton*. Awarded an MBE in 1983 for his services to nature conservation in Bedfordshire, he died in March 1991.

In July 1942 boys gained a total of 16 Cambridge Higher School Certificates, a record only beaten by three other schools in the country, two of which were public

schools. D.J.R. Lawrence gained an Open Scholarship worth £80 to University College, Hull, a State Scholarship, and a State Bursary to Gonville and Caius College, Cambridge. D. Payne gained an Open Scholarship worth £40 plus £30 maintenance, tenable at University College, Hull, and a State Bursary to King's College, Cambridge. D.L. Buttrick and R.H. Lewin both received State Bursaries for the Regent Street Polytechnic, London. M.V.W. Chote, briefly Head Prefect in 1942, was awarded an Open Exhibition to Emmanuel College, Cambridge to read modern languages. G.D. Nicholls received an Open Scholarship to Trinity College, Cambridge. P.S.J. Adkins gained a British Empire Open Scholarship of £50 per annum for a three years' Diploma Course at the School of Games, Athletics and Physical Education at Loughborough College.

During the autumn term fifteen senior boys met Mr Grayston and Mr Ridout at the Westminster Theatre, where they saw *Henry IV, Part I*, and were greatly entertained by the bewitching roguery of Robert Atkins' Falstaff. Atkins had spent his childhood in Luton, attending Christ Church School, then working for hat manufacturers, J.C. Kershaw and Co., before entering Sir Herbert Tree's Academy of Dramatic Art.

Chapter 9

The Lost Boys

In 1938 it seemed to many thinking people that another War was inevitable. Nationally and locally the Civil Defence were making preparations for every eventuality, but there was still enormous apathy amongst the majority of the population. By October thousands of gas masks were distributed to school children, and then adults. A few months later blackout was being tested, and on the night of July 6th, 1939, the Royal Air Force carried out an exercise over the whole of south-east England between midnight and 4 am next day to test its efficiency. Apart from a few minor flaws it seems to have been a great success.

On 3rd September, 1939, War was officially declared, and staff, senior boys and Old Boys braced themselves for the greatest conflict the world had ever known.

It is from the pages of *The Old Luton Modernian* and the files of *The Luton News* that we can glimpse something of the every-day lives and the gallantry that was the lot of the Luton boys.

Week after week throughout the war the eight pages of *The Luton News* carried columns of news and photographs of men and women from the Luton area who were serving in the services somewhere in the world. At first the news was optimistic, but soon the first 'reported missing' and 'lost in action' reports appeared. After a time the 'reported missing' notices might be replaced by 'now known to be a prisoner of war', giving relatives at home some hope of seeing their loved ones again. For others 'confirmed dead' was all too frequent. There was hope too when 'missing since the fall of Singapore' became 'a prisoner in Japanese hands'; what those at home didn't know of atrocities in the East was seldom revealed by those who had experienced them.

We have no figures to record how many Old Boys served in the Army, Navy or Air Force, or of the thousands who were employed in less conspicuous aspects of the

war-effort. We do know that at least 70 boys and one master lost their lives. To describe the Old Boys' War and their individual actions would need a book of its own, and so I have chosen a few incidents to represent them all.

Some of the first news came in *The Luton News* for November 1939, when the paper reported that Robert Lawrence (19) had left his job in the Education Office at Luton Town Hall to go to France with the RAF, where 'he found the French he learnt at School most useful.' 'When Rex Beales of the 'Green Man', Chalk Hill, Dunstable left Luton Modern School he worked in the experimental department of Vauxhall Motors. He is now a Sgt-Pilot in the RAFVR, finishing his training somewhere in England.' 'Two brothers, Edgar (20) and Manuel (21) Silver are now in the services. Both former Modern School boys and furniture salesmen, Edgar is with the RAOC and Manuel with the RAF.' 'Sapper A. A. Bourlett (son of Mr L.M. Bourlett, a master at the Technical College) was apprenticed to Commer-Karrier, Ltd. before joining the Royal Engineers, and Ronald E. Overhill of the RAFVR is now an RAF mechanic.' 'Sapper Ronald G. Sinfield (19) is in France with the Royal Engineers. He worked at Barton Airport until 1937, when he joined the Army.' In 1940 '2nd Lt. J.P.C. Seale, a former Head Boy of Luton Modern School, received his Army Commission in August. He has been posted to India to work with the Gurkhas.'

Whilst this was the good news, some of it soon turned sour. The first Old Modernian to die in the War was Maurice William Bagnall, on 29th April, 1940. A country boy from Flitwick, he was a Gunner in the Royal Artillery.

'George Herbert Farr, a Private in the Royal Corps of Signals, was accidentally shot dead in a train on 16th June, 1940. After leaving School in 1934, he was employed at the Luton Corporation Electricity Works, and joined the Territorial Army in the summer of 1939. September saw him in France, and he was among the first to enter Belgium and the last to leave Dunkirk.'

'Rex Beales was a Sgt-Pilot; he died on active service on 2nd August, 1940, as the result of a flying accident. Aged 24, he had been married for only four months.'

Aubrey Ernest Owles and Edward Francis Edwin were both Sergeant-Pilots in the RAFVR. Both were killed on active service in 1940. Owles, a graduate of the Institute of Mechanical Engineers, died on 31st August, aged 21, and Edwin on 14th November, aged 24.

Sergeant-Pilot Edward B. Douglas Jenkins died on active service on 28th December, 1940, aged 20. A keen sportsman at School, he had held the *Victor Ludorum* Cup for two years, 1937 and 1938, and at the time of his death held the Bedfordshire County Junior shot-put record.

To an observer, more than sixty years distant in time, six deaths in 1940 might seem a lot. But in 1941 the number rose to 14, in the following year 10, and in 1943, 12. The greatest losses were in 1944 when 21 were recorded, followed by 6 in 1945. The number of those who died of wounds and related illnesses after the War was over remains unrecorded.

Stories in *The Luton News* sometimes told of amazing escapes. After leaving school, John A. Smith became a Vauxhall apprentice. He joined the RASC, and in 1939 found himself with the BEF in France. He spent four of the longest days of his life on the beach at Dunkirk during the great evacuation. Later, in a ship bound for foreign service, he was torpedoed, bombed and machine gunned, and survived to tell the tale.

Robert Claude Verran (LMS: 1930–35) was not so lucky. A Sergeant in 148 Sqn. RAFVR, he was a member of a Wellington Bomber crew that carried out a number of major bombing raids in the Mediterranean, for which he was awarded the DFM on 23rd December, 1940. Three weeks later he was killed when his plane was shot down over Catania in Sicily: he was 21. He was buried in the Military Cemetery at Catania. His father received the DFM on his behalf from the King in October, 1941.

Pilot Officer Raymond John Tearle, aged 25, was accidentally killed whilst on active service near Sheerness. He had been admitted as a solicitor in 1937, and had learnt to fly at Luton airport. He joined the RAF in 1938.

Ordinary Seaman Richard Fulton Cunningham (LMS: 1924–31) was killed when the battlecruiser *HMS Hood* was sunk by the *Bismarck* on 24th May, 1941. He was 27.

When Eric A. Tew left the School in 1932 he travelled extensively as a member of the Edward Dunstan Repertory Company. Finding the stage a precarious living, he gained employment with Waterlow and Sons at Dunstable. In 1937 he joined the Navy and at the outbreak of war he was serving as a Sick Berth Attendant on the cruiser, *Calcutta*. His ship made several journeys to Dunkirk during the evacuation in 1940. It was then sent to the Mediterranean, where it was lost during the withdrawal from Crete, but Eric survived and became a prisoner of war.

At the outbreak of war Lt. Engineer Victor R. Bussereau offered his services to the Canadian Government, and was granted a commission in the Royal Canadian Navy. He was killed on *HMS Rajputana* on 13th April, 1941, aged 27.

Sgt. Frank L.T. Ireson was a wireless operator and air gunner in 83 Sqn, RAFVR, who had made many sorties into enemy territory. He was killed on 25th July, 1941, when the plane in which he was flying was shot down over Holland. He was buried on the most northerly Frisian island of Schiermonnikoog in the Netherlands.

Sgt. Denis F. Hawkes, aged 25 (LMS: 1927–32), and the crew of an Armstrong Whitley bomber of 78 Sqn. all died when it was shot down on 17th August, 1941. The pilot managed to avoid crashing onto the Dutch village of Ohe En Laak.

The body of Sgt. Navigator Anthony Richard Cain was washed ashore at Ellos on the west coast of Sweden. He was serving with 235 Sqn. RAFVR, when his plane was shot down on 15th June, 1941. He is buried in Kviberg cemetery, north-east of Gothenburg.

Sgt-Pilot James Emerton Cooper (LMS: 1930–35) was killed after serving with 91 Spitfire Sqn. for nine months. He is believed to have been the first pilot to shoot

down the new Messerschmitt 109F. He was on patrol with a brother airman over the south coast when ten Messerschmitts came out of the sky. In the ensuing battle Cooper shot one of the new machines into the sea, as did his friend. He had learnt to fly locally and made his first solo flight over Luton. He died on 9th September, 1941, aged 22.

Sgt. William J. King, (21) RAFVR, was awarded the DFM. He was stationed in the Middle East. In July 1941, he was a member of an aircrew that crashed on the north African coast, and was rescued by a Fairey Swordfish of the Fleet Air Arm. When the rescuing plane landed, Sgt. King and his colleagues made a dash for the Swordfish under rifle fire from some 200 hostile tribesmen. They managed to get away without injury.

LAC. Norman James Ficken, aged 20, was one of four killed in a plane which crashed off Prince Edward Island in Canada on 20th November, 1941. He had joined the RAF only five months before, and had been sent to Canada for training.

Pilot Officer Edgar G.T. Smith (LMS: 1933–37) was killed on his 29th operational flight over Germany, on 30th September, 1941. He was 20 years old, and is buried in the Kiel War Cemetery in Germany. Sgt. Philip E. Whiting of 49 Sqn. is also buried in the Keil Cemetery. Aged 23, his plane was shot down on 26 June, 1941.

Sgt. Joseph George Richardson (LMS: 1932–35) was killed in action, returning from operations over Germany with 101 Sqn., on 19th August, 1941. He was 20.

Gnr. Jack William Weedon (LMS: 1931–37) 77 HAA Regt., Royal Artillery died on active service on 4th September, 1941, aged 20. He was buried in Luton General Cemetery. His younger brother Douglas Henry Weedon, (LMS: 1934–39) of the 1st Bn. Hampshire Regiment, was killed in France on the day he landed, 13th June, 1944. Only 19, he was buried in the Bayeux War Cemetery.

On 8th February, 1942, the Japanese crossed the Johore Straits, at Kranji, 22 km north of Singapore, where the allies had a large, closely guarded ammunition magazine. On the evening of the 9th they launched a fierce attack which lasted several days, before the allies were forced to withdraw. Major Frederick James Randall (LMS: 1926–31) was seriously wounded at the outset and died in the Alexandra Hospital, Singapore, on 10th February, 1942, aged 26. The following day 2nd Lt. Rex Alec Holmes (LMS: 1925–29) was killed in the same conflict. He was 29.

The School was particularly shocked to receive the news that Pilot Officer Ronald Renshaw Flint had lost his life, along with the other members of the crew with whom he had been flying, on the night of 24th March, 1942. They were buried together in the Montrose Sleepyhillock Cemetery at Angus in the Scottish Highlands.

Ronald Flint had been born at Greenock in 1917, and a year or two later moved with his parents to Keighley, Yorks, where he later won a scholarship to Keighley

Grammar School and gained his School Certificate. He transferred to Luton Modern School in 1933, and appeared immediately at home. He was made a prefect in 1934, and Head Boy in 1935 and 1936. His ability on the Arts side was quickly recognised, and as the result of his Higher School Certificate in 1936, he was placed on the 'Reserve' State Scholarship list. He obtained an Honours degree in History at London University, together with a Teacher's Diploma.

Before leaving University he appeared before a Military tribunal, where his pacifist sincerity would have gained him complete exemption from military service. He preferred, however, non-combatant duties; but died as a member of an air-crew, not afraid to sacrifice his personal revulsion for war to his Country's need!

The death of Mr Thomas Plato Clark on 19th June, 1942, struck the School another heavy blow. He was killed in a ground accident whilst on active service with the RAF. A graduate of Queen's College, Oxford, he joined the Staff in 1930 to teach history, a subject about which he felt passionately. He took an active part in all school games, but especially enjoyed Rugger. He was buried at St Thomas' Church, Stopsley on 24th June, aged 34. Forty members of the School Cadet Force under their Commanding Officer, Capt. S.J. Pointing, formed a guard of honour. The pall bearers were senior boys: D.R.Brandon, D.R. Cook, P.R. Franks, C.M. Jacobs and B.V. Sealy. Fifteen members of staff, representatives of the Governors, the Old Luton Modernians Club and the North Western Polytechnic were amongst the many mourners. The lesson was read by the Headmaster, and Mr J. A. Cleaver played the organ. Two boys were overheard talking after the funeral. 'It's such a pity,' said one. 'Yes, because he was a good master,' added the other.

At a meeting on 27th August, 1942 the Old Luton Modernians' Club set up a Services Fund. With donations received from members, postal orders were sent to men serving in Britain, and cigarettes to officers, whilst those serving overseas, including prisoners of war, received a variety of gifts. Extracts from the many letters of thanks were printed in the Club's Magazine (at that time included as a supplement to the School Magazine).

'My sincere thanks to the Club for my delightful present. It was very welcome and much appreciated. I was also glad to get a copy of the Magazine. I was sorry to hear about Nobby [Mr T. P. Clark]. I always had a great affection for him. I suppose you read in *The Luton News* that I am now a proud father.' *R. D. Hill, Lt.*

'Thanks a million for the School mag., it certainly does bring back some of those happy days of the past, also some hurtful ones. You remember the old song, 'Just a little bit off the top will do for you' and Mr Woodcock's version of it?' *J. Hobbs*

Petty Officer Dennis Sydney Depledge, (LMS: 1930–34), an Engine Room Artificer on *HMS Ajax*, was killed in action and buried at sea in Gibraltar Bay on 1st January,

1943. He was about to be promoted to Chief Petty Officer. Aged 23, he had been a junior draughtsman at Skefko before joining the Navy in 1941.

In January 1943, Pilot Officer A.M. Hill (26) was the first Old Boy to receive the DFC. A fighter pilot during the Battle of Britain, he had completed two years general service with a night fighter squadron and had two confirmed victories to his credit. He was a prisoner during the latter part of the war. In civvy street he was a chemist with J. W. Green's brewery.

Flt. Sgt. G.E. Cornes (22) trained in Southern Rhodesia, gaining his wings in 1940. In February 1943, *The Luton News* reported that he has been awarded the DFM and promoted to Warrant Officer. The paper added that his older brother Wilfred had been with the Anglo-Iranian Oil Company for the past five years.

A month later the newspaper reported that Cpl. Frederick W. Hobbs (LMS: 1931–36) of the RAFVR, who had been missing since the fall of Singapore, had been evacuated to Java where he had been taken prisoner by the Japanese. He managed to send a card home saying that he was in excellent health, but he died at Sandakan Camp in Borneo on 23rd May, 1945. Pte. Alec Arthur Brown, (27) RASC, and Sgt. Aubrey A.B. Baker, RASC, were also taken prisoner after the fall of Singapore, but both fortunately survived.

The Luton News printed part of a letter from Ronald P. Hawkins, who had been captured in Crete, and sent to a POW Camp in Germany:

> 'The fruits of the labours of the Red Cross Collectors we see here in the regular arrival of parcels, books, games, etc., so you know it is not wasted. Every week, every day, we have proof.'

Sergeant Ronald G. Woodfield was the air bomber in a crew of seven, shot down over Denmark on 4th April, 1943. Today they lie side by side in the Fourfelt Military Cemetery at Esbjerg.

In July 1943 Pilot-Officer F.L.A, Morris (30) RAF, who had been at Luton Modern School and Dunstable Grammar School, was reported missing on his 30th operational flight over enemy territory. He miraculously reappeared and made more trips in one of the largest 4-engine Lancaster bombers used by the RAF.

Flt Sgt. Clifford L.B. Janes (LMS: 1924–31) was killed on active service in the Middle East on 26th July, 1943. He had been a director of H.C. Janes, Ltd., the firm that built the new School. After advanced flying training in Canada, he had gained his wings in 1941. An organ, dedicated to his memory, was presented to the School by his father in March 1949.

Lutonians were shocked to hear on the wireless on the evening of 30th September, 1943, that Stewart Sale (38), with two other front line war correspondents (A.B. Austin, *Daily Herald,* and W.J. Munday, *News Chronicle*), had died on duty with the Fifth Army near Naples. They were killed by a shell burst

whilst with leading units advancing beyond Novera. Sale left School in 1921, and joined the staff of *The Luton News*. He later acted as war correspondent for *The Daily Telegraph*. Here is part of an obituary by a Reuters colleague that appeared in *The Times*:

> '"I saw Berlin burn" was the first phrase of his fine story of the flight in a Lancaster bomber over Berlin on 16th January this year. It was typical of his character and the way he endeared himself to people that the crew with which he flew kept in the closest contact with him after the flight. So highly was his description valued that later he lectured to many RAF personnel on the experience of raiding Berlin. Early in August he went to Allied Headquarters in Algiers and, attached to the Fifth Army, his first dispatch told "how we landed at Salerno". From that day Sale was constantly in the front line. He was as capable and as conscientious as he was unassuming. He faced danger with the courage of a veteran British soldier.'

From time to time Old Boys met one another in unlikely places. In October 1943, Acting Sgt. R.H.J. Thompson (19) was undergoing flying training with the RAF in Gwelo, Southern Rhodesia, when he ran into the School's ex-PT master, Eric Harvey, who was a physical education instructor in the RAF. Both felt homesick after watching a film called *People's Land* with shots of the Warden Hills.

In October 1943, Flying Officer Ronald Wilfred King (29) RAFVR was serving with 224 Squadron and was awarded the DFC. Before the war he had been a civil servant attached to the Board of Agriculture and Fisheries. He underwent flying training in South Africa and was commissioned in 1942. The citation read:

> 'He participated in many operational sorties as navigator in a crew which destroyed at least two U-boats. In July last, his aircraft was so badly damaged by AA fire that for two minutes it was necessary to fly at sea level. Throughout *this* period *this* officer calmly continued his duties. At all times he displayed great technical ability and exceptional coolness and courage in the face of danger.'

A number of Old Boys died in air assaults over Germany in the first months of 1944. Flying Officer Jack Anstee, aged 22 (LMS: 1932–38); Flt Sgt. William Douglas James, aged 21 (LMS: 1934–39); and Sgt. Eric Gordon Waller, aged 20 (LMS: 1933–39), are all buried in the Berlin 1939–45 War Cemetery. Sgt. Brian Edward Clarke, aged 19 (LMS: 1935–40), had been on five operational flights and was credited with having shot down a rocket plane. He died over Brunswick. Sgt. William Maurice Gibson, aged 19 (LMS: 1935–40), died whilst returning from an air raid on Nuremburg. Sgt. Flt. Engineer George Douglas Champkin, aged 20 (LMS: 1934–39), was killed on his 11th operational flight near Bayern. He had been a corporal in the ATC, and joined the RAF in 1943.

Sgt. Alfred P.C. Kuster, aged 21 (LMS: 1935–40), died in Italy on 21st August, 1944 and was buried in Naples. Lt. Harold Arthur Cherry, aged 32 (LMS: 1923–29), also died in Italy whilst serving with the Royal Artillery attached to the Tactical Air Force, on 26th February, 1945. He was buried in the Salerno War Cemetery.

Lt. Richard Dockrill Hill (LMS: 1928–33) was stationed in Gibraltar in 1942 when he wrote to the *Old Luton Modernian* saying that he was looking forward to the time when he would be able to swap a few yarns over a 'beaker of the best'. He was with the Hertfordshire Regt. when he was killed in action, on 28th September, 1944, aged 27, and buried at the Faenza Cemetery in Italy. He had been a reporter with the Exchange Telegraph. His life is commemorated by a brass plaque in the High Town Methodist Church, Luton, where he had founded the Youth Club.

Flt-Lt. Maurice Dean Randall of Barton, aged 34 (LMS: 1922–28), was killed in a flying accident in India on 20th October 1944. He joined the RAF in December 1941, after some pre-service training with Luton 10F Squadron, ATC. Commissioned early in 1943, he went to India and took part in more than 150 operational flights. A popular member of the Old Luton Modernians' Club, he had been assistant editor of the old Boys magazine. He was buried in Ranchi War Cemetery in India.

Lt. Alan Underwood (LMS: 1929–33) was employed by Laportes before he joined the Birmingham City Police in 1936. He was awarded an MBE following an air raid in the city, during which he displayed great bravery. In 1943 he was given a commission in the Royal Marines. He collapsed and died during a voluntary night exercise on 23rd May, 1945, aged 28.

Lt. Jack Colin Crabtree, aged 20 (LMS: 1936–43), Head Prefect in 1943, was killed in action at Arnhem on 21st April, 1945. He joined the army on leaving School and received his commission the following January. His 2nd 'pip' followed in June. He was made Pioneer and Explosives Officer-Instructor, and in that capacity was attached to the King's Own Yorkshire Light Infantry, the 'Green Howards', when they went to the front in February 1945. C.M. Jacobs wrote in *The Old Lutonian*: 'He was admired by all at School. Boys in Form I and Form VI alike looked up to him. [He was 6ft 3ins tall and weighed 15 stone.] He, in turn, showed a very tender understanding towards all who came into contact with him.' Mr Webb wrote: 'He was loved by us all, masters and boys. We all feel better for having known him.'

Many Old Boys received awards and decorations, but no complete list is available. Nor do we know the names of all those who served in non-combatant posts, often doing work involving national security and entailing great danger. It is known that one or two did work of such secrecy that even now their stories may not be told.

The following awards were recorded in *The Old Lutonian* at the time:

Lt Alan Underwood, MBE.

Flt. Lt Edward S. Ellis, CGM, DFC.

Flt. Lt R. B. Birchmore, DFC and bar.
Flt. Lt Peter N. Aldred, DFC.
FO. Eric G. Dudley, DFC.
Flt. Lt Arnold M. Hill, DFC.
FO. Ronald W. King, DFC.
FO. Dennis Matthews, DFC.
Flt. Lt Ernest A. Sanders, DFC.
Flt. Lt G. C. Skelton, DFC.
Flt. Lt Roy Welch, AFC.
L. Cpl Sidney Faunch, GM.
Sgt Norman Adams, MM.
Flt Sgt G. E. Cornes, DFM.
Sgt William King, DFM.
Sgt Robert Verran, DFM.
Llt. Sgt Norman Thom, BEM (Military)
Flt. Lt W. J. Billington, mentioned in despatches.
Sgt Ernest G. Bell, mentioned in despatches.

It is appropriate at this point to mention the School Caretaker, A.R. 'Bob' Killick, who was born in London in 1911. In the late 1920s he ran away from home and, lying about his age, enlisted in the Grenadier Guards. Later he worked at Vauxhall Motors, before joining LMS in 1938. As a reservist he was called up in October 1939, joining the first battalion of the Grenadier Guards. In 1944 as a sergeant leading a patrol across a bridge at Louvain in Belgium he was struck behind the left ear by a richochet sniper's bullet. He was picked up by nuns who took him in a wheel-barrow to a local hospital where a Belgian brain surgeon saved his life. After months in hospital in Bromsgrove he was invalided out of the Army and returned to the 'battle-field' at Bradgers Hill. He remained a relatively sick man; but carefully nursed by his wife, and accompanied by his bull-dog, 'Ben', he continued working for the School until his retirement in 1976. He died on 10th July, 1987.

Two of Britain's leading 'back-room boys' were Old Lutonians. Dr Cyril Reid, an authority on nuclear fission, was engaged in atomic bomb research in Canada during most of the war. He left the School in 1934 to become a laboratory assistant at Rothamsted, and while there obtained a Royal Scholarship in Botany. Entering Imperial College, he graduated BSc with honours, ARCS, and later PhD. He was engaged on Government research after leaving Imperial College in 1939.

For the firing of V2 rockets from Cuxhaven, after the German surrender, known as 'Operation Backfire', chief technical superintendent was Dr William Henry Wheeler, director of projectile development in the Ministry of Supply, who left Luton Modern School in 1926. A specialist in fuel research, flame speeds was one of his studies.

The Prefects and Sub-Prefects, April, 1945. (back row) W.B. Strang, P.J.D. Gething, A.J. Wild, A.F. Trendall, A.J.W. Lawson, W.L.G. Gaskin, A.F.W. Pakes, (middle) P.D. Southgate, R.D. Whalley, P. Longbottom, A.T. Redman, B.R. Laurence, A.W. Thorpe, D.J. Wood, C.L. Tutty, (front row) G.W. Mandy, D.B. Fensome, G.S. Hawkes, M.J. Barber (Head Boy), C.A. Rushton, D.B. Hawkins, J.W.F. Farr. (*LN-LMC*)

Chapter 10

Business as Usual

'I joined the School in 1938 and was placed in a 'fast track' A-stream form. We were expected to take only four instead of the usual five years, before sitting our School Certificate exams. As I was a whole year younger than my classmates, I was very aware that the exams would take place shortly after my 14th birthday, something I regretted at the time but for which 4 years in the Sixth Form adequately compensated.'   [A.W. Thorpe]

Although the number of boys in the Sixth Form during the War was small, some, like Thorpe, spent three or four years there. This seemed to generate a closer bond of friendship between them than at any time before or since. Perhaps due to the unspoken knowledge that their futures were very much in the lap of the gods.

The Prefect system by 1943 had been in place for some years and was working well. The first step on the ladder, usually in the fast IVth or Vth years, was being chosen as Form Monitors, whose primary task was to keep the form in order until the arrival of a master. After that one progressed to Sub-Prefect, full Prefect, and if you were lucky Head Boy. Sub-Prefects were elected by a ballot of the upper school. Prefects were chosen by the Staff, and one promising Sixth Former at the time, who was sometimes in trouble, was vetoed by a single master who considered him an unsuitable role model. Sub-Prefects were recognised by the red ribbon bands worn a few inches above the cuffs of their jackets. Full Prefects had red ribbon all round the edge of their navy blazers as well as the cuff bands.

Head Boys proliferated during this period and it is difficult to tell how long they each held office. The *School Lists* and Magazines do not tally. The order seems to be P.R. Franks (1940–42); M.V.W. Chote (July 42 to Oct 42); A.S. Tweedie (1942); J.C. Crabtree (Spring 1943); G.D. Nicholls (1943); F.E. Stygall (1943); P.G.

211

Higgins (1944) jointly with M.J. Barber (1944–45); D.B. Fensome (1945–46); A.W. Thorpe (1946).

Thorpe gives us an insight into the duties of the office:

'As Head Boy I had a weekly meeting with KBW and Mr Godfrey, theoretically to tell them of any serious complaints from the boys and to learn what the LEA and other Government Departments were likely to impose upon the School. However, it was soon evident that the masters knew most of the boys' grumbles already, while the downward flow of future educational developments was strictly limited.

'The weekly Prefects' Meeting held in the Library was far more enjoyable, there being little to discuss that had not been thoroughly discussed and decided upon in the Prefects' Common Room.

'Prefects' Detention taxed us into trying to find worthwhile tasks for the detainees, like removing stones from the sports pitches and tidying the cricket Pavilion, but an attempt to help the caretaker shovel coke was – correctly, I think – vetoed by KBW, on the grounds of lack of protective overalls.' [Clothing coupons were needed to purchase clothes in those days of rationing. Outsize boys got extra coupons!]

Speech Day was held on Wednesday, 17th February, 1943. The guest speaker was Luton's MP, Dr E. Leslie Burgin, who told the boys they were privileged to be 'at the top of their form' in the most wonderful period of history, and they would be the envy of future generations. If they could select a day or time in history what day or time would they choose?

'Even before the last war the Germans were talking of 'Der Tag'. What is our 'Der Tag'? We must learn from the past, speculate into the future, but concentrate on the job of today. President Roosevelt's saying that our generation has a 'rendezvous with destiny' is true not only of Americans but of ourselves. Our war aim is to drive devilry from the world and to release the world from the reign of blaggardsim, and our peace aims are to bring about better and fairer conditions for the common folk everywhere, who are our brothers and sisters.'

After speaking with justifiable pride of the School's academic honours, mentioned in an earlier chapter, Mr Webb went on to praise the School Cadet Corps which was by then 200 strong. Three platoons had recently taken part in a Church Parade on Youth Sunday. The corps had its own open-air range not far from the School, and one platoon each week was able to use it. Some 60 boys between the ages of 12 and 14 who had recently joined the Junior Corps, and masters, other than officers, instructed them in signalling, field observation and first aid.

Derek Page was a member of the Cadet Corps who remembered with horror a

'Dig for Victory' was the wartime slogan. These pupils found themselves helping the war effort by hoeing turnips on Dunstable Downs in June 1942. *(LN-LMC)*

route march to Markham Hills beyond Streatley wearing new boots, and of being caught smoking with two friends on the way home from a parade. All three were made to stand in assembly next morning for having discredited the school.

The Headmaster also spoke of the many boys from the Upper and Middle School who had been engaged in a variety of farming activities during the previous summer holidays. Parties had also been sent out in term time to weed or lift vital crops when no other labour was available. They had lifted more than 100 tons of sugar beet.

In March 1943 Luton Education Committee tried to ban children of 12–14 helping with the forthcoming harvest. However, it was the Governors and not the Education Committee who had jurisdiction over the Modern School, and Mr Webb announced that boys of 12–14 and older *would* go harvesting again during term time, and on a more extended scale than in 1942. Boys were not allowed to work continuously for more than four hours, or to start work within 1½ hours of finishing school. It was an opportunity to serve the community which many boys wanted to take. Any boy who went for half a day and didn't like it, was not compelled to go back.

In May Luton celebrated 'Wings for Victory Week', challenging the town of New

Bedford in Massachusetts to a Savings battle, and setting a target of £1,425,000. First Year boys from the School undertook the distribution of posters during the Easter holidays. The School Savings Group, under the leadership of Mr Wareham, made an all-out effort to increase their previous year's total, and collected £1,037. [It had been £439.10s. in 1942]. The town collected £1,442,299 in all, but lost its challenge to New Bedford who raised £1,833,829.

One result of the War was a shortage of professional School cleaners and several boys were employed to help out in the main building. At the end of the day two boys from each class were 'volunteered' to sweep out their form rooms, leaving the dust in a neat pile ready for collection outside the door. Thus was born the 'Brush Brigade', whose chalked posters decorated the right-hand side of the blackboard each day. Woe betide any boy who missed his turn on the rota.

> After School, when work is done,
> And every boy has homeward gone,
> There are a few who are made to stay,
> And toil and toil and toil away.
> These are the lads of the Brush Brigade,
> Borrowing brooms, with their own mislaid,
> Shifting desks and sweeping the floor,
> Emptying baskets and cleaning the door;
> These are the jobs of this gallant Brigade.
> And after all this bother and strife
> Do they get paid? No! Not on your life.
> [C. B. Alderman]

Sports Report, 1943

The Soccer season began well, and the teams enjoyed some of the best weather for years. The 1st XI played more matches than in any previous season on record, and in order to avoid unnecessary travelling, only played games against local teams, whose average ages were higher than the School boys, and in five cases were adult teams. Only two out of fifteen matches were lost. Their success was due chiefly to the fitness and toughness of the team as a whole, combined with the special abilities of individuals – Crabtree's heading and kicking at centre half, Sealy's shooting power in the centre, Hobbs's speed on the wing and Irvine's determined tackling. The team were anxious to get Wednesday fixtures and appealed for any service teams who might be available.

147 competitors finished in the Inter-House Cross-Country Competition on 17th December, which was won for the Seniors by J.R. Beaumont, and (Juniors) by P.R. White. The Hornets were the winning house.

B.V. Sealy captained the Cricket 1st Eleven, with P.G. Higgins as vice-captain. During the season they played seven matches, winning three, losing three and drawing one. In the annual match against the Old Luton Modernians on 24th July, the Old Boys scored 116 (Wickson 21, East 21 not out, Sealy 7 for 48); the School 80 (Pakes 19 not out). The Williams Cup for House Cricket was won by the Wasps.

At Sports Day on Saturday, 22nd May, J.D. Ward equalled the Open 100 yards record of 10.24 secs. and L.M. Hine broke the Under 14 High Jump record with a jump of 4ft 6½ in. E. Hobbs and P. Heanue tied for the *Victor Ludorum* Cup. The Richardson Cup (field events) was awarded to P. Heanue and the new Waller Cup (track events) to J.D. Ward.

During June Mr Squire organised a Mass Physical Training Display in front of the Cricket Pavilion in which every form in the School took part. Loved by many, and loathed by others, all of whom were forced to take part, it raised £41 for the Red Cross Prisoners of War Fund.

Mr Godfrey's third annual Red Cross Athletics Contest on 4th June, despite adverse weather conditions proved quite a success, raising £140 1s 4d. for the charity. Vauxhall Motors AC were the winners, and the School gained second place.

After the Bedfordshire Junior and Colts AAA Championships at Wardown on Whit-Monday, 'Crusader' wrote in the *Tuesday Pictorial*:

> 'It would be interesting to know if there has ever been in the history of sport a record such as that created by Luton Modern School at the Championships held at Wardown on Monday. I certainly know of no parallel.
>
> 'Of the 15 championship challenge cups to be won, the School went home with 14! The solitary award was won by an Old Luton Modernian who left the School as late as December last.
>
> 'As a result the School hold for another year the "Arnold Whitchurch" Challenge Trophy, which they first brought to Luton from Bedford in 1938 and again last year.
>
> 'There is a gentleman called Godfrey who has seen a lot of hard work run to waste in previous years, but he is now getting a handsome reward for his patience and perseverance as sports master at the School.'

Morville Chote echoed the sentiments of the last paragraph. 'C.J. Godfrey was a great influence in my athletic life and we became close friends after I left School. He well deserves the tribute to the role he played in the success of the School in athletics. Though not an athlete himself, he was a good, stern coach in track and jump events. He managed to get Geoff Dyson, the national coach, to visit and talk to us.' Jack Waller was practising throwing the javelin. Mr Godfrey was training the sprinters nearby, and had left his megaphone on the edge of the throwing area. As Jack was about to throw he turned to his colleagues and said with a grin 'Watch me hit Piggy's

megaphone!' Amazingly, he hit it, though he had no intention whatsoever of doing so. He was petrified, as Mr Godfrey turned to him and said 'Good shot, Waller!'

Rugby in 1942 had been a phenomenal success, and it seemed that 1943 might be an anticlimax. D. B. Fensome quietly and efficiently took the captaincy. J.A. Heanue was at full back, and L. Hine partnered M.J. Barber at centre three-quarter. S.A.J. Pakes worked hard and perseveringly as scrum-half. D.I. Macdonald's reputation as a hooker saw him joining the forwards. D.J.F. Hill and A.T. Redman as wing-forwards were an excellent pair, together with J.R. Beaumont and J.F. Edwards, both valuable discoveries, and S.A. Moss, a keen player from the last year's Under 15 XV. G.L. Edmonds was the obvious choice for fly-half, though he was later incapacitated by a hand injury. The School won against the Old Boys, but unfortunately *The Lutonian* did not record the results of any of the other matches!

More Problems

A sub-committee, appointed to inspect the School building in search of defects, reported to the Bedfordshire Education Committee in September and estimated that a further £4,000 were needed for repairs. Parts of the flat roof over the library had been repaired, but other areas needed to be tackled. The Chairman of the Committee, Mr V.E. Goodman, expressed horror, saying 'We don't feel that the School will ever be right, and there will be constant need for repairs right the way through.' The Headmaster had informed the committee that 'the rooms were never the same size – they were affected by the time of year.' Posterity was being handed down a considerable amount of expense.

The Education Committee were more worried about the cost of implementing the new Education Bill – the 1944 Education Act, and in particular the cost of running the two Luton Secondary Schools and the Technical College. Sir Thomas Keens, the Chairman, estimated on the figures for 1943, that Luton would contribute about 43 per cent to the cost of higher education in the County. 'It is assumed that Luton's contribution will amount to £34,000 approximately. The expenditure on higher education at Luton Modern School, Luton High School and the Technical College involves a cost to the rates of £28,500.'

In July the Education Committee arranged a series of lectures for elementary, senior and secondary school staffs on sex-education in schools. This was at the instigation of the Ministry of Health, who were anxious to increase the awareness of VD amongst some senior pupils. Prior to this time all Old Boys who have been questioned are adamant that no sex-education was taught at the Modern School. 'Sex education? – none, but we got the hang of it all at a fairly early age!' It is easy to see why. Botany had been the chosen subject taught for years by Rex Clayton, and the only biology teaching of any kind that boys received was for one term in the 1st Year. In the 1940 Inspection it had been suggested that botany should be replaced

by biology, as boys found it more interesting, and in August of that year Francis C. Minns was appointed to teach the subject. Minns had spent three years as a research assistant to the great Professor J.B.S. Haldane. With Clayton's appointment as Careers Master it was possible to ease him out of his 'kingdom' gently! It was some time before Minns established his subject and was able to enter students for examinations. Even so, it is apparent that whilst the sex life of birds and bees got a mention, the study of human sex, except in the Sixth Form, had little or no part to play.

K.B. Webb recalled: 'Minns was an ex-Etonian. He found a dead sheep on Barton Hills, and brought it back in an attaché case on the bus, and it ponged, and he was reproached for it. He defleshed it and used it as a teaching specimen in Biology.'

On the 23rd June the School Rabbit Club held a Show with 42 entries. Mr Brewster, Secretary of the Luton Fur and Feather Club, judged the exhibits, and Mrs Minns, who presented the prizes, commented that rabbit keeping meant fur for clothing as well as meat for food. B.F. Schlueter (IIIc) won the best in the show and judge's fancy awards with his Havana Rex. Other award winners were for Chinchilla: A.F. Trendall (Va); Dutch: S.A. Pakes (Vc) and Fancy: M.E. Birchmore (IIIc).

Mr Minns was also kept busy as Chairman of the newly formed Tight Lines Club. Fishing matches were held at Cheddington, with L.S. Shepard making the heaviest catch of the season. The Field Club, of which Minns was also Chairman, had a rather lean summer, with only one outing, to Bedford Modern School Museum.

With blackout in the School it was possible for early evening activities to resume. The Literary and Scientific Society listened to lectures by outside speakers on 'Germany before 1933 and after; Indian Politics; Health Services after the War; and Soviet Russia.' Senior boys also took part in a 'Brains Trust' chaired by F. E. Stygall. A talk by an Old Boy, Kenneth Peddar, inspired a group of boys to build a reflecting telescope. Supervised by Mr Cooke, with components bought by the School, Phillip Gething, Paul Schagrin and Denis Mardle produced a very satisfactory piece of equipment and a concrete pillar to support it was set in the north-eastern corner of the School field. After a few months and numerous difficulties, the project had to be abandoned and the telescope was sold to the boys for two pounds. Phillip Gething went on to work at the Royal Greenwich Observatory and at Herstmonceux.

Dr Leslie Burgin, MP, was Question Master for a 'Youth Brains Trust' held in the Hall in June. The 'brains' consisted of Browning, Stygall, Sealy and Verdcourt and four girls from the High School.

A Spoken English contest was instituted during the year through the generosity of Dr Leslie Burgin. To be held annually, an award would be made for the two best all-round speakers in prose, poetry and speech-making in three sections of the School: years 1 and 2, 3 and 4, and 5 and 6, each forming a separate group with its own award. In 1943 the first awards went to F.E. Stygall (senior); D.I. Burrows (intermediate) and P.D. Saunders (junior).

In August 72 cadets and 6 officers from the School Cadet Corps attended a ten-day Camp in Gloucester, a Band consisting of 15 fifes and 7 drums was formed, and a rifle team chosen to enter the *News of the World* firing competition for Army Cadets.

Boys of the School belonging to the Town Squadron (10F and 1979) of the ATC, formed a School Flight under the direction of F/O B.J. Cooke, and used the School for instructional purposes. Classes in Mathematics, Signals, Aircraft Recognition and Navigation were given by Messrs. Finlay, Giddy and Howard.

At this time in the School's life, new teaching staff seemed to come and go every term; only one, Stanley R. Giddy, BSc, appointed in September to teach Maths and Science, was to stay for the duration of the School.

The School's assistant secretary, Miss Marjorie Hartley, left in July to take up a career in nursing. She was succeeded by Miss Olga Peters, who was destined to serve the School until its end, and continue with the Sixth Form College. The Headmaster's Secretary, Miss J.M. Oakley, was married just before Christmas, and was presented with a cutlery service and cheque, from the boys and staff respectively.

Two hundred and fifty parents and guardians attended the first meeting of the L.M.S. Home and School Association on 6th October. Mr Webb outlined the aims of the Association, which were to form a bond between home and school, to discuss subjects of interest to all who have to deal with children, and to work together in various projects that arise.

The parents spoke of the difficulties of obtaining clothes for rapidly growing boys during wartime, and it was decided to pool outgrown clothing. Messrs. Briggs and Co. agreed to receive and distribute articles from their shop in George Street. It was noted that the Girls' High School had operated a similar scheme since before the war.

Also in October, Mr Webb wrote to the Governors:

> 'The Masters wish me to request you in their name to give your serious and immediate attention to the desirability of changing the name of the School, deleting the word 'Modern' and either calling it Luton School or Luton Grammar School.'

This was because of the specialised meaning of the word 'modern' in the Government White Paper on Educational reconstruction. Mr Webb told the Governors that he had great difficulty in explaining to candidates for staff that Luton Modern School was a 'proper' secondary school. In February 1944 the Governors recommended that the name should be altered to Luton Grammar School.

Just before the end of the autumn term an Orchestral and Choral Concert was held in place of the usual Christmas play. As well as items performed by the orchestra and choir, their were several solo items, both vocal and instrumental. £5 15s was collected for the New Instrument Fund.

The following item appeared in *The Lutonian* for July 1943:

'A very fine zoo has grown within the School walls and there is now on view a fine collection of beasts and birds including woodcocks, partridges, martins, otters, a pig and a frog.'

1944 – A Year of Change

Christmas 1943 had been like every other wartime Christmas in Luton. The churches had been full during the daytime, but blackout prevented most evening gatherings. There had been the usual second rate pantomimes: 'Dick Whittington' at the Alma, and 'Jack and the Beanstalk' at the Grand Theatre, neither with any 'stars' of note. The senior boys and girls from the Modern and High Schools had done their fair share of delivering the Christmas mail. Food was scarce and presents utilitarian.

Members of the Fifth and Sixth Forms, together with their counterparts at the High School, and masters and mistresses of both Schools, met for a Social Evening on 29th January, 1944. As well as dancing and a variety of community games, other amusements, such as short plays and a quiz were organised. This was the first Social of its kind, but it proved so successful that it would become an annual event.

On 4th February, 650 people attended the Fourth Grand Concert to be held in the School Hall. The artistes were the famous BBC singer, Robert Easton, bass; the cornetist and trumpeter, Harry Mortimer, accompanied by Old Lutonian Arthur E. Davies (LMS: 1910–12). (It was revealed during the concert that they had first appeared together aged 8 and 9!). Augustus F. Lowe, a popular local organist, played the piano, and 12 years old School pupil, Geoffrey T. Ford, boy soprano, sang a selection of popular songs. £56 was raised as a result of the concert, bringing the total in the Organ Fund, which was invested in War Savings to £244.

At Easter two plays were presented to parents, other Luton schools, and boys of the School. *The Monkey's Paw*, by W.W. Jacobs, was produced by Mr Parry, and Mr Martin was responsible for *The Boy Comes Home*.

Speech Day was held on Wednesday, 23rd February, 1944, in the School Hall, which, as usual, was packed to capacity.

Lord Soulbury, former President of the Board of Education, was the Guest of Honour, and distributed the prizes. Fifty-nine Cambridge School Certificates were presented, and 18 Higher School Certificates. A State Scholarship and Governors Leaving Exhibition was awarded to G.D. Nicholls, and State Bursaries to D.A. Bage, K.W. Gladman and B.Verdcourt. J.A. Browning and G.W. Pearson gained entry to King's College, Cambridge. Short University Courses were offered to P.H. Gilder, E. Hobbs, A.R. Jeffs, C.K. Miller, B.V. Sealy and A.S. Tweedie. F.H. Mead obtained an Engineering Cadetship at Birmingham Technical College. An Indian Army

Cadetship went to R.C. Trendall, and RAF Apprenticeships to D.J. Annely, D.C. Barford, S.E. Beverley, and B.A. Knight.

Lord Soulbury told the School that they would be confronted at the end of the war with some very difficult tasks. A new heaven and a new earth would not arise immediately from the ashes of destruction. Feuds and the desire for revenge would be rampant; the appalling bitterness of the struggle and the memories of the outrageous cruelties would long remain in men's hearts, and the moral, mental and physical scars of the conflict would be visible and inflamed for many years to come.

The Head told parents that all the boys were engaged in the unusual afternoon activity of cleaning the School, and it was possible that some of them might be hiding their light of domesticity under a bushel. These comments were picked up in a Canadian newspaper, the *Brantwood Expositor*, which wrote on 16th March, 1944:

> 'There is a shortage of women cleaners in Luton (England) Schools, and the boy students undertook to sweep out classrooms after hours. Then their teacher, in a speech, let their parents know all about it, 'in case parents would like to make use of this domesticity.''

A month later Mr Webb advised the Governors that the School had only one temporary caretaker and no cleaning staff. 'I wonder if we got a chit from the Medical Officer saying we are in danger of plague, we might get somebody?' The boys were doing all the cleaning of their classrooms and laboratories, and the Head had even had a vacuum cleaner plugged into the staff common room 'in hopes'!

The Spring term was a busy one. The Second Spoken English Competition was held in April, M. Marsh-Edwards, P.D. Saunders and G.T. Ford winning the Upper, Middle and Lower School prizes respectively.

Several boys from the School worked in their spare time at the Britannia Engineering Works. The Manager wanted it placed on record that the essential Admiralty work on which they were engaged could not have been completed on schedule without their assistance.

On 11th May, Senior Masters and Old Boys were saddened to hear of the death in Sheffield of Mr William Otter, aged 76. Except for a break between his retirement in 1933 and 1941, when he returned to help in the Handicraft Department, he had been a member of staff from 1904 until his demise. As a boy in Lincoln he had studied at the Municipal Training School, and after acquiring various qualifications began teaching in 1893 at St Albans Technical College. He came to Luton in 1897 and worked for the Authority at various jobs, before joining the staff of the Modern School. He was buried in Luton General Cemetery after a service at Christ Church.

In November, Mr Raymond Otter, son of William, visited the School to present a Silver Cup from his two brothers and himself, (all Old Boys), for Junior Inter-House Competition in Association Football, in memory of their father.

Speech Day, 23rd February, 1944. J.C. Crabtree, receiving a prize from Lord Soulbury, Minister for Education. Fourteen months later, Crabtree was killed in action at Arnhem. (*LN*)

The School sustained another loss with the death on 2nd June of Alderman John Henry Staddon, aged 83. He had been a Governor of the Modern and High Schools and the Technical College for many years. A prize for Citizenship was established in his name.

In May the Governors were asked to consider adding a brick extension to the overcrowded dining room, and two extra single-storey classrooms over the shelters at the back of the school, linked to the main building by a corridor. By the end of the year the plans had been abandoned, and a prefabricated kitchen building acquired. On 5th June it was discovered with great pleasure that the drinking fountains in the yard were working for the first time for over four years!

It would be wrong to ignore a matter which upset a number of boys, mainly during the war period: that of anti-Semitism. From the mid-1930s a number of Jewish families fleeing from persecution in Europe, came to England and settled in Luton. There was also a large influx of felt hat firms, mainly Jewish owned, from London's East End. A number of their sons joined the School and followed its daily routine, with the exception of attending the act of worship in morning Assembly. What was it like to be in an 'ethnic minority' at the Modern School? Ronald Law (né Zakon), the son of a Polish born hat manufacturer, was a pupil from 1939–45. 'They were the happiest days of my young life,' he has said. 'The School was my third parent.' He remembered having 'Jew' chalked on his raincoat, whilst a friend had 'Jew, Jew,' carved on his desk. In a playground rough and tumble he was called 'a dirty Jew', and 'Bert' Fensome stood up for him and thumped the offender. He considered these of minor importance. When he went on to St Bartholomew's Hospital, where he trained as a General Practitioner, possibly the first from Luton Modern School – he was unable to get an interview for employment until he changed his name! One of his School contemporaries has confided, "We always snow-balled the Jewish boys."

Michael Freedland (1946–51) has written:

'Before I got to sit in a Bradgers Hill desk, I remember looking with envy at boys older than I who suddenly appeared at the local synagogue at Moor Path wearing smart new caps with red and gold badges. When my own brown envelope dropped on the doormat, all I could think of was wearing one of those caps with pride when next I went to Saturday morning Sabbath prayers.

'Actually being in the School wasn't quite so exciting. There were never more than a dozen of us at any one time. We knew who was who by the boys who attended the Jewish assembly. We used one of the form rooms during normal prayers time. Before I arrived at the School, Mr Samuel Finlay, who was on the Staff, said a couple of prayers and talked with us. After he left the School, we said them on our own and were remarkably well-behaved.

'Our services came with the blessings of the local Jewish minister, a rather

severe but, I always believed, very kind man called the Revd. Harry Ritvo, whose only son Lionel was in the year below mine. He was a man of whom we had great experience, because he not only conducted synagogue services at Moor Path, but was also Headmaster of the local Hebrew Classes, the Jewish equivalent of Sunday School. He met Mr Webb, and talked over what we needed – mainly to wear our school caps during our services.

'A master with a reputation, outside the School, of being an anti-Semite, came into the form room on one occasion: "Take your caps off," he insisted. We explained and he walked out. Two days later he came again. "Still wearing those caps!" he said. "Take them off!" Once was bad enough, twice was difficult. When he said it three times, one of us protested to the Head. He didn't come again.

'There were other 'coded' occasions. I went for a careers interview with Mr Clayton, and told him I would like to try for the diplomatic service. He didn't so much reply as sneer. "*You* couldn't possibly do that," he said. "You should try banking." It was a strange suggestion to make to a boy who had scored five per-cent in his last maths exam, and then the penny dropped: Jews and banking!

'A maths master once told me he was surprised to hear from his colleagues that I wasn't 'quite the moron' he thought I was – on the basis, I suppose, of those scores. The next day, when something in class had distracted me, there was a swish from one end of the room to the other – the master's gown rustling in his own wind – and the feeling of a bullet tearing through my left ear. This was a powerful man and he unleashed all his energy with a slap that I can still feel and a warmth not matched by my feelings for this man – who these days would face prosecution. It wasn't the smack that hurt, it was a final comment: 'I suppose you are going to snivel now, Freedland. You people always do!' And that four or five years after the Holocaust.

'It would be unfair to think only of anti-Semitism. The School went to a considerable trouble to accommodate us. Not only did we have our daily services, but we were always allowed to stay at home for Jewish holidays and Saturday mornings were sacrosanct for us. Saturday morning detentions became three after-school detentions. There were always the odd anti-Jewish remarks by others in the form, but I'm sure the Welsh and Irish boys had the same sort of ribbing directed at them, too. It was the kind of thing boys did.'

After an apprenticeship with *The Luton News,* Michael Freedland worked in Fleet Street, became a freelance journalist, wrote definitive biographies of Irving Berlin, Al Jolson, Fred Astaire, Errol Flynn and numerous other show-biz personalities, and has presented many musical programmes for the BBC.

Sport and Other Activities

The Cross-Country Club had a fairly successful Spring season with races against Bedford Modern School, Hertford Grammar School, St George's, Harpenden and Bedfordshire and Hertfordshire Boys' Clubs, winning the contests against the latter two. In the last of these fixtures, which was a courtesy run, J.R. Beaumont (Capt.), G.R. Lomax and S.A.J. Pakes all broke the School record. The School Junior Team, captained by W.A.G. Startin, secured second place in the Junior race.

Sports Day was held on Saturday, 20th May, 1944. At first the weather looked unpromising, but later in the afternoon the weather improved and all the events passed without rain. The standards were high, though only one record was broken. R.E. Harris broke the (u.14) 880 yards record in 2 mins. 28.24 secs. D.B. Fensome and J.R. Beaumont tied for the *Victor Ludorum* Cup with 30 points each, and also won the Richardson (field) and the Waller (track) Cups respectively. The Powdrill Cup for Athletics was easily won by the Wasps. The School were also successful in again winning the AAA Bedfordshire Junior and Colts Championships at Wardown.

In Association Football the 1st XI, captained by E. Hobbs, played eleven matches, won five, drew two and lost four.

The 1944 Cricket season was only moderately successful, five matches out of the twelve played being won. D.J. Wood and P. Longbottom were best with the bat, and S.R. Thurlow and Longbottom with the ball. P.G. Higgins captained the side extremely well and set an example as an ever alert fieldsman. The season finished with the first annual match against a Parents' XI: the score is not recorded.

The 1st XV, under the excellent leadership of D.B. Fensome, enjoyed another extremely rewarding Rugby season, suffering only one defeat, and that by the least possible margin. It scored 212 points to 12 and its line was only successfully crossed once, by Shepherd in the Old Boys' match.

The Second Gymnastics and PT Display took place on the School Field on 16th June, raising £23 for the Red Cross Prisoners of War Fund. Mr Squire, with unceasing energy, controlled proceedings from a vantage point on the cricket pavilion roof. Massed exercises were performed by the junior and senior boys to music provided by Mr Bridger and the School Orchestra, seated on the pavilion steps. A boxing display, directed by Mr W. Chapman, included a blind-folded round that caused much amusement. There was a hand-ball exhibition, followed by pyramids, Swedish form rotations and tumbling, supervised by Mr S.R. Giddy. At the end of the proceedings, Sir Henry Buckland, of the Crystal Palace, presented medals to the six best gymnasts in the School: Juniors: D.W.E. Bateman and J.G. Wynd; Middle: C.H. Gaudin and A.C. Brown, and Seniors: V.F. Turton and E.K. Wilkinson.

On the 30th June the Fourth Annual Red Cross Athletics Contest was held at the School. Six teams took part from Vauxhall, Electrolux, Luton ATC, the RAF, the

Storm clouds brewing over the Second Physical Training display on 16th June, 1944. Sir Henry Buckland was guest of honour. (*LN-LMC*)

Old Boys and the School. The Vauxhall team were the easy winners. The evening was interspersed with PT displays performed by various forms. A cheque for £142 was presented to the Mayor of Luton for the Red Cross Prisoners of War Fund.

The public were encouraged to spend their 'Holidays at Home' during the war, and the Town's Entertainments Committee organised numerous attractions. On 5th July, 1944, as part of the arrangements, a junior section of the School Dramatic Society presented the workman scenes from *A Midsummer Night's Dream* as their contribution to a concert provided by schools of the locality, at All Saints' Church Hall. The workmen were played by C.B. Alderman, L. Davis, R.M. Culling, M.C. Cray and S.J. Flemming. G.T. Ford and T.A. Stedman were cast as Titania and Oberon, Puck by D.W.E. Bateman, and Peaseblossom by D. Clark. At the last moment Mr Parry was obliged to step into the part of Bottom, and Mr Martin manufactured an ass' head to fit him.

Mr Arthur W. Martin left the School in July for Falmouth Grammar School. During eight years in the Art Department he had earned the respect, esteem and

affection of boys and staff alike. He was remembered not only for his art-classes and teaching of art-history, but also for his polished productions of end of term plays.

Mr Ronald Ridout also left after three years, to take up the Senior English post at the Northern Grammar School, Portsmouth. A young man of original views, he was particularly anxious to make young people word-conscious and articulate. To this end he went on to write many enlightened text-books for use in schools. He was Guest of Honour at the Old Lutonians' dinner in December 1959.

Membership of the Cadet Corps, which at the beginning of the year stood at 130 cadets, dropped in the autumn to 110. The Annual Inspection by Col. Mander took place on 29th June, and a small contingent attended the summer camp in Ampthill Park. The culmination of a cadet's training was War Certificate 'A'. Since the Corps began, 110 candidates had been successful in Part I of the Certificate, and 64 in Part II. In due course the majority of the latter joined some branch of the armed forces and proved the value of their earlier training. At Whitsun all thirty members of the ATC visited Luton Airport and enjoyed a flight of 25 minutes, during which they performed a navigational exercise in map-reading.

Interesting news of an Old Boy, T.S. Skillman, MA, AMIEE, reached the School from Australia early in the year. Leaving the L.M.S. for Cambridge in 1921, he had a share in the telephone development of many countries and became an acknowledged expert on remote control. From 1938 he worked in conjunction with the Post Office to install the Sydney-Newcastle 'Carrier Cable', believed at the time to be the most advanced and complex installation of its kind in the world. His own Company, Communication Engineering Pty, Ltd., manufactured much of the equipment needed.

Chapter 11

Luton Grammar School

When the School closed at the end of the summer term in July 1944, an era ended. Luton Modern School ceased to exist, except in the memories of 3,788 former students and 146 members of staff. In September the doors re-opened as Luton Grammar School. The event passed unrecorded in the School Magazine and the local newspapers.

In July 71 boys had left the School; their places were taken by 139 newcomers in September, bringing the number of pupils on roll to the very large figure of 654. With the exception of Scholarship winners, the majority of entrants were still fee-paying. The new Education Act, published on 3rd August, 1944, contained Clause 61, which stated – 'No fees shall be charged in respect of admission to any school maintained by a local authority.' This came into force for the Grammar School, High School and Junior Technical School on 1st April, 1945, much to the relief of the majority of fee-paying parents. All admissions would now be open to merit rather than a parent's ability to pay.

There were four new members of staff in September. Mr Martin's successor was Ronald W. Smoothey, who had trained at the Guildford Art School, and Goldsmith's College. He was joined by Mr Robert M. Stump who had spent his early life in Switzerland, and came to teach art and handicrafts. Many boys remember watching him ski-ing down the slopes of Bradgers Hill during a suitably snowy spell in 1945. Mr George D. Howells also came to teach handicraft, and was an authority on the Film Industry. Mr Geoffrey Clarke, BA, arrived in November to teach English; he also proved to be a first-class Rugby referee.

The Literary and Scientific Society had a busy autumn. Mr H.H. Watson opened the season with a useful lecture on 'The German Enigma'. Mr George Howells spoke on 'The Film Industry', and a month later, as a sequel, he showed a number of early

films ranging from French comedy to Chaplin, and to the famous 'Odessa Steps' sequence from 'Battleship Potemkin'.

The Lit. and Sci.'s most popular event was the Mock Election on 17th November, called to mark the newly-created Luton Grammar School Constituency. Five nominations were handed to Mr Findlater, the Returning Officer. These were J. Berridge, Communist; D. Hodgson, Socialist; O. Rosalki, Independent; W. B. Strang, Conservative; and A.J. Wild, Liberal. After a week of excited campaigning, polling took place resulting in Wild's election with 52 votes. The Socialists took 37 votes, Communists 26, Conservatives 12, Independents 4. There were two spoiled papers.

The Spring term saw the formation of a Boxing Club under the supervision of Mr W.H. Chapman. Enthusiasm quickly developed and the Club soon had thirty members. The Captain, D.J.F. Hill, scored a noteworthy success at Dunstable early in the season when he beat an ATC opponent over three rounds.

The School Library at this time still relied for its stock to a large extent on donations from past and present students and staff. Amongst books received were 300 volumes from the Library of Pilot Officer R.R. Flint, who had been Head Boy in 1935–36, and died on active service in March 1942. They were all suitably inscribed in his memory. The Library was run by a small team of boys under the supervision of the real 'boss', Mr Findlater.

Looking back at all the activities taking place at this time it is hard to remember that the country was still at war. Luton had certainly not escaped from bombing as numerous reports and photographs recorded in the local newspapers. War-time restrictions permitted them to refer only to 'German air raids on a south Midlands town', but news travelled fast and everyone knew where the bombs had fallen. One particular raid stands out in most Old Boys' minds:

> 'Like a bolt from the blue, a V2 caused part of the Biscot Road district to disappear just before 10 am on Monday, 6th November, 1944. It landed in Biscot Road between the dispatch department of Commer-Karrier, Ltd. and adjoining houses, and shook the town. Houses nearest the scene disintegrated in a manner the like of which had never been seen in Luton. They disappeared in a fine red dust, carried away across Wardown Park in the gentle breeze. The death toll of 19 was the second highest of any Luton incident. In addition 196 people were injured.'
>
> [from *Luton at War*, 1947]

The explosion was only a mile from Bradgers Hill (and less than ¼ mile from the Girls' High School who were fortunately on holiday). The writer, in his first term at the Grammar School, has a clear memory of diving under his desk for safety, and seeing Mr R. Phillips struggling to do the same. Keith Norcott, in IIb, was on the balcony parade with Mr Root's Latin class. 'There was suddenly an almighty

explosion outside. We all shot under our desks just as the blast hit the large windows, some of which shattered and showered the floor with glass. Fortunately none of us were hurt and we simply carried on working.' Lower VI were in the Library, where 'Dr Dony was taking a history lesson, perched on the wide window sill. Suddenly there was the sound of a distant explosion, and the small window flipped open, knocking the good Doctor off his perch.' [D. I. Macdonald].

The School Orchestra was in demand during the autumn term. One evening in November they entertained Service personnel at the Public Hall in Harpenden. On the afternoon of Wednesday, 13th December, a concert was held in the School Hall. Geoffrey T. Ford sang at both concerts, and at the end-of-term concert Michael Marsh-Edwards, Victor E. Raymond (violins) and Donald I. Burrows (piano) played solo items. These boys also provided solo items at Friday morning Assemblies.

At the end of 1944 Cllr. H. C. Janes promised £1,200 to pay for an organ to be installed in the School Hall as a Memorial to his son Sgt. Pilot Clifford L. B. Janes, who lost his life on active service in the Middle East in July 1943. Its installation on 30th March, 1949 was to prove an inspiration for many young musicians.

Mr Francis C. Minns, who joined the School in 1940 to teach biology, left in December 1944 to become Senior Biology Master at Manchester Grammar School. A popular master, he helped organise the Field and Angling Clubs, raised a flourishing hive of bees, and administrated the Rabbit Club.

The Final Countdown

C. Wynne Parry, in his Editorial for *The Lutonian* of February 1945, wrote that although it was the fifth year of bitter conflict, the School was carrying on much more normally than many similar institutions in Britain and Europe. He went on:

'However, the comparative smoothness of School life may blind us to the changes which are being made in the Educational System of the country. In April 1945, an Act is due to come into force which will make the term "Elementary Education" finally obsolete, and which will call all post-primary schooling, *i.e.* all schooling for children of 11 plus, "Secondary". In consequence the term "Secondary" will no longer be the preserve solely of Schools of the type of ours. There are those who will regret this change; they represent a social snobbery which must not be allowed to linger. It behoves us to be as glad to mix, on the games' fields and elsewhere, with other types of Secondary Schools, as we are to meet boys from the academic "Grammar" Schools. We shall now have two loyalties to maintain: one towards Schools of our type, so that we maintain and increase the fine record of the past, in examination successes and in other respects, and the other towards education in general, so that we welcome a further step which is being taken towards the completion of a national system.'

The year began with the appointment of Mr William N. Thorpe, BSc to the Geography Department, and in March, Mr Ralph Scurfield, BSc to succeed Mr Minns as Head of Biology.

At Whitsun the boys of the North Western Polytechnic, which had shared the School's premises since the outbreak of war, returned to their own quarters in Kentish Town. The two schools had worked side by side with remarkable ease for five years, and had enjoyed a friendly rivalry. Their participation in the nightly fire-watching duties had been particularly appreciated.

With the departure of the Polytechnic boys, and less pressure on Mrs Sankey and the kitchen staff, it was possible to extend the length of the dinner break, thus allowing boys who wished, to go home to lunch. As it coincided with a further cut in the family food ration allowances, it was not possible to take full advantage of the opportunity to return home.

For the first time since the War began, the School held evening performances of its Play. On the evening of 26th and 27th March, Sheridan's *The Rivals* was performed before very large audiences from whom it received an enthusiastic reception. Acting honours went to M. Marsh-Edwards for his portrayal of the fussy, overbearing, class-conscious old Aunt, Mrs Malaprop, and to D.B. Hawkins, who was most convincing as the dictatorial and impatient father with a keen sense of humour, Sir Anthony Absolute. R.J. Sales entered fully into the spirit of the sentimental young woman, Lydia Languish, whose taste had been fashioned by reading third-class novels. The play was produced by Mr C.W. Parry, with scenery by Mr R.W. Smoothey. A profit of £45 was presented to the Red Cross Prisoners of War Fund

At Speech Day on Wednesday, 21st February, the Headmaster drew attention to the 52 Cambridge School Certificates, with their 23 Matriculations, and 11 Higher School Certificates gained in the 1944 examinations. He pointed out that the number of pupils and choices of courses in the Sixth Form had increased to a very high figure, but he regretted that at all levels of instruction there was overcrowding. The School had not been able to extend its premises as its numbers had grown. By the Ministry of Education's own standards the School was at least eight class-rooms short.

Lord Luke of Pavenham was the guest speaker, and distributed the prizes, which included State Bursaries to N.V. Smith at the City and Guilds College, London and M.J. Barber at Sheffield University.

The start of the 1945 football season was delayed by bad weather, making it necessary to cram ten 1st XI matches into seven weeks, and winning all but three. The team was captained by Morgan J. Barber.

The new Education Act which came into force on 1st April required all children to receive a secondary education appropriate to their ability and aptitude. Consequently, it was necessary for them to take a selection test at eleven plus. The

The Dramatic Society's all-male production of *The Rivals* in March, 1945. D.B. Hawkins and M. Marsh-Edwards appear in the centre of the cast, as Sir Anthony Absolute and Mrs Malaprop. The proceeds went to the Red Cross Prisoners of War Fund. On the last night Mr Webb presented a cheque for £45 to the Fund's local secretary. (*LN-LMC*)

Bedfordshire Education Committee decided that children would take a two stage examination in their ten plus year, repeated where necessary in the eleven plus year. The first stage consisted of a 45 minute verbal reasoning test taken in November in their own Primary Schools, and a second stage, covering English, arithmetic and verbal reasoning, taken (by about half the candidates) at the Grammar or High Schools the following February. Children not selected at ten plus, had a second attempt the following year. In addition, a similar test was available to children at 13 for admission to the Luton Technical School. There had been some opposition from Primary Heads who thought that children should be tested between 11–12 instead of 10–12. Both K.B. Webb and Helen K. Sheldon were agreed that it was the bright child that mattered. They thought it deplorable that any youngster might be held

back on account of age. 'A child of 10 with the mental ability of a child of 13 should be in the higher school.'

> How much we all expected
>> Of the Education Act,
> With all its many clauses
>> Each one with good things packed!
> More and better teachers,
>> More and better schools,
> And even more and better 'Techs',
>> With more and better tools.
> But when the First of April came
>> They hadn't got the schools;
> They'd only cut our holidays
>> And made us April Fools.
>> [M. Marsh-Edwards]

Victory in Europe

Boys arrived at School on VE-Day, Tuesday, 8th May, 1945, not knowing if the School was in session or not. The Caretaker, Albert Killick, assisted by prefects, was sent to raise the Union Jack on the School roof. They found that the pulley at the top of the flag pole was jammed. A ladder was fetched and a volunteer sought to climb the pole. R.D. 'Jim' Whalley accepted the challenge, made the nerve-racking ascent, released the pulley, and hoisted the flag to cheers from the playground below. After a brief Assembly the School was closed for the rest of the day, and the 9th was declared a holiday. Many students made their way to the centre of Luton where great crowds had gathered as soon as the news was announced. 'Complete strangers joined hands to dance in the Palais Glide, British and American troops mingled with carefree camaraderie among the jostling and cheering throng.' The revelries went on for hours. As one Sixth Former observed, 'It's a good thing this only happens every twenty-five years!'

Sports Day, scheduled for Saturday, 12th May, was postponed until Wednesday, 16th May, due to the VE-Day celebrations. The weather was exceptionally fine, performance standards were high, and three records were broken. L.M. Hine broke the Open Long Jump record with a distance of 19 ft. 7 ins; P. Longbottom the Open Hammer record, with a throw of 133 ft. 2½ ins, and the Grasshoppers' Senior Relay Team (4 x 110 yds) set up a new record by winning in 50.36 seconds. The Powdrill Cup was won by the Wasps. L.M. Hine and A.T. Redman were joint holders of the *Victor Ludorum* Cup. The School again won the Bedfordshire Junior and Colts Championships at Wardown on 19th May; and came first in three field events at the

The Third Physical Training Display, 9th June, 1945. The junior boys seated in front of the cricket pavilion listening to Lt.Col. Part. Heavy rain prevented the mass exercises finalé being performed. (LN-LMC)

Midlands AAA Junior Championships at Beeston, Nottingham, on 7th July. D.B. Fensome (Captain) won the Shot and Discus, and D.J.F. Hill won the Javelin. Mr J. Dalrymple of Birchfield Harriers helped coach the field events once more.

Out of 13 matches played during the 1945 Cricket season, nine were won, one was drawn and three were lost. It was memorable for Captain Derek J. Wood's outstanding batting average of 41.3 and his unbeaten aggregate of 372 runs.

The Third Physical Training Display took place on Saturday, 9th June, in far from ideal weather for such a function. The high wind was a source of danger to the participants and irritation to the members of the Orchestra, whose music and stands were liable to be blown away by sudden gusts. Some of the new items attracted great

The orchestra accompanied the Physical Training Displays from the pavilion steps. The conductor, Ronald Bridger, is in the foreground. J.W. Findlater, M. Marsh-Edwards, C.W. Parry and D F. Gallimore are seated behind him. (C.E. Wareham)

interest, and the Musical Ride on Cycles was exceedingly popular. The Rope-Climbing was also spectacular; Mr Squire having taught the boys most of the tricks that would have been seen at a circus. An untimely shower of rain, which sent all the spectators to the shelter and made the grass extremely slippery, prevented the final display of Junior Mass Exercises, much to the evident delight of most of the Juniors.

Mr Squire appeared in a different light in November when he led a dozen senior boys on a fascinating tour of lesser known, central London.

The summer was marred by tragedy when a Fifth Year boy, Peter H. Wadsworth, found the pressure of impending examinations too much and took his own life, although Mr Webb had agreed to the postponement of his exams for a year.

During 1945 the Cadet Corps, having lost the Polytechnic boys, was reduced to 53 cadets. Major Pointing had resigned after three years service, and command was taken by Lieut. W.H. Chapman. At the end of July the boys enjoyed the rigours of a fortnight's Camp at Kessingland, mid-way between Lowestoft and Southwold.

The Literary and Scientific Society listened to lectures on 'The Art of Stage Make-Up' by Mr Smoothey, and 'India' by Lieut. Col. R.H. Milne. There were debates proposing the abolition of the death penalty, and blood sports; the former was carried by one vote, the latter defeated. Visits were made to Luton Electricity Station, J. W. Green's Brewery, and the Cement and Lime Works at Houghton Regis. Members also enjoyed a Balloon Debate, and a Mock Trial in which J. Berridge was charged with corrupt practices at an election, and sentenced to parse and analyse two-thirds of Karl Marx's book, *Das Kapital*.

During the summer of 1945 the Home and School Association and the Old Lutonians agreed to work together to raise funds for a covered, warmed swimming bath for the School as a Memorial to those who died during the War. By the end of the year £700 had been collected, but thousands more would be needed.

In July four members of staff left the School: Mr Paul Morpurgo, Mr Stanley MacGregor, Mr Samuel Finlay and Mr Basil Cooke. Mr James Findlater officially retired but continued with part-time work. They were succeeded by Mr Albert J.G. May, Mr Eric Sansome, Mr Redmond 'Baffer' Lane and Mr Herbert 'Herbie' J. Bryant. Mr Bryant was appointed Head of Physics and Mr May became Senior Maths. Master in succession to Mr Godfrey.

The appointment of Mr A.J.G. May, known to many boys as 'Charlie', was a great inspiration to all mathematicians. Dr J.R. Greenleaf has written: 'He truly walked on water. His command of Maths was outstanding. His love of the subject was infectious and it has remained with me for 45 years. He was one of the giants of the classroom.' Ray Robson has added: 'Being a mathematician he was and is my hero. Anyone who can multiply two four figure numbers together in his head is a bit ahead of me. I called to see him one day whilst I was at Imperial College, and mentioned a problem that I didn't know how to start let alone finish. It was to prove that partial dx over dx equals partial dy over dy equals partial dz over dz. Charlie sat

One of the Musical Concerts organised by Mr Godfrey in aid of the School Swimming Bath Fund, on 2nd January, 1946. The artistes were Stanley Riley, bass, and Margaret Rees, soprano, both BBC Singers; Harry Mortimer, trumpet and cornet, and Augustus Lowe, piano. (*LN-LMC*)

and thought for a moment, took out a piece of paper and wrote down the proof!'

The 1945 Rugby season has been long remembered for the remarkable performance of the 1st XV in scoring 407 points to 10 in ten matches. Nine of those matches were won; only in the last against Bedford Modern School 2nd XV, was the School defeated, and that by the narrow margin of one dropped goal to one try. Owing to that defeat the team failed to equal the record of the 1942 team, though they far surpassed it in the number of points scored. D.B. 'Bert' Fensome captained the team until called-up in November; he was ably supported by A.T. Redman, his Vice-Captain. 'George' Thorpe, one of the team, attributed much of the success to the inspirational coaching of Ronald Bridger, 'who thought nothing of suspending our best player who missed mid-week training to keep a date with his High School girlfriend.' Perhaps the regular posse of half a dozen young ladies who supported the home games also helped.

A lively Biology Club was formed in September, enthusiastically supported by Mr Ralph Scurfield. A large membership enjoyed talks, films, and cycling weekends to nearby Youth Hostels. Mr Howells promoted the School's own Film Institute, and large crowds were attracted to see *The Great Train Robbery* (1903) and *Nanook of the North* (1922). A School Newsreel was also made, grainey video copies of which still survive, showing athletics, cricket, potato pickers and characters from *The Rivals*.

On 29th October, the Luton Airport Orchestra gave a concert of light music to aid the School's Memorial Swimming Bath Fund. It included a piano recital of music by Liszt and Schumann, played by Ralph West, the first Luton Modern School boy

to take music in his School Certificate. Baritone soloist James Flicker and conjuror Richard White also took part.

The autumn term ended with the traditional School Orchestra Concerts on 18th and 19th December, which included solo performances by D.I.Burrows and J.T. Hill (piano), V.E. Raymond (violin), and B.J. Smith (clarinet). P.G. Knowles and B.C. Patrick played a violin duet and the Brass rendered a piece in four-part harmony.

With the new year came the return of three masters who had been absent for five years on War-Service: Mr Arthur Root and Mr Eric Harvey in February, and Mr Henry B. Williams in May. Mr Squire returned to London.

Speech Day fell on 20th February, 1946. Instead of a single special guest, addresses from three Old Boys, one from each of the Services, commemorated the first prize-giving since the end of hostilities. The speakers were Major J.R. Sears, RA, Flt. Lt. A.M. Hill, DFC, and Lieut. R.C.P. Stoneham, RNVR. Perhaps remembering boring Speech Days in the past, they amused the boys with reminiscences of School life that were light and direct, and made them readily acceptable to their audience, for which they were enthusiastically applauded.

The guests took turns in presenting the certificates and prizes. In July 1945 there had been 85 Cambridge School Certificates, 35 with matriculation, and 29 Higher School Certificates. Mr Webb said that the School had adopted a policy of endeavouring to let the curriculum fit the boy. The curriculum was an individual School responsibility, and they offered a choice of 19 subjects for the School Certificate. In addition to passes in the usual formal subjects, a number of candidates successfully presented topics for the first time – geology, economics, Spanish and navigation. M. J. Barber's distinction in geology was the only one in the country. P.D. Southgate gained a Royal Scholarship and a State Scholarship to Imperial College. M.J. Barber secured an £150 Open Geological Scholarship to Imperial College; W.B. Strang received an Open Scholarship at Trinity Hall, Cambridge; B.R. Laurence an Open Exhibition to Gonville and Caius College, Cambridge and G.S. Hawkes, a State Bursary tenable at Imperial College. Entrance to Universities: N.S. Thom, King's College, Cambridge; J.W.F. Farr, City and Guilds College, London; P. Longbottom, Queen Mary College, London. Entrance to Medical Schools: H.E. Rowley, P.J. Schagrin, R. Zakon – all to St Bartholomew's Hospital; C.L. Tutty, St Thomas' Hospital; D.B. Hawkins, Westminster Hospital.

Senior boys were taken to the Grand Theatre on 21st February to see a rather hastily prepared production of *The Merchant of Venice*, performed by the Rock Theatre Company, and produced by Terence O'Brien, who played Shylock. Next day, the actor, Robert Speaight, visited the School and spoke to senior forms about performing Shakespeare, in the 17th century, the early 20th century and in the 1950s.

The School's own actors took to the stage for three evenings in April, when they performed Arnold Bennett's *Milestones*. The play, which deals with the fortunes of a

wealthy family living in Kensington Gore, takes place over three periods of time, mid-Victorian, late-Victorian and early Edwardian. It requires the actors to age over the three Acts, something which even professionals find difficult. The School cast coped well, and particular credit went to the three principal characters. The resolute John Rhead was excellently acted by M. Marsh-Edwards; his equally determined sister Gertrude Rhead was played by P.D. Saunders, whilst D.W.E. Bateman charmed everyone with his exquisite performance as the young Rose Rhead, who retained his excellence as Rose became first mother and then grandmother.

All Head Teachers were allowed to spend 2s. per pupil on their School's 'Victory' celebrations. On 5th June everyone watched a performance of *The Family Upstairs*, presented by the Fortescue Repertory Company on the School stage. It was described as an American family drama. No Old Boys interviewed for this book had the slightest memory of it! Junior boys were also entertained by Mr White, the conjuror, who made a deeper impression on his young audience.

On June 6th 'Victory' was celebrated more seriously in a semi-religious service. A.J. Hucklesby played piano music by Coleridge-Taylor and Chopin, creating the necessary atmosphere for a 'broadcast' by boys from IVb surveying the outstanding international events of the period from 1870 to 1946, designed to explain how the present international situation had developed. The item was devised by Dr Dony and relayed from the Gym. Following it, the Headmaster said that we could do far worse than to let the three flags which make up the Union Jack stand for freedom, love and truth. We should not throw away the opportunities which peace had brought, but aim always at upholding those three qualities to make Britain, in the best sense, a land of 'hope and glory'.

> The shouting dies, a vision yet remains,
> An airman now beyond the ken of mortals;
> He died – for what? For freedom, love and truth,
> The brotherhood of man, the family, the home,
> For all he meant by Peace.
> The War he fought in had at last its ending,
> But where is Peace, the vision of his dying?
> In Council Chamber, factory, field and street,
> Men fight with words, and vilify each other;
> Famine and plague and death all ride the earth,
> The spectre War looks on with glowing eyes.
> That young man lying now in foreign earth,
> He died for Peace, and dying handed on
> His sacred charge of brotherhood to us;
> We must not, shall not, fail him!
>
> [D. F. Harrowell]

A new innovation on 1st June, 1946, was a Fair and Fête on behalf of the Memorial Swimming Bath Fund, in which parents and friends, Old Boys, Staff and present pupils co-operated. The attendance exceeded 12,000 and more than £1,100 was taken for the Fund. Throughout the sunny afternoon and evening there were many events for young and old. A Bazaar held in the Gym soon resembled Woolworth's on a Saturday night. Mrs Sankey ran a tea-room in the Hall, and there were a variety of refreshment stalls around the field. The School Orchestra played for three hours. A fun fair included a roundabout, games of skill and various side-shows. The Gym Club gave a PT display, and there were races for children, a seven-a-side Rugby tournament and Clock Golf. Inside the School various exhibitions had been organised including Art, a 'Museum', Pets' Exhibition, model trains and aeroplanes. Many visitors stayed into the evening to dance to the music of Edgar Allison and his Band.

In Sport the 1st XI Football team had a most successful season, winning all their ten matches. The Cricket season was rather short. Moderate success was achieved, mainly due to the sound batting of the Captain, Derek J. Wood, who three times topped the half-century, and after leaving School went on to play with distinction for the Luton Town 1st Team. Prospects for the 1st XV Rugby team were not very high at the beginning of the season, but under Redman's captaincy they gained in

OPPOSITE Scenes at the Fair and Fête in June 1946. (LN)
BELOW The 1st Rugby XV, 1946. (back row) Mr R. Phillips, G.J.W. Thorpe, L.S. Shepherd, K.E.C. Riches, V.E. Raymond, A.L. Ironmonger, R.V. Vaughan, M. Horsler, H.E. Mason, B.V. Selwood, Mr R. Bridger, (front row) S.R.B. Thurlow, S. Cameron, R.W. Kelly, A.F.W. Pakes, A.T. Redman (Captain), L.M. Hine, D.E. Wood, B.H. Rance, R.T. Mills. (LN)

Scenes at the Fair and Fete

1. The junior roundabout which was kept in motion by Old Boys.
2. Football Alley, with Mr Bracey in goal.
3. The P. T. Squad.
4. Alderman John Burgoyne with President Tom Smalley in the centre of a crowd visiting the Bazaar.
5. Another scene at the Bazaar.
6. The P. T. Squad again.
7. The younger generation on the roundabout.
8. Part of a never ending queue at the ice cream stall.

confidence and eventually scored 205 points to 33, only losing two games.

On Sports Day on 29th May, records were broken in the 100 yds (u.12), the 880 yds Open, the Long and High Jumps Open, the Hammer Open and the Javelin (u.15). A.P. Horn was *Victor Ludorum*. A.F.W. Pakes, D.J.F. Hill and A.F. Trendall all won gold medals in the Midland Counties AAA Junior Championships at Wolverhampton on 8th June. The School team also led the Beds. AAA Junior and Youths Championships at Wardown on 15th June, coming first with 164 points, to their old rivals Bedford Modern School, who were 2nd with 104 points.

The Literary and Scientific Society had a visit from Mr William Warbey, MP for Luton, who spoke on 'Impressions of Westminster', and Mr H.B. Williams lectured on 'Mines and Minesweeping', a subject he knew at first-hand. Members visited a number of local firms, as well as Rothamsted Experimental Station and the Dunstable Meteorological Station. A joint social with members of the VIth Form at the High School was held in March. The Chess Club played six matches against other schools, and won three of them. S.B. Rosalki and D.G. Taylor represented Bedfordshire in the inter-County Championships. Members of the Biology Club cycled to Felixstowe for a weekend, staying at Youth Hostels.

At the end of the summer holidays a mixed party of Modern School boys and High School girls went pea picking in pouring rain on a farm at Shefford!

Instances of boys in serious trouble were fortunately rare. Mr Webb always endeavoured to help them, irrespective of whether they had done wrong or gone astray. He recalled two boys breaking into a grocery store and stealing various items. He got them and their parents into his room, and it was very clear that they sincerely regetted what they had done. He persuaded them to make full restitution to the shopkeeper, but, when it was offered, the grocer said that he was fully covered by his insurance, and wouldn't accept it. Mr Webb found that most frustrating.

A fortunately rare incident had occurred in March 1946, when a boy found himself in Court, having been expelled from School for stealing sweet coupons. Although neither the School nor the boy were named, *The Luton News* tried to dramatise the story, saying that the Headmaster was being heavy handed and jeopardising the boy's career, as he would be unable to take his School Certificate. The following week an exceptional letter appeared in the newspaper signed by 'The School Prefects' in support of the Headmaster's action and accusing *The Luton News* of sensational reporting. They added 'We have known him [the boy] for five years – the magistrates only a few minutes.' The LEA 'confirmed the action taken by the Headmaster.'

Mr Webb was faced with a problem of a different kind in September. New Staff were finding it impossible to obtain accommodation in Luton. Mr William H. Chapman, with a wife and child, was homeless, and a number of bachelors were in most unsatisfactory lodgings. Boys took letters home, asking if parents knew of anyone with rooms to let. In desperation Mr Webb wrote to the Director of

Education, suggesting that the County Council requisitioned or bought a house for their use. Mr Lucking replied 'Where are we to find free or desirable residences in Luton?' Nothing happened, but somehow the problem eventually resolved itself.

Three new masters joined the School in September. Mr John Ririe succeeded Mr Eric F. Harvey as instructor in Physical Education. Mr Holland B. Evans, an ex-army chaplain, soon nicknamed 'Major', joined Dr Dony for the teaching of history. Mr Hugh H. Gilbert came to teach general subjects.

In Memoriam

On Sunday, 10th November, 1946, a Memorial Plaque, dedicated to those who had died in the Second World War, was unveiled in the Office foyer of the School. A grey slab of stone, measuring 6ft 3ins x 3ft 3ins, and beautifully inscribed in black Roman lettering, carried the names of the seventy young men, and the words:

LUTON GRAMMAR SCHOOL

1939 IN MEMORIAM 1945

SEE THAT THEY DIED NOT IN VAIN

In the top left hand corner was carved the School badge and motto, coloured in crimson and gold. Parents and relatives of the dead, together with Old Boys, Governors and friends, joined with the masters and boys of the School in a moving service. After the Headmaster had described the purpose and nature of the occasion, the names of the Master and sixty-nine Old Boys who died was read by Ronald Mead, himself a former prisoner of war.

'Let us now praise famous men', from Ecclesiasticus is not an easy passage to read, but the Head Prefect, A.F. Trendall, gave it its full meaning. The singing of the hymn, *'O God our help in ages past'*, was memorable for the treble voices of the Boys' Choir rising in descant above the full-throated voices of the congregation. It was followed by Alderman John Burgoyne's reading of the passage from the Book of Wisdom, 'The Souls of the righteous are in the hand of God'.

Mr J.W. Findlater's moving interpretation of Laurence Binyon's poem *'For the Fallen'* seemed to change the prevailing sadness into thanksgiving.

'There is music in the midst of desolation
And glory that shines upon our tears.'

Prayers were taken by the Headmaster, followed by the reading of a passage from the Revelation of St John by a bereaved parent, Mr Herbert C. Janes.

The last hymn, *'These things shall be: a loftier race'*, by A.J. Symonds, was followed by the Blessing, and the first part of the service concluded with the Boys' Choir singing, *'O God use the love that is in me'*.

The relatives of the fallen then followed the platform party to the Office foyer

where the Plaque was unveiled by the President of the Old Boys' Club, Tom Smalley. A short dedicatory service was taken by another Old Boy, the Revd. Laurence Brown, after which the whole School filed silently past the monument, eyes to the left, leaving many of those watching and those taking part, in tears.

The placing of the Memorial in the Office foyer was intended to be temporary, until such time as it could be moved to the Memorial Swimming Baths. When the Baths project was abandoned in favour of Tennis Courts it was felt that moving the plaque might damage it and so it remained in the foyer. With the development of the Sixth Form College, the foyer area has been enclosed. The Memorial remains *in situ* in the corridor, facing the wooden Memorial to the 1914–18 War. Their positions are cramped, insignificant and largely ignored by most who pass them by.

During the winter a number of white and pink chestnut trees were planted in the School grounds to commemorate the ending of the war in the Far East, using money left over from the 'Victory' funds.

For many weeks boys in the Art classes under Mr Smoothey's skilled direction had been constructing a variety of marionettes, from simple insects to juggling clowns.

Young visitors admire Mr Smoothey's marionette show which performed in the Hall on 16th December 1946. (*LN*)

Others had been building a large portable puppet theatre, writing sketches, painting scenery, and designing lighting effects. Together they produced a magical show that entertained children and adults alike on 16th December, with a butterfly ballet performed to 'The Rustle of Spring', a circus with a whip-cracking Ringmaster and sea-lions that caught balls on their noses, and a tale of skeletons and giants.

At Christmas the School Orchestra gave two concerts, for the School, and for parents and friends. As well as music by the Orchestra conducted by Mr Bridger, solos were played by V.E. Raymond (Leader), and D.I. Burrows, a duet by P.G. Knowles and B.C. Patrick, a quartet by V. Raymond, J.T. Hill, J.M. Southgate and Mr Parry, and a trio by D.W.E. Bateman, Southgate and Burrows.

The winter term, 1946, was one of the wettest on record, though the weather had failed to interrupt many activities. School broke-up on the 20th December with its usual end-of-term Carol Service. Many boys were again employed at the General Post Office and Drill Hall sorting and delivering the Christmas Mail.

Luton Takes Control

In 1947 control of the Grammar School and High School passed from the Bedfordshire County Council to the Luton Education Committee, which became a divisional executive with virtual control of all education within the Borough. A reconstitution of the Governing Body followed the change in administrative arrangements: it was now composed of 23 members, six of whom were appointed by the Local Education Authority, 12 by the Luton Borough Council, one by the Luton Rural District Council and the remaining four were co-opted. The same body governed all the Luton secondary schools for boys, and once a term the Headmaster of the Grammar School attended a meeting with the other headmasters in one of the schools concerned.

On 29th January, 1947, the old School Governors met for the last time before handing over to Luton. Ald. H.G. Brightman, presiding, said 'We are all sorry to lay down the reins, and we wish the new Governors success in their management of these schools. I believe they are amongst the foremost in the country, and the successes which have been achieved have been truly outstanding, for which the credit must go to the Headmaster, Headmistress and Staff.' It was noted that Lady Keens had been a governor for twenty years and Ald. John Burgoyne even longer. Speaking of the Grammar School, the latter observed, 'I believe this School has a magnificent future and that if Mr Webb stays in Luton that future is wonderfully assured.'

There were 678 boys on the School Roll when the new year began. Alan F.W. Pakes was Head Prefect, with a team of twelve Prefects, twenty Sub-Prefects and twenty-one Monitors to assist him.

Mr Ronald W. Smoothey left after only eight terms, but had made a deep impression on the School and all those he taught. His Assistant, Robert W. Stump,

also left to take up an appointment in his native Switzerland. One of their most talented students, Dennis L. Farr, CBE, has written:

> 'The really important influence on me was Ronald Smoothey, who, unlike R.S. Clayton, the Careers Master, had heard of the Courtauld Institute of Art, London University, and suggested to me that I might find it a congenial place to study art history, a subject then scarcely heard of outside a small circle of artists and *cognoscenti*. Stump always struck me as a most amusing man, and he and Smoothey made a lively duo. I was very sad when they left at the end of the Spring term, 1947. In 1995 I had an invitation to see a memorial exhibition of Mr Smoothey's work at the Guildford museum. I met his widow, whom I remembered from my sixth-form days. His paintings were surrealist, and I remembered thinking the style hadn't changed since the 1940s.' [Dennis Farr was Director of the Courtauld Institute from 1980–93]

Ronald Smoothey's successor was James 'Gusty' Gale, from Market Harborough Grammar School, and John H. Phillips, from Cardiff Technical College, replaced Robert Stump. Mr Jack Ashworth also joined the Staff to teach Biology. Mr Webb has commented:

> 'I offered Mr Ashworth the post, at which point he said, 'You may have noticed that I am a little bit ill and I must tell you before I accept that I've got multiple sclerosis, which will pull me down; but if you will put up with me as I am, I'll do my best.' He came and in that spirit he worked well. The boys did not play him up, in spite of the fact that he had to sit rather still, and it came to the time when they had to carry him round, which they did readily and without complaint. There was a boy that they also had to do that for, Denis Mardle. He developed polio at 15, and spent two years at the Royal National Orthopaedic Hospital, before returning to the Sixth Form.'

Speech Day, on 12th February, 1947, was the first since the death of Ald. Harry Arnold, Chairman of the Governors for many years. There were several new faces amongst the Governors, following the change of Education Authority, but the traditions remained unaltered. Introducing his somewhat pessimistic report, the Headmaster warned that 'a toneless world of undifferentiated mediocrity, where no one is recognised as being any better than anyone else at anything, will not introduce the century of the common man.'

Mr Webb felt that the right education for any child was the type that discovered,

OPPOSITE Ink and line drawing by Dennis L. Farr (U.VI Arts) illustrating the *Nonne Preestes Tale* by Chaucer, from *The Lutonian* of February 1947.

"This cok brak from his mouth delyverly ,
  And heighe upon a tree he fleigh anon ;
  And whan the fox saugh that he was gon,—
  ' Allas ! ' quod he, ' O Chauntecleer, allas !
  I have to yow,' quod he, ' y-doon trespass ;
  But, sire, I dide it in no wikke entente,
  Com doun, and I shal telle yow what I mente ' "

" Nonne Preestes Tale " — *Chaucer*

Boys at Speech Day, 1947, listening to the Mayor of Luton, Cllr George F. Seaward. (*LN*)

nourished, strengthened and exercised its special and peculiar excellences, bringing him to the common treasury for the service of mankind. He spoke of the difficulties of 'call-up' and National Service preventing a boy proceeding to college. This enforced gap in his studies presented problems for a boy with a good Higher School Certificate who left the Forces at 21 to proceed to college or his life occupation. Mr Webb felt that it was something that needed to be met on a national scale.

At very short notice the Mayor and Mayoress, Councillor and Mrs Seaward, agreed to attend, and Mrs Seaward distributed the numerous awards. In 1946, 87 boys had gained Cambridge School Certificates, 54 with matriculation exemption, and 27 had obtained Higher School Certificates. Three State Scholarships and two Royal Scholarships was an unprecedented record. The State Scholars were P.J.D. Gething, (Imperial College, London), B.R. Laurence, (University College, London), and W.B. Strang. The Royal Scholarships went to P.J.D. Gething and A.F. Trendall, (both Imperial College, London). In addition W.B. Strang was awarded a Laming £100 Open Scholarship, tenable at Queen's College, Oxford; and A.F. Trendall

received a London Inter-Collegiate Examinations Board Major (£100) Scholarship in Geology, tenable at King's College, London. D.G. Alexander gained entrance to University College, Hull; G. Smith to Manchester University, D.J. Wood to Cambridge University, and two boys, M.R. Marsh-Edwards and B.J. Smith, went to Trinity College of Music, London. At the end of June the boys received an extra three days holiday, earned for them by the successful examination candidates.

The Dramatic Society presented *The School for Scandal* on 24th–26th March, 1947. Acting honours went to P.D. Townsend, P.D. Saunders, T.S. Bunker and R.V. Vaughan. Mr Parry wrote: 'Townsend impressed by the naturalness with which he portrayed the humourless, dogmatic and yet harassed Sir Peter Teazle, Saunders reproduced all the sourness and bitterness of Crabtree, while Bunker and Vaughan, as the contrasted brothers, played very long parts with polish and distinction. Of the other actors, D.A. Webb played the elderly Sir Oliver Surface with great credit, while H.M. Swallow delighted the audience with his imitations of the Jewish money-lender, "honest Moses". Mr Henry B. Williams was responsible for the excellent production, and Mr Ronald Smoothey and his helpers for the clever scenery.' As a result of the production nearly £67 was handed to the School's Memorial Swimming Bath Fund.

The School's second Fair and Fête took place on 17th May. As D.L. Farr observed, 'On that hot Saturday afternoon the populace of Luton seemed to have but one objective. They thronged the highways and were in a truly festive mood, the wealthier amongst them careering past in their opulent "baby" Austins. A magnificent spectacle awaited them.' Ideal weather rewarded the organising committee representing the Home and School Association, the Old Lutonians' Club, and members of the school staff and boys. On the School field was a fun fair, a PT Display, a seven-a-side Rugger tournament, where the Old Lutonians' beat Luton Town Club by 10 points to nil, and a fancy dress cricket match. Inside the School were a model railway exhibition, model aero display, tropical and freshwater fish, cartoon film shows, bazaars, a flower shop, an art exhibition (silhouettes drawn for a moderate fee), a display outlining the School's history, lots of refreshments, and an evening dance. The day's efforts produced a further £722 7s 5d for the Memorial Swimming Bath Fund.

To mark her retirement after twenty-eight years as Headmistress of the High School, Miss Helen K. Sheldon visited the Grammar School on the morning of 25th June. The Headmaster and Head Boy, D.B. Slope, both paid tribute to the part she had played in fostering closer ties between the two Schools by socials, debates and in other ways. She was presented with a wall-mirror and a book-token from the School and Staff. Miss Sheldon expressed her thanks in a charming speech and showed no signs of the alarm she said she felt at the ordeal of addressing an exclusively male audience. 'Whenever I look into this mirror,' she observed, 'I will not see myself. I will see all the boys of Luton Grammar School!'

Some Light Relief

During the summer holidays from 28th July to 5th August, a party of 33 boys, led by Mr Parry and Mr Watson, and accompanied by Mrs Watson and Mr Parry's father, made the School's first post-war journey to Switzerland. The party stayed at Montreux, where they bathed in the lake, rowed or climbed the nearby hills. Excursions included visits to the Great St. Bernard Hospice where they were introduced to some of the famous St. Bernard dogs; a day spent in Geneva during which they visited the former League of Nations building, being used in 1947 as the European Centre of the UNO; and a final day tour by funicular railway to the spectacular summit of the Rochers de Naye, overlooking Montreux. Laden with watches, cameras and films, the party had to run the gauntlet of the Newhaven Customs officers, who took some toll of the party before they were eventually allowed to board the train back to Luton.

The abnormal weather conditions at the beginning of 1947, and fuel restrictions, caused numerous activities to be cancelled. The Literary and Scientific programme was somewhat affected, although the joint debate with the High School went ahead on 24th February. The topical subject for debate was 'That Woman's Place is in the Home'. M. Wynter proposed the motion whilst Janet Cook opposed it; their respective seconders were Pamela Brown and T.S. Bunker. After much plain speaking from both sides and the floor of the House, the motion was carried by the narrow margin of 45 votes to 39.

On 17th May the Aero Club journeyed to Northolt Airport, where they were shown around the Meteorological Office, reception and customs buildings, and saw King George VI leave in his Viking aircraft for York. During the day they identified 51 different aircraft. The Biology Club dissected numerous small creatures, and listened to talks by members on 'Butterflies and Moths', 'Crime detection by Blood Analysis', 'Snails', and 'Morbid Anatomy'. A visit to the British Gelatine Works put most members off jelly for life, a trip to the sewage works when the wind was in the wrong direction was almost as off-putting, but Mr Chandler's Dairy Farm at Streatley proved more consumer-friendly. R.A. McDonald led an expedition when several birds' nests with eggs were found, including a robin's, blackbird's, hedge sparrow's, thrush's and a jay's, whose egg suffered an unfortunate mishap . . . The Chess Club had one of its most successful years, the Senior and Junior Tournaments being won by D.V. Mardle and C.C. Glenister respectively. During the season 14 matches were won and 6 lost, including one against the otherwise unbeaten Luton Chess Club.

The Railway Club's programme included a visit by 18 members to the Swindon locomotive works, and debates on 'The Nationalisation of the Railways' and 'The Best Type of Locomotive for Express Traffic'.

Sport in 1947

The Football season had been badly affected by the weather; the 1st XI, captained by Jim Anderson, played only two games, and the 2nd XI three games: all were won.

Cross-Country Running was also somewhat curtailed due to runners getting stuck in deep snow-drifts. The School narrowly lost to Bedford Modern, but came first in three-cornered contests with St George's and St Albans, and with St Albans and Ranelagh Harriers. The team was also second in the County Championships; D.E.J. Taylor and L.H. Holland being chosen to represent Bedfordshire in the English Counties Championship at Nottingham.

The Athletics season was also short, but the weather for Sports Day on 14th May was unusually fine. K.E.C. Riches, winner of the Open High Jump, broke the only record with a jump of 5ft 0¾in. At the Bedfordshire Junior Championships the team won 5 cups but failed to retain the Arnold Whitchurch Trophy.

According to Wynne Parry, the Cricket season, 1947, ranked with the leanest and most disappointing in the history of the School sides, particularly in respect of the 1st XI. Three crushing defeats, during which the side only just succeeded in reaching a score in double figures, expressed eloquently the lamentable performances. Alan F.W. Pakes proved a courteous and gentlemanly Captain, increasing the confidence of his men whenever he was able to play. Mr Glyn Owen never spared himself in his coaching, although his health was below par, and Mr Chapman did the lion's share of supervision; but it was a season best forgotten.

Things were much better for Rugby. Dudley Wood captained a team of old stalwarts and new blood, with J.G. Thorpe as hooker and P.J. Allen and M.R. Pattenden (and later P.N. Brown) creating a useful pack. The 1st XV won six of its eight games, and drew one against the Old Boys.

In September Alan E. Silvester, U.VI Arts, was lucky enough to be part of the Public Schools' Exploring Society's six-week expedition to Newfoundland. After five days sailing by boat to St John's, they travelled inland by train and truck to an area fittingly named the 'Barrens', where they surveyed vast boggy plains traversed by rivers, lakes and covered with coniferous forests. It was a land inhabited by moose, caribou, bear and beaver, where they force marched across bogs, waded through streams and struggled through dense undergrowth, all the time striving to preserve their plane tables [used for surveying] from injury.

On 30th October Mr Scurfield took most of IIIc and some U.VI Zoologists by coach to the Dairy Show at Olympia. Most of the third year boys with urban backgrounds were out of their depth, and spent the day competing against each other to see who could collect most free leaflets and samples!

The School Dramatic Society made history on four evenings in December 1947, when for the first time it combined with the High School Dramatic Society in a production of G. M. Sierra's play, *The Romantic Young Lady*. With the support of a

new Headmistress, Mrs E. Evans, and the enthusiasm of the producers, Miss Kathleen Hudson and Henry Williams, it was generally agreed that the experiment was a great success. It was to be the dawning of a golden age for drama in the two Schools. The production raised £60 for the Memorial Swimming Bath Fund.

The Expanding School – 1948

The number of boys on the School roll reached 727 in September 1948, but wartime austerity measures were still in force, and little could be done to relieve the overcrowding. Classes were held in every spare corner, including the balcony parade, prefects' common room, and even the projection room.

There were numerous staff changes during the year. Mr Eric Sansome, 'Ted', rejoined the School in January. At Easter, Mr Ralph Scurfield, Head of Biology, left for Doncaster, and was succeeded by Mr Herman E.W. Chalkley, an Old Boy who had been Head Prefect in 1932–3. In July Mr Wareham moved internally from the Science department to become Head of Handicrafts. His place was filled by Mr Stanley H. Matthews. Mr John Ririe left, making way for Mr John A. Muse. Mr Reginald Hulme, 'Slug', joined the Handicraft staff, and Mr Herbert Nickols became Head of Music. Mr Pointing and Mr Bridger moved to pastures new.

Mr Pointing, 'Tintacks', joined the School in 1933 and created a new workshop at Bradgers Hill in 1938. He was a keen badminton player, and much in demand as MC at Home and School Association socials and whist drives. As CO, he was the driving force behind the School Cadet Corps during the war and was always on hand when odd jobs needing skilful hands had to be done.

When Ronald Bridger joined the School in 1940, music was a Cinderella subject. After eight years he raised it to Higher School Certificate at advanced standard. Denis Wick described him as 'kind and knowledgeable' and Peter Isherwood has observed that 'he had quite a deal of influence on those who were musical – especially if they were interested in Rugby.' With the whole-hearted co-operation of a number of masters, he increased the efficiency of the Orchestra far above the standard found in the average grammar school. As a fierce disciplinarian he was not a popular master with younger, non-musical, boys, who failed to appreciate his 'Rudiments of Music'. Those who met him on the Rugby field found a very different man, South Africa trained, with a wealth of experience that, together with Ronald Phillips, he passed on to the School teams, revitalising their games. The more surprising for a man who chain-smoked all his life!

The School produced a number of talented musicians at this time, partly nurtured by Ronald Bridger, but mostly the products of private music teachers such as Leslie Dawson, a local violinist. His Grammar School pupils included David and Michael Southgate and David Bateman. Bateman went to the Royal College of Music and played in the Royal Philharmonic Orchestra under Sir Thomas Beecham.

After teaching violin at Harrow and Eton, he became Head of Strings at Oundle School.

Donald Ivan Burrows, who left in 1948, played the School organ, and was an assistant to Dr K. Abbott at Luton Parish Church. He studied at the Royal College of Music and the Royal College of Organists, in due course becoming organist at Saffron Walden Church, Director of Music at Warrington College of Education and then at Christchurch College, Canterbury, finally becoming Staff Tutor and Reader in Music at the Open University. He died of cancer in December, 1991.

On 9th February the Luton Girls' Choir, conducted by an Old Boy, Arthur E. Davies, and members of the School gave a concert in aid of the Memorial Swimming Bath Fund. D.I. Burrows, D.G. Wick, and B.J. Smith performed items, accompanied by R.D. Cleaver, and then Haydn's Trio in E flat was given by the 'Miniature Trio', Burrows (piano), D.W.E. Bateman (violin) and J.M. Southgate ('cello). The remainder of the programme was in the capable hands of the Girls' Choir and some of their soloists. The School Hall was packed to capacity and the Swimming Bath Fund benefited by £80.

Speech Day on Wednesday, 11th February, was addressed by Sir Frederick Mander, Chairman of the Bedfordshire Education Committee. Sir Frederick gave his assurance that with the intensive widening of educational facilities in the country the endeavour of the Beds. Education Committee would be 'to level up', not 'level down', the county's schools. 'We will do this not only for the parents and boys, but to a large extent for the sake of the nation as a whole. People everywhere are asking for more education, but behind that demand lies the danger that quantity will replace quality.' He concluded by defending 'the old school tie'. 'It is something to be worn round the heart not the neck.'

Although the War was over, National Service was still in force. Mr Webb informed parents that a recent Government ruling had said that boys might stay on at school to take Higher School Certificate or university scholarship exams until the end of the year in which they became 19, not 18 as previously. Following such a postponement of call-up, there could be no deferment. Call-up must follow.

D.C. Price was the only boy to be awarded a State Scholarship in 1947, although ten others were accepted for entrance to University, Medical and Dental Schools over the following two years.

Mention has already been made of Denis Mardle. In an obituary in *The Times* in 2000, his school friend Phillip Gething described him as a talented mathematician, who passed his School Certificate just before his 14th birthday in 1943, and developed infantile paralysis a year later, remaining badly disabled for the rest of his life. After two years in hospital, and with encouragement from Mr Webb, he returned to the sixth-form, where burly friends carried him up and down stairs when necessary. He concentrated on maths and School Certificate Latin, gaining a State Scholarship and Royal Studentship, and admission to Christ's College, Cambridge.

Mr Webb had meetings at the College in June 1948, to finalise the special arrangements necessary for him. He was a brilliant chess player, and it was at an Oxford v Cambridge match that he was spotted by C.H. O'D. Alexander, who was then head of the cryptanalysis (decyphering encoded text) division of GCHQ. He joined the Eastcote establishment in 1952 as a research mathematician, and, moving to Cheltenham, quickly moved up the ladder, eventually becoming chief mathematician in 1973. From 1982–89 he was head of the cryptanalysis division, with responsibilities in planning and staff management. He was appointed CBE in 1988. He died on 31st July, 2000, aged 70.

During the morning of 1st March the whole school watched a screening of Laurence Olivier's 1944 film, *Henry V*, shown to help the older boys with their English examination preparation. A fortnight later class IIIc presented the historical play *Nelson* by L. du Garde Peach to the Junior School. K.E. Nortrop played Nelson, and M.B. DuCane was Admiral Lord Howe. Production was by J. Dyer with D.A. Webb.

A fortnight later Mrs Alston, HMI, spent two days in the School. She expressed concern at the very small number of boys taking Latin in a Grammar School. The PT staff could not persuade her of the need for a specialist Athletics master; and she expressed horror at the shower provision in the gym changing room, and at the sight of six L.VI boys playing football in long trousers.

'Treasure Island' was the theme of the School's third Fair and Fête on 8th May. To create this impression a sand model of Stevenson's Island was built over the top of the air raid shelters, and beside it was a map where treasure hunters staked their claims to cash prizes. There were two showings of a full-length colour film of *Treasure Island*. The most popular side-show was 'Bash the Bobby', in which visitors had to knock off the policeman's helmet. When the Headmaster acted as the 'Bobby' there was a stampede of small boys anxious to take a pot-shot without fear of recrimination! A gymnastics display also included a bicycle football match. The Fair raised another £589 for the Memorial Swimming Bath Fund.

Term ended with a very popular Orchestral Leaving Concert in honour of Ronald Bridger, conducted by Mr Woodcock. Forms I and II sang Easthope-Martin's "Come to the Fair". Messrs F. Walker, H.H. Watson and C.W. Parry played a trio-arrangement of the "Andante" from Mendelssohn's Violin Concerto, and Mr Watson also obliged with a cello solo. The highlight was provided by D.I. Burrows and D.G. Wick, who played the very fast last movement of Mozart's "Horn Concerto".

During the summer holidays Denis Wick (trombone) and Michael Southgate (cello) travelled to Sherborne in Dorset to take part in the Music Teachers' Association summer school for under 19s. Whilst they were there they took part in recording music for the BBC.

Sport and the Olympic Games

In 1948 a fairly strong 1st Football XI was built up, and of nine matches played, six were won, two lost and one drawn. Bernard H. 'Bunny' Rance captained a very young team that showed promise for the future.

The Senior Cross-Country season was poor, but the Juniors had an excellent time, winning all four of their matches, with excellent running by Dennis Dunn, John Lawrence and Frank Bailey. In the County Championships Derek Gill and John Lawrence were the first two men home.

Five records were broken on Sports Day on 5th May, by B.E. Stimpson in the Mile Open; J.J. Hewitt in the High Jump Open; D.E. Wood with the hammer; M.J. Bracey in the 880yds (u.14) and the Senior (4 x 110yds) Relay Team. B.V. Selwood and B.E. Stimpson tied for *Victor Ludorum*. C.H. Fox won the (u.15) Discus, Javelin, Hammer and Shot. At the County AAA Championships the School won six events, and came second to Bedford Modern School for the Arnold Whitchurch Trophy.

The Cricket season was much more encouraging than in 1947. The 'old hands', Dudley E. Wood (Captain) and S.R.B. 'Butch' Thurlow, did much useful work, and newcomer Malcolm Jones had a splendid season. According to C.W. Parry 'Jim M. Worker kept wicket excellently, and R. E. Boyd had improved tremendously as a stumper. Barry D. Robinson did some excellent work off the field as Secretary and on the field as a batsman. T.J. Brown was the sheet-anchor of the side and he was certainly one of the most correct batsmen that the School ever produced.'

The 1948 Rugby season was a chapter of accidents from beginning to end. Before term began there were four casualties and from then on A.L. Ironmonger, J.G.W. Thorpe, J.D. Newman, R.V. Vaughan and D.E. Wood were all away for periods extending from three weeks to a whole term. When not injured the veterans gave excellent service; M.R. Pattenden, P.J. Allen, R.V. Vaughan, R.W. Kelly, S. Cameron and D.E. Wood (Captain) were the backbone of the 1st team without whom success would have been impossible. Even so they managed to win 8 of their 10 games.

There was excitement during the summer, when it was announced that an Old Boy, Lt. Morville Chote, had been selected to represent Great Britain at throwing the javelin in the 1948 London Olympic Games. It was 20 years since another Old Boy, Brian Oddie, had taken part in the 1928 Olympic Games. At Cambridge in 1943, Chote had thrown 163ft 6ins, qualifying for a full Blue standard of pre-war times, and membership of the Achilles Club. Following military service in India and Bangalore, he returned to England in 1947, just prior to Indian Independence, and rejoined the British athletics scene. He became the first Englishman to throw more than 200ft, with a throw of 203ft 3ins, beating his long-time Bedfordshire rival, Malcolm Dalrymple (son of Mr 'Jock' Dalrymple, the School's athletics coach in the 1930s), by 9ins. Both young men were chosen for the British team in the Olympics,

The joint High School - Grammar School Dramatic Society's production of *Pygmalion* by George Bernard Shaw, 14–17th December, 1948. (left to right) David Webb (Pickering), Sheila M. Dean, Joan Scrivener, Geoffrey Ford (Higgins), Patricia Kershaw, Dianne Hudson (Eliza), Joyce Chapman, Reginald Vaughan. (*LN*)

but sadly neither managed to qualify.

In September David J. Atkinson (U.VI Sc.) went to Quebec, Canada with the Public Schools Exploration Society (now the British School Exploration Society), where he experienced eating squirrels, sparrow hawks and woodpeckers, and enjoyed aqua-planing on Lake St John. The only outside news he heard during six weeks was that the violinist, Albert Sandler, had died, and that England were all out for 52!

The Dramatic Societies of the Grammar and High Schools joined for a production of Bernard Shaw's *Pygmalion* on the evenings of 14–17th December, 1948. The play, on which the later musical *My Fair Lady* was based, was much more demanding than the previous year's *Romantic Young Lady*. H.D.W. reviewed the play in *The Luton News*:

> 'It is a good, and as one would expect, scholarly *Pygmalion*, most of the players keeping well within their parts. They do not get all the laughs that would be drawn from a more experienced company, and are a little at sea in the less comic and more argumentative parts of the play. Dianne Hudson takes Eliza Doolittle's rise from the gutter to the garden party without faltering, and Geoffrey Ford makes a flamboyant attack on the role of the petulant Professor Henry Higgins.'

Gretchen Butcher alternated with Dianne Hudson as Eliza Doolittle. David Webb, as Colonel Pickering, was an excellent foil to Geoffrey Ford's Professor Higgins, but

to many, the *pièce de résistance* was Peter Townsend's performance as Alfred Doolittle, the Cockney dustman, the victim of 'middle-class morality'. The production was again by Kathleen Hudson and Henry Williams.

The following Easter, after the success of *Pygmalion*, the joint societies entered a one-act play competition in Harpenden. They chose a thriller called *Shall we join the ladies?* by J.M. Barrie, and were delighted when they won the junior trophy.

Through the Dramatic Society and the Literary and Scientific Society the barriers between the Grammar School and the Girls' High School were slowly breaking down. Mrs Evans' rule was still strict, but it was no longer a mortal sin for a girl to speak to a boy in the street, provided of course that more than a modicum of decorum was observed. Wardown Park was a convenient after-school trysting place, the downs at Chaul End more private, egg-heads preferred the Public Library, but on Saturday mornings the *only* place to meet was the Bute Street Milk-Bar with its 'contemporary' décor, juke-box, Coca-Cola and espresso coffee machine.

Food was under consideration at the end of the winter term. The County Council informed Mr Webb that the cost of School lunches must be reduced from 2s 6d per week to 2s 0d to bring them into line with the rest of the County schools. Mr Webb anticipated trouble from parents thinking that it would mean a reduction in quality and quantity. Fortunately no complaints were recorded.

Mrs F. Sankey, the Canteen Supervisor since 1940, retired at Christmas. She was most embarrassed to be called onto the stage at the end of term Assembly, to be presented with a coffee percolator by R.V. Vaughan, the Head Boy. She was not certain if the three hearty cheers she received from the boys were because they were glad or sorry that she was leaving!

In December 1948, the Head Prefect, R.V. Vaughan, presented a coffee percolator to Mrs Sankey, who retired, after being canteen supervisor for eight years. (*LN*)

The Memorial Organ – 1949

Late in 1947 workmen from John T. Garrett and Sons, the Builders of Cowper Street, Luton, removed the central window on the east side of the Assembly Hall and constructed an organ chamber in its place. This they had completed by March 1948, but installation of the organ was delayed due to Board of Trade regulations. It seemed to take an interminable time until 14th January, 1949, when the first consignment of the actul organ parts were received. The rest swiftly followed, and six weeks later Mr Henry Willis, the organ builder, came to check the instrument. The console was placed close to the stage on the west side, and the intricate electrical wiring ran under the stage so as not to damage the Hall's sprung floor.

The dedication of the organ was probably the most important event of 1949. On 30th March, a gathering of parents and relations of Old Boys joined with the boys of the School for a solemn and impressive service, during which the organ was dedicated to Clifford Lloyd Brown Janes, an old boy of the School who was killed on Active Service near Tripoli in July 1943.

The service was opened by the Headmaster, who described the purpose of the gathering and said something of Clifford Janes as a boy. This was followed by the hymn 'For those we love within the veil, who once were comrades of our way', and afterwards the Head Boy, Reginald V. Vaughan, read a passage from Bunyan's *The Pilgrim's Progress*. Councillor H.C. Janes then made the presentation. He spoke of his son, saying that as a boy at Park Square he had enjoyed playing the old organ there. From his youngest days he had been thrifty, and by the time of his death he had saved an appreciable sum of money. That money was the beginning of the organ fund, and the organ was truly his memorial. 'Clifford was not conscripted. He was a volunteer. He was one like so many others who in the early days of the war felt that everything must be forsaken in order to fight for freedom.'

The Plaque was unveiled and read by Mrs Marjorie White, eldest sister of the boy to whom the organ is dedicated. At the conclusion of the ceremony, Dr John H. Burgoyne, a school friend of Clifford Janes, played Walford Davies' 'A Solemn Melody', after which Cllr. Herbert R. Waller, speaking on behalf of the School and the authorities, accepted the organ. Prayers were then said by the Headmaster and the assembly sang Isaac Watt's hymn, 'O God, our help in ages past'. After God's blessing had been asked, the 'Marcia Religiosa' from Rheinberger's Sixth Organ Sonata was played by Dr Burgoyne as the assembly left the hall.

The Memorial Organ was dedicated on 30th March, 1949, to the memory of Clifford L.B. Janes, who was killed on active service on 25th July, 1943. Clifford's friend, Dr J.H. Burgoyne, is seated at the console (below), in front of Herbert C. Janes, who presented the organ, and Herbert R. Waller, an Old Boy and Governor. (*LN-LMC*) The pipes are located on the east wall of the Hall (right). (Inset opposite) Flt. Sgt. Clifford Janes, who was always in mischief at school. (*R.. Janes*)

The plaque on the Organ is inscribed:
TO THE GLORY OF GOD
AND IN ABIDING MEMORY OF
CLIFFORD LLOYD BROWN JANES
KILLED ON ACTIVE SERVICE 25 JULY 1943
THIS ORGAN IS THE GIFT OF HIS FATHER H. C. JANES

The Memorial Organ had once stood in a London church. It was the work of Henry Willis and Son, the most famous of organ builders, who rebuilt it before it was installed in the School in 1949. Such delicate precision instruments need constant care and attention, and it was overhauled and again partly rebuilt in the summer of 1963 using the remainder of the School's Memorial Fund. In 1996 advantage was taken of the opportunity to restore the instrument by substituting three stops on the great for rather brighter stops to make it more suitable for the performance of 18th century music. These new stops are trumpet (8´), larigot and sesquialtera (2 ranks). The restoration was once more generously supported by the Janes family.

The only Staff change during 1949 was the appointment of Mr G. Charles Grimshaw to take physical training and games. Miss Dorothy Baxter, the Headmaster's secretary since 1945, left in June to marry Brian Brightman (LMS 1936–42). Her place was filled by Miss Olga Peters, who was joined in the office by Miss Margaret Luhr. Mrs Dorothy Monk began her appointment as the new Canteen Supervisor in January. Mr W. Roberts, head groundsman, retired after twenty-two years. During that time he had converted rough grassland, single-handed, into a cricket table at Chaul End, and attempted the same at Bradgers Hill, where the clay and flints were always against him.

Speech Day was held on 9th March, when the distinguished visitors were Sir Bernard and Lady Paget. Sir Bernard's advice to the boys was 'Always learn to understand the other person's point of view, though not necessarily agreeing with it.'

The Headmaster, in his address, lamented the fact that 1950 would be the last year in the long and useful life of the old style School Certificate. An age bar would operate, prohibiting boys from sitting it if they were not 16 by 1st December, 1950. In 1951 the General Certificate of Education would replace both School and Higher School Certificates and boys would have to be 16 by 1st September, 1951, to take any subject at any level. 'I would say that the chronological age of a boy is no better criterion of his readiness to do work of a certain quality and take an examination of a certain standard than is the length of his foot,' Mr Webb wryly observed.

He spoke of the successes in the 1948 Higher School Certificate gained by Denis V. Mardle and Victor E. Raymond under the greatest of physical disabilities. The State Scholarships of Mardle, D.C. Price and K.G. Henson, and the Scholarship of P.D. Townsend to Trinity College, Cambridge, together with the Royal Scholarship of D.G. Gray received special mention.

The School shared a little reflected glory from 16 years old Denis G. Wick, its self-taught expert trombonist, who, having received the highest marks in Great Britain in the Grade VII music exam of the Associated Board, had been awarded the Gold Medal of the Royal Academy of Music. Wick went on to study at the Royal Academy for a year, but found it unfulfilling, so joined the Bournemouth Symphony Orchestra at 19, and progressed by way of the Birmingham Symphony Orchestra to

Cross Country Team, 1949. (back) P.B. Hart, F.H. Bailey, D.J. Atkinson, P.E. Hall, G.G. Francis, J.M. Sells, (front) C. Alderman, D.G. Gill, R.A. McDonald, (Captain), J. Lawrence, B. Buckingham. (*LN*)

the London Symphony Orchestra, with whom he played for 31 years, for the greater part as principal trombone.

Sam R.B. 'Butch' Thurlow captained a very successful 1st XI Football team in 1949. Out of ten matches played, only two were lost. The 2nd Eleven completed a third season unbeaten. The team had been captained for two years by B.E. Smith.

The Cross-Country runners faced an average season in seven matches against other schools, winning 4 and losing 3. In the Bedfordshire AAA Championships on 26th February, the Youths (14–16) came first, with arch-rivals Bedford Modern School second. The Junior team (16–19) came 4th, with Derek Gill the individual winner. Grasshoppers won the Wild Cup for inter-house cross-country.

Boxing, a sport that had been quietly practised at the School since 1944, came to prominence on 25th March, 1949 when the first Inter-House Tournament was staged in the Hall. Mr Chapman and Mr Muse were amply rewarded for the time and energy they had devoted to promoting the sport. The Amy Shore Cup for Inter-House Boxing was won by the Wasps. The Cup had been presented by Arthur P. Shore, a great friend and supporter of all School events, who ran a small Nursery

Garden at the foot of Bradgers Hill. Jim Bazely was the very active Captain for the 1949 season. The Secretary was Clive J. Howe, who had boxed since the age of 9, and went on to become Chairman of the Vauxhall Motors Boxing Section for 24 years. He was Team Manager of the England ABA team from 1972 until 2002. In 1986 he was elected President of the European Amateur Boxing Association. In the same year Dudley Wood became Secretary of the Rugby Football Union and Jack Walters, Chairman of the British Athletics League and a member of the European Club Championships Organising Committee.

Sports Day, on 26th May, 1949, was held under almost arctic conditions, resulting in times and distances recorded being below expectations, inspite of intensive work on the part of the new sports master, Mr John Muse. Even so, three new records were established and two equalled. In the One Mile (Open) 1st Derek G. Gill (4 min 50.6 secs) and 2nd John Lawrence both broke the School record. Ronald W. Kelly broke the Weight record with a put of 43ft 9ins., and the Hornets Senior Relay (4 x 110 yds) was run in a record 49.6 secs. Gill, in the 880 Yards Open, and Harry Maughan, in the (u.14) High Jump, both equalled the School records. Maughan had four firsts in Under 14 events. R.W. Kelly scored the maximum number of points permissible to become *Victor Ludorum*.

In 1949 the 1st XI Cricket team lost only two matches against other schools, and the standard of play was encouraging. Barry Robinson proved a very enthusiastic and efficient Captain both on and off the field. Sam 'Butch' Thurlow left at the end of term, having played in the 1st XI for six season and taken nearly 200 wickets – an all time record in the School's history.

Due to the initiative of J.M. Southgate and a few other senior boys, the Inter-House Swimming Sports were revived on 22nd June, 1949. The Open Air Baths were far from ideal from a temperature point of view, and sport on the whole was of a very poor standard, only serving to reinforce the School's need for it own pool.

The 1949 season was calamitous for Rugby, the 1st XV winning only three games out of nine, and those by small margins. The injuries were calamitous also. Reg V. Vaughan, the captain, played in the first match only and Aubrey Ironmonger, the vice-captain, only in the second half of the term. Peter Bonner, who was playing very well, broke his leg in the second match. The home game against Dunstable was the most satisfying of the season: fast and open with a score of 24–5. Ironmonger took over the captaincy in mid-season and proved a tower of strength to the team from then on, kicking the opportune dropped goal by which the team also won the return match at Dunstable 3–0. The School pack was out weighted against the Old Boys: the final score: School 0, Old Boys 41.

During the year a special necktie, to be worn by holders of Colours in any sport, was introduced. The design consisted of narrow stripes of red and yellow on a blue background.

On 7th May, Mr Godfrey organised a concert in aid of the Victoria League. The

artists, who gave their service freely, were Eileen Croxford (Cello), Edith Lewin (Singer), Harry Mortimer (Cornet and Trumpet) and Augustus Lowe (at the Memorial Organ).

The School Library continued to function efficiently with its team of nine Librarians. Different forms used it as a reading room during lunch breaks, where they could consult the wide range of magazines. Readers may remember *The Illustrated London News, The Listener, Mechanics, Boys' Own Paper, The National Geographic Magazine, The Children's Newspaper, John o' London's Weekly, Hobbies, Discovery, La France* and *The Bedfordshire Magazine.* Mr S. C. Hayne presented the complete 24 volume set of the *Encyclopaedia Britannica*, in memory of his son John Hayne, who was at the School from 1941–46.

Clothes rationing came to an end in 1949 and it was decided to reintroduce the School Uniform from September 1950. In fact the rule about wearing the uniform had never been rescinded, but, of course, no attempt was made to enforce it during the war years. As clothes wore out, parents were asked to replace them with regulation articles. The Prefects, it was noted, were setting an excellent example; nine out of seventeen were in uniform for the official 1949 Prefects' photograph.

A discordant note was sounded in July when the Council announced that it proposed to build houses on the land surrounding the School. Mr Geoffrey Clarke, in his Editorial for *The Lutonian*, wrote:

> 'The playing field appears very large – out of school hours! When, however, it is remembered that the school was designed for 450 boys and now houses 700, the size does not appear too great. Some day we hope to have a swimming bath and tennis courts, and space will have to be found for them. If houses have been built round the school field, the space can only come from the present playing area. And is the present uninterrupted view of Stopsley Common and Warden Hill of no value? Would the backs of houses, tool-sheds and clothes-lines be as good to look at?'

Opposition was mounted by Mr G.L. Hey, a chemist and former Stopsley Councillor, and David A. Webb (Prefect) wrote to *The Luton News*, observing that:

> 'The beauty of the view is continually remarked upon by visitors. With plenty of other land available, why 'hem in' as lovely a situation as that of Luton Grammar School?'

Old boy David F. Harrowell (LMS 1940–48) wrote from King's College, London, to the newspaper, supporting David Webb's letter and observing that 'the area was being destroyed by 'get rich quick' builders.' Not everyone agreed; one writer pointed out that the boys did not spend enough time at the School each day to enjoy

the scenery. Others, he suggested, should be allowed to see it from new houses.

Looking back, from 2004, we can see how lucky those of us who were students in 1949 really were. Bushmead Road, constructed in 1937, was originally intended to become a trunk road linking the A6 with the A505 east of Stopsley. The war stopped that development, but the road existed, and it was inevitable that houses would eventually be built along both sides, and in adjoining Fairford Avenue. No one in 1949 could have envisaged the great sprawling Bushmead development that would eventually engulf the land to the north in the 1980s and 90s, or the horrendous accretions that would deface Turock's 'Modern School' design of 1938 in order to extend the Sixth Form College. Gone are the corn fields, the green lanes and the cross-country course, for ever.

Three boys, D.A. Webb, W.D. Waller and B.E. Smith were members of a Luton Youth Club team which took part in a spelling contest with other Youth Club teams in a BBC programme called, 'Oh for a Dictionary!' The contest was a 'knockout' one and the Luton competitors survived for three rounds.

In the last week of the summer term 'Major' H.B. Evans took a party of boys, mostly from IVc, to London for a tour of the Houses of Parliament, guided by Mr William Warbey, Luton's MP. After a picnic lunch on Parliament Green, during which a few boys visited Westminster Abbey, the party proceeded to the Colonial Exhibition, it being Colonial Month in London.

During the summer holidays Mr Parry took a group of 16 boys to Tours, in the Loire valley, staying in a vast 13th century castle-like structure called the Hôtel de la Croix-Blanche. Jeanne, the motherly lady who waited at table, was quick to christen Mr Parry, in his black blazer and beret, 'le petit homme noir'. Visits were made to numerous châteaux, of which Chambord, with its fantastic chimneys, made the greatest impression. That it was only four years since the war was very evident. Many buildings were still in ruins, and bridges over the Loire destroyed. At Chaumont a temporary rope footbridge crossed the river, and the party quickly discovered that walking in step made it swing violently from side to side.

In August Peter L. Isherwood, 17, passed the ATCL examination for organ playing at the earliest age permitted. He had played the organ since he was 13, and had won a silver medal for piano at Trinity College when he was 15. In his free time he was assistant organist at Christ Church, Luton.

On three consecutive Tuesdays in September the School Hall was used by the BBC to broadcast a programme before an invited audience, called 'First House', featuring the Luton Girls' Choir, with Louis Steven, violinist, Ivor Dennis, piano, and Augustus Lowe playing the Memorial Organ.

The Sixth Form were privileged to listen to a talk on 'Penal Reform' by Miss Cicely M. Craven, JP, secretary of the Howard League. Speaking before the abolition of capital punishment for murder in 1965, she described the State as corrupt, since it treated criminals in the same way that criminals treat their fellow-men. She

David Webb's set for the ambulatory in Rheims cathedral. A scene from Shaw's *St Joan*,
performed at the School, 13 – 16 December, 1949. (l. to r.) the Dauphin (J. Dyer), Dunois (R.V.
Vaughan), Joan (Gretchen Butcher), Archbishop (P.L. Isherwood), La Hire (K.L. Earey), Bluebeard
(C. Somers). (*LN-LMC*)

stressed that the object of punishment should not be retribution but correction, and
she talked of reforms already being carried out in a few open prisons in Britain and
in Sweden.

Members of the Lower Sixth found themselves potato picking for Mr Shaw at
Manor Farm, Stopsley, during the first week in October.

The Literary and Scientific Society paid its annual visit to the High School to
debate the motion that 'The Pilgrim Fathers landed on the Plymouth Rock. In the
opinion of the house it would have been better if the Plymouth Rock had landed on
the Pilgrim Fathers'. Proposed and seconded by Audrey Bone and D.G. Gill, and
opposed by W.D. Waller and Jean Spink, the motion was defeated by a large
majority. A Balloon Debate, Mock Election and Brains Trust were all well supported
during the year.

The Joint High School and Grammar School Dramatic Societies presented what
was probably the most ambitious of all their productions on 13th–16th December,
1949: George Bernard Shaw's *St Joan*. Rather strangely, the 'review' of the
production in both Schools' magazines was by one of the producers, Kathleen
Hudson, and was felt by some to be rather biased. She wrote: 'The major part of Joan

was beautifully played with great sincerity and simplicity by Gretchen Butcher. All the other main parts were for the boys. David Webb, as Bishop Cauchon, gave an equally sincere performance, using every speech and movement of his body to display the fanaticism and zeal of ardent Roman Catholicism. Geoffrey Ford was admirable as the dilettante Earl of Warwick, though less believable perhaps as a leader of men. Peter Isherwood as the arrogant Archbishop of Rheims, and John Hopkins as the Inquisitor, with his difficult seven minute speech during the Trial Scene, were both thoroughly convincing. James Dyer invented oddities and exaggerated some of his own to achieve the extreme characteristion required to portray a very good Dauphin. The clever and simple settings, also by David Webb, were effective as well as being practical.' Henry Williams co-produced the play.

The year ended with a screening of the Australian film *The Overlanders* (1946) on 22nd December, followed in the afternoon by the annual Carol Service and dismissal. The familiar band of helpers went off to the General Post Office to help sort and deliver the Christmas Mail.

Senior boys helped sort Christmas mail throughout the War and for some time afterwards. This picture dates from December, 1949.(LN-LMC)

Chapter 12

The Challenge of the Fifties

There was a mood of anticipation in the air when the century reached its mid-point. Britain was beginning to emerge from post-war austerity and the Festival of Britain was about to take the country by storm. Jeffrey Greenleaf, (LGS 1952–59), has written:

'In the early 50s few people owned cars or television. Refrigerators, washing machines, and vacuum cleaners were almost unknown. During those years we were to see the introduction of all of these to a mass market. Those years marked the introduction of the transistor, jet airliners, the breaking of the sound barrier, and the first venture into space with the launch of the Sputnik. Harnessing atomic energy from fission, and also from fusion by means of the Zeta torus, promised unlimited cheap clean power. This was a time of immense optimism for the opportunity and power to be provided by science. At Luton Grammar School this was supported by some outstanding teaching in mathematics and the sciences, resulting in high levels of enthusiasm and achievement.'

But for the School the Spring Term, 1950, began on a sad note. One of the junior boys, Keith Batchelor (IIb), was killed in a cycling accident in Upper George Street at 6pm on Tuesday, 10th January. The following Friday morning the whole School filed past a wreath, which staff and School friends took to Keith's funeral on 14th January. Keith had been a keen boxer, and his father presented a Cup to the School for Junior Inter-House Boxing in memory of his son. In March the Grasshoppers were the first house to hold it. R. Ashby of V Sc. 2, who had been ill for some months, died in hospital on Good Friday.

Sadness of another kind was recorded with the retirement of James William

Mr J.W. Findlater as seen by A.W. Martin.

Findlater who had served on the School staff for 34 years. Born in Newcastle in 1884, 'Finny' had joined the School as Senior English Master in 1916. He had officially retired in 1945, but carried on part-time until July 1950. With degrees from the Universities of Durham and Cambridge, he first taught history at Bede Collegiate Boys' School, Sunderland, from 1907–16. In his early years in Luton he also taught history, but this was dropped soon after Thomas P. Clarke joined the staff in 1930, and he concentrated on English. He was an excellent teacher and gentle disciplinarian, and enjoyed playing in the School orchestra. Ronald Phillips wrote:

'we used to see him in the chair by the Staff Room fireside, pipe in mouth, steadily correcting a batch of exercises. He knew the value of attention to detail and did not neglect the dotting of 'i's and crossing of 't's. Slipshod or shoddy work of any kind, whether in the mechanical details of handwriting or in the composition of a Sixth Form essay, was abhorrent to him.'

His wife, Dora, died after a long illness in 1928, and it was not until the beginning of the war that he remarried, his new wife being the mother of the Head Boy, Derek W.H. Sharp and his brother Brian N.H. Sharp. 'Finny' was killed in a road accident at Coleshill, near Birmingham, on 14th August, 1954, and was mourned by T.A.E. Sanderson and many of his colleagues and old boys, who attended his funeral which was conducted by Canon Davison.

J. W. F.

Funny! I can't believe it . . .
To meet his end on the Open Road he loved
So well to cycle to the North Countrie.

He taught us, crude and callow youth,

To love the things he loved;

Particularly Shakespeare as I recollect.

(No easy job that was).

And Literature –

Palgrave's 'Golden Treasury' and some History.

But that's not all. There emanated

(When Finny, fancy free,

From his radiator leaning meanfully)

Something else. We couldn't always place it

Until long afterwards. What was it?

He had the gift of getting the talent

Each of us had to give in his small way.

(That's your true teacher!)

Once, I remember, in our class mag.

Which he inspired ('The Flying Post'),

He wrote our epitaphs

In comic verse so apposite.

Now we've got to write his . . .

What can we say?

"God bless him".

[Abridged, E.M.O. 1914–20]

Captain S.H. Starey, DL, County Commissioner for Scouting, was the Guest of Honour at Speech Day, on 15th February, 1950. After the Headmaster's report, Mrs Starey distributed the prizes.

In the 1949 examinations 83 Boys gained School Certificates and 42 Higher School Certificates. David J. Atkinson was awarded the Royal Dutch-Shell Scholarship in geology at Imperial College, London. It was the only one awarded that year, but the second to come to Luton Grammar School, M.J. Barber having received it in 1945. Mr Cleaver's determination to teach geology, which had only been on the syllabus for the past five years, was well rewarded. B.E. Smith had been placed on the reserve list for a State Scholarship. Eight boys had been accepted for University entrance.

Medical and dental inspections were carried out at regular intervals during the life of the School, usually in the PT Instructor's room. At intervals throughout Wednesday, 1st March, 1950, a procession of boys made their way to the Corn Exchange (now demolished, at the south end of George Street) to be X-rayed as part of a nation-wide scheme to identify and eradicate tuberculosis.

On 26th May, the film *Great Expectations* was screened in the Hall for the benefit of School Certificate candidates, who were joined by classes from the High School.

The Senior boys visited the Odeon Cinema to see Lawrence Olivier's *Hamlet*, and many older boys visited London theatres as members of coach parties organised by Miss Hudson of the High School. These included *Hamlet, Peer Gynt, Ring Round the Moon,* and Olivier in a brilliant production of *The School for Scandal.*

The most flourishing part of the Home and School Association was the Tuesday Old Time Dancing Class. In October 183 people attended a Social, the largest number ever, and severely taxed the caterers, as only 30 had bought tickets in advance.

Only three months after the triumph of *St Joan,* the joint Dramatic Societies presented *Housemaster* by Ian Hay on 14–17th March. It was to be a swan-song for Kathleen Hudson as the Schools' producer, and a vehicle for David Webb to show his remarkable talent as an actor. It was the first time that members of staff and students had appeared in a production together and it worked extremely well. David's performance as the Housemaster, Mr Donkin, was so convincing that many people in the audience were unaware that the actor was a boy, and some, confusing the names, believed that it was the Headmaster! Miss Hudson wrote:

> 'His voice, gesture, hesitations of manner, and most of all his rigidity of body, all helped to convey a sense of age. It is not enough to look old in feature and sound old in voice, if the body has the vigour and elasticity of youth. Every time the Housemaster sat down, his body expressed the setness of age. As was to be expected of David Webb, he "made" almost every one of his laughs, by expertness of timing and judicially pointed phrasing. It was an epic last performance.'

David Sturman performed superbly as Old Crump, as did Margaret Thomas and Mary Blake as the two girls, Rosemary and Chris. The twins, Button and Bimbo, played by Jacqueline Hargraves and Kenneth Gregory, enjoyed life enormously. The staff actors were more than competent, Miss Wood was a breezy delight, Henry Williams uncharacteristically tight-lipped and sarcastic and Geoffrey Clarke looked exactly like Charles Hill, Luton's newly elected MP.

During the Easter Holidays eight of the most senior boys joined students from all over England on a 'Cultural Holiday' in Paris organised by Huntingdon Grammar School. The objects of the course were to see and learn something of Paris and the French, and to do a little work under professors of the Sorbonne and the staff of the Lycée Saint-Louis. Most of the boys felt that they had improved their French, and had helped the waiters at the Lycée Lakenal in Sceaux, where they stayed, to learn such useful English phrases as 'I love you' and 'a kees'.

News of School Societies was thin on the ground in 1950, *The Lutonian* only containing news of four of them. The Chess Club enjoyed a reasonably successful season, with two of its members, H.M. Swallow and C.G.H. Abrahams, being chosen to represent the County team. The Railway Club paid a visit to the Stratford

Housemaster by Ian Hay, performed by staff and pupils from the Grammar and High Schools, in March 1950. (l. to r.) J. Hopkins, Jacqueline Hargreaves, I. Plummer, K. Gregory, Miss J.M. Wood, H.B. Williams, Margaret Thomas, Mary Blake, B. Robinson, D. Webb. *(LN)*

locomotive works and running sheds. Sixty-eight players entered the Table Tennis Club Championship, which was full of surprises as one by one the 'strong' players were laid low. D.J. Lowe of IIIa (age 13) was the youngest player to enter the Final, where he was beaten 3–0 by G. Bard of Vb. A new group, the Archaeological Society, was formed in February, and visited various ancient monuments in south Bedfordshire. During a very wet spell at the end of August, eight boys joined a training excavation at Dorchester-on-Thames in Oxfordshire. Rained out of their tents, they 'camped' in a nearby mill for a fortnight, and helped to uncover a neolithic henge monument, some 5000 years old.

In Football the 1st XI played well as a team. With no *prima donnas* the whole eleven were more uniformly matched than usual, which may have accounted for the good standard of play. The game against the Old Boys, which was drawn 4–4, proved the most exciting, though unfortunately Roy I. Brittain, the captain, missed it through illness.

The Cross-Country team, under Derek Gill's captaincy, had its most successful season to date, suffering only one defeat – at the hands of St Albans in a three-

Association Football 1st XI, 1950. (back row): the Headmaster, C.G.H. Abrahams, M.J. Sansome, G. Bewes, J. Clifford, K.T. Norcott, P. Gillis, Mr Grayston, (centre) A.W. Wilkins, B.D. Robinson, R.T. Brittain (Captain), M. Jones, G.M. Rowlands, (front) W.H. Hosler, A.A.G. Evans. (*LN-LMC*)

cornered fixture run in Luton. The greatest achievement was to provide the first seven men home in a race against Hertford Grammar School. Gill won six of the seven races in which he ran, and M.J. Bracey and P.B. Hart provided excellent support.

Considerable interest was shown in Athletics in 1950, and this was evident on Sports Day, on 24th May, when no fewer than twelve records were broken. Three were by Brian A. Clark in the Discus, Javelin and Shot, and Mick Bracey ran the 880 yds (u.16) in 2 min 9.6 secs which was 0.4 secs faster than the Open record, set up by Gill. The *Victor Ludorum* was J. Clifford, who broke the Open 440 yds record in 56.2 secs. There was less success in the Bedfordshire AAA Championships, but the School had two County Champions in Clifford (Junior 440 yds) and Gill (Mile).

Mr Parry considered the 1950 Cricket season one of the most successful the 1st XI had enjoyed in the past decade. Only one match was lost of the fourteen played. Mr Glyn Owen, the Coach, considered the batting potential greater than he had ever known, and he wasn't mistaken. Captain Barry Robinson scored over 300 runs, and several younger batsmen scored freely. A.T. Andrews was the most consistent of the newcomers, whilst Geoffrey Bewes, Rex Fardon and the Norcott brothers (Keith and Raymond) all made useful scores. Chief bowling honours went to Vice-Captain Malcolm Jones and Anthony A.G. Evans, who took nearly a hundred wickets between them, and the fielding of Hugh M. Swallow at short-leg was often brilliant.

The Swimming Sports were held at the Open Air Pool on Tuesday, 18th July. Mr

OPPOSITE The joint Schools' production of Shakespeare's *Twelfth Night*, December 1950. (*LN*)

Grimshaw had arranged a more ambitious programme than any before. Entries were more numerous, though the general standard lagged far behind that of the Waller Street Baths days. This was the first year that 1st form boys had had swimming lessons during PT and OG periods. The Old Boys' Cup was won by the Hornets.

Mr Grimshaw was also instrumental in setting up a Basketball Club, but without the proper equipment the School team was always at a disadvantage, and were soundly thrashed in games against Hertford Grammar School.

The 1950 Rugby season was a difficult one. The 1st XV was not well equipped for defensive play. The two wing threes were neither of them strong in defence and the first full back was definitely weak, until replaced by Brain Shortland who was more reliable. The main burden of the defence fell upon the captain, Barry Robinson, who bore it extremely well. In five games out of eleven the School did not score a single point, but matters improved in the last five matches with the score of 25 points for and 30 against.

The United Nations flag flew over the School throughout the week commencing 23rd October and special services relating to the work of that organisation were held.

1950 ended with the Joint Dramatic Societies presentation of Shakespeare's *Twelfth Night* on 4th to 7th December. Miss Hudson having left the High School, Miss Gladys Brown joined Mr Williams as co-producer. The anonymous reviewer in *The Lutonian* (probably C.W.P.) wrote:

> 'The Aguecheek of David Sturman was delightful; he was acting all the time he was on the stage and never fell into the rigid immobility which so often afflicts youthful actors when they are not actually speaking. Peter Isherwood made an excellent Malvolio and was so much the vain and pompous prig that we all rejoiced at his undoing at the hands of Maria and Sir Toby. Haydn Thompson played Sir

Toby with gusto and Pamella Jollye was a vivacious Maria; their doings below stairs were an admirable foil to the romantic behaviour of their betters. John Lawrence as Orsino "mooned" effectively and Pamela Smith gave us an Olivia full of charm and dignity. Janice Swallow played Viola and spoke some of Shakespeare's most lovely lines beautifully. Cyril Somers acquitted himself well in the role of the fool, Feste, and gave great pleasure by his singing of the charming lyrics.'

Cyril Somers, whose singing in morning assembly was equally memorable, later joined the Covent Garden Opera Company. In 1959 he began a 12 year association with the prestigious BBC Chorus. One of the musicians accompanying the play was Dudley Whiting. Out of School he was one of the Troubadour Trio, who won the All-England Cup for trio playing in the British Federation of Mandolin and Guitar Championships held in St Pancras Town Hall: Whiting also won the All-England Cup for mandolin solos, scoring ninety-four marks out of a possible hundred. He also made a number of broadcasts.

Festival of Britain Year – 1951

'Conceived among the untidied ruins of war and fashioned through days of harsh economy, this Festival is a challenge to the sloughs of the present and a shaft of confidence cast forth against the future.'

[Festival of Britain, Official Programme]

Opened by the King and Queen in London on the 2nd May, and with exhibitions and activities taking place all over Britain until the end of September, it promised to be an exciting year. Unfortunately for the older boys at the School the opening of the Festival coincided with examinations. For those in Years I and II it was a chance to travel by special train to London. On a gloriously sunny 15th June they visited the South Bank exhibition with its 27 acres of pavilions displaying British achievements in science, technology and industrial design. In the Dome of Discovery they watched the return of radar impulses that had been beamed from the top of the nearby Shot Tower and reflected from the moon. Little did they know that within their lifetimes man would walk on the moon and photograph the surface of Mars.

Some forty boys, accompanied by Messrs. Parry, Partridge, and Watson, spent Easter in Paris. France was in the grip of a nation-wide transport strike and Army lorries were being used for transport. As well as visiting the traditional sights of the city, they met some interesting characters, including one who claimed to have shot down Goering in the Great War, and another who plied them with quantities of drink and cigarettes and invited them to come and stay at his home in the summer.

A graphic account of the Paris holiday in *The Lutonian* was written by Ian Brodie, assisted by David Oldroyd. Brodie left School the following year to become a

reporter on *The Luton News*, and progressing as a reporter and foreign editor by way of the *Daily Sketch* and *Daily Express* to editor of the *Scottish Daily Express*. As a foreign correspondent he worked in Moscow, Vietnam, and New York. After a spell with the *Daily Telegraph* in Los Angeles and Washington, he completed his career as *The Times* correspondent in Washington, and was honoured by the Queen with an OBE for 'services to journalism'. He now lives in Bethesda, Maryland.

Leslie Watkins left the School in 1947 to become a journalist with *The Luton News*, the *Daily Sketch* and *Daily Mail*. A successful writer of fiction based on fact, his books included *The Killing of Idi Amin*, *The Unexploded Man*, dedicated to C.W. Parry, and the highly controversial *Alternative 3*. He emigrated to New Zealand in the mid-1980s.

Neil Shand left LGS in 1950 also to work on *The Luton News*, prior to joining the *Daily Mail* and *Daily Express*. He eventually broke into TV, at first in Current Affairs and later as a comedy script writer for Spike Milligan, Ronnie Corbett and Kenny Everett.

Another boy of the School, Roger Jones (L.VI Sc.), left Southampton with his family on 23rd December, 1950, bound for Sydney and a new life in Australia. He described his journey at length for the School Magazine. His story of what happened next is typical of hundreds of Old Lutonians who made their way to countries of the Commonwealth. Roger Jones took up surveying, working for the Victoria Dept. of Lands and Survey, and then for the State Electricity Commission of Victoria. In 1962 he moved to New Guinea, 'a virtually untouched land, where we camped in the jungle, reconnoitred routes for roads in country where you were battling to walk much less drive a vehicle. I supervised their construction, sought out places for airfields and worked out ideas for small hydro-electric schemes. I was almost a law unto myself.' With a growing family and a need for good schools, he returned to New South Wales and the Water Resources Commission based at Bega, which acted as a consulting service for farmers and graziers requiring advice on all aspects of water supply. He retired at 55, and became a lay preacher and acting Pastor of his local Presbyterian Church.

One of Roger Jones' contemporaries, Phil Patterson, was the first man to sail across the Atlantic in a trimaran (which he had designed himself). With a friend, he sailed from Fort Chimo in north Quebec 3,750 miles to Ardrossan in Ayrshire, taking 55 days.

On Speech Day, 7th February, the prizes and trophies were presented by Mrs Walton, and afterwards Captain F. Michael Walton, RN, who until recently had been Director of the Naval Weather Service and had commanded *H.M.S. Diadem* from 1946 to 1948, addressed the gathering, particularly delighting the younger boys with stories of his cat's adventures at sea.

Sixty-six candidates gained School Certificates in 1950, twenty-nine qualifying for Matriculation exemption. Forty-one boys gained Higher School Certificates.

The Cricket 1st XI, 1951. (back) R.R. Chambers (scorer), C.D. Warren, J. Gurney, R.D. Clark, A.J. Osborn, J.J.M. Gillespie, C.C. Glenister, T.C.E. Wells. (front) T.J. Andrews, M. Jones, B.D. Robinson (Capt.), K.T. Norcott, G. Bewes. (*LN*)

M.J. Mitchell and J.H. Towle won State Scholarships, and K.J. Tilling was placed on the reserve list for a State Scholarship. N.E. Bowker qualified for a Scholarship but was too old to hold it.

In April Mr Webb attended a conference on 'School Broadcasting' as the delegate of the Incorporated Association of Headmasters. Speaking before the days when every school had a tape or cassette recorder, he suggested that the BBC should make recordings of their school broadcasts available, so that lessons might be used at other than scheduled times, or for revision purposes. He felt this would be of special value in the study of foreign languages.

Sports Day, 9th May, had to be postponed due to continuous rain, but was held the following day when Mrs Muse presented the trophies. Due to the increase in the number of events from 38 to 51 the whole day was devoted to the Sports. The Pole Vault was introduced for the first time, and B.M. Webster (u.16) achieved a height of 7ft 3ins. The only record broken was by Brian Keech in the Under 13 High Jump with a height of 4ft 5¾ins. Derek Gill was *Victor Ludorum*. At the County AAA Championships at Wardown Park D. Gill, P. Isherwood and B.A. Clark won the Mile, Discus and Shot respectively. At the Luton Schools' Sports the junior boys (u.15) won the Championship Shield which was presented to the captain, Brian C. Sweeney, by the Mayoress of Luton, Mrs R.C. Oakley.

Richard C. Oakley was the first Old Lutonian to be elected Mayor of Luton, on 25th May, 1951. He left Luton Modern School at Christmas, 1914. His father, Albert Oakley, had been Mayor in 1903 and his uncle, Edwin Oakley, was Mayor on

three occasions. He was first elected to the Town Council as an Independent in 1938, but moved to the Conservatives 'to serve the town better as a member of a larger group.' Trained as a chemist, he set up in business as a ribbon dyer, known as Oakley and Jennings, Dyers of Collingdon Street.

The 1st Football XI had only six fixtures. A heavy 2–6 defeat at Bushey was suffered in pouring rain on a very sticky surface. Due to injury, the School, captained again by Barry Robinson, were never able to field their strongest team, and the season ended with 3 wins, 2 defeats and a draw.

The indefatigable Barry Robinson was once more captain of Cricket in 1951. It was considered a reasonably successful season, though the team was not quite so good as that of 1950. Even so, the first five batsmen all scored over 100 runs. Robinson began the season in brilliant form, but a bad patch towards the end prevented him surpassing Derek Wood's aggregate of 372 back in 1945.

Tom B. Vaughan became captain of the 1st XV Rugby team in September. Twenty-four boys were juggled around during the season, trying without much success to find the 'best-fit' team. Though only three out of eleven matches were won, valuable experience was gained.

By April 1951 £4,180 had been raised to provide the School with a Memorial

An exciting moment during a 1st XV Rugby Match against Northampton Grammar School in October 1951, when the School lost 0-33. A. Golding with the ball, is supported by J. Gurney, G. Wray, M. Wallace and L. Young. The Referee is the Scottish International, Dr H.M. Murray.

(LN)

Swimming Pool. The Fund's Joint Management Committee – The Headmaster, three members of the Home and School Association and three members of the Old Lutonians' Club – decided unanimously that it was impossible to build a swimming pool in the foreseeable future owing to the high cost and shortage of materials. The estimated cost was £75,000 and due to the Government giving priority for cement supplies to houses, it was impossible to obtain a building licence. The Committee explored at length alternative suggestions of a running track, additional classrooms, a bursary fund to assist boys at and after leaving the School, and tennis courts.

Following an extraordinary general meeting of the Old Lutonians in April, it was agreed that six hard tennis courts should be accepted as the best alternative memorial to the Boys and Master who fell in World War II, provided that £75, donated to the Fund by Luton Amateur Swimming Club, should be devoted to swimming at the School.

Barry D. Robinson was Head Prefect in 1950–51 and had to supervise the relocation of his colleagues from their eyrie overlooking the playground in the Prefects' Common Room at the end of the Upper Corridor, opposite the Library, to the Arctic Regions of the G.I.R. – the Gym Instructors' Room, next door to the Gym Changing Rooms. It lacked the privacy of the old room, as the PT Masters had to pass through it to enter their own room. Lined with wooden lockers, and filled by a large table and chairs used for lessons, and also used for daily ping-pong tournaments, it was decidedly cramped. In 1951 it was occupied by 14 Prefects, and at times 15 Sub-Prefects, the latter keeping their belongings on the Balcony Parade.

Boys took the first General Certificate of Education (GCE) examinations in July. In the past students had taken the School Certificate, requiring passes in six subjects, and graded very good, credit, pass and fail. Five credits usually meant matriculation exemption. Subjects were taken for the Higher School Certificate at subsidiary, ordinary and advanced standards. One, two or three points were awarded for passes in those standards, and Certificates were awarded for a minimum of six points together with a pass in a General (English) Paper. State Scholarships were awarded on the results of that examination and Universities granted exemptions on it from their Intermediate Degree, First Medical, Dental and Veterinary Examinations.

The new General Certificate of Education replaced both the previous exams. Candidates had to be 16 on 1st September of the year they took the exam. The old School Certificate credit became the new ordinary standard. One or more subjects could be offered and a certificate was issued for even one subject. Holding the GCE in itself meant very little. Its merit depended on the number and quality of its entries. Higher School Certificate grades were replaced by only two standards – advanced and scholarship. The old Matriculation examination was replaced by what was known as the Minimum University Entrance Requirements. Six subjects – three specified – of the GCE were required, two of them being at advanced standard.

Mr Donald E. Sutcliffe joined the English department in September and almost

immediately took over the Editorship of *The Lutonian* from Mr G. Clarke, who had succeeded Mr Parry as Editor in 1947. Mr Parry claimed to be the first Editor to run the Magazine at a loss, a tradition splendidly maintained in subsequent years. From 1948 only one magazine was issued each year, though it grew larger, with Mr Woodcock, and later Mr Muse, editing the sports' pages.

The Railway Club celebrated Festival Year with a memorable outing to the locomotive depots at Peterborough, March and Cambridge, all in one day. With a very tight schedule, they caught all their connections and arrived home safely, confounding the fears of those who said it couldn't be done. Whether it would be possible in 2004 is open to debate!

The Table Tennis Club won four of their six matches against other Clubs. The sixty-five entrants for the Club's Championship Tournament were eventually whittled down to two finalists, Eric Caldecourt and John Lawrence. Caldecourt won convincingly in three straight games, 21–8, 22–20, 21–16.

The Music Club listened to recordings on a brand new Decca Electric Gramophone, which was able to play both long-playing and standard 78rpm records. An Old Boy, Donald I. Burrows, delighted the Club when he brought two of his fellow students to play at the School. This was a trio consisting of Julian Bream, guitar, John Underwood, viola, and Burrows, piano.

The Literary and Scientific Society's annual debate with the High School considered the motion 'That it better to win the one hundred yards open than an open scholarship'. The motion was heavily defeated. The two societies also held a 'Top of the Form' competition in the style of the popular radio show. On March 8th a 'Brains Trust' team consisting of members of the Commonwealth answered questions on the United Nations affairs and topical problems. Mr Webb was the Question Master. The meeting, which was open to the High School girls, closed with votes of thanks from D.G. Gill and E. Gaskin.

The Archaeological Society got into trouble in July when it excavated a neolithic burial mound on Galley Hill, with the permission of the tenant farmer but not the Ministry of Works, who were guardians of the site. A photograph of one of the four skeletons uncovered got into the *Daily Telegraph*, alerting the authorities. Dr Dony, ostensibly responsible, narrowly escaped the Tower of London!

The sixth joint production of the Dramatic Societies of the High School and Grammar School took place on 3rd to 6th December. It was the spirited choice of Molière's famous comedy *The Miser*, adapted by Miles Malleson. Acting honours went to David Sturman as Harpagon, who was on the stage for most of the evening, In his speech, his physiognomy and every movement, he lived the part of the cunning old miser. This was to be H.B. Williams' last production with Gladys Brown.

Mr Williams left to become Second Master at Halesowen Grammar School. He had been at Luton Modern School since 1935, except for his years of war service. He

At the end of the summer term, 1951, the Archaeological Society excavated part of a barrow on Galley Hill, Streatley. Four skeletons of Roman date were uncovered. The diggers are J.M. Hopkins, E.C. Caldecourt, J. Dyer and J. Lawrence. (*LN-LMC*)

was appointed to teach English and French and help with Rugby football. He coached the Under 15 team which later became the unbeaten 1st XV of 1942. In 1941 he joined the Royal Navy, serving on a sloop scouring the North Sea, until it was torpedoed. Working below deck, he was lucky to escape. After the war, as well as heading the English department and running the Library, he was responsible for eight Dramatic Society productions, four of which were with Miss Hudson and two with Miss Brown.

Whilst at Epsom College, the Headmaster had taught a weekly lesson for VIth formers on Current Affairs. This he continued when he came to Luton, meeting the senior boys for wide-ranging discussions on a variety of topics. In October he published *A Source Book of Opinion on Human Values* (Tower Bridge Publications, 7/6d.). A reviewer in *The Luton News* wrote:

'More Lutonians are enrolling for evenings classes in philosophy than in any other subject. It illustrates the desire of ordinary people to know more about life's values, in a world where the voluminous nature of the subject makes it one of the most exacting to master. Kenneth B. Webb has been quick to interpret this new trend towards serious thought, and has done modern society a service by making available *A Source Book of Opinion on Human Values*. The book collates, in a manner easy to read and absorb, the words of great thinkers of all times on this particular branch of philosophy – human values.'

A number of Old Boys were in the news. G. L. Bond, an assistant Secretary at the Board of Trade, was awarded a CBE. A.C. 'Tony' Brown was on the staff of the *Daily Mail*. David Cox had joined the photographic staff of the *Daily Mirror*. Brian Sales was on the reporting staff of the *Manchester Evening Chronicle*. Robert J. Cunningham had joined the *Bristol Evening Post*. Phillip Gething was working at the Royal Observatory, Greenwich. C.W. Read (LMS 1918–26) had been appointed Director of Education for West Sussex. Alec Trendall (LMS 1937–46) was a geologist with the Antarctic Expedition, 1951–52, and had to be rescued from a crevasse. E.W. Bruce Hill was also in the Antarctic between 1949 and 1953 as a member of the Falkland Island Dependencies Survey, and at one time helping to establish a sledging base at Hope Bay, Graham Land. In 1955 the Queen awarded him the Polar Medal for his services to the Survey. Herbert R. Waller, Vice-Chairman of the School Governors, was to be High Sheriff of Bedfordshire. Dudley Wood became the School's first Rugby Blue. Arthur B. Allen (LMS 1917–21), a teacher for 27 years, was ordained a priest in the Church of England in Gloucester Cathedral. For many years he edited the *Old Lutonian Magazine*.

Farewell to 'Froggy'

Harold Hugo Watson retired in July 1952 after thirty-four years teaching French and German to generations of schoolboys at Luton Modern and Grammar School. Born in 1887, he joined the School in 1919 as Head of the French department, after teaching in France and at Loughborough Grammar School. Sometimes known as 'Sir Hugo', to most he was known as 'Froggy'. A versatile man, prepared to tackle most problems, he became the Staff Room handy-man. He loved music and played an important part in forming the School orchestra, always being available to play the cello, violin, piano or double bass. Best of all, he loved teaching French. 'When roused he erupted with volcanic violence, but the fury was usually of short duration and soon subsided, leaving little trace of upheaval. His bark was worse than his bite and it was not in his nature to bear malice.' Many tales were told of Froggy's diverse interests. Morville Chote recalled that he made wine in his cellar. One day it exploded and he came to School with sticking plaster on his face. His few years of

retirement were dogged with ill health, and he died on 13th January, 1958, aged 70.

Stanley H. Matthews left the staff in July after four years to become Senior Physics master at Maltby Grammar School, Yorkshire, and John H. Phillips, who came to Luton in 1947, moved to Chatham House School, Ramsgate, as Head of Art. Their places were taken in September 1952 by Robert C. Gibson (Languages); Richard J. Payne, (Physics and Maths); Kenneth G. Ainsworth (Art and Handicraft) and David McKechnie Smith (PE for one year, whilst G.C. Grimshaw was on a course). Thomas Russell Key, from Burnley Grammar School, was appointed Head of English from April 1952.

Speech Day was held on 13th February, 1952, with Councillor C.A. Sinfield in the Chair. After the Headmaster had presented his report, Mrs Charles Hill presented the prizes and trophies. Dr Charles Hill, MP for Luton, then adressed the gathering, his speech being delivered with the accustomed admixture of humour and common sense which had come to be associated with his name. Two boys, J. Lawrence and B. Pitkin, had been awarded State Scholarships.

At Easter ten senior boys from the School and thirteen girls from the Technical School travelled to Brünnen in Switzerland with Mr and Mrs Geoffrey Clarke and Mr and Mrs Eric Whitaker. As the only guests in the Hotel Mythenstein, they enjoyed an hilarious as well as educational holiday. In July about 100 boys again joined forces with their compatriots from the Technical School, this time to St Mary's Bay Holiday Camp, near Dymchurch.

The Memorial Tennis Courts were completed during 1952 and became a popular addition to the School's amenities. A very enjoyable match was played during the Summer Term against the High School. One of the Courts was marked out for basketball, a game that had become very popular in the School.

On 16th May, the School was shocked to hear of the death of Peter Graham Cooper, (1945–52) following a cycle accident at the Old Bedford Road – Stockingstone Road cross-roads. Appointed a sub-prefect a week earlier, he was a very popular member of the VIth Form, with the prospect of a brilliant career ahead of him. For most of the Upper Sixth who were present at his funeral, it was their first contact with the death of someone of their own age, and they felt it deeply. Peter had been a keen basketball player, and a cup, inscribed 'Peter Cooper House Basketball Trophy', was presented to the School for annual competition.

A younger boy, Peter Foster, (1949–52) died on 12th February. He had suffered from a diabetic complaint for some time, and his quiet serenity in the face of affliction had endeared him to all who came into contact with him.

A group of senior boys were listening to a BBC Schools' Broadcast in the Library, on 6th February, when it was interrupted by the announcement that King George VI had died. The Headmaster was immediately informed, and a special Assembly was convened at 2.15pm. On the 15th February, the day of the King's funeral, a special short service took place and 2 minutes silence was observed.

Dr Charles Hill, MP, was the Guest at Speech Day on 13th February, 1952. (*LN*)

Senior members of the Student Christian Movement in the School joined forces with parties from the High and Technical Schools for a two day conference on 'The Relevance of Christianity in Modern Life' held at the High School. Dr W.E. Duncanson, Reader in Experimental Physics at University College, London, and the Rev. Wilfred Wade, Minister of Kenton Methodist Church, provided thought provoking talks, which were followed by discussions led by the three Head Teachers.

Between 9.30 and 12.30 on 5th May, nearly 400 boys were X-rayed in a mobile unit parked outside the School, as part of the drive to eradicate tuberculosis and other chest diseases. A week later they were pictured again, but that was for a less serious panoramic School photograph.

The Chess Club received a well-deserved boost on 15th May when Mr Church and Mr Sweby of the Bedfordshire Chess Association delivered a shield awarded by the British Chess Federation to the school that had done most to promote the interests of chess in the 19 southern counties of England. The last time it had been in the area was in 1915 at St Albans School.

Highlight of the Literary and Scientific Society's year was a Mock Election which, after two weeks of frantic electioneering, was won by Les Young (Conservative), with a narrow majority over Ray Sinfield (Socialist). Richard Clark (Liberal) forfeited his deposit of one pair of braces. The joint debate, held with the High School, explored the motion that 'In the opinion of this house the introduction of jazz is regretted'. Defended by Avril Crosbie and Les Young, and ably opposed by Tom Vaughan and Doreen Phillips, the motion was heavily defeated.

The 1st XI Football team struggled to win four of their eight matches, though the excellent 9–4 score against Bushey Grammar School avenged the previous season's defeat, and everyone enjoyed the exciting 5–4 win over the Old Boys in a very strong wind. J. K. Doodson was captain for the season. The 2nd XI lost their five year unbeaten record against St Christopher School, Letchworth, in the first match of the season when they lost 1–2.

The Cross-Country teams had a busy, but only mediocre, season. The Seniors, captained by Harry Maughan, had too many 'tail' runners, giving insufficient support to the stronger boys. The Colts team, with Norman Edwards at the helm, were more successful, Edwards coming first in all his runs.

Sports Day, on 21st May, 1952, was the finest on record, both for weather and many worthy performances. Guest of honour was the Olympic Coach, Geoffrey Dyson. No less than 18 records were broken and 5 equalled. A.C. Gregory was singled out for special mention by Mr Muse for his performances in the (u.15) 100 yds, 220 yds and the Long Jump.

At the Luton Schools' Sports at Wardown on the 17th and 19th June, the School comfortably retained the Senior Championship Shield. Gregory broke the Luton Schools' Long Jump record with a leap of 18 ft 8½ in. and W.N. Edwards won the non-Championship 880 yds. in 2 min. 8.8 secs. Both were picked to represent

Bedfordshire in the English Schools' Championships at Bradford.

The Cricket season began with some difficulty, the 1st XI having lost their stalwarts, B.D. Robinson and M. Jones. It was not until the arrival, mid-season, of C.J. Hayes and R.J. Spencer from the 2nd XI to open the innings that everything changed. Not one of the last five matches was lost, and three were won, the team finishing the season with a greater number of victories than the strong 1951 side. A.J. Osborn captained the side, supported by J. Gurney, his vice-captain.

The Inter-House Boxing Tournament finals were held in the Hall on 27th November. During the evening Mr Froud of the Technical School gave a short but interesting talk on refereeing and on school boxing in general. Bees won the Shore Trophy and the Keith Batchelor Cup.

The 1952 Rugby 1st XV were little better than their immediate predecessors, due, it was said, to the lack of good players in the top forms. Bruce E. Potter captained the side, which lost six of its nine matches, won two and drew one. The season came to an abrupt end owing to snow and frost from 28th November, causing the Old Boys match to be cancelled for the first time ever.

A party of 100 boys and seven masters travelled to Twickenham on Tuesday, 9th December, to watch Dudley Wood play for a triumphant Oxford against Cambridge in the annual University Rugby match.

On 26th September the staff were called together to receive instruction in the use of the School's first tape recorder. A week later they were shown how to use still and sound projectors; all innovations which were considerably under used.

At the Annual Dinner of the Old Lutonians' Club, held on a very foggy 6th December, two presentations were made. The first to Mr Webb, on behalf of the School, was a portrait of the first headmaster, Mr T.A.E. Sanderson, painted by Mrs Sylvia Smedley. It was presented, in his presence, by the Old Boys to hang in the Assembly Hall. The second to Mr H.H. Watson was an electric coffee percolator to mark his retirement.

The joint Dramatic Societies' play for December 1952 was a gentle Spanish comedy by Los Quinteros, *A Hundred Years Old*. It was the first time a joint play had been performed at the High School. It centred around the preparations for the hundredth birthday of Papa Juan, a kindly old gentleman played by David Sturman, who excelled in elderly roles. Janet Richfield was outstanding as the cross-tempered Filomena. The quiet anxiety of Helen Wynter as Dona Marciala, contrasted with the amusing eccentricity and senility in her husband, Don Evaristo, played by James Dyer. David Oldroyd looked the romantic hero, Trino, that he played with elegance and complete self-possession. Gladys Brown and Russell Key were the producers.

Using £300 left over from the old 'Organ Fund', a new Bell and Howell film projector was purchased for the School, which could be operated from the projection room. A large screen, which descended electronically from a box just behind the blue stage curtains, was installed, and for the first time the School was properly equipped

to show full length films. To celebrate, the whole School watched the film *In Which We Serve* during the morning of Friday, 19th December. After lunch, the traditional Christmas Carol Service brought to a close the autumn term.

Coronation Year – 1953

Coronation Year was celebrated at the School by the issue to the boys of a souvenir of their own choosing from either a mug, beaker or spoon. The 1st–3rd of June was declared a national holiday, during which familes watched proceedings on their new black-and-white television sets, or ventured to London by the early trains to try and catch some part of the procession. A Coronation Thanksgiving Service was held at the School on 5th June. Next day, Saturday, 6th June, a Coronation Procession was held in Luton, and twelve boys from Years III, IV, and V, together with a Prefect and Sub-Prefect, were chosen to carry flags. On the following Monday morning most boys from the School filled the balcony of the Savoy Cinema to see a special showing of the Coronation film *Elizabeth is Queen,* which cost them 6d. each.

In early February Mr K.B. Webb and Mrs Eileen Evans were quizzed about the problem of early leavers, and were asked to comment on the fact that in Great Britain 22% of grammar school pupils left school before reaching the age of 16 plus. Mr Webb observed that the number of boys who left the Grammar School before 16 was lower than the national average. Mrs Evans said, 'Very few girls, in comparison with figures for the whole country, leave before completing their education. Local firms understand the need for a grammar school education, and they and the Youth Employment Service seek to dissuade girls from leaving early. It is a great temptation for Luton girls to leave at 15 because there are so many well-paid jobs available, but in fact the percentage is so low locally – about 10% compared with the 22% national figure – that it speaks well for the good sense of Luton people.'

By January 1953, Mr Jack Ashworth's insidious multiple sclerosis was making his work almost impossible, and so for the first time since 1919, a lady, zoologist Mrs D. Phillipson, joined the staff as his part-time replacement. Eventually, in October, he had to admit defeat and tender his resignation. He bore his affliction with indomitable courage and amazing fortitude for a further five years, dying on 11th July, 1958, in Manchester.

The Lutonian praised the achievements of the School's musicians, congratulating Peter Isherwood, who had won an open organ scholarship to Selwyn College, Cambridge, in 1951, and had recently been successful in the Music Tripos, Part I. After being responsible for music at Wellington College, Somerset and the Colchester Royal Grammar School, he became the youngest Music Adviser in the country, a task he combined with Director of the Coventry School of Music. Geoffrey Ford, Head Prefect, who left in July 1950, went to the Royal Academy, and, after national service at Kneller Hall, became Head of Strings at Charterhouse

School and also ran the School's newly built Ben Travers' Theatre, where he produced some eighty plays. Congratulations also went to David Oldroyd, who led the cellos in the 'A' Orchestra in a music course held at Sherborne School, and Julian Webb, deputy leader of the violins in the National Youth Orchestra of Great Britain which played under Sir Adrian Boult in the Edinburgh Festival. Webb, the younger son of the Headmaster, went on to his father's old college, Trinity, at Cambridge, and later taught at Manchester University, where he was a member of 'The Ad Solem Ensemble'. He became Senior Lecturer in Music at the University of East Anglia. He recently retired after 32 years as conductor of the Norwich Philharmonic Orchestra.

A number of the School's musicians were founder-members of the fifty-strong Luton Youth Orchestra, conducted by Michael Marsh-Edwards, the School's first BMus. from Trinity College of Music. The orchestra performed its first concert at the South Bedfordshire College of Further Education on 21st February.

A musician in a different *genre* left School in 1953. Graham Collier joined the Army as a trumpeter, training at Kneller Hall. Subsequently, he won a scholarship to the Berklee College of Music in Boston, USA, studying with Herb Pomeroy and becoming the first British graduate. Returning to Britain, he formed an ensemble known as Graham Collier Music, to play his own compositions. He was the first recipient of an Arts Council bursary for jazz, and wrote music for ensembles ranging from wind quartets to symphony orchestras, as well as music for films, plays and television. He is the author of several books. In the early 1980s, he developed the six-year jazz degree course still running at the Sibelius Institute in Helsinki, Finland. He is also a professor and director of jazz studies at the Royal Academy of Music. He was awarded an OBE by the Queen in 1987 for his services to the world of jazz.

The Annual Speech Day was held on 16th February, 1953. The Headmaster reported that in recent years old boys had been, or were, at every university in England, as well as the University of Wales and St Andrew's in Scotland. The Revd. R.L. Roberts, MA, Vicar of Sharnbrook, and a former Headmaster of Blundell's School, Tiverton, addressed the assembly, and Mrs Roberts distributed the awards and prizes. Mr Roberts received tumultuous applause when he asked for the usual half holiday and an additional whole day to mark Dudley Wood's performance in the University Rugby match at Twickenham. State Scholarships for 1952 were awarded to A. Golding and D.F. Sturman.

In February Donald Stott was lucky enough to spend a month at the Outward Bound Training School in Eskdale on a mountaineering and rock climbing course.

The Home and School Association and the Old Lutonians' Club organised an Open Day on 27th June. Between 400 and 500 parents and friends were entertained by a series of sporting events: School v. Old Lutonians at cricket; a tennis tournament between teams of masters, boys, parents and Old Lutonians; Basketball, School v. Old Lutonians, etc. An exhibition of hobbies, submitted by boys and parents, was also on view, as were a number of exhibitions staged by the School Societies.

Part of the audience that attended Speech Day, 1953, with file of recipients of awards at far side.
(*LN-LMC*)

The Literary and Scientific Society listened to a fascinating Presidential Address by Mr Donald Sutcliffe called 'Travellers' Tales' which ranged from Mandeville's Anthropophagi to Shipton's Abominable Snowmen. The joint debate with the High School considered the motion that 'In this new Elizabethan Age the costume and customs of the first Elizabethan Age should be revived'. It was proposed by David Sturman and Avril Crosbie, and opposed by Nora Martin and Les Young: the motion was heavily defeated.

The Film Club showed a number of films, including *The Ghost Goes West*, starring Robert Donat. The new projector and screen helped create a real 'cinema' atmosphere in the Hall, but the suggestion that the organ console be sunk in a pit, to emerge in soft, coloured lights during the interval, was not taken seriously.

The Archaeological Society listened to a series of lectures, visited Verulamium, and provided an exhibition for Open Day. During the summer members took part in excavations at Waulud's Bank, Leagrave, helping to establish its neolithic date.

A new group, the Natural History Society, was formed in March, and carried out an ecological survey of Bradgers Hill, and studied a number of ponds in the area.

The routine of School life was rudely disturbed on the morning of 17th March when a Uniform check was carried out. A large number of boys were caught without the regulation coloured shirts, socks or caps and were given a short time to produce the offending items with their *own* names stitched inside, or a valid explanation.

On 20th March the Handicraft Room was broken into at night. Some £10 worth of Savings Stamps and a sum of money for handicrafts was taken. A month later the burglary was repeated, but on that occasion only mess and damage occurred.

An interesting architectural argument developed in the local press in April, following a talk by the distinguished architect, Sir Albert Richardson, President of the Royal Academy, to a group of Surveyors in Bedford, during which he condemned the box-like containers of contemporary architecture. He said that architecture had been reduced to a matter of straight lines, with the Government playing Box and Cox on questions of accommodation and dimensions, with materials selected from catalogues where architects had no imagination at all, and the result was a well-known cheap sort of exhibitionism. The Editor of *The Luton News* wrote: 'Look at the Luton and Dunstable Hospital or Luton Grammar School and compare them with Luton High School. Look at almost any post-war schools in Luton and the plans for the new Luton and South Bedfordshire College of Further Education. Each building mentioned above is admirably designed for the purpose it serves, but, apart from Luton High School, is it good to look at? It is not.'

Old Lutonian, Dennis L. Farr, by then studying at the Courtauld Institute, challenged the newspaper, saying:

'Professor Richardson is most certainly right in saying that "set regulations are stifling our imagination" but to infer that imagination is lacking in the design of modern buildings is both misleading and unfair. Modern architects are no longer the dangerous revolutionaries of thirty years ago, but Romantics frustrated by the Government's inept building policy.

'*The Luton News* by comparing Luton Grammar School and Luton High School do a disservice to the argument. Luton High School is merely a rather large box with other small boxes joined on at right angles, while the Alexandra Avenue facade is heavy in effect with its thin veneer of giant pilasters and pediment designed in a bloodless neo-Georgian style. Yet it is conceded that the Grammar School is at once well designed for its purpose and has an immediate appeal to the eye.

'How can it be said, therefore, that it is neither good to look at, nor possible to live with this building for very long and like it? What are the standards of discrimination?'

In March the Dramatic Society presented the all male play, *Journey's End,* by R.C. Sherriff. David Sturman, in his last appearance on the School stage, played the

A serious moment from *Journey's End* by R.C. Sherriff, performed in March, 1953. 2nd Lieut. Hibbert (J. Sansom), 2nd Lieut. Trotter (R. Dolden), Captain Stanhope (D. Sturman) and Lieut. Osborne (C.A. Johnson). (*LN*)

irascible, nerve-stricken, whisky-doped Captain Stanhope, with considerable maturity. John Potter made a great impression as the 'death or glory' Colonel. The audience enjoyed Rodney Dolden's performance as the good-natured Trotter, and warmed to John Sansom's sympathetic treatment of the officer who had lost his nerve for the firing line. Robin Pyburn played Raleigh, the young and ingenious public-school officer, and Peter Vaughan was a weighty, efficient sergeant-major. Anthony Johnson caught exactly the spirit of the mature and unperturbed Lieutenant Osborne, a school-master turned officer. He reminded many of the School's senior staff of their colleague, T.P. Clarke, who had been killed in 1942. The play was produced by Russell Key.

At Easter 1953, twenty-seven boys, accompanied by Mr Parry and Mr and Mrs Partridge, enjoyed a tiring week in Paris, walking what seemed like hundreds of miles, to visit every 'sight'. Heights were a great attraction, and the towers of Sacré-Coeur, Notre Dame and Eiffel were scaled. Everyone agreed that for an educational holiday it had proved very enjoyable.

With J.K. Doodson as captain, the prospects of a good Football season were bright. Five of the 1952 Under Fifteen XI were promoted to the 1st XI and worthily held their places, obtaining 42 of the 57 goals scored. The table of results – played

8, won 8, 57 goals for, 6 goals against – was probably a record for the School Eleven. One of the team, A.C. 'Tony' Gregory, played for Luton Schoolboys who reached the 6th Round of the English Schools Trophy, and for England Schoolboys versus Scotland Schoolboys at Wembley under the captaincy of Duncan Edwards (who was killed in the Munich-Manchester United Air Crash in 1958). Gregory played soccer professionally for Luton Town (First Division) from 1956–61 (including the FA Cup Final of 1959), then for Watford Town from 1961–66. During his career he collected four caps for England Youth and three for England Under 21s. He

A.C. Gregory, one of the School's most successful footballers, seen here receiving a medal from Lord Luke. He collected 7 England caps (Youths and U.21s) and played for Luton Town (1st Div), 1956-61, and Watford Town, 1961-66. (LN-LMC)

said that he was influenced at School by Mr W.H. Chapman, who made him train when he preferred not to do so, and Mr H.B. Evans, who gave him a great deal of encouragement.

Norman Edwards, the School's Cross-Country captain, showed his skill again, both in the Ranelagh Schools' Race, where he came second, and in the County Championships (14–16 years), run on the School course, where he came first. In the Wild Cup competition he set up a new senior course record of 21 min. 7.48 secs. M.J. Mardle and A.G. Cundick provided strong opposition and were well backed up by R. Pyburn and D. Crosby.

For a second year running, Sports Day, 20th May, was held in glorious weather. Twelve records were broken and five more were equalled. Tom Odham, Tony Gregory and John Stevens had good reason to be proud of their track, long jump and field achievements, as did R.F. Young, D.E. Randall and M.J. Graves in the pole vault. At the Luton Schools' Sports the boys retained the Senior Championship Shield for the third year, and the new Coronation Cup, awarded on a 'points-per-eligible-pupil' basis. On the results of the Luton Schools' Sports and the County

AAA Championships, eight Grammar School boys were chosen to compete in the English Schools' AAA Championships at Uxbridge. Of those, Tony Gregory won the 220 yds title.

The 1953 Cricket season was one of the most successful for some years. The first ten matches played by School teams were won, and only five games lost in the whole season, two of those by the (u.15) XI when fielding a weakened side. The 1st XI were very strong in batting, but weak in bowling, with no one to support captain A.J. Osborn for sustained periods. John Gurney was an outstanding batsman who failed by only 21 runs to beat Derek Wood's aggregate of 372 made in 1945.

The first full season of tennis was played in 1953, with half a dozen stylish players. D.W. George and J.E. Phillips, the number one pair, were strong, though occasionally a little erratic; R.F. Tout and M.E. Dawson the second pair, both with a service that needed attention to develop it into a powerful weapon of attack; and finally Hucklesby and Olney, the 'babies' of the team. Of 8 matches played, they won 5, drew 1 and lost 2.

John Gurney captained the 1st XV Rugby team from the centre; E.J. Nash led the forwards from the lock position, and J.K. Doodson and R.W. Devey were a ready-made pair of halves. The season's record of winning 11 games out of 13 was a just reward for hard training and keen team spirit.

For Lower VI Science the autumn term began with a week spent potato-picking. 'We were the envy of most of the School, but I am not sure that we enjoyed the working "holiday" as much as other people might imagine. The pay was very good, but the work was back-breaking and seemed never-ending.'

The choice of Bernard Shaw's *Major Barbara* as the joint-schools' play for December 1953, was a brave one, since it is a difficult play to appreciate. But the Schools had a ready made Andrew Undershaft in Anthony Johnson, and he impersonated the armament king magnificently. Rex Boston, as Adolphus Cusins, was convincing as he tried to challenge the millionaire's outlook with his Greek philosophy, and Rodney Dolden, as Charles Lomax, once again delighted the audience in a comic rôle. David Watkins was most convincing with his unctuous repetition of pious platitudes. Rita Kelly, in the title rôle, had a most exacting part, but somehow didn't enter sufficiently into it, especially when appearing as the Salvation Officer on duty. Sheila Golding as the domineering old Lady Undershaft and Christine Livesey as her daughter Sarah were both convincing. Gladys Brown and Russell Key again produced the play.

It had become the custom for the VIth form to hold a Social at the end of the Autumn Term to which members of the High School were invited. In 1953 it was held on 16th December, two days before the end of term. Mr R.C. Gibson agreed to act as MC and a mixture of games and dances were well under way.

Unbeknown to the revellers an ill-conceived practical joke had been prepared, without due thought as to the possible consequences, and it went dreadfully wrong.

According to *The Saturday Telegraph*:

'An empty gas mask container with a lighted 'fuse' made of paper soaked in salt-petre was thrown into the crowded hall . . . on Wednesday night during the joint Sixth Form Social. Fortunately nobody was injured, and disciplinary action has been taken against four boys. There were 200 boys, girls, masters and mistresses in the hall at the time. Suddenly the lights went out, and the container was thrown from the balcony. A good deal of confusion ensued. One boy involved was dressed in a hooded costume resembling those worn by the Ku-Klux-Klan in the United States. He also wore rubber gloves reaching above his elbows. The container was incapable of causing damage other than by fire. The fuse caused slight burning to the hall floor and to the shoe of a spectator who tried to put it out. The Headmaster, Mr K.B. Webb, declined to comment.'

The story was all round the Schools the next day, the figure on the platform had been identified, as had his accomplices. One of them, David Conquest, has given his account of the story:

'The plot was fairly simple, and, of course, extremely juvenile. At a predetermined time, all the lights in the hall were to be turned off by Simon Luxemburg. This was a signal for another member of the group to activate the fire alarm system. Another two members of the group, under the cover of darkness, would descend to the front of the balcony and drape a banner over the balustrade with the legend 'Up the Revolution' or some such. From behind the curtain, Freddie Allen should have appeared with a 'bomb' made from a tin with a spluttering fuse, the sort you see in children's comics, place the 'bomb' on the front of the stage, shout a suitable revolutionary slogan and disappear back behind the curtain. The lights would then be switched on, whereupon the banner would be seen, the 'bomb' discovered to be harmless, and everybody would have a good laugh.

'Unfortunately, Fred panicked and lobbed the 'bomb' into the dancing throng. This of course caused a bit of alarm for those closest, although I understand that nobody was actually struck. However, as we learned later, the fuse, in its spluttering, scorched the highly polished hall floor.

'We all legged it round to the front entrance of the hall, to try to appear uninvolved, but of course Fred had been recognised and it didn't take too long to uncover the whole plot.

'The following day we all attended, individually with our parents, to Mr Webb's study to have the riot act read.'

Altogether, six boys were involved in the plot, and each was dealt with separately. The Governors met on 20th December, and it was decided to suspend Allen for two

weeks, but allow him to complete his Sixth Form course. One of the other boys chose to leave immediately; the rest were suspended for the last two days of term, but remained at School to complete their courses.

Fifty Years On – The Golden Jubilee

On Sunday, 19th September, the fiftieth anniversary of the opening of the Luton Secondary School on Park Square was celebrated by a Service of Commemoration in the Assembly Hall. The programme was a happy blend of a formal, religious service of thanksgiving, with less formal reminiscences contributed by speakers from the platform: Sir Frederick Mander, JP, Chairman of the Bedfordshire County Council; Alderman John Burgoyne, OBE, JP, Chairman of Governors; Mr T.A.E. Sanderson, MA, the Founder Headmaster; and two Old Lutonians, E.H.T. Hoblyn, MBE, PhD, ARCS, (School number 1646) and Mr W. A. Gething, BSc, (School number 297).

The visitors, who included Dr Charles Hill, MP, and Mrs Hill, Sir Herbert and Lady Janes, members of the County and the Borough Education Committees, and former members of the staff of the Luton Secondary School, were welcomed by Mr K.B.Webb.

After the singing of the hymn: 'Our Father, by whose servants, our house was built of old', the Headmaster introduced Sir Frederick Mander. He had, more than any other one man, affected the conditions of service of teachers in the schools and the general arrangements of the national provision of education. Sir Frederick spoke of 'The School', which, he said, need not fear comparison with any other. Its foundation was one of the fruits of that 'best hated' Education Act of 1902. He spoke of the contribution made by Grammar School boys to university life, commerce, industry and the professions, which, he said, was incalculable. 'But great as the past has been,' he concluded, 'there are still new fields to conquer. Let us hope that the best is yet to come.'

Alderman John Burgoyne spoke on 'Governors'. With very few exceptions, he said, he could claim to have known all the Governors who had served the School in the past fifty years. The original governors, with great pride, associated themselves with Mr Sanderson's work and strove for a cause which was founded on the idea that the refining and training of the mind of a child was honouring God. Those men adopted the idea and nurtured it, and by so doing, 'set the cause above renown; they loved the game beyond the prize.'

Mr T.A.E. Sanderson had been asked to speak on 'The earliest days, the Staff, the Motto' and anything else he could think of. Much of this has already been quoted in the earliest chapters of this book. He said that he would always be thankful for having been blessed with a loyal staff, in particular Mr John Hoblyn, Mr John 'Jimmy' Forbes and his invaluable secretary, Mr John Jeffs.

At that point, Old Lutonian, Alan John Osborn, Head Prefect in 1953, (School number 4138), read the 'Parable of the Sower' from the Gospels according to St Matthew and St Luke.

Another Old Lutonian, Dr E.H.T. Hoblyn, spoke on 'Staff'. His father had been a master at the School from 1904 to 1915 and a Governor from 1926 to 1933. He asked that there be greater appreciation of the value of human contact between master and pupil, for that which was not appreciated could not be well used. 'As we take off our hats to the first fifty years, let us be happy in the knowledge that the present staff have already taken off their coats to a bright new future.'

Former pupil, W.A. 'Billy' Gething (1908–1912), talked of 'Parents'. A boy's education went on during the whole of his waking hours, he said, and much that was done in school could be undone if parents did not understand that they should have a share of the work. Through their sons the education of the parents was continued, and he said that he spoke in the name of all parents when he took part in the School's Jubilee Celebration with a great sense of thanksgiving.

Rex S. Clayton (School number 254), who was absent through illness, should have spoken on 'Professions and Occupations'.

The Headmaster next asked the Mayor, Cllr. Hedley C. Lawrence, to lead the assembly in prayer. During that part of the service prayers were also spoken by Frederick Buckingham, BSc, (School number 9) whose name at that time headed the Honours Board outside the Hall; the Second Master, Mr Cyril J. Godfrey, BSc, and a present-day boy of the School, I. Morris (School number 5112 – IIa). The proceedings were brought to a conclusion by the singing of the School's end-of-term hymn, and a final prayer and blessing by Old Lutonian, Revd. Raymond S. Wilkinson, AKC, HCF, (School number 2259).

> God be with you till we meet again;
>   By his counsels guide, uphold you,
> With his sheep securely fold you:
>   God be with you till we meet again
>
> God be with you till we meet again;
>   'Neath his wings protecting hide you,
> Daily manna still provide you:
>   God be with you till we meet again.
>
> God be with you till we meet again;
>   When life's perils thick confound you,
> Put his arm unfailing round you:
>   God be with you till we meet again.

God be with you till we meet again;

Keep love's banner floating o'er you,

Smite death's threatening wave before you:

God be with you till we meet again.

[Dr J. E. Rankin]

The many guests then had the opportunity to renew old acquaintances, and to visit an Exhibition of items connected with the School's first fifty years arranged by Dr Dony in the Geography Room.

Writing of the Jubilee in *The Lutonian* for Autumn 1954, Mr Webb said:

'Old Boys are in many countries fulfilling many responsible tasks. Let us pay tribute; but then let us turn at once and look at the future.

'At every point of the scientific frontier – in agriculture, medicine, biology, chemistry, physics and geology – rapid and exciting advance is possible, and indeed likely, in our lifetime; and the use of atomic power, vast systems of irrigation, and plants for the harnessing of hydro-electric energy, will change the face of the continents.

'I confidently expect Old Boys to play a full part in discovering new facts, and in applying them for the good of their fellows.

'Look, however, at our life on this spinning, crowded planet from another angle. Politically, we live in a state not far removed from international anarchy and the next fifty years will see various experiments in co-operating at various levels.

'For the shaping of the necessary political machinery and for planning co-operatively the best use of natural resources, men of balance and integrity, kindness and intelligence, must be living witnesses to the existence of a World Community and a World Citizenship; and all that they can know of the story of Man, his religions and his arts, will be of value.

'I pray that our School will send forth a steady stream of such men who, in every continent and in every calling, will act as human bridges of under-standing and goodwill between those of different colour, code or creed.

'Only so can we serve the needs of our day and generation and discharge our obligations to those fore-runners at the foot of whose names, inscribed in red on the War Memorial, stand the words:

"See that they died not in vain".'

January, 1954, began with reports of near arctic conditions, particularly at the eastern end of the School, where heating engineers were called in to try to defrost Mr Cleaver and the Geography Room. So seriously was the problem taken, that Dr John Corbett, the Director of Education, called personally to deliver two oil heaters.

On the morning of 11th January, Mr Donald Richmond, who had joined the

The Memorial Tennis Courts were officially presented to the School on 26th June, 1954.
K.B. Webb is seen with Sir John Burgoyne, Cty.Cllr. T.H. Johnson, Cty.Ald. H.R. Waller, L. Carr
(Pres. Old Lutonians) and W.G. Barrett (Hon. Sec. Home & School Assn.) (*LN-LMC*)

School in September 1953 to teach Art and Handicraft, presented for Forms V and VI Bernard Shaw's play, *Arms and the Man*. It was the prescribed GCE play, and gave some young actors, as well as old hands, a chance to show their ability.

Late in January the Home and School Association organised a Junior Brains Trust at the High School. The Panel consisted of VIth Formers: Marjorie Horley, Stella Atkinson, Ruth Garrett, A.J. Osborn, J. Gurney and C.A. Johnson, and Cllr. Leslie G. Bowles took the Chair. A question on compulsory National Service caused some controversy, though all agreed that two years away from study could be harmful to a university undergraduate. The boys on the panel thought that girls should be made to take an intensified compulsory course in cooking and housewifery!

Saturday, 26th June, saw the culmination of the Memorial Tennis Courts Scheme, when the Courts and newly completed Pavilion were formally handed over to Ald. John Burgoyne (representing the Governors) and County Cllr. T.H. Johnson, Vice-Chairman of the County Education Committee. Mr L. Carr, President of the Old Lutonians, and Mr W.G. Barrett, Secretary of the Home and School Association, made the presentation. C. Cllr. Johnson said, 'The present generation of this School, and the coming generation, will remember with gratitude not only

A tournament to mark the official opening of the Memorial Tennis Courts on 26th June, 1954. The area, once the school vegetable garden, is now a car park.

those people who provided this memorial, but the Old Boys who gave their all for their country.'

It is a sad irony that within twenty years the tennis courts would become a car park. By way of retribution a Garden of Remembrance for the Second World War dead was eventually laid out at the Sixth Form College, with, at its centre, a sundial fashioned from two cornice stones removed from the Modern School at Park Square, and erected to the memory of T.A.E. Sanderson, the first Headmaster. The sundial was originally presented to the School by the Old Boys' Association in June 1963, and stood in front of the clock tower, but in later years it was subjected to vandalism and moved for its own safety.

Speech Day in Jubilee Year was held on 17th February, when the High Sheriff of Bedfordshire, County Alderman Herbert R. Waller, MBE, Vice-Chairman of the Governors and an Old Boy, took the Chair. The address was given by Air Marshall Sir Victor Goddard, KCB, CBE, DL, Principal of the College of Aeronautics, Cranfield, who discussed the question of realities, with particular reference to the uncertainties of what were thought by physicists to be realities. He believed school provided a link between the spiritual and material. Lady Goddard distributed trophies and certificates to a formidable list of prize-winners. The examinations of 1953 had resulted in the School's highest ever number of State Scholarships which were awarded to G.A. Carter at Reading University, C.A. Johnson at St John's

College, Cambridge, A.J. Miller at Manchester University, P. Robinson at Nottingham University and P.R. Vaughan at Imperial College, London. Open Scholarships were awarded to C.A. Johnson and F.R.D. Goodyear at St John's College, Cambridge.

From 3rd to 5th March the Dramatic Society staged Nicolai Gogol's comedy, *The Government Inspector*. With a cast of 26, and all parts played by boys, plus many back-stage workers, the Producers, Russell Key and Donald Richmond, had quite a formidable task, which they solved memorably. Rex Boston was at ease in impressing the ladies with his gallantry and deceiving the officials by his boasting, and Rodney Dolden was splendid as his shrewd and loyal servant. Anthony Johnson was not quite at home as the Mayor, but it would have been hard to find anyone better for the part in the School at the time. Goodge, as the Judge, brought the necessary self-importance and ponderousness to his part. Richards assumed the gait and bearing of the Mayor's daughter with skill, whilst Sansom, as the vulgar middle-class woman spoilt by wealth and the prospect of promotion, filled the audience with repugnance – a tribute to his acting skill.

The Literary and Scientific Society had one of its leaner years, though in 1954 it made history by having its first lady President. Mrs Diana Phillipson, deputising for Mr Ashworth, delivered a fascinating address on 'The lives and habits of British Birds', illustrated with tape recordings. The Joint Debate with the High School considered 'That in the opinion of this House Everest was just not worth climbing' – a motion that was duly defeated. At the end of the season Old Lutonian, David J. Atkinson, lectured on his experiences with the Prince Charles Foreland expedition, vividly recapturing the atmosphere and interest of Antarctica.

Michael Root receiving his prizes from Lady Goddard on Speech Day, 1954. (*LN-LMC*)

The Archaeological Society undertook a small excavation on a Roman site in Runfold Avenue, Limbury, in very bad weather. Members helped on an excavation at Barton Hill Farm at Streatley, and three boys dug on a Roman Auxiliary Fort in Radnorshire for Cardiff University. One of the latter, William H. Manning, after studying at Nottingham University and the Institute of Archaeology, London, was destined to become Professor of Archaeology at Cardiff University from 1983–2000.

The Natural History Society concentrated on field meetings and enjoyed visits to Maulden Woods, where a member managed to fall into the water, and Flitwick Moor, where they saw Heath and Marsh Orchids and the beautiful Bog Bean. David Bowler and Derek May led the pond life section on expeditions to Pearly Pond from where much live material was collected for the school aquarium.

Dr John G. Dony was honoured by the Town Council on 23rd February, when he was presented with a specially bound copy of his *Flora of Bedfordshire*, which had been published by Luton Corporation the previous year, and to everyone's surprise had completely sold out.

An unusual feature of *The Lutonian* for 1954 were reviews by two students of books written by members of staff. John T. Sansom enthused about Dr Dony's *Flora of Bedfordshire*. The results of 18 years research and recording, it was far more than a list of Bedfordshire plants. It looked in depth at environmental factors like climate, geology and soils, and recorded, with locations, every wild plant present in Bedfordshire. For the specialist it was a superb piece of scholarship and Sansom was justifiably full of praise.

Not so, Francis 'Frank' R.D. Goodyear, whose arrogant review of Wynne Parry's translation from the Latin of *Three Comedies of T. Maccius Plautus* reflected more badly on the reviewer than the translator. Mr Parry had gained much pleasure from translating the *Comedies* but had taken certain liberties with the text to which Goodyear objected. His comments, though perhaps correct, were unkind and unwarranted in the School Magazine. Goodyear was a fine classical scholar, who became a Fellow of Queen's College, Cambridge, and from 1966–84 Hildred Carlisle Professor of Latin at Bedford College, University of London. From the closure of Bedford College until his sudden death in 1987 he was Visiting Professor at the University of Witwatersrand.

Mr David G. Barker, BSc, and Mr Clive B. Folland, BSc, were both appointed in September to join Mr John Lovell in the Biology Department.

The 1954 1st XI Football team was slow to 'click' together. Scoring was somewhat erratic, but with the hard work of Doodson (Captain), Devey and Head, only two matches out of nine were lost. The 2nd XI, captained by R.F. Tout, enjoyed an unbeaten record for the season, winning all nine of their matches.

The Senior Cross-Country team, captained by A.G. Cundick and trained by Mr Partridge, had a very successful season, being beaten only twice in eleven fixtures; once by a very strong Old Boys team led by the Cambridge Blue, John Lawrence,

The 1954 Athletics team that won the Luton Schools' Sports Shield and Coronation Cup, with Mr G.C. Grimshaw and the Headmaster. (*LN-LMC*)

and once by Watford Grammar School. In the Youths (16–18 years) section of the Beds. and Hunts. Championships they won the cup, with six Grammar School runners finishing in the first ten. In the Eastern Counties at Goldington, D.K. Head, the second Colt to finish, received a silver medal.

Sports Day was held on 26th May in glorious sunshine, when the boys all wore their new house vests for the first time. These were white with bands of red, yellow and red round the chest, and were trimmed with individual house colours at the neck and shoulders. Nineteen records were broken and three equalled, of which 13 were connected with track events.

It was a fitting reward for his keenness and leadership that the Captain of Athletics, Donald Stott, should break the Open 880 Yards record in 2 min. 8.8 secs. Others who contributed worthy best performances were J. Gurney (100 and 220 yds Open), T. Odam (100 and 220 yds u.16) and R.F. Merchant (100 and 220 u.15). In the Pole Vault T.C.E. Wells and D.E. Randall cleared 9ft and 9ft 2ins. respectively, and J.E. Stevens won all four u.16 Field events.

At the Bedfordshire AAA Championship T.C.E. Wells needed to win the final event of the day, the Pole Vault, for the School team to gain the Arnold Whitchurch Cup. After a cliff-hanger of a contest he cleared 9ft to secure the event and the Cup by one point. At the Luton Schools' Sports the Championship Shield and the Coronation Cup were easily won for another year. The match with the Old Boys on 7th July was not so easy, with experienced opponents like Jack Walters, Tony

Gregory, Mick Bracey and John Lawrence to compete against. The Old Lutonians won by 112 points to the School's 95 points.

The Cricket season was only moderately successful, and the 1st XI played more as a loose collection of talented units than a well-knit team. Several senior players, like J. Gurney and D.G. Gilder, failed to reach their 1953 form. A.J. Osborn, in his third year as Captain, was for a long time out of luck with the bat, though he did more than his share with the ball: perhaps the strains of Head Boy, Cricket Captain and examination worries were getting too much. The greatest promise was shown by A.J. Evans, D.J. Hills and J.E. Stevens.

Two boys, David Hucklesby and David Olney, represented Bedfordshire in County Junior Tennis matches. In a season during which the School played fifteen extremely pleasant games, one or two stood out: two needle matches against Flitwick, the second followed by a near midnight feast at Mrs Olney's; the struggle at Watford, and, later, at Laporte's to preserve an unbeaten record; and the tenacity of the Parents in the July fixture against the Home and School Association.

The Rugby season, captained by E.J. Nash, started well with a run of five victories against less fit and experienced sides. Then the 1st XV ran into trouble against Hertford and Kettering. The second half of the season was notable for the game with the Old Boys. With a team strong enough to dictate the tactics, the Old Boys threw the ball about at every opportunity and it is to the credit of the School that they responded in similar fashion. J.W.V. Barrett, the School hooker, had an excellent game and gave his three quarters a plentiful supply of the ball. The final score was School 6, Old Boys 19. For the second successive season the 2nd XV, coached by Mr H.E.W. Chalkley, and with D.J. Bracey as captain, produced an unbeaten record.

VIth Former Peter R.W. Robinson gained a Cadet Hundred Badge in an inter-Service Cadet Force rifle meeting at Bisley in October. He was one of eight members of the Beds. ACF under the control of and coached by Major 'Bob' Ellis.

On 18th November 32 boys were presented with cycling proficiency certificates, pennants and badges at morning assembly by Cllr. G.L. Matthews, who was joined by Sgt. W.H. Coppock and PC Alexander on behalf of the Road Safety Committee.

At the beginning of December 1954, the combined Dramatic Societies presented their annual play, Oliver Goldsmith's *She Stoops to Conquer*. It was a happy, lively performance which did great credit to Russell Key and Donald Richmond, its producers, and the latter also as set designer.

Sheila Golding and Christine Livesy shared the part of Kate Hardcastle which they both played well: Sheila perhaps the more lively and Christine the sweeter. Valerie Bland, as Constance, acted cleverly with Tony Lumpkin when love or irritation had to be feigned. Elizabeth Hey, as Mrs Hardcastle, was particularly good in her two 'catastrophes'. Robin Pyburn was very impressive as the elegant Young Marlow, and was well supported by Derek May as George Hastings. David Oldroyd and David Day took the parts of the elderly Sir Charles Marlow and Mr Hardcastle

seriously, surprising the audiences with their powerful voice control. John Sansom as the key figure, Tony Lumpkin, was first-class, his acting exhibiting the excellent stage-craft that the producers had come to expect from this experienced young actor.

The performances were marred by two events, neither of which were in the control of the cast or production team. On the second night the audience in the balcony were disruptive and some had to be evicted. On the last night two Old Boys, at that time at University, played a childish hoax on the audience which severely embarrassed the Headmaster and was in extremely poor taste. A week later they made a public apology in *The Luton News.*

The Autumn term ended with a coach load of boys travelling to the Varsity Rugby match on 7th December, members of the Dramatic Society visiting London on the 14th to see a performance of *The Match Maker*, and the longest day of the year being celebrated with an Old Time Dance in a beautifully decorated hall. The School Orchestra gave a concert conducted by Mr Woodcock which revealed the talents of its soloists. David Oldroyd caused some laughter with a performance of Saint-Saens' Elephant, from the *Carnival of the Animals*, and B. Router demonstrated the versatility of the trombone in *Lucy Long*. In both these items D. Grant proved himself an able and sympathetic accompanist. The School broke up for the holidays on the 23rd, after the traditional end of term Christmas lunch and Carol Service.

A Quiet Gentleman

The School suffered a great loss on New Year's Day, 1955, with the sudden death following a heart attack of Mr William H. Chapman whilst he was walking in New Bedford Road. A native of Windermere, Mr Chapman came to Luton in 1942 after several years teaching in Bishop Cotton's School in India. Wynne Parry described him as a man of many parts, who identified himself with almost all activities of the School, to which he was devoted. During the War he had been an officer of the School's Cadet Corps, and afterwards he had sponsored the aero-modelling club, organised school boxing and assisted in a big way the School's soccer and cricket. He also found time at a mature age to read for a London University BSc degree, which he took externally in 1954.

The School held a special Memorial Service on 5th January, at which Mr W.N. Thorpe said a prayer and Mr Wynne Parry read from Bunyan's *The Pilgrim's Progress.* The funeral took place later that day at St Andrew's Church, and was attended by 23 members of Staff, a dozen senior boys, Governors, Old Boys, members of the Education Committee and many others. Next day the boys of Mr Chapman's class, 1a, sent flowers to his widow and daughter.

Another Memorial Service was held at Luton Parish Church on 11th February; this was for Miss H.K. Sheldon, former Headmistress of the High School, who had

died in Epsom on 2nd February, aged 72. The Headmaster, senior Staff, the Head Prefect and Second Prefect joined the High School representatives who were in attendance.

The spring term began with six inches of snow, making travel to and from School difficult. An Old Boy, Michael R. Phillips (1943–50), was appointed to the Staff in January to teach mathematics; he was only the third ex-student to return as a master.

The Home and School Association was troubled by falling numbers. The annual 'Any Questions' evening, during which almost any master was available to be consulted, was probably the most popular fixture; followed closely by a river trip from Maidenhead to Windsor, which included a tour of the Castle. The Association also provided prizes for Spoken English, medals for Athletics, and assistance in individual cases where boys were in need of financial aid. During 1954 it presented the School with a set of hurdles costing £120.

In Soccer the 1st and U15 XIs were unbeaten. Under John E. Stevens' captaincy, the former contained some experienced players and also some youngsters of great promise, including David J. Hills, who was chosen to play for London Schools against Glasgow Schools. The Under 15 XI won the Wix Trophy final (played on Hitchin Town FC Ground) against Old Hale Way School, Hitchin, by 5 goals to 1, Captain R. Day scoring 4, and J.C. Tait 1 goal.

In Cross-Country the teams ran in 19 meetings and did averagely well. Conditions were often atrocious; four inches of snow and flooding at Hertford Grammar School and thick fog and treacherously icy ground at Stratton School. In the Ranelagh Harriers Schools' Cup captain P.R. Robinson came 22nd in a field of 111 runners.

At Cricket the School won 24 matches and lost 18. In the 1st team, G.F. Taylor was the most promising batsman, always giving the innings a good start and performing creditably at the wicket. J.E. Stevens was usually his opening partner, showing a sound defence. A.J. Evans was a good fighting captain who never relaxed his concentration, and whose batting and bowling were the steadiest in the side.

In Swimming the team came second in the Luton Schools' Gala, and did it on the enthusiasm of a handful of boys. The Invitation Relay (4 x 1 length), swum by J.G. Booth, W.J. Dickens, B.S. Haddon and R.F. Chivers, won them the Dillingham Shield. The House Swimming Championships were won by the Grasshoppers.

In Tennis 10 matches were played of which five were won and five lost. Roger Tout and David Olney, the School's first pair, lost only one set during the season.

Four new records were broken on Sports Day on 18th May, in spite of heavy rain and snow overnight and a strong north wind on the day itself. All jumps and field events had to be made into the wind, allowing only one record to R.F. Merchant in the (u.16) Discus. Track events were also affected. D.G. Bond equalled the Open 440 yds record and went on to become *Victor Ludorum*. The Bland brothers were rewarded for their hard training, and two House relay teams set up new best times.

The Tennis team, 1955. (standing) B. Phillips, Mr C.E. Wareham, S.J. Maynard, (seated) F. Wallder, D.B. Olney, R.F. Tout, T.C. Ray, D. Horne. (*LN*)

In the Luton Schools' Sports the under 15 boys won the Championship Shield for the 5th year in succession, and a new cup, the Tripp Trophy, awarded for an outstanding individual performance, went to William O. Williams for superb hurdling. In the County AAA Championships the team just lost the Arnold Whitchurch Trophy to Kimbolton School, but gained 6 first, 8 second and 4 third places.

Rugby enjoyed a very good season; 42 games being won out of 62 played. The 1st XV were unbeaten in their 14 matches and scored 355 points at the cost of 65 against them. There was a tremendous team spirit, due in no small measure to the loyal and enthusiastic band of parent supporters and the inspiration it gained from its experienced and exemplary captain, 'Jumbo' J.E. Stevens. A stuffed elephant in the School rugger colours was presented to Stevens by the parent supporters, with the wish that it would become a tradition for each rugger captain to hold 'Jumbo' during his term of office. At the end of the season a number of boys played for the

newly formed Bedfordshire Schools' Rugby Union.

School Clubs and Societies were proliferating. Participation in one or more often helped a boy to find himself and thence his career; or to simply have fun. However, so many boys were involved with dramatics or athletics, that they often had little time left to participate in other activities.

The Literary and Scientific Society found that in debate frivolity is generally more successful than serious discussion, and bore this in mind when selecting the motion for the Joint Debate with the Girls' High School, 'that this House prefers the Devil to the Deep Blue Sea'. It certainly did! A Mock Election, during General Inspection week in mid-July, returned D.R. May (Liberal Conservative) with a considerable majority. J. Sansom (Soc.) provided the only credible opposition. D. Lintern (Welsh Nationalist) proved the worth of his policy that Wales is for the Welsh.

The Archaeological Society visited Someries Castle and Verulamium Museum, and some of its members took part in excavations at Barton Hill Farm, Streatley, and at Snail Down, near Everleigh in Wiltshire, during the summer holidays.

The Natural History group had a number of field meetings on Bradgers and Warden Hills, and listened to talks on subjects as diverse as myxomatosis and the preservation of butterflies and moths. Messrs. Lovell, Barker and Dr Dony offered considerable enthusiasm and guidance.

Mr Eric Sansome led the Student Christian Movement Group, which joined with the High School for a Christmas Service of Lessons and Carols, and a Service of Lessons and Carols tracing the events in Christ's life from Palm Sunday to Easter Day. Two of the group helped Mr Ashworth by working in his garden. A number of speakers talked about their own denominations, including James Gale, Wynne Parry and the local Jewish Rabbi.

The School's annual Speech Day on 15th February was addressed by County Alderman F.G. Simms, JP, Chairman of the Bedfordshire Education Committee, who said that he was tired of the current tendency towards the adverse criticism of youth. He felt that the boys of 1955 compared favourably with those of previous generations. Every boy should have ambition and remember that one's education was never completed: the future of the country depended on them.

The Headmaster was worried about the effect that out of school jobs had on boys' school work. In a count made at the end of the summer term, 109 boys worked before morning school; 47 after school, 78 on Saturday mornings and 28 all day Saturday. He felt that this could only be detrimental to the boys concerned.

Mrs F.G. Simms presented the prizes, which included State Scholarships for D.C. Glover to the London School of Economics, and F.R.D. Goodyear to St John's College, Cambridge.

During the School Year 1955–56 Nicholas F. Gardner (L.VI Sc.), son of the Borough Librarian, spent a year at Benson High School, Portland, Oregon, USA, having obtained an American Field Service scholarship. The AFS was a private

organisation, with no political or religious affiliations, which aimed to increase understanding between nations and allow scholars to tell each other about their own countries. Students lived as a member of an American family, sharing the home, school and holiday life of the household. 650 students took advantage of the scheme and they all met together in Washington at the end of the year after a lightning tour of the country and a reception at the British Embassy. Gardner found the experience so beneficial, that the School subscribed to it for many years.

David Oldroyd was chosen to play in the National Youth Orchestra. He wrote:

> 'I was thrilled and would not have missed a minute of it. The first full rehearsal was the greatest moment, when 120 people plunged together into the splendour, bombast, excitement and, at times, unearthly beauty of the Benvenuto Cellini Overture.
>
> 'We gave two concerts: one in the Usher Hall, Edinburgh, as part of the Edinburgh Festival, and one in Glasgow, which was broadcast. I shall never forget the tense atmosphere as we came into the Usher Hall, packed to the roof-top, and struck up the chords of 'God Save the Queen'.
>
> 'At Easter we went abroad and gave concerts in Brussels and Amsterdam. Before leaving, we had strenuous rehearsals in Canterbury with Sir Malcolm Sergeant, culminating in a concert in the Festival Hall, which was televised.'

Oldroyd did not enjoy his years at Luton Grammar School and having himself taught in four senior schools, considered it 'a mostly bad school, a reflection of a mundane town that lacked a spiritual soul'. After Cambridge and eleven years of teaching chemistry in London and New Zealand, he became a lecturer in geology at the University of New South Wales, and later held a Professorship in their School of Science and Technology Studies, where after retiring in 1996 he is now Honorary Visiting Professor. His books on the history of geological research include *The Highlands Controversy* (1990) and *Earth, Water, Ice and Fire: 200 Years of Geological Research in the English Lake District* (2002).

From 23 to 25th March boys of the School performed *The Tempest*. 'Mr Donald Richmond lived with the play day and night for three months, conceived and largely designed the set, and made or directed the making of nearly all of the costumes.' Mr Herbert Nickols composed some delightful music including an impressive overture.

'As Calaban,' wrote Wynne Parry, 'John Sansom had all the poetry, primitive greatness and primitive littleness of this masterly creation of the dramatist; his gestures were intelligent and his articulation always clear. David Watkins (Stephano) showed how much real humour there is in Shakespeare, and made the most of his bottle and his lines. Frank Wallder acted with that merriment, lightness of touch and ease which the part of Trinculo required. The audiences were charmed by Guy Rowston as Ariel, and could hardly believe that he was a young and small boy. And

An all-male production of *The Tempest* was staged in March 1955, produced, designed and dressed by Mr D.E. Richmond. Here are the sailors: D. Bracey, D. Cheshire, D. Cooper, J. Cunningham, L. Fedigan, M. Hill, B. Router, A. Smith, J. Stevens, G. Taylor. (*LN-LMC*)

Prospero? Ian Cooper presented a noble and praiseworthy effort, that must have left him well-nigh exhausted after the last performance.'

It was in April 1955 that 'The September Players' were formed. A group of former High School and Grammar School actors, mostly at University, who believed that live theatre had something the cinema could not provide, aimed to produce a play every September at either the High or Grammar School. With David Sturman as Chairman, and Helen Wynter as Producer, they gained the support of the Head teachers and Lady Zia Wernher. Their first production, Ibsen's *The Wild Duck*, was performed from 21st September for three nights. In 1956 the group performed *Berkley Square*, and the following year, Pirandello's *Henry IVth*. Later productions were staged at the High School or the Luton Library Theatre.

Many of the Schools' former actors had prominent parts including David Hanson, David Sturman, Anthony Johnson, John Sansom, David Oldroyd, Sheila Golding, Patricia Farr and Valerie Bland. Of these, only one boy, David Hanson, is believed to have followed a theatrical career, after having read History at Nottingham and trained as a teacher at Exeter. He worked for some years in Repertory at Leatherhead, Guildford, Scarborough, Perth and Edinburgh, and played 'professional gentlemen' in television series, such as *Reginald Perrin* and *Within These Walls* (by Stopsley dramatist Kathleen Smith). In 1982 he was appointed lecturer in drama and English literature at Burapha University in Thailand, where he died in 1998.

The following summer (May 1956) another group of old students, called 'Thespians', performed *Much Ado About Nothing* in the open-air at Houghton Regis.

From 1947 it had been possible for children to be late-transferred between secondary schools by the introduction of a thirteen plus test and interview. This had taken place annually at the Luton 'higher' schools. On 6th May, 1955, preliminary tests were held for 13-year olds who had failed to gain entry to the Grammar and High Schools at 11. They were open to boys and girls born on or after 2nd September, 1941 and not later than 1st September, 1942. Their parents or guardians had to be resident in Bedfordshire. The applicants for the Grammar School were interviewed on 12th June. In 1954 some twenty children had been transferred at 13.

The Inspectors Call

From 23rd to 26th May, 1955, the School underwent a full General Inspection. Mr Webb recorded 'A full battery of Inspectors sat-in on Assembly, Monday to Wednesday. Used the Projection Room as their private room. Had their lunches with the staff.'

The following paragraphs are taken from their twenty-two page Report:

'This county grammar school for boys has experienced considerable change since 1940, when it was last inspected.

'The number of pupils has increased from 435 to 688; fee payers, who were then in the majority, and the ten-year-old boys, who then made up almost half the annual entry, are no longer accepted. 90% of the present pupils live within the borough of Luton, and it has the comfortable assurance that profitable and interesting employment for the leavers is available locally. This latter circumstance is, no doubt, a strong reason why some two-thirds of boys leave before they have had the advantage of a course in the Sixth Form. It is very disappointing that of the dozen or so boys who enter annually at 13 few reach the Sixth Form and many leave before completing a year in form five.

'The proportion of boys going on to universities continues to increase even

though the numbers (46 of the 376 leavers in the years 1952–1954) are still markedly below the national average for similar grammar schools. In this period the largest number of leavers took up apprenticeships (110) and other large groups went to accountancy and banking (45), national service (44), laboratory work (31), trades (30), and municipal and post office services (25).

'A new kitchen and an extension to the dining room are soon to be built and then, except for a shortage of washing facilities, the accommodation will be admirable for a grammar school with a three-form entry, the size for which this school was planned and to which it may eventually revert. The building is not really adequate for the present numbers and if the school is to have a permanent entry of four forms it will need a larger laboratory for advanced work and it will be desirable for it to have a second art room, a second library or reading room, and more storage space. The present solution to the pressing shortage of teaching space is to use the library and balcony parade for class teaching. This cannot be regarded as satisfactory so long as the dining room and assembly hall remain unused for the greater part of the day.

'In view of the number of boys taking advanced courses in mathematics, it would be advantageous to set aside for Sixth Form study of the subject a room in which the special equipment might include at least one calculating machine. It is doubtful whether the electrical wiring in the classrooms permits a proper use of modern teaching aids.

'The annual grant from the Authority to the school Library has been £125 per year. This sum, which has to cover new books, replacements, repairs and the purchase of periodicals, is hardly sufficient for the needs of 700 boys. The actual use of the Library as a place of study is very limited indeed. For more than thirty periods of the week the room is used as a teaching space and even the Sixth Form have very limited opportunities to use it for reading or private study. The Library can never become the centre of intellectual life in the school, until alternative space is found for the teaching of the forms who now use it.

'The assistant staff of 35 masters, well led by the various heads of departments, is a forceful and competent teaching unit, numerically adequate for the length and diversity of the courses in operation. A certain lack of scholarship and sparkle in the classroom and a marked tendency to limit the objective of teaching to examination requirements may not be unrelated to the fact that not more than half of its graduate members hold good honours degrees or their equivalent, only about half their total number have had experience in teaching in comparable schools elsewhere, and only eight masters are under 40 years of age. The greatest care will have to be exercised in making new appointments if the balance of academic distinction, appropriate experience, and age is to be redressed without harmful delay.

'Great care has been taken to ensure that the curriculum should combine the

basis for a sound general education with the maximum opportunity for boys to work on the subject of their choice. Since the excellent apprenticeships available in Luton usually depend in value upon the level at which the candidate has satisfied his examiners in mathematics and science, it is not surprising to find those subjects, particularly science, generously treated, albeit somewhat at the expense of flexibility in the curriculum as a whole.'

The teaching of individual subjects was found on the whole to be satisfactory. Mathematics was one of the strongest in the school and could become even stronger. Art could be made more purposeful: 'pictures might be painted to decorate the very long corridors.' Latin, which had caused so much trouble at the time of the 1940 inspection was still taught by Mr Root. 'The grammar is drilled methodically. The lessons lack something of liveliness and breadth, qualities which might go far to establish a wider interest in the subject. Much would be gained if more use were made of Latin reading matter from the earliest stages.' In Science 'The Sixth Form has far outgrown the capacities of the advanced laboratories for physics and chemistry, and some solution will have to be found if high standards of practical work are to be maintained.' Perhaps the most scathing report was on Mr Herbert Nickols' Music lessons, where 'in the first three years he appears to be preoccupied with the future requirements of the comparatively few boys who will offer music as an examination subject, and the lessons heard with the first, second and third year forms followed a uniform pattern of written exercises on notation, with a little singing of traditional songs. There is scanty evidence of progression in this narrow field, the repertory of songs is small, and the quality of singing is poor.' This was exactly the pattern of music lessons under Ronald Bridger, ten years before. The only difference was that Bridger was a disciplinarian: Nickols was gentle and sensitive. In 1949 the county Music Organiser had spent a day with Mr Nickols, as a result of which Ronald Bridger had returned to demonstrate how to control and teach a class, and Mr Webb had a serious talk with him about preserving order and being more systematic in the basic music course. Bridger's demonstration music lesson had been repeated ever after with the younger boys, and it must have been a merciful relief when, in July 1956, Mr Nickols was able to retire to Cornwall. He was a man of ready wit, unfailing courtesy and infinite kindness. The School was shocked to hear of his death on Sevenoaks railway station on 10th June, 1963, during a spell of very warm weather.

The Inspectors' Report concluded:

'The School can record substantial progress during the last 15 years. Higher academic standards have been attained, the volume of advanced work has been expanded, and more enthusiasm has been aroused for physical activity. There is now a solid foundation on which to build and it may be expected that before long

the teaching will lay greater emphasis on scholarship, as distinct from examination preparation, that the Sixth Form courses will attract a greater proportion of the boys, and that the standards of character and social training will be compatible with those highly responsible positions in the adult world for which so many of the boys are fitted by intellect.'

Within a month of the Inspection Miss Hughes, the School Meals Advisor, was in School with plans for the new Dining Room, and a week later Mr Smith, from the Borough Architect's Department, had called to discuss a new Advanced Physics laboratory with the Headmaster. The Staff met to discuss the implications of the Inspectors' Report on 14th November.

We may at this point pause to mention bullying. This subject has come up frequently in discussions with Old Boys. When questioned, Mr Webb said 'there was no bullying at the Grammar School, the boys were beyond that.' One former student has written: 'Mr Webb seemed to me to be disengaged, as if he hardly knew what was really going on in the School. There was terrible bullying at times, but he never seemed to make the slightest effort to stamp it out. Terrible things went on in the changing rooms. You will remember the misery of being driven out into the cold in winter to that awful playground. And the fights. *That was the worst part of it all.* You could get a bully picking on someone. Eventually a bloody fight would start. After about five minutes someone would come out and stop it. Both combatants would be blamed, and that was never fair. Why did Mr Webb not put a stop to those barbaric practices? He never seemed to care. Some poor boys like A—— and G—— had a terrible time being bullied. Such things should not have happened in a civilised school.' Most of the Prefects ignored what they saw. Those who tried to be more positive were seen as wimps. Masters who intervened (with some notable exceptions) usually found it more convenient to issue detentions, rather than investigate the cause. For boys who did not conform, dared to *not* like sport, were considered too academic by their peers, had an eccentric hobby or some slight physical defect – Luton Grammar School was not always a happy place.

During the morning of 7th July, Mr Rex Clayton, the Careers Master, suffered a stroke and Dr Joachim was called. He returned to School in September, mornings only, but was unable to sustain the pressure. Absent for the remainder of the School year, he retired in August 1956.

On Sunday, 10th September, 1955, an Old Lutonians' Masonic Lodge was consecrated. Founded by six Old Lutonians and a Master (W.N. Thorpe), it held its meetings at the Luton Masonic Centre on the corner of Church Street and Waller Street. Archie Wickson was the driving force, and many Old Lutonian Freemasons expressed a wish to join: 'The loyalty and love which we feel for the 'Old School', in whatever form it may be, will surely be strengthened now that so many of us will unite as brethren in our own Lodge.' Following the formation of the Sixth Form

College in 1966 members resolved to accept former male students of the College. This proved less productive than expected, and the Lodge is now 'open' to non-Old Boys, and meets five times a year at The Pavilion, Bowling Green Lane, Luton.

When the School returned after the summer holidays, on 13th September, they were greeted by an IRA flag with crossed rifles flying from the flagpole. White-washed across Mr Godfrey's window were the words 'THE IRA STRIKES AGAIN!' Painted over the windows of the Gymnasium, Woodwork and Geography rooms were nicknames of masters. As soon as the slogans were seen by the Caretakers, they got to work removing them; though not before most of the boys had enjoyed the joke, and a freelance photographer had recorded them for *The Luton News*.

The Joint School Play in December was J.B. Priestley's *Time and the Conways,* performed at the High School. It was a play designed to give full scope to the ladies of the cast, the men filling in the background. Valerie Bland captured the delightful freshness of the young Carol, and Rochelle Saunders was convincing as the simple, sensitive girl who marries not very successfully into a self-important family. Patricia Henrey as Hazel had plenty of vitality and Angela Connolly made effective contrasts between the grave and the gay; her sadness at the close, wrongly attributed by her 'mother' to over-excitement, was very moving. Joanna Chapman, as the completely undiscerning mother, and Moya Miller, as the self-important school-Marm, played their roles so well as to make us thoroughly detest such women. The boys, Alvin Turner, Desmond Turner, Simon Luxemburg and Robin Musson, managed the difficult task of under-acting remarkably well. The producers were Gladys Brown and Russell Key.

The Old Lutonians held their 25th Annual Dinner at the School on the evening of 3rd December. The guest of honour was Mr Dorian Williams, a well-know television commentator on horse-jumping events, and Master of the Whaddon Chase Hunt. Earlier in the day the School XV had beaten the Old Boys by 14 points to nil in the annual rugger match.

The winter term ended much as usual. Thirty-six boys went with Mr Muse to Twickenham to watch the Varsity Match on 6th December. Three days later the VIth Form social in the School Hall passed off without incident. Mr G.C. Grimshaw left the PE department, his place being taken by Mr M.J. Beadle. The whole school watched the semi-documentary Robert Flaherty film *Louisiana Story* (1948) during the morning of 21st December, and in the afternoon joined in the annual Carol Service, before departing for the Christmas holidays.

Mr R.S. Clayton as seen by 'Bryant'.

Chapter 13

1956 to 1960

The School was delighted to receive the news that its Chairman of Governors, Alderman John Burgoyne, OBE, JP, had received a Knighthood in the 1956 Queen's Birthday Honours 'for political and public services'. Sir John had devoted many years to the service of the School.

Mr Rex S. Clayton officially retired on 31st August, 1956, due to serious illness. His career was unique in the history of the School. He entered as a boy in January 1908, with the number 254, and left in July 1914. He was soon in the Royal Artillery, serving on the Somme and Arras fronts and the notorious Ypres Salient. His health broke down at the end of the War, and he never fully recovered. Many who knew him saw his personality change too. With a BSc from London University, he joined the School staff in 1919 and taught chemistry and botany at various levels, and was made the first Careers Master in 1940. He threw himself into this latter task and set many boys on paths to their future careers. He knew all the local Heads of Industry, and was conversant with the straightforward paths to University entrance. For boys who were prepared to follow the normal routes his help was second to none. For boys who preferred a different pattern, an unusual career, often in the arts, he was likely to falter.

When Dennis Farr wanted to study the history of Art, it was Mr Smoothey, not Mr Clayton, who guided him towards the Courtauld Institute. He gave K.T. Norcott 'no usable advice'. A.W. 'George' Thorpe received 'no advice at all'. Professor David Oldroyd had the misfortune to be 'taught' chemistry by him for two years to O-level in 'Physics with Chemistry'. 'For many weeks we did nothing but learn how to put stools down silently from off the benches! We did almost no practical work. In the end the 'teaching' became no more than having the syllabus dictated to us, and even that was not completed before we sat the exams. It was a deplorable state of affairs,

and Mr Webb *should* have been aware, and done something about it. I got a grade 3 in O level, and nearly all the marks must have come from the physics side. The physics teacher, Mr S.H. Matthews, was very good.' Phillip Gething recalled Clayton as 'a rather short man with tinted glasses, who seemed to be in a state of permanent complaint about boys and their manners. His nickname was 'Jellybelly' and I think this was due to his constant whinges rather than any shortcomings in his digestive system. He had nearly been Head Boy: time after time he told us it was a close thing between 'Leighton and Clayton'.

Mr Donald Richmond left in 1956 after three memorable years. He had thrown himself into School life, and made a tremendous impact, particularly upon Drama. 'Perhaps his greatest triumphs lay in the conversion of all kinds of unlikely material – human and otherwise – into works of art. His infectious enthusiasm and all-round competence enabled him to create a variety of stage personalities from boys of only average acting ability, while with those with aptitude his success was outstanding.'

Seven new members of staff joined the School in September: Mr P.J. Ingram, BSc, Mr K.J. Williams, BSc, Mr A.C. Hauke, GRSM, LRAM, Mr G.W. Barraclough, BSc, Mr M. Sharman, NDD, Mr A.E. Bowen, BA and Mr R.J. Griffiths, BSc.

The Guest for Speech Day, 7th March, 1956, was the former Chairman of Skefko, the Right Honourable Lord Glyn of Farnborough, MC, DL, whose duties as Chairman of the Select Committee on Estimates took him away to Westminster before the proceedings had concluded. Mr Webb warned his audience against becoming too 'gadget minded' in the age of automation, and empasised the need to preserve the abiding values from becoming lost in the new world of technology. He wanted boys with the best brains to be educated to the top of their bent, and to go to the jobs that needed them and which they alone could do. Industry needed more and ever more of the best young men, but the professions needed them just as much.

Lord Glyn spoke of the dangers of complacency in a highly competitive world. Expressions like 'I couldn't care less' had to be eradicated. He thought that in the future there might be a war fought, not with nuclear weapons, but with brains: a fight for survival. The country that had technicians would also get the trade.

Alderman E.K. Hickman, Mayor of Luton, presented the prizes and awards. In the GCE examinations at ordinary level, 105 boys had between them gained 564 subject passes. At the advanced level 41 Sixth Form boys gained 103 subject passes. D.G. Bond had been awarded a State Scholarship to Imperial College. His result was outstanding: passes in 5 subjects, when 3 was the common number. He had been Captain of Athletics, was *Victor Ludorum*, and a member of the Rugger 1st XV. R. Pyburn, then at Manchester, was on the reserve list for a State Scholarship,

In February the Chairman and Vice-Chairman of Governors, together with Dr Corbett (Director of Education), interviewed four senior members of staff for the post of Careers Master. The applicants were Mr G. Clarke, Mr E. Sansome, Mr W.N. Thorpe and Mr H.E. Woodcock. So difficult was the choice that the

Headmaster wisely distanced himself from the interviews. In the end Mr Harold Woodcock, who had joined the School in 1923, was offered and accepted the position. He commenced in April 1956, with an increase in salary of £140 per annum.

The School was closed on 24th February for the admission examination. A note records that also present were Form IVc, and eight boys who truanted in order to see the England v. Spain football match at Wembley, or on television.

For his final dramatic production at the School Mr Richmond chose *A Servant of Two Masters*, a farce by Carlo Goldoni. It was staged on 14th, 16th and 17th March, with an all male cast. David Watkins was exceptional in a very long part, playing the servant, Truffaldino, with all the necessary agility. The scene in which he served a meal to his two masters went without a hitch, which was a triumph, not only for himself, but also for the Stage Manager, David Wallington, and his backroom boys. Guy Rowston as the serving-maid, Smeraldina, was at times almost incredibly funny. It was a brilliant move on Mr Richmond's part, to put together on the stage the tallest and shortest boys in the school as waiters.

On 6th June, 350 boys from the upper School, accompanied by ten masters, visited the cinema to see Olivier's *Richard III*, the set play for the coming year.

The 1st XI football team enjoyed a very successful season and played soccer of a very high standard. The team, which included seven of the previous season's Wix Trophy players, maintained its unbeaten record. David Hills was the outstanding player, scoring 27 goals, thus exceeding all recent totals since A.W. Thorpe in 1946. Peter Evans was selected to play for the London Schools (u.16) against the Glasgow Schools at Glasgow on 12th May. Mr Wally Shanks of Luton Town Football Club was the FA Coach to the School for six afternoons. R. Day and R.D. Pearman took advantage of the FA coaching course at Lilleshall.

Snow, sleet, rain, mud and bone-hard ruts will put anyone, but the most hardy runner, off Cross-Country. The 1956 season was far from successful. The demands of other School activities made it almost impossible at times to field a full team, and the Colts (u.15) team was largely made up of 12-year-old boys. In a road relay at Queen's Park, D.F. Cooper completed the last mile with a broken toe, and in a creditable time. Donald Bracey captained the senior team.

For a number of years the School sent some its most promising athletes to the National Coaching Course under Mr Geoffrey Dyson at Motspur Park during the Christmas holiday. At the beginning of 1956 they were able to send eight boys, and their training clearly showed during the Athletics season. For the first time Sports Day, on 16th May, saw the introduction of a 75 yards hurdles race (2ft 6in) for the u.14 age group, and the Hop, Step and Jump for the u.16 and Open groups. Guest of honour was Old Boy Brian Oddie, Olympic 5000 metres finalist in 1928. *Victor Ludorum* was Captain of Athletics, John E. Stevens, who achieved a fine shot put of 47ft using the latest O'Brien style, and adding over a yard to R.W. Kelly's record of

1949. Tom Odam, Vice-Captain, was runner-up with three firsts including a new High Jump record of 5 ft 4 ins. Michael J. Bland gained five firsts, three of which brought new records.

In the Luton Schools' Sports where championship scorers had to be under 15, the School was not strong enough to ward off a challenge from Icknield School who beat them 59 points to 52. The School team were comfortable winners in the Five Schools' Meeting where the older boys could play their part. In The Bedfordshire County AAA Championships the team broke five County records, gained 9 firsts and regained the coveted Whitchurch Trophy. John Stevens and Tom Flitton went on to gain National Standards at the English Schools' AAA Championships.

John 'Jumbo' Stevens went on to train as a Doctor at St Bartholomew's Hospital, London, before moving to South Africa, where he was indirectly associated with Dr Christian Barnard's Heart Transplant team.

In Cricket the excess of wins over losses looked fairly impressive, but the sides were all rather erratic and unpredictable. Three stalwarts of the 1st XI played their last seasons, and the School owed a great deal to Captain, A.J. Evans, G.F. Taylor, and J.E. Stevens, with his heavy commitment to athletics. David Hills bowled well and G. Gazey was a reliable stock bowler. The 2nd XI always played interesting cricket, with Barker, Bird and Gibbs as the star players. M.J. Gibbs was the first player from the School for three years to win a bat under the 'Star' scheme, and it was good to see him receive his colours after years of unobtrusive loyalty.

In Tennis, S.J. Maynard and E.G. Day were a very steady first pair and finished the season with a balance of 110 games in their favour. The Wasps were the winners of the Gething Cup.

In the Luton Amateur Swimming Club Gala the Pike Trophy for the Boys (u.16) Invitation Relay (3 x 33 yds.) was won by J.G. Booth, W.J. Dickens and B.G. Haddon. A combined Grammar School and High School team competed against Luton Amateur Swimming Club at the High School on 30th June, and won by 61 points to 56.

The 1956 senior Rugby teams had a successful season. The 1st XV had a run of eight victories and then ran into trouble, losing two matches against Hertford and Kettering and against two clubs, the Old Boys and Saracens Gypsies. Hertford clearly won by denying Luton possession of the ball – a very sound principle, and the Old Boys were definitely after blood, and under A.W. Thorpe's astute captaincy they got it in full measure. 'Experience and determination overcame youthful exuberance and physical fitness quite easily in this "match of the season" at Bradgers Hill.'

Another party of 37 boys, together with Mr Parry and Mr and Mrs Partridge, spent Easter in Paris, staying at the 'Institution Vaysse' in the Pré St Gervais district. They viewed the principal monuments, made trips to Fontainebleau and Versailles, and shopped in 'Au Printemps'. On the Tour Eiffel they met an Old Boy, Richard

Clark, who was an assistant in a Paris Lycée; and one evening a number of them went to the 'Bouffes Parisiennes' to see a performance in French of *Pygmalion*.

Four members of the Natural History Society came second in a competition organised by the Wild Flower Society, in which they recorded 647 species. Kingswood School at Bath won with a collection of 764 species.

On 22nd March the Student Christian Movement Group held a Conference attended by about 180 pupils from the High School, Secondary Technical School and the Grammar School. Their speaker was John Ferguson, MA, BD, lecturer in Classics at Queen Mary College, Chairman of the Fellowship of Reconciliation, and a member of the British executive of the UNA. In speaking about 'Christianity and Modern Problems' he said that he considered the most vital problems to be food, colour, communism and the new status of women – in that order. Mr Ferguson answered a barrage of questions in a frank and lively manner, and was thanked for a stimulating and challenging evening by Maureen McGlashan and Michael Root.

For the second year in succession the School had been honoured by the award of a Field Scholarship by the American Field Service. On 7th August, David Reilly sailed from Zeebrugge to spend a year at Moorhead Senior High School, Minnesota. He, and a fellow Exchange student, a vivacious New Zealand blonde called Jenny Lynch, were given the best possible year that they could have wished for. David soon had many speaking engagements, press interviews and television shows; he also had his own radio record show: "This is Dave Reilly, the lackadaisical limey, bringing you records for your listening pleasure over KVOX, 1280 on your radio dial." The highlight of his trip was meeting President Eisenhower at the White House.

Some Old Lutonians

There was interesting news of Old Boys during 1956. Pilot Officer John Gurney (1946–54) received his wings as a National Serviceman. They were presented to him by Princess Alexandra, together with the Pilots' Course Aerobatics Trophy which he had won in a Vampire T11. He trained under the RAF Provost-Vampire scheme, and had completed 120 hours with De Havilland Vampires T11 and Mk V at RAF Oakington in Cambridgeshire. John went on to gain his BA Hons. in English from St Edmund Hall, Oxford in 1959. After a period in teaching, he became Senior English Lecturer at Bedford College of Higher Education from 1969–85. He then retired, becoming a freelance writer with a number of books of poetry, including thirty-six verse plays to his credit. He died in October 2002.

Brian C. Sweeney (1947–52) was also granted a National Service Commission in the RAF, and had become a Pilot Officer in the Technical (Engineering) Branch.

Dr William D. Waller (1942–49) – younger son of County Alderman H.R. Waller – had recently qualified at Gonville and Caius College, Cambridge for his MB and BChir. He already had his BA and MA. Whilst at Cambridge he was

President of the Medical Society. He had spent four years at Westminster Hospital, London.

Peter R. Vaughan (1945–53) had gained his BSc Eng from Imperial College, and had been awarded the Unwin Medal and premium for being the best student of the year. He went on to work on the Kainji Dam project in Nigeria, before joining the academic staff of Imperial College and becoming Professor of Ground Engineering from 1987–94. He became a Fellow of the Royal College of Engineering in 1991.

Peter D. Townsend (1941–49), married the actress Elizabeth Seal, star of the West End musical, *Pyjama Game*, on 11th February, 1956. Mr Webb sent them a congratulatory letter from the School, which was read out at the reception.

Mr G. E. K. 'Gekko' Walsh, Head Boy in 1936, called at the School on 8th March, whilst on six months leave from his District Officer's post in Northern Rhodesia, where he was the link between officialdom and the local tribespeople. He had been in Northern Rhodesia for nine years, and spoke two of the local languages.

News reached the School in October of the death of Anthony C. Davies (1947–52), who was killed in a motor cycling accident near Nicosia, in Cyprus. In his last years at School he had been captain of boxing, played in the 1st XV, and was a member of the School Athletics and Cross-Country teams. He was a sergeant in the RAF.

On 10th March, 1956, Tony Gregory (1948–53) made his first 'promising' home League appearance for Luton Town in a match against Bolton Wanderers: neither side scored. A more experienced sportsman, Trevor Bailey, the England Test Cricketer, visited the School on 15th March and spoke to a packed audience of school boys from all over the town in the afternoon, and parents in the evening.

A Harvest Festival service was held at the end of September, to which boys were invited to bring fresh flowers, fruit and vegetables. These were auctioned by the Home and School Association, the proceeds going to a deserving cause.

Some of the senior boys had harvesting imprinted on their minds. They had helped Mr C.H. Shaw at Manor Farm, Stopsley, gather 13 acres of potatoes during the first week of October. The crop was described as big enough, but not a heavy yield.

Remembrance Day was marked by a special service on 12th November to which Old Boys and parents were invited. Lessons were read by the President of the Old Lutonians' Club, Mr Ronald S. Bailey, and the Head Prefect, David A. Watkins. The whole School then marched past the War Memorials.

A Christmas Bazaar and Hobbies Exhibition organised by Messrs. G. Clarke and J. Muse for the Home and School Association was a great success, raising £214 19s 5d, and thus enabling the Association to pay off the balance on a Trophy Cabinet, which they were presenting to the School. They had also made a considerable contribution towards the cost of the Honours Board, and purchased a further set of hurdles which had been used on Sports Day.

The annual Junior Brains Trust was held at the High School with a panel of Sixth Form students: Maureen McGlashan, Pauline Thorpe, Hilary Tompsett, D.A. Watkins, B.D. Patterson and B.N. Martyn. In spite of the dangers of the venue the boys more than held their own.

The joint Schools' Play at the end of November was *Tovarich*, a very free adaptation of Jacques Deval's original French comedy about the Russia-in-Exile movement. The experienced actors, Patricia Henry, Valerie Bland, Robin Musson and the most mature Elizabeth Hey, all gave polished performances. There were a number of new faces, all of whom the reviewer, Wynne Parry, found most effective. He singled out Michael Anderson as Gorotchenko, 'the mailed fist within the velvet glove' for the elegant ease and control with which he played the rôle. Gladys Brown and Russell Key again produced the play.

At the beginning of December the Bedfordshire Education Committee announced that they were amending their Awards Scheme, by deleting the requirement that students must be British subjects to be eligible for grants and scholarships. Mr K. B. Webb found this unacceptable, and pointed out that Bedfordshire students sometimes received awards to enable them to study abroad. They did not expect to receive awards from their 'host' countries – but if foreign students were to be eligible for awards in Bedfordshire, it was possible that the scheme would be abused. What was to stop a student from Switzerland coming to Bedfordshire, receiving an award and returning to Switzerland immediately his course was completed? The Chairman of the Awards Committee lamely replied that the Committee would have to see that no such abuse occurred.

The term ended on 21st December with a disastrous screening of *The Last Days of Dolwyn*, (1949), written and directed by Emlyn Williams. It told the true story of a Welsh valley flooded to make a reservoir. In spite of starring Dame Edith Evans and Richard Burton, it did not go down well with the boys, who found it stiff and stagey. They demonstrated their boredom well before the end.

The Year of *Sputnik*

It had been realised for many years that the School had to keep parents informed of their sons' progress, hence the termly scarlet Report Books. Many parents felt that this was not enough: they wanted face-to-face contact with the masters who taught their boys. The matter had been partly remedied by 'Any Questions' evenings, organised by the Home and School Association. In February 1957 this was taken a step further, when, after an 'open' session in the Hall, parents were able to talk with Heads of Departments and their colleagues in various parts of the building.

The Annual Speech Day was held on Wednesday, 20th February. In a lengthy report, the Headmaster likened life to an educational journey. Once a boy embarked on the Grammar School 'train' at 'Station 11-plus' the train was designed to take him

through to 'Station 18-plus' or, sometimes, '19-plus' in a continuous journey. "If people jump off the train at 16 or, worse still, at 15, without exceptionally good reasons, they have not only prevented someone else from going the whole journey, but they have not seen those wider views which lie between Stations 16 and 18." Grammar School boys, he said, were needed in every field of modern scientific and industrial development, but there were not enough of them to meet all demands. "The proportion of our sixth form on the science side is just over 70 per cent, and cannot well be higher without robbing such professions as the Church, the law, banking, accountancy, librarianship, music and arts teaching. The total number in the sixth form ought to be half as big again, if the needs of the nation are to be realised."

The Headmaster reported that in 1956 a total of 110 fifth-form boys had gained passes in 528 subjects in GCE. At advanced level 50 boys had gained 109 passes. State Scholarships had been awarded to M.W. Root, Imperial College, London; C.J. Webb, Manchester University; M.C. Johnson, Birmingham University, and reserve, S.C. Luxemburg, Imperial College, London. A record further eighteen boys had gained entrance to university, or comparable courses, somewhere in Britain.

Prizes and awards were distributed by the Mayor, Cllr. F.W. Bates, an Old Lutonian. The Guest of Honour was Sir Norman Kipping, JP, Director-General of the Federation for British Industry. Sir Norman reviewed the industrial progress made in this country over the previous fifty years. Half the people employed in industry today, he said, were making things which were unimagined fifty years ago. He guessed that in five years' time people would be making things unthought of in 1957. He went on to stress the disadvantages of specialisation: a man needed to have breadth of life in order to understand other men's business and to understand other peoples on whom we depended for our export market.

Instead of the usual full-length play in March, it was decided to experiment with a series of one-act plays and sketches. This enabled members of the Junior Dramatic Society to show their performing skills in the first of these, *The Bishop's Game*. Michael Anderson and David Page enjoyed themselves in the well-known sketch *The 'Ole in the Road*. The acting in *The Football Club Supper* was very clever, and ably supported by the two speaking parts, those of Keith Thompson as the butler and Melvyn Butcher as Lord Fitzwoolley. The last play, *The Fourth Man,* was the most satisfying of all. Jonathan Lutley held the team of actors together, ably supported by David Brown as the fruity-voiced caricature clergyman, and John Cunningham as the schoolmaster.

On 18th April fourteen boys and Mr Parry set sail, in a heavy mist, for Ostend and Brussels. The party visited the Brussels Museum and Art Gallery 'which Mr Parry found very interesting.' They toured the city and noted with interest the speed with which civil marriages were conducted in the Town Hall – four in fifteen minutes! Ghent and Bruges were enjoyable, but best of all they liked the clean city

of Middleburg in Holland, where they bought presents. Few of them were likely to forget the very rough sea crossing home.

On 19th April another group of twenty boys from the School and twenty-seven girls from the 'Tech' went by coach to Bönigen in Switzerland, led by Mr and Mrs Clarke and Mr Ellis. There were no real language problems, although one boy managed to order three quart bottles of cider and one glass. The crowning event was the ascent of the Jungfraujoch (12,000 feet) by train. Whilst some of the boys spent their spare time with the girls, others preferred to play rugger at the lakeside, where a fisherman was on hand to recover the ball.

There were some original and praiseworthy performances at the First Annual Concert given by the School Orchestra and Choir on 5th June. Reviewing the concert in *The Luton News*, Mary Paul wrote:

> 'The concert commenced with three pieces from the orchestra, a 'Processional March', in which the attack was excellent; the Minuet from Mozart's Symphony No 41 C Major which was severely mauled – here the orchestra overstepped themselves, one of Mozart's earlier works would perhaps have been a better choice; and a Hungarian Dance by Brahms.
>
> 'Two organ solos were well played by D.G. Cambridge. They were a Choral Improvisation by Karg-Elert and Bach's Fantasia in C Major. The Grammar School possesses a very promising musician in this young organist.
>
> 'The best individual performance of the evening was unquestionably that of the oboe Concerto in B flat by Handel, which was played by David R. Grant, with D.G. Cambridge at the organ. The soloist displayed a technical mastery which was most impressive, and he should do very well if he intends to take up music seriously.
>
> 'The most successful songs from the choir were a group of Hungarian folk songs and a fantasy on 'Old Mother Hubbard', which were sung extremely well and with delightful humour.
>
> 'A great deal of the success of the evening was undoubtedly due to the lively personality of Mr A.C. Hauke, the Music Master, and Mr C.W. Parry, who played some of the accompaniments.'

The Student Christian Movement hosted a Christian Conference in April, also attended by members of the High School and Technical School. The speaker was the Revd. Gibson Clarke who, as Secretary of the Churches' Committee on Gambling, had been a member of two Royal Commissions to investigate Betting and Gambling.

The Literary and Scientific Society's traditional Friday meetings suffered from lack of support, due to the insistence of the PE staff that the Rugby players could not do with less than five evenings a week for training. Only the debates seemed to attract a reasonable attendance. The motions, that this House 'preferred Statistics to

Shakespeare', and 'had faith in Her Majesty's Ministers' at the time of the Suez Crisis, were both carried; but at the Joint Debate with the High School the House soundly defeated a motion that 'Modern Youth is Degenerate'.

The Natural History Society held a large number of meetings: eleven indoors and six in the field. Lecturers included a vet, an official from the Agricultural Engineering Establishment at Silsoe, and a Senior Scientific Officer from the Meteorological Office at Dunstable. Visits were made to Flowers' Luton Brewery, the Luton Sewage Works, and Kew Gardens. Professor Colin J. Humphreys has written:

> 'I particularly remember the history teacher, Dr John Dony, who interested me in botany. At weekends he would lead four boys* from the School up hills, down dales, into marshlands, on the look out for both common and rare wild flowers throughout Bedfordshire. I remember our team entered a competition run annually by the Wild Flower Society for school groups throughout the United Kingdom. Between March and October 1956 we recorded 792 species, and won a small prize for coming first. At the time I knew hundreds, if not thousands, of Latin names of botanical species and I am sure this experience influenced me in my subsequent decision to be a scientist, although not a botanist! In the sixth form I had the difficult decision of deciding what subjects to take and, with great reluctance, I omitted A-Level Biology, thinking I could do it as a hobby, whereas studying Physics as a hobby was more difficult!'
>
> *[J. Harper, C.J. Humphreys, D. Stanbridge and J.D. Stephen]

Since gaining a State Scholarship in 1959 to Imperial College, London, Colin J. Humphreys is now Goldsmiths' Professor of Materials Science at Cambridge University and President of the Institute of Materials, Minerals and Mining. He was a past president of Christians in Science, and his book *The Miracles of Exodus* (2003) has caused much interest in theological as well as scientific fields. He was recently honoured with a CBE.

There was a large entry for the annual Open Table Tennis Championship during the Spring Term. The Final, played between M. Kaye and M.H B. Peters, was one of the most exciting of recent years; Kaye eventually running out the winner. In eight matches against other schools, five were won and three lost.

The School Football teams enjoyed a long, mild Spring Term, allowing them to play a total of 44 matches. For a long period of the term the three inside-forwards, R. Day, W.P. Evans and M.J. Gibbs, were almost level as goal scorers. Then Day had a day of prolific goal scoring, which he repeated until it almost became a habit, and he finished the season with 37 goals, only two fewer than 'George' Thorpe in 1946. The team remained unbeaten for the third successive year, and their total of 89 goals was a new record for a 1st XI. Captain, Tony Hall, was a splendid example to the other players. R.J.H. Barker was chosen as reserve goalkeeper for the London

The Cross-Country Team, April 1957. (back) Mr H.E. Bowen, D.J. Wagon, K.R. Halstead, R.F. Matthews, R. Bates, R. Peck, R.C. Easton, (front) D. Turner, D.F. Cooper, D. Bracey, M.J. Bland, D. Watkins. (*LN*)

Schools against Glasgow Schools in the match on Chelsea's ground on 8th April.

By running the Inter-House Cross-Country Championships in the Autumn Term, some hidden talent was discovered in time for the Spring season. Captain, David Bracey, D.F. Cooper, D.S. Turner, E.J. Lutley and R.C. Easton all put up some good performances and gained their colours. Bracey's achievements in races at Ranelagh and Queen's Park, and in the Eastern Counties Championships, showed that he was a long distance runner of considerable ability. Mr H.E. 'Hank' Bowen took over management of the team from Mr Partridge, who retired after five years service.

Due to the long Spring term, Athletics training started well before the Easter holidays, and a number of boys benefited from the AAA course held at the School on 11th May. There was a fresh northerly wind, and a hard, dry track for Sports Day, on 29th May. Even so, six records were broken, including the Open Relay (4 x 110 yds) won by the Wasps in 46.8 seconds. Tom C. Flitton was *Victor Ludorum* and his Captain, Tom Odam, was runner-up.

The School finished 2nd to Kimbolton School in the County AAA Championships. John G. Booth put up a new championship record in the pole-vault of 9ft 3½ins. W.O. 'Bill' Williams, though beaten by a faster sprinter but inferior

hurdler, gained a Midland Counties standard in the Youths 110 yards Hurdles.

In the Luton Schools' Sports the School were not strong enough to hold off Icknield, who showed their superiority in the track events for the second year running. Individually, E.J. Reynolds showed good style over the hurdles, G.F.K. MacRae's Western Roll was much admired and J.W. Flippance and P.A. Auch were worthy champions in the long jump and javelin respectively.

For Cricket the Summer Term was a short but interesting one. The consistently high scoring of the 1st XI, which topped the hundred on six occasions, was a feature of the season. Five players scored more than a hundred runs, and special mention was made of the spirited hitting of R.D. Pearman and the splendid concentration shown by R.J.H. Barker. M.J. Gibbs had a very successful season; a very consistent bowler, he achieved a hat-trick in the final match. A. Hall was at all times a good captain, firmly controlling his side. The 2nd XI had one of its best seasons, with R.V. Colyer and R.J. Hill proving an excellent opening pair.

The School Lawn Tennis team, under the captaincy of S.J. Maynard, had a very successful season, winning 10 of its 13 matches, with 3 further matches rained off.

Like most other School activities, the Rugby season was hit by the Asian Flu epidemic, and a few games had to be cancelled. Statistically the 1st XV were not as successful as in the two previous years. Five games out of thirteen were lost. Of those which were won, most were comfortably achieved. The exceptions were against St Albans CGS, and Hitchin GS which was a tremendous battle. So well did Hitchin perform that Luton were always in arrears and the game looked lost. Captain, Tom Flitton, however, thought otherwise and in the closing minutes of the game led his team in an all out effort, throwing the ball about in every conceivable position. It was fitting that he should crown this great effort with a personal try that will long be remembered by those who were present. The score 8–6, tries – Rumble, Flitton; conversion – Blackbourn.

Some New Buildings at Last

The Spring term of 1957 saw workmen building urgently needed extensions to the School. In answer to the demand for more and more scientists, a new Advanced Physics laboratory was being constructed at the end of the Handicraft block, as well as two and a half new classrooms at the office end of the bottom corridor. The dining-room and kitchen were also being extensively enlarged and modernised.

By the Autumn Term, when most of these extensions were completed, the number of boys in the School had risen to 770, making the relief barely noticeable. Only on one day when 268 boys were absent with Asian Flu was the congestion briefly eased. The new Physics laboratory wasn't quite ready to move into, and the new kitchen was experiencing teething troubles, which lasted for some months.

In October the School celebrated its annual Harvest Festival, the produce being

The Home and School Association Christmas Bazaar and Hobbies Exhibition, 1957, raised £213 for School funds. Young visitors enjoying the Railway Club's exhibits. (LN-LMC)

auctioned off in the evening by the Home and School Association. The Bazaar and Hobbies Exhibition on 23rd November raised £213, which the HSA used to defray the cost of a Cricket Score Box and Pavilion Clock. The Score Box was in place by the 1958 season, but some delay was experienced in the placing of the clock.

Following a week of Poppy selling, Remembrance Day was commemorated on 11th November. As tradition required, the President of the Old Lutonians, Mr E.G. Setchell, read the lesson.

During the term the senior boys had listened to two stimulating lectures. The first by Dr Howe discussed 'Education in Empire'. In the second Miss Robbins of the Cavendish Laboratory at Cambridge opened the boys' eyes to the future with a talk on the work her Radio Group was conducting on satellites and the ionosphere for the International Geophysical Year.

Terrence Rattigan's play *The Winslow Boy* was produced by Russell Key for the

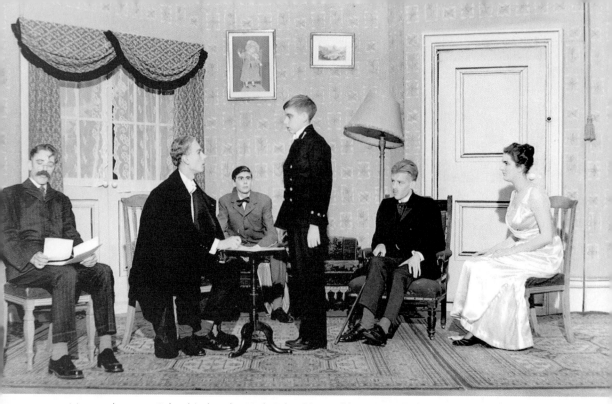

Not strictly a joint Schools' play, the High School loaned four young ladies to appear in Terrence Rattigan's *The Winslow Boy*, in November 1957. (l. to r.) Desmond (John Cunningham), Sir Robert Morton (Martin Woods), Dickie Winslow (Peter Bryant), Ronnie Winslow (Guy Rowston), Arthur Winslow (Jonathan Lutley), Catherine Winslow (Joanna Chapman). *(LN-LMC)*

Dramatic Society on 6th–8th November, 1957. Guy Rowston had the difficulty of playing the Cadet, Ronnie Winslow, who was some three or four years younger than himself, but he did so with skill. As the elderly and infirm father of 'the boy', the task for Jonathan Lutley was even harder, but he contrived to remain in character throughout, and his performance showed thoughtfulness and understanding. Martin Woods combined a correct demeanour, polished diction, sufficient aloofness and occasional sharpness to give a convincing portrayal of the distinguished barrister, Sir Robert Morton. The High School 'loaned' four very competent and experienced actresses. The audiences approved the broad comedy that Jill Halliday extracted from the part of the middle-aged maid, Violet. Angela Connolly and Joanna Chapman were sympathetic and dignified as the principal ladies, Grace and Catherine Winslow, and Rosemary Godfrey successfully depicted the gossiping reporter, Miss Barnes.

At the end of term, Mr Hauke, the Music master, revived the old custom of holding a concert for first year boys, which provided some excellent entertainment. A few days later, 43 first year boys were presented with Cycling Proficiency pennants. On the morning of 20th December, the whole School thoroughly enjoyed the 1950 comedy film *The Happiest Days of Your Life*, starring Alastair Sim and Margaret Rutherford. A Carol Service in the afternoon brought another year to a close.

And so to 1958

1958 was heralded in with the sad news of the death of Mr Harold H. Watson on 13th January, aged 70. His funeral three days later at St Andrew's Church, Luton, was attended by many of his former colleagues, Old Boys and Staff from the School.

Later in the year, on 11th June, Mr Jack Ashworth died in Manchester. A graduate of Manchester University, who served in the British Army in the Second World War with the rank of Captain, he joined the School staff in 1947 to teach biology. He had great teaching gifts and was a shrewd judge of character. He had had considerable experience as a chorister and he loved good music and plays. His nature was gentle and gracious, his sense of humour was rich, and to talk to him on any subject was always an enlightening and ennobling experience. For those who knew him, his life remains an object lesson in the patient bearing of intense suffering, a rebuke to our disgruntlements, and an inspiration to us to face the future with equanimity. The School intended to honour his memory annually on his birthday, 31st October, as Ashworth Day. Mr Ashworth was cremated in Manchester on 15th July, and Mr Giddy represented the School at the funeral service.

Wednesday, 19th February, 1958, was Speech Day. In making his report, Mr Webb likened going to a Grammar School to taking out an insurance policy. 'If we pay our premiums for a planned number of years, we take, at the end, the planned sum of money which is greater than all we invested – and is frequently accompanied by bonuses, promised but not guaranteed in amount. If we decide to stop investing

The new Physics laboratory, opened in September 1957. (C.E. Wareham)

our premiums after a few years only, and take what the company will give us, we do not get back even all we have paid. The boy who leaves at 16 has not had a Grammar School education. He has had part of a Grammar School Education.'

Speaking of the School itself, he said that the past year had been a very successful one. Two State Scholarships had been obtained by J.W. Bryant and T.B. Taylor, both to Imperial College, London. 109 boys had taken GCE at Ordinary level, gaining 561 subject passes. Whilst the national English language average mark was 53.6, for Luton Grammar School it was 76.4. In mathematics the national mark was 57.6: for the School it was 78.1. Forty Upper VIth form boys gained 108 subject passes at Advanced level. During the last year twenty-one boys had gone into universities or comparable courses, four had gone abroad and others entered trades, clerkships, laboratories, the Civil Service, the Armed Forces, banking, insurance, journalism and accountancy. Forty-eight went into apprenticeships – nine of which were the new commercial apprenticeships.

Mrs David Ennals then distributed the prizes. Afterwards Mr David Ennals, at that time Secretary of the United Nations Association, delivered a brilliant speech which dealt with the undeveloped peoples of the world.

He pointed out that within the next 24 hours the world's population would increase by 85,000. Most of those people would be black, brown, yellow, and not white, coming from Africa, Asia and Latin America. Many would die before they had the chance of reaching adulthood. Few would have a proper education. That was why there was a need for young, educated Britons to offer their services and help their fellow men in some way. Tom Flitton, the Head Boy, thanked Mr and Mrs Ennals and all the visitors.

The junior and middle school actors performed two plays on the 13th and 14th March. *The Knave of Hearts* by Louise Saunders, was a lively and colourful romp, produced by Mr Sutcliffe, whilst *The Farce of Maître Pierre Pathelin*, translated and staged by Mr Bowen was most successful because the actors let themselves go.

Various long-established School Societies were ticking along, following much the same pattern as in previous years. The Literary and Scientific Society heard a Presidential Address on the life and work of Louis Braille from Mr Bowen. There was a Balloon Debate with the High School, in which the final aviators were Salome and Sir Isaac Newton: this interesting combination was short lived and Salome was duly precipitated to the 'sharks' below. At another meeting at the High School David Reilly described his year at an American school. There is no record of the customary Joint Debate. Incidentally, David Reilly was also invited to talk about his American experiences to the Luton Rotarians on 12th June.

The Natural History Society was well patronised, presenting lectures by Mr Lambton Wilkinson of the National Coal Board, Mr E.H. Grice-Hutchinson of the Rothamsted Experimental Station and Mr John Lovell on the bird life of Scolt Head Island. Field visits were made to the Municipal Nurseries at Stockwood Park, the

British Gelatine Works, and jointly with the Archaeological Society to Totternhoe Knolls. For the second year running the Botanical Group won the Wild Flower Society's competition.

The 1958 Football season was notable for a 1st XI which won all its eleven matches and had three successive captains! R. Day was captain until February, when he left school, and the mantle fell on M.J. Gibbs. In mid-March he met with a serious injury whilst playing hockey, and W.P. Evans took over the leadership. According to Wynne Parry the team was magnificently fit, and more than a match for heavier and older opponents. Experienced players like Gibbs, Evans, Pearman, Flitton and Blackbourn had a steadying effect on the newer members of the team.

The senior Cross-Country team packed well, with such runners as P. Coleman, A.P. Roe and P. Meredith peaking during the season. D.F. Cooper proved a keen and enthusiastic captain. The highlight of the year was the under 16 team winning the J.S. Davison Trophy in the Eastern Counties Boys' Championship at Peterborough. The scoring three, of W.F. Lythgoe (5th), Coleman (6th) and Roe (10th), were first team, out of 209 runners and 26 teams. They easily beat their great rivals, Bedford Modern School, who were placed second. The under 16 team came a commendable first in the Luton Inter-Schools' Championships.

The School's athletes had a very successful and varied season ending with the selection of four boys who had reached National Standard to represent Bedfordshire in the English Schools Championships at Durham. The boys honoured were M. Blackbourn (Long Jump), M.W. Harry (110 yds. Hurdles), G.F.K. MacRae (High Jump) and W.F. Lythgoe (880 yds.)

Sports Day, on 14th May, was cold and showery, but eight records were broken or equalled. Tom Flitton, the School's captain of athletics, beat his own hop, step and jump record by nearly a foot, J.G. Booth became the School's first pole vaulter to clear 10 feet, and Michael Blackbourn at long last beat M. Hine's Long Jump record set in 1945, with a leap of 20 feet 9 inches. The School came second to Icknield once again in the Luton Schools' Sports, although the Upper Senior Relay team repeated their success in winning the Napier Trophy.

Michael Blackbourn breaks the long jump record with a leap of 20 ft 9 ins in May 1958.

In Basketball a team of senior boys, playing under the name of Luton Scorpions, entered the North Herts-South Beds League. Ably captained by M.H. Wernicke they acquitted themselves very well, winning half of their twenty league fixtures.

With the newly presented scoreboard in the background, and under the virile captaincy of Peter Evans, the 1st XI cricket team started off most auspiciously, with four consecutive wins. These games were followed by two splendid draws with Bedford School and the RAF, a narrow defeat by the Luton Town Colts, and a real festival game to celebrate Dunstable Grammar School's seventieth year, the result of which was a tie. Of the seasoned players, both Evans and M.J. Gibbs performed well. M. Hall, R.J. Hill and F.E. Plancherel were reliable and effective all-rounders. T.K. Washington and G.C. Wynn were among the stars of the side.

It was not the best of seasons for the 1st XV Rugby team. Leadership was clearly lacking, and the pack was directed to follow the orders of W.J. Dickens, the inspiring scrum leader. This understood, the forwards became the force expected of them. Scores were low but the defence was sound and the season concluded on a happier and more successful note.

On 3rd June a medical team visited the School offering every boy an anti-polio injection. It is ironic that on the day of the injections, one fifteen-year-old boy, Keith F. Newman, was absent with a cold. On 16th November, after only three days of serious illness, he died suddenly from a particularly virulent strain of poliomyelitis. A quiet, retiring boy, full of innocent fun, he had been expected to gain a creditable GCE. After a service at the Ceylon Baptist Church, he was buried at the Rothesay Road cemetery. The School was represented at his funeral by the Headmaster, Mr Parry, friends from the VI form and a group of his form mates from Vd.

Foreign Travel

On All Fools Day, 1958, a party of twenty-one Grammar School boys and seventeen girls from the Technical School, conducted by Mr and Mrs Clarke, and Mr Ellis, left Luton for Baveno, on Lake Maggiore, in Switzerland. The account printed in *The Lutonian* was written by two keen naturalists, D. Stanbridge and J. Harper. 'The area was forested, the cover providing good hunting grounds for the smaller birds such as hawfinch, redstart, nuthatch, and our own chiffchaff. There were many flowers, such as noble liverwort, squill, spring sedge and alternate-leaved saxifrage.'

Another party of boys spent a week in Paris with Mr Parry, where their guide, Monsieur Long, 'took us to Les Invalides, where we saw not only the enormous marble tomb of Napoleon, and many of his art treasures, but also various tanks and guns, and even an ancient aeroplane. We have a fine snapshot of an Irish bar in Montmartre with the legend "Broken English spoken here".'

In March Mr John Cleaver took a group of Sixth Form geographers and geologists to visit the Ordnance Survey Offices at Chessington, where they were able

to see most of the stages of map production. In June another group of boys and masters travelled to the Petroleum Engineering Exhibition at Olympia, at the invitation of Dr E.H.T. Hoblyn, the Director of the British Chemical Plant Manufacturers Association, and an Old Boy of the School.

During the week of 27th October, many of the boys queued outside the Gym Instructors' Room for a medical inspection, and a week later most of them travelled to the Technical School for a visit to the Mass X Ray Unit.

The joint Schools' play was staged at the High School on 19th–21st November. The choice was Thornton Wilder's *Our Town*. It was a play with a large cast, that gave many people an opportunity to make a small contribution: its scenery was of the simplest and the presence from time-to-time of scene shifters during the action made the performances more intimate. The main character is the Stage Manager who from the beginning takes the audience into his confidence: Jonathan Lutley underplayed him to great effect, commending his town and its people to the on-lookers. The play treats of everyday experiences, home-life and school, love, marriage and death, the affairs of everyday and the mysteries of eternity with restraint, delicacy and sensitivity. It was probably for these reasons that the actors and the audiences found the performances so satisfying and enjoyable.

Music in the School was not neglected during 1958. The Second Annual School Concert was held on 11th June. As in the previous year, there was still a tendency to be too ambitious with the choice of programme, but the choir in particular sang beautifully, and the combined efforts of choir and orchestra in the final item, *Non nobis Domine*, received a great reception from the audience.

P.T. Griffiths was the fourth old boy to join the National Youth Orchestra, following in the footsteps of J.B. Webb, D.R. Oldroyd and B.F. Router.

A new venture on 17th December was the first evening Carol Service, which was well attended by parents and friends. The choir sang well, due to Mr Hauke's patient guidance at practices and also to the reliable and tasteful accompaniment of David R. Grant. Grant also played the introductory and post-service music on the organ. After the first carol, 'Once in Royal David's city', the Headmaster spoke the bidding prayer. The service then continued with alternate readings by the Chairman of the Governors, the President of the Old Boys, a parent, the Head Boy, and others; and carols sung by the choir and congregation. A retiring collection was taken in aid of the National Fund for Poliomyelitis Research, in memory of Keith Newman.

For the first time at Bradgers Hill a lighted tree stood in the Hall foyer during Christmas week. On the last morning of term the boys watched, with much approval and delight, the Ealing Studios black comedy, *The Ladykillers* (1955), starring Alec Guinness. In the afternoon the traditional Christmas Carol Service was held. Later that evening many families joined the Home and School Association for a very successful and seasonal Old Time Dance.

One master, Mr Reginald Hulme, left the staff at Christmas, after ten years in the

handicraft department. A first-rate craftsman, he trained many boys in the way they should go, and produced some excellent artisans. Unfortunately, for those who did not share his ability, he had a caustic tongue, which did not endear him to every student who passed his way.

Destruction at Park Square

During 1959 the old Modern School building on Park Square was demolished to make way for the new College of Technology, which would in due course form the core of the University of Luton. Many old boys and girls genuinely grieved to see the building where they had spent their schooldays swept so completely away.

At the beginning of the year there were 864 boys on the School roll. There seemed never a time when the building was not overcrowded. Plans were in place to build a further three science laboratories and an extra classroom. Mr Webb and the Science staff burnt the midnight oil working on the finer details of the new laboratory plans.

There was another outbreak of Asian Flu in January, but although many boys and staff were ill, it did not reach the epidemic proportions of the previous year.

The annual Speech Day took place on 18th February, 1959. The Hall was packed to capacity, and for the first time, due to lack of space, the Junior School had to remain in their classes.

In presenting his report, the Headmaster stressed that the 11-plus examination need not be a bar to any Luton child succeeding academically. 'Transfer which is now working from the Secondary Modern School to our sixth form, the various exams taken in the Secondary Modern School, and the open door of the College of Technology, mean that no local boy is barred by being sent to one type of school at 11 years of age, from all hope of academic achievement for the rest of his life. The kind of wild language reported in some places is definitely not true in Luton.'

He went on to say that the size of the Sixth Form and the dictates of the time-table prevented many boys from taking the wide range of subjects that were desirable, and they accepted the specialisation they were forced to take with regret. He felt that the School had made some effort to address this problem. He added, 'For the odd one or two who count anything but physics, mathematics and chemistry as a waste of time, I suggest they learn the lesson of this epitaph: "Here lies John Smith. Born a man . . . and died a grocer".'

Little did Mr Webb realise that this last statement would cause a storm amongst the Grocery fraternity, and letters of censure appeared in the local press and from as far afield as Somerset. He hastened to explain himself, saying that the moral he was trying to point was that to be a whole Man is more than fulfilling a certain occupation. He was speaking against the narrowing effect of an exclusively vocational education. 'Our education prepares us for what we do for Pay, what we

do for Pleasure and what we do for Posterity also. A man is less than a man if the sum of his life is contained within his occupation.' Curiously enough, the Duke of Bedford, speaking at Dunstable Grammar School's Speech Day in 1956 had used a similar epitaph, substituting 'dustman' for 'grocer', and had aroused the wrath of the Transport and General Workers Union!

Reviewing a successful year, academically as well as on the sports field – 154 boys gained 773 subject passes in 'O' level GCE, and 33 gained 89 advanced passes – Mr Webb said that never before had the school had such a large Sixth Form.

More than 80 per cent of the subjects taken by 35 boys in the fourth year in GCE 'O' level, as an experiment, were successful. Two boys had gained State Scholarships, the present Head Boy, Derek J. Wagon, and A. Livingston. Wagon had been accepted for Gonville and Caius College, Cambridge in October, and Livingston was already at the Royal Veterinary College, London.

The guest speaker for the day was the distinguished scientist, Professor Owen A. Saunders, Dean of the City and Guilds College of London University, and an old friend of the Headmaster. He stressed that science had never played such an important part in the world as at the present time, but that was not to the discredit of classical education. One should have a wide outlook, not the narrow one which some scientists had. To be successful a man must have character and imagination.

At the beginning of March a decisive football match between Luton Town and Blackpool was to be played at Kenilworth Road on a Wednesday afternoon. A large number of boys petitioned the Headmaster for permission to attend the match. After a hasty consultation with senior staff on the day before, he decided not to release the boys. This resulted in 13 boys truanting and a noisy demonstration in the playground at morning break from those unable to go.

The School ventured into pastures new on 18th–20th March with a production of a Gilbert and Sullivan opera, *H.M.S. Pinafore*. As well as boys from the School, the cast included five members of staff and two girls and a mistress from the High School. Produced by Mr Michael Sharman with Mr Adolph Hauke as his Musical Director, the production proved a great success. Prior to the performances the whole cast and orchestra had spent the previous Saturday rehearsing from 9.30 till 5.00pm. Mr Sharman, the First Lord of the Admiralty, ruled the 'Queen's Navee' with great aplomb. As Captain Corcoran, the man who hardly ever used a big, big D, Mr Webb was convincing, especially when towards the end he became a saucy sailor with remarkable facility. Natalie Webber, as Josephine, the Captain's daughter, had a clear, sweet voice and a pretty modesty entirely becoming to her part. Miss Christine Broomer was a more than adequate Little Buttercup. At the last performance the trio in Act II, comprising Josephine, Captain Corcoran and Sir Joseph Porter received five encore calls. The delightful scenery was designed and painted by Mrs M. Sharman.

Mr Webb called one statutory Staff Meeting each term, although others were

The full cast and part of the orchestra which took part in *H.M.S. Pinafore* in March 1959.
(*LN-LMC*)

convened if there was a need. Many old boys have remarked that they always felt that the Head didn't know what was going on in his School. Members of staff have refuted this, saying that he invariably spent morning break in the staff-room with them, discussing any cause for concern that might have arisen. He was always accessible to staff and boys alike, and tried to instil in parents the knowledge that they could always come and talk to him.

On Monday, 27th April, the staff met to make a momentous and long overdue decision, an alteration to School Rule 16 – Official School Dress. It was decided to abolish the requirement to wear the School cap. The news was greeted with elation by the boys. For many older lads it had been a cause of constant embarrassment and ridicule, at a time when such head gear had long been out of fashion. Sixth Formers could be eighteen or nineteen years old, and yet had still been expected to conform. Many masters, including Mr Godfrey, had long been aware of the situation, and conveniently looked the other way. It is said that a spate of small celebratory fires were reported around Luton at about that time! T.P. Smith has pointed out that wearing the School cap, even at sixteen, often allowed a boy to get away with half fare on the local buses!

At Easter, Mrs Dorothy Monk, who had been in charge of the kitchen for eleven years, decided to retire. She had been very popular with all members of the School.

Her assistant, Mrs Wallace, also retired after sixteen years' service. One of Mrs Monk's greengrocery lists survives from 1949, showing her weekly order to Fredk. Foster, Carpenter and Undertaker of Offley, for 4 bushels of apples at £1 per bushel. Mrs Harrison was appointed to take Mrs Monk's place.

The School's Easter excursion was to Montreux in Switzerland. Mr Parry, together with Mr and Mrs Partridge and their daughter, led 41 boys from years IV to VI. They stayed in a Youth Hostel right on the shore of Lake Geneva. Excursions took them to Champéry in the genuine Alps, from where they ascended by téléférique to Planachaux. A longer excursion took them to Gruyère, the centre of the cheese industry. On the final trip they went by railway to Rochers-de-Naye, where they witnessed the last Slalom of the season and were amazed at the speeds recorded.

Guy Rowston (L VI Arts) won first prize in an essay competition set by the Council for Visual Education. The prize was presented in London by Sir Hugh Casson, the distinguished architect, at the Building Centre during April. Guy was subsequently interviewed in the 'Town and Country' radio programme on the BBC Home Service.

The start of the Football season was delayed by snow and fog, and the 1st XI never really got its act together. That it managed to win eight of its thirteen games and draw one, was something of a surprise. The 2nd XI did rather better, losing only two of their ten games. Two boys, D.W. Rigg and B.J. Wanstall, attended the FA Course for Schoolboys held at Lilleshall; whilst five boys and three masters attended a series of lectures on the Laws of the Game, which looked in particular at the problems facing referees.

The Cross-Country season was a frustrating one, although both teams were stronger than the results showed. Jeffrey Greenleaf started in splendid form, breaking the Bedford Modern School course record. W.F. Lythgoe broke his ankle before the season but devoted much time coaching the Under 13 pack. In the Luton Inter-Schools Championship the Under 16 and Under 13 teams came first, with I.S. Aldridge and P.N. Tomlin individual winners. For the first time the School competed in the English National Championships at Peterborough, which all agreed was a worthwhile experience. E.J. Lutley had proved a most valuable team captain.

The summer of 1959 was outstanding for its fine weather, and the athletics performances were almost as commendable. Many mornings of the Easter holidays had been given up to strenuous training with Cyril Godfrey and John Muse. There was a keen struggle for standard points for the Jenkins Cup before Sports Day, with Grasshoppers ahead; a lead which they held to win the Powdrill Cup, and shared the Relay Cup with the Hornets. The *Victor Ludorum* Cup was also shared by M.F. Blackshaw, an improved sprinter, and W.O. Williams in the throwing events; each scored two firsts and a second. Of eight records broken, M.R.C. Towl's triple success with the discus, javelin and hammer in the Under 16 group was outstanding, and

The impressive march-past of the School's athletes at the Luton Schools' Sports, at Wardown, on 22nd and 25th June, 1959. Sadly, this was a year when results did not match up to appearances.

(*LN*)

earned him the Richardson Cup. Four boys were chosen to represent Bedfordshire in the English Schools' Championships in Cheshire, J.G. Booth (Pole Vault), W.F. Lythgoe and J.H. Fossey (440 yards), and C.E. Rumble (Long Jump).

The 1959 Cricket 1st XI was the first to go unbeaten since Chote's team of 1942. A settled team was fielded almost from the start. It had retained its bowling mainstays, M.J. Gibbs and Captain, M. Hall, and its opening batsmen, R.J. Hill and G.C. Wynn, had definitely matured. Hill and Wynn, by scoring 368 and 369 runs respectively, surpassed the achievements of B.D. Robinson in 1950 and 1951, and of J. Gurney in 1953, and nearly equalled the 372 scored by D.J. Wood in 1945. The 2nd XI was defeated only once in eleven games.

Statistically, the 1st XV Rugby team had its poorest season for some years. Ten matches were played, 3 won and 1 drawn, 85 points being scored against the opponents' 96. As John Muse wrote at the time, 'Statistics do not reveal that this team was composed of a splendid group of fellows, keen to learn as well as practise, pleasant to deal with and happy and cheerful in adversity. That was in no small measure due to the leadership of W.O. Williams and his two officials, B.J. Wanstall and M.F. Blackshaw.'

In Tennis the School was outclased in all its matches. In Swimming a small list of fixtures was carried through. The Dillingham Shield was won, the School came second in the Pike Trophy and second (to Icknield School) in the Inter-Schools' Gala.

Old Boys and masters were saddened to hear of the death at the age of 74 of Mr W. Roberts on 10th June, 1959. He had been the School's first groundsman, serving the School from the time when it got its first playing fields at Chaul End until his retirement in 1949. He lived for the School and its games, especially cricket, and by his quiet firmness he enjoyed the respect of many generations of boys.

The 3rd Annual School Concert was held on 10th June. The programme, devised by Messrs Hauke and Parry, followed the usual pattern of orchestral and choral items interspersed with instrumental solos. C.J. Humphreys played the piano, D. McGregor and J.D. Salmon gave violin solos, P.E. Bryant and R.J. Gregory performed a duet for two clarinets, D.R. Grant gave an organ solo, and B.E. Clark, one of the trebles in the choir, sang two delightful songs. The main orchestral item was Hubert Clifford's 'Kentish Suite', which, like the curate's egg, was good in parts. The concert finished with the choir and orchestra united in a performance of Parry's 'Blest Pair of Sirens'. 'Music the like of which we have not previously heard in this Hall', the Headmaster recorded. Much of the credit for this piece went to the trebles, most of whom had only been in the choir for about eight months.

Jeffrey Greenleaf, who left at the end of the summer term, has written:

'I recall Mr Geoffrey W. Barraclough who took us for chemistry. When our A and S-levels were over, he then gave us a course of fascinating chemistry lectures that went way beyond the syllabus on topics he considered interesting and with the

The Wind Section of the School Orchestra, 1959. (LN-LMC)

purpose of broadening our interest in chemistry. Thus our final term in 1959 went right through until mid-July. How different that was from today when most people in Upper VI, having finished A-levels, leave school in June. What a wasted opportunity! Indeed, I remember many instances throughout the VIth Form when staff chose to go beyond the limits of the syllabus – with the purpose of broadening our interests and of keeping the subject interesting.'

When the School opened for the Autumn Term, it was to the expectation of using the three new laboratories for Biology, Chemistry and Physics. Typically, they were not ready, and it was some weeks before they came into operation.

Partly due to the large number of boys in the School, nine new masters were appointed during the year. These were Mr R. Bedford, DSC (Handicraft), Mr G.B. Privett, BSc and, Mr A.S. Hill, BSc (both Maths and Physics), Mr M. Alpert, BA (Modern Languages), Mr J. Marsden, BSc (Chemistry and Physics), Mr B.M.A. Scott, BA (Mathematics), Mr R.S. Acton, BA (English), Mr D.J. Serby, BSc (Chemistry and Biology), and Mr J.J.M. Gillespie, DLC (Handicraft), an Old Boy.

The various School Societies enjoyed another season. The Literary and Scientific Society listened to a variety of speakers including Dr Charles Hill, MP, who spoke to some 150 boys and masters on his work as the Minister responsible for co-ordinating Government Information Services under the title 'Boosting Britain', punctuating his discourse with admirable humour. The Revd. E.H. Pyle of Cambridge talked on 'The New Ghana' from his experience of four years as a resident. Mr Ronald Mead, of Skefko Ltd, came twice to talk about Electronic Computers. Joint meetings with the Archaeological and Natural History Societies brought talks on 'Crete and Mycenae' and 'Radar Studies of Bird Migration'. Members of the Society also visited the new Luton Post Office in Dunstable Road, and toured Messrs. Olney's Hat Factory in York Street.

The Table Tennis Club held its annual Open Tournament between Christmas and Easter, the winner being M. Kaye, who defeated his younger brother L.T. Kaye, 21–13, 21–15 and 21–18, thus becoming the first player to win the cup for three successive years.

The Student Christian Movement Group held an evening meeting – a 'squash' at which they were joined by members of the High School branch and by friends from the Young Life Campaign. Two physicists from Welwyn spoke on 'The faith of a Scientist', and then answered questions. Later, over the supper table, there was much animated discussion, and members were reluctant to leave.

For the Chess Club, it was their most successful season for some years. The School team finished second to Challney in the Luton Schools Chess League, winning 12 matches out of 14. In a knock-out competition R.A. Parry beat A.P. Bennett, the Club captain, in the final.

Once again the Natural History Society had a very full programme of nineteen

meetings. The highlight seems to have been the day excursion to Scolt Head Island off the north Norfolk coast. Mr D.G. Barker, suitably clad in deerstalker and Norfolk jacket, led the party across the creeks and mud flats, allowing them to examine the flora of the salt marsh and the fauna of a creek bottom. Everyone, the botanists, ornithologists and 'bug-hunters' all had a very rewarding day. For the third year running the Botanical group won the Wild Flower Society's annual diary competition, recording 744 plants: just 13 more than their rivals, Kingswood School, Bath.

On Wednesday, November 11th, the Headmaster conducted the annual Commemoration Service for Old Boys who lost their lives in two World Wars. Owing to the unavoidable absence of the President of the Old Lutonians, Mr Reg. Matthews, the Secretary, Mr R. Mead, took his place and read the lesson. A Poppy collection during the week raised £9.

The Admirable Crichton by J.M. Barrie was the choice for the joint Dramatic Societies winter production from 11th–13th November, 1959. With an equal number of major parts for male and female actors, and a large number of supporting players, this was an ideal vehicle for displaying considerable talent. Crichton was a difficult part. It was not one that lent itself naturally to Guy Rowston's style, and he did not start with the physical advantages of it. It said much for his versatility that he fulfilled the part so well. In the island scenes he was not perhaps as dominant as he should have been, but he played with feeling the romance with Lady Mary (Elizabeth Horwood). Gladys Brown and Russell Key were once more the producers.

The New Boys (including the 13 plus entry) gave a concert for parents and friends on 27th November. It was held in the Dining Room 'to take away the formality of the event'. The choir performed a number of songs, varying from the beautiful 'Blow the wind southerly' to the amusing 'There was a funny little man'. Then followed a number of solo items including violin performances by A.J. Duncan and B.S. Cumming. W.P. Grant and P.A.D. Welburn, accompanied by A.R. Parr, played the 'Skye Boat Song'. A group of boys from 1a recited four humorous poems including 'The blind man and the elephant'. The choir closed the programme with 'Men of Harlech'. Tea and buns followed, provided by Mrs Harrison.

On the evening of 16th December the second annual Carol Service was held in the School Hall. Its format differed little from the first. Familiar lessons and carols alternated with lesser-known carols sung by the choir, and organ music opened and closed the service. After the blessing spoken by the Headmaster, Mr Douglas Serby played Bach's Fugue in B Minor. The choir, which was augmented by several parents, was directed by Mr Hauke. A retiring collection raised a goodly sum for World Refugee Year.

Term ended with a Staff dinner on the 17th December, and a breaking-up Carol Service for the whole School the following afternoon. The showing of an end of term film seems to have been discontinued.

Into a New Decade

Speech Day was held on Wednesday, 17th February, 1960. The Guest of Honour was Mr Deryk E. Mumford, MA, Principal of the Cambridgeshire Technical College and School of Art, whose wife distributed the prizes. In his report for the year the Headmaster said that in spite of extra laboratories, the School was still very crowded. With 867 boys on the School roll in September, 1959, it had been necessary to create five classes in the third, fourth and fifth years. This meant that the number of forms containing more than 31 boys was reduced to ten. Sixth Form numbers, at the same time, had risen to 161, of whom 48 were on the Arts side. This was the result of the very considerable success achieved in the GCE O-level examinations by Form IVa, two years running: the great majority of those boys going straight to the Sixth Form. 139 boys sat for the O-level in 1959 and gained 676 subject passes – an average of 4.9 subjects per boy. Fifty-one boys had secured 122 advanced level G.C.E. subjects. Four boys had gained State Scholarships: J.R. Greenleaf, Imperial College, London, C.J. Humphreys, Imperial College, London, (October 1961), R.F. Matthews, Brasenose College, Oxford, (October 1961), and D.R.A. Mowse, Manchester University. D.R. Grant won the Sir John Goss Organ Scholarship of the Royal Academy of Music. Nineteen other boys were admitted to universities and colleges, and eight student apprenticeships had been awarded.

The School collected £75 for World Refugee Year which ran from June 1959 to May 1960. A concerted effort to raise money was organised by the Student Christian Movement Group. Films were shown, every boy in the school heard a tape recording about refugees, an exhibition of photographs depicting some of the camps and their occupants was displayed, and, in the week commencing 15th February, fifty-eight pounds were donated. Two boys, H.I. Hammond and H.R. Owen, represented the School at the World Refugee Year rally held in the Albert Hall on 30th May. They had a most entertaining and satisfying afternoon in the company of the Archbishop of Canterbury, Princess Alexandra, Harold Macmillan, Hugh Gaitskell and some 5,000 others.

Three masters left at the end of the Summer Term and four replaced them. The latter were Mr A.B. Davies, History and Economics, Mr P.G. Hudson, Maths, Mr C.F.P. Porter, Maths and RI, and Mr R.K.J. Trend, Physics. The Assistant Secretary, Mrs Christine Nortrop (née Robinson), left the School Office on 31st March. She was succeeded by Mrs J. Fountain.

On the 17th and 18th March, the thriving Junior Dramatic Society performed two plays, *The Crimson Coconut* and *Shivering Shocks*. The former had two casts, one for each evening. The parts of Jack Pincher, the detective, and Mr Jabstick were played with equal success by both casts (M. Major and D. Atkins; P. Parker and G. Watson respectively). The make-up department produced two bewitching young ladies, one brunette the other a red-head, to play the part of Nancy (C. Grant and

T. Burgoyne). D. Burrows was memorable for his remarkable performance as Madame Gliserinski, with an erotic and totally unmanageable feather boa.

The lurid drama, *Shivering Shocks*, was played with gusto in a rather large and remarkably bare 'country' cottage. Specially memorable were R. Ward as a drunken taxi-driver, P. Vaughan's convincing if somewhat fluctuating Irish accent as 'The Shepherd', and the remainder of the cast who played gallantly in a play demanding speed and verve.

Between the two Junior plays, the Senior Dramatic Society had inserted their production of Galsworthy's *The Little Man*, which was delivered with the accustomed polish expected from more experienced actors. C.R. Pryor, in the title rôle, produced the right degree of meekness, whilst R.W. Woodham and R.P. Goodwin were a credible German and American respectively.

The Home and School Association held a Careers Evening on 30th March, with representatives of various organisations, including the Police, the Co-op, Marks and Spencer, and Insurance. A number of boys and their parents took advantage of he opportunity to get their career questions answered.

The end of the Easter term was marked by a showing of the 1953 Disney film *The Living Desert*, which the critics found over-gory, but the boys seemed to enjoy!

On Saturday, 9th April, Mr and Mrs Webb were invited to the opening of an exhibition of paintings by Henry Trivick (LMS: 1919–24), at Luton Museum, by another Old Boy, Dennis Farr, who at that time was an Assistant Keeper at the Tate Gallery. Trivick studied and later taught lithography at the Central School of Art and Crafts and at the Regent Street Polytechnic School of Art. He collaborated with his great friend, Stanley Spencer to produce lithographs from Spencer's drawings, and executed murals for the liner, Queen Elizabeth II. Many national art galleries and Luton Museum hold examples of his work. He died at Bourne End, Buckinghamshire, in 1982.

Luton Museum also houses a number of paintings by Edward Callum, FRSA, ROI, who left the Modern School in 1918. Taught by Freddie May, he went on to study at Goldsmith's College, and the Coventry and Warwick School of Art. During the war he designed camouflage for the RAF, and later became secretary of the British Army Art Society. His forte was landscape and architectural painting.

Firmly established as one of the highlights of the school year, the fourth annual musical Concert took place on 4th May. The orchestra opened each half with two groups of pieces. Of these, Gray's 'Merriment', heavily biased towards the string players, was the best rendered. D.E. Bazley and R.A. Chalkley, both second formers, played the March in G from the 'Casse-Noisette' suite by Tchaikovsky, and B.E. Clark sang two delightful treble solos. M.I. French, the leader of the orchestra, gave an animated rendering of the Allegro con spirito from Mozart's Violin sonata in G. C.J. Humphreys' performance of Mendelssohn's Andante and Rondo Capriccioso was very accomplished. The orchestra joined with the choir for a cantata by Schubert

entitled 'The Song of Miriam', in which D.E. Bazley had the arduous task of being treble soloist; and the rousing performance by the choir, orchestra and himself provided a glorious climax to the evening. All the musicians, together with Mr Hauke, the music master and conductor, and Mr Parry who arranged and accompanied the solo items, were warmly and enthusiastically praised.

A poem called *Mathematical Nightmare* appeared in the 1960 issue of *The Lutonian.* It must have summed up most Grammar School boys' nightmares:

> The rhomboid whistles to his mate,
> The pale cosecants crawl;
> The quadrants and quanternions chase
> Each other round the wall.
> The tangents in the treetops still
> Their quarrels carry on.
> After the common multiple
> Shuffles the polygon.
> Along the equilateral roof
> The coefficients ooze,
> The small surds play round the square
> On the hypotenuse.
> What makes the wee isosceles,
> So suddenly fall dumb?
> Hush, by the rectilinear ways
> The logarithms come!
>   [Abridged: A. E. Prime, L.VI Arts)

A Staff Meeting held in February agreed on the design for Sixth Form neckties. These would be dark blue with a number of small versions of the School badge printed (not embroidered) on it. At the same time the option of white or grey shirts was opened up to the whole school. Previously only the Sixth Form were allowed to wear white. In the days before the universal use of washing machines, most mothers preferred grey, as they could be worn longer before showing the dirt!

The 1960 First XI Football team lacked the ability and confidence to score goals. There was some good football, individual players worked hard, but the team took too long to work together. Captained by M.F. Blackshaw, by the end of the season, after eleven games, the score read 25 goals for and 34 against. In contrast the 2nd XI had a good season, losing only one of its eleven games, and scoring 64 goals to 15 against.

In 1959–60 the senior Basketball team had a reasonable fixture list of school matches for the first time. The record of 9 matches played, 6 won and 3 lost, gave a fair indication of the team's ability, with old stalwarts like R.J. Hill, (Captain), D.F.

Myhill and G. Ciantar playing regularly.

Sports Day, on 25th May, was held in glorious sunshine. Three records were broken and two equalled. Of these, the one that gave most satisfaction was N.J. Pugh's javelin effort of 162 ft. 9 ins., which improved by about 5 feet M.V.W. Chote's best performance back in 1942. Major Chote was quick to write and congratulate Pugh. Another was by a very promising young athlete, R.W. Dade, with a (u. 14) high jump of 4 ft 10½ ins., and the third was also in the high jump, the Open, by E.J. Reynolds with 5 ft 4½ ins. The *Victor Ludorum* was J.H. Fossey, who combined track events with jumping. His success was well merited, having given excellent service to athletics throughout his school career. Five boys from the School were selected to run for the county in the National Championships at Shrewsbury: K.P. Jones (sprints), W.F. Lythgoe (440), J.H. Fossey (relay), R.K. Smitham and R.R. Fear (hammer).

The outstanding performance of the 1960 Cricket season was undoubtedly the captain, R.J. Hill's, achievement of the magnificent aggregate of 431 runs. He was a graceful and attractive player, with a wide range of strokes, and an unruffled temperament, whatever the state of the game, He was honoured by being made captain of a Luton and District side which played the Huntingdonshire Youth XI. In batting the 1st XI was very strong, with little or no 'tail', and the hundred was topped on several occasions The bowling was not as penetrating as it had been in earlier seasons. A lot of work was thrown on to J.D. Mackey, R.A. Hill and T.A. Irvine, and when they lost their initial 'bite' the bowling tended to become negative and defensive. The 2nd XI played with plenty of keenness and determination, and gained an unbeaten record.

The School's small band of swimmers joined with Dunstable Grammar School to beat the boys of Luton Amateur Swimming Club by one point in a match in May. R. Robinson, G. Wright and K.P. Andrews won the Pike Trophy for the under 16 Medley Relay; and R.F. Holmes was 1st in the 100 yards breast stroke (15–18 years) at the ESSA Divisional Championships in Reading.

The 1st XV had a slightly better record in 1960 than in the previous year, winning five of the twelve games played and scoring 73 points against 89. On the few occasions when the team turned out at full strength it looked a well-balanced capable side, but there were too many injuries for it to settle down. Captain and blind-side wing forward, R.C. Jefferson, had tremendous energy and used his experience and tactical knowledge to lead the pack and encourage the team as a whole. He played for the Bedford RFC Schools' XV during the Christmas holidays. C.E. Rumble was the team's 'trump card' outside the pack. With his fine physique and powerful running he was a problem to any schoolboy defence. Without his co-centre, D.T. Rickard, he had all too often to go on his own. He played in all the representative games as far as the East Midlands Schools' XV.

At Easter, 1960, Mr Parry took fifteen boys to Brussels for a week. In the capital

they stayed in a rather grim hotel, but were soon seeing the sights of the city and discovering that almost every statue, monument and building had a legend woven around it. They visited Bruges and Ghent, where most of them bought Tyrolean hats, including a white one for Mr Parry, which he dutifully wore for the rest of the tour. On the last day they visited the Grottoes of Han, where, after walking for an hour, they climbed into small boats and were rowed along an underground river. Just as they were leaving the caves there was an almighty explosion: a small cannon had been placed at the entrance to the grottoes, where the sound was magnified by the echoes.

In June Mr and Mrs Clarke took a party to Otz in Austria. The journey was eventful, the coach getting stopped for speeding on the autobahn and for scraping paint off a stationary car in Munich! Time was spent in Ulm and Salzburg where they visited a salt mine. At Castle Hellbrunn they discovered that the grounds were rigged up with trick water sprays. Everyone got soaked apart from Mr Clarke, who had been there before.

Two members of Upper VI Science, D.I. Ritchie and K.C. Lockwood, decided to take themselves to Italy and Yugoslavia for six weeks. Their account of the journey in *The Lutonian* was hair-raising, but didn't seem to stop other students from making similar excursions. They were flooded out of their tent near Rijeka, engulfed in dust beyond Zadar, exorbitantly charged almost two shillings [1960s price] for a small, Hovis-sized loaf in Split, and in danger of losing their passports and being arrested near Dubrovnik.

The Archaeological Society, which had been semi-dormant for a year, was revived in 1959–60. Lectures by masters, boys and guest speakers dominated the programme, but the highlight was a coach excursion on a cold, February day, to Avebury and Stonehenge in Wiltshire. At Avebury the group circumnavigated the great stone circle, visited the museum, and then made their way through mud and flood to the West Kennet long barrow, where James Dyer, the founder of the School society, said a few words. After lunch on top of Silbury Hill, the party travelled on to Stonehenge, and concluded with a brief stop at Woodhenge.

The Natural History Society listened to a number of lectures, including one by Mr Beard of the Forestry Commission. They later visited his nursery at Maulden Woods. Dr Dony gave a Presidential Address on 'Wild Flowers of the Chalk'. The Botanical Group won the Wild Flower competition for the fourth year in succession. Members visited the Meteorological Office at Dunstable, and braver ones ventured to the Luton Slaughterhouse, which proved somewhat gruesome at times. The most interesting meeting was held at Walberswick in Suffolk. Mr Read, of the Suffolk Natural History Society, led the a party over the marshes, where they saw bearded tits, heard a bittern booming and found a large patch of Sea Pea.

The Chess Club had its most successful year since it entered the Luton Schools' Chess League. Their record was impressive: played 16 matches, won 15 and drew 1.

Games for 82, against 14, thus regaining the League Trophy. Each regular member of the team scored over 80% success, and all six were awarded colours. They were Bennett, Parry, Bell, Maple, Coeshall and Brown.

The School's oldest society, the Literary and Scientific, had a very varied programme which included lectures on life in Hong Kong; John Howard, the prison reformer; Oxygen Therapy and Resuscitation; and two years teaching in a State University in the USA. Visits were made to the Water Works, Rothamsted Experimental Station and a Luton Town Council meeting. In a debate J.D. Stephen and M.F. Blackshaw were of the opinion that 'the line ought to be drawn somewhere'. Messrs G. Ciantar and C.W. Parry failed, though narrowly, to persuade members that the opposite was the case. Perhaps the highlight of the season was a mock trial in which Robert Charles Jefferson was accused of looking at the world through cracked spectacles. The office of His Honour the Judge fell upon Dr Dony's shoulders, that of the Prosecuting Counsel to Basil A. Allsopp, and Defending Counsel to J.R. Sparrow. After a lengthy and highly amusing trial the defendant was found not guilty of the original charge, but His Honour found him guilty of wasting school time by having a hair cut, and consequently condemned him to writing an essay on 'Sleep' for C.W.P.

The Harvest Festival service was observed on 7th October, and was followed in the evening by the Home and School Association's AGM and sale of produce. Remembrance Day was marked by a service and march-past of the War Memorials.

Thomas A.E. Sanderson, the School's first Headmaster, died on 4th November after a long illness. He was 92 years old. Mr K.B. Webb, accompanied by some of the staff and J.D. Stephen, the Head Prefect, attended his cremation service at Bedford.

On 11th December a Memorial Service was held in the School Hall for the late Headmaster. It has already been described at the end of Chapter 4.

The School Orchestra played two short pieces by Charles Woodhouse sufficiently well to win the challenge cup at the St Albans Music Festival on 12th November. They returned to the city two weeks later to receive the cup and repeat their pieces at the Prize-Winners' Concert.

From 16th to 18th November Mr Sharman produced *A Midsummer Night's Dream* by William Shakespeare. The choice was greeted with some scepticism – boys playing the parts of girls, and fairies! Why not? They did it in Shakespeare's day. But it was also the set play for A-level GCE, and that clinched it!

Wynne Parry, reviewing the production, felt that even the most carping critics would have been silenced by the hempen homespuns, the mechanics in their *pièce de résistance*. Martin Webber, both with and without his magnificent ass's head, made this part 'Bottom's play'. Who was more fitted than he to contradict not only Quince but even the Duke? And even when he was dead he still acted, for he managed to provide Thisbe with a sword with which to complete the 'lamentable tragedy'. Guy

Rowston, as Quince, was by now the School's most experienced actor, rightly choosing to under-act. He read the Prologue with intelligent un-punctuation, and then with self-effacement typical of himself in real life as well as of his rôle, made way for the other actors.

The fairies might have looked cherubic, but they were real boys, capable of fighting and tripping each other up. Christopher Grant as Puck was full of life. Ian Slack as Oberon brought the best out of Shakespeare's lovely lines. Titania (M. Stevens) had a rich speaking voice, but needed to move with more grace. The music provided by Mr Hauke, and the beautiful scenery and costumes by Mrs M. Sharman, gave to airy nothing a local habitation and a name.

The Old Lutonians held their 30th Annual Dinner at the George Hotel on 17th December, 1960. The President, Mr Leslie Button, welcomed the guests, including the speaker, Mr H.B. Williams, now a Headmaster, and formerly head of the English department at the School. For many of those present it was their first chance to see the President's Collar and Jewel which had been presented by a past-president who wished to remain anonymous. The name of every new President would be added to the chain. At the suggestion of Sir John Burgoyne, a casket had been made to hold the collar. It had been carved from part of a beam rescued from the old School on Park Square, and had been fashioned by Mr Talbot, Head of the Building Section and his staff, with the kind permission of Mr Stephenson, Principal of the Luton College of Technology.

On the 21st December, the School held its annual Carol Service. It took the usual form of a selection of carols and readings by boys of the School. The High School girls were also invited to attend and occupied the whole of the balcony. The Editor of the School Magazine observed, "Many eyes turned upwards as their angelic voices floated down to those below."

The School closed for the Christmas holidays at noon on the following day.

House meetings were introduced in the 1960s, usually conducted by enthusiastic members of staff, as illustrated by this meeting of Grasshoppers about 1962. T.R. Key, W.N. Thorpe, J.G. Dony and H.B. Bryant. (M. Bagshaw)

Chapter 14

The Final Years

Term began on 9th January, 1961. In the afternoon a reunion of Old Boys from Universities and Colleges was held. Coffee and biscuits were served and Masters and their ex-pupils enjoyed a nostalgic get-together. Two evenings later the Staff celebrated the start of the New Year with a dinner.

Shortage of space was foremost in the Headmaster's mind in February, and he spent much time discussing extensions with the Borough architects. Much of the Sixth Form work was done in small groups, sets or divisions, and a plan was devised to build a block of six division rooms adjoining the Gym Instructors' Room and Prefects' Common Room. It would be another eighteen months before they materialised.

Speech Day was held on 15th February, 1961. Although the junior forms attended their usual classes owing to lack of space, the hall was crowded with boys from the upper School, their parents and friends.

After welcoming the guests, the Headmaster began his report with some figures. The numbers of boys on roll had risen from 833 in 1958, to 867 in 1959 and 895 in 1960. The VIth Form started off with 172 boys in September 1960, of whom 59 were Arts and 113 Science students. For some years the proportions had been heavily weighted on the science side, and it was pleasing to see an appreciable increase in Lower VI Arts. The number of boys staying for a 3rd year in the VIth was 32. This comparatively large number resulted from the repeated success of the fast track taking GCE O-levels in four years. These large numbers pressed heavily on the School's accommodation, and many places never intended as teaching spaces were in regular use as such. Mr Webb felt that the quality of school life, for boys and masters alike, suffered, and that a little spaciousness would add graciousness to all their lives.

In July 1960 82 Upper Sixth boys had gained 169 Advanced level GCE subject

passes and 72 Ordinary level passes (allowed where boys narrowly failed). 28 Scholarship paper entries gained a grade 4 or better. From Lower VI 13 A-level passes were gained in Economics and 8 Ordinary level in A-level attempts.

Two State Scholarships were awarded: one to Basil A. Allsopp for work in science. He had already started at Imperial College, London. At the present time (2004) he is Professor of Molecular Parasitology at the University of Praetoria. The other was to J. David Stephen for work in languages. He had earlier been placed second in a French essay competition open to his age group throughout Great Britain and had won himself a week's holiday in France. He became Head Prefect in September 1960 and had secured a place at King's College, Cambridge, for October 1961. Prior to that he spent seven months teaching in Spain. Since his time at University, Stephen has held numerous foreign and commonwealth appointments. He was the Representative of the United Nations Secretary General, and Director of the United Nations Office for Somalia from 1997 to 2001. In 2002 he was appointed Head of the United Nations Peace-building Support Office for Guinea-Bissau.

Guy Rowston of Upper VI Arts won a nationwide competition sponsored by the Council for Visual Education for an essay on 'The Street I like best'.

The Mayoress of Luton, Mrs J. Couldwell, distributed the prizes, after which the Vicar of Luton, Canon William Davison, who was shortly to retire, spoke to the boys.

For two evenings in March the Hall was taken over for a production of *The Shoemaker's Holiday* by Thomas Dekker. This was the story of Simon Eyre, a shoemaker who supplied the Lord Mayor of London with his footwear and eventually became Lord Mayor himself. Good-natured, cheerful, loyal, he excused the diversity of the action by linking the two more serious sides of the play, the pathetic story of Ralph and Jane, and the story of romantic love threatened by unsympathetic parents.

G.W. Fletcher, as Eyre, dominated the play; gruffly and effectively bawling his way, 'as merry as a pie', throughout. Equally successful were P.L. Titterington and T.I. Burgoyne as the jolliest of Eyre's journeymen, who really 'lived' their parts. In contrast were the more serious characters, Margery, Eyre's wife (V.J. Attwood); Ralph, the third journeyman (A.J. Wilson); and Jane, wife of Ralph ((D.M. Simmons). I. Slack, the reviewer, gave the acting bouquets to Master Hammon (M. Stevens) and Jane, for the most touching scene in which they spoke together in the seamster's shop, when Hammon pretended to Jane that Ralph was dead. Guy Rowston had designed a spectacular and ingenious set. The play was produced by Mr Robert Acton.

A vocal and instrumental Concert was held in the Hall on the evening of 10th May. It opened with two organ pieces played by P.J. Orme, and a vocal duet by C. Woodbine and P.J. Southwell (both Ia). L.A. Harding then played Arne's Violin Sonata in B flat major, displaying a technical skill far in advance of his sixteen years.

Treble, A.R. Parr, sang Handel's 'Let the bright Seraphim'; J.L. Thorogood played Beethoven's Piano Sonata in G, Op. 14 No 2; and the first half ended with a violin solo by J.O. Blanch: 'Idyll' by Elgar.

After the interval D.R. Goodwin played organ solos by J.S. Bach and Karg-Elert. Trio in D by Pleyel was played by L.A. Harding, R.C. Smith (violins) and Mr Parry (piano). The audience then enjoyed the rare sound at a school concert of a counter-tenor: I. Slack, singing two pieces by Purcell. A highlight of the evening was a very polished performance of 'The Golden Sonata' by Purcell, played by a Quintet led by H. Owen on the piano, with L.A. Harding and D.J. Burrows, violins, C.K. Eames, cello and H.I. Hammond, double bass. M.I. French accompanied by Mr Hauke then played the Violin Sonata in F by Handel with great warmth of tone and musical insight. The concert drew to a close with a performance by H.R. Owen of J.S. Bach's Prelude in B Minor; and concluded with G.T. Jameson's rousing trombone solo; 'Lucy Long'.

During 1961 the School received news of recent Old Boys. John Apps (1949–55), who had gained 1st Class Honours in Geology at London University, had won a three years' scholarship to Harvard University, Massachusetts. He also won the Royal Society of Arts' Silver Medal for his Thesis on Spanish Mines; the Le-Neve Foster Prize for outstanding work by a third-year student; the Cullis Testimonial Award and Fullbright Travel Award.

J. Phillips joined the Voluntary Service Overseas and was teaching 156 boys in an Anglican Mission School in the Solomon Islands. School started at 8 am and ended at 12 noon. 'Morning prayers begin at 6 or 6.30, then boys work in the gardens in the bush – for Missions in these parts grow their own food; they also have goats, pigs, chickens and cows. The Station has a Desert Island atmosphere complete with coconuts, palms, coral reef, white sand and, in addition, crocodiles and sharks.'

On 25th February the Bedfordshire Cross-Country Championships were held on the School course. The School won the Under 16 trophy, which the Headmaster was on hand to present. The Juniors (14–16) came first out of 38 teams in the Eastern Counties match, and two boys represented the county in the 19–21 group, in a five-county contest, which Bedfordshire won. Peter Meredith captained the Club, and Wasps won the Wild Cup for the inter-house Championships.

Starting with a nucleus of experienced players, the 1st XI Football team had a very successful season. Only two of the twelve games played were lost, 35 goals were scored and only 16 conceded. Much of the team's success was due to the unobtrusive leadership of N.J. Pugh, who was always constructively critical of each match, and never averse to experimenting with the re-positioning of players. The School was well represented in the Town's Boys' teams. P.N. Tomlin and T.S. Wiles played regularly for the Under Fifteen XI, the latter as captain. J. Bevis and M.J.F. Kingham acquitted themselves well in the Under Fourteen XI.

Sports Day was held on 17th May, but took on a somewhat different aspect. Due

to an unrecorded incident, spectators were banned for the day. Senior boys were appointed to do the jobs normally done by masters on the field, and school lessons continued for non-competitors as usual. Only the relays were run after 3.35 pm when spectators could choose to watch if they wished to do so. Among individual achievements, R.K. Smitham added nearly 17 feet to the School record, by throwing the (Open) Hammer 179 ft 4½ ins. T.S. Wiles broke the (u.15) 80 yds. hurdles record by one-fifth of a second. N.J. Pugh narrowly failed to beat his own javelin record due to an unfortunate cross-wind. K.P. Jones, *Victor Ludorum*, broke the 220 yards (Open) record in 24.0 secs. P. Meredith set a good example to his House (Hornets) by winning the Mile, 880 and pole vault, and running second in the 440: not records but a thorough day's work.

The athletes had a good season, coming first in the Five Schools' Meeting, and winning six events in the Luton Schools' Sports. In the Bedfordshire County Championships K.P. Jones set a new county Junior record for the 220 yards in 22.7 secs., and C.E. Rumble jumped 21 feet in the Junior long jump. In the Bedfordshire Schools' AAA meeting R.K. Smitham threw the Junior hammer 141 ft 1 in. As a result he was chosen to throw at the All-England Championships at Chesterfield, where he came second, and went on to throw in an international match against Wales and Scotland in Cardiff. His colleague T.S. Wiles won the 80 yds hurdles.

The 1961 Cricket season was highly successful. In the fifteen games which the 1st XI played, the School won the toss twelve times, and captain R.A. Hill always put the visitors in to bat first. His team were a good bowling side: he personally bowled very few loose balls, and gave nothing away as captain. T.A. Irvine shared the brunt of the attack with him, and when they tired they were worthily followed by M.F. Smith and M.J. Clark. R. Cox's aggregate of 350 runs ranks with the best in the School's history, not only because he was always looking for runs but also because of his beautiful style.

'The senior Rugby teams were disappointing, the juniors were more successful and showed promise for the future. That, in a sentence,' according to Mr John Muse, 'summed up the 1961 season'. The 1st XV lost their first six matches. The 2nd XV was also mediocre, occasionally showing flashes of promise. To complete the troubles the 3rd XV lost all its matches, though in their defence it should be said that half their opposition were either club sides or first teams of less established rugger schools.

On Easter Sunday, 1961, Mr and Mrs Partridge and Mr Parry took a party of 31 boys to Paris, where they stayed at a private boarding school, the Institution Vilbert. The weather was good and the pattern of the week was much as in previous years. In the grounds of Versailles, some boys went rowing on the canal, where, having cast off unaided, they felt indignant, when called back by the boatman demanding his 'pourboire'. One lad lost his bulging wallet, but neither the Commissariat de Police, the Bureau d'Objets Trouvés, nor the British Embassy was able to help him.

Two boys, M.R. Webber and A.M. Champkin, attended the annual East Anglian

Conference for schoolboys on 'The Church and the Layman' at Ridley Hall. Its main purpose was to encourage in adolescents a sense of vocation, whether their future was to be clerical or lay. It turned out to be a most lively, humorous (at times) and enlightening experience, and the Luton boys found the lectures first-rate and the contacts with boys from other schools, both public and state-run, especially valuable.

Early in the year Sir John Burgoyne retired from the School's governing body and from other public offices. Knowing of Sir John's interest in music, the Headmaster invited him to attend Assembly which included the end of term concert on 21st July. Mr Webb outlined Sir John's service since 1931 onwards, recalling his Mayorality from 1938 to 1944, his great work in the cause of National Savings, and doing for the people of Luton what Churchill had done for the nation during the war years. He spoke of his incalculable contribution to education in the town through the schools and College, to his Knighthood and to his close links with the Boy Scouts and other voluntary organisations. To mark his long association with the School, Mr Webb asked Sir John to accept his 'School Colours' – a plaque of the coat of arms, engraved on the reverse side. Music played by the orchestra and choir included 'Sons of Light' by Vaughan Williams, the Coronation Anthem, 'Zadok the Priest' by Handel, the 'Homage March' by Grieg, and an oboe solo by M.K. Ayres.

Sir John, moved by the occasion, thanked everyone for making it one of the most memorable days of his life. His philosophy in life, he said, was a very simple one, 'We are here to help one another'. He complimented Mr Hauke and all the musicians for their ambition in tackling really difficult music and their exceptionally high level of achievement. Sir John subsequently established a Trust, the interest on which provided annual prizes for boys of exceptional musical talent, and a House Music Trophy to be competed for each year.

The following masters left during the year: at Easter Mr B.M.A. Scott; in July Mr K.J. Williams, Mr G.N. Crapnell, Mr J.A. Pool, and Mr M. Alpert. In September 1961 there were seven new appointments: Mr E.C. Cranwell, BA (Maths), Mr P. Lawson, BSc (Maths), Mr J.H. Lightfoot, (Science), Mr V.S. Page, (Handicraft), Mr D.E. Stancombe, BSc (Science), Mr G.R. Winter, MA (Languages), and Mr W.P. Evans, DLC, a former pupil, (PE). In October Mrs Evelyn Springate was appointed the new Cook Supervisor in the School Kitchen.

Harvest gifts of fruit, vegetables and flowers, donated by the boys' families, were arranged on the stage on the 6th October. The following day the annual Harvest Festival service took place, and in the evening after the Home and School Association's AGM, they were auctioned, raising £34.

A 'Top of the Form' Quiz was arranged between the High School, the Technical School, Dunstable Grammar School and Luton Grammar School on 18th October. It proved a rewarding and entertaining evening, the High School being the winners.

On 11th November, 1961, the service of commemoration to Old Boys who lost their lives in two world wars, was held in the Hall. The Orchestra opened the

proceedings with a good rendering of Purcell's 'Air and Rondo in D. Minor'. The Headmaster conducted the service, and the President of the Old Lutonians, Mr Stanley Wood, read the lesson. The congregation then filed past the Memorial plaque, whilst the choir sang two anthems, 'I will lift up my eyes', by Bach, and 'Thou wilt keep them in perfect peace', by Wesley. Many parents of the fallen were present.

The Home and School Association Funds were swollen by £309 following the annual Bazaar and Hobbies Exhibition, held on 25th November. Messrs P. Shea and J. Marsden, supported by a keen group of boys, helped organise the event.

The Literary and Scientific Society began the year with lectures on 'Esperanto' by Mr M. Lewin; 'Meteorology' by Mr Boyden of the Dunstable Meteorological Office; and 'The Geography of Oil' by Mr Young from Esso. On 10th February, a retired High Court Judge, Sir Hugh Hallett, MC, described his experiences as one of Her Majesty's Judges, and intrigued his audience with a number of exhibits. Mr R.H. Squire, who taught PT at the School during the war, returned to speak of his experiences in the entertainment world. Visits were made to the local Telephone Exchange and to the National Physical Laboratory at Teddington.

The Natural History Society enjoyed a field meeting on 3rd June, led by Dr Dony, that began on Therfield Heath near Royston, and then progressed to Wicken Fen, near Soham in Cambridgeshire. As was to be expected with the Doctor as guide, the theme of the meeting was essentially botanical, though Mr Lovell and Mr Barker were on hand to answer more general questions. In the annual Wild Flower Competition, the School was beaten into second place.

The Chess Club had another good year. The Under 15 team won the Luton Schools' League again. For the first time the 'over 15' age group entered a team of seven boys in the *Sunday Times* Schools' Chess Competition. This was a knock-out competition, and the School were successful for several rounds, before being beaten by Magdalen College School, Oxford, when nearing the zone final. The Luton Co-operative Society presented a Cup for Inter-House Chess. J.S. Maple, the captain, was awarded his full School colours.

Medical Inspections were held in early November. A special Staff meeting was called on 17th November to draw masters' attention to the lax discipline that was developing within the School and they were asked to clamp down on it immediately, and also to see that the School's 'traffic' rules were obeyed. With so many people in the building, congestion was becoming a major problem at times.

The High School and Grammar School Dramatic Societies chose *The Golden Fleece*, a little known play by J.B. Priestley, for their production on 15th–17th November, on the High School stage. It was a straight-forward play in which the characterisation was clear-cut and obvious, the dialogue witty and easy both to speak and to appreciate, and the action direct. It could be enjoyed for its immediacy, with no need to search for hidden meanings.

The girls were full of vitality, and spoke and moved with clear purpose. Linda Craddock (Miss Weeks) could charm or wither at a glance. Angela Frary was suitably imperious and intolerant as the wealthy Lady Leadmill, and Sandra Else was an excellent foil to her as the more kindly and less demanding Mrs Tagg. Malcolm Spowart as Tagg, a man spoilt by his wealth, affected the Yorkshire accent very well, but was not always as aggressive as he might have been. Michael Smart, as Sir Richard Garnett, a milder man, played his part with quiet effectiveness. Of the three principal characters, Roger Woodham was impressive in the part of Lotless, the loquacious hotel porter, acting with obvious relish. Alongside him Jane Musson had the part of Molly Cudden. Her acting was mature and she knew how to suit her behaviour to changing moods and circumstances. Frederick Rodgers, as the young Dr Alec Rothbury, had to appear diffident, awkward, and somewhat disappointed in both love and his profession. It called for under-acting, which he did with considerable success. Production was once more by Gladys Brown and Russell Key.

The sixth New Boys' Concert took place in the dining hall on 15th November. It was attended by many parents and a good proportion of boys. The choir opened the evening by singing 'The British Grenadiers', and they were followed by two piano solos by A.P. Stephen. Violin, clarinet, and cornet soloists, a recorder group and verse-speaking group followed. The choir brought the proceedings to a close by singing 'The Traction Engine' by Marchant, and 'Just as the Tide was Flowing', a traditional tune. Mr Hauke conducted a fine concert, but admitted that perhaps 'The Traction Engine' was 'in need of a little oil'!

On the last day of term, 21st December, in a change to recent tradition, the annual Carol Service was held as part of morning assembly. The choir sang very well and the school responded in a pleasing way, lustily joining in the old favourite carols. P.J. Orme played the opening organ solo, and led the singing admirably.

'Three Times Round the World'

'The year 1962 will be remembered by some for its great progress in rocketry; for the fact that men have orbited the earth at great heights at very great speeds with considerable precision, and that unmanned satellites in very fair numbers are continuing to hurtle round us.

'I think it is realistic to feel that no results of this kind of research are likely to ease the lot of the average man very much for a long time to come.

'The average human is half-naked, permanently hungry, illiterate and dies young. This, and the struggle of millions to survive their poverty and their suffering, is the fundamental historic event of our time.'

These were the Headmaster's salutary words in the 1962 edition of *The Lutonian*. On 20th February, Colonel Glenn had orbited the world three times, but had it

made the world a better place? Mr Webb felt that everyone should co-operate to alleviate world poverty and hunger with ideals like the Freedom from Hunger Campaign.

At Speech Day, 23rd February, the guest speaker was the distinguished Old Boy of the School, Dr Alfred Caress, who was Research and Development Director of ICI. He had been at the School from 1915 to 1922 when he went to Cambridge. Six years later he joined ICI and was the person responsible for the development of Perspex.

The Headmaster began his Report by regretting the absence from the platform of Mr Willet Ball, JP, familiar to many hundreds of boys as 'the Governor who always wore an open neck white shirt'. He had resigned after many years of loyal service, due to age and failing powers, and the assembly sent him their best wishes.

The number of boys on the School Roll for 1961 was 885. The VIth Form started with 54 in the Arts and 105 in Science. Sixteen boys had joined post O-level from Secondary Modern Schools. Mr Webb repeated once again the need for more room. 'I long to give the VIth Formers more civilised quarters than an open pigeon hole for books and room to stand up; to teach Technical Drawing somewhere else than on the Dining Room's wobbly tables; to enlarge the library facilities either by having junior and senior libraries or by having a separate magazine or reading room; and to give the staff a locker or a desk or a cupboard each in addition to their staff room. Six division rooms, urgently needed for the past two years have been cleverly planned on paper and we anxiously await their materialisation. I hope it is noted that this will further reduce the playground area, once planned for 450–500 boys, and already appreciably diminished by earlier extensions.'

In the 1961 summer 257 boys sat GCE Ordinary level subjects and 119 one or more subjects at A-level. Some of the latter were in Lower VI and took Economics with a high level of success. Some of the former taking O-level were in the VI or in other IVs than IVa. 149 boys in the Vs and IVa had an average of just over 5 subjects each; and the 91 boys in Upper VI achieved an average of just over two A-level subjects each. Four State Scholarships were awarded: to C.J.D. Adams and D.J. Blythin chiefly for good work in Geology, to J.M. Chapman for Physics and Chemistry and to R. Westerman for Maths and Physics. The first three went to London University (Adams at Queen Mary, and the others at Imperial College), and Westerman to Trinity College, Cambridge (October 1962). Peter J. Orme won an Organ Scholarship to Sidney Sussex College, Cambridge – the School's third organ scholarship since 1951. He also received the first Sir John Burgoyne Prize for Music.

After Mrs Caress had distributed the awards, Dr Caress addressed the assembly, pointing out that science was necessary in education. Scientists had to be educated people. He also thought that boys studying the Arts should know something of science. He said that he had great faith in the younger generation. "They jive and twist to 'pop' music and 'square' is no longer a geometrical figure. I know you find

not only a more exciting world, but a very much more dangerous one and I know you face it with confidence." Dr Caress concluded by asking for an extra day's holiday to commemorate Colonel John Glenn's historic space flight.

The Head Prefect, D. R. Webb, thanked the guests and presented Mrs Caress with a book.

The year had begun with a concert at the School by present and former music students calling themselves the Juventus Quintet. Consisting of H.R. Owen (piano), D.J. Burrows (1st violin), L.A. Harding (2nd violin), C.C. Davis (cello) and H.I. Hammond (double bass), they were joined by guest soloists Peter Orme (organ) and Natalie Webber (soprano). Their programme was well-balanced and displayed the considerable talents of all who took part.

The Junior Dramatic Society performed three plays for parents and boys of the Lower School on 14th February. These were *The Treasure Hunt* produced by Mr Cranwell, *The Grand Chan's Diamond* produced by Mr Acton and *The Night Rider* produced by Mr Shea. It was seen as a good introduction to acting in front of a large audience, and the young players did surprisingly well.

Open Evening on 7th March took the form of an 'Any Questions' evening, with parents meeting members of the School Staff. Those whose problems could not be dealt with in the time, were invited to return for a fuller discussion at a later date.

The Home and School Association held a Celebrity Lecture in March when Mr Dorian Williams, a well-known TV commentator on equestrian matters, spoke on 'TV behind the scenes'. A new venture arranged by the Association was a Social Evening on 6th April, rewarding parents who had carried out duties of stall holding, supplying refreshments and decorating the Hall for the annual bazaar, together with the whole of the School Staff. They were entertained by Rex Cooper, a conjuror, and Henry Ellcock, pianist. Later in the year the Association spent half a day visiting some of the Oxford Colleges, under the guidance of Mr G.W. Barraclough. Book Prizes on Speech Day and medals for the school sports day were also provided by the HSA and, where needed, various Societies and Clubs of the School received financial assistance. A grant of £200 was made for the purchase of a new printing machine, which was used by the boys to print tickets and programmes.

The main musical event of the year took place on 17th and 18th May. The School choir and members of the School orchestra, with some friends of the School, performed Burnand and Sullivan's *Cox and Box*, and Gilbert and Sullivan's *Trial by Jury*, in the School Hall. *Cox and Box* called for a fast pace, and with only two principal characters it required skill to hold the audience. Bob Minney of the Luton Amateurs was a lively Sgt. Bouncer, and ex-Grammar School boy Malcolm Singer was excellent as the eccentric James John Cox.

Malcolm Singer, who was at the School from 1951–57, originally went into banking, enjoying music as a hobby. Later he spent three years at the Royal Academy of Music, before becoming a freelance singing teacher and broadcaster.

In *Trial by Jury* the Usher was sung by Michael Sharman, (the producer), whose 'Silence in Court!' boomed across the chorus every now and then. Kenneth Webb did not stand out as much as the part of the Judge required, but he clearly enjoyed what he was doing. The show was really stolen by Malcolm Singer as Counsel for the plaintiff. Angelina, the heroine, was played by Natalie Webber, an old girl of the High School (at the time studying at the Royal Academy in London). The male chorus was excellent, but the bridesmaids, who included a number of High School girls, lacked force, though they were a very pretty sight. Adolph Hauke was the musical director.

In Football the 1st XI had a good season in 1962, losing only three of its twelve matches, during which they scored 45 goals. One of the games lost was against Bushey Grammar School, for the first time in many years; but the defeat was reversed in the return match. The School had a very sound defence, there being complete understanding between goal-keeper and backs. At centre-half L.T. Kaye worked hard both in defence and in attack, keeping his forwards well supplied. G. Allen, G.C. Day and J. Game provided the spearhead of the School's attack. J.R. Wintle, on the wing, took advantage of every opportunity for a shot at goal. His centring was strong and accurate and contributed in no small measure to the final tally of goals.

Playing as the 'Luton Nomads', in the second division of the Luton League, the enthusiasm of the School Basketball team was suitably rewarded by taking first place and winning a cup and individual medals. In the inter-house competition for the Peter Cooper Cup, Wasps were strong in all age groups and were the easy winners.

The Groundsman, Mr A. Graffham, retired at Easter after twelve years of loyal service to the School. He was succeeded by Mr Frank Reid.

Sports Day was held on a warm, sunny 30th June. In spite of the favourable weather only two records were broken; A. Rising added 1 ft 8 ins to the (u.16) Shot and R.K. Smitham beat his own Open Hammer record with a throw of 184 ft 9¾ ins. In the Open events, M.W. Haynes (H) scored 28 points to be runner-up to *Victor Ludorum*: K.G. Roberts (G) who gained the highest possible score, (last achieved by R.W. Kelly in 1949). In the Luton Schools' Sports the School team won the Championship Shield after a very close fight with Rotheram and Beech Hill Schools.

The 1962 season was not one of the best for the School's cricket teams. The 1st XI played a number of its home matches on grass, and fewer on the bituturf wicket, and it was interesting for the veteran spectators to compare the conditions. R. Cox, the captain, fielded magnificently at all times, and R.D. Mumford was a reliable wicket-keeper. The batting was not always stable, and depended a great deal on Cox, though R.L. Root, B.J. Wiseman and Mumford all defended stoutly, R.W. Spall made considerable progress, and J.R. Wintle and S.J. Coeshall got runs quickly when required to do so.

With Mr I.R. Rendell taking an interest in Swimming, a reasonable amount of

The Luton Schools' Athletics Championships, 1962. (back row) A.F. Harris, E. MacKenzie, R.E. Hearn, R.M. Wells, D. Brown, D.T. Wootten, P.J. Oddy, (standing) R.A. Smith, G.R. Yeates, R.N. Jenkins, R. Stacey, S.W. MacPhail, A.J. Bonnington, A.F. Compton, G. Bibby, D.P. Poulton, (sitting) D.C. Earl, G.B. Whittaker, M.A. Syrett, Mr W.P. Evans, J. Bevis, A.J. Duncan, A.N. Potts, (front) D.R. Hamel, D.C. Lumb. (L.N.)

progress was made, with eight members of the team of thirteen reaching the finals of the Luton Schools' Gala. R.J. Skellam gained 4½ points and N.C. Evans 4 points. Evans set a very good example as captain and was keenly assisted by R.R.Q. Neale. Hornets won the Inter-House Gala by a staggering 154 points.

The 1962 1st XV Rugby team, apart from a nil-all draw against Dunstable, lost to all its school opponents and failed to cross the line into the bargain. In club games they had their only successes, winning three against modest opposition and being beaten heavily (3–51) by a strong and mature Old Boys side. 'In the circumstances,'

John Muse observed, 'it would be improper to criticise individuals, who were unfortunate to come through the lower school when coaching was not in the healthy state it is now.'

Four Masters left at the end of the summer term having been appointed Heads of Department in other schools. Messrs G.W. Barraclough, D.G. Barker, R.K.T. Trend (a former Old Boy) and C.F.P. Porter.

Mr Geoffrey W. Barraclough had taken Mr Clayton's place in the Chemistry department in 1956, and was soon involved in School activities, including the Under 15 Rugby side, and inter-house seven-a-side Rugby. He worked for three years on the committee of the Home and School Association. Mr David G. Barker came in 1954 and saw the completion of the new Biology laboratory. As a botanist he was an enthusiastic President of the Natural History Society. He took over Under 15 cricket on the death of Mr Chapman, and ran the side for eight years.

Six new Masters joined during the year. Mr I.R. Rendell (PE), Mr R.H. Barter, BSc (Biology), Mr M.R. Dupont, BSc (Maths), Mr T.C. Flitton, BSc, an Old Boy, (Physics), Mr R.A. W. Rhodes, BSc (Chemistry) and Mr B. Shaw, BSc (Physics).

Mr Pierre Lanza, as the French Assistant, and Miss Ursula Sander, the German Assistant, spent the year (1961–62) at the School. Their places were taken for 1962–63 by Mr Pierre Trompeau and Mr Dieter Hampel.

When the School returned after the summer holiday, the new annexe had been completed. It consisted of six classrooms, mostly for VIth Form teaching, a new Prefects' Common Room and a book store. These new additions reduced the use made of various non-teaching spaces for teaching, and allowed most Sixth Form study periods to be taken in the Library. What had been the old Prefects' Common Room became the book store. The new Common Room was built adjacent to it, and partly along the east side of the gymnasium. It was lit from above.

The School was saddened to learn of the sudden death of 17 years old James A. Cosgrove of Upper VI Science on 14th September. An experiment at home, in which he had put a plastic bag over his head, had gone tragically wrong. A number of his School friends and members of staff attended his funeral at The Vale, Stopsley, on 22nd September. On 10th November a second year boy, Christopher H. Czapiewski (age 12), was killed when he was struck by a car on the New Bedford Road near Streatley. He had been cycling with his headlamp turned off, probably to conserve the battery. He was buried in Biscot churchyard after a Requiem Mass. The School's Assistant Caretaker for ten years, Mr A. E. Williams, died after a long and painful illness on 24th September. A native of Tredegar, he had been to school with the politician, Aneurin Bevan, and they began work together in the mines at the age of 13.

The Harvest Festival service was held on 5th October. In the evening the produce was sold and the proceeds went to organisations caring for the elderly.

All Luton schools had a holiday on Friday, 2nd November. Queen Elizabeth II

visited the town and toured the recently opened Central Library. Sadly, it poured with rain all day, depriving many citizens of witnessing a very rare event.

On 7th November the New Boys' Concert was held in the Dining hall. It was a chance to spot new talent, and the general quality of performance was very good, only slightly marred by the inevitable nervousness. The Junior Choir opened the programme with two traditional songs, 'The Nightingale' and 'All through the night'. Piano, violin and clarinet solos followed. Trebles S.G. Smith and P.R. Outen sang 'Flight of the Earls' and 'Lonely Woods' respectively. The Recorder Ensemble played a number of pieces and Mr E. Cranwell had produced a verse-speaking item. The evening closed with the Choir's rendition of Britten's 'Tragic Story' and Parry's 'England'.

The Headmaster conducted the usual service to commemorate Remembrance Day on 11th November. The President of the Old Lutonians, Dr Jack Burgoyne, read the lesson, and the choir sang Wesley's 'Thou wilt keep him' and Bach's 'I will lift up mine eyes'. Fewer than ever relatives of the dead were able to attend, but many old boys and friends of the school were present as the boys once more filed past the Memorial plaques.

From 14th–16th November the School Dramatic Society presented *M. Perrichon Goes Abroad*, a comedy by Eugene Labiche and Edouard Martin, in the School Hall, with a further performance on 17th at the new Library Theatre in Luton. Probably due to the fact that hardly anyone had ever heard of the play, the audiences were some of the smallest the School had witnessed. Although the cast included six young ladies from the High School, it was not the traditional joint-production. The greatest applause each evening was reserved for Philip Bonner, who had the leading part, and he certainly deserved it. As an example of stamina alone his performance was magnificent. The two principal ladies were also excellent, especially Ann McIntosh as Madame Perrichon. Malcolm Spowart as Armand, the young banker, gave his best performance yet in school dramatics. It was a difficult part, which he handled with skill. Timothy Burgoyne played Daniel with plenty of verve and even ebullience. Mrs Sharman's sets were most pleasing, and the School was once again indebted to Michael Sharman for a very enjoyable entertainment.

On 25th November the Christmas Bazaar and Hobbies Exhibition proved to be a big success, and a total of £322 was raised for the Home and School Association Funds.

'Members of the Railway Club provided, manned and operated a splendid collection of working models. The Geography Room became a veritable Clapham Junction for the occasion and was filled with the whirr of the little trains busily making their journeys around two separate track layouts. Around the room too, stood many varied exhibits of railway interest lent by members and friends of the Club.'

The first week of December was one of heavy frost in Luton, and further afield, in London, dense smog. Many minor School events were cancelled. By the last day of term there was also snow and ice to contend with. Everyone enjoyed the Christmas Carol Service which began with the choir singing 'Once in Royal David's city'. This was followed by the Bidding Prayer, read by Mr Webb. The choir sang 'Torches, Torches' by John Joubert, and the Head Prefect, I.R. Carter, read the first lesson. Four more carols, two lessons and a prayer completed the proceedings. After a good lunch, school broke up, and the boys dispersed amongst a flurry of snowballs.

Snow and Ice

The New Year, 1963, began with heavy snow and ice. Low temperatures meant that the field could not be used for matches until 9th March nor the playground until after half-term in February. Following tradition there was a reunion for Old Boys at Universities and College on the evening of 8th January, but due to the weather it was poorly attended.

Many parents and friends of the School gathered in the Hall for Speech Day on 15th February, 1963. The lower school continued with their normal work while the seniors listened to the Right Honourable Dr Charles Hill, who as usual made a stirring and humorous speech. At the time Dr Hill was Member of Parliament for Luton. A few weeks later he was elevated to the House of Lords and adopted the title of Lord Hill of Luton.

The Headmaster delivered his review of the past year's work and progress. He said that for the last few years the number of boys on the School Roll had been about 890 in September, dropping to about 865 or 870 in January. In September 1962 the Arts VIth totalled 64 of whom 12 were 3rd year and the Science VIth contained 110 boys of whom 20 were 3rd year. The School were glad to take 15 boys with GCE Ordinary levels from local Secondary Modern Schools, and he stressed the successes of their predecessors as Prefects, Head Prefect and at Universities. In the summer of 1962 a total of 367 boys sat for one or more subjects in the GCE at O or A-level. 144 boys in the Vs and IVa shared 738 O level passes or an average of just over 5.1. One member of IVa, S.C. Gregory, passed all his eight subjects at the high distinction mark of Grade 1. 199 A-levels were gained by 86 boys in U.VI: an average of 2.3 subjects each. Awarded on the GCE results were two State Scholarships, one to K.C. Bowler in Maths and Physics. He also won an Open Entrance Scholarship to Imperial College, London. The other went to R.P. Whymant for Modern Languages. He was already the winner of an Alliance Française prize. He had spent most of the last term in Germany, returning to win an Open Scholarship to Magdalene College, Cambridge.

Thirty-six boys went into full-time higher education, of which 22 went to university to study science and mathematics, 5 to universities for Arts degrees, 5 to

Training Colleges, and 4 to Colleges of Further Education. Thirty-two boys went into industry, mostly engineering. The Law, Accountancy, Banking, Insurance, Architecture and Surveying received 23 boys: seven of them held commercial apprenticeships. Thirteen boys had laboratory posts; 8 went into HM Forces, 2 the Merchant Navy, 14 into clerical jobs and one into agriculture.

After the Headmaster's report, Mrs Hill distributed the prizes. Dr Hill then delivered his speech which as usual was pregnant with prudent advice, wisdom and humour.

From his seat in the body of the Hall, Sir John Burgoyne presented a House Championship Cup for Music to the Headmaster. The Mayor of Luton, Ald. Leslie Bowles, expressed thanks on behalf of all those present to Dr Hill and Sir John.

At Easter a party of 16 boys, led by a science master, Mr John H. Lightfoot, sailed on the ship *M.S. Devonia* to Morocco. After one day in Lisbon and five at sea, they disembarked at Tangier. The port resembled a fairground, with peddlers and beggars, story-tellers and jugglers, hawkers and sellers, all seeking the party's undivided patronage. During three days of tramping round the Medinas and Casbahs and pounding round the Moroccan countryside in a primitive Moroccan bus, they soon discovered that the brightly coloured brochures and postcards that lured travellers to Morocco were far from typical. A rather different picture was obtained first-hand, of narrow dirty streets, desperately overcrowded, and extreme poverty.

During the Spring term the Music department launched an enterprising series of three lunchtime recitals, the proceeds of which went to the Freedom from Hunger Campaign. The charge was 6d. per boy and 1s. each master. The first of the series on 12th March was given by Roger Windmill on the organ. He played music by Hurford, Haydn and Purcell, and gave a short talk on the working of an organ. A week later Lawrence Harding and Donald Burrows (violins) played pieces by Pleyel, Monty and Dvorak, followed by a talk on the construction of the violin. The last concert in the series was a recital of Consort Music involving a dozen musicians. The attendance at the concerts was disappointing but in all about £3 was collected.

The Luton Concert Orchestra, whose members included a number of present and past pupils of the Grammar, High and Technical Schools, gave a concert in the Hall, on 9th March, conducted by another former student, Bryan Summerfield.

In March the Home and School Association held an 'Any Questions' evening, which proved very popular and allowed parents to question members of Staff on a host of different subjects. In the same month, with Mr I.R. Rendell as Staff Representative, a Grand Dance was organised in the School Hall, which made a profit of £19 8s 0d. for the Freedom from Hunger Campaign.

A letter appeared in *The Luton News* in March 1963. It was headed:

GRAMMAR SCHOOL GENTLEMEN

'An astonishing thing happened to me while I was waiting for a bus near Luton

Grammar School. I turned the corner from Bradgers Hill Road, to the bus stop, and was faced by a four-deep crowd of boys from the Grammar School. Thinking I wouldn't stand an earthly chance of getting on the bus, I meekly took my place at the end of the queue.

'Then a Prefect came up to me and politely suggested that I should go to the front of the line, as this was the custom. Feeling like the Lady of the Manor, I did so, and was very flattered by this kind thought.

'We seem to spend most of our time moaning about teenagers, but give less thought to the times when they can be perfect little angels.'

On the 20th March two coaches took 60 boys and masters to Twickenham for the annual Varsity rugger match.

The Senior Cross-Country team had a successful season, in spite of deep snow which lay on many of the courses for much of the Spring term. Home and away fixtures were kept to a minimum. By the 14th March it was possible to host the Bedfordshire Schools' Championships on the School course. R. Moore (captain) ran well throughout the season and together with M. Haynes, J. Taylor, G. Slack and P. McAleer was chosen to represent the County in the National Schools' Cross-Country Championships. Unfortunately, the County team failed to arrive at Coventry in time for the start, due to a transport slip-up. Mr W.P. Evans stimulated a lot of enthusiasm in the 1st and 2nd years with the result that a strong Junior team was fielded, and for the first time a number of Under 13 colours were presented.

As with the other winter sports, the Football season was memorable mainly for the severe weather, with many fixtures cancelled. The record of the 1st XI was not impressive. The main weakness lay in the forwards, particularly on the left flank. This was overcome by moving J.E. Brown to inside-left and K. Jenkins to outside-left. Defence was strengthened by bringing S.J. Coeshall as a fourth half-back to play with S.A. Evans, E.P. Clutten and D.S. Tudball. The forwards held their own, and G.C. Day (captain) and J.R. Wintle played some excellent football, finding the net frequently. On 4th April a Staff team beat the 1st XI 2–0.

The Senior Basketball team lost only one of its ten games, and the captain, P.L. Green, was the most prolific scorer. Wasps won the Peter Cooper inter-house cup.

In 1963 the English Schools' Athletics Association changed the rule governing the age of competitors. The new date for calculating their age was 1st September. This meant that boys could be as much as seven months older in each age group, and many would be competing in the same age group as in the previous year.

Sports Day was held on a fine 22nd May. Eight new records were created and three equalled. The most outstanding effort was C.J. Harrison's (u.16) Hammer throw of 158 ft 0½ ins. which added no less than 34 feet to M.R.C. Towl's throw in 1959. *Victor Ludorum* was the captain of athletics, Michael W. Haynes, who qualified for seven finals. The day ended with the relays, which produced three of the

records and rewarded the seniors who had spent so much time coaching the teams. Wasps easily took the Relay Cup and the Powdrill House Championship Cup with a margin of 99 points. The Bedfordshire County AAA Championships took place in the same week as Sports Day, leaving competitors with insufficient time to decide which events to enter. Apart from winning the Boys (13–15) relay, individual successes were in the field events. In the County Schools' at Bedford, A.C. Riches (hammer) and M.A. Syrett (220) gained national standards. At the Luton Schools' Sports the captain, M.A. Syrett, broke the records for the 220 and 440 and won the Tripp Trophy for the best boy athlete. D.R. Fryer's high jump broke the School's (u. 13) and the Luton Schools' lower senior records. The School took the Championship Shield. At the end of the season, five boys were chosen to represent Bedfordshire in the English Schools' Athletics Championships at Chelmsford, namely A.C. Riches and A.J. Duncan (both hammer), M.A. Syrett (440), and G.B. Whitaker and R.M. Wells (long jump). All did very well, but none reached the final three in their events.

The cricketers had a moderately successful season. The winter weather had played havoc with the bitumen wicket, so all home matches were played on grass. Out of 42 matches played, 19 were won and 19 lost, with 4 drawn. The 1st XI's play improved as the season progressed. The regular bowlers, J.R. Wintle, J.E. Brown and S.J. Coeshall, played well, and had the batting been of the same consistency as the bowling the team might have been unbeaten. Wintle, the captain, bowled especially well in a match in which he made history by beating Bedford School 2nds for the first time, when he took 8 wickets for 20 runs. Fielding was weak, but C.J. Harrison was commended for his throwing to the wicket, and the reliable wicket-keeping of G.C. Day was a real asset to the side.

Swimming was usually based around the Luton Schools' Gala and the Inter-House Gala, but in 1963 six swimming fixtures were arranged against other schools and clubs. The team had moderate success, winning three and losing three. The most pleasure came from beating Bedford Modern School at their own pool. In the Luton Schools' Gala the team came second. Several boys were chosen to represent Luton in the Bedfordshire Schools' Championships. R. Robinson, the School captain, gained second place in the Senior Men's Breaststroke and P. Clarke a first in diving. The School's Senior team was then chosen *en bloc* as the Luton Schools' Senior team in the Divisional Championships, and Robinson was chosen to compete in the Nationals.

The programme of the Student Christian Movement Group contained plenty of variety, including films, discussions, a Brains Trust, addresses by outside speakers and special visits. One of the highest attendances was recorded for a speaker from the Marriage Guidance Council. 120 people from the High School, Technical School and Grammar School attended a Conference at Bradgers Hill, on 28th March, addressed by a young Lutonian, who was an Assistant Minister at a church on a large

housing estate in Bristol, the Revd. Brian Phillips. He called his talk 'Teds and an Unsquare Faith', and it was illustrated by a film of a modern passion play, properly entitled 'A Man Dies' but popularly called 'Christ in Jeans'. It was the story of the temptation and crucifixion of Christ, with much of the dialogue and many of the songs in a modern idiom. The members found it enjoyable and stimulating.

The Archaeological Society had been revitalised with David H. Kennett and Terence P. Smith at the helm. Lectures were given by Mr P.G. Laws, the County Planning Officer, on '800 years of Design', Mr F.W. Kuhlicke, Curator of Bedford Museum on 'Saxon Architecture', and Mr J. Moss Eccardt discussed 'Prehistoric Hertfordshire'. A novel idea to increase membership was a Brains Trust on the last day of the Spring Term for all the first forms. A large party visited sites in Wiltshire during the summer, others cleared rubbish from Someries Castle, and during the holidays quite a number took part in excavations locally and further afield. On Speech day the Headmaster observed 'It is only a few years ago that J.F. Dyer and W.H. Manning were boys at School infecting others with their enthusiasm in this field. The newly established erudite *Bedfordshire Archaeological Journal* does them credit.' David Kennet was to edit that Journal for seventeen years. After reading Archaeology at Cardiff University he became a recognised authority and writer on Anglo-Saxon pottery and rural society in the later middle ages. Terence P. Smith read theology at St John's College, Cambridge, and is an authority on early brickwork, and author of *The Medieval Brickmaking Industry in England, 1400–1450*.

The highlight of the Natural History Society's year was a lecture entitled 'The Genetic Code' given by Dr Kalmus, an expert researcher in genetics. It was attended by 70 boys, and 24 girls from the High School. During the year Mr E. Meadows gave an illustrated talk on 'Seabirds of the Norse Isles', Dr Holden of Rothamsted spoke about the larger British Fungi, and Mr Lingard described animals of the woods and streams. Field meetings took the group to Stockwood Park nurseries, Flitwick Moor, Leagrave Marsh, and Blakeney Point. The team for the Wild Flower Society's annual competition came second to Stamford High School, and recorded 563 flowers.

The Chess Club entered a comparatively young team into the Luton Schools' League (confined to players under 16 years of age). By the end of the season the team was only a few points behind Old Bedford Road School, who, having a very strong team, won all their matches. The most successful School player was G.N. Jepps who, playing on the top board, won all his games. The House Chess Cup was won by the Grasshoppers. The senior team was beaten 3½ to 2½ by Bedford Modern School in the first round of *The Times* tournament.

The Railway Club was very active. Apart from their display at the Hobbies Exhibition, they watched films and listened to Mr E.C. Lewis, the Station Master at Aylesbury Town Station, who spoke on railway operations and his responsibilities as a Station Master. Once again the annual outing went to the Great Western Railway

Museum and the Locomotive Works at Swindon.

The Headmaster was delighted with the School Concert that took place on 10th May. The boys all wore white shirts for the occasion. The orchestra was conducted by Mr Hauke, and began rather shakily by playing four pieces from 'The Yeomen of the Guard'. S.G. Smith sang two treble solos, and pianist Desmond Bazley played Liszt's 'Consolation' with great feeling. A Brass Quartet, Violin Duets and Clarinet Quartets followed. A.J. Pryer played the 'Trumpet Voluntary' accompanied by Roger Windmill on the organ.

> 'The Finale,' wrote A.R. Parr, 'in the shape of "Schwanda the Bagpiper" accelerated wildly as it was played through, much to Mr Hauke's distress, and was crowned by a vicious thump on the tympani by the percussionist, John Gosling. Unfortunately, it came one beat after the remainder of the orchestra had finished playing. The audience "encored" and, nothing daunted, Mr Hauke raised his baton and recommenced at a more leisurely tempo, to finish the concert in a very pleasing, not to say, memorable manner.'

On 12th June the first part of the House Music Competition for the Sir John Burgoyne Cup was held. It was limited to 1st and 2nd year entrants, but senior boys were allowed to train the junior choirs, and Miss Fuller of the High School judged the results. These were Bees 45, Hornets 40, Grasshoppers 37 and Wasps 33. On 15th July Mr Michael Marsh-Edwards, conductor of the Luton Symphony Orchestra, then judged the solo items, awarding the Grasshoppers 75 points, Bees 61, Hornets 59 and Wasps 33. Grasshoppers, the overall winners, were the first house to receive the Cup.

On 29th September, the Old Boys' Association presented a sundial to the School in memory of Mr T.A.E. Sanderson. Constructed of stone from the old Park Square building, it was placed on the lawn outside the main entrance.

On the last morning of the Summer Term the caretaker arrived to find slogans white-washed onto the windows of the School, and the sundial, presented only three weeks previously, daubed with pink paint. Bins had also been placed on the clock tower. The whitewash and bins were removed before morning Assembly, but the sundial needed professional attention. A typical end of term jape, perhaps, yet a photograph of this early morning incident taken by a free-lance photographer appeared in *The Luton News*, as a previous prank had done, back in September 1955.

Three members of Staff left in July, Mr M.R. Dupont who had taught maths for a year, Mr E. Cranwell who covered English and History for two years, and Mr J.D.C. Grayston. Mr James 'Pip' Grayston had joined the School in 1941 to teach mathematics. It was from his rank in the Cadet Corps that he had acquired his nickname. He took charge of the middle school soccer as soon as he arrived, and later succeeded Mr Cooke in running the senior side. He often played cricket in adult

teams against the School, and kept wicket in a 1943 match, when the Staff scored sixty-seven and then dismissed the 1st XI for twenty-three. He was a fine teacher, with beautifully neat handwriting and blackboard work. He left to teach at the Luton College of Technology.

Four new Masters joined the Staff in September. These were Mr A.R. Cator, NDD (Handicraft); Mr M.J. Holst, BA (Art and Music); Mr W.G.B. Oram, Bsc (Mathematics) and Mr D.V. Law, BA (Handicraft).

The Revd. Ivor M. Clemitson and a civil engineer, Mr Stearn, visited the School on 23rd and 24th September to talk to IVa and the Vth and VIth years about voluntary work overseas. Ivor Clemitson was an old pupil (1942–50) who had studied at the London School of Economics, majoring in government and politics. After working in industry, he attended Bishop's Theological College, Cheshunt, from where he was ordained and became Curate in an industrial parish in Sheffield. Later he was appointed the first Industrial Chaplain to the Diocese of St Albans. In 1974 he was elected Labour MP for Luton East. (He was the first Church of England priest to sit in the House of Commons). He lost his seat by a narrow margin in 1979. After some years in teaching he retired to France, where he died in 1997.

The Grammar School has no long-standing record of Old Boys entering Parliament. The only other MP known to the writer is Dr Desmond Turner, ARCS (LGS: 1951–57), Labour Member for Brighton Kemptown since 1997.

The Harvest Festival Service was celebrated on 4th October. The choir sang two anthems, one of which was Mandero's 'Praise the Lord, O Jerusalem'. This had a very rousing opening and final section which was sung to great effect. Afterwards, members of the WVS and Vesper collected half each of the produce for distribution amongst the needy of the town.

The Remembrance Day Service was held on 11th November, when more Old Boys than usual were able to attend. Past-President of the Old Lutonians, Leslie Button, read the lesson in the absence of A.W. 'George' Thorpe who was in Geneva. As the boys filed past the Memorials the choir sang Bach's 'Jesu, Priceless Treasure' and Wesley's 'Thou will keep him'.

From 13th to 15th November the joint School Dramatic Societies presented Sheridan's *The Rivals*. It had last been performed at the School eighteen years previously with an all male cast. The roles of Sir Anthony Absolute and his son Jack were played by Philip Bonner and Michael Stevens, both experienced actors who interpreted their parts proficiently. Martyn Kempson as the 'country idiot', Acres, brought a great deal of life to the character. Anthony Susman got the most out of the extremely awkward and unrewarding part of Julia's lover, Faulkland. Peter Titterington *was* Sir Lucius O'Trigger, an Irishman the audience could believe in. Mary Childs was a delicious Mrs Malaprop, revelling in her own malapropisms. Avril Moss as Lydia Languish, the reader of third-class novels, was perfect for the part, and Lynn Smith gave a commendable performance as her cousin Julia. Michael Sharman

and Gladys Brown were the producers, and Alan Cator designed the set.

The annual Bazaar and Hobbies Exhibition was held on 23rd November. Six boys, together with Messrs Acton, Davies and Rendell, formed an organising committee and took responsibility for the whole event from the Home and School Association. Parents were still very much involved. As well as the usual side shows and exhibitions, the special attraction was 'The Cavern'.

> 'We borrowed the Art Room from a naturally reluctant Mr Gale. Mr Cator, the History master, who did not know us very well, volunteered to be the master in charge. *The Luton News* kindly supplied paper to cover the walls; this was painted and adorned with slogans in many languages. The two groups performing in the afternoon were Bryan and the Hangmen, and the Raving Cannibals. About 500 people came to 'The Cavern' during the three sessions: a real atmosphere was obtained – due to the lack of ventilation.'

A fresh west wind helped to make the balloon race a success. Labels were later returned from as far away as East Germany, Poland and Lilley! The day finished with dancing to 'Johnny Starr and the Midnights'. After all the bills had been paid, almost £485 was given to the Freedom from Hunger Campaign.

The annual School versus the Old Boys Rugby match took place on 7th December. It was the last time the Old Boys played as the Old Lutonians RFC. They disbanded under that name, since more than 35% of the players were not members of the parent club. For the game the Old Boys chose a team of which each member was a past or present Captain. The final score was 10–14 to the Captains.

The Carol Service was held on the morning of 20th December, with Sir John Burgoyne in attendance. It proved an enjoyable end to term and beginning of the Christmas festivities.

Sixty Years On

1964 saw the appearance of a new-style school magazine with a magisterial photograph of Mr Godfrey, in a familiar pose, dominating the cover. Many readers felt that the old magazine was solid, but rather stuffy, and that it needed a shot in the arm. Whilst this might have improved its popularity and sales, it was a bitter blow for future historians, but was soon to get worse! The new Editor, Mr Robert S. Acton, decided to replace letter-press printing with photo-lithography. This was done partly for cheapness and partly so that illustrations could be used more freely. The new illustrations included facetious cartoons alongside more serious scraperboard, linocut and pen-and-ink drawings, and a wider selection of photographs. The size, for three issues only, was increased to 250 mms x 175 mms. The useful 'School Notes' section, chronicling important events in the School year, disappeared, to be

replaced by not always accurate reports of three or four selected events. At a critical time in the School's history, this was a tragic decision. No longer was it possible to read the names of prize winners, GCE successes and University entrants.

The new year started on 7th January, with the annual reunion of Old Boys at present at University. The attendance was good, the weather having proved unusually mild.

Two days later, the Mayor of Luton, Alderman Leslie G. Bowles, visited the School to receive a cheque for £556 10s 7d from Andrew C. Riches, the Head Prefect, for the Freedom From Hunger Fund. The School's total contribution to the Fund collected over the whole of 1963 was £658 16s 9d.

The Headmaster travelled to Cranwell on Sunday, 12th January, for an important meeting, not returning to Luton until Tuesday. At midday on Monday he was called to the telephone to be told that Mr. H.E. Woodcock had been found dead at his desk a few hours earlier. To say that the whole School was stunned was an understatement. The atmosphere for the next few days was uncannily subdued, but in a building full of young life, it was not long before things appeared to get back to normal.

Harold Evelyn Woodcock was 64, a Yorkshireman, and had joined the School staff in January, 1923. His colleague, Wynne Parry wrote:

'He was one of the most vigorous personalities on the School staff. Of magnificent physique, impressive build and infectious cheerfulness, he entered whole-heartedly into every department of life of the School, and he was completely selfless in his devotion. In his younger days he had played Rugger, Soccer and Cricket with distinction, and had helped to run the boys' teams, and up to the end he continued to act as a judge at the Athletics meetings and to umpire Cricket matches. He had umpired every Old Boys' match for forty-one years.

'Until the appointment of a full-time Music master in 1940 Mr Woodcock had organised the Music of the School, and he continued to conduct the Orchestra until he became Careers Master in 1956. He was fond of piano playing and of singing, and his fine, accurate baritone voice could always be heard giving balance to the hymn-singing at Morning Assembly.

'For over thirty years he was Sports Editor of the School Magazine. He kept a record of every match played in every sport, and of colours awarded. As a teacher of French and, in the early days, of Geography, he was a tireless worker and a prolific marker. He knew how to mete out punishment with a strong voice and a still stronger hand, but his punishments were never administered in malice or sadism, and were generally accepted cheerfully by the transgressors. He had a rich sense of humour and an amazing ability to give to boys a nickname which was completely appropriate yet never gave offence. Stern though he could be, he was very good-natured and fundamentally almost unbelievably kind.

'He was the ideal choice for Careers Master. If possible, he worked even harder

Mr H.E. Woodcock (front right) at the Old Lutonians' Dinner in 1954. To his left are C.W. Parry, Keith Woodcock, James Gale and Ian Brodie. (*LN*)

in that capacity. On most days he was at his desk by 8.30 in the morning, and was still to be seen working in his office when the caretaker came to lock-up in the evening.'

On Mr Webb's return to School on Tuesday afternoon, there was a whirl of activity. Mr Woodcock's desk had to be cleared, and his ongoing appointments and arrangements taken care of. It was imperative for the boys that a successor should be found immediately. The obvious answer was C. Wynne Parry.

Many colleagues, Old Boys, friends and students joined Mr Woodcock's family for his funeral at Christ Church on 18th January. At the same time, arrangements were put in hand for a Memorial Service to be held at the School on Monday, 27th January.

At the Memorial Service the Lessons were read by Mr C.J. Godfrey and Mr C.W. Parry; the hymns chosen were 'Lord of All Being', sung to one of Mr Woodcock's

favourite tunes, 'Maryton', 'The God of Love', and 'Lord of All Hopefulness'. The Choir sang the chorale 'Jesu, Priceless Treasure' and the Nunc Dimittis.

Dr Edward Hoblyn said: 'It was probably in his last seven years as Careers Master that he did some of his finest work. I could but wish that more schools had men of his calibre in this important position. Mr Woodcock was a complete, dedicated, efficient, cheerful, friendly and, most important of all, utterly approachable schoolmaster.'

Mr Ernest Irons, Commandant of 'E' Division of the Special Constabulary, added: 'He joined the Special Constabulary early in the war as a constable, but by his efficiency and devotion to duty he was soon promoted to the rank of Sergeant and then to Inspector. I couldn't have asked for a more loyal colleague. All through the war he was on duty every night, and that meant until seven o'clock in the morning. He was called upon to deal with casualties and accidents, and the manner in which he dealt with them earned him the admiration of all his colleagues. It is true that recently he has been more concerned with administration but as recently as the last election he was engaged in crowd control at the counting of the votes when at one time matters developed in a rather ugly manner – no mean effort for a man of his years.'

In the 41 years that Mr Woodcock had been on the staff of the School he had been absent for only a fortnight for illness, and the only assembly he had ever missed was on the Monday that he died.

After consultation with his family the School set up an annual H.E. Woodcock Travel Scholarship, to help senior boys to attend courses abroad or just to travel. The nucleus for the fund was the considerable sum which the boys collected, greatly in excess of what was needed, to buy a wreath.

At Speech Day on Wednesday 12th February, 1964, the Headmaster delivered his annual report in which he spoke of 1963 as a year of sound and solid, but not spectacular, achievement. There had been a much needed playground extension, and plans were slowly beginning to move towards a new staff room, a new gym or suitable alternative, and better provision for library, reading room, technical drawing and art and craft teaching.

There were 190 boys in the Sixth Form in September, 1963; 68 on the Arts side. Accommodation provided by the new division rooms had been a great help and Mr Webb felt that the School could now cope with any likely increase in VIth Form numbers. Nineteen boys with GCE ordinary levels had come from Secondary Modern Schools, 5 to L.VI Arts and 13 to L.VI Science, and one to Remove.

In the 1963 examinations, the average number of GCE O-level passes had gone up from 5.1 to 5.9. Boys entered for a massive 1,337 subjects at O-level, and 872 were gained making a 65.2% pass rate. At Advanced level 90 boys in U. VI gained 190 passes and 7 A-levels were gained by boys in L.VI. Of the 12 boys who had come to the School at 16+ from Secondary Modern Schools and left in July, two had 4 A-

levels, five had 3, three had 2, one had 1 and one had none. Of all boys who left the School in July, fifty had found places at universities or similar centres.

State Scholarships were abolished in 1962. Two boys were awarded Entrance Scholarships to Imperial College London: R.J. Lowin and T.L. Rogers (October 1963). M.K. Ayers was awarded an Exhibition to study mathematics at Sidney Sussex College, Cambridge for October 1964, and D.J. Burrows would go to Trinity Hall College, Cambridge. Both Ayres and Burrows were musicians, playing in the School orchestra, and both made careers in teaching. Burrows taught music for some time in Abingdon. He began part-time studying with the Open University and was their first student to gain a PhD in music. He later obtained a lectureship at the Open University and is currently its Professor of Music. An acknowledged biographer and authority on Handel, he was awarded the prestigious City Prize from Halle (at that time in the GDR) in recognition of his various Handel projects. Readers will find it remarkable and perhaps confusing, that the School has produced two talented musicians with almost identical names and both teaching at the Open University: Donald I. Burrows from 1940–1948, and Donald J. Burrows, 1957–1963.

Two senior boys profited greatly by Travel Awards from the Luton Prisoners of War Fund; another had the autumn term in Germany; a fourth spent the 1963–64 academic year at the Moravian School, Los Angeles, on an American Field Service Scholarship. R. Moore was chosen as a member of the British Schools' Exploration Society's Expedition to northern Finland, where serious scientific work was undertaken under what most folk would have considered pretty desperate conditions.

Lady Pearson then presented the prizes, after which Sir Reginald Pearson, former Deputy Chairman of Vauxhall Motors Ltd, the guest speaker, was invited to address the School. He suggested the boys should develop a love of study, pointing out that the true function of education was to help us make an intelligent contribution to society and to appreciate life. To this end we should develop an inquiring mind and make the most of our opportunities at school in this direction. He concluded by asking for an extra day's holiday for the pupils.

The Speech Day programme listed all the prize winners, examination and sporting successes. It is appropriate at this point to single out one of them: Geoffrey C. Brown, one of 'Jock' Cleaver's last pupils, who was reading geology at Manchester University. By 1970 he had obtained his BSc and PhD, and had become an authority on granitic rocks. He joined the Open University in 1973 and by 1982 was Professor in the Department of Earth Sciences. By then his research interests had shifted from granites to monitoring volcanoes using microgravity. This sort of information could help give advanced warning of eruptions, and it had the potential to save thousands of lives in areas where populations were densely packed on the rich soils of volcanic regions. In January 1993, Geoff Brown was attending an International Conference

on volcanology in the northern Andes at Pasto, Colombia. The town was 5 miles from the centre of the volcano, Galeros. On 14th January, some tourists and delegates mounted to the rim of the crater and cautiously descended into the steaming interior. After an hour it was time to leave. One of them, Professor Stanley Williams, described what happened next in his book *Surviving Galeros* (Little, Brown, 2001):

> 'I had asked the tourists to start down, and was preparing – with José Arlés at my side – to leave myself. Then rocks started tumbling off the inside walls of the crater – first one, then a handful, then a cascade. In my mind there was no doubt that this was either the prelude to an earthquake or an eruption. In Spanish and English I shouted, "Hurry up! Get out!" I vaguely remember seeing Geoff Brown on the opposite rim of the crater and gesturing to him to flee.
>
> 'After that I remember turning. I remember the volcano shaking. I remember dashing madly downhill, the world around me a jouncing tableau of boulders and scree. I had no idea where my colleagues were, saw nothing but the charcoal universe of the cone.' Geoffrey Brown was never seen again.

Two senior masters, Mr Godfrey and Dr Dony, were amongst others due to retire in July, so much of the Headmaster's time at the beginning of the year was taken up with interviewing potential candidates. On 17th March Mr John T. Pye, BSc, a Maths specialist, was offered the post of Deputy Headmaster, taking effect from the Autumn Term. Mr H.B. Evans was promoted to Head of History and Economics, and Mr I.W. Arthur, BA, was appointed to join the History department in September.

County Borough Status

Mr Webb made his last appearance at a meeting of the Bedfordshire Education Committee on 6th March. He had been attending regularly since 1947. On 1st April, 1964, after years of struggle, Luton finally achieved County Borough status. This meant great changes in secondary education within the town, which Anne Allsopp has described in detail in the Girls' High School companion volume to this book. Briefly, in the early 1950s the Borough Education Officer proposed what became known as the Corbett Plan. In it the Grammar, High and Technical School would be retained as selective schools with a much reduced intake of about 8% who would follow a 'fast track' GCE O-level course over four years. All the secondary schools (the word modern would be dropped) would have at least one GCE O-level stream. If pupils from those schools obtained the appropriate GCE O-level passes and could cope with a GCE A-level course, they could, if they wished, transfer to one of the sixth forms at the selective schools. It was a political hot-potato. The

minority Tory group on the Council opposed it on the grounds that it was part of the Labour Party's plan for comprehensive education and a philosophy of levelling down. The Labour politicians said the aim was not to level down the grammar schools but to lift up the secondary moderns. It was expected that the Corbett plan would commence in September 1964.

On Tuesday, 28th April, seven HM Inspectors arrived at the School for four days, ostensibly to see how it would fit into Dr Corbett's programme of re-organisation. They hoped that their findings would be of help in connection with the two other selective schools, particularly as the transfers into the sixth form from non-selective schools were likely to increase.

The Inspectors reported back a week later. They emphasised the fact that both the School and the Education Committee might need to change their attitude to sixth form work and to the treatment of members of the sixth forms. The needs of the School were summarised as follows:

1. The present building was too small, even for current needs. Some adaptation of the building might be helpful in association with the needs for a sixth form study area.
2. There should be a second art room.
3. There should be two handicraft rooms and one drawing office. Only as much technical drawing should be done as was necessary for:
    a) potential University students doing the mechanical sciences tripos or the equivalent;
    b) students pursuing craft studies to a high level.
4. Music. There should be a storage room and a few individual practice rooms, as well as a fairly large one, to accommodate small orchestral groups or ensembles. There should also be a second music classroom.
5. The Science laboratory technicians needed their own workshop with a bench.
6. The Biology department needed a proper greenhouse.
7. The sanitary fittings were below standard for the numbers. There were 10 wash basins short, and these should be sited close to the W.Cs.
8. The demands of modern Physics and Chemistry required special grants for equipment. Arrangements should be made to spend £1,250 over the next three years.
9. The Library grant should be increased from £250 to £500, and there should be a specific grant for suitable middle-school fiction. The Library stock needed winnowing, and some of the older, seldom-used material put into store. Paperback books should be bought for general study in the sixth form.
10. Another Staff room was required.
11. Provision for the sixth form might be considered in terms of a sixth form block with separate junior and senior sixth form common rooms served by a joint tea bar.

Musical Chairs

During the Spring Term there was much activity amongst the School's musicians who were busy rehearsing for the House Music Competition and School Concert. The former took place on Monday, 20th April, and was judged by Mr Robin Black from Dunstable Grammar School. The competition was held in the presence of all first and second form boys, from whose ranks the choir and several other entrants were drawn. There were five classes of entry: choir, junior violin, senior violin, junior piano and senior piano. Out of a possible total score of 200 marks, the Grasshoppers came first with 152 marks, Hornets 144.5 marks, Bees 106 and Wasps 87.5, making Grasshoppers the first winners of the Sir John Burgoyne Trophy.

On 5th May, the School Concert attracted a large audience, and was one of the most ambitious ever undertaken. Unfortunately it overran by many minutes and at least one item had to be cut from the programme. *The Luton News* reviewer, M.M. Horton, wrote of 'a really workmanlike orchestra, which produces good, strong tone, especially in the brass section, efficient percussion work, and balanced woodwind and string sections. Two woodwind ensembles playing a gavotte by Bach and a trio by Mozart revealed careful attention to intonation. A.H. Swann, playing from memory, displayed confidence, good tone and careful phrasing in the Allegro moderato from Reiding's Sonata in B minor for violin and piano, and D.E. Bazley, as a soloist in his own right, also showed himself a confident and well prepared performer in an arrangement for piano and orchestra of one of Mozart's sonatas. The trebles of the School choir contributed three songs, of which 'Sunlit Paths', with its novelty third verse, proved the most popular.' Three masters, Alan Cator (horn), William Oram (clarinet) and Adolph Hauke (piano) joined together in a lively rendering of the third movement of Brahm's Trio in E flat, rudely waking a few of the audience who had nodded off. Two Old Boys, Jasper Thorogood and Peter Orme, both organists, gave fine, but over-long performances, and were a good advertisement for their old School. In the finale, the 'Little Symphony' by Wilkinson and Mussorgsky's 'Great Gates of Kiev', the orchestra, conducted by Adolph Hauke, came into its own again, the last work being particularly impressive.

Good weather at the beginning of 1964 helped the 1st XI Football team to enjoy a much better season. Fifteen matches were played, of which thirteen were won and two lost. The defence, though conceding 25 goals, were in terrific form for most of the season. Strength lay in the half-back line of J.E. Brown, S.A. Evans and E.P. Clutten, all of whom played with intelligence and great vigour. Most of the goals scored came from the partnership of G.C. Day (captain) and R.A. Smith. Day was once again an inspiration to his side: his play was direct and keen and brought the best out in all his forwards, especially Smith. The 2nd XI were also successful, playing nine games and losing only two of them.

It was not a very good season for the Cross-Country teams. The Wild Cup for

Inter-House competition was won by the Bees. In the Luton Schools' Championships held at Icknield School the intermediate team won the Adamant Cup for the first time. A.J. Montgomery gained second place, and was chosen to represent Bedfordshire in the National championships, where he came a creditable 46th.

Sports Day was held on 13th May, when eight records were broken. J.E. Brown was *Victor Ludorum*. In the County Championships, the relay teams took two firsts and a second; A.N. Potts and R.E. Hearn both won trophies for the Youths 220 and High Jump respectively. Six boys were chosen to represent the County in the National Championships at Hendon. G.B. Whittaker (long jump) and I.R. Thompson (880) failed to qualify, D. Brown and M.A. Syrett (both 220) got through the first round, and R.E. Hearn (high jump) reached the final pool and earned a National Standard. A.J. Duncan came fifth in the hammer. In the Luton Schools' Championships the School's middle and junior athletes retained the Shield for the third successive year, together with the Coronation Trophy. R.E. Hearn went on to run for Great Britain in a number of international events, and in 1974 was selected to run the 400m in the Commonwealth Games in New Zealand, but failed to qualify due to injury.

Two new Cricket nets were erected and the original one improved, but they came too late for their benefit to be felt during the 1964 season. 52 games were played, 22 won, 16 lost, 10 drawn and four abandoned due to rain. The 1st XI were on the whole poor, winning only 3 of their 16 games. Both the bowling and batting were weak, and, in the former, only J.E. Brown, the captain, and E.P. Clutten made any impression. Of the batsmen only G.C. Day, A.L. Wright and, in the latter part of the season, T. Crouch made many good scores.

After regular winter training at the Waller Street baths, the standard of swimming had improved and under the captaincy of R. Robinson, a good team spirit developed. The School was again runners-up to Rotheram School for the Dillingham Shield, and third in the Pike Trophy, at the Luton Schools' Gala.

After an unsettled start, the 1st XV Rugby team showed a degree of competence and confidence that had not been seen in the past ten years. The 1964 team displayed the right combination of talent, loyalty and dedication to training, that enabled it to win fourteen of its sixteen games and lose only two. After an unsettled start the team went from success to success. When playing in ideal conditions against R.G.S., High Wycombe, the handling and determined running were a joy to watch and M.A. Syrett's three tries underlined his ability when given the ball quickly and with room to get into his stride. Captain, A.R. Nicholas, had every reason to be proud of his team. By his special skills as hooker and dynamic forward play, he set a high standard for others to follow. The Under 15 team went into the age group having been undefeated at Under 13 and Under 14. At the end of the season they remained undefeated, (a unique junior record), and thirteen of the team represented

The 1964 under-15 Rugby side were unbeaten at under-13, under-14 and under-15. (back row) E.D. MacKenzie, M.A. Sharp, G.A. Dixon, D. Brown, R.W. Summerfield, B.K. Burridge, I.R. Thompson, Mr W.P. Evans, (middle) D.R. Fryer, A.S. Browne, A.F. Harris, G. Collinson, P.M. Barrett, (front) A.S. Montgomery, M.E. Parker, H. Taylor, K.I. Gillies. (*LN*)

Luton Schools against Bedfordshire Secondary Schools, winning 8 points to 6.

The highlight of the Literary and Debating Society's year was the Mock Trial, presided over by Judge Jefferies Dony. P. Harrison of U.VI Arts was charged with 'being biased against the Beatles'. Kitchen and Martin of U.VI Arts led the prosecution and defence respectively and quite respectably. The jury gave a semi-unanimous verdict of guilty and Judge Dony sentenced Harrison to listen to Beatles records and wear his hair in a 'Beatle Cut'. Dr Dony, on the eve of his retirement, was thanked for the many times he had presided over Literary and Scientific functions.

The Natural History Society was as active as ever, with lecturers from Rothamsted talking on Beekeeping and Orchids. Old Boy Mr R. Moore returned to talk about his experiences on the 'outward bound' expedition to Finland. The Society's team came first in the Wild Flower Society's annual competition, recording a total of 853 species. On a very warm 30th May, 28 members visited Woodwalton Fen, in Huntingdonshire, owned by the Nature Conservancy. They were guided round by another Old Boy, Dr Terry Wells, who worked for the Conservancy. By the time they

had been shown the extremely rare Fen Woodrush, all the gnats, midges and other obnoxious insects in the fen had converged on the party and were busily biting and sucking.

The newly formed Photographic Society enjoyed visits to the Vauxhall photographic studio and the Kodak processing station in Hemel Hempstead, where they watched as the giant organisation received thousands of exposed films and processed them in bulk, knowing always (usually!) which film belonged to whom.

The Railway Club enjoyed visits by coach to five British Railways Motive Power Depots in the London area and the Museum of British Transport at Clapham. A small group watched the Highland Railway locomotive 'Jones Goods' 4-6-0 being used for film-making on the disused Hitchin-Bedford line near Cardington.

Younger members of the Dramatic Society performed two one-act plays in front of their peers on 22nd April. *Shivering Shocks* was the juniors' production, giving S.R. Chambers, as the Captain, a chance to shine. A more senior group performed *Rough Justice*, a court-room drama, with R.E. Eade very convincing as the poacher, Ned Fouracres.

The Home and School Association had a good year. The Parents' 'Any Questions' evening on 4th March was well attended, as was a dance a few evenings later, which made a profit of £11 10s 0d. In May there was a highly successful Car Rally Treasure Hunt, and on 13th June some 140 parents and boys attended the Royal Tournament. During the year the Association made several grants of money to assist school activities, including cricket nets, a record player, £30 worth of books for the School Library, £100 worth of instruments for the Orchestra, book prizes for Speech Day and medals for Sports Day. Financial help was also given to boys attending special courses, and in cases of welfare when brought to their notice by the Headmaster.

On 9th July, 1964, all the Staff attended an enjoyable Dinner at the Halfway House in Dunstable Road. It celebrated the retirement of four loyal and long-serving colleagues, C.J. Godfrey, R. Phillips, J.G. Dony and (in December) G.R. Howard.

Farewell to 'Piggy'

"Why man, he doth bestride the narrow world like a Colossus", is a most apt description of Cyril John Godfrey. 'Piggy' was born on 25th November, 1900, at Clifton, a small village east of Shefford, Bedfordshire, and attended All Saints' Village School. He was a pupil at Bedford Modern School between 1913 and 1918. However, that education and his life changed for ever as a result of a bizarre accident when he was 14 years old. His father was a master builder. Cyril was helping him with some carpentry in his workshop one day, when his father clipped off the head of a nail. The piece of metal flew through the air and passed right through the boy's left eye, causing tremendous pain. He was rushed to Guy's Hospital, where he spent

the greater part of the next two years, missing much of his schooling. His mother refused to let the surgeons remove the damaged eye at the time, in the forlorn hope that the sight might be restored. From then on he could see nothing on his left hand side. Cyril had been a crack shot in the Bedford Modern School rifle team. After the accident he could only shoot rabbits: useful in wartime. Perhaps boys would have excused his apparent fierceness had they known that he was in pain throughout his life.

He matriculated at Bedford in 1918. For two terms he was employed at Luton Modern School as a temporary Junior Master, teaching maths in middle and lower forms at a wage of £40 per term. In October 1919, he went to University College, London, where he gained his BSc Hon. 3rd Class in Chemistry in November 1922. Mr Sanderson had no chemistry post to offer him at the Modern School, but mathematics was available. He accepted that, although they both knew that he was untrained in mathematics. Sanderson was a sound judge of his staff! He started full-

Four long-serving members of staff retired in 1964, C.J. Godfrey, J.G. Dony, R. Phillips, and G.R. Howard. Between them they had taught at the School for 140 years! (*LN*)

time at the School in January 1923, and finished on 31st August, 1964. He died in February 1969, aged 68, and his ashes were buried at the Stopsley crematorium.

His colleague, Wynne Parry, wrote that all who were associated with Mr Godfrey in any way, knew him as a splendid organiser and a first-rate disciplinarian. He always showed a remarkable sense of fair play, and treated offenders as well as the better behaved pupils as though they were human beings whose dignity deserved to be respected. Punished they might be, and they certainly left his room sadder if not wiser men, but they were never humiliated. Small boys might walk in fear of him, and even bigger boys would not dare take liberties with him, but as they grew older they learnt to respect him, and with senior boys he was always extremely popular.

Mr C.J. Godfrey as seen by
R.W. Smoothey

Few boys realised that he had a strong sense of humour. He could also be tremendously kind. Many boys who had difficulties in their lives, infirmity or bereavements perhaps, found him caring and considerate.

Mr Godfrey, himself, wrote that his 25 years in charge of athletics gave him a rich reward and a host of happy and amusing memories. He recalled during the war starting races with his grandfather's double-barrelled 12 bore gun, which, aimed into the sky, could be heard all over Stopsley. One sports afternoon he asked his boy-assistant how things were going, meaning his supply of blank cartridges. The boy looked up at a flock of birds overhead and remarked dryly, 'Nothing's come down yet, sir!' Morville Chote, one of his many protégés, said that he was one of the greatest influences in his athletics life and became a close friend after he left School. He added that although C.J.G. was not an athlete himself, he was a good, stern coach in track and jump events. An observation with which many of his fellow athletes concurred.

Ronald Phillips, 'Pills', was born in 1900, on a farm at Kingham, in the Oxfordshire Cotswolds. He was one of five brothers who all became teachers. He started at the village school at the age of four, and recalled sitting on the Infant Teacher's knee whilst she was teaching. For some reason he burst into uncontrollable laughter and was made to stand in the corner. The Headmaster came in and sent the infant Ronnie to his room, where he was caned on both hands. He progressed to Burford Grammar School, [where pupil D.C. Glover later became Head], and

graduated in English from Keble College, Oxford, where he was a keen Rugby player. He began his teaching career at Kirby Lonsdale, Cumbria. He came to Luton Modern School in 1927, after suffering a nervous breakdown following a traffic accident. He lodged with Rex and Margaret Clayton in Stopsley until the latter's death, when he returned to the family home in Kingham. Initially appointed to teach English and history, he also taught physical training, and for more than thirty years organised Rugby at the School.

Throughout his career we was interested in the problems of Religious Education, and was himself a magnificent example of a scholar, a Christian and a gentleman, with infinite compassion and deep humility. Unfortunately, he suffered from an inability to control a large class. K. B. Webb has said 'he was such a dear man, and his word was law on the rugger field, but he had such difficulty looking after a class. He would try and *teach* the boys all the time, instead of giving them something to do.' Working with small examination groups or sixth form English students gave him much more satisfaction and pleasure. A lovely man; he had cherished memories of the School, and thought nothing of motoring from Kingham to Luton for the Old Boys' reunion dinners until he was 90. He died on 31st December, 1995, aged 95.

John George 'Doc' Dony's story has been outlined in Chapter 8. He was a man of infinite enthusiasm for history, economics and public affairs, and his beloved botany. Many generations of boys can testify to his qualities as a teacher, his thoroughness, his gifts of illustration, his power to convey difficult ideas in simple terms, his refreshing classroom manner and his up-to-dateness. All will remember his invariable cheerfulness, his jaunty air, his purposeful gait, his buoyancy, his enjoyment of a joke, and his support for Luton Town Football Club.

George Robert Howard, 'Growler', grew up in Peterborough, and studied at Sheffield University where he gained his MSc. He came to Luton Modern School in January 1928, where he taught chemistry for 36 years. Under his expert teaching large numbers of pupils rose to high positions in University and Technical College, in Industrial Chemistry and Chemical Engineering, and in the Scientific Civil Service. Dr J.H. 'Jack' Burgoyne described him as an

Mr G.R. Howard according to
James Gale

outstanding teacher of advanced chemistry. Those boys who found the subject difficult were less inspired. A.W. 'George' Thorpe remembered him more for his cricket coaching than chemistry. Mr Howard had been in charge of cricket throughout the war years, when the pavilion was partly a classroom, partly a storage room for inflammable chemicals, and very subordinately a place for cricketers. He trained some very fine sides, including a bowler who took 79 wickets in a season: an all-time School record.

The Summer Term ended on 17th July. A mysterious note appears in the School Log book: 'Mischief the next to last night caused me to cancel staff match in school-time and final concert and say School would lose a possible one day's holiday. But atmosphere on last day was good.' The staff *v.* boys cricket match took place after school with the result: Staff 102 (J.E. Brown 6–32); School 58–8. The final concert did not take place. As to the mischief? Someone, not entirely unconnected with the concert, had super-glued the Headmaster's chair to the stage.

Eight new members of Staff joined the School in September, Mr J.T. Pye, BSc, Deputy Head; Mr I.W. Arthur, BA, History and English; Mr A.J. Bailey, BSc, Mathematics; Mr C.J. Carmell, BA, Languages; Mr H.B. Luke, BA, English; P.M.E. Maddocks, Handicraft; Mr P.W. Norton, PE; Mr J.D. Stephen, BA, Languages.

The Annual Harvest Festival service was held on 2nd October, all the produce being shared between the WVS and Vesper, a local organisation founded by Dr Douglas R. Snellgrove, that provided employment and aid for the elderly.

The New Boys' Concert took place on the 4th November, and began with the choir singing 'The Lass of Richmond Hill' and 'Who is Sylvia?' Then followed a piano solo by A.V.B. Bishop, a Recorder Group ensemble, and a violin solo by G.M. Averill. A group of first year boys performed an amusing recitation and mime called 'The Delights of a Picnic' by Jack Lindon. J.E. Cook, I.M. Sutherland and D.A. Howlett played piano, tenor horn and trombone solos. An extremely good concert ended with three contrasting pieces from the choir. The final song 'Moses Toeses' was sung with great difficulty by those unable to twist their tongues fast enough!

The School Orchestra, with 38 members, had a busy time in November. They entered for the St Albans Music Festival, playing 'The Great Gate of Kiev', a thundering, majestic piece by Mussorgsky, with which they achieved third place. On 11th November, Remembrance Day, they played a new work called 'Adagio in A minor', specially written by Mr Hauke, in memory of Harold Woodcock, for so many years the Conductor. At the Bazaar and Hobbies Exhibition on 28th, almost continual music was provided in the Dining Hall, orchestral items alternating with solo performances on the piano and electronic organ. The Home and School Association, who organised the Bazaar, raised some £300 for their funds.

Chapter 15

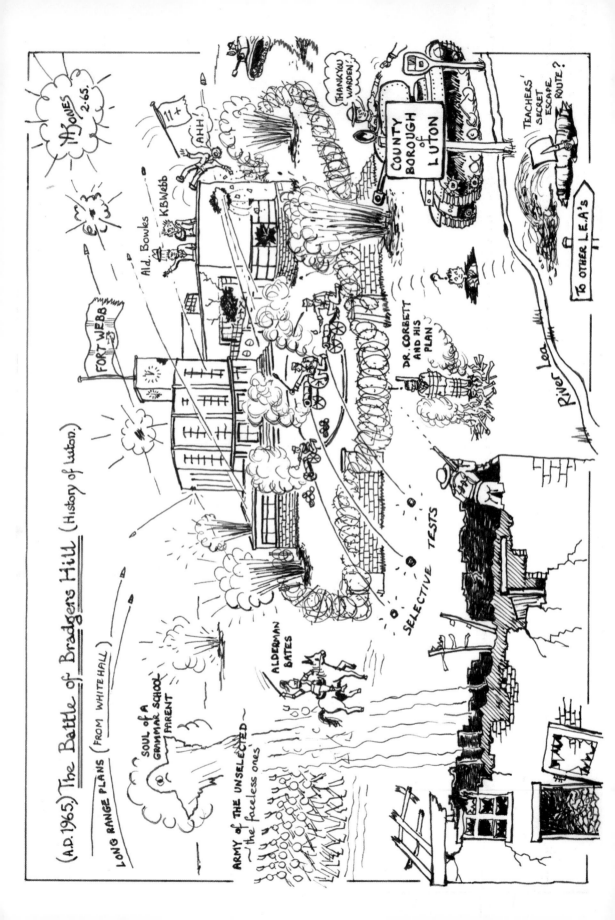

The Bombshell

The Headmaster was called to a meeting of the teacher members of the Joint Consultative Committee on 9th December, 1964. Alderman Bates informed them that the Labour group had decided to abolish selective schools in Luton and establish common secondary schools to the age of 16, capable of taking pupils up to O-level standard. Two Sixth Form Colleges would then cater, without an academic bar, for all pupils over the age of 16, and offer A-level work.

R.D. Whalley, at that time teaching at the Technical School, said that for some time there had been numerous whispers and asides amongst the town's teachers. 'The idea, of course, was to go Comprehensive and the move towards a comprehensive system of education was almost universally accepted in the profession, for the injustice of the tripartite system had become only too apparent over the twenty years since the 1944 Butler Act.'

The idea had its merits. The students at the Colleges would all be on A-level work, able to motivate each other better and form a more mature student body. The best qualified staff with specialist equipment could be concentrated there.

There were also disadvantages. The students would only spend two years at the Sixth Form Colleges, allowing little time to develop any sense of loyalty to them. Changing schools at that important time in their educational lives might have a detrimental effect on some pupils. Staff in the High Schools, having worked hard to achieve good O-level results, would see their brighter charges going off to another establishment with no chance of doing any sixth form teaching themselves.

The Joint Consultative Committee (JCC) was the mechanism by which the Local Education Authority (LEA) consulted with the teachers in their employment.

LEFT The Battle of Bradgers Hill, as seen by History master, Ivan A. Jones (1965).

Membership of the JCC was dominated by the National Union of Teachers (NUT), but in 1964 the National Association of Schoolmasters (NAS) and the Joint Four Committee, largely representing secondary teachers and headteachers, were given one seat each. Three working parties were rapidly set up to consider the various forms of comprehensive education, but there was not enough time or encouragement for thorough working-party techniques or consultations. In January the JCC made its proposals which were almost entirely based on those of the NUT, and which were not dissimilar from those of the NAS. Only the Joint Four working party, whose members were mainly in the selective schools, voiced dissent. The proposals, devoid of any detail, were approved by the Luton Borough Council by 23 votes to 12 on 12th February, 1965.

From the announcement on 9th December, Mr Webb had found himself embroiled in a flurry of meetings. He was clearly not prepared to accept the proposals without a fight, and was in demand to voice his opinions at every opportunity. At the Old Lutonian Club's annual dinner on 12th December he made little public reference to the problem, the main business of that occasion being to present gifts to the retiring masters. By the end of the following week, however, he had lost his voice! When School broke up for the Christmas holidays on the 18th, his Deputy, Mr Pye, had to take most of the Carol Service and read the colour awards list. The choir and orchestra, under the direction of Mr Hauke, had worked hard to see that the year ended on a bright note.

School resumed on 6th January. The annual 'Universities Reunion' took place in the evening, with more than 40 boys currently at university attending.

On the 2nd February, 1965, the BBC descended on the School to record a new quiz programme, 'Sporting Chance', in which a team of boys competed with a team of experts on sporting activities. Four boys represented the School: John Young, Michael Syrett, Trevor Crouch and Stephen Evans. The experts were Messrs Peter West, Alan Clarke and Maurice Edelston. John Snagge, famous for his commentaries on the Boat Race, was the Question Master. In spite of loud applause from the audience of boys, parents and staff on many occasions during the evening, and after a well-fought contest, the School team lost by 58 points to 79. Contestant Stephen Evans later achieved fame as co-producer of the film *The Madness of King George*.

On 5th February the Home and School Association called a meeting to discuss the future of the School, which was attended by more than 500 parents. Only eight votes were cast against a resolution expressing complete opposition to the Council's proposals for reorganisation and promises were made to fight them by all legal means. Mr Gordon Vowles has written in his book *A Century of Achievement* (2003):

> 'An Action Committee was formed, support was elicited from parents' associations
> at the High and Technical Schools and a petition sent to the Secretary of State. The
> Headmaster of the School, Kenneth Webb, was staunchly opposed to the

proposals: he was fearful of the slow death of the Grammar School from the bottom upwards and had serious misgivings about a break being imposed at the age of 16 for those moving into a sixth form.'

On the evenings of 10th–12th February the Dramatic Society presented Robert Bolt's play *A Man For All Seasons*, produced by Michael Sharman. It was almost the first time that a serious, modern play had been performed by the School, and on the whole it was well received. Malcolm Brown was excellent as the fatalistic, man of the world, Sir Thomas More. Richard Tiley, playing the Common Man, coped admirably with an extremely long part. Geoffrey Kitchener gave a sympathetic and natural portrayal of Thomas Cromwell, as did Philip Bonner as the Duke of Norfolk. The ladies, played by girls from the High School, were adequate.

The Assembly Hall was filled to capacity once more on 17th February for the annual Speech Day. The Guest Speaker was Mrs Eileen Evans, retiring Headmistress of the Girls' High School, whom Mr Webb described as 'young in heart, wise in counsel, gay in spirit, and a champion of all that is best in school life'.

In his report the Headmaster noted with concern the relative swing away from technology and science, and towards economics, literature, language and philosophy shown by the applications for admissions to colleges. For the most part pupils had been academically and athletically successful during the school year. In September 1964 there had been an entry of three Forms of 30 eleven-year olds, instead of the usual four Forms of 36 boys. The others who might have come had been distributed in local Secondary Schools. Mr Webb felt that both masters and boys would profit from smaller classes. In September the total number on Roll was 848, with 210 in the Sixth Forms (82 Arts and 128 Sciences) and 27 in the Remove. The GCE O-level pass rate remained static but satisfactory at 5.9 subjects per boy in IVa and fifth-form candidature, while at A-level the average was well over two subjects passed per candidate. S.C. Gregory had been awarded an Open Exhibition to Magdalene College, Cambridge where he would study Biochemistry. Thirty-nine other boys had been accepted for places at Universities or other Colleges of Further Education. Another six had been awarded Student Apprenticeship Dip. Tech courses. A younger boy, Michael Stevens, was spending a year at a High School in New Trier, Illinois, on an American Field Service Scholarship. Mr Webb mentioned that the H.E. Woodcock Travel Scholarship Fund stood at £743 and he hoped that it would soon be providing assistance to boys wishing to see something of the world.

After a brief introduction from the Mayor, Councillor Beckett, Mrs Evans presented the prizes and trophies. She then gave a refreshingly unbiased view of education for one so intimately connected with it. She stressed the need to avoid the error of thinking that cleverness and knowledge are virtues and thus good. Wisdom is born of knowledge, but the essence of wisdom is a sense of proportion and humility embracing consideration for others and a respect for natural order. Casting

her mind over the various changes she had seen during her teaching experience, Mrs Evans observed that the most recent, the age of self-expression and the expert, appeared to her to have failed in that it had produced the destructive form of argument or concept. She made a telling point in referring to acceptance of authority: the destructive view held by many did not allow for the idea of community discipline, which she saw as the guide for more responsible, mature citizens.

After her speech, Mrs Evans was thanked on behalf of the School by the Head Boy, B. J. Wiseman, who also presented her with a brief-case, in recognition of her kindness to many generations of boys of the School.

In order that there was more time for questions, the Parents' 'Any Questions' evenings were split into two sessions, on 24th February and 23rd March. As always, the evenings proved very successful, giving parents the opportunity to question individual masters concerning their boys' education. The one question that couldn't be answered was 'what is the future of the School?' It was assumed that it would become one of the two proposed sixth form colleges. If so, which would be the other, the High School or the Technical School?

The Luton News for 4th February, 1965, carried an Editorial headed 'What's more alarming?' In it, the Editor, Norman North, wrote:

> 'The very thing that has alarmed all thinking parents is the failure of any of the protagonists of this switch in education policy to tell them anything about this scheme beyond vague, sweeping phrases . . . To force the issue in this manner is not the behaviour of a body that has taken into account its responsibilities to all its citizens.'

On 1st March the Joint Four Committee wrote to the Secretary of State for Education asking him to intervene over Luton's Secondary re-organisation plans.

When the School broke up for the Easter holiday on 9th April, Mr Webb noted in the School Log: 'Without detailing dates, Luton Borough Council put to the Department of Education a development plan involving no further entry to the Selective Schools, and the Secretary of State wrote telling them to put it off, publicly announce the plans for closing the Luton High School, (2 months for protest), and to run their eleven plus.'

A special meeting of the Town Council on 7th May reported the receipt of a circular letter (10/65) from the Secretary of State welcoming local education authorities' decisions to re-organise education on comprehensive lines which would preserve all that was valuable in grammar school education. 'It is important that new schemes build on the foundation of present achievements and preserve what is best in existing schools.' Formal notice was issued by the Council of its intention of discontinuing the Girls' High School. This resulted in the receipt of ten objections

and a petition of protest. It was later announced that, initially, only the Grammar School would become a Sixth Form College.

A meeting of parents of boys and girls attending the Grammar and High Schools met at Bradgers Hill on 10th May, and approved four principles that they wished to work for, namely: selection in education; parental choice; minority rights; and the parents' right to be consulted.

For some years the Old Lutonians' had met for an annual 'London Lunch' at the Connaught Rooms. On 14th May, Charles Fox, the President, who had travelled from Derby, welcomed 22 members and guests. The Headmaster always tried to be there, and in 1965 he was accompanied by Mr J.T. Pye, the new Second Master, and Mr Herbert Bryant, President elect. The Lunch provided an opportunity for Old Boys who were unable to keep in touch with affairs in Luton to meet informally with old friends. After the Lunch Mr Webb gave a résumé of recent events at the School and provided an up-to-date account of the proposals to turn it into a Sixth Form College.

The Sir John Burgoyne House Music Competition took place in April. Entries were allowed from all age groups, and the adjudicator, Miss Alfreda Lewis, Head of Music at the new Putteridge Bury College of Education, had a very difficult task. The winning House was Wasps with 165 marks out of a possible 200.

The School Concert, on the evening of the 18th May, was considered one of the most ambitious for many years. It began with three orchestral pieces. These were followed by a magnificent organ solo from John Gosling, playing Bach's 'Prelude and Fugue in G minor'. John Britten, leader of the orchestra, was equally versatile on the violin. His sensitive performance of Bridge's 'Spring Song' and the joyous Bach Gavotte in D, were both beautifully accompanied by Mr Hauke on the piano. Another Sixth Former, Colin Smith, showed what an accomplished pianist he was, by playing the opening movement of Beethoven's 'Piano Sonata in F minor op. 2'. The second half of the concert was devoted to Parts I and II of Haydn's Oratorio 'The Creation'. Performed with augmented orchestra and choir, and three guest soloists, Margaret Slater (soprano), Geoffrey Deakin (tenor) and Malcolm Singer (bass), it was a triumphant success, and enormously enjoyed by the audience. M.H. Horton, Music Critic of *The Luton News*, wrote: 'A few years ago the idea of staging such a work in a school concert would have been unthinkable; it is a measure of the school's progress that the impossible has become reality.'

After a successful Football season in 1964, and with six of that year's team remaining at School, everything pointed towards a high standard of 1st XI soccer in 1965. Mr W. Peter Evans, their trainer, was not disappointed, as the final record of played 13, won 9, drew 2 and lost 2 proved. He wrote that the strength of the team lay in the half-back line of S.A. Evans (captain), E.P. Clutten and P.J. Southwell. N.R. Boult was a fast, reliable full-back, and with A.L. Wright's determined approach on the other flank, and the safe-handling of T. Crouch in goal, it was not

surprising to finish the season with only 13 goals scored against the team.

The Cross-Country runners had a better season, with Messrs G. Gorton and W.P. Evans willing to run with them on training nights. The Inter-House races took place before Christmas 1964 so that the talent was sorted out before the season-proper began. The individual winners were Senior: R.D. Orpwood (W), Intermediate: I.R. Thompson (W) and Junior: R.T. Cawdell (G). Grasshoppers won the Wild Cup. In the County Championships, the Boys' team ran second to Bedford Modern School with A.J. Montgomery in individual 3rd place, but the Youths' team reversed the order by good packing, with Orpwood 9th, C.J. Stevens 10th and M.E. Pratt 11th. In the Luton Schools' Championships held on Stopsley Common, the Intermediate team won convincingly, with Montgomery and Thompson leading the field. Montgomery, Thompson, Orpwood, A.J. Bonnington, R.R. Raw and Pratt were all chosen to represent Bedfordshire in the English Schools' Championships.

Sports Day (19th May) was cold, but the threatening rain kept off. The Open Mile Final was held on the preceding Friday, and Ian R. Thompson, a (u.16) athlete, ran a fine race to win in 4 mins. 41.1 secs, beating D.G. Gill's record of 1950 by 9.3 seconds. 'This surely promises well for Thompson in the future,' J.A. Muse wrote prophetically in *The Lutonian*. On Sports Day seven more records were broken. The outstanding one was C.J. Harrison's senior javelin throw of 158 ft 5½ ins, beating his previous best by over 20 feet. A.N. Potts and M.A. Syrett (Captain) fought a close battle for *Victor Ludorum*, both finishing with 30 points. At the Luton Schools' Sports the School retained the Championship shield for the fourth successive year, and the Coronation Trophy. The finals of the Luton Schools' clashed with the County Championships, so for once the Whitchurch Trophy was out of the

The 880 yds under-15 race on Sports Day, 1964. I.R. Thompson leads from D.C. Lumb, the eventual winner. In 1974 Thompson won the gold medal for the marathon in the Commonwealth Games in Auckland. (*LN*)

question; even so School athletes managed 8 firsts and a 2nd: a rare achievement. Eight athletes represented the County in the English Schools' Championships at Watford. Only C.J. Potts and Tim Watson passed the qualifying stage. Watson gained fifth place in the hurdles final.

In Cricket, the 1st XI, under the capable captaincy first of B. J. Wiseman, and then of T. Crouch, had on the whole a good but rather wet season. Only one school side, St Albans, beat them and the other two defeats were at the hands of the Staff and the Luton Town Strollers. During the early season Crouch and J.D. Young made some useful scores, whilst C.J. Harrison, as well as topping the batting averages, took the greatest number of wickets. P.J. Hamel's wicket keeping was always exemplary, and his batting was steady.

The senior Tennis teams had a far from successful season, having played 11 matches, won 5, lost 5 and drawn 1.

Swimming training continued during the winter before school and seemed to bear fruit. Four new junior records were established and the School team finished 2nd behind Rotheram in the Luton Schools' Gala.

LEFT The Swimming Club, 1965-66. (back row) A.P. Davies, C.B. Chalkley, R.C. Muse, J. Hull, M.B. Ayres, C.V. Dunnington, A. Slessor, G.R.L. Windle, R.J. Hilliard, N.D.North, (centre) S.G. Regulski, E.H. Trantum, R.A.G. Willis, Mr I.R. Rendell, J.H. Britten, D.T. Lowther, D.L. Howlett, (front) D.A. Howlett, G. Dunnington, J.D. Potten, S.M. Peck. (*LN*)

The 1965-66 Rugby XV. (back row) Mr J.A. Muse, G. Collinson, D.A. Smith, P.G. Davie, W.J. Wood, A.J. Bonnington, P.J. Hamel, P.J.R. Sankey, (middle) P.J. Southwell, N.R. Boult, G.B. Whitaker, S.J. Fryer, A.J. Duncan, M.A. Syrett, P.B. Salmon, (front) H. Taylor, A.F. Harris. (*LN*)

For the second year running all the Rugby teams had a highly successful season. The 1st XV, captained by S.J. Fryer, played 15 games, won 13, lost 1 and drew 1, and scored 405 points while ceding 49. The game lost was 5–6 to High Wycombe Grammar School and that drawn was 0–0 against the Old Boys; both played in atrocious conditions. The Under 15 XV won all its 10 games, scored 208 points and ceded 8. In all, the School's seven XVs played 70 games and won 50. Eight 1st XV boys, Fryer, Whittaker, Boult, Duncan, Southwell, Syrett, Wood and Salmon, played for the County XV and in no small way contributed to its unbeaten record in the holiday games.

School Clubs and Societies were as active as ever during 1965. The Literary and Scientific Society began its 41st season with a visit to the Sundon Park works of SKF Ball Bearings Ltd. The first speaker of the year was Mr Hardy, Chief Assistant planning officer to the Borough Engineer, who talked about the future development of the Luton town centre. Dr J.F. Hindle, FRCS, of the Luton and Dunstable Hospital described the design and use of the new Casualty Department at the hospital. Mr G.N. Crapnell talked about his experiences of teaching in Zambia for three years. Three debates were held, two jointly with the Technical School and one with the High School. The motion for the first that 'This House believes that the re-introduction of some form of National Service is immediately desirable' was soundly defeated. There was considerable surprise at the result of the second, that 'This

House is of the opinion that selective schools must go'. The motion was carried by 52 votes to 34, and caused some comment in *The Luton News*. The debate with the High School considered that 'This House is of the opinion that school meals are satisfactory in both quantity and quality' – the motion was defeated by an almost unanimous vote. The final meeting was Mr R.H. Barter's Presidential Address on 'Flight Procedure'.

The new Junior Society watched films, held a Stamp Exhibition, a Quiz Evening, a Brains Trust (starring Messrs Luke, Jones, Giddy and Hudson) and made visits to the London Planetarium and the Imperial War Museum – 'where they almost lost Ian Pirks somewhere in the building'.

On 15th February a small group of Sixth Form boys formed 'The '65 Society' which held meetings on the second lunch break every Monday. A wide range of subjects were debated including Blood Sports, Vietnam, Local Government, Trade Unions, Red China and the frightening prospect of an Ugly Britain. Two Brains Trusts were also held, producing lively comment on Communism, beer and steel nationalisation.

The Student Christian Movement Group held a dozen meetings, ranging from a visit to the Mormon Church being built in Cutenhoe Road, talks by masters and a clergyman, and the tape-recorded testimony of a converted American gangster, to a joint 'Squash' (assembly) and conference with the High and Technical Schools. At the 'Squash' the Revd. J. Johansen-Berg spoke to an audience of sixty on 'Breaking down barriers', and some thirty boys attended a series of three lectures at the High School by the Revd. Bryan Green in which he discussed 'A basis for teenage morality'.

Numbers attending meetings of the Natural History Society generally flagged during the year. An exception were the 70 people, including 27 from the High School, who enjoyed a celebrity lecture given by Dr K. McQuillen of Churchill College, Cambridge on 'Cell organelles'. Dr Lloyd-Evans talked about 'Bird Ringing', and Mr Lingard brought some of his own animals to illustrate 'British Wild Life'. The team entering the Wild Flower Society's annual competition again came first, having recorded 593 flowers. A party of thirty members and three masters visited Scolt Head Island, Norfolk, where the highlights were the ternery – hundreds of terns nesting on sand-dunes – a shelduck's nest in a rabbit burrow, and the rare matted sea-lavender.

Membership of the Archaeological Society was also on the decline. A number of members gave talks, including C.J. Potts on 'Nimes', T.P. Smith on 'Prehistoric Britain' and Old Boy, David Kennett, on 'Medieval Pottery'.

Large parties of boys travelling abroad during the summer holidays seem to have come to an end, although a mixed group of ten boys from the Grammar School, nine girls from the High School, and about as many from Hatfield School, together with masters, mistresses and hangers-on, did make a three week visit to Russia in 1965.

They travelled through the divided Berlin, on to Warsaw (the city they enjoyed most), Minsk and Moscow. They found the cities depressing: just like most western cities, but much less prosperous. There was far less traffic than in the west, and much of it was either public or military transport. In Moscow the Black Market was rife: the official exchange rate was 2.5 roubles to £1 sterling, but in the Market 6 roubles to £1.

A very different trip was organised by the Home and School Association to Dovedale in June. More than a hundred parents and youngsters filled two coaches, for a very pleasant, sunny outing.

Whilst the normal daily routine of the School ran its course, the staff were busily making arrangements for the new school year. Numerous meetings were held at which the Heads of Departments planned the constitution and allocation of the second three form entry and all that entailed. John Muse was getting a new Sports Hall and went off to Harlow to choose equipment. Mr Bryant took a party of boys to the National College of Agricultural Engineering at Wrest Park, Silsoe, and first year boys were awarded their cycling proficiency pennants. At the end of the summer term the Staff beat the 1st XI at cricket: the Staff 89 (J.A. Muse 59); School 36.

Seven members of staff left on 16th July. Amongst them Mr D.E. Stancombe, who had spent four years teaching biology, returned to his old School, Hitchin Grammar. Messrs D.V. Law and W.G.B. Oram, after teaching History and Maths respectively for two years, left for promotion.

One man, John Alfred 'Jock' Cleaver, had completed thirty-nine years as Head of Geography and (later) Geology. A native of Derbyshire and a graduate in chemistry from Sheffield University, he was an enthusiastic geographer, who had inspired generations of boys. Group Captain Alan E. Silvester (1940–47) was strongly influenced and encouraged by him (and his colleague W.N. Thorpe) and his recommendation had helped him get a place on the Public Schools' Exploration Society's expedition to Newfoundland. 'Jock' established Geology as an A-level subject, enabling boys like M.J. Barber and D.J. Atkinson to achieve Royal Dutch-Shell Scholarships to Imperial College. No man could have felt more satisfaction than he through the successful careers of his old pupils, scattered throughout the continents and holding important positions in academic, governmental and industrial circles. The move from his cramped quarters at Park Square to the well equipped Geography room at Bradgers Hill, with suspended globe, maps and charts, a tracing table, many geological specimens and an epidiascope, gave him a new lease of life. As a young teacher he had been a good wicket-keeper, and later umpired or scored at the Staff versus School matches. He loved music, played the piano or double bass at Morning Assembly, and was the organist at St Thomas' Church, Stopsley, for many years. After retirement, his health was not good and he gradually became both deaf and blind. He bore his difficulties with amazing cheerfulness, and was regarded with affection by most of those he taught.

The Last School Year

The Autumn Term began on 8th September, with another three form entry in the First Year.

In spite of the uncertain future there were six new members of staff during 1965. Mr G.H. Gorton, MA (Languages) – in January; and in September Mr D.A. Kendell, MA (History); Mr D. Green, BSc (Maths); Mr M.A. Siddiqi, MSc, LLB (Maths); Mr R.L. Humphrey, BSc (Geography, Geology); and Mr J.J. Mitchell, BSc (Science).

Sadly, it was to be another term of deaths. Mr John M. 'Jimmy' Forbes died on 7th October, aged 87. Many Old Boys and colleagues attended his funeral in Luton two days later. He was appointed to teach Maths at Luton Modern School in January 1909, was promoted to Second Master in 1919 and retired in 1939.

On 13th October Ronald Bridger died at his home in Old Welwyn. He had taught music at the School from 1940 to 1948.

Rex S. Clayton was an Old Boy of the Luton Modern School, a Prefect and Captain of Soccer and Cricket, a master at the School from 1919 until he retired 1956, and the School's first Careers Master. He was a semi-invalid from the time he retired until his death at his home in Stopsley on 30th November. There was a large number of Old Lutonians and School staff at his funeral on 6th December. The Headmaster read the lesson.

Mr Frank Reid, the School's third Head Groundsman, died on the School field on 18th October. He was a loyal, friendly and conscientious man. His position was filled the following January by Mr Gutteridge.

The 35th Annual Dinner of the Old Lutonians' Club was held at the Halfway House Hotel, Dunstable, on 5th November, 1965, with the President, Mr H.J.C. 'Herbie' Bryant, in the Chair. Speaking to the assembled members Mr K.B. Webb said, when referring to the re-organisation of Luton's educational system upon a comprehensive basis, 'I believe it to be an unwise and unjustified step, which Luton may come to regret – to pull down before they are sure they can build up.' Mr Webb emphasised that he was very much for the extension of educational opportunities, but he believed that the proposals to kill the three selective schools, keeping everyone in common schools to the age of 16 when they would have a chance to join a different establishment was an inflexible policy, unsupported on educational grounds by any evidence whatsoever. An essential feature of Grammar School education was the continuity of education through the teenage years up to 18 or 19.

Mr Webb remarked that he had consistently advised against the plan, and was engaged professionally trying to have it further delayed or changed. He had helped and he would help all he could to see that if it was to be, then young people should be harmed as little as possible. 'My decision to leave next year,' he concluded, 'is in no way associated with the proposed re-organisation. My wife and I decided in the

Summer of 1964 that I would give it another two years.'

Other speakers also criticised the plan. Dr Hugh M. Swallow, the president-elect, said that with the advent of Sixth Form Colleges the influence of schoolmasters as builders of citizens would end. The school master would become a mere 'purveyor of learning'. Dr Alfred Caress, Research Director of ICI, said the whole plan was 'utterly ludicrous' and described it as 'a foolish and wilful change which I hope everyone will resist'. Tom Byfield, a founder member of the Old Lutonians' deplored the prospect of Luton Grammar School and the Luton High School 'fading into obscurity', and it was a deep regret to him that one of the architects of the scheme was an Old Boy of Luton Grammar School.

The Remembrance Day Service on 11th November followed the time-honoured pattern, solemn music, prayers and the Headmaster's address: 'Old and young pause together and take a look backwards at the way we have come, and consider the doubtful doom of humanity, and the part we ourselves must play.' The relatives of those who had died who were still able to attend were most anxious that they would continue to be invited to share with the School in that very special experience.

The GCE examinations began on 22nd November. During half an hour, as 120 candidates were trying to get to School, there was a sudden fall of snow; four inches caused chaos, and a delayed start.

The Home and School Association's Annual Bazaar and Hobbies Exhibition took shape over the 26th–27th November. For the School, Mr Peter G. Hudson, with a team of boys, was in great demand organising exhibitions, finding spare tables and chairs, unloading vans, and generally making sure that everything ran as smoothly as possible with the minimum of fuss. At the end of the day, which concluded with a dance, a clear profit of £290 had been made for the Association's use.

Mr Webb found himself in great demand as a speaker at this time: to the High School Speech Day, Richmond Hill Special School 'Nativity' play, and the annual Prize Givings at Vauxhall, Hayward Tyler and SKF. On 9th December he chaired a Brains Trust at the School on 'Problems of Growing Up'. There were four guest panellists: Mrs Eileen Evans JP, the ex-Headmistress of the High School, Mr B.T. Henman JP, Chairman of Luton Juvenile Court, Mr P. Pantry, Senior Probation Officer, and Mr R. Shackleton, Children's Officer for Luton.

The Prefects held a dance in the Hall on 11th December, which Mr Webb hailed as 'a very good do'. They had sold 400 tickets at 4 shillings each and made a profit of £50.

Mr Haydon Luke produce the last 'Grammar School' Play which was performed for three nights from 15–17th December. Probably the most ambitious production since Shaw's *St Joan* in 1949, it was John Arden's *Serjeant Musgrave's Dance*. This was a modern play in an historical setting, said to have been sparked off partly by an incident in Cyprus when, in reprisal for the murder of a British soldier, several 'terrorists' were killed.

Mr Robert Acton reviewed the play for *The Lutonian*. He wrote: 'It would be near-impossible to find any schoolboy in Britain, let alone Luton Grammar School, with the theatrical experience, physical stature and authority of voice to render the title-part convincingly. 'Black Jack' – puritanical, fanatical, mad perhaps – was a tremendously demanding role. Steven Lowe, whose first experience of acting this was, had to be congratulated for the success with which he avoided the pitfall of allowing his character to appear ludicrous. David Rees, Brian Marshall and Owen Moulton were very convincing and well contrasted as the three privates. They gave sincere performances without ignoring the humorous possibilities of their parts. Moulton's portrayal of Hurst was, for me, the most impressive of the three – remarkable for its intensity of feeling. Andrew Baxter delighted the audience as the bargee. Both Carol Conway and Eileen Boothroyd ('released' by the High School) gave clear and effective performances; Annie's scream at the sight of the skeleton provided one of the most electrifying moments. John Gosling's Parson was amusing, without being a caricature, and the clarity of his diction deserved congratulation. I think this was one of the most enjoyable and deeply rewarding productions the Dramatic Society has ever presented.' In his Log Book K.B. Webb summed it up: 'Different and difficult, but it all worked out very well.'

The new year, 1966, began without the traditional University Students' reunion. The Old Lutonians' Club Committee held a Dinner at the Royal Hotel, Tring, on 17th January, attended by some 18 members. The President, Mr Bryant, presented a set of recordings of classical music to Mr 'Jock' Cleaver as a retirement gift.

The nucleus of a new and exciting Luton Schools' Orchestra gave its first public concert at the School on Monday, 21st February. Five schools were represented, the Grammar School, High School, Technical School, Rotheram School and Dunstable Grammar School. Adolph Hauke was the conductor, John Britten the leader, and it was augmented by several experienced local players. The idea of creating the orchestra came from the young players themselves, who formed their own committee, and gave up most of their half-term holiday in order to prepare the concert.

The orchestral programme included the minuet from Mozart's 'Linz' Symphony, the first movement from Schubert's Symphony in B flat (No 5), 'The March of the Bowmen' by Curzon, the intermezzo and alla marcia from Sibelius's 'Karelia' Suite, and Moussorgsky's 'The Great Gates of Kiev' from 'Pictures from an Exhibition'. The evening was enlivened by the singing of Mr Malcolm Singer, baritone, and the Ionian Singers, a group of VIth form boys and High School girls, conducted by Mr Hauke, who contributed a group of madrigals, freshly and carefully performed, and the vocal part of Faurés gentle Requiem. A small group of singers from the Grammar School Junior choir, and some of the masters, provided the chorus work for the Requiem.

Friday, 4th March, 1966, was memorable in a number of ways. It was the last

Speech Day of Luton Grammar School before it changed to a sixth-form College in September. It was also the Headmaster's last report before his retirement after 26 years at the School. The two guest speakers were both Old Boys of the School.

After welcoming the many guests, Mr Webb paid tribute to a number of masters who had recently left or had died. He then went on to inform his audience that the new Sports' Hall was almost complete, but from the point of view of accommodation, the school still had many inadequacies, especially for technical and art subjects, the library and reading room, and more civilised quarters for the staff and sixth form.

The School numbers had diminished with the second intake of approximately 90 boys in September 1995, instead of 140. The total in September had been 768, of whom rather more than one third, namely 265, were in VIth Form courses or in their sixth year in the school. Sixteen had joined the VIth Form from other Luton Secondary Schools. In the Upper Sixth the ratio of Science to Arts was a little more than 2 to 1, namely 99 to 43. Mr Webb continued:

'May I take a peep back to my first Speech Day in 1941? I was able then to report 58 School Certificates, comparable roughly with the GCE at O-level; and 5 Higher School Certificates, comparable with GCE at A-level.

'Today I can report 112 boys in Upper VI gaining an average of 2·5 A-level subjects each: Grade A in 9 subjects, 7 distinctions in Scholarship level papers. 112 compared with 5 – and it is one of my regrets that I cannot know 112 as well as I could 5! Another 24 boys took A-level in Lower VI. The total number of School candidates sitting an O-level exam in July 1965 was 253, and while I am sorry about the failures the over-all results are up to our usual high average.

'The 'paper-chase' for qualification in which we are obliged to participate does not blind us to the fact that in the end *qualities* matter more than qualifications.

'A few individual successes are worthy of mention. In September Michael Stevens returned to School from his scholarship year in America. In October S.C. Gregory went up to Magdalene College, Cambridge, on his Exhibition for Biochemistry. In the summer A.M. Susman won a fortnight's holiday in Germany by his entry in an Essay Competition under the auspices of the Council of Europe. Unfortunately he could not take it up as he was in the School party going to Russia. In December he won an Exhibition to read law at Trinity Hall, Cambridge. Another boy N.R. Pashley won an opportunity of a different kind, a place in the British Schools' Expedition to Northern Norway.

'Travel scholarships from the Trust Fund established in memory of Mr H.E. Woodcock were awarded for the first time. They helped four senior boys to attend courses abroad. Others were helped by the Luton Prisoner of War Fund, as was an Old Boy, R.P. Whymant, still at Cambridge, who last summer was able to spend a month in China, whose language he is studying.

The Headmaster's Final Speech Day, 4th March, 1966. Mr Webb with his guests, Mr F.W. Mullinger and Major M.V.W. Chote, Second Prefect and Head Prefect respectively in 1942. (*LN*)

'Boys have been on party holidays abroad, on field courses in biology and geology, short courses in Hospital administration or an introduction to industry; and for the first time a large group spent a long, hard day at ICT on computers. This is a subject which warrants immediate serious thought and financial backing by the authority.

'Until recently in this country we have spent a smaller percentage of our national revenue on education than some other industrialised nations. Some folk, even now, are opposed to spending more. Leaving aside the major costs such as building and salaries, if we look at money over which the Headmaster and staff have some control, namely the allowance we can spend on books, stationery, materials, furniture, apparatus, equipment, games, educational visits, library; and divide the total by the number of boys and the number of school days in the year, the answer is approximately 8 pence per boy per day, something between the price of 2 or 3 cigarettes, yet his free bottle of milk and the subsidy on his school dinner comes to twice as much. I think it is surprising how well we do for so little.'

In completing his final report, Mr Webb paid tribute to all the masters who had worked with him over the past twenty-six years and given him their loyal support. To these he added the names of Mr Bob Killick, the Head Caretaker, who had joined the School in 1938, and except for his service in the war, from which he returned to his duties, though seriously wounded; and his Secretary, Miss Olga Peters, whose ever ready, cheerful, competent helpfulness over every school event was invaluable.

> '*Next* to finally, I want to thank governors, administrators and others, who have been sympathetic to some of our special difficulties and who have gone out of their way to give me immense encouragement.
>
> '*Really* finally, I should like to thank generations of boys and young men because they have helped me to look to the future with hope, indeed confidence. So very many seek to live their lives by ideals of honesty and service, though the few others sometimes get more notice. So very many deserve respect and admiration for the way they meet disaster or difficulty.'

The Mayor, Alderman F. Goodyear, then introduced the two guest speakers who afterwards distributed the prizes and awards.

The first was Major Morville V.W. Chote (retired), who had been Head Prefect in 1942, and the second was Mr Frank J. Mullinger, also an old boy of the School. He was Second Prefect in 1942, and in 1965 was Headmaster of Ludlow Grammar School. Both recounted memories of their own school experiences and amusing stories of some of the staff, which soon won over many in the audience.

So ended an enjoyable and satisfying final Speech Day for Luton Grammar School.

The Shape of Things to Come

On Monday 7th March, the Heads of the three selective schools were called to the Education Office and told of the plans for Reorganisation in September, 1966. There would be no new intake of Ist year pupils. Years II and III would all go to the Technical School at Barnfield Avenue, Years IV and V would complete the next two years at the selective school that they were already in, and the Lower VI of the whole of Luton would be the start of the Sixth Form College at Luton Grammar School.

A fortnight later the Director of Education, Dr Corbett, and the three selective school Heads met to discuss the plans for September. It was estimated that there would be one Sixth Form of about 390 students. Two days later the Director spoke to the Grammar School staff and attempted to allay their fears for their futures.

Staff were told that the Grammar School had been chosen as the new Sixth Form College as, amongst other advantages, it had the best science laboratories and technical drawing facilities. Since it was a thirty-year-old single-sex school, where

technical drawing was done on hand-held boards in the dining hall, teachers at the High and Technical Schools found this hard to believe. The latter school was nine years old, co-educational, with better workshops and laboratories; but also some severe architectural problems.

Mr Webb informed the Staff that as incumbents they would have priority in the 'job stakes' over the staff of the other two selective schools. This seemed to be a logical assumption, and staff in all three schools either accepted it, or made applications for jobs outside the Authority before re-organisation was completed. Mr Webb and Dr Charlesworth of the Technical School had both decided to retire, and Miss Irvine, the Headmistress of the Girls' High School, was offered the post of Vice-Principal of the Sixth Form College when it came into being.

On 25th April the School entered the space age – for an hour or two. The British Interplanetary Society and the National Aeronautics and Space Administration of America arrived at the School with a travelling exhibition of models of almost every conceivable type of space vehicle, which, when set up, occupied the whole of the front of the School stage. At the centre was a working model of a satellite revolving round the Earth. Introducing the models was Dr W.F. Hilton, Executive Secretary of the International Academy of Astronautics, and Squadron Leader R. Dawson, a senior lecturer at the RAF College, Cranwell. They spoke to members of the IVs, Vs and VIs. During the lecture, which was richly punctuated with working demonstrations, Dr Hilton dealt with the basic problems of launching satellites and keeping them in orbit. The scientific principles of space flight were also discussed – the role of models and experiments being shown to be extremely important before a proper launching could take place. The boys watched an American film simulating the landing of men on the moon using an Apollo Spacecraft designed to carry three astronauts. [This was three years before the Apollo project that landed Armstrong and Aldrin on the moon on 20 July, 1969]. The audience was obviously enthusiastic and asked questions for more than thirty minutes. Some boys were very reluctant to leave a subject they clearly found fascinating.

There was a meeting at the School on 10th May for prospective pupils and their parents, interested in the Sixth Form College. They were addressed by Dr Corbett, and Mr Webb, Miss Irvine, Headmistress of the Girls' High School, and Dr Charlesworth, Head of the Technical School, were in attendance.

Meanwhile, throughout May, a series of meetings were held for parents of boys already at the Grammar School, to inform them of what would be happening to their sons when the change-over occurred in September. Many of them were *not* happy.

The Mass Radiography Unit arrived at the School on 16th May, and every boy was X-rayed as a precaution against tuberculosis and other chest complaints.

On the same very hot day, Mr H.J. Bryant drove Mr Webb and Mr Pye to the Old Lutonians' London Lunch. Fifteen Old Boys were present and Mr Webb

recorded 'a fine meeting, with much good will'. He spoke to them of the chaos of trying to run the School at that time, due to the change-over to a Sixth Form College. Dr Hoblyn raised the question of the fate of the various Trusteeships, the tennis courts, the sundial, the organ, and various Scholarships donated to the School by Old Boys. He suggested that where possible movable objects might be placed in Luton Museum. Mr Harold White felt that if items were left within the School premises they might instil a sense of tradition in future students. The Head agreed with him, as did the assembly, and the Club pledged itself to watch closely all future developments at the School.

Whether by coincidence or a conscious effort, the sporting year 1965–66 was one of the most successful ever.

In Football the 1st XI played 17 games, won 12, drew 3 and lost 2. The team were eager for possession at all times by all players, and frequently tried to attack from defensive positions. The middle line of P.J. Southwell and N.R. Boult (Captain) worked tremendously hard and was well-supported by link-man, D.R. Hamel, whose ball-control and agility compensated for his lack of stature. Top-scorer and spearhead of the attack, W.J. Wood, proved the value of a player who was striving for the whole eighty minutes.

No record was published of the 1966 Cross-Country season. Suffice to say that the Hornets won the Wild Cup, and the Meredith Cup for individual performance went to A.J. Montgomery.

The Open Mile race was run before Sports Day. Ian R. Thompson looked likely to beat his own record, but conditions were unfavourable. Against a strong wind down the back straight and with little pressure from behind, he had to make all the running and his moment of glory failed to materialise. With a time of 4 min. 39·3 secs., he was 1·8 seconds outside his previous year's record. On Sports Day itself, Thompson not only broke the record for the 880 yards (u.17) in 2 mins. 5·7 secs. but improved the Open record by 0·3 secs. In March 1968, as a member of the Sixth Form College, he came 3rd in the English Schools Cross-Country Championships. After leaving college Thompson pursued his athletics career, crowning it by winning the gold medal for the Marathon in the 1974 Commonwealth Games in Auckland, New Zealand. This was questionably the greatest athletic achievement of any Old Boy of Luton Modern or Grammar School.

Three other records were broken and three equalled on Sports Day on 19th May. A.N. Potts took the 220 yds. record in the first event of the morning. Tim S. Watson clipped half a second off the 80 yards hurdles record. Efforts in the field events were not quite so impressive, except for Nicholas J. Page, who managed to throw 125 ft. 10 ins. in the Under 16 discus. The *Victor Ludorum* was A.N. Potts, who won all three of the sprints.

The Bedfordshire County AAA Championships took place two days after Sports Day, where the School had the distinction of regaining the coveted Arnold

Whitchurch Trophy. Tim Watson set up a new Bedfordshire record in the hurdles, and D. Brown and Ian Thompson both had double firsts in the sprints and middle distance events respectively.

Knowing that this was the last time the School would compete in the Luton Schools' Sports, the boys pulled out all the stops. Not only did they win the Championship Shield for the fifth successive time, but they also won the Coronation Trophy for the third year running, and S.P. Clydesdale took the Tripp Trophy for the best individual performance in which he equalled the 100 yds record and broke the 220 yds. The final result was 1st, School 103 points; 2nd Rotheram 67 points; 3rd Stopsley 47 points.

Seven boys represented the County in the English Schools' Championships at Blackburn. The brightest hope, Watson, met with a serious accident in training and could not compete. The others all performed creditably, but none got further than the semi-finals.

In Cricket, the 1st XI, ably captained by Peter Hamel, bowled and fielded well and never allowed its opponents to feel they were having an easy time; but on the whole it was not the best season. The main weakness lay in the side's batting which was terribly fragile, and it could have done with one or two commanding batsmen. Of the bowlers, P.G. Davie, the vice-captain, was the most successful as well as the most hostile and amassed a creditable total of 53 wickets. G. Collinson topped the batting averages but never fulfilled hopes of a lot of runs. Hamel frequently had to carry the batting burden as well as the captaincy and inevitably his performance suffered.

The Senior Tennis team had its most successful season, winning eleven out of twelve matches against local schools and clubs. This was achieved by a stable team playing a steady and effective type of tennis. Some of the credit for this must be shared by J.P. Timms, the captain, and W.J. Wood, the secretary. The School won their first round in the Glanville Cup, a national knock-out tournament for all types of secondary schools, but were soundly beaten in the second by Ratcliffe College and Ipswich G.S.

With access to the new swimming pool in Bath Road, the School swimmers had their best season ever. In the 38 years existence of the Luton Schools' Gala, the School had never won. 1966 being their last chance, the boys made every effort. Gary Dunnington was quite outstanding and had two firsts in the First Year Breaststroke and Butterfly. In the Second Year events, D.A. Howlett was first in the Freestyle and also had a second and a third, while the Seniors (third and fourth years) were inspired by their captain, C.V. Dunnington, to win the Freestyle Relay and to take several places. The School won with 52 points, three more than rivals Rotheram.

School Societies do not seem to have been very active in 1966. The Railway Club continued to meet every Wednesday to exchange magazines and watch slide shows. In January fourteen members, accompanied by Mr I.W. Arthur, visited Motive

Power Depots at Basingstoke and Eastleigh, and the Eastleigh Locomotive Works. In all cases it was found that the stock of steam railway locomotives had sadly depleted. In early June the club visited Derby, Crewe and Stoke-on-Trent. A considerable number of steam engines were seen, in contrast to the previous visit. Among those inspected was 'The Lion' of 1838 vintage used in the film *The Titfield Thunderbolt*.

The Natural History Society identified 70 different species of Fungus in a foray in the grounds and woods around Rothamsted Experimental Station. In June they were given a guided tour of the Wild Fowl Trust at Slimbridge, and the Westonbirt Arboretum with its magnificent display of rhododendrons, maples, sycamores and magnolias. Members joined with the Literary and Scientific Society for a lecture by Dr P. Kilburn, who compared the merits of British and American National Parks, and a talk by N.R. Pashley (U.VI Sc.A) on his recent expedition with the British Schools Exploration Society to Lapland, which he illustrated with a film made by the party.

The '65 Society continued its lunch-time meetings with discussions, debates and brains trusts. A principal aim of the Society was to provoke, and so a number of films consistent with that policy were shown, ranging from an appeal for medical aid to North Vietnam and to the National Liberation Front of South Vietnam, to a film on Apartheid issued by the South African Embassy.

The Bishop of Bedford spoke to a joint meeting of the Student Christian Movement groups of the Grammar, High and Technical Schools on the subject of 'Is Christianity Relevant?' Other talks were given by the Revd. Larner on 'What is Life For?' and Mr James Gale on 'The Quaker Contribution'.

The School Concert took place on the 20th May, to a packed house. It opened with the orchestral extracts from 'The Yeoman of the Guard'. This was followed by Colin V. Smith's rendition of Chopin's Nocturne in C Major – made difficult as the piano was out of tune. The Clarinet Trio played a Bach Fugue, and then there was some delightful singing by the First Year Choir. In the second half there was a pleasant bassoon solo from E. Slack, called 'The Fairy Clock'. John Gosling's organ solo, Bach's Fugue in E Flat, was impressive, and P.R. Outen, S.J. Welch and A.R. Parr gave a polished performance of Handel's Sonata in E. Messrs A. Hauke and A.R. Cantor apologised in case the audience found their item a collection of strange noises, before they played 'Duo Concertant' by Milhaud. An innovation was music for the bagpipes, excellently played by A.L.M. Stewart.

The concert closed with the choir, orchestra and organ joining together in Blake's 'Jerusalem'. When the piece had finished and the applause died down, Mr Hauke reminded the audience that this would be the last Grammar School Concert in its present form, since the structure of the School would be radically altered next year. He invited the audience to join the choir in singing 'Jerusalem' once more. This they did with gusto, and the concert closed in an atmosphere of damp eyes and nostalgia.

It was announced in June that the first Principal of the Luton Sixth Form College

would be Mr Brian D. Dance, MA. He paid a brief courtesy visit to meet Mr Webb and see the School on 14th June.

On 20th June all the First and Second Year boys marched to the Technical School in Barnfield Avenue, where Mr Webb met them and their parents and introduced them to Dr Charlesworth who would be their Headmaster until July 1967.

Three days later Mr Webb was called to the Town Hall to receive a certificate from the Mayor on behalf of the National Savings Movement. It commemorated the fact that the School had been a continuous member of the Savings Movement for fifty years.

There was an almost desperate note in the Head's Log Book on 4th July: 'Pneumatic drills all day in lavatories: converting them for girls!'

On Tuesday, 5th July, the Home and School Association held a Farewell Evening for Mr and Mrs Webb. A portrait of the Headmaster, painted by Mr Maurice W. Finch, art master at the Luton College of Technology, was presented to Mr Webb by Mr J. Stephen on behalf of the Association. Mr Stephen said, 'This is an historic meeting for two reasons. It is the last meeting of the Luton Grammar School Home and School Association, and it gives us an opportunity to give our thanks to Mr Webb after his twenty-six years of headmastership.'

Replying, Mr Webb said that he was very appreciative of the gift and asked Ald. Hedley Lawrence, Chairman of the Governors, to receive the portrait on their behalf. Mr Webb also expressed appreciation of the presence of Ald. Fred Bates, Chairman of the Luton Education Committee, because at times they had not always been in agreement over education policy. 'While I remain in some form of conflict of opinion over the education plan,' said Mr Webb, 'I have consistently worked to make my own judgement look foolish – in other words, to give the Sixth Form College the best possible start I can.'

Ald. Lawrence added that 'We can concede to one another that what we have both sought to do has been, we believe, for the well-being of the children.'

Mr J.W. Lowe, Secretary of the Home and School Association presented a radiogram and a cheque for £115 to Mr Webb. A bouquet was given to Mrs Webb by Mrs Daphne Edler. Mr Lowe revealed that, under Mr Webb's chairmanship, the Association had raised about £8,000 for the School's use.

At that point Ald. Lawrence presented a gold watch to Mr Webb to mark twenty-five years of service to the Education Authority. The gathering was then joined by the Mayor and Mayoress, Cllr. and Mrs Sam Gonshor, who had left a reception at the Town Hall in order to pay tribute to Mr Webb.

The Staff held a dinner on 8th July, chaired by Mr Pye, at which they said goodbye to fourteen of their younger colleagues, and then made presentations to three senior masters, Mr Eric Sansome (1945), Mr Charles E. Wareham (1931), and Mr Enyr Jones (1930). Mr Albert Partridge, as the most senior member of staff (appointed 1929), then made a presentation to K.B. Webb of a tape-recorder. [The

only other remaining member of staff who had preceded Mr Webb was Mr Arthur Root (1931).]

Mr Eric Sansome, 'Ted', was born in Leicestershire, and attended Loughborough Grammar School, where he was taught French by 'Froggy' Watson. He worked for some years in the textile industry and was also a Minister in the Independent Methodist Church. After studying part-time he graduated as a BA of London University in the mid-1940s. He briefly taught Latin at Luton Grammar School in 1945 until Mr Root was demobilised, and returned again in 1948 to teach Latin, Religious Knowledge and French. Always a gentleman, he was a stickler for good manners, warning his 1st year class in 1952 that, when they started smoking, they must remember not to address a lady with the cigarette in their mouths. He was on less sure ground when he informed a new arrival with a strong Yorkshire brogue that he would have to learn to speak with a Southern accent. When the Memorial Tennis Courts were opened, Mr Sansome took charge of tennis within the School. He was also responsible for the Student Christian Movement group, and became Head of Religious Knowledge in 1965, after Mr Parry's promotion to Careers Master. His son, Michael, was an old Boy of the School (1943–51) and became an Inspector of Schools in Hertfordshire, and later Director of Education for Harrow.

Charles E. Wareham, 'Pants', was born in York in 1907 and educated at Bishop Holgate's Grammar School. He graduated with a BSc in Physics from Leeds University. He taught for three years in Stockton-on-Tees, before moving to Luton Modern School in 1931 to teach physics, chemistry and physical training. When Mr S.J. Pointing retired from teaching handicrafts in 1948, Mr Wareham retrained and took over that department. Shortly afterwards he introduced Technical Drawing to the School syllabus. He was a Yorkshireman who preferred tennis to cricket, and took over the School Tennis Club from Mr Sansome. He was a very versatile musician, playing the violin in the School orchestra for a number of years, later learning the clarinet and oboe. He died, aged 96, in March 2003.

Enyr Jones, 'Jonah', was a Welsh-speaking Welshman who was versatile in many tongues. He spent his early years in Argentina where he learnt Spanish. He returned to University College, Swansea, where he was awarded his BA in modern languages. After a spell teaching in Yorkshire he came to Luton Modern School in 1930 where he taught languages and history. He took the first ever School party abroad in 1938, to Norway. He persuaded boys to write to pen-friends in countries whose language they were

Mr Enyr Jones drawn by James Gale.

learning. In particular, he encouraged them to read and love Spanish writers. A number of them, like Dr Robert Gurney (1951–59), devoted their lives to Spanish studies. For five years Mr Jones edited the School magazine. He was an Executive Member of the Association of Assistant Masters for some years and a representative of Bedfordshire at the annual policy-making Council for well over thirty years. Active on the left wing of politics since his college days, he was better known locally as a Director of the Luton Co-operative Wholesale Society. During the war he was a special constable, on duty every third or fourth night, but always at School punctually in the morning.

At a Luton Town Council meeting in July, the chairman of the Labour controlled Education Committee, Ald. Frederick Bates, was asked why so many Grammar School masters were leaving. He said that four older men were retiring, and 14 of the young teachers were moving to other schools. He believed that this did not compare unfavourably with the position at the end of previous summer terms. *The Luton News* wrily observed that in 1965 one Grammar School master had retired and five resigned to take teaching jobs outside the town.

Elliot's Mobile Computer Class Room spent the whole of 12th July at the School, giving most boys their first taste of the world of computers. The visit cost the School £50, but most of the boys and staff who had sampled its activities considered it money well spent.

On Thursday 14th, the School Swimming House-Championships were held at the Waller Street Baths. The First and Second year boys, and the Sixth Form, went as spectators and were treated to some exciting competition. 'A splendid do!' Mr Webb recorded.

"A Lovely End"

Everything came to an end the following day, Friday, 15th July, 1966. It began with a telephone message at about 8.30 a.m. The Police had been informed that there was a bomb in the School. Whilst it was almost certainly a hoax, precautions had to be taken. No one was allowed inside the building until the police and senior staff had made a cursory search. This completed, the boys made their way into their class-rooms, where they searched their own desks.

In spite of the disturbance, the final morning Assembly was delayed by only five minutes. With eighteen masters leaving, the boys had been hard-pressed to collect enough money for farewell presents. On their behalf, Michael Syrett, the Head Boy, gave a gift to each of the fourteen who had been at the School for a relatively short time, including Mr Sharman, who had completed ten years.

Michael Sharman had joined Mr Gale in the Art Department in 1956. A Yorkshireman with an interest in sports, he helped run the 1st Football XI for some years, and played Cricket in most staff matches, and for Luton Town Club for a few

seasons. His first loves were Art and Dramatics and eventually he devoted himself almost full-time to painting, design and the theatre. Not only did he produce a number of outstanding plays and (with Mr Hauke) light operas for the School, with scenery designed by Mrs Sharman, but he also contributed to the theatrical life of Luton, and (with Mr Freddy Benson) was one of the driving-forces behind the Luton Arts Council.

Morning Assembly was followed by a VIth Form Revue, which, Mr Webb observed, included 'some good skits, and one miserable piece of inaudible slapstick!' It was reviewed by Andrew Stephen for *The Lutonian.* A number of sketches attempted, with varying degrees of success, to portray staff as seen by the boys, emphasising their peculiarities. 'Some were very predictable: an Irish teacher for example "running through the board", whilst others, like the irate Science master moaning at Lab. Stewards, were unrecognisable. Three masters, Messrs I.R. Rendell, J. Marsden and P.G. Hudson appeared in a "Red Riding Hood" story, which amused many of the younger pupils. A group of musicians performed three Beatle songs, arranged for their "Chamber Orchestra".' Towards the end of the concert 'some masters made a brave attempt to enliven the proceedings, and sang an ingenious adaptation by Wynne Parry of "The Vicar of Bray". The Headmaster joined in and was shortly singing a solo – as the Judge in an excerpt from "Trial by Jury". Members of the staff sang the choruses, and the performance was repeated with slightly amusing word-changes.'

A History of Our Education – In Verse or Worse

1   In gay King Edward's spacious days,
    When Balfour led the nation,
     We saw created LEAs
    For secondary education;
   Scholarship child or 'passed to pay'
    To Luton Modern wended,
  Where Sanderson, ('The Boss'), held sway
    And to no man unbended.

Chorus:
    And this is fact that we'll maintain,
    And make the world acknowledge,
   That in that short but glorious reign
   There was no sixth-form college.

2   When sober George became our King,
    The word 'co-education'

Acquired a most unpleasant ring,
Like 'prior consultation'.
To meet the wrath of ladies spurned,
Regardless of the revenue
The Council left no stone unturned
In Alexandra Avenue.

Chorus:

And this is fact that we'll maintain,
And make the world acknowledge,
That in that long and noble reign
There was no sixth-form college.

3   An Edward might the throne ascend,
Doomed soon to abdication,
Or brother George to ruling bend;
We still had education.
Some shone at Maths., and some at games,
And some with brush and hammer,
While Logic, ever strict on names
Changed 'Modern School' to 'Grammar'.

Chorus:

And this is fact that we'll maintain,
And make the world acknowledge,
That though those days brought stress and strain,
There was no sixth-form college.

4   And now, as time its cycle turns,
A gracious Queen upholds us,
While still the torch of learning burns,
And education moulds us.
Yet though on earth men promise heaven,
Who cannot be but pensive?
For legion are the meanings given
To one word – 'comprehensive'.

Chorus:

But this is fact that we'll maintain,
And make the world acknowledge,
That whatsoever party reign,
There'll be no sixth-form college.

C. W. P.

After lunch the boys and staff of Luton Grammar School gathered in the Hall for the last time. Head Boy, Michael Syrett, made four final presentations, to Mr E. Sansome, Mr C.E. Wareham, Mr E. Jones and the Headmaster, each of whom said a few words. [As has already been said, Mr Webb received his main present of a radiogram from the parents and boys at the Home and School Association's Farewell Evening on 5th July.]

The afternoon ended with the singing of the School hymn. Mr Webb went to the door and shook hands with most of the leavers. His last entry in the School Log Book read: 'A lovely end to twenty-six years of Headmastering'.

Kenneth B. Webb

Kenneth B. Webb celebrated his hundredth birthday on 10th March, 2004, receiving cards and messages of goodwill from many of his Old Boys. Sadly, he died three months later on 15th June.

In April 1966, through the columns of *The Luton* News he had written a 'thank-you' letter to generations of Old Boys, which concluded with the words 'I shall ever be grateful for the enrichment my life has had, and I trust will go on having, through twenty-six years' association with Luton Grammar School, the colleagues I have served with, and the boys grown into men I have known.'

In compiling this book many Old Boys, masters and friends have described their memories and expressed their regard for the Headmaster. For the younger boys he was always a distant figure, rarely seen outside his office, except for morning assembly. Only in the Sixth Form did pupils feel that they got to know him better.

For Frank Stygall, (1937–44) [after Mr Gauntlett] 'Kenneth Webb was a very welcome change: tall and imposing, relatively young, a strong personality, very approachable, and liberal (with a small L). He had, he believed, to refrain from showing bias as between the political parties; but he was certainly "progressive" (my impression was that he was Centre and quite possibly slightly Left of Centre). In most ways he was an ideal Headmaster.'

A.W. 'George' Thorpe (1938–46) 'liked Mr Webb from the start, and grew to appreciate the way he respected our views. He was no-one's fool and provided the right degree of discipline needed without stamping his own ideas on others. The old cliché 'an iron fist in a velvet glove' just about sums him up. I suspect that he would have preferred the boys to concentrate more on education than sporting achievements, but he realised that to try and change the system would have been resented by boys and masters alike. I especially welcomed the Friday morning debating sessions in his study with the Upper Sixth students – there were only about a dozen of us – when his aim seemed to be to impart knowledge of national and international matters of significance before we went forth into a grown-up world. His respect for the United Nations and the need for international co-operation on a

scale hitherto unknown must surely have sewn seeds of intellectual enlightenment in some of us present.'

Professor Colin Humphreys (1952–59) remembered 'sometime when I was in the fourth or fifth year, Luton Football Club did well in the FA Cup. I think a cup replay match was due to be played in Luton during the week. K.B. Webb announced in morning assembly that he would not be giving a half-day holiday and would take a very dim view of any pupil who was absent on that afternoon. I wrote him an anonymous letter saying that if the United Nations Organisation had a public meeting in Luton that afternoon, I felt sure he would have given time off for all those pupils who wanted to attend, and to my mind an FA Cup replay was at least as important as a meeting of the United Nations. At the next assembly Mr Webb announced that he had received an anonymous letter from a pupil, and that he knew who had sent it and he wished to see him in his study afterwards! I thought I had carefully disguised my handwriting, nevertheless I went along to his study and he greeted me with, "Humphreys, I knew this letter was from you!" He then told me how much more important UNO was than Luton Town Football Club, but I was not totally convinced.'

Professor Derek C. Glover (1950–54) talked with K.B.W. in 2001 about the annual Remembrance Day service. 'I saw it in a different light when he explained the heartache he had experienced at the loss of so many of his boys with so much wasted potential – and he was able to list their names and recall his last conversations with them. In many ways they were so much more grown up than we were at that time.'

Deric B. Hawkins (1939–45) observed that Mr Webb always related well to his pupils and appeared to get on well with his staff. He had an extraordinary memory. When Hawkins and his wife attended the Old Lutonians' dinner on K.B.W.'s 90th birthday, Mr Webb greeted him by name and referred to his "extra curricular" activities getting in the way of his academic work!'

Sir John Burgoyne, OBE, wrote in *The Old Lutonian* for August 1966:

'I can easily remember my first meeting with Mr Webb. It was when he appeared before the Governors, with Mr Harry Arnold in the chair, to support his application for the post of Headmaster. How well he did present himself and his case! Although he was a little flushed and nervous, his spoken English, together with a wide ranging vocabulary and an exceptional facility for calling up the right word, was all very attractive to the listener. [K.B.W. had won the Oration Prize at Cambridge.] My own impression was then, and still is, that the applicant's written credentials which we had before us were exceedingly good, but not half so convincing as that personal display of self-confident ability to direct aright the life and work of a grammar school.

'Between then and now have gone twenty-six years which began in the drab days of war; seventy-eight terms in which work has been done and success with

distinction has brought gladness to innumerable homes and conferred invaluable benefits on the social and business life of Luton. There is no accepted method by which we can fairly evaluate the work of Mr Webb. We only know that what the records say of him, what we have heard of him, and what we have seen of him is enough for his good name and our warm regard.'

C. Wynne Parry joined the School one term after Mr Webb. His honest opinion could always be trusted. He wrote of the Headmaster:

'Mr Webb's humanity and his essential kindliness are among the most immediately recognisable of his qualities. Eminently approachable, he has been a clear interpreter of the aims of the School to parents and governors, to Old Boys, University Boards, employers and their federations, HM Inspectors, and, not least, to the more contentious of the boys themselves. Possessed of an agile brain, which

The Headmaster and 48 Staff, July, 1966. (back row), W.P. Evans, M.A. Siddiqui, J.J. Mitchell, H.B. Luke, C.J. Carmell, P.M.E. Maddocks, G.H. Gorton, D. Green, R.L. Humphrey, M. Sharman, A.R. Cator, R.W.A. Rhodes, W.J. Hazelton, I.W. Arthur, M.J. Holst, G.N. Crapnell, (middle row) J.V. Ephgrave, A.B. Davies, W.G. Messer, T.C. Flitton, I.R. Rendell, R.S. Acton, A.E. Bowen, T.R. Key, J.A. Muse, J. Marsden, R.H. Barter, A.C. Hauke, J.H. Lightfoot, D.E.Sutcliffe, J. Lovell, P.G. Hudson, (front row) H.B. Evans, R. Lane, A.J.G. May, G. Clarke, D.F. Gallimore, C.E. Wareham, E. Jones, J.T. Pye, K.B. Webb, A.C. Partridge, A. Root, C.W. Parry, S.R. Giddy, W.N. Thorpe, H.J. Bryant, E. Sansome, J. Gale. (LN)

preferred to move constructively rather than indignantly, and believing that in most situations there is a way of action which a calm and unruffled temper will disclose, he has won victories over obstructive opponents by his informed opinion and his eloquent debating, and has maintained happy relations with staff and pupils by his enthusiasm, good humour and kindly interest.

'To those who have read something of the philosophical implications of

modern physics it is not surprising that a man brought up in the joint disciplines of the Christian faith and the university department of physics should show particular interest in philosophy and educational theory. In education he has always believed strongly in the importance of the individual and the increased flexibility of the time-table, with its variety of choices for pupils from a comparatively early age, has reflected this belief.

'It has been his proud claim that in almost every field (the great exception which he has persistently mentioned is creative writing) he can point to former pupils who are holding positions of great responsibility and meeting experts at the highest level.

'The greatest satisfaction for a Headmaster as he lays aside his gown must always be the intangible, the imponderable. The after-success of boys whom one might have been tempted to write off as "my failures", the letters from all parts of the world describing fascinating careers for which the foundation is gratefully acknowledged to have been laid at Bradgers Hill, the recollection of difficulties overcome by determination and good humour, these are the most lasting rewards.'

Chapter 16

Epilogue

The first Principal of the Luton Sixth Form College was Mr Brian D. Dance, MA. Educated at Kingston Grammar School, where he was Head Boy for two years, he won an Exhibition to Wadham College, Oxford, as a Sheriff Scholar in History. After graduating in Jurisprudence, he became a Solicitor's Articled Clerk and passed the Law Society's Intermediate Examinations. He endured fifteen months of boredom, and decided that he would prefer to return to his first love and teach history. The offer of a post at his old school started him on his teaching career. In 1959 he moved to Faversham Grammar School as Senior History Master, and in 1962 he went on to Westminster City School, one of the largest and most successful Grammar Schools in the London area. He was Headmaster of Cirencester Grammar School prior to coming to Luton. A keen, all round sportsman, he was also a lover of classical music, stamp-collecting and old cars.

Miss M.E. Irvine, BA, the last Headmistress of the Girls' High School, was appointed Vice-Principal of the new College.

The first day of the Sixth Form College term began on 7th September, 1966. There were 255 admissions to the First Year Sixth, and interviews began immediately to work out the appropriate courses for each student. In the afternoon Mr Dance called the new students together, and addressed them on his vision and aims for the College.

About 320 boys remained from the Grammar School; in years IV and V and the senior Sixth forms. R.D. 'Little Pop' or 'Jim' Whalley has chronicled this period of the School's history:

> 'The fourth and fifth year pupils left in the College with no younger pupils
> beneath them became overnight the "babies" of the establishment and we all felt

that this affected their attitude by making them more immature. They were considered a nuisance and an encumbrance in the function, running and organisation of the Sixth Form College and they also tended to get the blame for any discipline problems that arose. The youngsters who moved across to the Technical Grammar had the problem of a change of school and teachers.'

A number of staff from the former Grammar School were required to teach the second and third years from the old school who were now in the Technical School building, so they had to travel back and forth between lessons. Some of the older pupils had to travel from the VIth Form College to the former Girls' High School for lessons, and arrangements had to be made with Hillside coaches for their daily transport. This all caused major problems with time-tabling the students.

R.D. Whalley had been Head of the Craft Department at the Technical School, and was appointed Head of the reciprocal department in the College. He has written:

'There was satisfaction and dissatisfaction amongst the staff as some, like myself, gained Head of Department status and others, who had been Heads of Departments in their schools, lost their status on moving to the College. W.E. Bowen, who had been Head of English at the Tech., lost out to Barbara Harrison, who had been Head of English at the Girls' High School and became Head of English at the College. The Maths Department at the College was split into Pure and Applied Maths and R.G. Blacker got the Head of Applied Maths, whilst the sitting tenant, A.J.G. May, remained Head of Pure Maths. History was also split into Early and Modern and Frank H.C. Maggs of the Tech. got the Early, whilst H.B. 'Major' Evans retained the Modern. A year later, a third historian, Ivan A. Jones, moved across from the High School and became Head of Economic History. The subject was split three ways, each with its own stock book and capitation allowance! J.F. Sanson, who had been Head of Science at the Tech., lost out to Nicholas Crapnell as Head of Chemistry. Although status was lost, salaries were protected, but the loss of status is always difficult to bear.'

What was life like for the younger Grammar School boys who were left at their old school? One of them was Pierre Cowlard who recalled:

'I was one of the fourth formers as the school welcomed its first Sixth Form College cohort. I remember feeling that we were something of a nuisance – a bunch of kids to get out of the way before the College could get on with the real work. Many of the older and traditional teaching staff at the Grammar School that were not enthused by the political decision made their feelings known to the pupils, and many left the school to find alternative roles or retire. I was clear that

they had been let down and that years of culture and tradition were being dismantled. I feel that our particular cohort got a poor deal and was "sacrificed" to some extent.'

And what of those who were transferred to the Technical School? Robert Knowles observed:

'At the age of 11, we had joined a school with a good reputation but imbued with slightly stuffy tradition, where most of the 'masters' wore gowns, facilities were showing their age, desk graffiti dated back to the 1940s and so did many of the text books.

'At the end of my second year and in the fast-pack aiming for O-levels in four years, my form was relocated unceremoniously to the Technical School, renamed Barnfield High. It meant new uniforms [optional], revised travel routes, modes of transport and quite a different regime. It also meant girls.

'My form of 18 boys was kept together and segregated from the rest of the LGS, LHS, LTS refugees. It had two effects. We enjoyed dedicated attention from the best of the teaching staff who relished the prospect of achieving good results from students who responded to their efforts. I have fond memories of 'Dilly' Dilkes (maths), Bill Davies (French) – we once filled his pipe with a shredded pencil rubber, but he didn't notice, 'Ma' Clarke (English), Mr Ellis (who led an inspirational geography field trip to Derbyshire) and Mr and Mrs Harding, who stoically endured a coachload of testosterone-packed teenagers on their first trip to France. But the rest of the school despised us as a privileged elite, and we spent two years in splendid isolation, which served only to bond all 18 of us into a mutual support group. The outcome was that we amassed something like 120 O-levels between us and at the end of our fourth year transferred *en bloc* back to the fledgling Sixth Form College to start A-levels.

Steven Crooke has slightly different memories:

'I attended Luton Grammar School in 1964 and was quite happy there for two years, until Harold Wilson decreed that it was far too good for us, and so we were shifted *en masse* to what was the Technical School at Barnfield and became Barnfield High in 1966. Two years later, in 1968, we were shifted back *en masse* to the Luton Sixth Form College to complete our school studies (some of us had been "fast streamed" so we jumped from the 4th year straight to Lower Sixth – a reverse Remove?). Fortunately, we regained a lot of the old Grammar School masters when we rejoined the Sixth Form College. I seem to recollect that the ones that were thrust upon us at Barnfield were not quite ready for such a bunch of pimply eggheads!'

There were a fortunate few who had reached the Grammar School Sixth Form in 1966, and were able to continue their studies, mostly with staff that they already knew. Philip Eden (1962–69) was already fascinated by meteorology before he reached the Sixth Form, but, with plenty of encouragement from Mr Alun 'Taffy' Davies who taught geography and economics, he got to Birmingham University, gaining his BA (Hons) in Geography and MSc in Meteorology and Applied Climatology. A Fellow and Life Member of the Royal Meteorological Society, and with his own Weather Consultancy, he has written a number of 'weather' books, and is well-known for his forecasts in the *Daily* and *Sunday Telegraph* and on BBC Radio 5-Live.

Professor Sir Alec Jeffreys (1961–67) was passionately interested in science from a very early age, largely due to his father's enthusiasm. At the Grammar School it was the influence of Mr Roy H. Barter, the Biology Master, who had the greatest impact on him.

'This impact really started during my A-level studies once the School had mutated into a Sixth Form College. The high point was definitely becoming a laboratory assistant and having my own preparation and research space. Roy Barter was enormously encouraging, going out of his way to help me in my studies and give me access to weird and wonderful specimens – including a starfish (out of a bottle) for dissection! I also remember with fondness one of my physics teachers, a Pakistani gentleman by the name of Dr S.U. Haq, who completely opened my eyes to the potential of doing science by the pure power of thought, in the fashion of Einstein and his ilk.

'My specific interest in genetics really only crystallised later at university, though I do remember being taught the basics of DNA, RNA and protein at the Grammar School which really fuelled my imagination, showing as it did how chemistry and biology are inextricably entwined.

'Of my various successes at the School I take particular pride in Latin. I found this a totally tiresome subject and in retrospect felt very sorry for Mr Root, who obviously regarded me as a thoroughly irksome student, particularly after I gained totally miserable marks in my mock O-level. Probably out of sheer spite, I pulled out all the stops just before the real O-level, absorbing huge amounts of Latin vocabulary and grammar into my short term memory, and managed to get

Alec Jeffreys, LGS and VIth Form College, 1961 - 1968, discovered the DNA genetic fingerprint in 1984. He was appointed Professor of Genetics, Leicester University, 1987, and received a Knighthood in 1994.

the joint top Latin O-level for the entire year!

'Another important figure was Mr Brian Dance, the College principal. Up to that point my vague thoughts about university were directed either to a red-brick establishment or conceivably Cambridge. It was Mr Dance who brought me into his study on a very memorable occasion, and basically told me that I was going to Oxford since he was determined, as an Oxford man, to see someone from the Sixth Form College following in his footsteps. That was the one meeting that altered the course of the rest of my life!

'Looking back on my time at the Grammar School and Sixth Form College, I am enormously indebted to everyone there for the tremendous and, to use an old fashioned word, scholarly education that they gave me.'

Alec Jeffreys was awarded a Postmastership in Natural Sciences at Merton College, Oxford in 1968, and went on to gain BA, MA and DPhil. Elected a Fellow of the Royal Society in 1986, he became Professor of Genetics at Leicester University in 1987, and in 1991 Wolfson Research Professor of the Royal Society at Leicester University. It was on 15th September, 1984, that he discovered the DNA genetic fingerprint which showed that the tissue of every living thing has its own singular individual pattern. His discovery has been used extensively to establish the guilt of criminals. Since then he has received a host of prestigious scientific honours and awards, and in 1994 a Knighthood from Her Majesty the Queen.

Jeffreys' colleague, W.J.H. Gardiner, won an Open Exhibition for Natural Sciences at Sidney Sussex, Cambridge in 1968.

David Renwick was two years younger than Jeffreys, joining the School in 1963.

'I have vivid memories of being taken down to one of the approved outfitters in the town, to get kitted out with the new School uniform and sports gear in my house colours (green for Grasshopper). Looking back the place had a kind of public school feel about it: the tradition of rolling "new boys" down the grassy bank at the edge of the playing field [the forgotten air-raid shelters]; the end of term "pranks" (one year I seem to remember a master's car was taken apart and reassembled on the roof by the music room); and the rigid hierarchy of monitors and prefects.

'On my first day there I remember seeing burly sixth-formers quake in their boots as the diminutive, elderly Second Master, Mr Godfrey, barked at them on their way to assembly. My cousin, three years ahead of me, took me through the School list, briefing me on all the masters and their nicknames. Many were simply known by their first name, others seemed quite eccentric: the Irish maths master called "Baffer", and the appropriately named Mr Giddy, who I can recall dangerously shaking a piece of phosphorous about in front of me while explaining how volatile it was.

'During my third year we were all fans of Peter Cook and Dudley Moore on TV, and there was a great enthusiasm for that post-satire period of British comedy. By the time I reached the fourth form most of the boys in my class were avid fans of *I'm Sorry, I'll Read That Again,* so much so that I organised an outing to see some of the shows recorded, along with an episode of *The Frost Report* in 1967. It was from that moment on that I became interested in the idea of writing comedy myself, though I remember our form master, Mr W.G. Messer, commenting in my school report that I was "decidedly weak" at English, so my tutors clearly couldn't see much potential at that stage. It was a bizarre time. Luton Grammar as a separate entity had ceased to be, and the building had been designated one of the first Sixth Form Colleges in the country. Suddenly the place was filled with boys and girls in "civvies", while we were still filing down the corridor in our red and gold ties and blazers. And the sudden introduction of girls in mini-skirts was a real shock to the system at that age. Some of the masters never quite seemed to adapt – even when I reached the sixth form they persisted in calling the boys by their surnames and the girls by their first names, it was a habit they just couldn't shake off.

'I became heavily involved in an independent magazine called *Spasm* (a kind of "hippie" alternative to *The Lutonian*), contributing mostly humorous pieces as it gradually evolved into more of a rag magazine.

'Because I quite liked writing, the Careers Master, Mr Parry, steered me into applying for a couple of journalism posts, so when I left I became a reporter and sub-Editor on *The Luton News,* where I stayed from 1970 to 1974.'

Readers will know Renwick best as the creator and script-writer for the brilliant television comedy series *One Foot in the Grave* (1989–2000) and the murder mysteries of *Jonathan Creek* (1997–2004). He was also responsible, with Andrew Marshall, for *The Burkiss Way* and *If You See God, Tell Him.* Inevitably, one wonders if any of his characters were based on members of the School staff.

And how did the staff fare in the Sixth Form College? The old staff room was not big enough for the increased staff so the Lecture Room next door was converted to a second staff room. R.D. Whalley again:

'When we "intruders" arrived, the old staff room was still being used as it had been since time immemorial. The easy chairs, already worn out years previously, were placed down one wall, and staff sat, in order of seniority, ready to move up one if a death or retirement took place. Woe-betide anyone who sat in the wrong place. The table in front of the fireplace was reserved by the "Bridge" group, led by John Muse, who played regularly at break and dinner-times. They blocked the fire from everyone else in the room and required a silence in order to concentrate. Since this group constituted the most senior members of the staff and everyone else was

deemed subservient, they had their way and silence prevailed whilst they played.

'The High School staff also had their hierarchical structure, with junior members of staff only expressing opinions when asked and nearly always saying "My Head of Department says this or that".

'We of the old Tech. staff, were more fortunate for we had taught mixed classes and our staff was mixed also. It was into this staid, rather old-fashioned and certainly hostile to each other, situation, that we joined these two staffs to form the new Sixth Form College staff.

'It was like mixing chalk and cheese. The hallowed ground of the old staff room was too much for those of us from the Tech, and so we, along with the ex-High School staff, took over the new Lecture Theatre staff room. We soon had the ice broken and they were laughing and joking with us. Gradually, some of the younger members of the Grammar School staff moved over to our room, and with the retirement of the older staff we soon became integrated, and new staff who joined the College never knew the divisions that had existed in those early days.'

The Old Lutonians held their 36th Annual Dinner at the Halfway House, Dunstable, on 16th September, and, although there was the usual gaiety associated with such reunions, there was also a sombre underlying note, and many nostalgic memories. "It is a sad thought," said Major M.V.W. Chote, "that the Old Lutonian Club as we know it today may have to experience a severe change. As old masters and boys of the Luton Grammar School pass on, the old boys and girls of the College may join together in an entirely different club."

It was not the first time the Club had had to change with the School – and not the first time the School had been co-educational. "I remember," said the Revd. Arthur B. Allen, "the earliest days of the Luton Modern School. Boys and girls then sat side by side in the same classroom."

Presentations were made to Messrs Wareham and Jones on their retirement, and to Mr K.B. Webb.

Mr A.S. Bennett, President of the Old Dunstablians, wished the new venture every success. [His own School would become co-educational in 1970]. Dr Hugh Swallow, President of the Old Lutonians, said, "It is up to us to cool our tempers and help the new school grow in reputation, whatever the change in name may be. We must urge all Old Lutonians to mould the new college into a great school."

Following much behind-the-scenes work, the Inaugural Meeting of a re-formed 'Old Lutonians' Club' – which incorporated the Former Pupils' Associations of the Luton Modern School, Luton Grammar School, Luton High School and former members of the Luton Sixth Form College – was held at the Sixth Form College on 27th May, 1968. The Chair was taken by Andrew Colley (Old Boys' Association), who was supported by Mrs Erica Swallow (Old Girls' Association) and Miss Shirley Willock (Sixth Form College).

The College attempted to retain some of the School traditions. The annual Harvest Festival services were held at the College in 1966 and 1967, but were not continued after the last Vth year Grammar School boys had left. At the Annual General Meeting of the Home and School Association on 5th October, Mr Dance was elected Chairman and Miss Irvine Vice-Chairman. The meeting approved the inclusion of Sixth Form College parents as members, but rejected links with the ex-Grammar School boys' parents transferred to the Technical School: a rather short-sighted decision when some of the latter would be back at College in less than a year. The annual Bazaar was held in 26th November and was well supported, raising £170.

The Remembrance Day Service on 11th November, 1966, was well attended by relatives of the fallen, former staff and Old Lutonians. Being something of a traditionalist, Mr Dance continued to hold a service in the Hall for a further two years, and then the ceremony was reduced in size and moved to the area by the memorial plaques. After his departure it was dropped from the College calendar.

One old School custom, the annual visit to the Varsity Match at Twickenham, was upheld on 6th December, 1966, when the Principal and Mr Muse accompanied a large party of students to watch an exciting game.

On the 8th, 9th and 10th December the Dramatic Society performed Arthur Miller's play, *The Crucible*. It was a difficult play for a relatively inexperienced cast to attempt, and an unappreciative element in the first night audience did not help their confidence. Fortunately this was remedied by the third night, which did the actors much credit. David Rees and Shirley Willock, as the two central characters, John Proctor and Abigail Williams, gave polished performances. 'Rees brought over the powerful dominance of Proctor, emphasising how his struggle is one with himself rather than as the result of the actions of others, an almost unique factor in this play. Abigail Williams is the principal trouble-maker in the community, she has such charm and is so convincing a liar that she deceives all.' Shirley Willock played the part with highly creditable skill and professionalism. 'The play was one in which it was important for the whole cast to work intimately with each other and this is where the production was really successful. Mr Godfrey Samuel, the producer, was to be congratulated for a most rewarding evening's entertainment.'

Shortly before Christmas W.P. Merrick heard that he had been awarded an Exhibition in Natural Sciences to Pembroke College, Cambridge.

The College's first term ended on 21st December with a very successful Carol Service in the morning, attended by the Chairman of Governors, Alderman Lawrence. A collection for Oxfam raised £7 5s 9d. At midday there was a sherry party for the Staff attended by the Director of Education, Dr Corbett. In the afternoon there was a Final Assembly, which included the presentation of colours, and the College said farewell to Mr Robert Acton (English) who had completed almost seven years in Luton, and Mr R.W.A. Rhodes (Chemistry) after four years.

In *The Old Lutonian* for August 1968 Mr Dance was asked to write his impressions of the first year of the Sixth Form College.

'Frankly,' he wrote, 'my impressions are somewhat blurred, partly because so much has happened in these early months, and partly because one is writing at some distance in time from the actual events. Many emotions are mixed in my thoughts about the College: satisfaction that it is actually working; annoyance at inevitable compromise; amazement that one has become unwillingly a sort of pundit; pleasure at some remarkable successes – the list is only just begun.

'There is no doubt that the actual opening of the College was, in the words of the Duke of Wellington, "a damned close run thing". Time was against us, and uncertainty in the air, yet staff and students alike approached the new project with the sensible view that here was something on which everyone's future depended, and so it had better succeed. To both these groups my gratitude ought to be limitless for I alone could have done nothing. It would be foolish to minimise difficulties and occasional conflicts, but the vast majority responded well. Indeed I believe that there will always be something special about our "founder members".

'The amount of interest aroused by the Sixth Form College has brought an embarrassing flow of visitors and enquiries to Luton. Many of my Headmaster colleagues seem increasingly to be convinced that the Sixth Form College offers the best chance of maintaining academic standards.

'The examination results (by which we must to a large extent be judged) have so far confirmed these opinions. Open Scholarships and a large number of University places have been won. But we should not be concerned with academic affairs alone. Co-education is proving a benefit, and I believe is fundamental to the life of the College. Sporting standards and Dramatic productions have been at a high level, and I look forward to the day when musical activities are similarly supported. Above all the College Council members have shown a high degree of responsibility and have justified my confidence in them as young adults rather than as school children.

'I have always said it will take ten years to create the Sixth Form College: five years to start it, and five years to rectify the mistakes. It is a relief that the first year is over, but it is no exaggeration to say that I have drawn more encouragement from the friendliness and support of so many Old Lutonians, both at Club functions and on other occasions. It is my sincere hope that the reorganised and enlarged Old Lutonian Association will start well and be a source of strength to the College.'

Those Who Are Left Grow Old

Twenty-nine members of the Grammar School staff remained at the College after 1966. Many had given long and loyal service to the School. Some were due to retire within a year or two, others preferred working with younger pupils and soon left, a few found teaching girls difficult and even embarrassing, but a number who had spent all their teaching lives in the monastic atmosphere of a boys' school, thrived on the new experience. There is only room to mention a few of them.

Mr A.C. Partridge, as sketched by James Gale.

Albert C. Partridge, 'Birdie', had joined the Modern School in 1929, when he was 20 years old. He had been educated at King Edward VI School, Nuneaton, where he was captain of the 1st XV Rugby team and *Victor Ludorum* in athletics in 1926. Awarded two Scholarships to Birmingham University, he gained a BA (1st Class Honours), and was a member of the University Harriers and Athletics teams. At Luton he joined Messrs Watson and Woodcock in the modern languages Department, becoming Head on Mr Watson's retirement. In 1966 he was the only former LGS Head of Department who was offered security of position beyond his 60th birthday. In spite of having a daughter, and taking parties of girls abroad, he was not happy teaching mixed classes. When it was proposed to make changes in his Department during 1970, with which he did not agree, he hastily submitted his resignation and left at Christmas, refusing any formal farewell from the College. In 1988, his health failing and a widower, he moved to live with his daughter in the French Alps.

Arthur Root, 'Spud', had joined the School to teach Classics in January 1931, when he was 24. Born in 1907, he was a native of Leicestershire, and read Classics at Keble College, Oxford. A keen football supporter, he coached the middle school sides for many years, including the Under 15 team that won the Wix Trophy in 1955. A good-humoured, equable and imperturbable gentleman, he weathered the purge of Mr Gauntlett in 1939, and five years in the Armed Forces. In appearance he seemed to have found the secret of perpetual youth, and was absent through illness for only three days in the whole of his teaching career. He retired in 1967.

Conrad Wynne Parry, 'Harry', was born in December 1914, and educated at Pembroke Dock County Secondary School (1926–32), followed by King's College, London (1932–35) and Reading University (1935–36). He taught at Adelaide College, Ilfracombe and in Swindon, before coming to Luton Modern School in

January 1941. He taught religious education, English and French, but in his earlier days had been called upon to cover history, geography and mathematics. In 1964 he was appointed Careers Master and Director of Studies, and, when the College opened, Head of Boys' Careers. In spite of suffering from chronic asthma, he loved sport: his interests ranging from boxing, football, rugger, athletics and best of all – to cricket. A Cricket Trophy was presented in his name. His Christian ethics were a dominant part of his philosophy, and he was an Elder of St Ninians Presbyterian United Reform Church in Luton.

His Church and the School were Wynne Parry's life. He called himself a 'square', but in no sense was this true. His resilience and vitality lasted until the day he retired, and a thousand Old Boys (and Girls) will remember the quiet astute observation delivered with a twinkle in his eye. In preparing this book, the name of Wynne Parry has occurred more often than any other in correspondence with former pupils, and it has always been with warmth and affection. He was the one member of staff that almost every boy could turn to, if he were in trouble or distress. Michael Freedland has written 'that wonderfully kind man, Mr C.W. Parry – who I can only hope, if there is another world, is enjoying happiness and health there to the full. He told a friend that he hoped we Jewish boys kept to our traditions because we had such a wonderful heritage.' He retired in July 1979, and died suddenly just one year later.

Denis Gallimore, 'Rubber Neck', was born in 1910. He gained his MA at Sheffield University, and Diplomas from the Universities of Poitiers and Rennes. He joined Luton Modern School in September 1941, to teach English and French. He often seemed distant and shy, but he enjoyed most sports, played the piano and violin, was an accomplished ballroom dancer and an authority on Dixieland jazz. J.D. Stephen (1953–60) has written: 'Denis Gallimore taught me French every year up to O-level and his teaching – his meticulous and methodical approach to language, both English and French – provided the grounding for my subsequent studies in languages and for much of my subsequent work. In the United Nations, "drafting" is important, as well, of course, as language skills: and Denis was my mentor. As a teacher he was without parallel.' He retired in 1974, and died in February 1990.

Robert Stanley Giddy, 'Stan', was born in 1908. He attended Devonport High School from 1920–27, and University College, Exeter 1927–30, where he gained his BSc (London). He taught at Sir Josiah Mason's School, Erdington, Birmingham until 1943, when he joined Luton Modern School to teach science, maths and PT. A shy, eccentric and excitable person, 'Stan' was liable to explode in more ways than one (especially when handling phosphorus – year after year)! 'Ye gods and little fishes' was a favourite expletive. Soon after he joined the School it was discovered that he had an inoperable brain tumour. He agreed to pioneering cobalt treatment. Apart from the permanent loss of hair at the side of his head, it proved successful. He was long connected with the Railway and the Film Clubs. Unmarried, the pupils

were his only family. He retired in 1968, suffered a stroke 12 years later, and died in 1989.

Geoffrey Clarke, 'Nobby', joined the School staff in November 1944. Born in 1905, he was educated at Kingswood School, Bath; Westminster Training College and London University, where he studied classics. He taught at the Priory School for Boys in Shrewsbury from 1930 until he came to Luton to teach English. He was a pleasant, friendly and good-natured master, who, being a realist, believed that all boys were pleasant provided you did not ask them to do any work. His interests were wide, including dramatics (one recalls his performance in *Housemaster* in 1950), cricket, cross-country, which he ran for several years, and bridge, which he taught to many boys. He edited the School magazine for some years. He also organised a number of foreign holidays, helped by his wife, Christine Clarke, who was senior mistress at the Technical School. He retired in August 1968, and died following a heart attack in July 1971.

William Newby Thorpe, 'Crumpet' or 'Ned', was born in 1907, and educated at Raines Foundation School, London from 1919–26. He was Head Boy of the school and played in the Rugby 1st XV. He gained his BSc at the London School of Economics, taught briefly in Goole, and then spent 14 years at Truro School (a boys' boarding school). Coming to Luton in 1945, he taught geography and economics, and helped coach soccer, rugby and athletics. He was a fine and caring teacher, though somewhat under the shadow of 'Jock' Cleaver, his Head of Department.

Albert J.G. May, 'Charlie' or 'Daisy', was born in 1907, and educated at Corporation Grammar School, Plymouth (1919–25) where he was Head Boy. He obtained his BA (Hons) in maths at University College, Exeter in 1928. He taught in Derby, Minehead and Isleworth before coming to LGS in 1945. A brilliant teacher (see page 234), he was a senior examiner in GCE for many years. He was a man of few words: but what he did say was always relevant. He did a great deal for School Chess and some of his best players reached County and National Honours: whilst others were to be found at GCHQ, Cheltenham. He retired to the west country in 1967.

Herbert J.C. Bryant, 'Herbie', was the affable Head of Physics. He joined the School in 1945 at the age of 38. He was educated at St Olave's Grammar School in London, and the Royal College of Science where he obtained his BSc and ARCS in 1929. He taught at Bishop Vesey's Grammar School, Sutton Coldfield (1930–44). Geologist, Prof. David Oldroyd has written 'Bryant was a first-rate physics teacher, well organised, well-informed, kind and helpful. In fact he was too good! He made me think I wanted to be a physicist.' A number of Old Boys are convinced that they were accepted at Imperial College, mainly on the strength of his recommendation!

Every post-war Old Boy has memories of Redmond Lane, 'Baffer'. He came to LGS in 1945 when he was 33 years old, with a BA degree from the National University of Ireland. His right arm had been paralysed since birth. His Irish accent

was broad and, to many, incomprehensible. His strict Catholic schooling had given him a dogged determination to keep on teaching, even when it was clear that the whole class was lost. 'He succeeded in making a complicated subject completely unintelligible.' He became unjustifiably a figure of fun, the butt of a thousand stories. *The Lutonian* for 1952 records the monotony of one of his geometry lessons being broken by a squawk. Form 1a, knowing its origin, broke into laughter. 'And what are ye a-lookin' in y'r dask fer, Mandy?' enquired Baffer. 'D'ye t'ink a rabbit's goin' ta pap its h'ad oota de dask?' At the end of the period Mandy tried to remove the culprit into his satchel, but he was caught and had to explain. The answer was a jackdaw, found on the way to School by M.R. Mandy and A.A. Pestell. Many will remember him for the Biscuit or Bun Fund which he ran with the help of the Prefects in order to swell School Funds. For those lucky enough to 'know' him, he had a rich Irish sense of humour, and it was a delight to see him coming to the climax of the narration of a good joke. He resigned from the VIth Form College in 1967, and moved across to Denbigh High School, where he was very unhappy and unsettled. The Grammar School had been his life. He died tragically beneath a bus in Harpenden.

Holland Bowen Evans, 'Major', was born in Corwen, Merionethshire, in 1908. He was educated at Ruthin Public School and Jesus College, Oxford, where he obtained his degree in Modern History in 1930, and was a keen member of the boat club. He was ordained in the Church in Wales, becoming a Curate at Wrexham and tutor to theological students at St Michael's College, Llandaff. During the war he was an Army Chaplain, seeing service in North Africa, Sicily and Italy. He came to Luton Grammar School in 1946 to teach history and some divinity. He succeeded Dr Dony as head of History in 1964. A warm and sincere man, Old Boys will remember his piercing blue eyes. Colin Dawson writes, 'He was a very likeable man with a ginger moustache, who knew his subject, but his tedious style made it extremely difficult to listen to him.' Yet he was enthusiastic for new ideas, and introduced individual history 'projects' long before the Plowden Report made them popular. He encouraged his Form to produce their own plays, and even take the first faltering steps into archaeology. Greatly interested in Rugby football, he coached the under-15 team for many years. In 1973 he retired to Pentraeth on Anglesey, where he died in 1985.

Art master, James Gale, 'Gusty', was born in Newcastle-on-Tyne in 1906, and won a scholarship to Rutherford College. He left in 1923 to work for the Great Northern Telegraph for six years. Obtaining his BA Hons in Fine Arts at Durham University in 1934, he was awarded the Constable Prize for Landscape, and a travelling prize to study art in London. The following year, with a Teaching Diploma, he became art master at Gateshead Secondary School. Being a Quaker and conscientious objector, in 1942 he was dismissed from his post. For the next year he worked as a caretaker at Bootham School, York. From 1943 until the end of the war

he taught art at the Friends' School, Wigton, Cumbria. He became Head of Art at Market Harborough Grammar School from 1945 till 1947, when he moved to LGS, retiring in 1968. 'Gusty' was a delightful man with very strong principles. He had control problems in the classroom, and boys took advantage of his pacifism, knowing that he would not strike them. He was an excellent artist, talented in many aspects of the discipline, and generous to a fault when it came to sharing his time and knowledge. He loved 'inventing', though some of his projects would have done credit to Heath Robinson. He was famous for dropping off to sleep in the staff room at the end of the day, and a tale is told of the caretaker, unaware of his presence, locking him in for the night. He died in 1984.

John A. Muse, 'Pussy', was probably the first master to bring a modern, enlightened approach to physical education at LGS. Born in 1916, he attended Spalding Grammar School from 1936–39, before moving on to Goldsmith's College, where he obtained his Teaching Certificate and PT Diploma. He was on the staff of Highfield Secondary Modern School, Chatham from 1939–48, then served as a Major in the Infantry during the war. He was a lively and enthusiastic sportsman who realised that not everyone found pleasure in physical exertion, yet he managed to persuade even the most reluctant boy that he needed to find some form of exercise to keep himself fit. He seemed to know the rudiments of every sport going, and his expertise was in great demand from numerous organisations at county and national level. How he found time to fit in the hours of team training, circuit training, and athletics coaching during the Easter holidays (with C.J. Godfrey) perhaps only his family could tell. In 1967 he became PE Adviser to Luton, and in 1974 Adviser for Bedfordshire.

Donald E. Sutcliffe joined the English department in 1951. After military service he had graduated at Southampton University. He was an enthusiastic and lively teacher, with a strong interest in drama. He retired due to ill health in 1969.

Thomas Russell Key was born at Church Farm in the village of Newnham, Northamptonshire, in 1907. As a boy he attended Daventry Grammar School, proceeding to Reading University to read English, obtaining his BA in 1931 and MA (externally) in 1935. He taught at Leigh Grammar School, Lancashire (1931–35), and Burnley Grammar School from 1936 to 1952. During the war he was an Education Officer in the RAF. As Head of English at LGS he was much involved in drama, and loved anything to do with books. Jeffrey Greenleaf has spoken of the 'occasion of pure magic when he read us "Reynard the Fox" by John Masefield, and had our Vth form class utterly spellbound for a full and memorable lesson.' He was fascinated by archaeology. 'I will come and dig for you,' he would say. He would arrive, lean on a shovel for an hour or two, and then decide that it was time he was off on some other project. He loved local history and produced *Flitwick, A Short History* in 1973. After his retirement in 1968, he returned to Newnham, where he became engrossed in tracing the medieval parish boundaries. In his latter years he

lost his sight, a dreadful affliction for one who loved reading, and he died in 1989.

John Lovell, 'Shovel', joined the School in 1954 to teach biology. An old boy of Knaresborough Grammar School, he graduated at Leeds University in botany, and won his university colours for hockey. He taught Biology at Darlington and Fakenham Grammar Schools, before coming to LGS. A competent and dedicated teacher, whose department grew to be the largest in the College, after English and mathematics. The Natural History Society flourished under his guidance. He retired in 1977, and died in December 2000.

Music in the School was revitalised in 1956 when Adolph Covel Hauke, 'Harry', joined the staff. Born in 1920, he had attended Grammar Schools in Willesden and Bec between 1932 and 1937. After various 'clerical' jobs, he was a Flight Sergeant in the RAF until 1947. He then trained for three years at the Royal Academy of Music, becoming a silver medalist. A very popular master, he persuaded many reluctant schoolboys that they could enjoy music, and had something to offer to the choir or orchestra. Although he retired from the College in 1981, he continued to work for a further ten years at the Arts Education School at Tring, providing music for ballet classes. He is still active in 2004.

Mr Dance wrote: 'Arthur Eric Bowen ['Hank'] was not an orthodox schoolmaster, though always pleasant and co-operative. His real interest was his pupils.' He tried to share with them his many pursuits, such as numismatics, archaeology, art and literature. Born in 1916, he had attended the County School for Boys, Bromley (where he was taught by Dr J.A. Corbett, Luton's Director of Education). He graduated in Modern Languages at King's College, London, and held the Diplôme aux Études Supérieures. At LGS he coached the cross-country teams. In 1966 he became lecturer in English at the Dunstable College of Further Education. He died eleven years later when his bungalow at Aley Green burnt down.

One person who served the School and College longer than any other was Miss Olga Peters, who joined the Office as Assistant Secretary in 1943, when she was 18, and became Headmaster's Secretary in 1949 in succession to Miss Dorothy Baxter. She weathered the transfer to the Sixth Form College, retiring in 1988 as College Bursar. Her working life was devoted to the School and also to the Girl Guide Movement, where she was an adviser on the organisation of Guide camps, and could demonstrate her fascination for natural history. She died in March 1996, aged 71.

Envoy

The life of the Luton Modern and Grammar Schools spanned only sixty-two years, yet during that time some 7,102 pupils passed through the portals – from the first, A.E. Parry in 1904, to the last recorded in the School List, P. Zakis in 1965. During that time they were taught by 250 full-time teachers.

Some of the earliest students spent only one or two years at Park Square, but from

1906 E. BUCKINGHAM. ALLEN ENGINEERING SCHOLARSHIP.
1910 A.T. REEVE. ROYAL SCHOLARSHIP, IMPERIAL COLLEGE, LONDON.
1913 F. M. LEIGHTON. OPEN SCHOLARSHIP, SELWYN COLLEGE, CAMBRIDGE.
OPEN SCHOLARSHIP, TRINITY HALL, CAMBRIDGE.
1914 C. J. NIXON. MITCHELL SCHOLARSHIP, CITY AND GUILDS TECHNICAL COLLEGE FINSBURY.
1920 S. J. GREGG. STATE SCHOLARSHIP, IMPERIAL COLLEGE, LONDON.
1921 T. S. SKILLMAN. STATE SCHOLARSHIP.
OPEN SCHOLARSHIP, CLARE COLLEGE, CAMBRIDGE.
A. CARESS. OPEN SCHOLARSHIP, TRINITY HALL, CAMBRIDGE.
1922 A. CARESS. STATE SCHOLARSHIP.
1923 R. F. J. BROWN. MARMADUKE LEVETT SCHOLARSHIP, SELWYN COLLEGE, CAMBRIDGE.
1925 H. R. BARNELL. TATE SCHOLARSHIP, DOWNING COLLEGE, CAMBRIDGE.
W. H. WHEELER. OPEN EXHIBITION, EAST LONDON COLLEGE.
OPEN SCHOLARSHIP, ST. CATHERINES COLLEGE, CAMBRIDGE.
STATE SCHOLARSHIP.
L. E. PROSSER. OPEN SCHOLARSHIP, KINGS COLLEGE, LONDON.
1927 W. G. WREN. ENTRANCE SCHOLARSHIP, IMPERIAL COLLEGE, LONDON.
1928 E. H. T. HOBLYN. ENTRANCE SCHOLARSHIP, IMPERIAL COLLEGE, LONDON.
1930 J. H. BURGOYNE. ENTRANCE SCHOLARSHIP, IMPERIAL COLLEGE, LONDON.
1933 H. E. W. CHALKLEY. ENTRANCE SCHOLARSHIP, IMPERIAL COLLEGE, LONDON.
1934 E. R. ROBERTS. ENTRANCE SCHOLARSHIP, IMPERIAL COLLEGE, LONDON.
ROYAL STUDENTSHIP, IMPERIAL COLLEGE, LONDON.
E. J. WHITMORE. ENTRANCE SCHOLARSHIP, IMPERIAL COLLEGE, LONDON.
ROYAL SCHOLARSHIP, IMPERIAL COLLEGE, LONDON.
STATE SCHOLARSHIP.
1935 I. E. TWEEDIE. ENTRANCE SCHOLARSHIP, IMPERIAL COLLEGE, LONDON.
1936 I. E. TWEEDIE. ROYAL SCHOLARSHIP, IMPERIAL COLLEGE, LONDON.
STATE SCHOLARSHIP.
1937 R. D. KITCHENER. ROYAL STUDENTSHIP, IMPERIAL COLLEGE, LONDON.
1938 M. HOLDSWORTH. ROYAL SCHOLARSHIP, IMPERIAL COLLEGE, LONDON.
1941 J. H. S. KENT. STATE SCHOLARSHIP, EMMANUEL COLLEGE, CAMBRIDGE.
A. R. EMERY. OPEN EXHIBITION, UNIVERSITY COLLEGE, HULL.
STATE BURSARY, KINGS COLLEGE, LONDON.
G. A. EMERY. STATE BURSARY, CITY AND GUILDS COLLEGE, LONDON.
P. R. FRANKS. OPEN EXHIBITION, UNIVERSITY COLLEGE, HULL.
1942 P. R. FRANKS. OPEN EXHIBITION, EMMANUEL COLLEGE, CAMBRIDGE.
STATE BURSARY.
D. L. BUTTRICK. STATE BURSARY, REGENT ST. POLYTECHNIC, LONDON.
B. H. LEWIN. STATE BURSARY, REGENT ST. POLYTECHNIC, LONDON.
D. J. R. LAURENCE. OPEN SCHOLARSHIP, UNIVERSITY COLLEGE, HULL.
STATE SCHOLARSHIP.
STATE BURSARY, GONVILLE AND CAIUS COLLEGE, CAMBRIDGE.
D. PAYNE. OPEN SCHOLARSHIP, UNIVERSITY COLLEGE, HULL.

1942 D. PAYNE. STATE BURSARY, KING'S COLLEGE, CAMBRIDGE.
M. V. W. CHOTE. OPEN EXHIBITION, EMMANUEL COLLEGE, CAMBRIDGE.
G. D. NICHOLLS. OPEN SCHOLARSHIP, TRINITY COLLEGE, CAMBRIDGE.
P. S. J. ADKINS. OPEN ATHLETICS SCHOLARSHIP, LOUGHBOROUGH COLLEGE.
1943 D. A. BAGE. STATE BURSARY, QUEEN MARY COLLEGE, LONDON.
K. W. GLADMAN. STATE BURSARY, QUEEN MARY COLLEGE, LONDON.
G. D. NICHOLLS. STATE SCHOLARSHIP.
B. VERDCOURT. STATE BURSARY, READING UNIVERSITY.
F. H. MEAD. ENGINEERING CADETSHIP, BIRMINGHAM TECHNICAL COLLEGE.
1944 M. J. BARBER. STATE BURSARY.
N. V. SMITH. STATE BURSARY, CITY AND GUILDS COLLEGE, LONDON.
1945 M. J. BARBER. ROYAL DUTCH-SHELL SCHOLARSHIP IN GEOLOGY, IMPERIAL COLLEGE, LONDON.
W. B. STRANG. OPEN SCHOLARSHIP, TRINITY HALL, CAMBRIDGE.
G. S. HAWKES. STATE BURSARY, IMPERIAL COLLEGE, LONDON.
B. R. LAURENCE. OPEN EXHIBITION, GONVILLE AND CAIUS COLLEGE, CAMBRIDGE.
P. D. SOUTHGATE. ROYAL SCHOLARSHIP, IMPERIAL COLLEGE, LONDON.
STATE SCHOLARSHIP.
1946 P. J. D. GETHING. ROYAL SCHOLARSHIP, IMPERIAL COLLEGE, LONDON.
STATE SCHOLARSHIP.
B. R. LAURENCE. OPEN EXHIBITION, GONVILLE AND CAIUS COLLEGE, CAMBRIDGE.
STATE SCHOLARSHIP, UNIVERSITY COLLEGE, LONDON.
R. J. SALES. OPEN EXHIBITION, KING'S COLLEGE, CAMBRIDGE.
W. B. STRANG. OPEN SCHOLARSHIP, QUEEN'S COLLEGE, OXFORD.
STATE SCHOLARSHIP.
A. F. TRENDALL. ROYAL SCHOLARSHIP, IMPERIAL COLLEGE, LONDON.
LONDON INTER-COLLEGIATE OPEN SCHOLARSHIP, KING'S COLLEGE, LONDON.
1947 D. C. PRICE. STATE SCHOLARSHIP.
1948 D. C. PRICE. STATE SCHOLARSHIP.
ROYAL SCHOLARSHIP, IMPERIAL COLLEGE, LONDON.
D. G. GRAY. ROYAL SCHOLARSHIP, IMPERIAL COLLEGE, LONDON.
D. V. MARDLE. STATE SCHOLARSHIP, CHRISTS COLLEGE, CAMBRIDGE.
ROYAL STUDENTSHIP.
G. B. HENSON. STATE SCHOLARSHIP, LIVERPOOL UNIVERSITY.
P. D. TOWNSEND. OPEN EXHIBITION, TRINITY COLLEGE, CAMBRIDGE.
1949 D. J. ATKINSON. ROYAL DUTCH-SHELL SCHOLARSHIP IN GEOLOGY, IMPERIAL COLLEGE, LONDON.
1950 M. J. MITCHELL. STATE SCHOLARSHIP, IMPERIAL COLLEGE, LONDON.
J. H. TOWLE. STATE SCHOLARSHIP, IMPERIAL COLLEGE, LONDON.
1951 R. L. CHAMBERS. OPEN RUSSELL SCHOLARSHIP UNIVERSITY OF ST. ANDREWS.
STATE SCHOLARSHIP.
J. M. HOPKINS. STATE SCHOLARSHIP, UNIVERSITY OF WALES.
P. L. ISHERWOOD. OPEN ORGAN SCHOLARSHIP SELWYN COLLEGE CAMBRIDGE. (STATE SCHOLARSHIP)

1951 J. LAWRENCE. STATE SCHOLARSHIP, QUEENS' COLLEGE, CAMBRIDGE.
B. PITKIN. ENTRANCE EXHIBITION IMPERIAL COLLEGE, LONDON. (STATE SCHOLARSHIP.)
1952 A. GOLDING. STATE SCHOLARSHIP, UNIVERSITY COLLEGE, LONDON.
D. F. STURMAN. STATE SCHOLARSHIP, PEMBROKE COLLEGE, OXFORD.
1953 G. A. CARTER. STATE SCHOLARSHIP, READING UNIVERSITY.
C. A. JOHNSON. STATE SCHOLARSHIP.
A. J. MILLER. STATE SCHOLARSHIP, MANCHESTER UNIVERSITY.
P. ROBINSON. STATE SCHOLARSHIP, NOTTINGHAM UNIVERSITY.
P. R. VAUGHAN. STATE SCHOLARSHIP, IMPERIAL COLLEGE, LONDON.
C. A. JOHNSON. OPEN SCHOLARSHIP, PEMBROKE COLLEGE, CAMBRIDGE.
F. R. D. GOODYEAR. OPEN SCHOLARSHIP, ST. JOHN'S COLLEGE, CAMBRIDGE.
1954 D. C. GLOVER. STATE SCHOLARSHIP, LONDON SCHOOL OF ECONOMICS.
F. R. D. GOODYEAR. STATE SCHOLARSHIP, ST. JOHN'S COLLEGE, CAMBRIDGE.
1955 D. G. BOND. STATE SCHOLARSHIP, IMPERIAL COLLEGE, LONDON.
1956 M. W. ROOT. STATE SCHOLARSHIP, IMPERIAL COLLEGE, LONDON.
C. J. WEBB. STATE SCHOLARSHIP, MANCHESTER UNIVERSITY.
M. C. JOHNSON. STATE SCHOLARSHIP, BIRMINGHAM UNIVERSITY.
1957 J. W. BRYANT. STATE SCHOLARSHIP, IMPERIAL COLLEGE, LONDON.
T. B. TAYLOR. STATE SCHOLARSHIP, IMPERIAL COLLEGE, LONDON.
1958 A. LIVINGSTON. STATE SCHOLARSHIP, ROYAL VETERINARY COLLEGE, LONDON.
D. J. WAGON. STATE SCHOLARSHIP, GONVILLE AND CAIUS COLLEGE, CAMBRIDGE.
1959 D. R. GRANT. SIR JOHN GOSS ORGAN SCHOLARSHIP, ROYAL ACADEMY OF MUSIC.
J. R. GREENLEAF. STATE SCHOLARSHIP, IMPERIAL COLLEGE, LONDON.
C. J. HUMPHREYS. STATE SCHOLARSHIP, IMPERIAL COLLEGE, LONDON.
R. F. MATTHEWS. STATE SCHOLARSHIP, BRASENOSE COLLEGE, OXFORD.
D. R. A. MOWSE. STATE SCHOLARSHIP, MANCHESTER UNIVERSITY.
1960 J. D. STEPHEN. STATE SCHOLARSHIP, KING'S COLLEGE, CAMBRIDGE.
B. A. ALLSOPP. STATE SCHOLARSHIP, IMPERIAL COLLEGE, LONDON.
1961 C. J. D. ADAMS. STATE SCHOLARSHIP, QUEEN MARY COLLEGE, LONDON.
D. J. BLYTHIN. STATE SCHOLARSHIP, IMPERIAL COLLEGE, LONDON.
J. M. CHAPMAN. STATE SCHOLARSHIP, IMPERIAL COLLEGE, LONDON.
R. WESTERMAN. STATE SCHOLARSHIP, TRINITY COLLEGE, CAMBRIDGE.
P. J. ORME. ORGAN SCHOLARSHIP, SIDNEY SUSSEX COLLEGE, CAMBRIDGE.
1962 K. C. BOWLER. STATE SCHOLARSHIP.
ENTRANCE SCHOLARSHIP, IMPERIAL COLLEGE, LONDON.
R. P. WHYMANT. STATE SCHOLARSHIP.
OPEN SCHOLARSHIP, MAGDALENE COLLEGE, CAMBRIDGE.
1963 R. J. LOWIN. ENTRANCE SCHOLARSHIP, IMPERIAL COLLEGE, LONDON.
T. L. ROGERS. ENTRANCE SCHOLARSHIP, IMPERIAL COLLEGE, LONDON.
M. K. AYERS. EXHIBITION, SIDNEY SUSSEX COLLEGE, CAMBRIDGE.
1964 S. C. GREGORY. OPEN EXHIBITION, MAGDALENE COLLEGE, CAMBRIDGE.
1965 A. M. SUSMAN. OPEN EXHIBITION, TRINITY HALL, CAMBRIDGE.

The School Honours Board stood outside the Assemble Hall. Its original white plastic letters were later replaced by smaller painted lettering when it appeared to be getting too full. The Board was 'wiped clean' in 1985. (*Beds.C.C. Photographic Unit*)

the 1950s, eight or nine years was not unusual. For the first thirty years most of the pupils were fee-paying, although there was always a small percentage of scholarship winners. This meant that initially the majority came from middle class homes that had some understanding of academic standards. The scholarships enabled the more able children, irrespective of background, to enjoy a more challenging higher education.

The 1944 Education Act abolished school fees (in 1945); text books and equipment were provided free of charge, and LEAs gave financial help for families unable to afford uniforms, meals or transport.

The Luton Modern and Grammar Schools provided boys with systematic preparation for university, technical, and a wide range of commercial occupations, at the same time setting a high standard of personal and civic responsibility. As well as work, out of school activities opened up a vast spectrum of sport and leisure pursuits, including dramatics, public speaking and debate, singing and music. Boys were introduced to foreign travel, pen-friends and exchange visits. The school was a busy place for those willing to take advantage of it. Family circumstances, the need to earn a living, or simply boredom with learning, necessitated many boys leaving at the end of year five. For those who were privileged to stay longer, the rewards could be abundant. Small VIth Form groups with an enthusiastic master, enjoyed a special learning relationship, that was impossible in a class of thirty. It was there that the seeds of many future careers were undoubtedly sewn.

It was not just the building, but the people in it, that made the School. The first students in the old hat factory at Park Square were just as enthusiastic as those who moved to Bradgers Hill in 1938, or left on the last day in July 1966. They each carried with them a tradition, a sense of belonging to something that had grown so big that it embraced the world. It wasn't Eton or Harrow, and had never intended to be, but it had prepared each of them to follow their chosen careers, and to make of them what they would. Out of 7,000 Old Boys, only a handful have been mentioned in this book, and the writer is conscious that many men, outstanding in their chosen fields, have gone unrecorded. Old Lutonians have played their part in industry, commerce, science, the Military Services, education, the Church, entertainment, and a hundred other disciplines. *Ubi semen, ibi messis.*

The Old Lutonians' Club no longer exists, except in the hearts of many. Former members still meet to play golf or bridge, and they play rugby, but not as the Old Lutonians. The Masonic Lodge meets five times a year, but is now 'open', accepting non-Old Boys. Around the world, small, ever diminishing groups of Old Lutonians meet each year for a drink and a chat, where they can remember Finny, Froggy, Piggy, Wynne Parry and KBW, and tell stories of the unbeaten 1942 Cricket team, N.J. Pugh's javelin throw of 1960, balloons floating out of the organ chamber during morning assembly, Cyril Somers singing Schubert's *Heidenröslein*, and Tony Router's rousing rendition of *Lucy Long*.

Luton Modern School
ROLL OF HONOUR

1914–1918

George Hine Adcock
Ernest Allin
Archibald Christopher Allwood
Hedley Angel
Charles Thomas Barnard
Ernest Isaac Barrow
Harry Berry
Arthur William Biggs
William George Bowles
Thomas Victor Brown
Charles Frederick Burley
Sydney Ewart Cannon
Horace George Dunham
Richard Cyril Eads

Augustus Fensome
Reginald Thomas Franklin
Johnson Julian Harris
Arthur Haworth
John Hayden Healey
Arthur Haddon Hill
Gilbert Horsler
Thomas Huffington
Harold David Joad
Daniel William Juett
James Herbert Reginald Lendrum
Arthur Jesse Little
Arthur Thomas Mahon
Leonard Arthur Maynard

Herbert George Merchant
Robert Charles Morsley
Cyril John Nixon
Aubrey Julian Pearce
Frederick Lewis Pedley
Charles Leslie Pyne
Frank Cowper Rimmer
George David Smith
Joseph Smith
Eric William Squires
Sidney Charles Squires
Reginald Sydney Strange
Ronald William Tearle
Thomas Coates Johnson Wing

1939–1945

Jack Anstee
Maurice William Bagnall
Maurice Edgar Barker
Rex Beales
Ivan Ronald Briden
Victor Roque Bussereau
Anthony Richard Cain
Rex Canham
Edward George Carter
Douglas George Champkin
Howard Arthur Cherry
Brian Edward Clarke
Thomas Plato Clark
James Emerton Cooper
Jack Colin Crabtree
Richard Fulton Cunningham
Dennis Sydney Depledge
Kenneth Drage
Edward Francis Edwin
George Herbert Farr
Vernon Clifford Farr
Norman James Ficken
Ronald Renshaw Flint
Derek Noel Flitton

William Maurice Gibson
John Antony Goodwin
Paul John Betts Gosling
Ralph Halliwell
Denis Farmbrough Hawkes
Raith John Cable Hazleton
Richard Dockrill Hill
Frederick William Hobbs
Rex Alec Holmes
Frank Lewis Thomas Ireson
Francis Charles Jackson
William Douglas James
Clifford Lloyd Brown Janes
Edward Douglas Jenkins
Ernest Arthur Kingham
Alfred Peter Charles Kuster
James Lawrence
John Sydney McGeorge
Philip Alfred Neville
Aubrey Ernest Owles
George Sharman Painting
Eric Horace Parrott
Frederick James Randall
Maurice Dean Randall

Derrick Sydney James Richards
Joseph George Richardson
Stewart George Sale
Peter Sears
Maurice Silver
Edgar Gordon Smith
Douglas Philip Swain
Raymond John Tearle
Philip Edgar Thomas
Eric Frank Underhill
Alan Ernest Underwood
Edward Upton
Robert Claude Verran
Eric Gordon Waller
Douglas Henry Weedon
Jack William Weedon
Ronald Horace Welch
Richard Strickland Westrope
George Robert White
Philip Edward Whiting
John Raymond Williams
Ronald George Woodfield

Select Index

A

Acton, Mr R.S., 338, 348, 367, 420
Acts, Education, 2, 3, 216, 229, 230, 429
Adams, N., 209
Adkins, P.S.J., 193, 195, 200
Air Raids, shelters, etc., 149, 150, 156, 179–80, 181, 252
Airship R101, 59, 82, 87
Air Training Corps, 218, 226
Alderman, C.B., 214, 225
Aldred, P.N., 209
Aldridge, I.S., 335
Allen, A.B., 28, 49, 77, 80, 104–5, 161–2, 279, 419
Allen, F.C., 291
Allin, E., 54, 63
Allotments, 30, 36, 180
Allsopp, B.A., 345, 348
American Field Scholarships, 304, 317, 371, 385
Anderson, M.L. 320
Anstee, J., 207
Anti-Semitism, 222–3
Any Questions? 302, 319, 355, 377, 386
Apprenticeships, 309
Apps, J., 349
Archaeological Society, 269, 277, 278, 286, 298, 304, 328, 338, 344, 364, 391
Ark, The, 25, 32
Arnold, Ald. H., 22, 32, 78, 122, 143, 147, 153, 163–6, 187
Arthur, Mr I.W., 372, 381, 401
Ashby, R., 265
Ashworth, Mr J., 244, 284, 327
Athletics, 41–2, 87–8, 113–4, 123–6, 184–5, 215, 260, 270, 274, 282, 289, 299, 302–3, 315–6, 323–4, 335, 343, 349–50, 356, 362, 375, 388, 400–1
Atkinson, D.J. 254, 267, 297, 392
Austin, William, 98

B

Badge, 14, 17–18, 76, 93
Bagnall, M.W., 202
Bailey, R.S., 318
Baines, Mr H.E., 148, 165
Ball, Willet, 354

Barber, M.J., 212, 230, 236, 267, 392
Barford, Ald. M., 93, 98, 133
Barker, Mr D.G., 298, 339, 352, 358
Barker, R.J.H., 322, 324
Barraclough, G.W., 314, 337, 355, 358
Barrett, J.W.V., 300
Barrow, Mr E.I., 36, 52–3
Barter, Mr R.H.,358, 391, 416
Bartlett, Sir C.J., 129, 195
Basketball, 271, 280, 330, 342, 356, 362
Batchelor, K., 265
Bateman, D.W.E., 237, 243, 250
Bates, Ald. F.W., 105, 320, 383, 403, 405
Baxter, A.R.W., 395
Baxter, Miss Dorothy, 258
Bazaar, Hobbies Exhibitions, 318, 325, 352, 359, 367, 381, 394
Bazley, D.E., 341–2. 365, 374
Beales, R., 202
Beaumont, J.R., 214, 224
Bedford, Duke, Duchess of, 4, 22, 32, 333
Bedford Modern School, 57, 104, 125, 155, 224, 240, 249, 253–4, 329, 335, 363–4, 378
Bedfordshire A.A.A.,123–5, 194, 215, 224, 240, 253, 259, 270, 290, 299, 303, 316, 323, 350, 363, 400
Bedfordshire Education Committee, 372
Bell, E.G., 209
Bennett, Mr A.S., 419
Bennett, C.C., 9, 25, 65
Berry, H., 55
Bevis, J., 349
Bicycles, sheds, etc., 12, 150
Billington, W.J., 209
Biology Club, 235, 240, 248
Birchmore, R.B., 208
Blackbourn, M., 324, 329
Blackshaw, M.F., 335, 336, 342, 345
Bland, M.J., 302, 316
Bland, Valerie, 300, 307, 319
Blythin, D.J., 354
Bombs, 178, 181, 228
Bond, D.G., 302, 314

Bond, G.L., 9, 40, 65, 279
Bonner, P.R., 359, 366, 385
Booth, J.G., 302, 316, 323, 329, 336
Boston, R., 290, 297
Boult, N.R., 387, 390, 400
Bourlet, Mr A.F., 77, 79, 80, 160
Bowen, Mr A.E., 314, 323, 328, 427
Bowler, K.C., 360
Bowles, Ald. L.G., 295, 361, 368
Boxing, 228, 259, 265, 283, 318
Bracey, D.J., 300, 315, 323
Bracey, M.J., 270, 300
Bradgers Hill, 122, 147ff
Brains Trust, 195, 217, 277, 295, 319, 391, 394
Bray, C., 84
Breed, Nellie, 9, 35, 63
Bridger, Mr R.P., 178, 185, 187, 224, 233, 235, 243, 250, 252, 309, 393
Brightman, B.G., 258
Brightman, H.G., 105, 243
Britannia Engineering, 220
B.B.C., 192, 252, 262, 274, 280, 335, 384
Britten, J.H., 387, 395
Brodie, I.E., 272–3
Brown, D., 375, 401
Brown, Miss G., 271, 277, 283, 290, 311, 319, 339, 353, 367
Brown, G.C., 371–2
Brown, J.E., 362, 363, 374–5, 381
Brown, L.A., 96, 242
Brown, M., 385
Brush Brigade, 214, 220
Bryant, Mr H.J., 234, 387, 392, 393, 399, 424
Buckingham, F., 9, 19, 62, 66, 293
Bullying, 310
Burgin, Dr E.L., MP., 129, 195, 212, 217
Burglaries, 19, 287
Burgoyne, J.H. 'Jack', 81, 96, 105, 256–7, 359, 380
Burgoyne, Sir J., 105, 148, 153, 181, 182, 192, 241, 243, 292, 295,313, 346, 351, 354, 361, 365, 367, 374, 387, 409
Burrows, D.I., 217, 229, 236, 243, 251, 252, 277, 371

Burrows, D.J., 341, 349, 355, 361, 371
Bus services, 150
Busserau, D.F.R., 82
Busserau, E.V.R., 82, 202
Butcher, Gretchen, 254, 264
Butcher, M.E., 320
Button, L.W. 104, 366

C

Cadet Corps, 57–9, 75, 187–8, 205, 212, 218, 226, 234, 300, 301, 365
Cain, A.R., 203
Caldecourt, E.C., 277
Callum, E., 341
Camera Club, 112, 119, 133
Cameron, S., 253
Careers Masters, 165, 168, 189, 313, 314, 368
Caress, A., 95, 354, 394
Caretakers, 19, 32, 102, 142, 358
Carol Services, 180, 284, 311, 326, 331, 339, 346, 353, 360, 367, 384, 420
Carr, J.E., 142, 153, 155
Carter, G.A., 296
Carter I.R., 360
Cassel, Sir Felix, 129
Cator, Mr A.R., 366, 367, 374
Cedars School, 85, 90
Chalkley, H.E.W., 96, 103, 250, 300
Chambers, S.R., 377
Champkin, A.M., 350
Champkin, D.G., 141, 207
Chapman, Joanna, 326
Chapman, Mr W.H., 198, 224, 228, 234, 249, 259, 289, 301
Charitable Trusts, 2, 10, 72
Charities, 59–60, 132, 185, 215, 230, 340, 361, 367, 420
Charlesworth, Dr S., 399, 403
Chaul End, 83, 86, 97, 121–3, 337
Chennells, E.J., 99, 104
Cherry, H.A., 208
Chess Club, 113, 240, 248, 252, 268, 282, 338, 344, 352, 364
Childs, Mary, 366
Choir, 112–3, 187, 190, 192, 197, 218, 241, 321, 331, 337,339, 341, 353, 355–6, 359, 366, 374, 381
Chote, M.V.W., 125, 155, 158,

181, 184, 185, 193, 195, 197, 200, 215, 253, 279, 343, 379, 398, 419
Ciantar, G., 343, 345
Cinema, *see* Films,
Clark, B.A., 270, 274
Clark, B.E., 337, 341
Clark, Mr T.P.,79, 172, 179, 205, 266, 288
Clarke, B.E., 207
Clarke, Mr G., 227, 261, 268, 280, 314, 318, 321, 330, 344, 424
Clarke, P., 363
Clayton, Mr R.S., 12, 28, 40, 42–3, 47, 53, 72, 165, 167, 168, 174, 198, 216, 244, 293, 310, 312, 313, 380, 393
Cleaver, Mr J.A., 79, 100–101, 172, 190, 205, 267, 294, 330, 371, 392, 395
Clemitson, I.M., 366
Clifford, J., 270
Clubs, small societies, 113, 160, 217, 248, 268, 304, 377
Clydesdale, S.P., 401
Coeshall, S.J., 345, 356, 362, 363
Coleman, P., 329
Colley, A., 419
Collier, J.G., 285
Colours, school, 123, 191, 260, 299
Commonwealth Games, 400
Competitions, 49–50, 191, 217, 220, 351
Comprehensive Schools, 373, 383, 386
Computers, 405
Concerts, 46–8, 185, 218, 219, 235, 252, 260, 321, 326, 331, 337, 339, 341, 348, 353, 355, 359, 365, 374, 381, 387, 402
Connell, R.J., 95
Conquest, D.K.W., 291
Cooke, Mr B.J., 79, 160, 164–5, 174, 218, 234
Cooper, D.F., 315, 323
Cooper, I.M., 306
Cooper, J.E., 203
Cooper, P.G., Cup, 280, 362
Corbett, Dr J.A.; Plan, 105, 294, 314, 372–3, 399, 420
Cornes G.E., 206, 209
Coronations, 46, 47, 284
Cosgrove, J.A., 358

Cowlard, P.J., 414
Cox, D., 279
Cox, R., 350, 356
Crabtree, J.C., 193, 195, 208, 214
Cranwell, Mr E.C., 351, 359
Crapnell, Mr G.N., 390, 414
Cricket, 41, 84, 123, 158, 184, 193, 214, 224, 233, 238, 249, 253, 260, 270, 275, 283, 290, 300, 302, 316, 324, 330, 336, 343, 350, 356, 363, 365, 375, 381, 389, 392, 401
Cricket table, 41, 180, 258
Crime, 19, 102, 240, 287
Crooke, S., 415
Crosbie, Avril, 282, 286
Cross-Country, 42–3, 193, 214, 224, 249, 253, 259, 269, 282, 298–9, 302, 315, 323, 329, 335, 349, 362, 374–5, 388,. 400
Crouch T., 375, 384, 387, 389
Croxford, Eileen, 261
Cundick, A.G., 289, 298
Cunningham, J.D., 320
Cunningham, R.F., 203
Cups, trophies, 103, 128, 155, 184–5, 193, 224, 259, 303, 363, 375, 401
Cycle proficiency, 300, 326
Czapiewski, C.H., 358

D

Dade, R.W., 343
Dalrymple, J., 113, 124, 233, 253
Dalrymple, M.J.W., 113, 253
Dance, Mr B.D., 403, 413, 417, 420, 421
Davie, P.G., 401
Davies, A.C., 318
Davies, A.E., 192, 219, 251
Davis, C.C., 355
Davison, Rev. W., 148, 348
Dawson, C.E., 425
Dawson, Mr L., 111, 113, 154, 250
Dawson, M.E., 290
Day, D.W., 300
Day, G.C., 356, 362–3, 374–5
Day, R., 302, 315, 322, 329
Death of pupils, 45, 127–8, 131, 234, 261, 265, 280, 330, 358
de la Mare, Walter, 115
Depledge, D.S., 205
Detentions, *see* Discipline,

Devey, R.W., 290, 298

Dickens, W.J., 302, 316, 330

Dillingham, R., 88

Dinners, school, 25, 75, 180, 255, 391

Discipline, 17, 46, 76–7, 160, 175, 178

Dolden, R., 288, 290, 297

Dony, Dr J.G., 10, 98, 179, 190, 198–9, 229, 237, 277, 294, 298, 322, 344–5, 352, 372, 376, 380

Doodson, J.K. 282, 288, 290, 298,

Drama, 47–8, 112, 114, 118–9 153–4, 186–7, 197, 219, 225, 230, 236, 247, 249, 252, 254–5, 263–4, 268, 271–2, 277, 283, 287–8, 290, 295, 297, 300–1, 305–7, 311, 315, 319, 320, 325–6, 328, 331, 339, 340–1, 345, 348, 352–3, 355–6, 359, 366, 377, 385, 394–5, 406, 420

Drill, *see* Physical Training

Duncan A.J., 339, 363, 375, 390

Dunnington, C.V., 401

Dunnington, G., 401

Dunstable Grammar School, 23, 37–8, 40, 333, 343, 351, 295, 419

Dyer J.F., 199, 252, 264, 283, 344, 364

Dyson, Sir F., 94

E

Eade, R.E., 377

Eames, C.K., 349

Earle, D.C., 190

Easton, R.C., 323

Eden, G.P., 415

Edmunds, Mr E.W., 8, 30, 33, 43, 65

Edwards, W.N., 282, 289

Edwin, E.F., 202

Elections, Mock, 100, 228

Electrolux, 197, 224

Elliot, Mrs, 125

Ellis, E.S., 208

Ellis, Mr R.H., 321, 330

Emery, A.R., 113, 184, 189

Emery, G.A., 113, 189

Emigration, 63–4, 72, 100, 273

Empire Games, 87

Employment, 129, 169, 192–3,

220, 284, 304, 307–8, 361

Ennals, Mr D., 328

Enticknapp, E., 102

Epidemics, 324, 332

Ernle, Lord, *see* Prothero,

Etiquette, 92, 361–2

Evacuation, 156, 158, 230

Evans, A.A.G., 270

Evans, A.J., 300, 302, 316

Evans, Mrs Eileen, 105, 250, 255, 284, 394

Evans, Mr H.B., 241, 262, 289, 372, 385, 414, 425

Evans, S.A., 384, 387

Evans, W.P., 315, 322, 329, 330, 351, 362, 387–8

Evening classes, Institute, 8

Examinations, 15, 18, 53, 111, 211, 230, 276, 307, 332, 347, 370

Exam successes, 62–3, 95–6, 129–31, 143–4, 156, 169, 184, 189, 199–200, 219, 230, 236, 246–7, 251, 258, 267, 273–4, 280, 296–7, 304, 314, 320, 328, 333, 340, 348, 354, 360, 370, 385, 396, 428

Expeditions, exploration, 60, 249, 254, 285, 371, 392, 396

Extra-curricular activities, 98– 100

F

Facer, F., 39, 40–3, 48, 52

Fair and Fête, 238, 239, 247, 252

Farm work, 192, 213, 240, 290, 318

Farr, D.L., 148–9, 158, 190, 192, 198, 244–5, 247, 287, 313, 341

Farr, G.H., 202

Faunch, S., 209

Fees, admission, 9, 29, 75–6, 90, 169, 227

Fensome, D.B., 212, 216, 222, 224, 233, 235

Ficken, N.J., 204

Field Club, 113, 119, 156, 190

Film Club, 119, 235

Films, 100, 252, 264, 267, 284, 286, 311, 315, 319, 326, 331, 341

Findlater, Mr J.W., 30, 80–81, 90, 99, 119, 135, 161, 171–2, 228, 241, 266

Finlay, Mr S., 179, 222, 234

Firewatching, 181

Fisher, H.A.L., 70

Fisher, Mr H.A.L., 70

Fletcher, G.W., 348

Flint, R.R., 117, 129, 130, 134, 135, 204–5, 228

Flitton, T.C., 316, 323, 324, 328, 329, 358

Football, 37–40, 65, 86, 127, 154, 184, 193, 214, 224, 230, 238, 249, 253, 259, 269, 275, 282, 298, 302, 315, 322, 329, 335, 342, 349, 356, 362, 374, 387, 400, 409

Forbes, Mr J.M., 30, 32, 36, 54, 73, 161–4. 393

Ford, G.T., 219, 220, 225, 229, 254, 264, 284–5

Foreign Travel, 115–6, 248, 262, 268, 272, 280, 288, 316, 320–21, 330, 335, 343–4, 350, 361, 370, 391, 396

Fossey, J.H., 336, 343

Foster, P.B., 280

Fountain, Mrs J., 340

Fox, C.H., 387

Franks, P.R., 180, 184, 189

Free places, 9, 74

Freedland, M., 222–3, 423

French, M.I., 341

Frost, Mr A.P., 30, 173, 197

Froud, Mr A.S., 283

Fryer, S.J., 390

G

Gale, Mr J., 244, 304, 402, 425–6

Gallimore, Mr D.F., 179, 188, 190, 423

Game, J. 356

Games, 13–4, 27, 28, 35–43, 75, 84. *see* individual sports.

Gardiner, W.J.H., 417

Gardner, Miss Clara, 8, 30

Gardner, N.F., 304

Gas masks, 150, 158, 160, 201

Gauntlett, Mr F.E., 107–9, 114–5, 117, 143–4, 152, 160, 163–8, 170, 178

General Cert. Education, 276, 347, 372, 394

Geology, 267, 349, 392

George, D.W., 290

George Vth, 134, 248, 280

Germans, nation, 51–2, 115

Gething, P.J.D., 63, 167, 217,

246, 251, 279, 314
Gething, W.A., 63, 292–3
Gibbs, M.J., 316, 322, 324, 329, 330, 336
Gibson, W.M., 207
Giddy, Mr S.R., 218, 224, 327, 417, 423
Gilder, A.L., 37
Gilder, D.G., 300
Gill, D.G., 253, 259, 263, 269–70, 274, 277, 388
Gillespie, J.J.M., 338
Gilpin, P.J., 127–8
Girl friends, 48, 67
Girl Guides, 58–9, 427
Girls' High School, 70–72, 90, 114, 117, 197, 219, 228, 240, 248, 254–5, 263–4, 267–8, 277, 280, 287, 290, 295, 297, 301, 304, 306, 311, 316, 317, 318, 321, 326, 328, 333, 338, 346, 351, 352–3, 356, 359, 363, 385, 386, 390, 391, 395, 399, 402, 419
Glenister, C.C. 248
Glover, D.C., 304, 379, 409
Godfrey, Mr C.J., 72, 81, 88, 92, 124–5, 164–5, 168–9, 173, 178, 185, 215, 260, 293, 334, 335, 369, 372, 377–9, 417
Golding, Shiela, 290, 300, 307
Goodwin, D.R., 349
Goodyear, F.R.D., 297, 298, 304
Gorton, Mr G.H., 388, 393
Gosling, J.R., 365, 387, 395, 402
Governors, 4, 22–3, 28, 32–3, 57, 73, 77, 83, 89, 140, 148, 163–8, 175, 180, 187, 196–7, 205, 218, 221–2, 241, 243, 291, 292, 314, 398, 403, 420
Graffham, Mr A., 356
Grant, C., 346
Grant, D.R., 301, 321, 331, 337, 340
Graves, M.J., 289
Gray, D.G., 258
Grayston, Mr J.D.C., 179, 188, 200, 365
Green, J.W., Brewer, 1, 5, 14, 93–4, 234, 265, 335, 337–8, 340
Greenleaf, J.R., 234, 265, 335, 337–8, 340
Gregg, S.J., 95

Gregory, A.C., 282, 289–90, 300, 318
Gregory, S.C., 385, 396
Grimshaw, Mr C.G., 258, 271, 311
Grover, G.H., 155
Gurney, J., 283, 290, 295, 299, 300, 317, 336
Gurney, R.E., 405

H
Hall, A., 322, 324
Hall, M., 330, 336
Hambro, H.C., 94
Hamburger, Dr H.L., 178
Hamel D.R. 400
Hamel, P.J., 389, 401
Hammond, H.I., 340, 349, 355
Hanson D.J., 307
Haq, Dr S.U., 416
Harding, L.A., 348, 355, 361
Harmer, F.G.; Cup, 128
Harmonium, 25, 81–2, 111
Harrison, C.J., 362, 388
Harrison, Mrs J., 335
Harrison, P., 376
Harrowell, D.F., 237, 261
Harry, M.W., 329
Hartley, Miss Marjorie, 185, 218
Harvest Festival, 318, 324, 345, 351, 358, 366, 381, 420
Harvey, Mr E.F., 152, 175, 179, 207, 236, 241
Hauke, Mr A.C., 314, 321, 331, 333, 337, 342, 346, 351, 353, 356, 365, 374, 381, 384, 387, 395, 402, 427
Hawkes, D.F., 203
Hawkins, D.B., 230, 409
Haworth, A., 55
Hayne, J. 261
Haynes, M.W., 356, 362
Head Boys, 121, 131, 159, 184, 202, 211, 247, 328, 333, 355, 360, 386, 398
Head, D.K. 299
Health, see medicals,
Heanue, J.A., 216
Heanue, P., 215
Hearn, R.E., 375
Hey, Elizabeth, 300, 319
Hickman, Ald. E.K., 314
Higher Grade School, 3, 11
High School for Girls, see Girls' High School.

Hill, A.M., 206, 209, 236
Hill, Dr C., MP., 280, 281, 292, 338, 360
Hill, D.J.F., 216, 228, 233, 240
Hill, E.W.B., 279
Hill, R.A., 343, 350
Hill, R.D., 208
Hill, R.J., 324, 330, 336, 342, 343
Hills, D.J., 300, 302, 315, 316
Hine, L.M., 232
Hine, M., 329
Hobbs, F.W., 206
Hoblyn, E.T.H., 81, 96, 132, 292–3, 330, 370, 400
Hoblyn, Mr J.B., 8, 30, 32, 83, 132
Hockey, 14, 43, 65
Holmes, R.A., 204
Holmes, R.F. 343
Home and School Association, 218, 234, 247, 268, 276, 285, 295, 300, 302, 318, 319, 325, 331, 341, 345, 351–2, 355, 359, 361, 367, 377, 381, 384, 392, 394, 403, 420
Hopkins, J.M., 264
Horton, M.H., 374, 387
Horwood, Elizabeth, 339
Houses, school, 37
Howe, C.J., 260
Howard, Mr G.R., 79, 81, 174, 380–1
Howells, Mr G.D., 227, 235
Howlers, 57, 120
Howlett, D.A., 401
Hucklesby, Ald. A.J., 4
Hucklesby, A.J., 237
Hucklesby, D.J., 300
Hudson, Dianne, 254
Hudson, Miss Kathleen, 250, 255, 263, 268
Hudson, Mr P.G., 340, 394
Huffington, Mr T., 54
Hughes, Miss J.D., 310
Hulme, Mr R., 250, 331
Humphreys, C.J., 322, 337, 340, 341, 409
Hunter, Mr H., 72

I
Icknield School, 316, 324, 329, 336, 375
Inspections, HMIs., 18, 27–8, 30, 44, 89–90, 161–2, 166–7, 169–75, 252, 307–10, 373

Ionian Singers, 395
Ireson, F.L.T., 203
Ironmonger, A.L., 253
Irvine, Miss M.E., 399, 413, 420
Irvine, T.A., 343, 350
Isherwood, P.L., 250, 262, 264, 271, 274, 284

J
Jackson, Miss F.M., 30, 72
James, W.D., 207
Jameson, G.T., 349
Janes, C.L.B., 206, 229, 256–7
Janes, Sir H.C., 134, 148, 229, 241, 256–7, 292
Jeffs, H.J., 32, 120, 134
Jefferson, R.C., 343, 345
Jeffreys, A.J., 416–7
Jenkins, E.D.B., 125, 202
Jepps, G.N., 364
Jewish boys, 222–3
Joad, Prof. C.E.M., 195, 196
Johnson, C.A., 288, 290, 295, 307
Johnson, M.C., 297, 320
Joint Consultative Committee, 383–4
Jones, Mr E., 79, 115, 117, 159, 165, 167, 173, 403, 404–5, 408, 419
Jones, Canon E.W., 79, 152, 156
Jones, Mr I.A., 382, 414
Jones, K.P., 343, 350
Jones, M., 270
Jones, R.G., 273
Jubilee, School's Golden, 292–3

K
Kaye, L.T., 356
Kaye, M., 322
Keens, Lady, 243
Keens, Sir T., 129
Kelly, R.W., 253, 260, 356
Kempson, M., 366
Kennett, D.H.W., 11, 364, 391
Key, Mr T.R., 280, 283, 288, 290, 297, 300, 311, 319, 325, 339, 353, 426
Killick, Mr A.R., 142, 147, 159, 209, 232, 398
King, R.W., 207, 209
King, W.J., 204, 209
Kingham, M.J.F., 349
Kitchen, J.E., 376
Kitchener, G., 385
Kitchener, R.D., 131, 144

Kuster, A.P.C., 208

L
Lacey, W. & Son, 43, 109–10
Lambert, K.J., 123
Lane, Mr R., 234, 417, 424–5
Law, R. (Zakon), 222, 236
Lawrence, Ald H.C., 293, 403, 420
Lawrence, J., 253, 260, 272, 277, 280, 298, 300
Leavers, early, 15, 94, 188, 284
Leighton, F.M., 40, 46, 62
Lightfoot, J.H., 351, 361
Lists, school, 114
Literary and Scientific Society, 99–100, 113, 116–8, 154, 190, 217, 227, 234, 240, 248, 263, 277, 282, 286, 297, 304, 321, 328, 338, 345, 352, 376, 390, 402
Livesey, Christine, 290, 300
Livingston, A., 333
Lockwood, K.C., 344
Longbottom, P., 224, 232, 236
Lovell, Mr J., 298, 328, 352, 427
Lowe, Mr A.F., 186, 192, 219, 261, 262
Lowe, S.J., 395
Lucking, Mr T., 241
Luhr, Miss Margaret, 258
Lutley, E.J., 320, 323, 326, 331, 335
Lutonian, The, 135–7, 277, 367, 368, 388
Luton, County Borough, 372
Luton Education Committee, 243, 403, 405
Luton Girls' Choir, 251, 262
Luton, history, 1–3, 101, 120, 255, 372
Luxemburg, S.C., 291, 311, 320
Lythgoe, W.F., 329, 335, 336, 343

M
Macdonald, D.I., 216, 229
Macdonald, R.A., 248
Macfarlane, Miss J., 14
Mackey, J.D., 343
MacRae, G.F.K., 324, 329
Magazines, School, 43–4, 135–7, 277, 367, 368
Magoon, Mr J., 179, 188, 197
Mahon, Rev.; Mrs., 73, 78
Mander, Sir F., 198, 251, 292

Manners, *see* Etiquette,
Manning, W.H., 298, 364
Maple, J.S, 345, 352
Mardle, D.V., 217, 248, 251, 258
Mares, Charles, Ltd., 91, 109
Marshall and Tweedy, 138, 148–9
Marshall, B.E., 395
Marsh-Edwards, M., 186, 191, 220, 229, 230, 232, 237, 247, 285, 365
Martin, A.J., 376
Martin, Mr A.W., 109, 135, 137, 154, 174, 186, 190, 192, 225
Masonic Lodge, 310, 429
Matthews, D., 209
Matthews, Mr. S.H., 280, 314
Maughan, H., 260, 282
May, Mr A.J.G., 234, 414, 424
May, D.R., 300, 304
May, Mr F.F., 8, 30, 108, 133
Maynard, S.J., 316, 324
McGlashan, Maureen, 317, 319
Medals, *see* Awards,
Medicals, 76, 90, 131, 161, 205, 267, 330, 352
Memorial organ, 256–8
Memorial services, 104–5, 241–2, 292–3, 301, 318, 269–70
Memorial Swimming Pool Fund, 234, 235, 238, 242, 247, 250, 252, 276,
Memorial Tennis Courts, 242, 276, 295–6
Memorials, War, 77–9, 241–2, 318
Merchant, R.F., 299, 302
Meredith, P., 329, 349, 350
Merrick, W.P., 420
Messer, Mr W.G., 418
Meteorology, 87–8, 416
Military Service, 51–60, 187, 201–9
Minns, Mr F.C., 178, 180, 190, 216, 229
Modern School, Park Square,
The Building: 29, 97
Demolition of, 322
Extensions, 120, 134
Great Hall, 23, 69, 71
Insurance, 25
Laboratories, 24, 97
Library, 28, 90, 119
Office, 120
Playground, 28

Curriculum: 15, 74
  Advanced courses, 72, 94
  Arts, crafts, 17
  Foreign languages, 15, 46, 74
  Homework, 75
  Latin, 15
Administration: 18, 89
  Absence records, 18, 76
  Aims and ethos, 18, 52
  Admission exam, 74, 230
  Assembly, 25, 110, 113
  Attendance, 74, 131
  Dossiers, boys', 115
  Military occupation, 36, 51
  Name of school, 28–9
  New School needed, 120–2, 129
  Noise, 27
  Opening of, 22
  Overcrowding, 121
  School lists, 114
  School calendar, 75
  Socials, 111–2. 119
  Testimonials, 132
**Modern-Grammar School,
  Bradgers Hill,**
The building:
  Architectural competitions, 21,
    136, 138–40
  Assembly Hall, 141, 147
  Blackout, 157, 196–7
  Boiler house, 142
  Buidling problems, 159, 184,
    216
  Camouflage, 159
  Construction, 141–2, 143
  Cost of school, 122, 136, 159,
    184
  Design, 287
  Extensions, 222, 310, 324, 358
  Gymnasium, 142, 152
  Kitchen, 195, 230, 308, 334
  Laboratories, 324, 338
  Landscaping, 136, 140, 242
  Library, 170, 228, 261, 308, 373
  Location, 138, 261
  Office, 185, 218, 258, 340
  Ratable value, 159
  R.I.B.Architects, 136
  Specifications, 138
  Sports Hall, 392, 396
  Staff Rooms, 181, 418–9
The Curriculum: 171–4, 309
  Art, 174
  Biology, 174, 373
  English, 171–2

French, 172
Geography, 172
Geology, 267, 349, 392
German, 173
Handicrafts, 174
History, 172
Latin, 171, 173, 309
Mathematics, 173–4, 342
Science, 174, 309, 373, 399
Sex education, 216
General:
  Christmas tree, 331
  Half-holidays, 197
  Hospital, school as, 178, 196
  Name change, 218, 227
  Overcrowding, 129, 230, 250,
    308, 340, 347, 354, 373
Monk, Mrs D., 334
Montgomery, A.J., 375, 388, 400
Moore, Mr A., 99
Moore, J.E., 148
Motto, School, 18, 93, 129
Morris, F.L.A., 206
Morris, I., 293
Mortimer, Harry, 219, 261
Moulton, O., 395
Mowse, D.R.A., 340
Mullinger, F.J., 187, 193, 195, 398
Mumford, R.D., 356
Murals, 190
Muse, Mr J.A., 250, 277, 282,
  318, 335, 350, 357, 388, 392,
  418, 426
Music, 111, 171, 175, 190, 284,
  309, 331, 333, 339, 341, 351,
  353, 355–6, 359, 361, 365,
  373, 374, 387, 395, 402
Music Club, 112, 277
Musson, J.G.R., 311, 319
Myhill, D.F., 342

N
Nash, E.J., 290, 300
National Savings, 59, 184, 214,
  219, 403
National Service, 246
National Youth Orchestra, 305,
  331
Natural History Society, 286, 298,
  304, 317, 322, 328, 338, 344,
  352, 364, 376, 391, 402
Navy, 54
Neale, R.R.Q., 357
Newman, K.F., 330, 331
Newman, R.S., 143

Newton, Prof W.G., 138–9, 140
Nicholas, A.R., 375
Nichols, Mr H., 250, 305, 309
Norcott, K., 228, 270, 313
Numbers, School, 76

O
Oakley, A.A., 4, 33
Oakley, E., 4, 33
Oakley, Miss J.M., 134, 163, 185,
  218
Oakley, R.C., 274–5
Oddie, B.C.V., 87. 95, 253, 315
Oddie, G.J.W., 87–8, 95
Odham, T., 289, 299, 316
Old Boys, Lutonians, Modernians,
  41, 65–8, 103–4, 151,161,
  163, 168, 180, 181, 184, 205,
  224, 242, 276, 283, 292–3,
  295, 300, 311, 316, 317, 318,
  325, 346, 347, 357, 360,
  365–8, 384, 387, 393, 395,
  396, 400, 419–20, 421, 429
Old Girls' Association, 67
Oldroyd, D.R., 272, 283, 285,
  300–1, 305, 307, 313, 424
Olney, D.E., 300, 302
Olympic Games, 87, 253
O'Meara, Dr J.M., 86
Orchestra, 112–3, 151, 154, 181,
  187, 197, 218, 224, 229, 233,
  236, 238, 243, 250, 252, 301,
  321, 331, 337, 241–2, 345,
  351, 355–6, 368, 374, 381,
  384, 395, 402
Organ, Memorial, 256–8
Orme, P.J., 348, 353, 354, 374
Orpwood, R.D., 388
Osborn, A.J., 283, 290, 293, 295,
  300
Osborn, Ald. C.H., 28, 33
Otter, Mr W., 8, 30, 80, 88, 92,
  102–3, 179, 220
Outen, P.R., 359
Owen, Mr G., 249, 270
Owen, H.R., 340, 349, 355
Owles, A.E., 202

P
Page, D., 167, 212
Page, D.A., 320
Page, N.J., 400
Pakes, A.F.W., 240, 243, 249
Panton, P., 187
Parents, 11, 78, 293, 319, 399

Parry, Mr C.W., 44, 79, 178, 190, 229, 230, 243, 247, 248, 249, 252, 262, 270, 272, 277, 288, 298, 301, 304, 305, 316, 319, 320–21, 329, 330, 335, 337, 342, 343, 345, 349, 350, 369, 379, 406–7, 410–12, 418, 422–3

Partridge, Mr A.C., 79, 124–5, 173, 272, 288, 298, 316, 335, 350, 403, 422

Pashley, N.R., 396, 402

Patriotism, 51–6

Pattenden, M.R., 253

Patterson, P.M., 273

Pearman, R.D., 315, 324, 329

Pearson, G.W., 187

Peters, Miss Olga, 218, 258, 398, 427

Phillips, J.E., 290

Phillips, Mr J.H., 249, 280

Phillips, Mr R., 6, 18, 36, 79, 81, 93, 98, 153, 160, 164, 167, 171, 228, 266, 379

Phillipson, Mrs D., 284, 297

Physical Training, 16–17, 26, 36, 37, 83, 175, 179,

P.T. Displays, 198, 215, 224–5, 233, 247

Pick, Dr F.W., 179, 190

Pitkin, B., 280

Playing fields, 13–4, 27, 36, 83, 86, 88, 97, 137–8, 258

Pointing, Mr S.J., 80, 174, 187, 205, 234, 250

Polytechnic, North Western,
Boys, 158, 179, 180, 181, 187, 197, 230
Girls, 158–9

Post Office Work, 152, 187, 197, 219, 243, 264

Potatoe picking, 263, 290, 318

Potter, B.E., 283

Potts, A.N., 375, 388, 400

Potts, C.J., 389, 391

Poulton, Miss E.St S., 30, 68

Pranks, 92, 179, 290–1, 301, 311, 333, 365, 381, 405, 417

Prefects, Monitors, 45, 46, 69, 77, 142, 159, 210, 211, 261, 276, 284, 310, 361–2, 394

Prefects' Common Room, 276, 358

Prime, A.E., 342

Prize Giving, see Speech Day.

Prospectus, 9, 73

Prothero, R.E., (Lord Ernle), 4, 17, 22–3, 28, 32, 41, 47, 94, 103, 132

Pugh, N.J., 343, 349, 350

Punishment, see Discipline.

Pupil Teacher Centre, 34

Puppet Show, 242–3

Pyburn, R., 288, 289, 300, 314

Pye, Mr J.T., 372, 381, 384, 387, 399, 403

R

Rabbit Club, 190, 217

Railway Club, 248, 268, 277, 359, 364, 377, 401

Rance, B.H., 253

Randall, D.E., 289, 299

Randall, F.J., 204

Randall, M.D., 208

Raymond, V.E., 191, 229, 236, 243, 258

Red Cross, see Charities.

Red Cross Sports, 185, 216, 232, 235, 238

Redman, A.T. 180, 216, 232, 235, 238,

Rees, D., 395, 420

Reeve, A.T., 62

Reid, C., 130, 209

Reid, Mr F., 356, 393

Reilly, D.W., 317, 328

Religious Instruction, 16, 79, 171, 193, 351, 380

Remembrance Day, 318, 325, 339, 345, 351, 359, 366, 381, 394, 420

Renwick, D.P., 417–8

Reorganisation, 272–3, 383–7, 398–9

Report Books, 161, 319

Reynolds, E.J., 324, 343

Rhodes, R.W.A., 358, 420

'Rhubarb and Custard', 67, 92

Richardson, Sir A., 287

Richardson, J.G., 204

Riches, A.C., 363, 368

Richmond, Mr D.E., 294–5, 297, 300, 305, 314, 315

Ridout, Mr R., 179, 200, 226

Rimmer, F.C., 54–5

Rising, A., 356

Ritchie, D.I. 344

Ritvo, Rev. H., 223

Roberts, E.R., 123, 130

Roberts, K.G., 356

Roberts, Mr W., 123, 142, 180, 258, 337

Robinson, B.D., 253, 260, 270, 271, 275, 336

Robinson, Miss Christine, 340

Robinson, P.R.W., 300, 302

Robinson, R., 343, 363, 375

Rodgers, F.L., 353

Roe, A.P., 329

Roll, School, 44–5, 94, 169, 178, 227, 243, 250, 324, 332, 340, 347, 354, 360, 396

Rogers, T.L., 371

Root, Mr A.,79, 164–5, 167, 168, 173, 179, 228, 236, 309, 404, 422

Root, M.W., 317, 320

Root, R.L., 356

Router, B.F., 301

Rowston, G., 305, 315, 326, 335, 339, 346, 348

Royal Flying Corps, 54

Rugby Football, 85–6, 127–8, 155, 184, 195, 216, 224, 235, 238, 249, 253, 260, 271, 275, 278, 283, 290, 296–7, 300, 303, 316, 324, 330, 336, 343, 350, 357, 362, 367, 375, 390

Rugby, Varsity Match, 283, 301, 311, 362, 420

Rules, School, 69, 75–6, 160

Rumble, C.E., 324, 336, 343

S

Sale, S., 206–7

Salmon, P.B., 390

Sanders, E.A., 209

Sanderson, Mr T.A.E., 5–8, 16, 18, 22, 25, 30–2, 35, 56, 65, 73, 78, 81, 93–4, 98, 103–6, 107, 114, 161, 266, 283, 292, 296, 345, 365, 378

Sankey, Mrs F., 180, 181, 230, 238, 255

Sansom, J.T., 288, 297, 298, 301, 305

Sansome, Mr E., 234, 250, 304, 314, 403, 404, 408

Saunders, P.D., 217, 220, 237, 247

Schagrin, P., 217, 236

Scholarships, American Field, 304, 317, 371, 385
Entrance, 9, 34, 230, 307, 332

Free Places, 9, 74
Leaving, 72
School Certificate, 74, 258, 276
Scurfield, Mr R., 230, 235, 249, 250
Seale, J.P.C., 130, 202
Sealy, B.V., 193, 214
Second Master, 72, 168, 372
Secondary Day School, 8–9, 13–14
September Players, 306
Serby, Mr D.J., 338, 339
Sharman, Mr M. 314, 333, 345, 346, 356, 359, 366, 385, 405–6
Sharp, D.W.H., 152, 153, 159, 184, 266
Shaw, Mr C.H., 193. 263, 318
Sheldon, Miss H.K., 16, 73, 98, 114, 118, 132, 154, 163, 231 247, 301
Shore, Mr A.P., 259
Silvester, A.E., 80, 198, 249, 392
Sinfield, R.C., 282
Singer, M.J., 355–6, 387, 395
Sixth Form, 262, 320, 332, 340, 347, 360, 370, 373, 408
Sixth Form College, 115, 242, 262, 296, 310, 383, 386, 398, 403, 413ff, 421
Sixth Form Socials, 219, 240, 290–1
'Sixty-Five' Society, 391, 402
Sjogren, P.A., 89
Skelton, G.C., 209
Skillman, T.S., 226
Slack, I., 346, 349
Slope, D.B., 247
Smalley, T., 242
Smart, M.R., 353
Smith, B.E., 262, 267
Smith, C.V., 387, 402
Smith, Mr D.McK., 280
Smith, E.G.T., 204
Smith, J.A., 203
Smith, S.G., 359, 365
Smith, T.P., 334, 364, 391
Smitham, R.K., 343, 350, 356
Smoothey, Mr R.W., 227, 230, 234, 242, 243–4, 247, 313
Snagge, Mr John, 384
Somers, C., 272, 429
Soulbury, Lord, 219–21
Southgate, J.M., 191, 243, 250–1, 252, 260

Southgate, P.D., 191, 236, 250,
Southwell, P.J., 348, 387, 390
Sparrow, J.R., 345
Speech Days, 56, 59, 60, 70, 93–5, 128–30, 143–4, 152, 182–4, 188–9, 212–3, 219–20, 230, 236, 244–7, 267, 273, 280, 285, 304, 327–8, 332–3, 340, 347–8, 353–5, 360–61, 370–71, 385–6, 395–8
Spooner, Mr F., 8, 22
Sports Days, 41–2, 87–8, 123–5, 155, 160, 184–5, 193, 215, 224, 232–3, 240, 249, 253, 260, 270, 274, 282, 289, 299, 302, 315–6, 323, 335, 343, 349–50, 356, 362–3, 375, 388, 400
Spowart, A.M., 353, 359
Springate, Mrs E., 351
Squire, Mr R.H., 198, 215, 234, 236, 352
Squires, E.W.; Cup, 128
Staddon, Ald. J.H., 4, 33, 148, 151, 165, 180, 222
Staff:
Accomodation, 240
General, 8, 30–31, 52, 72, 80, 164–8, 170, 250, 283, 308, 339, 347, 352, 355,377, 383, 392, 403–4, 414, 422–7
Meetings, 164, 166, 333, 342
New, 79, 197, 250, 338, 351, 358
Salaries, 33–4, 53, 72–3, 177–8
Common room, 418–9
Trade unions, 384
Stafford, Lucy, 30, 62
Starey, S.H., 267
Steff, M.H., 82, 87
Stephen, A.P., 353, 406
Stephen, J.D., 322, 345, 348, 381, 423
Stevens, J.E., 289, 299, 300, 302–3, 315–6
Stevens, M., 346, 366, 385, 396
Stimpson, B.E., 253
Stott, D., 285, 299
Student Christian Movement, 282, 317, 321, 338, 363, 391, 402, 404
Student teacher scheme, 35
Stump, Mr R.M., 227, 243–4
Sturman, D.E., 268, 271, 277, 283, 285, 286, 287–8, 306–7

Stygall, F.E., 80, 167, 181, 191, 199, 217, 408
Summerfield, B.D., 361
Susman, A.M., 366, 396
Sutcliffe, Mr D.E., 276, 286, 426
Swallow, H.M., 247, 268, 270, 394, 419
Sweeney, B.C., 274, 317
Swimming, 88–9, 128, 140–1, 260, 270–1, 276, 302, 316, 336, 343, 357, 363, 375, 389, 401, 405
Swimming Pool, see Memorial Fund,
Syrett, M.A., 363, 375, 384, 388, 390, 405, 408

T
Table Tennis, 113, 269, 277, 322, 338
Talbot, Mr A., 159, 162, 173
Taylor, G.F., 202, 316
Taylor, E., 83, 91
Tearle, R.J., 203
Technical education, 3, 122
Institute, 4, 90, 105, 114, 122
School, Junior, 134, 142, 197, 280, 317, 321, 351, 363, 390, 395, 398, 419
Tennis, 280, 290, 300, 302, 316, 324, 336, 389, 401, 402, 404
Tennis Courts, see Memorial,
Theatre visits, 154, 200, 236, 268, 301
Thirteen Plus, 307
Thompson, I.R., 375, 388, 400, 401
Thompson, Rev. M.W., 31
Thorogood, J.L., 349, 374
Thorpe, A.W., 179, 198, 211, 212, 235, 313, 315, 316, 322, 381, 408
Thorpe, Mr W.N., 230, 301, 310, 314, 424
Thurlow, S.R.B., 224, 253, 259, 260
Tiley, R., 385
Tomlin, P.N., 335, 349
Tout, R.F., 290, 298, 302
Towl, M.R.C., 335, 362
Town Hall, Luton, 17, 23
Townsend, P.D., 247, 255, 258, 318
Traditions, 17
Transport, 11–12, 150–51

Trapps Lane, 36, 38
Trendall, A.F., 192, 240, 241, 246, 279
Trials, Mock, 118, 234
Trivick, H., 341
Turner, D.S., 311, 323, 366
Turok, G.L., 148–9, 262
Tweedie, I.E., 129, 130

U
Underwood, A., 208
Uniform, 14, 25, 91, 109–10, 218, 261, 287, 334, 342
    caps, 14, 26, 76, 91–2, 109, 123, 334
    neckties, 260, 342
    sports kit, 38, 76, 123, 299
United Nations Assn., 271, 277, 317, 328, 348, 408

V
Vaughan, P.R., 288, 297, 318
Vaughan, R.V., 247, 253, 255, 260
Vaughan, T.B., 275, 282
Vauxhall Motors, 129, 132, 134, 224–5
Verran, R.C., 203, 209
VE Day, 232, 237
Visits, school, 49, 100–01, 272, 391, 392
Vyse Hat Factory, 5, 93

W
Wagon, D.J., 333
Waller, E.G., 207
Waller, Ald. H.R. 190, 256–7, 279, 296,
Waller, J. 167, 168, 215
Waller, W.D., 262–3, 317
Walmsley, Miss A., 4, 13, 33, 73
Walsh, G.E.K., 117, 318
Walters, J., 260, 299
Wanstall, B.J., 335, 336
Warbey, W., MP, 240, 262
Wareham, Mr C.E., 79, 83, 167, 173, 214, 250, 403, 404, 408, 419
Warren, G., 4, 22–3, 33
Warship Week, 192
War Weapons Week, 184
Watkins, D.A., 290, 305, 315, 318, 319
Watkins, L., 273
Watson, H.H., 56, 57–8, 72, 80,

88–9, 99, 115, 159, 171–3, 190, 227, 248, 252, 272, 279, 283, 327
Watson, T.S., 389, 400, 401
Webb, D.A., 247, 252, 254, 261, 262, 264, 268
Webb, D.R., 355
Webb, Miss E., 30–32, 55
Webb, J.B., 285
Webb, Mr K.B., 105, 164, 175–8, 180, 181–4, 188–9, 190, 193, 208, 212–3, 216–8, 220, 223, 230–1, 236, 237, 240–1, 244, 246–7, 251–2, 256, 258, 267, 274, 277, 278–9, 280, 283–5, 291–2, 294, 301–2, 304, 309–10, 314–5, 319–20, 327–8, 331–4, 337, 339, 340, 341, 345, 347, 349, 351, 353–4, 356, 359–61, 364–5, 368–70, 372, 380, 383–7, 393–4, 395–400, 403–6, 408–12, 419
Webber, M.R., 345. 350
Webber, Natalie, 333, 355–6
Weddings, 67
Weedon, D.H., 204
Weedon, J.W., 204
Welch, R., 209
Wells, T.C.E., 299, 376
Wernher, Mrs Alice, (Lady), 4, 13, 36
West, R., 235
Westaway, F.W., (HMI), 18, 30, 32
Whalley, R.D., 232, 383, 413, 418–9
Whalley, T.B., 123
Wheeler, A.T., 9, 37
Wheeler, W.H., 95–6, 209
Whipp, Mrs B., 159
Whitaker, Mr E., 280
Whitbread, Mr S.H., 22, 94
White, H.O., 190, 400
White, Mrs M., 256
Whiting, D.R., 272
Whiting, P.E., 204
Whitmore, E.J., 130
Whittaker, G.B., 363, 375, 390
Whymant, R.P., 360, 396
Wick, D.G., 250–1, 252, 258
Wiles, T.S., 349, 350
Wilkinson, Ald. A., 4, 33, 78, 83
Wilkinson, Rev. R.S., 293
Williams, Mr H.B., 109, 117,

144–5, 154, 171, 179, 236, 240, 247, 250, 254, 264, 268, 271, 277–8, 346
Williams, H.O., 4, 32, 33, 73, 78
Williams, W.O., 303, 323, 335, 336
Willock, Shirley, 419–20
Windmill, R., 361, 365
Wings for Victory Week, 213
Wintle, J.R., 356, 362
Wiseman, B.J., 356, 386, 389
Wix Trophy, 302
Wood, D.E., 160, 249, 253, 260, 279, 283, 285
Wood, D.J., 224, 233, 238, 247, 275, 290, 336
Wood, Miss J.M., 268
Wood, W.J., 390, 400, 401
Woodcock, Mr H.E., 79, 80, 112, 119, 135, 173, 175, 197, 252, 277, 301, 314–5, 368–70, 385, 396
Woodfield, R.G., 206
Woodham, R.W., 341, 353
Wooding, W.H., 52, 66
Woods, M., 326
Workers' Educational Association, (WEA), 97
World War I, 27, 40–2, 48, 49, 51–60, 77–9
World War II, 201–9
    Bombing, 178, 181
    Civil Defence, 201
    Declared, 156
    Firewatching, 181
Wynn, G.C., 330, 336
Wynter, Helen, 248, 283, 306

X
X-Ray, Mass, 267, 282, 331, 399

Y
Young, J.D., 384
Young, L., 282, 286,
Young, R.F., 289
Youth Hostel Assn. 115

Z
Zakon, R., *see* Law, R.,

J. S. Allen
Michael Bagshaw
Dr. Brian R. Baker
John Barden
Robert A. Barker
John Barton
Richard Barton
A. R. W. Baxter
Norman John Baynham
Robin Bland
C. J. Blanks
Peter B. Bonner
Alvar Bowley
P. G. Brown
Jean Bullimore
Donald Burrows
Melvyn Butcher
M. V. W. Chote
Stephen Crooke
Margaret Crosskey
     (née Godfrey)
Colin E. Dawson
Joan Don
Harry Earl
M.J.Eastaff
Philip Eden
Rex Fardon
Dennis Farr
John Farr
Douglas (Bert) Fensome
Michael Freedland
John B. Gentle
Dr. Phillip Gething
John J. M. Gillespie
B. J. Glenister
Derek C. Glover
Rosemary Grant
     (née Godfrey)
Jeff Greenleaf
Gwendoline D. Gribble
George Grover
Mary Kirk Harrison

S. J. Harvey
Vernon Hawkes
Deric B. Hawkins
Doug Head
David Henden
Michael Henden
David James Hills
Ann Holes
David Hucklesby
Colin Humphreys
Peter Isherwood
Robert C. Janes
Ivan Jones (staff)
Roger Jones
Royce Jones
Roy W. Joyner
Ron Kelly
Richard F. Kempson
David Kennett
Dr. Norman King
David Arthur Kitchiner
Stuart Kitchiner
Bob Knowles
Ronald Law (né Zakon)
Peter Lesniak
John Lewis
L.R.N. (Roger) Lewis
Edmund Lynch
Neil Marsden
Denis Martin
Roger Merchant
William Merrick
Peter & Patricia Morgan
     (née Charlesworth)
Barry P. Neale
James Newns
Keith Norcott
Bob Norman
John (Bertie) Osborne
Don Paul
Geoffrey Parkhouse
H. N. Pearson

Richard Powell
Arthur T. Redman
B. D. Robinson
Derek Robinson
Peter Robinson
Brian Roe
Michael Root
Guy Rowston
Graham Sanderson
Geoffrey Scales
Anne Simkins
     (née Kathleen Thursby)
Malcolm Singer
Leslie Horace Smart
Geoffrey Smith
James S. C. Smith
Terence Paul Smith
Ivan Solomons
Michael Southgate
Richard M. Stanghan
David Stephen
David J. Steward
Derek J. Thomson
A. W. (George) Thorpe
Richard Tiley
Colin Titmus
Tom Tomlin
Christopher L. Tutty
Alan Tweedie
Jack Waller
Johnny Ward
Steve Watson
Tim Watson
David Webb, RADA. Dip.
Julian Webb
R. D. Whalley
Colin White
Denis Wick
G. Wilkin
Graham Windle
Eric Wooding

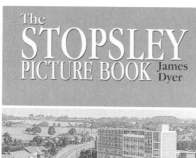

THE STOPSLEY BOOK
THE STOPSLEY PICTURE BOOK

James Dyer

The hamlet of Stopsley, two miles from Luton in Bedfordshire, has a history that stretches back some 300,000 years. Situated in a region initially dependent on agriculture, straw plaiting and brick making, it can be seen as a microcosm of life in almost any village on the northern edge of the Chiltern Hills.

The Stopsley Book tells the story of 20 farms, 16 schools and 4 churches within the civil parish which stretched from Someries Castle in the south to Galley Hill and the Icknield Way in the north. It looks in detail at almost every aspect of village life, particularly in the 19th and 20th centuries, and includes the work of the Parish Council, the weather, water and gas supplies, health care, policing, farm work, brick making and a wide variety of leisure pursuits. Based on thirty years of extensive search and interviews with local people, many now deceased; it is an exhaustive account of a community that still prides itself on its village spirit and individuality.

It includes a collection of 146 photographs, many of which have not been published before.

The Stopsley Book aroused such a great deal of interest in Britain and abroad that a number of readers submitted archive photographs of Stopsley and its surrounding area to the author. These are included in *The Stopsley Picture Book*, which contains 150 photographs and carefully researched captions, to supplement the original work.

A HATFUL OF MUSIC
The Dance Band Days in Luton, Dunstable & District

Stuart Goodyear

In 1939 Lutonian Stuart Goodyear was born into a musical household, whose father, also Stuart, encouraged him to embrace his love of music.

As a millennium project, Stuart was asked by the Luton Historical Society to write a page or two about the local "dance band days" of the last century, and drawing on his own involvement as novice pianist through to bandleader, was happy to undertake the challenge.

Starting in a modest way in the 1950s with fellow airport apprentices, his first band The Rainbow Melody Makers, rapidly became a larger and more polished dance band, and was subsequently renamed The Ray Miller Band. Remaining as leader of the band through to the 1980s, he became well connected with the local musical establishment, and has comprehensively collated his experiences during that time, although it soon became apparent that the finished article would be a book, rather than a dossier.

In a most fascinating personal and wider-ranging survey of musical days gone by in Luton, Dunstable and the surrounding area, Stuart has compiled a detailed impression of how he remembered the busy dance scene, and the many brilliant musicians who contributed to a period of live musical entertainment that will never return.

Deliberating over a title, he shortlisted "Batons and Bows" and "You've gotta lot to learn my boy", but thinks that a "Hatful of Music" just about strikes the right chord. The book contains over 300 photos of events covered over the years. People born and bred in Luton will be pouring over the nostalgia for weeks to come.

WERE YOU BEING SERVED?
Remembering 50 Luton Shops of Yesteryear

Bob Norman

The "nation of shopkeepers" has entered a new era. Our high streets have become impersonal, filled with efficient but bland chain-stores. Gone are the days of the privately-owned stores and shops, when personal service was paramount. Gone but, as far as Luton is concerned, and thanks to this book, not forgotten.

Bob Norman one of their number himself, knew many of those retailers personally. In retirement, he has supplemented his own memories by talking to past employees and family descendants of the original entrepreneurs.

So here are the stories of the traditional chemist, barber, baker, butcher, tobacconist, garage, clothier, jeweller and dozens of other specialists who really knew their trade inside out … and their customers too. A tribute to 50 of Luton's best businesses of yesteryear, profusely illustrated with private and archive photographs, almost all previously unpublished.

The author, Bob Norman was educated at Luton Grammar School.

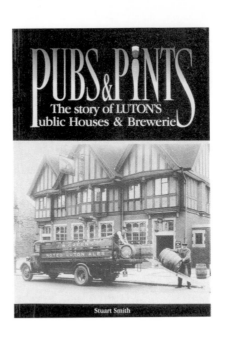

PUBS AND PINTS
The story of Luton's Public Houses and Breweries

Stuart Smith

Whilst the town of Luton is well documented in other ways, this book is the first comprehensive history of its important brewing industry and retail beer outlets – linked, staple trades in the area for over five hundred years.

The development of the modern public house from the early taverns and coaching inns closely followed that of the breweries, with the final decades of the last century seen as the high point in the number of houses licensed to sell beers for consumption on or off the premises. Since then the total has declined with the loss of around 40% during the last one hundred years, most of these losses occurring in the period from 1950 to 1970.

Although documentation dealing with the early breweries and public houses is extremely sparse, it is the intention of this book to try and record the history of each brewery and public house that has had its bearing on the social and drinking pastimes of Lutonians over the last one hundred and fifty years. A special feature of this book is the vast range of three hundred photographs – many old, rare and unusual.

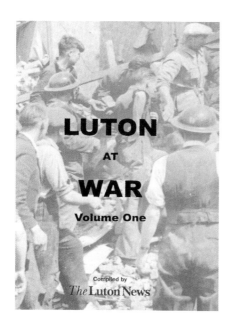

LUTON AT WAR
Volume One & Volume Two

Initially published by the Luton News in 1947, the story of how the people of Luton withstood the dark years of war between 1939 and 1945.

Luton and its population have changed so dramatically in the years since the war that now only a few will recall how the town stood up to the trauma of those war years.

Because of strict war-time censorship much of what occurred during those years was not mentioned in The Luton News. Once the war was over however, The Luton News set about the mammoth task of presenting a complete and vivid picture of war-time life. It tells of the long anxious nights, the joy and the sorrow that made even the most terrifying moments bearable thanks to the tremendous way in which the people joined to help each other.

Written and compiled by the staff of The Luton News at the time, it contains the most comprehensive and fascinating pictorial record. As well as being a moving personal account it is also a unique historical document.

This large format paperback is published in two parts.

THE CHANGING FACE OF LUTON

Stephen Bunker, Robin Holgate & Marian Nichols

The Changing Face of Luton traces the fortunes of the settlement and economy of the town from the earliest recorded arrival of people in the area to the present day. It looks at different aspects of Luton and its development rather than giving a straight chronological account of its history.

Luton's roots go back a very long way, yet in less than 200 years it has changed from a small market town to today's busy industrial and commercial centre. This transformation is described, helped by a range of excellent photographs, thereby answering many of the questions frequently asked, and perhaps raising more, about this intriguing town.

The three authors from Luton Museum are all experts in local history, archaeology and industry.

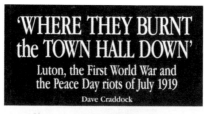

"WHERE THEY BURNT THE TOWN HALL DOWN"
Luton, The First World War and the Peace day Riots of July 1919

Dave Craddock

The weekend of 19/20th July 1919 was arguably the most momentous in the history of Luton. What began as an afternoon of peace celebrations marking the end of the Great War turned into riots that had by the Sunday morning left the Town hall a smouldering, gutted ruin with the military in control of the town. Yet over the years, the story of the riots has been largely neglected.

Drawing broadly on contemporary documents, witness statements and newspaper reports, the book gives a blow-by-blow account of the riots, their aftermath and subsequent trials. The hostility between the Town Council and ex-servicemen's organisations in the preceding months is also covered extensively, as is the impact of the First World War on Luton.

Features of this book include informative appendices containing a wealth of information and over 50 illustrations.

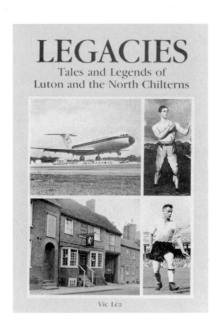

LEGACIES
Tales and Legends of Luton and the North Chilterns

Vic Lea

Vic Lea spent most of his lifetime researching and collecting famous and infamous historical tales of Bedfordshire and Hertfordshire. Following his best selling book, Echoes, here is a further choice of fascinating gleanings from his archives.

Recounted compulsively as only he could, Legacies offers twenty-five gripping sagas of yesteryear... bravery, murder, sport, riot, achievement, disaster, superstition, crime, devilry, transport, danger, intrigue... and many more such dramatic ingredients in an irresistible anthology of legacies from the past.

BARKING MAD
Cautionary Tails!

"I really enjoyed reading the chapters" ROLF HARRIS

Danae Johnston

BARKING MAD

Danae Johnston

Every dog lover between nine and ninety will enjoy following the exploits of Tom and Gill, two delinquent poodles. On their retirement, despite the risk to their prize-winning garden and resident cats, Danae and David rashly take on these canine comedians, their first dogs!

So naïve that they did not know how big the puppies would get, or even that they would need to be clipped at six weekly intervals, the pensioners were to learn everything the hard way – how to deal with scrape after scrape. When Tom jumped the garden fence and returned with one of the neighbours' chickens, for instance! When the dogs herded a flock of sheep into a pond on Christmas Day, or paid an unscheduled visit to a retirement home, or stole the cream from the Jersey milk as it cooled in a bucket on the farmer's kitchen floor, or chased a wallaby at Whipsnade Wild Animal Park – the mischievious adventures go on and on.

Author Danae is a Lutonian, and many of the dogs' exploits are in and around Bedfordshire. Her humorous cartoons and original pithy style make this book a must for all dog lovers. She is also a talented gardener and her garden "Seal Point" has appeared in magazines and on T.V. many times, the most notable being in 1999 when she won the title "B.B.C. Gardener of the Year for the East and South East of England." Many famous gardeners have been to her garden. Geoff Hamilton, back in 1986, Gay Search in 1998, and of course during the recent competition Adam Pasco, Nigel Colborn and Ali Ward as the judges, plus Charlie Dimmock and Alan Titchmarsh, who masterminded the whole show, were around. At certain times her garden is also open to the public to view for charity. And throughout Tom and Gill were never far away!

The Book Castle

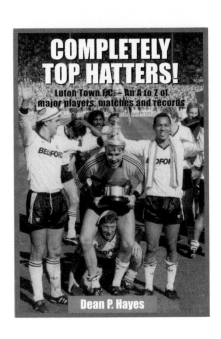

COMPLETELY TOP HATTERS
Luton Town F.C. – An A to Z of major players, matches and records

Dean P. Hayes

Packed full of information on players, managers, outstanding games, glorious and inglorious times, this is the essential guide for all Hatters fans.

Dean Hayes has compiled this encyclopaedia of Luton Town Football Club for all to enjoy. From abandoned matches to the Zenith Data Cup, from the biggest victory to the worst defeat, everything is included. Players' profiles include Joe Payne, Syd Owen, Bob Morton, Billy Bingham, Allan Brown, Bruce Rioch, Malcolm MacDonald, Ricky Hill and Brian Stein to name only a few.

The book includes statistics of major honours, championships, FA Cup performances, greatest number of appearances in a Luton shirt and much, much more.

"Completely Top Hatters – Luton Town F.C. – An A to Z" is a book for every Hatters fan and with its easy alphabetical system, a wealth of Luton Town facts are available in an instant.

EXPLORING HISTORY ALL AROUND

Vivienne Evans

A handbook of local history, arranged as a series of routes to cover Bedfordshire and adjoining parts of Hertfordshire and Buckinghamshire. It is organised as two books in one. There are seven thematic sections full of fascinating historical detail and anecdotes for armchair reading. Also it is a perfect source of family days out as the book is organised as circular motoring/cycling explorations, highlighting attractions and landmarks. Also included is a background history to all the major towns in the area, plus dozens of villages, which will enhance your appreciation and understanding of the history that is all around you!

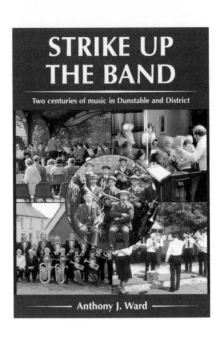

STRIKE UP THE BAND
Two centuries of music in Dunstable and District

Anthony J. Ward

In 'Strike Up The Band', the author traces the history of music-making in Dunstable and District from the earliest times where information is available, up to the present day. It is derived from a wider ongoing project by the author.

The book particularly emphasises the history and development of Brass Bands, Orchestras and other groups, recording their contributions to the changing life of the Town and District, and highlighting the various celebrations that have taken place over so many years. The book closes with a series of chapters on the three local Senior Schools in Dunstable with their bands, orchestras and music.

The design of the book is largely based on a collection of photographs and memorabilia, derived from the wide number of contributors having connections with the organisations featured in the book, featuring their recollections of events and personalities. The story of music-making in Dunstable and its surrounding villages is shown in the context of the history of the area and its citizens.

FORGOTTEN FAMILIES
of Hertfordshire and Bedfordshire

Evelyn Wright

This book tells the story of families once famous but whose fame is now mainly forgotten. They all lived in Hertfordshire and Bedfordshire in the 16th and 17th centuries, and include the Bechers of Renhold (of Becher's Brook fame), the Mordaunts of Turvey Abbey, Lady Cathcart of Tewin, the Bull family of Hertford, the Nodes family of Stevenage, the Docuras of Lilley and the Wicked Lady of Markyate Cell. All the families were related to each other, forming an intricate network over two counties: Hertfordshire and Bedfordshire. The author is one of their 20th century descendants. The book includes pedigrees showing the relationship between various families, and illustrations of many of the manor houses and mansions in which they lived.

Evelyn Wright was born in the village of Wingfield in Suffolk, and moved to Bedfordshire soon after her marriage in 1952. During a busy life bringing up five children, running a Nursery School and looking after elderly parents, she has always found time for writing. Evelyn is married to John Wright, a Chartered Surveyor, and they live in Aspley Heath in Bedfordshire.

THE CHILTERN AREA'S LEADING SERIES OF MAPS FOR WALKERS
by Nick Moon

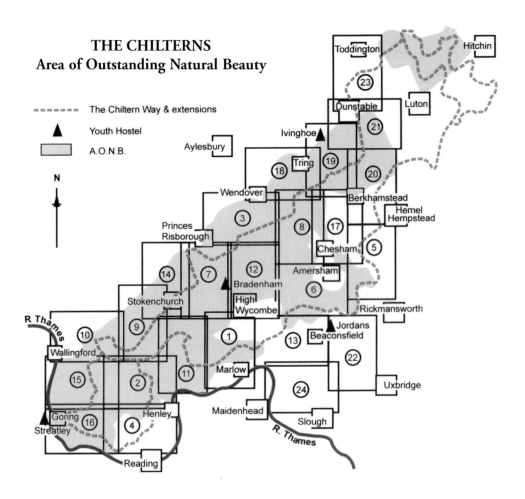

This expanding series of currently 24 maps at a scale of 2½ inches to the mile depicts footpaths, bridleways and other routes available to walkers, riders and cyclists across the Chilterns, as well as pubs, railway stations, car parking facilities and other features of interest. Several suggested walks also appear on the back of each map. New titles appear regularly and will soon extend coverage from the Thames in the south to Hitchin in the north.

COMPLETE LIST OF CHILTERN SOCIETY FOOTPATH MAPS

1. High Wycombe & Marlow
2. Henley & Nettlebed
3. Wendover & Princes Risborough
4. Henley & Caversham
5. Sarratt & Chipperfield
6. Amersham & Penn Country
7. West Wycombe & Princes Risborough
8. Chartridge & Cholesbury
9. The Oxfordshire Escarpment
10. Wallingford & Watlington
11. The Hambleden Valley
12. Hughenden Valley & Gt.Missenden
13. Beaconsfield & District

14. Stokenchurch & Chinnor
15. Crowmarsh & Nuffield
16. Goring & Mapledurham
17. Chesham & Berkhamsted
18. Tring & Wendover
19. Ivinghoe & Ashridge
20. Hemel Hempstead & the Gade Valley
21. Dunstable Downs & Caddington
22. Gerrards Cross & Chalfont St.Peter
23. Toddington & Houghton Regis
24. Burnham Beeches and Stoke Poges

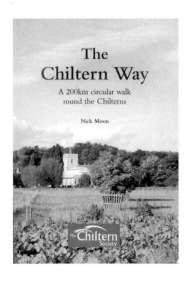

THE CHILTERN WAY
A 200km Circular walk round the Chilterns

Nick Moon

This book is a guide to the original circular long distance path through Bedfordshire, Buckinghamshire, Hertfordshire & Oxfordshire.

The Chiltern Way was established by the Chiltern Society to mark the Millennium by providing walkers in the twenty-first century with a new way of exploring the diverse, beautiful countryside which all four Chiltern counties have to offer. Based on the idea of the late Jimmy Parson's Chiltern Hundred but expanded to cover the whole Chilterns, the route has been designed by the author and has been signposted, waymarked and improved by the Society's Rights of Way Group.

In addition to a description of the route and points of interest along the way, this guide includes 29 specially drawn maps of the route indicating local pubs, car parks, railway stations and a skeleton road network and details are provided of the Ordnance Survey and Chiltern Society maps covering the route.

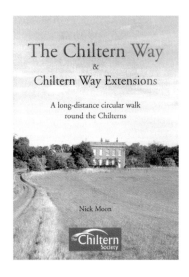

THE CHILTERN WAY
& CHILTERN WAY EXTENSIONS
A long-distance circular walk
round the Chilterns

Nick Moon

This is the new complete official guide to the now extended circular long-distance path through Bedfordshire, Buckinghamshire, Hertfordshire and Oxfordshire, whereby the society has responded to demand by incorporating further mileage both to the north and to the south of the original route.